T0321976

Analyzing the Strategic Role of Social Networking in Firm Growth and Productivity

Vladlena Benson
Kingston University, UK

Ronald Tuninga
Kingston Business School, UK

George Saridakis
Kingston University, UK

A volume in the Advances in E-Business Research (AEBR) Book Series

www.igi-global.com

Published in the United States of America by
IGI Global
Business Science Reference (an imprint of IGI Global)
701 E. Chocolate Avenue
Hershey PA, USA 17033
Tel: 717-533-8845
Fax: 717-533-8661
E-mail: cust@igi-global.com
Web site: http://www.igi-global.com

Library of Congress Cataloging-in-Publication Data

Names: Benson, Vladlena, 1976- editor. | Tuninga, Ronald, 1959- editor. |
  Saridakis, George, editor.
Title: Analyzing the strategic role of social networking in firm growth and
  productivity / Vladlena Benson, Ronald Tuninga, and George Saridakis,
  editors.
Description: Hershey, PA : Business Science Reference, [2017] | Includes
  bibliographical references and index.
Identifiers: LCCN 2016017589| ISBN 9781522505594 (hardcover) | ISBN
  9781522505600 (ebook)
Subjects: LCSH: Information technology--Economic aspects. | Social
  media--Economic aspects.
Classification: LCC HC79.I55 A524 2017 | DDC 658.4/038--dc23 LC record available at https://lccn.loc.gov/2016017589

This book is published in the IGI Global book series Advances in E-Business Research (AEBR) (ISSN: 1935-2700; eISSN: 1935-2719)

British Cataloguing in Publication Data
A Cataloguing in Publication record for this book is available from the British Library.

For electronic access to this publication, please contact: eresources@igi-global.com.

Advances in E-Business Research (AEBR) Book Series

In Lee
Western Illinois University, USA

ISSN: 1935-2700
EISSN: 1935-2719

Mission

Technology has played a vital role in the emergence of e-business and its applications incorporate strategies. These processes have aided in the use of electronic transactions via telecommunications networks for collaborating with business partners, buying and selling of goods and services, and customer service. Research in this field continues to develop into a wide range of topics, including marketing, psychology, information systems, accounting, economics, and computer science.

The **Advances in E-Business Research (AEBR) Book Series** provides multidisciplinary references for researchers and practitioners in this area. Instructors, researchers, and professionals interested in the most up-to-date research on the concepts, issues, applications, and trends in the e-business field will find this collection, or individual books, extremely useful. This collection contains the highest quality academic books that advance understanding of e-business and addresses the challenges faced by researchers and practitioners.

Coverage

- Virtual Collaboration
- Trends in e-business models and technologies
- E-CRM
- Web advertising
- E-business systems integration
- Global e-business
- Electronic Supply Chain Management
- Web 2.0
- Intelligent Agent Technologies
- Sustainable E-business

IGI Global is currently accepting manuscripts for publication within this series. To submit a proposal for a volume in this series, please contact our Acquisition Editors at Acquisitions@igi-global.com or visit: http://www.igi-global.com/publish/.

Titles in this Series

For a list of additional titles in this series, please visit: www.igi-global.com

Securing Transactions and Payment Systems for M-Commerce
Sushila Madan (University of Delhi, India) and Jyoti Batra Arora (Banasthali Vidyapeeth University, India)
Business Science Reference • copyright 2016 • 349pp • H/C (ISBN: 9781522502364) • US $205.00 (our price)

E-Retailing Challenges and Opportunities in the Global Marketplace
Shailja Dixit (Amity University, India) and Amit Kumar Sinha (Amity University, India)
Business Science Reference • copyright 2016 • 358pp • H/C (ISBN: 9781466699212) • US $215.00 (our price)

Successful Technological Integration for Competitive Advantage in Retail Settings
Eleonora Pantano (Middlesex University London, UK)
Business Science Reference • copyright 2015 • 405pp • H/C (ISBN: 9781466682979) • US $200.00 (our price)

Strategic E-Commerce Systems and Tools for Competing in the Digital Marketplace
Mehdi Khosrow-Pour (Information Resources Management Association, USA)
Business Science Reference • copyright 2015 • 315pp • H/C (ISBN: 9781466681330) • US $185.00 (our price)

The Evolution of the Internet in the Business Sector Web 1.0 to Web 3.0
Pedro Isaías (Universidade Aberta (Portuguese Open University), Portugal) Piet Kommers (University of Twente, The Netherlands) and Tomayess Issa (Curtin University, Australia)
Business Science Reference • copyright 2015 • 407pp • H/C (ISBN: 9781466672628) • US $235.00 (our price)

RFID Technology Integration for Business Performance Improvement
In Lee (Western Illinois University, USA)
Business Science Reference • copyright 2015 • 317pp • H/C (ISBN: 9781466663084) • US $225.00 (our price)

Integrating Social Media into Business Practice, Applications, Management, and Models
In Lee (Western Illinois University, USA)
Business Science Reference • copyright 2014 • 325pp • H/C (ISBN: 9781466661820) • US $225.00 (our price)

Electronic Payment Systems for Competitive Advantage in E-Commerce
Francisco Liébana-Cabanillas (University of Granada, Spain) Francisco Muñoz-Leiva (University of Granada, Spain) Juan Sánchez-Fernández (University of Granada, Spain) and Myriam Martínez-Fiestas (ESAN University, Perú)
Business Science Reference • copyright 2014 • 393pp • H/C (ISBN: 9781466651906) • US $215.00 (our price)

www.igi-global.com

701 E. Chocolate Ave., Hershey, PA 17033
Order online at www.igi-global.com or call 717-533-8845 x100
To place a standing order for titles released in this series, contact: cust@igi-global.com
Mon-Fri 8:00 am - 5:00 pm (est) or fax 24 hours a day 717-533-8661

Editorial Advisory Board

Table of Contents

Detailed Table of Contents

Chapter 1
The Management and Performance of Social Media Initial Public Offerings (IPOs): A Case Study
Analysis 1
Piotr Wisniewski, Warsaw School of Economics, Poland

Social media companies have increasingly used global stock exchanges to raise fresh capital needed to expand and commercialise their business models. Despite the soaring proliferation of social media interactions and improving economic fundamentals, many of the high-profile IPOs have underperformed on debut and in secondary trading. This chapter seeks to identify success and failure factors of social media stock market flotations from the operational, industrial and financial perspectives. The research features flagship social media IPOs comprised by the most representative social media Exchange Traded Fund (ETF), the Global X Social Media Index ETF (SOCL), which replicates the price and return performance of the globally recognised Solactive Social Media Total Return Index. The analysis sums up the early evidence of IPO organisation with regard to social media issuers and posits three decisive factors in this process related to: flotation timing, pricing and pre-IPO business integration. The research offers some practical recommendations for future social media IPOs as well as directions for further academic studies at the interface of social media industrial, economic and capital market activity. The following takeaways concerning social media IPOs emerge from the study: 1) Staging and timing: social media companies should mull flotations when a clear-cut path toward cash generation and accrual profits is observable (chronically cash deficient and unprofitable social media tend to underperform on debut and in post-IPO trading) and amid protracted bull markets so as to raise the odds of a propitious IPO climate; 2) Organisation and management: the success of social media going public decisions is a function of seamless IPO organisation (including conservative pricing, share dilution tied to envisaged liquidity and capital expenditure as well as trading and clearing system reliability); 3) Issuer characteristics: social media IPOs are facilitated by businesses commanding a dominant position on the home market, having a diversified core business (including exposure to non-media operations), coming on the stock market either as industry trendsetters or in the wake of successfully executed IPO benchmarks; 4) Factor coalescence: no isolated factor discussed in this chapter can fully explain the performance of a social media IPO – it is rather their combination and interconnectivity that can comprehensively attest to the success or failure of a going public strategy employed by a social media company. From the investment standpoint, the case study analysis demonstrates that a case-by-case (rather than sectoral) approach needs to be adopted for investors seeking to derive gains from social media IPOs, as passive exposure to the entire industry (e.g. via index tracking) is not per se a guarantor of market competitive investment performance.

Chapter 2

Lukasz Lysik, Wroclaw University of Economics, Poland
Karol Lopacinski, Wrocław University of Economics, Poland
Robert Kutera, Wroclaw University of Economics, Poland
Piotr Machura, Wroclaw University of Economics, Poland

Contemporary consumers obtained many possibilities to search for goods and they are very active in this field. Although specialists know that it's difficult to state how, where this process of search takes place. Multi-channel market place is a very complex environment where brand battle for the customer attention. This chapter helps to understand consumer behaviour and reveals many facts concerning mobile and social world of marketing. The authors present the idea of micromoments and their place in the mobile and social channel of communication with the market. Among definitions and examples explaining the idea of micromoments Authors also try to answer questions that can help to understand how micromoments should be handled. Main aim of this chapter is to present behaviour of a modern consumer and factors influencing his decisions as being a part of mobile consumer communities.

Chapter 3

Maria Hopwood, Sports Management Worldwide, USA
Hamish McLean, Griffith University, Australia

Social media engagement is changing the relational dynamic between organizations - and individuals - and their publics. This is particularly evident in the world of elite sport where the market value of an elite athlete is measured by their public reputation which is pinned on healthy relationships with stakeholders, such as fellow athletes, team managers, coaches and, importantly, fans. In fact, social media analysts have attributed much of Twitter's growth to early adopters in the sports world. As a continually expanding global business, sport has to grapple with the challenges of how to harness this uncontrolled medium to best advantage, particularly in times of crisis. This chapter examines the bond between fans and sport in the context of social media in order to examine how this relationship could foster forgiveness for elite athletes who confess to transgressions, thus having enduring implications for the athlete's sport and sport business generally.

Chapter 4

Kiru Pillay, University of Witwatersrand, South Africa
Manoj Maharaj, University of KwaZulu-Natal, South Africa

Online advocacy is big business. Online advocacy organisations need to structure themselves along business lines for fund raising, and to strategically utilise their online and traditional resources to achieve their goals. The growing influence of civil society organisations has been fuelled largely by an increase and ubiquity of emerging technologies. There is no evidence of a detailed analysis of social media led advocacy campaigns in the literature. The global environmental justice organisation, Greenpeace is used as a case study. The rise of online social media has provided the organisation with an alternative to traditional mass media. There have been some notable successes for Greenpeace. The most recent of which has been its efforts to halt the drilling for oil in the Arctic. Equally the Greenpeace campaigns have sometimes provoked the public ire, for example in their miscalculation of the fallout over their recent Nazca plains intrusion. It is clear that to attain any level of success the organisation needs to structure itself on sound business principles and strategies.

Chapter 5

Richard Bull, De Montfort University, UK
Monica Pianosi, De Montfort University, UK

Social media is a worldwide phenomenon with applications like Facebook and Twitter credited with everything from Obama's 2008 election victory to the Arab Spring. But alongside claims of a social media inspired 'revolution' lay more nuanced questions around the role and impact of digital tools, smartphones, and social media in 'every day' contexts. The chapter discusses the role and impact of social media in organisations through two case studies where social media and digital technologies were used to increase energy awareness and environmental citizenship within organisations. Encouraging findings are presented that show the potential of such tools to facilitate change within individuals and organisations yet a cautionary note is offered with regards implementing and measuring such campaigns. Results from the interviews are discussed revealing how claims of social media on participation can be tested, and recommendations offered on how to design interventions for future social media and environmental communication initiatives.

Chapter 6

Zdenek Smutny, University of Economics, Czech Republic
Vaclav Janoscik, Academy of Fine Arts in Prague, Czech Republic
Radim Cermak, University of Economics, Czech Republic

This chapter addresses the issue of privacy settings with a focus on Generation Y from a technological, social, generational, cultural and philosophical point of view. After introducing the issue of Internet privacy and other relevant areas—generational and cultural differences, the philosophical framework, the postinternet condition, the possibilities of processing and (mis)using personal data, and privacy policy— the authors present their perspective on the issue, drawing implications for individuals and organizations based on their own research and other relevant studies. The authors discuss the possible implications in terms of a prospective use of personal data by companies (e.g. for marketing and management) and possibility of processing user data. Such perspective will allow them to formulate a critical basis for further assessment of social networking and Generation Y's attitudes to privacy. The chapter concludes by outlining several recommendations concerning the commercialization of social networking services with respect to the constantly changing conception of privacy.

Chapter 7

Skaržauskienė Aelita, Mykolas Romeris University, Lithuania
Rūta Tamošiūnaitė, Mykolas Romeris University, Lithuania

Scientific society argues that human group demonstrates higher capabilities of information processing and problem solving than an individual does. Collective Intelligence (CI) is the general ability of a group to perform a wide variety of tasks. The new channels of social media enable new possibilities to be involved in collaborative activities for broader groups of people without limitations of time or geographical zones. The scientific problem in this chapter is defined is relationship between social media technologies and collective intelligence in networked society. The subject of the research are online community projects (collective intelligence ecosystems) which include social media tools allowing and encouraging individual and team creativity, collective decision making, on-line collaboration, entrepreneurship, etc.

Chapter 8

Nurdilek Dalziel, Staffordshire University, UK
Janet Hontoir, IFS University College, UK

By focusing on Facebook as an emerging Social Media (SM) customer services channel, this research provides an insight into social media service encounters. Data were collected from the Facebook pages of two British banks. Evidence is presented on the discrepancy between what customers expected of SM and what banks were prepared to offer, a discrepancy which resulted in customer frustration. The findings also demonstrate that, apart from banking regulation, a bank's own SM policies and the training and empowerment of its staff are likely to impact on the quality of firm-customer interactions on SM. It is challenging for financial institutions to develop strategies to address customer queries satisfactorily on their SM pages and at the same time to work within the rules of compliance regulations. Moreover, many customers who put up a complaint on SM are observed to have developed rather negative feelings about their banks and to have lost their trust, suggesting a lack of clarity about the limited role of banks' Facebook channel among customers.

Chapter 9

Daithi McMahon, Univeristy of Limerick, Ireland

Ireland has faced significant economic hardship since 2008, with the Irish radio industry suffering as advertising revenues evaporated. The difficult economic circumstances have forced radio station management to devise new and cost effective ways of generating much-needed income. The answer has come in the form of Facebook, the leading Social Network Site (SNS) in Ireland. Using Ireland as a case study, this chapter looks at how radio station management are utilising the social network strategically in a bid to enhance their audiences and revenues. Radio station management consider Facebook to be an invaluable promotional tool which is very easily integrated into radio programming and gives radio a digital online presence, reaching far greater audiences than possible through broadcasting. Some radio stations are showing ambition and are realising the marketing potential that Facebook and other SNSs hold. However, key changes in practice, technology and human resources are required to maximise the profit-making possibilities offered by Facebook.

Chapter 10

Andrew Duffy, Nanyang Technological University, Singapore

Under threat from social media and interactive Web 2.0, the traditional media industry seeks new models to maintain its viability. This chapter studies both consumers and prospective producers of one genre— travel journalism—to advocate a model that could help arrest the industry's decline and return to growth. It argues that one way forward for traditional media would be a new model of curatorship, in which a professional journalist collaborates with amateur contributors. It suggests that such a hybrid arrangement will be recognisable neither as professional newsroom nor as amateur social media, but a new model with features of both. This offers a way forward so that rather than contributing to the declining fortunes of the traditional media industry, as many journalists fear, social media can instead encourage progress.

Chapter 11

Micro SME documentary producers are challenged to understand, adapt and apply social media technology in the creative economies. This paper examines the technological premise of social media, applications and limitations in documentary filmmaking. Drawing from other fields such as psychology, the author proposes a Real- and Virtual World Networking Model (RVNM), theorizing on how documentary producers can connect via social media networking to generate strong system support for their documentary project. RVNM helps documentary filmmaker make sense of the complexity of social media from development to distribution in order to further stimulate significant growth within the creative industries.

Chapter 12

Tourism is one of the leading sectors based on other people's views and comments found on the Internet. Prior to deciding where they would like to go, individuals obtain information about the travel agencies they will use, the hotels they will stay at and the regions they would like to visit, plus the views and experiences of others in terms of these issues, which are largely shared via social media environments. Accordingly, it has become a necessity for establishments to follow the main social media platforms, such as Facebook, Twitter, Instagram and so on, and develop their goods and services in line with the comments shared on these platforms. In this study, how national and international airline companies implement the 4Ps of marketing (product, price, place, promotion) in social media environments is investigated through examples and analysed through data obtained via interviews.

Chapter 13

Social media tools are becoming an important presence in recruitment processes, transforming them. They allow an instant sharing of ideas, opinions, knowledge and experiences, creating a new "space-time" dimension that could be translated in a new way (additional) to "recruit" workers. Although there are many benefits and promises from social media, however several risks are associated with their use. The ambiguity related to legal and ethical issues of social media, at the same time, contains the enthusiasm related to the potentialities that social media offer. In particular, this chapter aims at analysing the perceived risks and benefits of social media by students to understand if it can be useful for University Career Services (referred to UCS) to use these tools in job placement. The analysis is conducted in five countries: Netherlands, Sweden, Lithuania, Bulgaria and Croatia. It can be useful for managers of universities and firms to understand whether the presence of Universities on social media by students and firms is positive or not.

Chapter 14

The mission of this chapter is to explore the role of social networking and knowledge management competencies combined with social networking strategies as an essential component and support for the development of co-innovation and business co-creation processes for future and potential entrepreneurs enrolled in higher education programs. Business students are active users of social networks but usually do not have clear business-focus priorities when devoting their time to social networking. Social networks enable virtual communities which allow knowledge sharing and collaborative learning a different stages of new business development. These networks have the potential to create ties for cross-border business initiatives that cannot be created in face-to-face networks. Innovative ideas often emerge from combining different sources of knowledge. Social networks can be used for action learning and cross-border knowledge sharing in the academic context in order to enhance cross-border entrepreneurship.

Chapter 15

Students are dedicated and innovative users of Social Media; in the context of Higher Education they use such media in a pragmatic fashion to enhance their learning. Higher Education institutions are thus in a position to facilitate their students' learning by embedding Social Media in their teaching and learning pedagogy. This chapter will discuss the Key Success Factors of using Social Media as a coordinating, managing, and learning tool to enhance students' education in the context of Higher Education. The Key Success Factors are mapped along the communication and activity flows of the student's study enterprise as viewed from an Actor-Network Theory lenses.

Since 2004 when Myspace was converted from a file storage service to a social networking site, social media has become an integral part of people's everyday experiences. Social media has also come to play an influential role in business. The purpose of this chapter is to introduce the Five-Sources Model of Brand Value that illustrates the importance of functional, emotional, self-oriented, social, and relational brand consumption experiences helping different organisations get a clear sense of where they can add value to their marketing communication strategies on social media. The model is consumer-centered and is grounded in consumers' experiences collected through interviews and Facebook focus group. This chapter is based on an on-going project that first started as a Masters research in 2011. It has continued with conferences and academic papers, in conjunction with consulting and lecturing on social media applications in New Zealand business and education context.

In this era of rapid technological change, Social Media has emerged as a key marketing practice in the ICT sector in India. In this chapter, the authors examine the emergence of Social Media as a marketing practice, its application in Relationship Marketing and Market Research and the influence of these on Customer Satisfaction in a B2B market. This research integrates Social Media with the widely prevalent Marketing Management and Relationship Marketing paradigms. A web based survey was used to collect data from a sampling frame of ICT firms in India. Factor analysis evidenced the emergence of Social Media as a unique and distinct factor. It also clearly shows the use of Social Media for Relationship Marketing and Market Research purposes by these ICT firms. Multiple regression analysis showed a significant positive relationship between the independent variables - Social Media, Relationship Marketing and Market Research and the dependent variable Customer Satisfaction.

Chapter 18

Being able to find information, people and expertise helps business to grow and remain competitive. Professional networking using the web 2.0 is providing entry opportunities into international markets, allowing professional workers to interact with both workers and companies in markets worldwide. For that reason our research seeks identify the Social Networking Sites (SNSs) used with business purposes by professional workers, as well as to test the importance given by workers of the Basque Country region in Spain, to the use of social networks, particularly SNSs, to find new professionals around the world and help the workers network. Business Networking is a valuable way to expand knowledge, learn from the success of others, attain new clients and tell others about the business.

Chapter 19

Social media accounts on various social media platforms represent the public-facing Web presences of egos (individuals) and entities (groups). On the surface, these may be understood based on their profiles, their shared contents and postings, and their interactions with other user accounts online. A number of software tools and analytical techniques enable further analyses of these accounts through network analysis, content analysis, machine-based text summarization, and other approaches. This chapter describes some of the capabilities of "manual" or semi-automated (vs. fully automated) remote profiling of social media accounts for insights that would not generally be attainable by other means.

Chapter 20

Patrick Winter, University of Marburg, Germany
Michael Schulz, University of Marburg, Germany
Tobias H. Engler, University of Marburg, Germany

Knowledge workers are confronted with the challenge of efficient information retrieval in enterprises, which is one of the most important barriers to knowledge reuse. This problem has been intensified in recent years by several organizational developments such as increasing data volume and number of data sources. In this chapter, a reference algorithm for enterprise search is developed that integrates aspects from personalized, social, collaborative, and dynamic search to consider the different natures and requirements of enterprise and web search. Because of the modular structure of the algorithm, it can easily be adapted by enterprises to their specificities by concretization. The components that can be configured during the adaptation process are discussed. Furthermore, the performance of a typical instance of the algorithm is investigated through a laboratory experiment. This instance is found to outperform rather traditional approaches to enterprise search.

Chapter 21

Kijpokin Kasemsap, Suan Sunandha Rajabhat University, Thailand

This chapter provides an overview of the challenges and benefits of social media across various industries. The use of social media has created the highly effective communication platforms where any user, virtually anywhere in the world, can freely create the content and disseminate this information in real time to a global audience. The chapter argues that professional and business applications of social media platforms can enhance business performance toward reaching strategic goals in the digital age. What are keeping various industries awake these days? Why are social media applications important to various industries? How do social media platforms apply for professional and business perspectives across various industries?

Foreword

Social media has indeed become a facet of life, the tools of which have become widely used, thereby reducing the costs associated with maintaining lines of communication and connections between and among stakeholder groups. Social media has been described as inherently different from other types of media given the characteristics of the social networks so engaged. One study has suggested that social media contributes to the "self-developing" and "self-awareness" dynamic which creates opportunities for interconnectivity and interaction which can be beyond the control of an organization. Certainly, social media is associated with a specific set of management and interaction principles, the analysis of which is associated with its own metrics. The distinct nature of social media as an agent of information acquisition and dissemination makes it difficult to apply established principles of traditional communication. Consequently, a new cadre of insights is required to determine the impact of the application of social media to any given situation. Competently navigating the platforms have become somewhat of a challenge for those organizations which are less adept to technology. Actually, the increased use of social media as a formally established mode of communication is no doubt a by-product of globalization. The pace at which information is obtained and disseminated today is phenomenal providing an excellent platform for fostering an entrepreneurial dynamic that is unlike any other that has been experienced in the past. Such platforms though, do pose threats to traditional businesses. The need for organizations to include social media as part of their communications and marketing strategies is no longer contested, with an increase in the application of the same by both the public and private sector. To date, social media has been used, successfully to support organizational knowledge management, work flow operations, collaborative work projects and stakeholder management. An imperative at this stage of modern technological development is to have a clearer understanding of the strategies in social platform adoption, measuring their rate of return and identifying the key success factors associated with its use and implications of the non-integration of the same into the business operations. Further, consider that different contexts of social media applications warrant differing approaches to their integration. In the first instance the strategic, in terms of potential and actual, role of social must be carefully assimilated, followed by a careful consideration of the best modality of integration and application of social media to the various opportunities and challenges identified. From this perspective, this book provides a collection of discussions which will prove to be an invaluable resource addressing challenges and highlighting best practices across a spectrum of industries: from journalism to creative industries, information technology and education. Indeed, via the in-depth discussions pitched on the wide range of issues associated with the application of social media at the organizational level, this book creates a rich account of the possibilities for business survival and development in a globalized world. It provides some details as to innovative applications of the same and the impact of such experiments. Indeed, it is recognized that the complexity of the social media platform offerings and the open channel nature of the stakeholder-firm communication in an ever globalizing world presents increasing challenges to firms. In this type of environment, firms must be weary that non-response can contribute to its marginalization in the market place. This book helps uncover the specific strategies for successful applications of social media for firm growth and expansion opportunities; as well as setting the foundation for a rich future research agenda on the topic.

Anne-Marie Mohammed
The University of the West Indies, Trinidad

Preface

Social media have earned their strong positions as communication media of strategic importance. One of the key steps in building and expanding a firm's social media presence is to identify goals and objectives and match them against the business strategy. A challenge is, however, created when business organisations seek to use social media in search of opportunities for business development and growth. We set the agenda for research efforts in this emerging field.

A global team of contributors from Europe, Australia, Africa, Asia and North America worked on this volume. A wide range of topics touching on social media applications in public and private sectors and their strategic implications were brought to light. We open the book with a discussion on the role of social media and identify questions which are arising in this continually evolving field—which is a subject of debate both in academia and in commercial circles. The following chapters comprise a rich account of the relevant issues: social media adoption, its strategic impact and emerging challenges.

Chapter 1: *The Management and Performance of Social Media Initial Public Offerings (IPOs): A Case Study Analysis* addresses how companies turn to stock exchanges in search of opportunities to expand and commercialise their business models. Despite the proliferation of social media and the improving of fundamentals, many high-profile IPOs have underperformed on debut and in secondary trading. This chapter seeks to identify the success and failure factors attendant on social media flotations from the operational, industrial and financial perspectives.

Chapter 2: *The Strategic Role of Consumer Moments of Truth: A Marketing Challenge in Mobile Communities* covers the challenges of the multi-channel market place as a complex environment where competing brands battle for the customers' attention. This chapter helps shed light on consumer behaviour on mobile platforms. The authors present the notions of micromoments mobile context and social channels of communication with the market. This chapter contributes to understanding the behaviour of modern consumers and the factors influencing their decisions in mobile consumer communities.

Chapter 3: *Social Media in Crisis Communication: The Lance Armstrong Saga* highlights the changing dynamics in the firm-consumer relationships on social media. This is particularly evident in the world of elite sport where the market value of elite athletes is measured by their public reputation. The latter criterion is grounded in the sound relationships which the athlete has with stakeholders, such as fellow athletes, team managers, coaches and, importantly, fans. As a continually expanding global business, sport has to grapple with the challenges of how to harness this volatile medium, particularly in times of crisis. This chapter examines the bond between fans and sport through social media in order to examine how this relationship could foster forgiveness for elite athletes who confess to transgressions; it further considers the commercial implications of the impact of this medium on sport.

Chapter 4: *The Business of Advocacy: A Case Study of Greenpeace* addresses challenges faced by online advocacy. The authors find that the growing influence of civil society organisations has been fuelled largely by the increase in and ubiquity of emerging technologies. There has not yet been any research on social media led advocacy campaigns in the literature; the chapter presents a case study of the global environmental justice organisation, Greenpeace. The rise of online social media has provided the organisation with an alternative to traditional mass media. There have been some notable successes for Greenpeace, including the recent efforts to halt the drilling for oil in the Arctic. Equally, the Greenpeace campaigns have, on occasion, provoked the public ire, such as, for example, in their miscalculation of the fallout from their recent Nazca plains intrusions. Based on an analysis of the Greenpeace strategy and experience, the chapter presents a review of sound business principles and strategies.

Chapter 5: *Social Media, Participation, and Citizenship: New Strategic Directions* discusses the role and impact of social media in organisations through two case studies which illustrate how social media and digital technologies were used to increase energy awareness and environmental citizenship within organisations. Interesting findings show the potential of such tools to facilitate change in individuals and within organisations. Results from the interviews analysis reveal how the claims of social media on participation can be tested. The chapter offers recommendations on how to design interventions for future social media and environmental communication initiatives.

Chapter 6: *Generation Y and Internet Privacy: Implication for Commercialisation of Social Networking Services* presents a multi-faceted view (technological, social, generational, cultural and philosophical) on the issue of Internet privacy for Generation Y. The chapter outlines several recommendations concerning the *commercialisation* of social networking services with respect to the constantly changing notion of individual privacy.

Chapter 7: *Social Media and Collective Intelligence: Online Communities' Perspective* argues that humans in groups demonstrate higher capabilities of information processing and problem solving than individuals. Collective intelligence (CI)—the general ability of a group to perform a wide variety of tasks—has been fundamentally altered by the new channels of social media. This chapter discusses the relationship between social media technologies and collective intelligence in a networked society. Insights into online community projects (collective intelligence ecosystems), which include social media tools allowing and encouraging individual and team creativity, collective decision making, on-line collaboration, and entrepreneurship are presented.

Chapter 8: *A Tale of Two Banks: Customer Services on Facebook* provide insights into social media service encounters. Data analysis from the Facebook pages of two British banks is presented in this chapter. Evidence of the discrepancy between what customers expect from social media and what banks were prepared to offer resulted in customer frustration. The findings also demonstrate that, apart from banking regulation, a bank's own policies, staff training and empowerment, impact the quality of firm-customer interactions on social media. It is a challenge for financial institutions to develop strategies to address customer queries satisfactorily and, at the same time, work within the rules of the compliance infrastructure. Moreover, many customers who posted a complaint on social media developed rather negative feelings about their banks and lost their trust, suggesting a lack of clarity about the limited role of banks' Facebook channel by its customers.

Chapter 9: *With a Little Help from My Friends: The Irish Radio Industry's Strategic Appropriation of Social Network Sites for Commercial Growth* uses Ireland as a case study. This chapter looks at how radio stations and their audiences are using Facebook as a conduit for interactions and how radio station management utilises the social network strategically in a bid to enhance their audiences and revenues. Radio station management considers Facebook to be an invaluable promotional tool which is very easily integrated into radio programming and gives radio a digital online presence, reaching far greater audiences than possible through broadcasting. Some radio stations are showing ambition and are realising the marketing potential SNSs hold. However, in this regard, key changes in practice, technology and human resources are required, which are highlighted in this chapter.

Chapter 10: *How Social Media Offers Opportunities for Growth in the Traditional Media Industry: The Case of Travel Journalism* describes how traditional media industry seeks new models to maintain its viability. This chapter studies both consumers and prospective producers in travel journalism and presents a model that could reverse the industry decline and return to growth. It argues that one way forward for traditional media would be a new model of curatorship, in which a professional journalist collaborates with amateur contributors. It suggests that such a hybrid arrangement would be a way forward; therefore, rather than contributing to the declining fortunes of the traditional media industry—as many journalists fear—social media could instead encourage progress.

Chapter 11: *Social Media in Micro SME Documentary Production* addresses the challenges faced by producers in understanding, adapting to, and applying social media technology to, the creative economy. This chapter examines the promise of social media, including its applications and limitations to documentary filmmaking. The author proposes a Real- and Virtual World Networking Model (RVNM), theorising on how documentary producers can connect via social media to generate strong support for their documentary projects. RVNM helps documentary filmmakers make sense of the complexity of social media from development to distribution in order to further stimulate significant growth within the creative industries.

Chapter 12: *The Role of Social Media in Shaping Marketing Strategies in the Airline Industry* describes tourism as one of the leading sectors owing its growth to people's online views and comments. Prior to deciding where they wish to go, individuals obtain information about travel agencies, accommodation, and the regions they wish to visit; in addition, feedback on experiences, both positive and negative, are shared via social media. Accordingly, it has become a necessity for organisations servicing the tourist industry to monitor main social media platforms, such as Facebook, Twitter, Instagram, and to develop their goods and services in line with the comments shared on such platforms. This study reports on how national and international airline companies implement the 4Ps of marketing (product, price, place, promotion) in social media environments.

Chapter 13: *Can the Use of Social Media be Useful in Universities' Career Services? An Overview of Five European Countries* explores the presence of Universities on social media and how it is applied in job placement search. Authors find that social media tools are becoming an increasingly important element in the recruitment process, and, for this reason—with a view to understanding whether the presence of Universities on social media is positive or not—it is intended to conduct an analysis of recruitment processes in five countries: the Netherlands, Sweden, Lithuania, Bulgaria and Croatia. The conclusions of the chapter show that, although there are many benefits and promises from social media, there are, at the same time, several risks associated with their use. The ambiguity related to the legal and ethical issues surrounding use of social media, at the same time, enables enthusiasm related to the potentialities that social media offer.

Chapter 14: *Strategic Role of Social Networking and Personal Knowledge Management Competencies for Future Entrepreneurs* explores the challenges of applying social networking to entrepreneurship learning. Knowledge sharing, development readiness, and tools for graduate young entrepreneurs are discussed, comparing business school students in Albania, Estonia and Finland. Authors find that social media are useful tools for personal knowledge management but young entrepreneurs need to develop networking competencies in order to share knowledge in online social networks for creating new business opportunities. Young entrepreneurs can overcome learning barriers in online social networks through e-mentoring and action learning in online teams.

Chapter 15: *Critical Success Factors of Using Social Media as Learning Tools in Higher Education* identifies the key success factors that facilitate integration of social media in learning process in Higher Education. Authors find that social spaces, collaborations communities, and reflection spaces are the three dominant social media types extensively used in the context of Higher Education. The conclusions of the chapter highlight that the successful use of a social medium depends on overcoming the cognitive assumptions of the user base for the utility of each social medium type.

Chapter 16: *Desperately Seeking Customer Engagement: The Five-Sources Model of Brand Value on Social Media* explores how consumers experience brands on Facebook and Twitter. Authors state that the brand consumption in social media settings is characterised by the consumers' functional, emotional, self-oriented, social and relational needs. The chapter concludes that the brand value on social media is, to a large extent, created and delivered, through consumers' interactivity with brands, and their involvement in the co-creation of brand experiences. It is written for businesses and organisations that want to understand how they can add value to their marketing communication strategies.

Chapter 17: *The Emergence of Social Media as a Contemporary Marketing Practice* investigates the key marketing practice in the ICT sector in India. This chapter examines the emergence of Social Media as a marketing practice, its application in Relationship Marketing and Market Research, and the influence of these on Customer Satisfaction in B2B markets. This research integrates Social Media with the widely prevalent Marketing Management and Relationship Marketing paradigms. The analysis of a survey of ICT firms in India shows the emergence of social media as a unique and distinctive factor; it also uncovers the use of Social Media for Relationship Marketing and Market Research in the ICT sector with an impact on customer satisfaction.

Chapter 18: *Getting New Business Contacts in Foreign Markets through Social Networking Sites: Perspectives from Professionals of the Basque Region in Spain* highlights how professional networking expands entry opportunities into international markets. This chapter seeks to identify the Social Networking Sites (SNSs) used for business purposes by professionals, as well as to assess how workers of the Basque Country region in Spain use new professionals around the world and network globally. Business Networking is a valuable way to expand knowledge, learn from the success of others, attain new clients, and tell others about the business.

Chapter 19: *Manually Profiling Egos and Entities across Social Media Platforms: Evaluating Shared Messaging and Contents, User Networks, and Metadata* explores how social media platforms represent public-facing footprint of individuals (egos) and entities (groups). At a first glance their digital footprints are based on their profiles, shared content, and interactions with other user accounts online. This chapter describes some of the capabilities of "manual" or semi-automated (vs. fully automated) remote profiling of social media accounts for insights that would not generally be attainable by other means, which can be used for hiring solutions, organisational knowledge networks, and intelligence discovery.

Chapter 20: *Finding Information Faster by Tracing My Colleagues' Trails: A Reference Algorithm for Enterprise Search explores* knowledge reuse as data volumes noting that the number of data sources is growing exponentially. In this chapter, a reference algorithm for enterprise search is developed integrating aspects from personalised, social, collaborative, and dynamic searches. Because of the modular structure of the algorithm, it can easily be adapted by enterprises to their specific requirements. The components that can be configured during the adaption process are discussed. Furthermore, the performance of a typical instance of the algorithm is investigated by a laboratory experiment. This instance is found to outperform rather more traditional approaches to enterprise search.

Chapter 21: *Professional and Business Applications of Social Media Platforms* offers an overview of commercial uses of this technology. Based on extensive review of literature this chapter provided a synopsis to a wide ranging role of social platforms in business settings.

The changes brought about by fast pace communication technologies extend to professional applications of social technologies. In particular, the effect of social media in marketing and organisational knowledge management is indisputable. However, challenges still remain with regard to social media applications for companies' growth, new market penetration strategies, reputation management, and talent acquisition. Social technology changes the way people work and the ways firms develop and grow. The impact of the social means by which employees communicate is undoubtedly changing organisations. Transformations of industrial networks and the ways firms interact and establish competitive differentiation, and pursue positioning strategies now involve social technologies. This is especially relevant to firms which compete using information and communication technology. The chapters in this book explore themes of social media strategies applied in the private and public sectors, covering a wide range of industries from sports to the airline industries. This book envisages providing an overview of the emerging trends in social technologies having an impact on growth and productivity of firms. Being under-explored in extant literature, this topic is very fresh and has recently become a subject of intense academic debate. We anticipate a great interest in the publication from various areas.

Introduction

THE STRATEGIC ROLE OF SOCIAL MEDIA: EMERGING TRENDS AND OPEN RESEARCH

In the emerging domain of social media use by organisations, key questions are raised for future research consideration. Though achieving a wide reach in public and private sector alike, social platforms are still a novelty from an academic perspective. We explore whether the emerging questions brought about by the proliferation of social platforms in organisational settings are fundamentally different from those arising in other contexts. We further consider whether social media platforms offer unique strengths and opportunities for firms' growth and productivity. We also open a discussion on the changes in methodology required for gaining a better academic understanding of the social networking phenomenon in the business domain.

It would be virtually impossible to attend a business fair, listen to news, or open an academic publication, and not to come across a reference to social networks. What is going on in the world is often mirrored in social media and ideas currently *trending* become the trendsetters of tomorrow. The use of social media for business is no exception. It may be presumptuous to say that social platforms are possibly the most significant descriptive technology in business over the current decade and also the next big step in the development of the digital economy. However, what does this big change mean to organisations? This is particularly important in light of the advent of big data and new unprecedented levels of business intelligence analytics (Agarwal & Dhar, 2014). Rather than relying on our interpretation of the social media phenomenon in business settings, we invited prominent researchers and practitioners in the field to contribute to this conversation. As the debate flourished, five questions surfaced which helped us frame our thinking on the domain:

1. Is the adoption of social networks by organisations a new way of doing old things or, rather, old wine in new bottles?
2. In what new areas in the workplace —both with respect to the public and private sectors—are social media applications emerging?
3. What strengths does the use of social media in professional settings bring to the enterprise and does it lead to a competitive advantage over rivals?
4. What significant developments have taken place in the development of the metrics of 'success', 'business benefits' and 'effectiveness' with regard to social media?
5. As academics (editors and reviewers) what methodological changes are needed with respect to evaluative assessments and methods of inquiry in this emerging domain?

While working on this book and constructing our world view of social media developments in organisational settings, we came across a vast array of transformational ways in which social media are used in today's professional world. The manner in which firms interact with its external stakeholders, including consumers, has seen tremendous changes. As noted in Blanchard's influential work, social media ROI is hard to compute; a much greater challenge in this context, however, is harnessing control of social media organisational channels and managing brands and organisational reputation (Blanchard, 2011). The public sector is no exception and, in this regard, governmental information flow relies largely on social media channels to increase its reach to citizens. Current research highlights the new ways the public sector has enhanced efficiency and productivity in government service delivery, spawning new labels for social media interactions such as "Citizen Sourcing," "Government as a Platform," and "Do-It-Yourself Government"(Linders, 2012). Other researchers draw attention to the contrasting nature of the impact that social media creates in personal and professional settings (Benson & Morgan, 2015).

This book intends to provide an overview of the emerging trends in social media and other technologies having an impact on growth and productivity of firms. The world is embracing new technologies in anticipation of further revenue opportunities, while a range of important issues surrounding the organizational implications of technology remains rather under-explored.

Up until a few years ago, very few general managers outside of the IT industry deemed themselves social media strategists. As social networking media seized the focal point on the business scene, the majority of companies embraced the new technology, seeking to leverage it for competition or revenue. Although the popularity of corporate Facebook and Twitter accounts has levelled off in recent years, most businesses have not sought to disengage from virtual communities. The gap between the early aficionados of social networking and those waiting to take the social strategy to the next level has actually widened.

The advances in IT and in online social networking in particular have had a significant impact on how people communicate and work. The shift towards ubiquitous technologies, facilitated by the proliferation of mobile devices, has transformed personal, organizational and industrial relations. Social technology is changing the way people work and the ways in which firms are developing and growing. The impact of the use by employees of social networking tools for communication is undoubtedly changing organizations. Transformations of industrial networks and the ways in which firms interact, establish competitive differentiation, and pursue positioning strategies, now involve social technologies. This is especially relevant for firms which compete using information and communication technology. A great potential for social technology monetization is largely underexplored by the current literature.

Research in the area of social technology strategy in organizational settings is thriving and we hope to open the debate for further exploration of this challenging topic.

CONCLUDING REMARKS

Chapters in this book addressing a series of issues on the application of networking and social media to organisations raise important issues of organizational adoption of social media in the private and public sectors. The topic is very fresh and has recently become a subject of intense academic debate. We envisage a great interest in this publication from various areas. Through an in-depth discussion of a range of issues touching on the impact of social media and technologies on organizations, we hope to create a rich account of how firms leverage social networking as well as provide an excellent reference point on the subject for policy makers, academics, and public and private sector firms.

REFERENCES

Agarwal, R., & Dhar, V. (2014). Editorial—Big data, data science, and analytics: The opportunity and challenge for IS research. *Information Systems Research, 25*(3), 443–448.

Benson, V., & Morgan, S. (2015). *Implications of social media use in personal and professional settings*. IGI Global.

Blanchard, O. (2011). *Social media ROI: Managing and measuring social media efforts in your organization*. Pearson.

Linders, D. (2012). From e-government to we-government: Defining a typology for citizen coproduction in the age of social media. *Government Information Quarterly, 9*(4), 446–454.

Chapter 1
The Management and Performance of Social Media Initial Public Offerings (IPOs):
A Case Study Analysis

Piotr Wisniewski
Warsaw School of Economics, Poland

ABSTRACT

Social media companies have increasingly used global stock exchanges to raise fresh capital needed to expand and commercialise their business models. Despite the soaring proliferation of social media interactions and improving economic fundamentals, many of the high-profile IPOs have underperformed on debut and in secondary trading. This chapter seeks to identify success and failure factors of social media stock market flotations from the operational, industrial and financial perspectives. The research features flagship social media IPOs comprised by the most representative social media Exchange Traded Fund (ETF), the Global X Social Media Index ETF (SOCL), which replicates the price and return performance of the globally recognised Solactive Social Media Total Return Index. The analysis sums up the early evidence of IPO organisation with regard to social media issuers and posits three decisive factors in this process related to: flotation timing, pricing and pre-IPO business integration. The research offers some practical recommendations for future social media IPOs as well as directions for further academic studies at the interface of social media industrial, economic and capital market activity. The following takeaways concerning social media IPOs emerge from the study: 1) Staging and timing: social media companies should mull flotations when a clear-cut path toward cash generation and accrual profits is observable (chronically cash deficient and unprofitable social media tend to underperform on debut and in post-IPO trading) and amid protracted bull markets so as to raise the odds of a propitious IPO climate; 2) Organisation and management: the success of social media going public decisions is a function of seamless IPO organisation (including conservative pricing, share dilution tied to envisaged liquidity and capital expenditure as well as trading and clearing system reliability); 3) Issuer charac-

DOI: 10.4018/978-1-5225-0559-4.ch001

teristics: social media IPOs are facilitated by businesses commanding a dominant position on the home market, having a diversified core business (including exposure to non-media operations), coming on the stock market either as industry trendsetters or in the wake of successfully executed IPO benchmarks; 4) Factor coalescence: no isolated factor discussed in this chapter can fully explain the performance of a social media IPO – it is rather their combination and interconnectivity that can comprehensively attest to the success or failure of a going public strategy employed by a social media company. From the investment standpoint, the case study analysis demonstrates that a case-by-case (rather than sectoral) approach needs to be adopted for investors seeking to derive gains from social media IPOs, as passive exposure to the entire industry (e.g. via index tracking) is not per se a guarantor of market competitive investment performance.

INTRODUCTION

Social media companies have only recently contemplated going public. Such novelty can be attributed both to the limited record of social media existence and their unproven business models. Additionally, public exchanges – owing to relentless pursuit of transparency, security and formalism – seldom provide a welcoming environment to trailblazing industries. Similar constraints have historically been faced by a multitude of innovative public issuers ranging from power generation to information technology companies. Consequently, the going public route remains a difficult choice for social media ventures seeking start-up or expansion capital.

The research undertaken in this chapter depicts the early evidence of social media initial public offerings (IPOs) with particular emphasis on IPO strategies and tactics from the operational, industrial and financial perspectives. The research methodology draws on a selection of global social media initial IPO cases capturing the zeitgeist of their going public decisions and portraying their aftermarket performance. Furthermore, a synthetic approach (based on a relevant exchange traded fund, ETF which quantifies the performance of leading global social media issuers) has been adopted to examine the industry from a uniform perspective.

A few limitations apply to such empirical pursuits. Firstly, the very definition of social media remains subjective and their classification varies from source to source. Secondly, it is difficult to identify a globally recognisable listed company whose core business is completely dominated by social media operations (social media companies tend to combine the use of traditional and non-media resources). Thirdly, the sample of companies used for the purposes of this research might not be adequately emblematic of a highly fragmented, dynamic and opaque industry. Fourthly, a global approach to social media implicates the use of data collected from various sources where – especially in emerging economies – transparency might be problematic. Lastly, the novelty of social media renders any far-reaching conclusions based on a narrow scope of available datasets precarious.

Despite such constraints, the research strives to identify critical drivers of a well-executed initial public offering (IPO) in the global social media space. It contains practical takeaways useful in assessing the rationale for upcoming social media listings.

BACKGROUND

Social media are emerging as one of the most innovative segments of information technology. Despite opaque economic fundamentals and limited records of existence in the public market domain, the outlook for online creating and sharing user generated content is generally viewed as promising. Figure 1 summarises the key drivers of social media's envisaged economic expansion.

The history of social media as a commercial concept is limited (in practice dating back to the turn of the millennium). Initially, social media had been viewed as grassroots collective initiatives with modest business relevance. Gradually, the sector has attracted commercial attention in two major ways (or their combinations):

- Social media as a facilitator of existing offline or online business operations, including the use of social media data in the investment management process (McGuire, 2013);
- Social media as an investment asset per se (through exposure to individual equities, but also collective investment forms, e.g. mutual- and exchange traded funds).

Additionally, the asset management industry has recently begun to eye opportunities provided by the widespread take-up of social interconnectedness (Stratford *et al.* 2013; Radeljic, 2013). Accordingly, by far more strategic emphasis is necessary from this industry to commercialise social media channels (McGuire, 2013). In accordance with concepts posited by Bültmann *et al.* (2012) the learning curve of asset management organisations gradually embracing social media (as the new frontier of business origination and development) is passing through the following stages (synthesised in Figure 2.):

- Awareness (noting growing consumer enthusiasm for social media use in other industries and at competitors),
- Discovery (launching business initiatives focused on a single social medium, e.g. Facebook),
- Development (initiating a single objective enabled by social media and crafting a tactical response around that objective),
- Experience (recognizing diverse opportunities provided by social media and formulating a set of dedicated objectives to address them),
- Championship (optimally and effectively interacting with various consumer audiences via social media and firmly embedding a social media strategy within the overall corporate strategy).

THE CASE FOR INVESTING IN SOCIAL MEDIA AND THEIR PUBLIC OFFERINGS

The potential of investing in publicly listed social media stocks or collective investment schemes remains constrained by the unparalleled newness of social media initiatives, their limited records of activity in incorporated form and in the public domain (including public markets). Given the novelty of investment in social media, the following challenges have been identified as critical in the process of investment due diligence (cf. Harvard Business Review, 2010):

Figure 1. Key drivers of social media's current and anticipated growth
Source: Own elaboration.

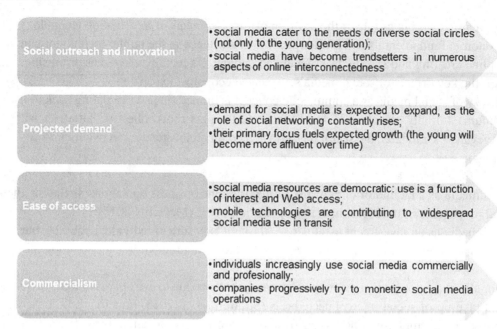

Figure 2. Stages of social media adoption by financial businesses (including asset management)
Source: Own elaboration of Bültmann et al. (2012).

- **Business Metrics:** This ground-breaking segment of online interconnectedness and content sharing requires commensurately trailblazing approaches to gauging operating efficiencies – their underlying methodologies are still in flux (cf. Kaske *et al.*, 2012);
- **Successful Monetisation:** Among the principal challenges to setting up and developing viable business models based on social media has been the indistinct potential for predictable value extraction – although some of the early social media initiatives have now begun to break even, many are still struggling to demonstrate immediate commercial soundness;

- **Ongoing Innovation and Virality:** Most social media companies are "hit driven", i.e. to remain competitive they constantly have to roll out new inventions (their business renewal being a function of organic research and development or successful merger and acquisition activity);
- **Customer Acquisition and Retention:** Another factor closely linked to the ongoing propensity to innovate – social media have to attract and satisfy an ever-sophisticated and demanding pool of high-tech savvy customers.

In view of the rising significance of passive investing (especially by way of exchange traded funds, ETFs), whose proliferation has defied the ebb and flow of other collective investment forms (TheCityUK, 2013), it is worth illustrating the fortunes of social media companies in aggregate, through a composite benchmark.

The most representative vehicle enabling investment exposure to worldwide social media is the Global Social Media Index (SOCL). Its (maximum 50) components comprise worldwide social media operations that fulfil two key prerequisites (Solactive, 2012):

- **Public Status:** The obvious precondition for inclusion into the index is prior admission to public trading and adequate stock market capitalisation and liquidity (free-float);
- **Global Outreach:** Not only should the SOCL components have domestic visibility (i.e. be leaders in their country of origin) but they are also expected to be able to draw audiences beyond their local market.

Both defining features imply the use of languages representing cohorts resident in large countries and/or dispersed globally. Table 1 shows the top 10 equities incorporated in the index (with their trading characteristics and as weightings towards the composite value).

The index offers interesting insights into the performance of listed social media businesses against the broad equity stock market (epitomised by three well established recognised indices, i.e. the Dow Jones Industrial Average, the Standard and Poor's 500 and the NASDAQ). The following observations are noteworthy in this respect (Figure 3.):

- **Inauspicious Debuts:** The social media segment got off to an unpromising start: most of the stocks trailed the broad equity indices during the initial phase of the prolonged stock market rally;
- **High Volatility:** Clearly, social media have exhibited a heightened variance (attesting to their unsettled fundamentals);
- **Recovery and Outperformance:** Despite the humble start, the social media segment has managed to overcome initial weakness and outrun the broad listed equity indices at year-end 2013 (a trend reversed beginning 2014).

The SOCL index can also be analysed more thoroughly and consistently through the prism of portfolio efficiency – combining returns with various metrics of investment risk, as per the (Post)Modern Portfolio Theory (Swisher & Kasten, 2005) (Le Sourd, 2007). It is evident that the globally listed social media stocks making up the SOCL index have substantially benefited from a sustained presence in the publicly listed domain. Following unimpressive debuts, they have recouped losses not only in absolute terms, but also began to narrow the gap in risk adjusted results (Table 2).

Figure 3. Solactive Social Media Index (SOCL) performance against the Dow Jones Industrial Average (DJI), Standard and Poor's 500 (S&P 500) and the NASDAQ in 3 April 2012-9 October 2015
Source: Yahoo! Finance charts [online] available from: https://beta.finance.yahoo.com/chart/SOCL [10.10.2015].

Table 1. Top 10 Components of the Solactive Social Media Index (SOCL) as of 16 October, 2015

Name	Ticker*	% of NAV	Market Price (US$)	Shares Held	Market Value (US$)
Facebook, Inc.	FB	12.94	97,54	101 394.00	9 889 970.76
Tencent Holdings Ltd.	700	10.02	18,92	405 005.00	7 661 126.84
LinkedIn Corp.	LNKD	8.40	197,90	32 460.00	6 423 834.00
Alphabet	GOOG	6.63	695,32	7 292.00	5 070 273.44
NETEASE.COM INC ADR	NTES	6.25	139,77	34 163.00	4 774 962.51
PANDORA MEDIA INC	P	5.76	19,91	221 091.00	4 401 921.81
NEXON CO LTD	NEXOF	5.02	13,62	281 572.00	3 836 343.20
SINA CORP	SINA	4.80	45,96	79 807.00	3 667 929.72
YAHOO! INC	YHO.HM	3.78	33,37	86 520.00	2 887 172.40
YANDEX NV-A	YNDX	3.37	13,60	189 310.00	2 574 616.00

Source: Solactive (2015) Social Media Index, Index Reporting, Solactive AG, Frankfurt a.M., Germany, pp. 1-2. (*)Ticker is a unique trading symbol denoting a particular stock.

Table 2. SOCL performance (absolute and risk related) for different periods ending on 16 October 2015

Category in US$	30 Days	90 Days	180 Days	360 Days	YTD	Inception
Performance	5.5%	-4.8%	-5.9%	0.6%	5.7%	32.1%
Performance (p.a.)	91.1%	-18.0%	-11.4%	0.6%	7.3%	7.3%
Volatility (p.a.)	21.7%	24.5%	21.5%	19.1%	18.7%	20.5%
High	130.86	138.70	143.76	143.76	143.76	155.27
Low	116.68	112.37	112.37	112.37	112.37	80.39
Sharpe Ratio	5.35	-0.42	-0.63	0.09	0.33	0.33
Maximum Drawdown	-6.1%	-19.0%	-21.8%	-21.8%	-21.8%	-28.1%
VaR 95\99	n.a.	n.a.	n.a.	-32.1%\-55.0%	n.a.	-34,3%\-57.5%
CVaR 95\99	n.a.	n.a.	n.a.	-47.5%\-66.9%	n.a.	-49.8%\-71.1%

Source: Index Reporting – Solactive Social Media Index, Solactive AG, Frankfurt a.M., Germany, available at: http://www.solactive.com/indexing-en/indices/equity/solactive-indices/ [retrieved: 19.10.2015].

An even more detailed analysis is possible at the level of individual stocks comprising the SOCL. As shown in Table 3, the global leaders in social media tend to be:

- **Neutral vs. the Index:** Their investment betas (β) are slightly higher than one (on average), although several defensive stocks can be demonstrated as well;
- **Overvalued vs. the Broad Market:** Social media companies command valuations much elevated than the vast majority of listed equities in other industries;
- **Volatile in Earnings, Cash Generation and Management Efficiencies:** Some social media companies have been operating at accrual losses, negative operating cash flows and are yet to prove their scale related efficiencies;
- **Working Capital Positive:** Most social media companies appear to have elevated levels of short-term financial liquidity.

SOLUTIONS AND RECOMMENDATIONS

Managing IPOs is more of an art than a science – notably in respect of issuers active in revolutionary industries. Despite a relative dearth of research into the specific organisation of social media flotations, most challenges faced by IPOs in trailblazing businesses are, in essence, universal. They usually boil down to lack of or insufficiently reliable price discovery prior to an IPO and limited operating histories of IPO candidates. These constraints are aggravated by industry specific issues (novelty, opacity and elusive commercialism).

From the technical standpoint, the IPO manager is caught between two mutually exclusive and equally uneasy extremes: delivering the highest possible IPO price for one client (i.e. the issuer – to whom it owes the IPO mandate) or rendering the IPO valuation affordable for the other client (i.e. the investor community – whose longstanding attention is the lifeblood of the manager's future deal flow), a dilemma empirically illustrated by Beatty & Ritter (1986). A great deal of adroit manoeuvring and visionary prescience are thus requisite to balance both pressing exigencies.

Table 3. SOCL components: risk, valuation, financial liquidity and management efficiency measures as at 19 October 2015

Company	β	P/E	P/BV	P/S	EV/EBITDA	CR	ROA (%)	ROE (%)	ROS (%)
Facebook	0.83	99.74	6.92	18.77	40.86	9.01	9.14	9.47	18.70
Tencent	1.14	45.71	88.58	101.00	237.45	1.48	10.53	30.41	29.69
LinkedIn	0.96	n/a	6.15	10.07	110.15	3.75	-0.56	-3.13	-4.36
Alphabet	1.03	31.33	4.06	6.52	17.42	4.85	8.53	13.86	21.79
Netease	0.56	22.61	4.53	7.88	17.78	3.46	10.46	21.99	34.57
Pandora	0.75	n/a	7.34	4.13	-103.00	3.28	-4.62	-9.89	-5.28
Nexon	1.10	17.69	1.89	3.83	7.87	5.75	9.19	11.80	22.18
Sina	0.95	15.06	1.30	3.32	138.23	4.41	-0.67	8.19	24.10
Yahoo!	1.75	4.65	0.94	6.45	49.52	5.39	0.18	30.02	142.49
Yandex	2.46	9.36	2.27	2.49	7.14	4.60	9.37	27.64	26.85

Source: Yahoo! Finance: http://finance.yahoo.com/ [retrieved: 19.10.2014].

β = beta coefficient, P/E = price/earnings ratio (price per share/earnings per share, P/BV = price/book value ratio (price per share/book value per share), P/S = price/sales ratio (price per share/revenue per share), EV/EBITDA = enterprise value (market capitalisation + total debt - total cash & short term investments)/earnings before interest, taxes increased by depreciation and amortisation, CR = current ratio (current assets/current liabilities), ROA = return on assets (net income/total assets), ROE = return on equity (net income/total shareholders' equity). ROS = return on sales (net income/total revenue). The multiples' calculation methodology further explained at Yahoo! Help Central (2015).

Ibbotson et al. in their seminal work (1994) identified three key anomalies associated with IPOs and their inefficiencies: short-run under-pricing (a global phenomenon although its magnitude varies internationally), cycles in volume v the under-pricing ("hot issue" markets and the significance of momentum) and long-run underperformance (generally inferior returns fetched by IPOs in the long term). These findings were developed by Rajan and Servaes (2002) who incorporated a market sentiment perspective. Counterintuitive information asymmetries existing in IPOs were examined by Lowry et al. (Lowry et al., 2010).

The Appendix contains the case studies of all the top SOCL components for which comprehensive data have been available. Although in the aforementioned context it would be premature to pronounce comprehensive judgment on the complexity of social media IPO management, the following observations can be inferred from the Appendix (cf. Shemen, 2013):

1. **Staging:** It can be postulated that many of the social media IPOs came on the stock market at stages when no clear path towards lasting operating cash flow generation or fundamental commercialisation (based on operating cash flow sustainability) could safely be plotted – their stockholders and managements need to balance out pressing refinancing exigencies with the uncomfortable message that a lacklustre or failed IPOs send to the aftermarket (Appendix: Facebook, SINA and Yahoo!).

2. **Timing:** As nascent, speculative, aggressive stocks, social media companies should be floated in a protracted bull market (no matter how distinctive their core operations, they remain highly vulnerable to downside volatility, especially in light of their fragile business models). IPO managers thus need to exercise caution in pre-IPO planning so as to complete a flotation in a propitious market environment (cf. Appendix: NetEase and SINA).

3. **Management:** Numerous social media IPOs have been priced rather aggressively (at the higher end of the valuation spectra) and have been plagued by technical problems (the most flagrant of these affected Facebook's IPO on the first trading day); other technical issues relate to IPO free floats (an oversupply of stocks bodes ill for the success of the IPOs) and the linkage between IPO proceeds and business expansion (consistency plays a big role here). Failed social media IPOs tended to combine a series of managerial lapses (cf. Appendix: Facebook, Alphabet, NetEase and Pandora Media).

4. **Core Business Diversification:** As sacrilegious as it may seem for an industry as promising as social media, the IPOs tend to profit from revenue diversity overlapping more established industries (whose monetisation is infinitely more predictable and which sometimes demonstrate healthy synergies with social media operations), cf. Appendix: Tencent and LinkedIN.

5. **First Mover Advantage:** Evidently, social media stocks breaking new ground in a given segment of the industry stand a bigger chance of attracting high-quality institutional investors (whose commitment is a critical aspect of post-IPO performance), cf. Appendix: LinkedIn and Yandex.

6. **Market Leadership:** As with other innovative industries, having a dominant share in a given market segment and the ability to use this leverage to affect the competitive landscape and market direction is a forte in social media's envisaged profitability and cash generation (cf. Appendix: Tencent, NetEase and Yandex).

FUTURE RESEARCH DIRECTIONS

Research on social media IPOs is only emerging and plenty needs to be accomplished to account of IPO strategic management in this unique context. Among intuitive areas where further studies are likely to be particularly beneficial are the following problems:

- **Specific Metrics:** Social media need industry specific valuation methodologies (a pivotal element of every IPO) whose sophistication would on the one hand surpass routine tools applied to IPO candidates from traditional industries, while on the other hand would maintain close relevance to cash generation and profitability;

- **Quantitative Studies on IPO Performance:** In the light of rising numbers of social media IPOs and their expanding records of trading, the critical mass needed to perform statistically meaningful analysis of IPO and post-IPO performance might soon be available and relevant studies should be pursued;

- **Isolating IPO Success Factors:** Thus far, it has been noted that several elements contribute to an auspicious IPO exercise, it would be informative to assess the independent effect of each of these elements on the going public process and aftermarket performance (which would result in practical recommendations for future IPO organisation);

- **Isolating Social Media Operations:** As avowed at the outset of the research, its results are somewhat compromised by activities of a non-core character – given the growing transparency of social media issuers (a by-product of regular and in-depth information disclosure) it might soon be feasible to isolate the social media economic factors and analyse them independently.

From a broader socioeconomic perspective, academic work on social media should not ignore the social dimension of these initiatives – including a catalogue of desirable and undesirable outcomes as well as estimates of their monetary impact (cf. Wiśniewski, 2015). Ultimately such studies should lead to a set of recommendations for socially responsible investment in this media genre. Other aspects of this research direction relate to the composition of a social media responsibility index – a form of active or passive ethical screening in investment activity involving asset allocations to social media.

CONCLUSION

Although it would be rash and incautious to judge the full effect of recent flagship initial public offerings (IPOs) by global social media companies, tentative conclusions can be postulated in such a context. They include the need for:

- **More Careful Time Management:** Several social media IPOs appear to have been ill timed – a more propitious timing of many of the flotations would have resulted in improved post-IPO performance and would have been better received by diverse investor classes;
- **Superior IPO Management (Overall):** Recurring book-building, pricing and technical mishaps surrounding the IPOs indicate that more seamless organisation and hands-on focus are requisite for the proper handling of future social media listings;
- **Pre-IPO Integration:** To some extent, the uneasy fortunes of several social media IPOs have arisen from inadequate prior integration of their business models (via organic or external growth); greater emphasis on pre-IPO preparation will go a long way towards minimizing many of the risk factors associated with the social media sector.

REFERENCES

Beatty, R. P., & Ritter, J. R. (1986). Investment Banking, Reputation, and the Underpricing of Initial Public Offerings. *Journal of Financial Economics*, *15*(1-2), 213–232. doi:10.1016/0304-405X(86)90055-3

Bloomberg. (2014). Retrieved April 1, 2014, from http://www.bloomberg.com/markets/stocks/http://www.bloomberg.com/markets/stocks/

Bültmann, R. (2012). Social Media – A Splendid Opportunity for Fund Promoters and Asset Managers, Performance. Bath, UK: Deloitte Financial Services.

Financial Times – Markets/Equities. (2014). Retrieved April 1, 2014, from: http://www.ft.com/intl/markets/equitieshttp://www.ft.com/intl/markets/equities

Harvard Business Review., (2010). *The New Conversation: Taking Social Media from Talk to Action*. Boston, MA: Harvard Business School Publishing.

Ibbotson, R. G., Sindelar, J. L., & Ritter, J. R. (1994). The Market's Problems with the Pricing of Initial Public Offerings. *Journal of Applied Corporate Finance*, *7*(1), 66–74. doi:10.1111/j.1745-6622.1994.tb00395.x

Index Reporting – Solactive Social Media Index. (2014). Solactive AG. Retrieved March 31, 2014, from: http://www.solactive.com/indexing-en/indices/equity/solactive-indices/

Kaske, F., Kugler, M., & Smolnik, S. (2012). Return on Investment in Social Media – Does the Hype Pay Off? Towards an Assessment of the Profitability of Social Media in Organizations. *45th Hawaii International Conference on System Sciences* (pp. 3898-3907). IEEE Computer Society. doi:10.1109/HICSS.2012.504

Le Sourd, V. (2007). *Performance Measurement for Traditional Investment - Literature Survey*. Nice, France: EDHEC Business School.

Lowry, M., Officer, M., & Schwert, G. (2010). The Variability of IPO Initial Returns. *The Journal of Finance, 65*(2), 425–465. doi:10.1111/j.1540-6261.2009.01540.x

MarketWatch. (2014). Retrieved April 1, 2014, from: http://www.marketwatch.com/investing/stocks?link=MW_Nav_INVhttp://www.marketwatch.com/investing/stocks?link=MW_Nav_INV

McGuire, S. (2013). *Social Media and Markets: The New Frontier (whitepaper) GNIP*. Boulder, CO: GNIP.

Radeljic, K. (2013). *Look before you tweet. How asset managers can use social media to their advantage*. New York: EY Financial Services.

Rajan, R., & Servaes, H. (2002). *The Effect of Market Conditions on Initial Public Offerings*. University of Chicago and NBER/London Business School and CEPR.

Shemen, J. (2013). *The Story Behind Social Media Valuations*. Stern School of Business New York University.

Solactive. (2012). *Guideline relating the Solactive Social Media Total Return Index*. Structured Solutions AG.

Solactive. (2015). *Solactive Social Media Index*. Solactive AG.

Stratford, P. (2013). Asset management and social media. In EY EMEIA Asset Management Viewpoint. London: Ernst & Young Global Limited.

Swisher, P., & Kasten, G. W. (2005). *Post-Modern Portfolio Theory*. FPA Journal.

TheCityUK. (2013). *Fund Management*. Retrieved April 1, 2014, from: http://www.thecityuk.com/research/our-work/reports-list/fund-management-2013/http://www.thecityuk.com/research/our-work/reports-list/fund-management-2013/

Wiśniewski, P. (2015). Intellectual Capital (IC) in Social Media Companies: Its Positive and Negative Outcomes. In A. Rospigliosi & S. Greeder (Eds.), *Leading Issues in Social Media* (pp. 71–88). Reading, UK: Academic Conferences & Publishing International.

Yahoo Help Central. (2015). Retrieved October 19, 2015, from https://help.yahoo.com/kb/SLN2347.htmlhttps://help.yahoo.com/kb/SLN2347.html

Yahoo Finance. (2015a). Retrieved October 9, 2015 from: http://finance.yahoo.com/q?s=socl&ql=1

Yahoo Finance. (2015b). Retrieved October 9, 2015, from: http://finance.yahoo.com/http://finance.yahoo.com/

KEY TERMS AND DEFINITIONS

Exchange Traded Fund (ETF): A security replicating an investment asset or a security, a form of passive investment.

Initial Public Offering (IPO): Flotation, listing, debut: the launch of a company on a regulated market.

Portfolio Efficiency: An optimal combination of highest possible returns and lowest possible risks (the latter usually measured through volatility).

ENDNOTE

[1]   The chapter is an elaboration of earlier research contained in the Proceedings of the 2nd European Conference on Social Media 2015: ECSM 2015.

APPENDIX

Facebook, Inc. ("FB"): Initial Public Offering (IPO)

Summary: FB's IPO was conspicuous among social media stocks for ineffective management– the catalogue of failures included: overaggressive pricing despite sagging profitability and cash generation, excessive stock dilution right before the IPO and egregious technical glitches (order execution) on the first day of trading. FB had also been plagued by fundamental pre-IPO weaknesses: low monetisation of its advertising business and concerns about user privacy.

Table 4. FB's IPO facts

Date (dd.mm.yyyy)	18.05.2012	Flotation Price	US$38.00
Stock Exchange	NASDAQ	Daily Price Change*	+0.61%
Initial Market Capitalisation*	US$140.20bn	30 Day Price Change*	-17.34%
Lead Manager	Morgan Stanley	Current price (08.10.2015)	US$92.47

Source: Yahoo! Finance datasets: http://finance.yahoo.com/q?s=fb&ql=1 [retrieved 10 October 2015]. *Based on the flotation price.

Figure 4. FB's share price performance (+143.87%) against the NASDAQ (+74.91%) in May 18, 2012-October 9, 2015 [logarithmic scale]
Source: Yahoo! Finance Interactive Stock Chart: https://beta.finance.yahoo.com/chart/FB [retrieved: 10 October 2015].

Tencent Holdings Limited ("700"): Initial Public Offering (IPO)

Summary: 700's IPO was primarily targeted at institutional investors and – despite being priced at the top of the range – was 158 times oversubscribed. The company (established in 1998 and headquartered in Shenzhen) has morphed into one of the leading Chinese Internet service portals. The IPO derived strength from 700's diversified operations (Internet, mobile, telecommunications, online advertising and other services) and a burgeoning home market.

Table 5. 700's IPO facts

Date (dd.mm.yyyy)	16.06.2004	Flotation Price	HK$3.70
Stock Exchange	Hong Kong Stock Exchange	Daily Price Change*	+12,16%
Initial Market Capitalisation*	HK$6.22bn	30 Day Price Change*	0.00%
Lead Manager	Goldman Sachs	Current price (09.10.2015)	HK$141.90

Source: Yahoo! Finance datasets: http://finance.yahoo.com/q?s=0700.HK [retrieved: 10 October 2015]. *Based on the flotation price.

Figure 5. 700's share price performance (+6400.00%) against the Hong Kong Hang Seng Index (+75.32%) in June 16, 2004-October 9, 2015 [logarithmic scale]
Source: Yahoo! Finance Interactive Stock Chart: https://beta.finance.yahoo.com/quote/0700.HK [retrieved: 10 October 2015].

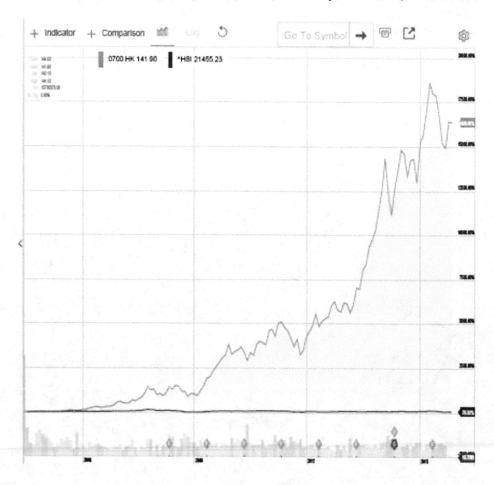

LinkedIn Corporation ("LNKD"): Initial Public Offering (IPO)

Summary: LNKD blazed a trail as a U.S. social media issuer amid concerns of an impending "tech bubble" yet buoyed by an interest from institutions scrambling to develop exposure to the nascent industry. Despite pricing at the high end of underwriters' expectations, demand for LNKD stock was bolstered by an elitist customer base (professionals) and a three-pronged revenue mix: online B2B advertising, premium B2C subscriptions and headhunting tools.

Table 6. LNKD's IPO facts

Date (dd.mm.yyyy)	19.05.2011	Flotation Price	US$45.00
Stock Exchange	New York Stock Exchange	Daily Price Change*	+109.44%
Initial Market Capitalisation*	US$4.5bn	30 Day Price Change*	+41.58%
Lead Manager	Morgan Stanley, Bank of America, and J.P. Morgan Chase	Current price (09.10.2015)	US$195.61

Source: Yahoo! Finance datasets: http://finance.yahoo.com/q?s=fb&ql=1 [retrieved: 10 October 2015]. *Based on the flotation price.

Figure 6. LNKD's share price performance (+109.96%) against the NYSE Composite Index (+20.92%) in 19 May 2011-October 9, 2015 [logarithmic scale]
Source: Yahoo! Finance Interactive Stock Chart https://beta.finance.yahoo.com/chart/LNKD [retrieved: 10 October 2015].

Alphabet Inc. ("GOOG"): Initial Public Offering (IPO)

Summary: GOOG, originally as "Google, Inc.", went public at the low end of pricing expectations and its debut was marred by scepticism over the Dutch auction mechanism of the offering as well as over GOOG's revenue stream and general business model. Few at the time believed in GOOG's ability to corner the search engine market, monetise the online advertising operation and expand via synergic mergers, acquisitions and partnerships.

Table 7. GOOG's IPO facts

Date (dd.mm.yyyy)	19.08.2004	Flotation Price	US$85.00
Stock Exchange	NASDAQ	Daily Price Change*	-41.04%
Initial Market Capitalisation*	US$23.10bn	30 Day Price Change*	-29.86%
Lead Managers	Morgan Stanley, CSFB	Current price (09.10.2015)	+635.14

Source: Yahoo! Finance datasets: http://finance.yahoo.com/q?s=fb&ql=1 [retrieved: 10 October 2015]. *Based on the flotation price.

Figure 7. GOOGL's share price performance (+14.04%) against the NASDAQ (+17.09%) in 19 August 2004-October 9, 2015 [logarithmic scale]
Source: Yahoo! Finance Interactive Stock Chart https://beta.finance.yahoo.com/chart/GOOGL [retrieved: 10 October 2015].

NetEase, Inc. ("NTES"): Initial Public Offering (IPO)

Summary: NTES' IPO faced a tough balancing act amid regulatory hassles (involving the Chinese administration and US watchdogs), choppy profitability and an underperforming secondary market. NTES, operator of China's most popular Internet portal, had initially approached the NASDAQ on 27 March 2000, however, had to pull the plug on its going-public plans. Despite the initial challenges, the ultimate flotation proved successful in the long term.

Table 8. NetEase's IPO facts

Date (dd.mm.yyyy)	30.06.2000	Flotation Price	US$15.50
Stock Exchange	NASDAQ	Daily Price Change*	-21.74%
Initial Market Capitalisation*	US$91.30	30 Day Price Change*	-61.29%
Lead Managers	Merrill Lynch	Current price (09.10.2015)	US$129.16

Source: Yahoo! Finance datasets: http://finance.yahoo.com/q?s=fb&ql=1 [retrieved: 10 October 2015]. *Based on the flotation price.

Figure 8. NTES's share price performance (+4161.30%) against the NASDAQ (+29.03%) in 30 June 2000-October 9, 2015 [logarithmic scale]
Source: Yahoo! Finance Interactive Stock Chart https://beta.finance.yahoo.com/chart/NTES [retrieved: 10 October 2015]

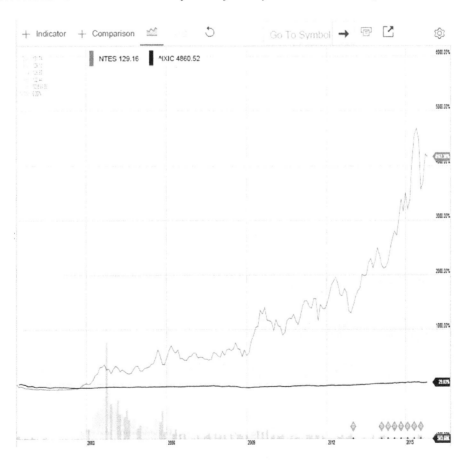

Pandora Media, Inc. ("P"): Initial Public Offering (IPO)

Summary: Demand for the IPO was boosted by a scarce initial free-float of P stock, its close relevance to P's expansion plans, and earlier high-profile social media flotations (including LNKD). In the run-up to the IPO, P had put out a series of solid earnings reports and forecasts. The IPO related risks included high costs of content acquisition and a structural customer shift to mobile applications (where P's visual ads play a lesser role).

Table 9. P's IPO facts

Date (dd.mm.yyyy)	15.06.2011	Flotation Price	US$16.00
Stock Exchange	New York Stock Exchange	Daily Price Change*	+8.88%
Initial Market Capitalisation*	US$2.56bn	30 Day Price Change*	+11.13%
Lead Managers	Morgan Stanley, JP Morgan Chase, Citigroup	Current price (09.10.2015)	US$20.90

Source: Yahoo! Finance datasets: http://finance.yahoo.com/q?s=fb&ql=1 [retrieved: 10 October 2015]. *Based on the flotation price.

Figure 9. P's share price performance (+55.97%) against the NYSE Composite Index (+26.32%) in 15 June 2011-October 9, 2015 [logarithmic scale]
Source: Yahoo! Finance Interactive Stock Chart https://beta.finance.yahoo.com/chart/P [retrieved: 10 October 2015].

Sina Corporation ("SINA"): Initial Public Offering (IPO)

Summary: SINA, the Chinese microblogging website akin to Twitter, managed to squeak through its IPO yet ended up raising less capital than planned amid souring sentiment towards technology issuers, concerns over Chinese censorship and anticipated competition from its industrial peers. SINA had displayed robust top line growth, however, its active user numbers had been disappointing and its profitability outlook seemed questionable.

Table 10. SINA's IPO facts

Date (dd.mm.yyyy)	17.04.2000	Flotation Price	US$17.00
Stock Exchange	NASDAQ	Daily Price Change*	+18.41%
Initial Market Capitalisation*	US$3.50bn	30 Day Price Change*	+127.24%
Lead Managers	Morgan Stanley, China International Capital Corporation	Current price (20.10.2015)	US$45.88

Source: Yahoo! Finance datasets: http://finance.yahoo.com/q?s=fb&ql=1 [retrieved: 20 October 2015]. *Based on the flotation price.

Figure 10. SINA's share price performance (+133.78%) against the NASDAQ (+42.92%) in 17 April 2000 – 20 October 2015 [logarithmic scale]
Source: Yahoo! Finance Interactive Stock Chart https://beta.finance.yahoo.com/chart/SINA [retrieved: 10 October 2015].

Yahoo! Inc. ("YHOO"): Initial Public Offering (IPO)

Summary: YHOO's IPO soared in initial trading despite serious concerns about the company's fundamentals and long-term profitability (it was operating at a net loss at the time and was warning about its future earnings outlook). Besides, analysts were cautioning investors against a repetition of the lacklustre IPOs by YHOO's direct competitors (Excite and Lycos), however, YHOO's brand appeared to be stronger and the company was being financed by Softbank.

Table 11. YHOO's IPO facts

Date (dd.mm.yyyy)	12.04.1996	Flotation Price	US$13.00
Stock Exchange	NASDAQ	Daily Price Change*	+153.85%
Initial Market Capitalisation*	US$1.00bn	30 Day Price Change*	-3.08%
Lead Managers	Goldman Sachs	Current price (09.10.2015)	US$32.52

Source: Yahoo! Finance datasets: http://finance.yahoo.com/q?s=fb&ql=1 [retrieved: 10 October 2015]. *Based on the flotation price.

Figure 11. YHOO's share price performance (+2522.58%) against the NASDAQ (+288.48%) in 12 April 1996-October 9, 2015 [logarithmic scale]
Source: Yahoo! Finance Interactive Stock Chart https://beta.finance.yahoo.com/chart/YHOO [retrieved: 10 October 2015].

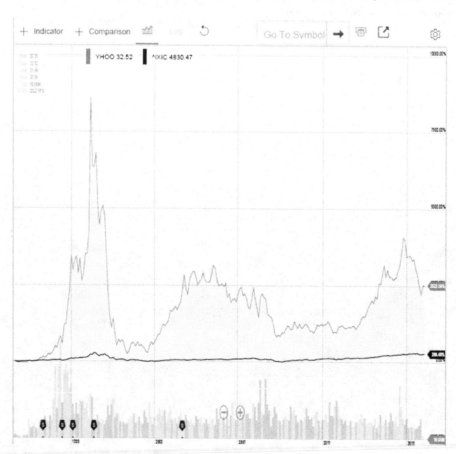

Yandex N.V. ("YNDX"): Initial Public Offering (IPO)

Summary: YNDX beat market expectations by raising 19% more than the target issue in the largest US based IPO since that of GOOG in 2004. The investors were transfixed by the potential locked in Russia's booming market for Internet services and a euphoric debut by LNKD just a couple of days earlier. On the fundamental side, the favourable outlook for YNDX stock was tied to the company's dominant position among search engines operating in Russia.

Table 12. YNDX's IPO facts

Date (dd.mm.yyyy)	23.05.2011	Flotation Price	US$25.00
Stock Exchange	NASDAQ	Daily Price Change*	+55.36%
Initial Market Capitalisation*	US$11.20b	30 Day Price Change*	+24.68%
Lead Managers	Morgan Stanley, Deutsche Bank, Goldman Sachs	Current price (09.10.2015)	US$12.37

Source: Yahoo! Finance datasets: http://finance.yahoo.com/q?s=YNDX [retrieved: 20 October 2015]. *Based on the flotation price.

Figure 12. YNDX's share price performance (-60.73%) against the NASDAQ (+73.78%) in 23 May 1996-October 9, 2015 [logarithmic scale]
Source: Yahoo! Finance Interactive Stock Chart https://beta.finance.yahoo.com/chart/YNDX [retrieved: 10 October 2015].

Yandex N.V. (YNDX) ★ Watchlist
13.53 -0.07(-0.51%) NASDAQ As of 4:00PM EDT

Chapter 2

Strategic Role of Consumer Moments of Truth:
A Marketing Challenge in Mobile Communities

Lukasz Lysik
Wroclaw University of Economics, Poland

Robert Kutera
Wroclaw University of Economics, Poland

Karol Lopacinski
Wrocław University of Economics, Poland

Piotr Machura
Wroclaw University of Economics, Poland

ABSTRACT

Contemporary consumers obtained many possibilities to search for goods and they are very active in this field. Although specialists know that it's difficult to state how, where this process of search takes place. Multi-channel market place is a very complex environment where brand battle for the customer attention. This chapter helps to understand consumer behaviour and reveals many facts concerning mobile and social world of marketing. The authors present the idea of micromoments and their place in the mobile and social channel of communication with the market. Among definitions and examples explaining the idea of micromoments Authors also try to answer questions that can help to understand how micromoments should be handled. Main aim of this chapter is to present behaviour of a modern consumer and factors influencing his decisions as being a part of mobile consumer communities.

INTRODUCTION

Behaviours, needs, expectations and decisions of modern consumer are progressively evolving along with technological and civilization development. Consumers are more aware of their purchasing decisions and take them on the basis of careful analysis and assessment of alternatives. They don't want to play a passive role of people buying products and services and evolving into the active prosumers.

DOI: 10.4018/978-1-5225-0559-4.ch002

This market trend is largely caused by the development and popularization of social media and mobile technologies that are redefining the previous models of consumer behaviour. The increasing flow of information, growth in significance of mobile communities, access to information anytime and anywhere meant that consumer behaviour has become more and more complex, and the decision-making process began to consist of increasing number of steps as well as took the form of the consumer journey.

The success of modern companies largely depends on their correct identification of such changes and timely adjustment of their marketing strategies to those changes as well as the improvement of their marketing communication with customers. Therefore, the modern company should lay emphasis on consumer behaviour research at various stages of the consumer journey. A very useful in this case may be the moments of truth (MOTs) concept, which directly arise from the popularization of mobile technology and social media. The concept of MOTs based on interactions in buyer-seller relationships. These moments build value to the customer, which may result in the subsequent sale. Thus, companies and marketers should interact with the consumer to create added value for her/him, to support her/him in the consumer journey and provide active support in their decision making process.

This is possible thanks to the correct identification and analysis of various types of factors, that in conditions of pervasive mobile technologies, influence on purchasing decisions within various stages of consumer journey. This requires market researching, analysing of the latest consumer trends, and based on this proposing new approaches and classifications. Therefore, within the chapter is presented an authorial model which includes technical and behavioural factors affecting on purchasing behaviour in mobile communities in the context of the individual MOTs.

Moreover, the authors analyzed a model in the context of the latest trend in consumer behaviour, which is based on the so-called micromoments. Micromoments largely enrich the MOTs concept and at the same time create significant challenges for companies and their marketing activities at mobile channels.

Therefore, the purpose of the chapter is to show the extent of the behaviour changes of modern consumers who actively use modern technologies and create mobile community. These changes will be discussed in detail in the context of the concept of consumer's moments-of-truth and micromoments and their impact on the shape of today's marketing strategies. The authors present how social and mobile technologies shaped the consumer purchasing process, as well as explain why the MOTs and micromoments concepts are so important for today's businesses marketing strategies. It is also shown how companies should adapt to new realities by shaping their marketing strategies and communication and sales objectives.

BACKGROUND

Consumer behaviour and their decisions are gradually evolving along with progressive technological and civilization development. Growing awareness of consumer rights, more transparent market and global competition make it more important for consumers to make purchasing decisions consciously, based on the analysis and assessment of possible offers.

The increasing number of sources from which they retrieve the information, makes, however, that consumers come into contact with more and more different kinds of stimuli. Hence, these stimuli may encourage consumers to impulsive purchase, especially for fast moving consumer goods (FMCG's) and services. On the other hand, in the case of the more important purchasing decisions, when the process is taking longer, consumers are exposed to stimuli for a longer period of time and under different situations. Contemporary marketing strategy should take into account recent changes in consumer behaviours, defined as "the dynamic interaction of affect and cognition, behaviour, and the environment by which human beings conduct the exchange aspects of their lives" (Bynum, 2008).

Since the first pulse (stimulus, needs, desires) consumer is guided along the purchase funnel, consisting of four steps (Barry, 1987):

- **Awareness:** The consumer is aware of a product or service,
- **Interest:** Consumer actively expresses interest,
- **Desire:** Consumer feels the need to purchase,
- **Action:** Execution of the action towards purchasing the chosen product or service.

New media, technologies and the increasing flow of information caused the purchase funnel to be composed of ever greater number of steps (including the stimulus before the first stage and loyalty after purchasing), and the consumer decision-making process took the form of "The Consumer Journey" (Court, Elzinga, Mulder & Vetvik, 2009).

Every day, consumers come into contact with all sorts of advertisements on television, radio, newspapers and the Internet. These stimuli may, however, lose their impact if the consumer does not take any direct decision towards the purchase (does not start the consumer journey). The complexity of the consumer journey in the digital age was discussed in Harvard Business Review by Edelman D.C. (Edelman, 2010). As early as 2010 Edelman noted that instead of focusing on how to allocate spending across media, marketers should target the stages in the decision journey.

What, however, in the case in which the company skillfully planning their activities in order to provide the right stimuli at the right moments? The cumulative effect of impressions (spot on TV, radio advertising, newsletter, animated web banner ads in web browser) may in this case play a strategic role in influencing consumer's behaviour.

Universality of technology and mobile devices caused that the consumers often have the device (smartphones, tablets) they can use anywhere, at any time, with access to the Internet and countless sources of information. It is thanks to mobile devices, that businesses and marketers have gained the tools to influence the consumer the exactly right moment. By using geolocation, we can accurately determine the user's position and display marketing message given to him only when he is in a location such as near the restaurant. On the other hand, the prevalence of social technologies (e.g. applications associated with social media, social login using an existing account at social networking site such as Facebook, Twitter or Google+) allows for the precise targeting of users, as users consciously (or unconsciously, but accepting the terms of the agreement) share with companies their personal information – such as favorite pages on social media, viewed videos liked places, their age, sex, geographical location and other information – depending on what conditions they agreed to. It is in fact a convenience for the consumer (one quick login for multiple applications), but at the expense of losing some privacy (payment for the convenience is made by providing data and personal information).

The number of touch points with the consumer increased with the development of new technologies, which raised the need for a structured approach to MOTs. The concept of MOTs is based on interactions in buyer-seller relationships (Shanker, 2008). These moments build value to the customer, which may result in the subsequent sale. Companies and marketers should interact with the consumers to create added value for them, to support them in the consumer journey and provide active support in their decision making process.

B. Solis describes the four essential moments for consumer behaviour (Solis, 2013):

1. **Zero Moment of Truth (ZMOT):** Presented by Google, focuses on what users will find on the Internet after searching, which was initiated by the stimulus. It is also important to enrich the information consumers find with directions to the next steps, which may lead him to the purchase funnel closure (e.g. a form on the website or quick navigation to point of sale).
2. **First Moment of Truth (FMOT):** Presented by Procter & Gamble (P&G), focuses on what consumers think and how they react to a product or service in direct contact with the product or service. It's their feeling about the product and the moment in which their expectations are faced with the actual receipt of the product. This is the moment in which a well-designed package can turn a visitor into a consumer.
3. **Second Moment of Truth (SMOT):** This is another moment resulting from reflections of P & G's. It focuses on what people feel, they see, hear and experience using the product over time. Significant here is the after-sales phase, including consumer support that can build a long lasting relationship with the consumer.
4. **Ultimate Moment of Truth (UMOT):** A moment introduced by B. Solis, emphasizes the importance of sharing information and experiences with other consumers. It also describes the problem of creating these moments, their planning, rather than as a reaction to information coming from consumers. It should be emphasized that it is UMOT can be ZMOT for the next consumer.

Thanks to smartphones and tablets consumers have gained permanent access to information and social media, while the companies – to some extent – permanent access to consumers. The era of digitization, democracy and plurality of the media caused that the users themselves choose which communication channels they want to use and how. Some people still remember the times without the Internet and mobile devices, we should, however, realize that for a growing number of consumers those facilities were "always". Modern consumers live in both real and virtual world, and they treat Internet and mobile technologies as an extension of reality, and not as a medium (Jerin, 2015). Their main characteristic is that they allow interacting in real time, so that consumers can comment, seek information and express their opinions, regardless of place and time.

Robertus T.H. claims that social media has a significant contribution for customer in decision-making process because many information and recommendation are provided by social media (Robertus, 2015). Therefore, involvement is social and mobile technologies can affect the consumer's opinion, behaviour or even interest. Knowledge and efficient use of MOTs should be one of the major areas of concern of the modern companies. It allows for full utilization of the potential of mobile consumer communities.

INFLUENCE OF CONSUMER BEHAVIOUR ON MARKETING STRATEGY

Contemporary companies are forced to compete in a global marketspace (more just than traditional physical marketplace, containing also virtual spaces for electronic business) by gathering and retaining satisfied customers and adapting to continuously changing market conditions. Given the above-mentioned situation managers should concentrate on planning and building the short- and long-term strategies to shape the company's businesses in order to meet market expectations. This applies both to company's internal business processes shaping as well as its cooperation with the external economic environment.

Between the company's overall strategy and marketing there are two-way relationships: marketing plays an important role in shaping of the strategy by providing a leading philosophy and input for strategic planning. It helps to identify attractive market opportunities and evaluate potential ways of their use. What is more, the major part of company's strategy deals with marketing variables – market share, market development and growth – these areas of interest overlap in both types of activities. determines the needs of customers and the company's ability to satisfy them, and these factors determine the mission and goals of the company.

On the other hand, the strategy establishes the role of marketing in the organization and is the starting point for the planning of marketing activities. Marketing strategies refer to actions aimed at achieving the objectives of the customer's satisfaction. The company may however formulate other purposes. In particular, it refers to companies whose objectives may focus on aspects of the development, increasing its value, creating capital groups or business alliances. A marketing strategy can be very loosely associated with the overall company strategy. What is more, in the case of separate business units of larger companies their independency can cause that they create their own marketing strategies. It is another matter when it comes to small companies where it can often be observed a cross-fertilisation between their overall development strategy and marketing strategy.

According to Kotler, the marketing strategy is "the way in which the marketing function organises its activities to achieve a profitable growth in sales at a marketing mix level" (Mongay, 2006). Marketers in the process of defining marketing strategies have to use customer-centric solutions (like Lauterborn's 4C (Lauterborn, 1990): customer value – the value for the customer, cost – the cost of which shall be borne by the customer, convenience – the convenience of purchasing, and communication – communication with the market) rather than traditional product-oriented marketing mix tools, the P's—product, place, price, and promotion. It led to the significant reorganization of the marketing function into complementary specialties, allowing focus on each element of the 4C and alignment with the customer's purchase journey (Ettenson, Corado, Knowles & Rethinking, 2013).

In other words, the marketing strategy should be defined as a short- or long-term plan to achieve the organisation's objectives, which includes selection of resources that should be allocated within marketing activities and ways of use these resources to take advantage of expected opportunities.

An important part of marketing strategy is answer to four important questions:

1. Where the company operates? Detailed market analysis and its segmentation for company's purposes, with indicating the most important segments for company's activity.
2. To whom the company wants to sell? Target groups' description, identification of customer segments and criteria of their evaluation, customers' needs, their pains and gains that need to be addressed through the company's value proposition; customer archetypes or personas, to understand the traits of the customer.
3. Who and to what extent is competitor on the market? Identification of other entities acting on the market, analysis of how others respond to the needs of the target group.
4. What is the value of company's offer? Description of the ingredients of the offer, what distinguish it – a clear and compelling reason why the product or service is different and worth buying, determination of pricing policy.

Marketing strategy should take into account recent changes in consumer behaviour. They concern all pre-purchase activities, purchase decisions and post-purchase behaviour in the marketplace of products or services. These behaviours are influenced by many factors of different kind.

Cultural factors as a whole spiritual and material heritage of society, customs, beliefs and patterns of behaviour handed down from generation to generation, have a big impact on consumption patterns of individual consumers and groups. The globalization of culture resulted in the creation of patterns of global consumption. The worldwide process of unifying patterns of consumption is caused by increased mobility of consumers who are learning from other cultures. On the other hand it is a result of the activities of global companies who are directing a unified offer to different cultural groups, affecting their experiences and purchasing preferences.

Social factors influence consumption too. People want to accentuate their social status and belonging to certain groups more than a few decades ago (Bynum, 2008). Consumers are sensitive to the demonstration effect, which makes them feel part of a particular group of reference or can differentiate and emphasize their individuality. The mere act of purchasing has gained social dimension and often goes hand in hand with satisfying such needs as interpersonal networking or spending leisure time with family and friends. Demographic factors affecting consumer behaviour patterns are: the age and stage of family life cycle. Consumers representing certain demographic group behave in a different way than others groups. It can also be observed a trend of changing roles in the household in making purchasing decisions. Very important is also the role of children in the process of purchasing specific products and services dedicated for adults (Lindstrom, 2009) (e.g. car industry, travelling).

Educational factors are also affecting consumer behaviour. Better educated citizens become consumers, who are aware of their rights and who can take advantage of available information to acquire high quality assets maximizing perceived value at a reasonable price. He or she is also more willing to share knowledge and experience with other users and companies. They also have abilities to use modern ICT tools to support them in making purchase decisions.

Consumer revenues is an economical factor influencing consumer behaviours. In developed countries there has been a long-term trend of growing prosperity. With an increasing number of people with incomes higher than the average, the structure of household expenditures is changing. The share of expenditures on food is decreasing while the share of expenditure on higher needs (leisure activities, health, luxury products and services) is increasing. At the same time there is a noticeable trend of polarization of revenues – making a gap between the most and least well paid.

The psychological factors that influence an individual's decision to make a purchase are categorized into the individual's motivations, perceptions, learning and his or hers beliefs and attitudes. A person can be motivated to buy a product for convenience, for style, for prestige, for self-pride or being at par with others (Yakup, 2014). Perception is how consumers understand the world around them based on information received through their senses. In response to stimulus, consumers subconsciously evaluate their needs and expectations, and then they use such an evaluation to select, organize and interpret the stimulus (Jablonski, Yakup, 2012). In every circumstance people's perception is conditioned by their prior experience (learning) and they seek to maintain balance or consistency by relating to and interpreting new stimuli in terms of past or learned stimuli (Blythe, 2008). Beliefs as well as attitudes are generally well-anchored in the individual's mind and are difficult to change as they are the basic part of their personality. It's important to understand, identify and analyze the positive attitudes and beliefs but also the negative ones that consumers can have on a brand or product. When the negative ones appears, companies should adjust their marketing activities in order to get consumers to change their product/ brand perception (Perreau, 2013).

These all factors connected with globalization and technical development cause that a change observed in consumer behaviour, the demand side of the market, has resulted in a change in the competitive strategy of firms, the supply side of the market (Clemons, 2008). They have to deal with such consumer trends as:

1. **Informed Consumer:** Well-educated and open to new experiences consumers, being aware of the potential of Internet and other ICT technologies, can use them practically during the entire process of making purchase decisions. More and more popular is also multichannel communication for gathering different kinds of information, making a purchase or leaving a post-purchase feedback.
2. **Engaged Consumer:** Modern consumers gradually depart from the typical pattern of passive receptors of purchased goods and services, and evolve into active prosumers. They not only make conscious and deliberate choices of goods and services as well as time, place and manner of purchase, but also play an active role in product design and marketing campaigns (Łysik, Kutera & Machura, 2014). Engaged consumer should be treated as a partner by company, which can make the use of his/her input.
3. **Pragmatic Consumer:** Consumers are becoming experts in search of information about the products and their acquisition. They expect attractive offers at affordable prices they monitor the market in search of good opportunities. The economic crisis motivated consumers to adopt more sustainable behaviour.
4. **Ecological Consumer:** The modern consumer is aware of the impact of human activity on the environment and they see the need to actively protect the earth's resources. Increasing importance is also attributed to the influence of external factors such as diet and lifestyle on the physical and mental condition.
5. **Mobile Consumer:** Consumers equipped with smart mobile devices have instant access to different electronic services. Such a situation cause that there is a need to ensure them the multichannel customer service 24 hours per day and 7 days per week. There is also a great opportunity for companies to use location-based and time-limited marketing offers.

Summarizing the specification of consumer trends it can be said that the objectives of companies, as well as motivations of individual consumers doesn't change so much in relation to previous market conditions – but a huge change can be observed in the scale of information and services available to all consumers. The richness of information sources ensure that everyone can find proper information of any type from official and unofficial sources, via different communication channels. The easy and effortless access to rich, up-to-date and accurate information has enabled consumers to make better choices based on many decision factors; if something they want is available in the marketspace, consumers now truly can and will find and purchase it, if the price is right. On the other hand, when consumers are able to optimize their choices, firms can now optimize their selection of offerings. Consumer choice drives corporate selection, corporate selection drives consumer choice, and both are driven by greatly enhanced information (Clemons, 2008).

Customer-centric marketing strategies should take into account recent phenomena and concepts associated with consumer behaviour. The impact of social media and mobile technology, as the leading technologies in recent years, on consumer behaviour manifests itself primarily in a personal character of contact with the company (personal mobile devices, personal profiles on social networking sites), spontaneity and immediacy. In addition, these technologies generate huge collections of heterogeneous data possible for the processing with big data technologies. These features should be taken into account when formulating a strategic action plan.

In the following sections mentioned changes in consumer behaviour will be discussed in detail in the context of the concept of consumer's moments-of-truth and micromoments and their impact on the shape of today's marketing strategies.

TECHNICAL AND BEHAVIOURAL FACTORS OF INFLUENCE ON CONSUMER BEHAVIOUR IN MOBILE COMMUNITIES ENVIRONMENT

The development of social and mobile technologies has caused that new concepts of consumer behaviour patterns have to be introduced and popularized. Alongside conventional factors described in the previous section of the chapter identifiable are also additional factors resulting from the technological environment of mobile communities. These factors shown in relation to stages of purchase decision-making process are basic part of model of consumer behaviour in mobile communities.

In this model the following kinds of factors are distinguished (Łysik, Kutera & Machura, 2014, November):

- Technical, related to offering innovative tools as well as social and mobile services,
- Behavioural, connected with the changes in the manner of performance of particular activities within the phases of purchase behaviours of the members of mobile consumer communities.

These factors, within the proposed framework, could be separated into factors (Łysik, Kutera & Machura, 2014, November):

- Having impact throughout the whole purchase process, irrespective of its particular stages (shared factors),
- Having impact only on its selected stages and demonstrating a significant relation with actions and decisions occurring at a given stage (Figure 1).

The first stage of each purchasing process is a stimulus, an initial factor that comes either from the close proximity network (social media) or from mobile communication channels. This is a time when a consumer run the process of initial consideration of a potential purchase. The next phase, and the most influenced by social and mobile technologies, is the phase of active evaluation and ZMOT. Consumer conducts in-depth analysis of the expected product or service – both through push-type information or through pull-type search for information and evaluate different propositions. The value of each of them depends on completeness and richness of information, source credibility, availability of users' reviews and opinions etc., that are delivered especially through social media, supported by mobile channels. After that the act of purchase take place (FMOT) and then the post-purchase behaviours (SMOT). In these two phases, the predominance of mobile technologies is evident, and social media play a supportive role. Proper combination of the two elements results in purchase closure and, at the same time, limits the extent of post-purchase dissonance (Łysik, Kutera & Machura, 2014). Important parts of the model are also loops back to earlier stages and choosing the right path depends on good or bad previous experiences in purchasing process.

As mentioned above, there are some factors that are present at each of the consumer decision process, including 5 behavioural and 5 technical factors.

Figure 1. Technical and behavioural factors in the original model of purchase behaviours of the members of mobile consumer communities
Source: Łysik, Kutera and Machura, 2014, November.

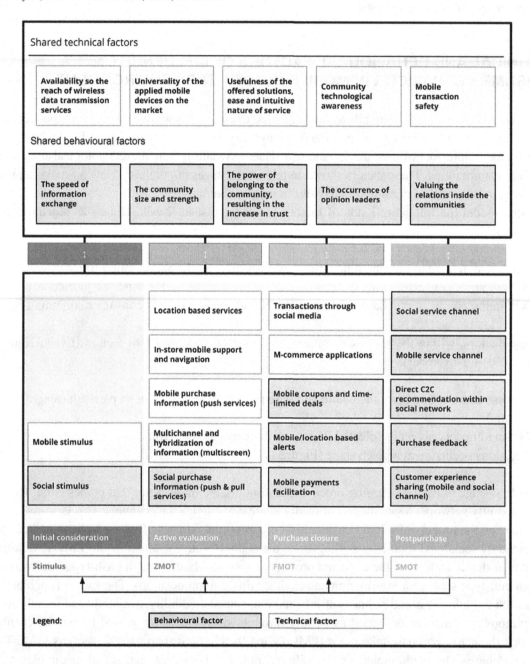

Among the shared technical factors can be distinguished:

- Availability of wireless data transmission services, that allow to freely communicate with one another and have mutual impact on purchase behaviours in a manner very convenient for consumers,
- Popularity of mobile devices influence the reach and extent of relations inside mobile consumer communities and the nature of relations taking place,

- Usefulness of the offered solutions for the end user (properly designed graphic interfaces, careful selection of information architecture), causing that users use them more willingly and more often,
- Technological awareness of the society directly defines the potential number of individuals who can belong to mobile communities, because the more technologically aware persons will be in the society, the more potential inter-consumer relations may take place,
- Mobile transaction safety is connected with awareness and trust towards the securities offered, as well as ensuring a safety to sensitive personal data.

On the other hand, shared behavioural factors group include:

- Pace of information exchange, which helps consumer to look at the product of his/her interest from various points of view and create a better picture of what he/she is looking for and assess, compare with his/her expectations,
- Quantity and impact strength of a given community, which cause that the information transferred gains better quality,
- Power of belonging to the community, where purchase decisions are to a bigger and bigger extent determined by relations and opinions created during the relation between the members of mobile communities,
- Occurrence of leaders, whose opinion has the biggest impact on purchase decisions by evaluating propositions, suggesting where to look for and how to gain more valuable information, which finally results in taking a more conscious purchase decision,
- Valuing relations, which are not equally important to consumers, as they choose, who is becoming an authority for them, usually persons from the closest environment inspire bigger trust than even the most recognized specialist.

Some technical factors have impact only at particular stages of the decision-making process of members of mobile communities.

Purchase decision process could be initiated by a mobile stimulus that may be in the form of a graphic advertisement, contextual text advertisement or the notification from the native mobile application. It may directly lead to the sales transaction or initiate further processes of the decision-making process.

At the ZMOT stage, the services using geolocation allow the consumers to easily search for information about the products and services located in a given geographic area. Mobile support and in-store navigation allows the access to more comprehensive information (technical data, video review) by means of the extended reality or help in the navigation around the store, using the current location of the consumer. Mobile purchase information (push services) is delivered to the consumer immediately at the moment of emission of this information by a given company and often include information about current promotions. The multi-channel nature and hybridization of information enable the transfer of the message simultaneously at various devices that the consumer uses. This results in the occurrence of the effect of synergy and accumulation of parallel messages due to which a given offer and/or brand becomes more recognizable for a consumer.

At the FMOT stage social transactions can take place, which are based on the use of social media and mobile consumer community networks in e-commerce transaction processes. For example, f-commerce service enables to make purchase transactions using Facebook mechanisms and the user actions are shared within the framework of the community, owing to which friends receive recommendations regarding products purchased by virtual friends. M-commerce applications enable the access to e-commerce services offered by smartphone, tablet and other mobile devices. As a result, the purchase procedure regarding a given product or service is streamlined and shortened, among others, owing to the application of the possibility of the use of mobile payments.

There are also identified a set of factors of behavioural nature, which occur dominantly only at selected stages of this process.

At the first stage of this process the occurrence of a social stimulus is a very important factor, which takes the form of a direct or indirect interaction with another member of the community or even with the group, on the basis of which a new need arose or the information about a new product was obtained. It may also come from recommendation mechanisms built in the social networking services.

At the ZMOT stage, with social purchase information coming from consumer social network it makes a significant change of the direction of search and assessment criteria. Purchase information may take the one-direction push or the pull form that mobilizes the recipient to perform given feedback.

FMOT stage is also influenced by some behavioural factors. Mobile voucher or a time limited transaction promotional offer to the consumer force the consumer to make a decision in real time and in the conditions of surprise and the lack of possibility of in-depth analysis of the offer conditions. In addition, at this stage, with the use of geolocation technology, particular messages – alerts based on location – may be sent to mobile consumers staying in defined space. Offering mobile payment systems allows for quick and easy finalization of the transaction at any place and time, shortening the whole purchase procedure, replacing traditional, more time-consuming payment forms.

Social channel of consumer service should be also considered as the factor of behavioural nature that influence especially on post-purchase experience (SMOT). Owing to social media tools it is possible to discuss with the consumer, listen to his/her needs and expectations and solve his/her problems with the consumption of the product or the service. Thanks to it there is possible to build positive consumer experience and loyalty. Simultaneously or alternatively a mobile channel could be used. Facilities in the form of dedicated mobile applications or mobile website versions oriented at customer service make the consumer gain new communication possibilities at any place and time.

Innovative customer service channels at the same time constitute a perfect tool for gathering post-purchase feedback. Consumers have their opinions on purchase procedure and product usage and share it with the company or other consumers. Feedback published via social media, have emotional load and correlated with the context in the form of data from the social networking service profile of a given consumer and comments and discussions under the entry brings a significant value for the company. The importance of high quality feedback within the framework of the mobile service channel, frequently gained in spontaneous situations and not burdened with the previous analysis of the transfer of given information, is worth emphasizing.

On-line social networks and tools helps in transferring direct C2C recommendations, positive or negative ones. They come from identified individuals and are much more credible than commercial information. It most often takes place by publishing and sharing one's opinion regarding previous cooperation with the offeror in social media, consumer portals or at the company website.

The model presented in the chapter covers the whole decision-making process and illustrate what factors are influencing it as well as at what stage these factors occur. In the meantime, some new concepts are developed. The most important seems to be another Google concept, extending the Google's MOTs concept – micromoments. The new Google's idea is close to author's concept of presented technical and behavioural factors, so it is worth considering what has been changed.

MICROMOMENTS: NEW MODEL OF MOBILE CONSUMER BEHAVIOURS AND A BIG CHALLENGE FOR BUSINESS

Mobile revolution, which can be observed for several years, is gaining momentum year-on-year and poses new challenges for business. Mobile devices have become an indispensable tool in the everyday life of consumers. It is also important that modern smartphones and tablets have growing possibilities so in many areas of private and professional life they begin to replace computers and laptops. Accordingly, the number of very active, or even addicted mobile users regularly increases. This is confirmed by global researches (Khalaf, 2014) regarding the use of mobile tools. They show that in 2013–2014 the number of users addicted to mobile applications ie. those who use them more than 60 times per day noticed a 123% rise (from 79 million to 176 million users). The number of users who use mobile applications less frequently, ie. 16-60 times per day was in 2014 as much as 55% higher (from 283 million to 440 million users). Also in the least active group, whose representatives open applications less than 16 times per day noticed a 23% growth (from 639 million to 784 million users).

Moreover, researches (Lanoue, 2015) show that the persisting development of the mobile market and increasing usage of mobile devices have a significant impact on how we use of such tools as well as shape the behaviours of their users. The number of websites visited through mobile devices grew by 20% in 2014 compared with the previous year. On the other hand, the average duration for that type of visits decreased by 18%. In addition remarkable fact that the conversion rate for mobile rise as much as 29% in the same period of time. The model of mobile users behaviours is changing very fast and companies should take it into consideration, draw conclusions and adapt to new realities.

Consumers live faster and faster, obtaining product information in real time from anywhere. They also make purchasing decisions in another way. Instead of a long browsing available offers, consumers more and more often swap these search for short but frequent web browsing using mobile devices. They do it in every free moment, wherever they currently are.

Thus, mobile technologies have led to revolutionary changes in the modern consumer journey smashing it into tens, hundreds and sometimes even thousands of so-called micromoments. They occur at various times and places, but ultimately they contribute to make specific purchase decisions.

Micromoments are usually short user interactions with tools such as a browser or mobile application. They are highly dispersed in time and can last a few seconds or more, but in the whole day may add up to even few hours. Micromoments aim to rapidly respond to different needs and therefore four basic types of them can be distinguished (Etherington, 2015):

- I-want-to-know-moments,
- I-want-to-go-moments,
- I-want-to-do-moments,
- I-want-to-buy-moments.

I-want-to-know-moments arise from the need to quickly acquire a knowledge about products, brands, ads, etc. These are the moments in which mobile users are looking for information that will help them make different types of decisions, including purchasing decisions. Decision-making process of the modern consumer looks completely different than it was a few years ago. The search for the best offer is no longer based on several hours of searching for information on a laptop with Internet access. Instead, the consumers in their spare time repeatedly reach for smartphone and find pieces of information that in the long term make up the desired answer.

For example, Luke wants to spend your next vacation in Tuscany, Italy. He wants to rent a house and a car. Because there is still five months to the holiday he decides to organize everything in detail. Luke is very busy, but during any free time (during lunch on the train, standing in a traffic jam, in the waiting room at the doctor) he takes his smartphone out and look for the most attractive offers on the Internet. He visits websites with offers of houses for rent, verifies the prices on price comparison websites, reads reviews about the regions of Tuscany on Internet forums, checks the assessments of chosen houses, looks for information about the weather, checks cars in the area and compares prices of flights by plane in various airlines. Finally, after two weeks and tens of several minutes micromoments Luke is pretty sure that the most suitable to his needs offer is small, lastly renovated house with a large terrace and swimming pool. House is located in Asciano in very recommended by Internet users region of Tuscany. Besides in this tourist resort you can cheaply rent a car as well as visit many restaurants recommended on culinary and touristic forums.

I-want-to-go-moments are moments where we want or have to go somewhere and we need immediate information about the interesting locations. The easiest way to obtain this type of information is a mobile device enabled geolocation, installed map and GPS navigation.

For example, Yvonne visited her friends who live in Paris. She did not know the city but being in the downtown she decided to go for lunch, then visit a shopping mall with designer fashion shops. She pulled smartphone out of her handbag and checked which vegetarian restaurants are close to her. She chose the one that was the most recommended by the Internet users, and then she went there directed by GPS navigation. During the lunch she checked how to get to the biggest shopping mall in the centre of Paris. Being there she used her smartphone once again in order to download the application with an interactive map which that eased her to find her favorite stores and brands.

I-want-to-do-moments arise from the need to obtain a rapid and useful information and advice on how to do things, e.g. to repair, install, cook, etc. During such type of moments, mobile users expect immediate assistance regardless of whether they are (at home, in the car or on the beach on vacation, etc.). The easiest way is drawing a smartphone from the pocket, typing in search phrases like "how to do something" and quick solving the current problem.

As an example, Thomas is in his garage and he wants to change the oil in his motorcycle as well as install the new silencer that he bought the day before. It turns out to be more difficult than he thought. There is no laptop in the garage, so he unlocks his smartphone, runs youtube.com and enters the search phrase "how to mount a Ixil silencer in the motorcycle Suzuki GSR". It turns out that the silencer manufacturer posted a video with instructions, which is very helpful. Thomas mounts the silencer according to instructions, and then he reviews motorcycle enthusiasts internet forum where they describe the details of how to change the oil.

I-want-to-buy-moments are associated with making the purchase decision, comparison of offers (often in the traditional place of sale), or making the purchase. These moments occur when the mobile user is sure that he or she wants to buy something right now, no matter where they are currently located.

It is important to note that I-want-to-buy moments are quite similar to the I-want-to know moments. Both of them are related to making a purchasing decision. However, in the first case the decision is made rather in the long-term perspective and leads to the gradual increase of knowledge about the product or service. In the second case, the purchasing decision is more spontaneous and more dependent on the context in which the consumer currently is.

As an example, Jacob went camping with friends for the weekend. On Sunday, it appears that his tablet is completely discharged, and nearby there is no electrical outlet. Jacob is very unhappy because he was waiting for important email from parents. Besides, he wanted to browse Facebook. Jacobs' friend said that he can borrow him an external charger so-called powerbank, which is able to completely charge tablet even up to five times. Jacob didn't know about this type of device so far. He is so impressed that he decides to buy it as soon as possible. Using the tablet he enters the products comparison websites and checks the prices and technical specifications for this type of equipment. In addition, he reads the users' opinions and their assessments. Finally he selects the product of Samsung with a capacity of 10,000 mAh. The next step is quick purchase in the online store. The entire purchasing process took less than half an hour.

Multitude, the frequency and variety of micromoments in consumers' everyday life cause that they redefine and enrich principles of consumer behaviour defined within the concept of MOTs. Extending this concept by separating the specific micromoments within the consumer journey gives the company new opportunities in reaching to the customers and shaping theirs behaviours.

Micromoments should be treated very seriously by companies because their existence is not accidental but very often a result of the consumer's involvement, aimed at achieving a particular objective or meeting a specific need. This may be a preliminary check of prices or product reviews, gaining knowledge about special offers, finding stores in the area or the purchase itself. Furthermore, increasingly stronger media convergence causes that such a micromoment may just be the beginning of the purchasing path continued later on completely different devices (laptop, computer, PDA, TV, console).

The success of modern companies largely depends on whether they can adapt to the new market reality which is determined by mobile micromoments. To make this possible it is necessary to change the company's strategy by focusing it on a new type of mobile consumer and his or hers needs revealed its needs made during the micromoments. This is not easy because the procedures, business processes and information systems in most companies haven't been designed for mobile users. Winning the individual micromoments requires a reorientation of the entire company to make them mobile ready (Schadler, Bernoff & Ask, 2014).

First, it requires a change in thinking about the consumer and about how the company should serve him and deliver their products and services. The company has to get to know and understand the specific mobile consumer behaviours i.e. what are their most common actions on mobile devices, in which locations and at what time they occur, how long they last and from what they come. It is necessary to correctly identify the possible occurrence of micromoments and the context in which they may occur. Thus, the company must get to know the behaviours of their customers in the mobile space. It can be: searching for information about a new TV, checking the train schedule, the will to book a table for the evening, buying tickets on-line, checking the reviews about the recent video game, etc.

Equally important is the micromoments' context, ie. the location, time of day, previous actions, the occurrence length, the state of mind etc. Micromoments are identifiable and somewhat predictable because they usually occur during everyday consumer activities such as morning shopping, waiting at the bus stop, driving to work, preparing dinner, a night out to the movies, etc. Therefore, the company can explore and analyze when, where and through what channels micromoments are initiated by consumers.

To better illustrate the convergence of the model introduced earlier in this chapter with new concept of micromoments, the authors attempted to create a new model showing these correlations. Figure 2 presents this model, showing the impact of both behavioural and technical factors on individual moments.

Figure 2. Occurrence of technical and behavioural factors considering micromoments
Source: Own Elaboration.

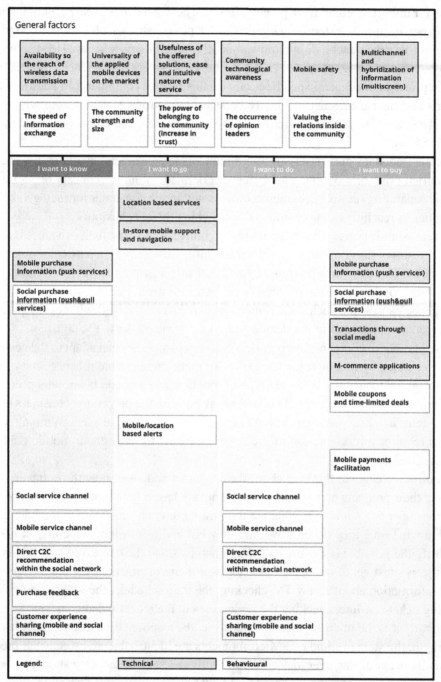

This approach will allow the company pre-determine when and where it can interact with the consumer, and respond to his or her need. It is also necessary to plan a possible to use methods of that interaction, such as: contextual advertising, search engine results, the results of products comparison websites and push notification, opinions about company / product on community sites etc.

Continuous readiness and correct prediction in what place and time as well as how it comes to interaction can result in winning micromoments by establishing relationship with the consumer. The result of such a relationship may be gaining valuable information about the consumer, enlisting the loyalty and satisfaction or ultimately the purchase company's product or service.

SOLUTIONS AND RECOMMENDATIONS FOR MICROMOMENTS HANDLING

Everyday more and more customers are switching from desktops to mobile channel through which they have granted access to all sorts of social groups (social portals, wikis, forums, blogs and other forms of group sharing tools). As mentioned in prior parts of this chapter mobile technology enables customer public evaluation of products and services delivered on the market. The importance of personal recommendation has always been an important factor in consumer journey but never it was that easy up to this day. The customer path across the purchase process is no longer linear or predictable. Therefore, brands needs to be ready to act proactively while gathering information across relevant channels.

This process of buying goods and services started with deep research of information concerning searched issue enabled by Internet and connected devices. Consumers had to find significantly long time spot during their day to perform many searches using their desktops to gather information as much as possible. Nowadays the only difference is that customers are capable of using advanced technology, mobile solutions, and confront their point of view with other members of global networks. This process is no longer attached to a certain place and time but is customer free time driven. This process can be described by a simple metaphor that consumers are no longer eating 3-meal course in a restaurant but are consuming whenever they have time to do so and in different places. In this case MOTs or so called marketing touchpoints, when customers interact with brands or offers, should be reconsidered as becoming more and more important. The traditional and already known model of web behaviour is no longer valid, customers become more conscious of purchase decision than ever before and they make it faster. The brands that accompany customers in these MOTs will attract their attention and interest and in the end their money.

According to Google ethnographic research (Lanoue, 2015) there are three insights important in designing winning MOTs: immediacy, relevancy and loyalty to needs. All of them can be simply defined:

- **Immediacy:** Portable devices become customers first point of interaction, they reach for them when realizing simples need like want to learn, find, do or even buy something. This behaviour is based on any impulse and the interaction is possible anytime and anywhere. Result of such a change is immediate response to customer need and expectation of quick gratification.
- **Relevancy:** Every time consumer is reaching for his smartphone looking for specific information in this impulse driven behaviour his expectations and impatience are high. The pursuit for relevant information becomes the main goal while everything else becomes less important.
- **Loyalty to Needs:** Combination of immediate effect expected by customers and relevancy results in high loyalty to personal needs among consumers. Only those services will be chosen that meets these requirements.

In these micromoments consumer expectations are higher than ever. The powerful computers we carry in our pockets have trained us to expect brands to deliver exactly what we are looking for – the moment we are looking. We want things right, and we want things right away. In fact, 69% of online consumers agree that the quality, timing, or relevance of a company's message influence their perception of a brand (Ramaswamy, 2015).

Marketing managers responsible for building relation with external environment, especially with customers, has to do deal with several issues that may influence the quality of purchase journey. Authors would like to present only selected which are as follows:

- Permission marketing,
- Big data,
- Search Engine Optimization (SEO).

One of the first issues that need to be considered while handling MOTs is the legal data collection, and the permission issues. According to many professionals this concept guarantees higher engagement rate, loyalty and willingness to share information than relation based on unsolicited communication.

Authors would like to put more emphasis on this ethical issue especially when it comes to customers who are aware what kind of information they're sharing. Conducting all the activities according to principles of permission marketing model guarantees transparency for customers and high rate people sharing information. Today social business is mainly all about Facebook, but not only, who is juggernaut on the market and is a source of plethora information about habits of contemporary consumers. Other social sources of actual customer behaviour are also important and the permission strategy should include them because they can help create the big picture of contemporary customer in different situations along the day. Allowing customers to log to brands services using Facebook connect platform is the first step of gathering useful information what more most of this gathered information describes real customer behaviour and reveal preferences. Proper mix of communication tools, which we can observe plethora (online and offline), can significantly influence process of building awareness among target audience and stimulate them to grant the permission. Organizations have to be aware that receiving permission is a process, which can be continued to learn more about customer through time allowing gathering more detailed information. Through time this process transform into a dialog and customers are more willing to share more information resulting in better handling of micromoments and effectively increasing conversion.

Permission marketing policy should guarantee person who is sharing it's personal information a certain "security" level that, first of all encourages him leaving this date and secondly keeps him sure that improper third party will not take advantage of this information.

Finally, responsible permission strategy enables users quick opt-out option. This issue of permission based MOTs correctly resolved influences all other aspects especially social identity, geolocation, big data and of course touchpoints, moments when the customer meets the offer.

Specialist designing MOTs to match the issue of permission need to consider factors mentioned in the model, especially focusing on: location based services, mobile location alerts, mobile/social push type information and all types of information shared by consumers.

Relevant data transformed into information is the foundation of MOTs handling strategy so proper handling of Big Data in terms of MOTs is a very important issue. Gathering complete information about customer behaviour is all about extraction and skillfully combining this data. That can help to create not only a profile of a customer, determine his preferences but also plan the customer journey. This holistic attitude towards consumer search behaviour can significantly help to successfully plan and place micromoments in consumer day. Taking into consideration data gathered about customer proper analysis may decide whether touchpoints will result in purchase.

Big data redefines process of consumers buying and retailers selling making it personalized and customized. Today's online shopping becomes substitute to yesterday's obsolete in-store purchase behaviour. Accessing and integrating data from multiple sources for analysis to analyse them can help develop "360-degrees" view on customer's interactions and experience across channels. This can help to predict and plan when customers are engaging with the brand to determine the appropriate strategy towards touchpoints. This vast knowledge extracted from relevant sources allows brands to effective interaction that results in convenient fulfilling of consumer's needs – offering him what he or she want, where he or she wants it in a convenient way for him/her. Applying predictive analytics can help companies to anticipate how customers will react on constantly changing market thus be prepared to respond in a proactive way. Successful application of this strategy depends on in-depth analysis of all possible sources of data about customer (shares, likes, status updates, comments and so on) gathered from both social and mobile channel. Monitoring and analysis of this raw data can help derive insights much faster and achieve greater intimacy with potential customers which leads in retaining focus on individual consumer preferences and consequently ensuring loyalty. Among many sources of information this presented below may be of great importance, according to authors, in big data analysis and development of segments of buyers:

- **Social Identity:** People tend to act according to actual situation and people they spend their time with. It's highly important to observe customers not only as individuals but also how they behave in a crowd and how it affects their decision. Because social life in these days is not difficult to observe people like to share their moments in life in different ways but this tendency can help anticipating potential touchpoints with brands. Another issue in this area of interest is also ability of organization to measure and identify influencers. Analysis of the occurring relation between influencers and rest of the network can be used to refine current strategy. These finding can affect in a positive way customer segmentation and also help in tracking valuable customer and prospects.
- **Geolocation:** Powerful source of actual behaviour about buyers that can be used while profiling map of real places where MOTs can actually work. Most of social media tools available on the market and majority of mobile devices grant access to this type of information, if the customer wills to share it. Appropriate strategy can help draw a map on which it will be easier to situate potential consumers and choose correct form of interaction (content and channel);
- **Wearables:** These activity trackers can be a powerful source of information that can enrich other sources of information about buyers If specialists match information from different sources and assemble them with those collected from wearable, which are always on, it can help establish what kind of emotions customer had with certain types of content or channel of information. This is hard knowledge about actual human behaviour that can help handle micromoments and design them to increase conversion.

All of the above mentioned may be used by organizations to model customers' propensity to buy, sharpen customer targeting and determine best context (time, localization, platform, emotion etc.) to deliver micromoment and finalize sales process.

Last but not least important factor that authors would like to take a closer look is the search engine optimization (SEO). It all starts with the search and oftentimes the process of buying begins somewhere in time with a question. Even higher-consideration purchases require search which can play a significant role in assisting along the consumer journey. Therefore, search may be considered as one of the key channel for organizations to leverage in order to take advantage of micromoments.

As mentioned before consumers are using primarily the mobile to search for relevant information and that is the key driver for SEO strategy handling micromoments. They reach for their mobile phone whenever they want to be informed or search for something. Mobile becomes determinant of consumer behaviour and there are different rules applying.

When it comes to Big Data specialist responsible for implementation of MOTs have to take into account factors connected with gathering information from adequate channels and especially focus on: location based services, customer experience sharing, social/mobile purchase information.

One of the most important thing to take care of is to be ready to have customers from different platforms, so a website that works on all devices is the best way to handle SEO strategy for micromoments.

Other crucial issue concerns word like "near me", "nearby", "closest", "specific location" which are becoming more and more popular and are occurring frequently in consumer searches. There is also and observable tendency in search procedure where consumer instead of looking for traditional result switch to maps (Google Maps). What is more these type of searches differ from their desktop counterpart because they are short termed, intent driven, geolocalized and valid only for a while.

Key point to apply successfully SEO strategy in to micromoments is to determine profile of "always-on customer". This profile may include:

- Demographics.
- Where customer can be interested in your offer?
- What can he be searching form?
- How the actual place and context influences his search query?
- Is the offer clearly visible on any device?
- Website or mobile app?

Answering to this questions can help to identify possible pains of your customer and answer resolve above issues. Segmenting customers is a key in establishing how different customers use different keywords depending if he or she is using traditional search on web or integrated services for specific products. Identifying places where customers can be interested in a given organization offer is the fundament in applying SEO strategy to micromoments. The localization determines not only the device but also influences context and in an effect type of key phrase customer is searching. Natural next step is to establish visual form of the touchpoint so it would be relevant and presented in a convenient way. Very important question that need an answer is wheather customer is using web or prefers dedicated search engines.

Finally, analysing touchpoints during consumer journey companies have to take into consideration different patterns of search among which most popular are:

- Last click, last recorded micromoment becomes successful and ends with purchase, it also means that the last channel is the most effective.
- First click, the credit goes to the first channel/micromoment that redirects to the website/offer, this is mostly affiliate model.

- U-click, when the first and the last channel are the most important, there can be made a simple distinction 1st channel represents sort of a need/interest/stimulus, while the last leads to a specific offer.
- Time decay, is when each channel brings the purchase closer, with every click and every new bite of information customer gets more convinced to convert.

What this means is that organization needs to make micromoments search matching consumer segmentation and take into consideration specific demands of search process.

Regarding SEO strategy specialist need to focus on these factors, mentioned in the model: social/ mobile purchase information and also recommendations shared by consumers.

FUTURE RESEARCH DIRECTIONS

For future research authors would like to explore the problem of micromoments in consumer journey. It is somewhat important to make market research on changes that occur in the web behaviour of consumers. This research would include both managers responsible for handling micromoments but also customers who are direct recipients. Authors would like to redefine and refine the model proposed in this chapter and add practical knowledge to the subject resulting from development of phenomena such as: localization based search (Google Maps), social search (based on social graph), advanced biometric devices, predictive algorithms, gamification. Areas worth consideration are consumer segmentation and in-depth analysis of new shape of consumer journey. This two important issues influence many decisions concerning how and when to deliver effective micromoments resulting with conversion. In further research authors would like to put more emphasis on relations taking place in mobile and social channels considered separately as well as merged.

CONCLUSION

The analysis presented in this chapter lead to a few important conclusions. Identified radical change in consumer behaviour and consumer purchase journey needs refined strategies in brand communication with the market. In the course of the purchase process, customers actively research product information on the Web (often with the use of mobile channels and devices), and contact friends and relatives to gather opinions on the product planned for purchase. At home, stimulated by broadcasts of TV/radio commercials, they employ additional devices (tablets, smartphones, etc.) to look up additional information on the advertised product. In this context, proper synchronization of information presented across multiple screens (devices), and particularly – the optimization of mobile channels – seem to constitute a precondition for reaching the customer in the most appropriate and effective manner. Improvements and refinements in this respect should involve the following:

- Optimization of mobile webpages,
- Continuous monitoring, testing and improving of individual elements of webpage display,
- Monitoring of user webpage behaviours,
- Designing coherent content for each channel of communication used,

- Emphasizing the need for intriguing, surprising and educating,
- Inclusion of gamification and viral elements, based on the assumption that highly entertaining content can stimulate consumer activity.

On the basis of a postulated model of behavioural and technical aspects of purchase behaviour, the Authors demonstrated and substantiated the role of micromoments in mobile consumer communities.

REFERENCES

Barry, T. E. (1987). The Development of the Hierarchy of Effects: An Historical Perspective. *Current Issues and Research in Advertising, 1987*, 251–295.

Blythe, J. (2008). *Consumer Behaviour*. London: Thomson Learning.

Bynum, R. (2008). The Myth Of Equality. *New English Review*. Retrieved September 30, 2015, from http://newenglishreview.org/Rebecca_Bynum/The_Myth_Of_Equality/

Clemons, E. K. (2008). How information changes consumer behavior and how consumer behavior determines corporate strategy. *Journal of Management Information Systems, 25*(2), 13–40. doi:10.2753/MIS0742-1222250202

Court, D., Elzinga, D., Mulder, S., & Vetvik, O. J. (2009). The Consumer Decision Journey. *McKinsey Quarterly*. Retrieved September 30, 2015, from http://www.mckinsey.com/insights/marketing_sales/the_consumer_decision_journey

Edelman, D. C. (2010).Branding in the Digital Age: You're Spending Your Money in All the Wrong Places. *Harvard Business Review*.

Etherington, T. (2015). *Micro-moments: how to survive the new mobile battleground for brands*. Retrieved August 27, 2015, http://www.marketingmagazine.co.uk/article/1359653/micro-moments-survive-new-mobile-battleground-brands

Ettenson, R., Corado, E., & Knowles, J. (2013). Rethinking the 4 P's. *Harvard Business Review*. Retrieved from https://hbr.org/2010/12/branding-in-the-digital-age-youre-spending-your-money-in-all-the-wrong-places

Jablonski, S., & Yakup, D. (2012). Integrated Approach to Factors Affecting Consumers Purchase Behavior in Poland and an Empirical Study. *Global Journal of Management and Business Research, 12*(15), 94–115.

Jerin, K. (Ed.). (2015). *Nowi mieszczanie, raport trendowy*. Retrieved September 21, 2015, from http://www.fpiec.pl/nowi_mieszczanie_f5_analytics.pdf

Khalaf, S. (2014). *The Rise of the Mobile Addict*. Retrieved September 6, 2015: http://flurrymobile.tumblr.com/post/115191945655/the-rise-of-the-mobile-addict#.VPA77_ mG-W5

Lanoue, S. (2015). *How to Win on Mobile: Understanding Micro-Moments and Consumer Behavior.* Retrieved from https://www.usertesting.com/blog/2015/07/02/how-to-win-on-mobile-understanding-micro-moments-and-consumer-behavior/

Lauterborn, B. (1990). New Marketing Litany: Four Ps Passé: C-Words Take Over. *Advertising Age, 61*(4), 26.

Lindstrom, M. (2009). *The real decision makers.* Retrieved: September 30, 2015 http://juicecompany.net/development1/the-real-decision-makers/

Łysik, Ł., Kutera, R., & Machura, P. (2014). Zero Moment of Truth: a new Marketing Challenge in Mobile Consumer Communities. *Proceedings of the European Conference on Social Media: ECSM 2014.* Academic Conferences Limited.

Łysik, Ł., Kutera, R., & Machura, P. (2014, November). Behavioural and technical factors of influence on purchase behaviour of mobile consumers. In *Proceedings of the 18th International Academic MindTrek Conference: Media Business, Management, Content & Services* (pp. 110-117). ACM.

Mongay, J. (2006). Strategic Marketing. A literature review on definitions, concepts and boundaries. MPRA Paper No. 41840.

Perreau F. (2013). *4 factors influencing consumer behavior.* Retrieved September 1, 2015, from http://theconsumerfactor.com/en/4-factors-influencing-consumer-behavior/

Ramaswamy, S. (2015). Outside Voices: Why Mobile Advertising May Be All About Micro-Targeting Moments. *The Wall Street Journal.* Retrieved September 3, 2015 http://blogs.wsj.com/cmo/2015/04/08/outside-voices-why-mobile-advertising-may-be-all-about-micro-targeting-moments/

Robertus, T. H. (2015). Grown Up Digital: Effect Social Media Usage on Consumer Behavior. Advanced Science Letters, 21(4), 1035-1038.

Schadler, T., Bernoff, J., & Ask, J. (2014).*The Mobile Mind Shift: Engineer Your Business To Win in the Mobile Moment.* Forrester Research.

Shanker, R. (2008).*Services Marketing.* New Delhi: Excel Books.

Solis, B. (2013). *What's the Future of Business: Changing the Way Businesses Create Experiences.* John Wiley & Sons.

Yakup, D. (2014). The Impact of Psychological Factors on Consumer Buying Behavior and an Empirical Application in Turkey. *Asian Social Science, 10*(6), 194-204.

KEY TERMS AND DEFINITIONS

Behavioural Factors: Influencing a consumer behaviour factors connected with the changes in the manner of performance of particular activities within the phases of purchase behaviours of mobile consumer communities.

Consumer Behaviour: The dynamic interaction of affect and cognition, behaviour, and the environment by which human beings conduct the exchange aspects of their lives.

Marketing Strategy: The way in which the marketing function organizes its activities to achieve a profitable growth in sales at a marketing mix level.

Micromoments: Short, highly dispersed in time consumer interactions with tools such as a browser or mobile application; they aim to rapidly respond to different needs i.e. to know something, do something, go somewhere or buy something.

Mobile Communities: The collectivity of people who share common values and needs, but most of all, a way of communication using mobile devices and mobile communication technologies; members of such communities use the network anywhere and at any time.

Moments of Truth: The stages of the consumer purchasing decision-making cycle that are associated with buyer-seller interactions; these moments build value to the customer, which may result in the subsequent sale.

Technical Factors: Influencing on consumer behaviour factors related to offering innovative tools as well as social and mobile services.

Chapter 3
Social Media in Crisis Communication:
The Lance Armstrong Saga

Maria Hopwood
Sports Management Worldwide, USA

Hamish McLean
Griffith University, Australia

ABSTRACT

Social media engagement is changing the relational dynamic between organizations - and individuals - and their publics. This is particularly evident in the world of elite sport where the market value of an elite athlete is measured by their public reputation which is pinned on healthy relationships with stakeholders, such as fellow athletes, team managers, coaches and, importantly, fans (Hopwood 2007). In fact, social media analysts have attributed much of Twitter's growth to early adopters in the sports world. As a continually expanding global business, sport has to grapple with the challenges of how to harness this uncontrolled medium to best advantage, particularly in times of crisis. This chapter examines the bond between fans and sport in the context of social media in order to examine how this relationship could foster forgiveness for elite athletes who confess to transgressions, thus having enduring implications for the athlete's sport and sport business generally.

INTRODUCTION

Social media – particularly the micro-blog Twitter – has provided sports fans with the opportunity to fulfil the eternal ambition of getting closer to their idols. This is particularly important in the world of elite sport where the market value of an elite athlete is measured by their public reputation which is pinned on healthy relationships with stakeholders, such as fellow athletes, team managers, coaches and, importantly, fans (Hopwood 2007). There are numerous examples, however, of athletes and sports organizations finding, to their sometimes heavy reputational and image cost, that strict protocols for social media usage need to be embedded at all levels of the organization, thus making it not quite the open

DOI: 10.4018/978-1-5225-0559-4.ch003

access communication channel for which fans might have hoped. Managing a crisis scenario which is played out in the full glare of social media is a real and present challenge for organizations. It is therefore essential that a comprehensive crisis communications management strategy is in place at all times.

Drawing on the case of cyclist Lance Armstrong who, despite a large following, turned his back on social media and opted to confess on American prime time television via the channel of a much publicized interview with Oprah Winfrey, the authors' research focusses on how the convergence of social and traditional media is impacting the sport/fan relationship. The findings of this research are therefore of relevance to anyone with an interest in the business of sport and social media relationship management within the wider public relations context.

This chapter focusses on the strategic and theoretical elements of crisis communication, as utilized by organizations generally, and attempts to demonstrate their application to social media crisis communication through the case study of Lance Armstrong's confession to doping on the Oprah Winfrey Show in January 2013. The objective for our research is to highlight the challenges faced by individuals and organizations of relationship management during a crisis when it is played out via social media. The reason for focusing on Lance Armstrong is that he is a prolific Twitter user and strategically used this medium as a way of reinforcing his web of deceit. He built up a global empire of supporters who have been devastated by his fall from grace and who continue, even two years after the confession, to share their grief and disappointment on Twitter. Though the case study is clearly sports business related, the authors' findings are applicable to organization communication within the wider context. The chapter considers how sports fans and elite athletes use social media and the associated pitfalls. As both authors' specialism is public relations, there is a discussion on social media relationship and reputation management and the use of social media in a crisis situation, referencing crisis communication literature. The Lance Armstrong case study is presented and its implications considered both within sport and the wider business context.

BACKGROUND

Fans, Elite Athletes, and Social Media

Sport is a reflection of society, both good and bad, and is compelling because of its ability to connect people emotionally rather than rationally. As Boyle (2013) observes: "[the] sporting discourse is often about emotions and opinions deeply held and readily expressed by athletes and fans". Dimeo (2007, cited in Lopez 2010) argues that sport has a war-like persona therefore

... is fundamentally about winning, hierarchy, elitism and losers get nothing. It encourages people to think of others as enemies. Bias and partisanship are actively promoted. It demarcates the best from the rest. It is all about physical and social superiority. It is a harsh system that is not just intolerant towards failure but explicitly rejects those who fail.

The battle-ground environment of sport unifies fans (Osborne 2013) who link their social identity to the on-and-off field performances of athletes and teams (Sanderson and Emmons 2014). This bond arguably can blossom into a religious-like fervor (Garratt 2010) and beyond with an "identification so intense that some fans are willing to engage in hostile and criminal acts towards opposing teams and players" (Sanderson & Emmon, 2014). Although there is no universal definition of a fan (Osborne 2013), scholars have explored fan motivation and how their allegiance develops in favor of certain clubs and athletes. For example, the revised Funk & James (2006) Psychological Continuum Model sets out the process of becoming a fan: awareness, attraction, attachment and finally allegiance. In their study of an Australian Football league fan, de Groot and Robinson (2008) note that the "feeling of belonging and closeness is achieved by fellow group members sharing important experiences and on this basis build their own identity". In a study of sport bloggers McCarthy (2014) found that they were motivated by a sense of community by sharing and meeting with like-minded fans and "somehow shaping, or shaping the narrative of sport". Blogging, they observe, allows fans to "regain a sense of common ownership of sport which has been lost" (2014). To sustain fan support, Taker (2012) argues that it is crucial for athletes and clubs to frequently interact with fans so they develop strong bonds with the team, which creates a ripple effect that attracts others to become involved. In the context of social media, fans expect content to be of maximum interest, which in turn will increase revenue generated by an engaged fan base (Taker, 2012). In reality, however, Taker (2012) argues that the sport industry often takes fan loyalty for granted rather than engage in genuine two-way symmetrical social media conversation. For example, in the UK, the Newcastle United Football Club Supporter Trust found only 3 percent of fans felt the club was engaging with them. The vital importance of fan engagement is evidenced by the emergence of groups such as The Fan Experience Company (UK) and Fan Engagement (the Netherlands), both of which are actively engaged on social media.

Building Relationships on Social Media

Social media has changed forever the sports communication paradigm. Arguably, it has empowered fans to become participants rather than placid observers (Kishner & Crescenti, 2010). Gantz, therefore notes:

Modern technology magnifies fan voices so they can be heard far and wide. Lurking or active participation in blogs and websites provides a connectivity and sense of extended community fans value. It democratizes sports and provides fans with a base of information and influence they would not have as individuals. These forums can break news as well as serve as a bullhorn expressing and galvanizing fan pleasure or disgust. (Gantz, 2012)

Twitter has been described as "…two-way talk which allows athletes to speak on their own terms" (Gregory, 2009). Athletes have also noticed that where once they were followed by fans on Twitter, they are now actively chased. When fans tweet athletes messages and they get a response, this is the modern equivalent to an autograph (Wertheim, 2011). The 140-character micro-blog Twitter is one of the most popular platforms for connecting fans (Highfield et al. 2013, Laird 2013, Hambrick et. al. 2010) while Facebook remains the top preference for following and discussing sport. Hambrick et. al. (2010) observe that Twitter is popular with athletes to connect directly and in real-time with fans without any filtering by public relations departments, clubs and traditional media gatekeepers. The choice of using social media, however, remains in the domain of the athlete. As Frederick et. al. (2014) note: "The athlete must choose to take down that wall, effectively transforming the everyday fan from voyeur to digital acquaintance". Athletes, therefore, become content generators "deciding not only what to discuss but how to discuss it and with whom to discuss it" (Frederick, 2014). The use of social media to engage with fans extends to referees, who are responding to questions about on-field decisions in an effort to build relationships (Glynn, 2013). As one referee noted: "For a long time there has been a view that we just turn up for games, make decisions that are viewed as wrong, take no accountability and then go back into our box" (Glynn, 2013).

Social media helps strengthen the bond between fans and the sport entity. A recognized fan state is known as 'basking in reflected glory' (Cialdini et. al. 1976), also referred to as BIRG-ing. This is a recognized state in which fans, through their association with a successful team or athlete, develop feelings of success and belonging, thus creating a stronger emotional bond between themselves and the sport entity. Social media, by its very nature, is proving to be a powerful enabler of this state which is a crucial element of fan engagement.

SOCIAL MEDIA IN A SPORT CRISIS

Social media platforms breathe life into a reputational crisis (McLean, 2013). With access to social media available on a myriad of mobile devices, it takes little time or effort for fans to voice their opinions in real-time and across borders. For example, Sanderson (2013) analyzed Facebook posts regarding a voluntary move by a football coach between teams. Fans of the team the coach departed responded with posts ranging from character assassination, threats and intimidation to rallying support for a future without the coach. Therefore, social media platforms become valuable tools in uniting a fan base (Brown & Billings, 2013), frequently to defend the reputations of athletes and "build community and promote preferred representations of athletes and sports figures" (Sanderson, 2013). Sanderson (2010) observes that elite athletes can counter negative media coverage by encouraging their social media fan base to support them. Seeking such support has benefits as Sanderson (2010) explains:

In such circumstances, it seems plausible that communicative exchanges between professional athletes and fans via blogs would empower professional athletes to be more open in their disclosures about such events, which may translate to fans expressing support for the athlete's openness.

Among the plethora of social media platforms Hambrick et al (2010) have found that Twitter is popular by allowing athletes, within the confines of a Tweet to connect directly and immediately to fans:

… instead of having their messages filtered through the public relations departments of sports organizations and mainstream media outlets. Online social networks have created a significant shift in the sports communications paradigm.

Fans also use Twitter to connect with athletes, other fans and the traditional media. Athletes have extended this symmetrical communication to encompass off-field personal activities, such as social events and channeling fans to personal pictures, blogs and other internet and social media content. Social media is therefore creating a personal world between athletes and their fans. Hambrick et. al. (2010) explain that "this interactivity element adds another dimension to fan perceptions regarding athletes as fans watch them engage in personal exchanges". Needless to say, athletes who conducted extensive interactivity with fans attracted higher numbers of followers on Twitter. This micro window into the life of an elite athlete helps strengthen the personal bond with fans and other interested publics. In turn, this engagement drives loyalty towards the athlete and/or team (Hambrick et. al. 2010). Fans are drawn to learn more intimate details about the athlete, creating and cementing a bond that may be resilient in a crisis. This changes the relationship dynamics as fans "are no longer observers, they are participants" Kishner & Crescenti (2010). Social media platforms, such as Twitter, become valuable tools in uniting fans who then seek to defend the reputation of the athlete or team (Brown & Billings, 2013). For example, when exploring social media support for troubled Boston Red Sox pitcher Curt Schilling, Sanderson (2010) found that "communicating directly to fans via blogs seems to be a strategy to quickly mobilize support networks that bolster the athlete during a personal crisis".

This chapter examines reputation management in the case of Lance Armstrong. The use of social media and tactics adopted at different stages of crisis management are of interest to this research. Hambrick et. al. (2013) observed that he maintained image repair strategies on Twitter both before and after the United States Anti-Doping Agency (hereafter USADA) investigation, but during and following the Oprah Winfrey interview, he chose not to mention it on Twitter. The authors' review of Armstrong's Twitter feed after the broadcast found no reference to the confession. Armstrong's usually engaging Twitter activity was silent for almost a month after the broadcast. It gradually returned to life in the Spring of 2013 with a mix of social and sport comments and a constant stream of Tweets in relation to his high profile in the charity work he engaged in for cancer and the Livestrong Foundation. It seems the 'confession' remained strictly off-topic. Interestingly, the authors found that in the days following the broadcast, social media posts on the confession reached around 1.5 million (Polipulse, 2013). Given the power of social media to maintain the support of fans and Armstrong's already strong following, it suggests that it was a missed opportunity for Armstrong not to have utilized Twitter for a period of questions and answers. Had he done so, this would have allowed fans an on-going personal and exclusive insight into his confession and an opportunity for him to understand and address their concerns on a more personal level. In other words, Twitter would have provided Armstrong with a real-time awareness of, and engagement with, fans. Sanderson (2010) observes that elite athletes can counter negative media coverage by engendering their fan base to support "their actions and views" with direct dialogue on social media platforms. Thus:

In such circumstances, it seems plausible that communicative exchanges between professional athletes and fans via blogs would empower professional athletes to be more open in their disclosures about such events, which may translate to fans expressing support for the athlete's openness. (Sanderson 2010)

The Armstrong Enigma

@lancearmstrong Imperfect guy in an imperfect world. Founded @Livestrong. Raised half a billion dollars to fight cancer. Raced bikes. Finally broke 80. Austin, TX · mellowjohnnys.com. (Lance Armstrong's Twitter biography 2013)

Lance Armstrong was undoubtedly a global sporting icon but an individual who, as his career and image burgeoned, polarised opinion. Until 1994, which was the year that he began working with Dr Michele Ferrari who was known to dope cyclists, Armstrong achieved moderate, but not outstanding success in his sport. In 1995, his winning streak began and he rose to 7th place in the world rankings and joined the French team *Cofidis*. In 1996, aged just 25, he was diagnosed with testicular cancer which swiftly metastasised throughout his body and from which he was not expected to recover. However, following aggressive treatment, by early 1997 he was in full remission. Just a year later in 1998 he got back on his bike and made his post-cancer comeback:

Sponsored by Nike, the US Postal Service (USPS), Discovery Channel, RadioShack, Anheuser-Busch, Oakley, Nissan, Trek-Bicycle Corp, Johnson Health Tech, SRAM Corporation, FRS, Easton-Bell Sports, Honey Stinger and 24-Hour Fitness Gyms, Lance built a team strong in cycle technology, sports gear, nutrition and capital. (Young 2013)

Against seemingly unbelievable odds Armstrong won the first of his seven consecutive Tour de France races in 1999 and became a living legend. He acknowledged this during his opening speech to the World Cancer Congress in Montreal in August 2012.Interestingly, this coincided with his announcement the previous week that he would no longer challenge USADA's drug charges against him. It also coincided with USADA's decision to throwout his competitive victories dating back to 1998, which included all his Tour de France wins. At this point, Armstrong was still spinning the yarn: "My name is Lance Armstrong. I am a cancer survivor. I'm a father of five. And yes, I won the Tour de France seven times". (Associated Press, 2012). Armstrong's inspirational and iconic status was further enhanced by his links with the Livestrong Foundation of which he is acknowledged as 'Our Founder' on the organisation's website (Livestrong.org, 2013).

He and Livestrong were indivisible; he was not merely a rider, he was a cancer survivor. He credited his fitness and willpower with his 'beating' cancer, which appeared to convey greater cult status. (Young, 2013)

As a cancer survivor, cycling phenomenon and prolific Twitter engager, Lance Armstrong helped to create and perpetuate for himself an image of the invincible sporting hero. What the millions of fans around the world did not or perhaps did not want to see was that underneath it all, Lance Armstrong was a cheat who used his power unethically (Young 2013).

Armstrong Goes Against the Flow

Player transgressions - on and off the field - directly threaten relationships with fans. Therefore, transgressions frequently result in players confessing and seeking forgiveness (Sanderson& Emmon, 2014). This strategy places fans in the position of having to make a choice about whether or not to forgive the transgression. Confession is one of the fundamental strategies to reduce negative stakeholder reactions to wrong-doing (McDonald, 2010, Coombs, 2012). One such approach to confession is the notion of self-disclosure, or stealing thunder, which emerged within the legal context where for defendants who fessed-up of their own accord to damaging information, the outcome had less negative impact than had it been brought to light by the prosecution (Williams et. al. 1993). The strategy is also found to reduce negative media coverage of a transgression by moving the media forward to a frame of "what comes next" (Wigley,2010).

On two nights in January 2013, Lance Armstrong, world renowned cyclist, cancer survivor, Olympic Bronze medalist and winner of an unprecedented seven Tour de France titles finally admitted to US chat show host Oprah Winfrey and a television audience of 4.3 million what many had long suspected – he had used banned performance-enhancing drugs (PEDs) throughout his professional cycling career. In a statement released within an hour of the interview's conclusion, Travis Tygart, CEO of USADA, the organization with whom Armstrong had been battling for many years against persistent allegations of doping, said: "Tonight, Lance Armstrong finally acknowledged that his cycling career was built on a powerful combination of doping and deceit" (USADA, 2013).

For more than a decade, Armstrong strenuously denied any involvement in doping and verbally attacked and sued anyone who suggested that he did. From winning his first Tour de France in 1999 – ironically hailed as 'The Tour of Renewal' as it was intended to bring the Race out of the shadows of doping accusations - until he finally gave up his fight with USADA in August 2012, Armstrong, as leader of the U.S. Postal Service cycling team was involved with what Tygart described as

... the most sophisticated, professionalized and successful doping program that the sport has ever seen ... a program organized by individuals who thought they were above the rules and who still play a major and active role in sport today (USADA 2012)

Why Oprah Rather than Twitter?

So, why did Lance Armstrong decide to finally admit to his transgressions and why did he choose the public forum of the Oprah Winfrey Show as his preferred communications channel? It is evident that Armstrong is an individual who is very used to being in control and controlling and his choice of media channels for his mea culpa reflect this. As a televised interviewee, confessing all to his friend Winfrey, he could both craft his message and his image. King (2008) argues that television talk show programs "selectively exploits and manipulates the confessional process" where celebrities can engage in a form of damage control. Televised confessions are designed and delivered to meet the demands of performance, competitive advantages and audience expectations. As King (2008) observes, "confessions on television are staged for entertainment without deep moral consequences. The tears and ardent pleas for forgiveness are tied to the occasion and quite often faked". It is suggested that by his use of Oprah Winfrey and Twitter as his confessional platforms, Armstrong felt that he could control his message and perhaps set the 'confession' agenda. Arguably the fundamental principles of crisis public relations are these: knowing your audience; crafting the message accordingly; communicating a credible message through appropriate communication channels with the ultimate objective of getting the audience onside: apologizing for a transgression and making amends. However, Armstrong's communication behavior since August 2012 suggests that he feels that such rules do not apply to him as he continued to use Twitter in order to snipe and attempt to belittle those with whom he had come into confrontation such as previous cycling team mate Tyler Hamilton (@lancearmstrong @Ty_Hamilton twitter exchange 7 November 2013) David Walsh, the journalist who had originally exposed Armstrong's deceptions and Emma O'Reilly, the team soigneur. Armstrong has never actually fully and unreservedly apologized for his taking of PEDs, maintaining throughout that the fault is with the sport of cycling rather than him the individual. This led to claims of arrogance particularly when he aligned himself with former President Clinton's rehabilitation, stating that Clinton was a "hero of mine" that he wanted to copy him in becoming "president of the world" and publicly stating that "I'm like Bill Clinton and people will forgive me" (Bates 2013).

Armstrong's use of Twitter was undoubtedly strategic. Due to his multi-dimensional image – elite cyclist, cancer survivor, humanitarian, living legend – Armstrong managed to develop distinctive character traits and personalities which appealed to varied publics, thus creating a number of varied fan bases. As Hambrick et. al. (2013) observe: "Twitter and other social media channels function as a mechanism to alternate between a variety of identity positions that may 'make sense' to fans." Armstrong's choice of Oprah Winfrey to host his 'confession' on her national US television programme, in fact, alienated many of his legion of fans on social media, where reaction ranged from disbelief to shock (News.com.

au 2013). The reason may be the bonding power of social media, in this case to build personal bridges between an elite athlete and their fans, who can be forgiving of transgressions but that extends only so far. A second point is that Armstrong's failure to apologize without reservation during his 'confession', and subsequently ignoring the issue on social media, intensified fan outrage. Almost one-third of the 1.5 million social media posts in the days following the confession "think of him differently" while 24 percent "think his career is over" (Polipulse, 2013). Ironically, it was social media that finally pushed Armstrong to confess. Choking back tears, Armstrong told Winfrey he had made the decision to come clean after his son defended him on the social media site Instagram against accusations of doping (Bacon, 2013). Even this display of emotion failed to convince some fans of his sincerity, with one Tweeting: "Lance Armstrong's tears have tested positive for narcissism" (Yadav, 2013). From a crisis communications perspective, it is essential that individuals and organizations, who are mindful of their image and reputation, give closer consideration to how and when they communicate with their publics, particularly when the platform of choice becomes social media. From the perspective of the sports personality this is even more critical. "Armstong has been a strong proponent of Twitter since its inception, and social media analysts have attributed much of Twitter's growth to early adopters in the sports world such as Armstrong" (Fisher 2009 cited in Hambrick et. al. 2013).

Since 'coming clean' in January 2013, Armstrong has shunned the media spotlight and reverted to using Twitter, though to a lesser extent than previously. An analysis of his current Twitter usage indicates that he focusses predominantly on his family, social and charitable activities. Much of his Twitter activity is devoted to supporting and encouraging cancer sufferers, an example perhaps of, his attempts to salvage relationships. There are also instances where he engages directly with fans who continue to ask him for an apology. For example, in one case responding to a fan who has written a blog in which he eloquently expresses his disappointment in the cyclist, Armstrong replied:

@Michael_Better Mike, read your piece & I don't take your words lightly. I am truly sorry for the disappointment and betrayal you feel. (Lance Armstrong Twitterfeed, December 10, 2013)

No outright apology, perhaps, but certainly an expression of regret. He is also using Twitter to communicate with journalists, wishing Paul Kimmage, one of those who originally exposed him, a happy New Year on 31st December 2013. In another move, on 8th January 2014 Armstrong chose to confirm, via his Twitter account, his willingness to co-operate openly and honestly with an independent commission into cycling's doping past.

However, it could be argued that the original crisis continues to smoulder. Though the social media backlash surrounding Armstrong's original confession in 2013 may have abated, the sport of cycling is struggling to move ahead. In direct response to the Armstrong scandal, in March 2015 the Cycling Independent Reform Commission (CIRC) published a report which found that doping is rife in the sport of cycling (CIRC, 2015) and the Stephen Frears film "The Program: the true story of the greatest deception of our time", released to UK cinemas in October 2015, shows very clearly that the cataclysmic Armstrong confession still holds the public's interest. The backlash of the confession on the sport of cycling reappeared on Twitter during the 2015 Tour de France which was won by British rider Chris Froome. On July 14th 2015, Lance Armstrong took to Twitter with this provocative tweet which was retweeted 5,402 and favorited 2,480 times:

@lancearmstrong 1. Clearly Froome/Porte/Sky are very strong. Too strong to be clean? Don't ask me, I have no clue. (Lance Armstrong Twitterfeed, July 14, 2015)

This provoked a lengthy exchange which continued throughout July and which rekindled the controversy surrounding Armstrong's cheating and his continuing role in damaging the sport of cycling's reputation. It is interesting to note that Armstrong adopted a similar strategy in response to this Twitterstorm as he did to the original one surrounding the Oprah Confession – he withdrew for the most part, responding directly to a handful of Tweets such as this one:

@danieljcastille July 14 Manchester, England

@lancearmstrong you destroyed the reputation of this great race and now you try to harm it further by accusing others? Please stop.

@lancearmstrong July 14

@danieljcastille I'm not accusing anyone. In fact, quite the opposite. I'm not interested (nor do I have the credibility) to opine there.

The fact that Armstrong admits here to not having the credibility to give an opinion on Twitter is an interesting tactic because he quite clearly is giving an opinion and would likely know that there would be a reaction to any Tweet he posted. This is, arguably, yet another example of him using Twitter in order to gain support from those fans that remain loyal to him.

Continuing with the cycling theme, Twitter was also used as a weapon against Chris Froome during the 2015 Tour de France. Froome and the whole of Team Sky rode the race against a tide of vitriolic verbal and physical abuse from cycling fans around the world who accused him of riding an unclean race, an accusation that could possibly have been further fueled by Armstrong's inflammatory Tweet of July 14th. The abuse was allegedly stoked by the French media who cast aspersions on the legality of Froome and Team Sky's performance through all available channels, including social media. As well as having urine thrown in his face and a fellow team mate punched, Froome constantly had to defend himself against unfounded allegations of doping and taking performance enhancing drugs, an issue to which he refers in his autobiography (Froome, 2014):

I am not a student of Lance Armstrong or that period in cycling. He doesn't interest me and that era doesn't interest me. . . You think I'm guilty. Can you prove it? No. I know I'm clean. Can I prove it? No. You heard it all before from Lance Armstrong. Well, I'm not Lance Armstrong. You won't get fooled again. Not by me you won't, ever.

In response to the pressure from Twitter and the media and in order to gainsay the accusations of doping, Team Sky took the unprecedented decision to release confidential rider data as a public relations strategy. In acknowledging the power and influence of social media, Tim Kerrison, Team Sky's head of athletic performance observed at a press conference that:

With great power comes great responsibility. If you have the power to influence what millions of people are thinking about a situation, you have the responsibility to make sure that your facts are accurate. (Suleman, 2015)

CONCLUSION

The authors argue that Armstrong's failure to engage with social media at the time of his 'confession' was a missed opportunity to capitalize on the empathy of fans, who feel valued when asked for forgiveness (Sanderson & Emmon 2014). As Sanderson and Emmon (2014) explain, fans can identify with mistakes, confessions and forgiveness. For loyal fans, forgiveness may be the only course of action. A key finding is that fans on social media are part of today's sport DNA and should not be ignored in the confession process when player transgressions happen on-or-off the field. Fans, this chapter suggests, should be fully engaged in the confession process, which may bolster the chance of forgiveness and the opportunity to salvage the relationship with genuine two-way dialogue. Social media provides the ideal platform for such engagement but effectively utilizing its undoubted benefits for mutually beneficial outcomes is a whole new ball game for the business of sport.

As observed earlier in this chapter, Lance Armstrong continues to be a focus of social media attention. One of the earliest examples of his use of Twitter for self-promotion was his now infamous "Back in Austin and just layin' around..." tweet which he posted on 10 November 2012, just days after he had resigned from the Chair of the Livestrong Foundation, has received 1,220,703 views and 782 comments both for and against the cyclist. The tweet shows Armstrong relaxing on a couch surrounded by the yellow jerseys from the seven Tour de France wins that had earlier in the year been expunged from the records. Comments posted include:

@dopestrongsux: when do they collect the jerseys? after you give back all the (now less than) honorary degrees??

@jdusvet: Lance is the man. And those drugs don't work unless the man is already a beast. Lance was a beast without them, but to stay on top, you have to level the playing field. He wasn't the only one, and they all knew it."(Mobli.com, 2015)

Despite this, Armstrong has maintained somewhat of a strategic approach to his image repair efforts. For example, to coincide with the World Anti-Doping Agency (WADA) Conference in Johannesburg he offered to give 100 percent transparency in return for the overturning of his lifetime ban from competitive cycling (BBC World Service, 11 November 2013). More recently, Armstrong continued to polarize opinion on Twitter by participating in the Tour de France One Day Ahead charity cycling event on July 16th, 2015. The Tour organizers called him 'disrespectful' for appearing on the Tour's route and his appearance created frenetic Twitter activity from which Armstrong, yet again, withdrew. What Armstrong consistently and continually fails to do is unreservedly apologize for his transgressions. Instead he persists in adopting the role of the victim, which arguably continues to alienate his, and cycling's, audiences and further diminish his credibility in the eyes of both the cycling and wider sporting community. His current Twitter biography illustrates his continuing defiance as he refers to being a "7 X TdF champ", a reference which interestingly does not appear in the earlier 2013 version and which appears to have been written to appeal directly to the legions of loyal fans on whose support he clearly depends:

Father of 5 amazing kids. Cancer survivor. Founder of @livestrong. 7 X TdF champ. (Lance Armstrong's Twitter Biography, October 2015)

Lance Armstrong "presents a fascinating moral dilemma as cycling tries to move on from its past." (Cary2015) His transgressions will undoubtedly continue to have repercussions not only within the sport of cycling, but more generally within the context of crisis communications. The message from this case is clear, social media's developing but critical role in sport public relations and sport business cannot be ignored and must be strategically managed as an integral element of 21st century crisis communications.

REFERENCES

Armstrong, L. (2013). Twitterfeed @lancearmstrong.

Armstrong, L. (2015). Twitterfeed @lancearmstrong.

Associated Press. (2012). *Lance Armstrong says he's champ.* Retrieved October 13, 2015, from http://espn.go.com/olympics/cycling/story/_/id/8315779/lance-armstrong-introduces-7-time-tour-de-france-champ

Bates, D. (2013). *Lance Armstrong: I'm like Bill Clinton and people will forgive me.* Retrieved October, 13, 2015, from http://www.dailymail.co.uk/news/article-2292248/Lance-Armstrong-Im-like-Bill-Clinton-people-forgive-me.html

Boyle, R. (2013). Reflections on Communication and Sport: On journalism and digital culture. *Communication & Sport, 1*(2), 88–99. doi:10.1177/2167479512467978

Brown, N., & Billings, A. (2013). Sports fans as crisis communicators on social media websites. *Public Relations Review, 39*(1), 74–81. doi:10.1016/j.pubrev.2012.09.012

Cary, T. (2015). *Too soon to forgive and forget but Lance Armstrong is right about hypocrisy and need for a grown-up debate: cycling's Voldemort remains a compelling story, for better or for worse.* Retrieved October 13, 2015, from http://www.telegraph.co.uk/sport/othersports/cycling/lancearmstrong/11668810/Too-soon-to-forgive-and-forget-but-Lance-Armstrong-is-right-about-hypocrisy-and-need-for-a-grown-up-debate.html

Cialdini, R. B., Borden, R. J., Thorne, A., Walker, M. R., Freeman, S., & Sloan, L. R. (1976). Basking in reflected glory: Three (football) field studies). *Journal of Personality and Social Psychology, 34*(3), 366–375. doi:10.1037/0022-3514.34.3.366

Coombs, W. T. (2012). *Ongoing Crisis Communication. Planning, Managing and Responding.* Thousand Oaks, CA: Sage.

de Groot, M., & Robinson, T. (2008). Sport fan attachment and the psychological continuum model: A case study of an Australian league fan. *Leisure/Loisir, 32*(1), 117-138.

Frederick, E., Lim, C. H., Clavio, G., Pedersen, P., & Burch, L. M. (2014). Choosing between the one-way or two-way street: An exploration of relationship promotion by professional athletes on Twitter. *Communication & Sport, 2*(1), 80–99. doi:10.1177/2167479512466387

Froome, C. (2014). *The Climb: The Autobiography*. London: Viking.

Funk, D., & James, J. (2006). Consumer loyalty: The meaning of attachment in the development of sport team allegiance. *Journal of Sport Management, 20*, 189–217.

Gantz, W. (2012). Reflections on Communication and Sport: On Fanship and Social Relationships. *Communication & Sport, 1*(2), 176–187.

Garratt, D. (2010). Sporting citizenship: The rebirth of religion? *Pedagogy, Culture & Society, 18*(2), 123–143. doi:10.1080/14681366.2010.488040

Glynn, P. (2013). *Super league referees answer fans' Twitter questions*. BBC. Retrieved October 13, 2015, from http://www.bbc.com/sport/0/rugby-league/22384383

Gregory, S. (2009). *Twitter craze is rapidly changing the face of sports*. Retrieved October 13, 2015, from http://www.si.com/more-sports/2009/06/05/twitter-sports

Gregory. (2013). *How sports fans engage with social media*. Retrieved October, 13, 2015, from http://mashable.com/2013/10/03/sports-fans-social-media/#DumUh1plUkqz

Hambrick, M., Frederick, E., & Sanderson, J. (2013). From Yellow to Blue: Exploring Lance Armstrong's Image Repair Strategies Across Traditional and Social Media. *Communication & Sport, 00*(0), 1–23.

Hambrick, M., Simmons, J., Greenhalgh, G., & Greenwell, T. C. (2010). Understanding Professional Athletes' Use of Twitter: A Content Analysis of Athlete Tweets. *International Journal of Sports Communication, 3*, 454–471.

Highfield, T., Harrington, S., & Bruns, A. (2013). Twitter as a technology for audiencing and fandom. *Information Communication and Society, 16*(3), 315–339. doi:10.1080/1369118X.2012.756053

Hopwood, M. (2007). The sport integrated marketing communications mix. In J. Beech & S. Chadwick (Eds.), *The Marketing of Sport* (pp. 213–238). Harlow: Pearson Education Limited.

King, B. (2008). Stardom, celebrity and the para-confession. *Social Semiotics, 18*(2), 115–132. doi:10.1080/10350330802002135

Kishner, I., & Crescenti, B. (2010). The Rise of Social Media. *The Entertainment and Sports Lawyer, 27*(4), 24–26.

Livestrong Foundation. (2013). *Our Founder*. Retrieved October 13, 2015, from http://www.livestrong.org/Our-Founder

Lopez, B. (2010). Doping as Technology: A Re-Reading of the History of Performance-Enhancing Substance Use. *Institute for Culture and Society Occasional Paper Series, 1*(4), 1-17.

McCarthy, B. (2014). A sports journalism of their own: An investigation in the motivations, behaviors and media attitudes of fan sports bloggers. *Communication & Sport, 2*(1), 65–79. doi:10.1177/2167479512469943

McDonald, L., Sparks, B., & Glendon, A. (2010). Stakeholder reactions to company crisis communication and causes. *Public Relations Review, 36*(2), 263–271. doi:10.1016/j.pubrev.2010.04.004

McLean, H. (2014). Crisis and Issues Management. In J. Johnston & M. Sheehan (Eds.), Public Relations Theory and Practice. Crows Nest: Allen & Unwin.

Mobli.com. (2015). *Back in Austin and just layin' around.* Retrieved October 13, 2015, from http://www.mobli.com/media/show/id/22700756?referer=tw17

Osborne, A., & Coombs, D. (2013). Performative Sport Fandom: an approach to retheorizing sport fans. *Sport in society: Cultures, Commerce, Media. Politics, 16*(5), 672–681.

Polipulse. (2011). *Amercia Reacts to Armstrong Confession.* Retrieved November 15 2013 http://polipulse.com/america-reacts-armstrong-confession

Sanderson, J. (2010). "The nation stands behind you": Mobilising social support on 38pitches.com. *Communication Quarterly, 58*(2), 188–201. doi:10.1080/01463371003717884

Sanderson, J. (2013). From loving the hero to despising the villain: Sport fans, Facebook and social identity threats. *Mass Communication & Society, 16*(4), 487–509. doi:10.1080/15205436.2012.730650

Sanderson, J., & Emmon, B. (2014). Extending and withholding forgiveness to Josh Hamilton: Exploring forgiveness within parasocial interaction. *Communication & Sport, 2*(1), 24–47. doi:10.1177/2167479513482306

Suleman, K. (2015). *PR war over Chris Froome doping allegations boils over during Tour de France 2015.* Retrieved October 18, 2015, from http://www.prweek.com/article/1357129/pr-war-chris-froome-doping-allegations-boils-during-tour-de-france-2015

Taker, I. (2012). *Social media & sport – the importance of interacting with, not just talking at fans.* Retrieved October 13, 2015, from, http://www.theuksportsnetwork.com/social-media-interaction

United States Anti-Doping Agency. (2013). *Statement from USADA CEO Travis T. Tygart Regarding Lance Armstrong Interview.* Retrieved October, 13, 2015 from http://www.usada.org/statement-from-usada-ceo-travis-t-tygart-regarding-lance-armstrong-interview/

USADA. (2012). *Statement from USADA CEO Travis T. Tygart Regarding The U.S. Postal Service Pro Cycling Team Doping Conspiracy.* Retrieved October, 13, 2015, from http://cyclinginvestigation.usada.org/

Wertheim, L. J. (2011). *Tweet smell of #success.* Retrieved October, 13, 2015 from http://www.si.com/vault/2011/07/04/106084755/tweet-smell-of-success

Wigley, S. (2011). Telling your own bad news: Eliot Spitzer and a testing of stealing thunder strategy. *Public Relations Review, 37*(1), 50–56. doi:10.1016/j.pubrev.2011.01.003

Williams, K. D., Bourgeois, M. J., & Croyle, R. T. (1993). The effects of stealing thunder in criminal and civil trials. *Law and Human Behavior, 17*(6), 597–609. doi:10.1007/BF01044684

Young, S. (2013). *Lance Armstrong – Everybody's doing it: A case study about a leader's ethics and use of power.* Retrieved October 13, 2015, from https://www.researchgate.net/publication/245024505_Young_-_Lance_Armstrong_2013_v1-4

KEY TERMS AND DEFINITIONS

Crisis Communication: The efforts taken by a company to communicate with the public and stakeholders when an unexpected event occurs that could have a negative impact on the company's image and reputation.

Early Adopters: People who start using a product or technology as soon as it becomes available. In turn, they encourage usage amongst others.

Fans: People who have a strong interest in or admiration for a particular person, thing or sport.

Image Repair Strategy: A five step process devised by William Benoit in 1995. This process is used by organizations and individuals to overcome reputational and image damage following a crisis situation.

Performance Enhancing Drugs: Performance-enhancing drugs (PEDs) are any substances taken by athletes to improve performance.

Social Media: Websites and applications, such as Twitter, that enable users to create and share content or to participate in social networking.

Stealing Thunder: Win praise and support for oneself by pre-empting someone else's attempt to detract, criticize or impress.

Transgression: Any act or action that goes against a law, rule, or code of conduct; an offence.

Tweet: A posting made on the social media website Twitter; a micro-blog of 140 characters or fewer.

Twitter: A globally popular social networking website.

Chapter 4
The Business of Advocacy:
A Case Study of Greenpeace

Kiru Pillay
University of Witwatersrand, South Africa

Manoj Maharaj
University of KwaZulu-Natal, South Africa

ABSTRACT

Online advocacy is big business. Online advocacy organisations need to structure themselves along business lines for fund raising, and to strategically utilise their online and traditional resources to achieve their goals. The growing influence of civil society organisations has been fuelled largely by an increase and ubiquity of emerging technologies. There is no evidence of a detailed analysis of social media led advocacy campaigns in the literature. The global environmental justice organisation, Greenpeace is used as a case study. The rise of online social media has provided the organisation with an alternative to traditional mass media. There have been some notable successes for Greenpeace. The most recent of which has been its efforts to halt the drilling for oil in the Arctic. Equally the Greenpeace campaigns have sometimes provoked the public ire, for example in their miscalculation of the fallout over their recent Nazca plains intrusion. It is clear that to attain any level of success the organisation needs to structure itself on sound business principles and strategies.

THE BUSINESS OF SOCIAL ADVOCACY

Early this century, Dahlgren (2005) recognised the increasingly strategic importance of mass media and emerging technologies in fostering public dialog. A consequence of this has been the transformation of the public sphere into technology-enabled spaces, where the current social narrative is able to circumvent geographic boundaries and time constraints, and increasingly the prevailing hegemonic discourse (Mason & Hacker, 2003).

The effect of a technology-enabled public sphere is contentious, with Poster (1995) as far back as 1995, arguing that Habermas' description of the public sphere as being made up of an homogenous group of people in symmetrical relations is not sustainable in cyberspace i.e. if the discourse exists as "pixels

DOI: 10.4018/978-1-5225-0559-4.ch004

on screens" then the question of talking and of meeting face-to-face is confused and complicated. Others like Benkler (2006) argue that it may strengthen democratic ideals with still others predicting that technology will splinter the public sphere (Sunstein, 2001). Dahlgren (2005) in particular draws attention to the fragmentation that occurs in the public sphere when opposing political views foster intolerance. The impact of the Internet on the prevailing political discourse is often difficult to describe with such attempts, often reduced to producing 'opposing anecdotal evidence' (Shirky, 2010a). Dalgren (2005) does note however, that the Internet and social media in particular should be considered long-term tools that can ultimately strengthen civil society and the public sphere.

The impact and consequences of social media adoption on society are only just being realised and studied in detail, and there is no universal agreement as to its effects. Blogs for example have made it possible for the general public to act as journalists, which in turn has shifted the discourse to outside of the mainstream media. Other less optimistic viewpoints point to the fact that people generally restrict themselves to points of view to which they already subscribe, for example in the news sites that they read, which Kerbel & Bloom (2005) pointed out, could splinter and ideologically polarise the blogosphere. In research conducted to determine if blogs are comparable to Sunstien's (2001) concept of the echo chamber, Gilbert, Bergstrom and Karahalios (2009) concluded that polarisation on the blogosphere differed according to genre of the blog, with blogs dedicated to technology and entertainment provoking the least amount of polarization as opposed to blogs dedicated to lifestyle and politics which caused higher levels of polarisation. In other research using social identity theory (SIT) and an interrogation of the blogosphere, Selva, Kuflik and Gustavo (2010) conclude that there has been an increase in the number of hate groups on the Internet with these groups often using blogs to establish an online presence.

Even the practical use of Web 2.0 does not provide any answers to the impact of the Internet on the prevailing social narrative with a noticeable difference in the strategic use of social media services by presidential hopefuls Barak Obama and Mitch Romney in the lead-up to the 2008 American elections. The Obama camp's strategy for example, provided real-time campaign information, which as Rigby (2008) states helped capture the zeitgeist of the supporters, while the Romney campaign in contrast was unable to influence the campaign based on information from its followers. This is credited with playing a significant role in ensuring an Obama victory.

This chapter reports on an analysis of the role of emerging technologies in social advocacy and examines three social media-led campaigns executed by the global environmental justice civil society organisation (CSO), Greenpeace. Specifically the following research question is posed: What are the implications of Web 2.0 adoption on civil society organisations?, and in particular What transformation does Web 2.0 adoption bring to civil society organisations?

Environmental justice organisations and Greenpeace in particular, have been leaders in the adoption of emerging technologies, with many campaign victories stemming from their ability to adapt to communicating with these new technologies. Greenpeace, since its inception in 1971 has employed high-profile media-orientated protest campaigns to bring environmental issues to the attention of the public. While the effectiveness of these traditional campaign methods are understood, the effectiveness of these methods when migrated into the virtual realm need to be investigated.

BACKGROUND

Civil society is made up a global network of organisations and behaviours that straddle both governments and the general public (Glasius, 2002; Kaldor, 2003). While they have diverse reasons for existing and are structured differently to for-profit organisations DeMars (2005, p. 41) states that "if business firms are private actors pursuing private profit, and governments are public actors pursuing public purposes, then NGOs have one foot in each camp." They vary in the way they attempt to achieve their goals, are staffed differently and serve different constituencies. What they have in common is that they all operate in the public sphere with a view to achieving public agendas.

The resurgence of civil society has been attributed to the sector's ability to exploit new emerging interactive technologies, and an ability to adapt its communication and mobilisation strategies in the emerging technological paradigm. Surman & Reilly (2003, p. 4) state: "As civil society, we are confronted with an opportunity – to use the Internet and other emerging network technologies to support our quest for global peace and social justice." Referring to the Greenpeace Argentina office Kinkade and Verclas (2008, p. 46) maintain that Greenpeace Argentina has become the leading environmental CSOs in Argentina and "…its grassroots organising, online advocacy, use of social media, and innovative use of mobile technology has enabled it to win remarkable legislative victories in Argentina."

Professionalising Civil Society

As a definitional starting point this chapter employs The London School of Economics Civil Society Project definition of civil society (quoted in Deibert & Rohozinski, 2008, p. 124), which states:

Civil Society refers to the arena of unforced collective action around shared interests, purposes and values. In theory, its institutional forms are distinct from those of the state, family and market, though in practice, the boundaries between state, civil society, family and market are often complex, blurred and negotiated. Civil society commonly embraces a diversity of spaces, actors and institutional forms, varying in their degree of formality, autonomy and power. Civil societies are often populated by organisations such as registered charities, development non-governmental organisations, community groups, women's organisations, faith-based organisations, professional associations, trades unions, self-help groups, social movements, business associations, coalitions and advocacy groups.

della Porta & Diani (2006) define professional CSOs by a number of characteristics including a full-time leadership team; membership to the organisation that requires only that a person sign up as a member; and attempting influence policies that affect a particular constituency, which the organisation represents. Organisations like Amnesty International and Greenpeace fit this mould of a professional CSO.

The growth of global civil society has been fuelled by an increase in resources, technology and money. The larger global civil society organisations (often referred to as transnational social movements) are made of numerous national offices, have memberships in the millions, and have strong levels of bureaucracy.

In support of the need for organisations to become more visible Yang (2009) argues that online activists have begun to adopt marketing strategies to promote both their organisations and theirs causes. Activism no longer has the image of the scruffy children of the 1960s but rather activists are more likely to be full-time employees of advocacy organisations, with possibly a scientific background, and a likelihood of having obtained post-graduate degrees in the field of politics and/or business.

Advances in interactive networked technologies has not only created new channels for distributing information but has also transformed the way organisations and individuals communicate, which has resulted in new forms of social involvement and relationships. Civil society organisations for example, are structured as a network of organisations and supporters, which reinforce the development of a collective identity (Van de Donk, Loader, Nixon, & Rucht, 2004). CSOs have become adept at filtering and amplifying knowledge, facilitating learning, convening different audiences and developing communities to ensure changes in the status quo i.e. they have become adept at exploiting the network organisational structure to enable more flexible and responsive behaviour (Arquilla & Ronfeldt, 1998; Aaker & Smith, 2010).

Networks are not new and there have been, presumably, social networks since the dawn of society, but it is technology-based networks – which first found their way into computing via the original development of the ARPANET – that have fundamentally altered the way society functions.

Civil Society: Networked Adopters of Technology

Communication, both internal and external, is core to the effectiveness of civil society, and it is this centrality of communications that promotes the adoption of technology by CSOs. As Internet and mobile telephone usage increases so does the ability of CSOs to develop their network structures and strengthen their capacity to connect with organisations around the world. It suggests that there is a virtuous cycle between the network society and civil society. The attractiveness of Internet technologies lies in its distributed, decentralised, and relatively cheap and easily deployable architecture, which matches the organisational and political logic of global civil society networks (Deibert & Rohozinski, 2008). Internet-based technologies provide a platform for communication between different types of organisations thereby facilitating a diversity of views, (Benson & Morgan, 2015). For example the functionality of blogs has changed traditional websites into public sphere platforms thereby creating what Benkler (2006) termed a 'writable Web'. boyd (2011) describes the concept of networked publics as public spaces restructured by and through networked technologies, within which a virtual collection of people, technology and practice interact.

Virtual Communities

Real-world networks contain groups of interrelated nodes with certain parts of the network having nodes that are more closely related to each other (communities) than nodes in other parts of the network, (societies) which corresponds to the distinction between communities and societies i.e. communities are those parts of a network where the nodes are more highly clustered. Communities are generally small stable groupings with members exhibiting strong personal links and intense direct person-to-person relationships which in turn provide sociability and a strong sense of group and social identity (Memmi, 2010; Wellman, 2001), while the links within societies are less intense, less personal and more functional than those of communities.

Virtual communities are social groupings that emerged as a result of the advances in information technology and in particular the Internet, social media and mobile telephony all of which provide the infrastructure and the platforms for the creation new knowledgeable communities that exist autonomously and united around issues that span local interests as well as global issues (Memmi, 2010; Rheingold, 2002).

The questions arise as to the nature of these communities: Are they simply traditional social groups in an electronic guise or are they a totally new phenomenon? Are virtual communities different from older virtual groups? What is their structure and are they cohesively densely knit groups or more loosely linked? Are they stable or do they evolve rapidly with time: what are the goals, needs and representations of participants in these communities; and can common goals be identified?

The advent of emerging interactive technologies that transcend boundaries, the ability to create virtual communities of interest, all within the concept of a globalised world has been described by sociologist Appadurai (2011) as global dimensions or 'scapes' that flow across cultural boundaries with 'technoscapes' being emerging technologies that diffuse globally at a rapid rate (witness the global diffusion of social networking services).

AN ANALYSIS OF GREENPEACE CAMPAIGN STRATEGIES

Two separate sets of in-depth interviews were held namely: interviews with members of Senior Management Team of five Greenpeace offices (Greenpeace Head Office in the Netherlands, India, Argentina, Digital Media Unit in the USA, and South Africa) and interviews with Greenpeace campaign managers, one from Argentina and two from Greenpeace International. In total 18 interviews were held as detailed in Table 1.

The interviews were held either in person or via a Skype call. Organisational documents were also collected, which as Yin (2003) argues are a good source of evidence in that they are stable, unobtrusive, exact and have broad coverage.

Three global campaigns selected for an in-depth analysis displayed an effective use of social media:

Table 1. Greenpeace offices interviews

Greenpeace Offices	Senior Management Team
International	7
Africa	4
Argentina	2
India	1
Digital Media Unit (USA)	1
Campaign Interviews	**Campaign Managers**
Argentina - Forest Law	1
International – Green my Apple	1
International – Unfriend Coal	1
Total	18

The Green My Apple Campaign: Taking on the ICT Companies

In 2006 Greenpeace initiated the 'Green My Apple' campaign, which was targeted at the electronics sector, to eliminate the use of hazardous chemicals in the manufacture of products and for the ethical disposal of electronic waste. Apple was targeted by virtue of it being the leading company in the sector. Apple eventually acceded to the campaigns demands and in 2007 its founder Steve Jobs (Jobs, 2007) issued the following statement:

Apple has been criticized by some environmental organizations for not being a leader in removing toxic chemicals from its new products, and for not aggressively or properly recycling its old products. Now I'd like to tell you what we are doing to remove toxic chemicals from our new products, and to more aggressively recycle our old products.

The most recent Greenpeace report into the electronics sectors, while noting that major advancements must still be made with respect to 'greening' the sector, acknowledges that significant progress has been made and notes specifically that there are more products free from the worst hazardous substances compared to 2006, when the original campaign was launched (Greenpeace, 2014).

The Forest Law Campaign: Protecting Argentina's Forests

Greenpeace's Forest Law campaign in Argentina (or La Ley de Bosques) which sought to reverse the effects of deforestation, applied pressure on the Argentinian Senate to approve a new Forest Law by urging people to vote for a new proposed Forest Law rather than for a particular candidate. The campaign used the Web, mobile phones, television coverage, and newspapers to convince people to sign a petition in support of the new law. The online activity was supported with direct action with activists setting up camp and occupying the trees from where they blogged and transmitted reports and updates. The new law was eventually passed in 2007 and included a one-year moratorium on the clearing of indigenous forests and also established a process of public hearings and environmental impact studies (Kinkade & Verclas, 2008).

A 2014 report in the Argentina Independent (2014) notes that loopholes in the original legislation have been closed allowing additional forested areas to be protected under the law. The campaign also seems to have galvanised a new generation of activists who have been encouraged to monitor a specific area of forest and inform relevant authorities of any significant changes caused by forest clearance; this use of crowdsourcing has meant that large quantities of data can be analysed in a short time (DMC, 2013)

The Unfriend Coal Campaign: A Focus on Clean Energy

Data centers are the fastest-growing contributor to the ICT sector's carbon footprint (The Climate Group, 2008) with Greenpeace in 2011 having rated Facebook's data centers as amongst the most polluting in the world (Sayer, 2011). The campaign against Facebook involved the setting up a Facebook page called 'Unfriend Coal' which asked supporters to pressure the social media company to re-examine its environmental policies. After nearly twenty months of campaigning, on 15th December 2011, Facebook and Greenpeace reached an agreement that saw the organisations agree to cooperate to promote clean energy options and to encourage power generation companies develop renewable energy alternatives (Meikle, 2011). The statement from Facebook (2011) said in part:

Facebook is committed to supporting the development of clean and renewable sources of energy, and our goal is to power all of our operations with clean and renewable energy.

An article in the Guardian newspaper (2014) reports the Greenpeace itself is highly complimentary of some of the leading technology companies, and specifically Facebook and Apple for using an increasing amount of renewable resources to power their data centers, with the research showing that Google in particular has been the most ambitious by buying wind energy that is then injected into the local electric grids where it runs data centers.

SOLUTIONS AND RECOMMENDATIONS

It is clear that Greenpeace has had to reinvent itself in the face of strong competition from emerging online advocacy organisations. To do this the organisation has embraced technology, but rather than discarding its traditional means of campaigning, and drawing attention to environmental issues, it has supplemented them with online methods that have broadened its appeal and reach. Thus Greenpeace has not competed with the WWW for the attention of its audience but has appropriated these technologies to supplement its traditional methodologies.

Placing Supporters at the Centre of a Campaign

Internal Greenpeace documents emphasise the need to move away from the traditional mode of one-dimensional one-to-many communications, to having 'conversations' with supporters where their actions and behaviours generate content that can be dynamically repurposed and which eventually lead to real-world activities (Greenpeace Internal Document3, 2011). The document argues that social media must be a tool that allows supporters to participate in a meaningful and engaged manner. This has to some extent been achieved by Greenpeace Argentina:

Each cyber activist helps us to reach our target. We start involving more and more people in the design and the way we push our campaigns. We evolve more when we start working with these social tools, where the people can organize themselves and create things in collaborative work. The last step we reached a couple of years ago where we moved from a centralized model. Like a big net of nets that we work in. Now we have a model where Greenpeace is not in the middle, but all the people, cyberactivists, volunteers and donors share some content and all the connections are between the people. We help people that are connected by Greenpeace by social media but also between connections, between cyberactivists and the other social media people so they receive the content from us or from other users, but the discussion that they are having will help other users to change the way we communicate or the way we create our campaign.

Greenpeace has modified its traditional approach to campaigning with Greenpeace at the centre, to an approach in which the supporters are at the centre of the campaign. The director of the media unit whose brief is to understand the role of social media in campaigning, notes:

I think that the organisation is going through a massive shift right now. Certainly one of the missions that I have through this digital mobilization lab is to figure out and demonstrate how we can campaign with supporters at the center of the work - a much more supporter-centric or supporter driven model.

Some elements of this strategy are evident in individual campaigns with the Forest Law campaign for example urging supporters to repackage information from the website and distribute as widely as possible. As one respondent stated, supporters were increasingly more concerned with the actual issues that the campaign was focussed on rather than on the organisation that was spearheading the campaign. As far back as 1999, Ronfeldt, Arquilla, Fuller, and Fuller (1999) in the course of analysing the Zapatista conflict in Mexico remarked that the information revolution favours the networked form of campaigning and that within weeks of the Zapatista campaign the conflict became less about the EZLN (the organisation) and more about the actual campaign. Increasingly, organisations must define campaigns based on what will resonate with supporters rather than what will resonate with the media.

Networks and Virtual Communities

Internal organisational networks are important sources of knowledge and as Rogers (2003) argues, highly complex organisations embody high-levels of knowledge and expertise amongst members. Within Greenpeace, recognition of this inherent knowledge has in part motivated the formation of the digital media unit which aims to "seek out and find those pockets of innovation and places where people are testing and trying new things and then to support that and grow and enable that to happen".

Individualisation in Online Communities

Technology-enabled networks and the ability to form online communities are important properties for CSOs and specifically for their campaigning objectives. Virtual communities are described as technology-enabled forms of support for a new form of sociability, different but not inferior to previous forms of social interactions (Castells, 2000). Networks and virtual communities are the backbone of citizen-enabled campaigning in the information age. The Forest Law campaign afforded the opportunity for Greenpeace Argentina to collaborate on a wide scale: firstly with volunteers and activists, and also with traditional media and other CSOs. This collaborative effort became, in the words of the campaign manager "the biggest online community in Argentina and Latin America."

The Internet and social media affords individuals and online communities the ability to join groups and engage in conversations based on very specific personal preference referred to by Negroponte (1995) as the 'Daily Me' and by Sunstein (2001) as the 'Daily We'. This has the potential to polarise the discourse and while this behaviour has always existed (e.g. people choosing newspapers and magazines that mirror their opinions) there is now a difference in degree; emerging technologies increase the individual's control over content. While the evidence points to virtual communities being fairly homogeneous in terms of values and viewpoints, in practice this has not been the experience within Greenpeace with one respondent stating that Greenpeace has seen some diversity in its online supporter communities, particularly on Facebook, with groups that instinctively should not be tolerant of each other "holding together as a community." He further notes that these diverse communities straddle "bible belt US, that believes in the stewardship of the planet and yet Greenpeace protecting the whales, protecting the seals, they see this as consistent with the Christian mission and they like Greenpeace and its great."

Strong Ties, Weak Ties and Clickactivism

Clickactivism or the purely online activity of supporting a cause or campaign exclusively in cyberspace is the domain of online organisations like Avaaz, but increasingly it is a tactic that has been employed by established CSOs as well. White, (2010) writing in the Guardian argues that organisations increasingly ask less and less of their members, which has the potential to reduce activism into a series of petition drives based on current events. A Greenpeace manager commented that clicktivism is not always a low-risk option arguing that in parts of the world where there is no focus on civil liberties, the clicking of a button or the signing of a petition implies that the person's name is digitally recorded with a time stamp, allowing access to the clickactivist's personal identity by the authorities.

Clickactivism is closely related to the concept of strong and weak ties and has been vigorously debated with respect to online activism and in particular with regards to the use of social media in campaigning. All social networks contain either weak or strong connections (or ties). Strong ties involve frequent contacts, emotional intensity and solidarity while weak ties are casual, superficial and do not enable the formation of communities but are nevertheless important for the circulation of new information (Memmi, 2010). Gladwell (2010) writing in the New Yorker magazine provoked a flurry of responses when he suggested that cyberactivism associated with social media, is built around weak-ties which is a low-risk option that very rarely leads to high-risk activism, and does not achieve any meaningful change. He uses various examples of activisms and advocacy from the American civil rights movement through to the Italian extremist group, the Red Brigades, to argue that traditional activism and activists show a strong-tie phenomenon. In the case of the Red Brigades, almost seventy percent of recruits had at least one good friend already in the organisation and the same is true of many of the men who join the Mujahideen in Afghanistan. Even spontaneous revolutions like the bringing down of the Berlin wall were at the core strong-tie phenomena.

In a counter-argument to Gladwell, Shirky (2010) argues that changing public opinion requires two steps: in the first step ideas, thoughts and debates are transmitted by the media, and in step two these are then re-transmitted by friends and family. It is in this second social step that political opinions are formed. In both these steps, the Internet and social media in particular can make a difference. Shirkey (2010) further contends that political activism has to be accompanied by a civil society literate enough and densely enough connected to discuss the issues being presented, and mass media alone does not change people's minds. In response an interviewee argued that Gladwell's article ignored the value of social media in amplifying a campaign:

… what's frustrating about that article for a number of people in this space is that he grossly undervalues or refuses to acknowledge the role of social media communications at all. It's not a binary thing right? So when you look at Egypt, of course it was not a Facebook revolution, it did not happen because of Facebook but it could not have happened without Facebook and social technologies to enable people to see that they were not alone, to be able to share information that previously they could not have.

One example of a web-based CSO is the global organisation Avaaz (which means 'voice' in many Asian and Middle Eastern languages) whose stated aim is to "close the gap between the world we have, and the world most people everywhere want" (Avaaz, 2014). Avaaz is the biggest online CSO in the world, with a membership of 41 million people (Avaaz, 2014). The existence and growth of the organisation is due mainly to the emergence of new communication technologies, in particular the Internet. The use of the Internet as its main campaigning tool gives the organisation an element of agility and flexibility, which in turn allows it to effectively mobilise on a global scale. Avaaz campaigns span a wide range and include human rights issues, the environment, and poverty alleviation. Nobel Prize winner and environmental campaigner Al Gore describes Avaaz as "inspiring, and has already begun to make a difference" (Avaaz, 2014). While it is true there are mixed views on the actual role of social media in various protests and actions, the role of social media is more likely to be one of creating the material conditions for coordination and cooperation amongst activists. Activists use the tools of the day to frame views and coordinate their actions and it would be impossible to analyse any number of recent protests actions without discussing social media. Online social media is an additional weapon in the arsenal of the activist.

A particular strength of weak ties is the ability to engage with new ideas. For example, weak ties between one person in a closely knit group and an acquaintance (weak tie) in another group becomes not merely a trivial acquaintance, but rather a crucial bridge between the two densely knit clumps of close friends. These distinct groups would not have been connected to one another at all were it not for the existence of these weak ties (Granovetter, 1983).

Small World Theory and Social Networking Density

Another closely related concept is that of small worlds (also called small world patterns or networks). A small world is a graph with both local clustering and short distances between nodes; short distances promotes accessibility, while local clustering and redundancy of edges prevent disconnections and promotes reliability and accessibility (White & Houseman, 2003). Two characteristics of small world networks are that when balanced properly they let messages move through the network effectively, and secondly in small world networks large groups are sparsely connected (Shirky, 2008).

These dense and sparse characteristics of small world networks manifest themselves in social networking communities. In a report by the Pew Internet and American Life Project (Pew Reserch Center, 2012) it was found that with respect to the density of people's friendship networks, people's friend's lists on Facebook are only modestly interconnected i.e. a fully connected list of friends would have a density of one (everyone knows everyone else). As an example of what this means, if you have ten friends (n), the number of possible friendship ties among everyone in your network is forty-five (possible ties=n*(n-1)/2), while the average Facebook user's friends list has a density of 0.12. This means that 12% of a person's Facebook friends are friends with each other.

Civil society organisations can exploit small world networks by adopting both dense and sparse connections i.e. by first encouraging small groups to connect tightly, and then aiding the connections between these groups (Shirky, 2008). Small world theory has been adopted by Greenpeace with small groups of cyberactivists connecting to each other to form a larger network.

Ladders of Engagement

Getting supporters to increased levels of engagement and action has long been a focus within civil society. For example, the organisation Groundwire (2012), which advises CSOs in their use of the Internet, uses the concept of the 'Engagement Pyramid' to describe the process of actively getting supporters to higher levels of involvement in campaigns. In this process supporters theoretically traverse from being mere observers to eventually being leaders of campaigns. Greenpeace's version of this concept is the ladder of engagement. They argue that the easiest way for the organisation to pursue this increased level of engagement is to simply ask supporters; the challenge is not so much that supporters are not willing to do more but that the organisation's members do not want to invest the time required to develop creative ways in which supporters can meaningfully impact the campaign.

A Final Note

A respondent argued that clickactivism does not give the person participating the feeling of experiencing anything new and that the 'experience' is forgotten within a couple of minutes, suggesting that the campaign has made very little serious impact on that particular person's outlook. The 1963 American Civil Rights March led by Martin Luther King in Washington DC is presented as an example of 'real' activism and the respondent states "that issue is about experiencing, it is something that in a way shook your soul for ten minutes, for a whole day, it doesn't matter. It is not something that passed by without leaving an impression in your soul. This is the thing that I think Avaaz has taken this very lightly. I tend to consider this kind of cyber activism as zombie activists, because these people they click, simply because they click."

Weak or strong ties notwithstanding the importance of a human network in advocacy is well recognised. For example, during the Burmese monks protest in 2007, and despite an Internet penetration rate of 0.1 per cent and government censorship, reports and images were sent at regular intervals by activists and everyday citizens with increasing levels of engagement appearing seemingly without any concerted effort. As Sigal (2009, p. 15) states "Additionally, local groups and activists in Burma that previously lacked a public presence gained access to telecommunications and media tools and became visible and influential players on the national and the global stage. Long-time Burma-watchers found themselves communicating with groups of activists that appeared to have sprung fully formed out of nowhere."

With social networks being used predominantly to maintain pre-existing ties, whether strong (close friends) or weak (acquaintances) the question that arises is 'what really is new with emerging interactive social media technologies?' The answer may be that these new systems make relational structure explicit. However, it is not yet apparent whether this new paradigm fundamentally changes human motivations and social relations (Memmi, 2010).

FUTURE RESEARCH DIRECTIONS

Social Media Adoption in Civil Society Organisations

One of the purposes of social media adoption by civil society is to expand the public spaces for citizens to voice opinions. Research into how CSOs, through their use of social media, provide alternate discourses and agendas would be instructive.

There has been an almost exponential increase in the number of citizens-led protest around the world, all seemingly aided to a large degree by the use of social media, so much so that Time magazine declared 2011 as the Year of the Protestor (Stengel, 2011; Anderson, 2011). This study notes the distinction between civil society and their use of institutionalised advocacy for the most part, and popular protest led by social movement and mobs whose modus operandi is more instinctive, immediate and often violent. With the increasing importance of civil society and social movements in socio-political life, aided by an increase in technological resources available, the possible points of convergence and divergence that exist between these two social groupings demand greater critical investigation.

Furthermore, based on the wave of socio-political changes taking place globally, in response to the deep divisions that exist in society, and aided in part by emerging collaborative media technologies, this study finds it incumbent that future research be undertaken into the role of these technologies in civil society.

The evaluation of advocacy and its associated effect on policy and legislation is notoriously difficult to evaluate. If advocacy is intended to effect changes to policy or indeed enact new policy then the effectiveness of advocacy campaigns should be a simple matter of evaluating changes to policy brought about by advocacy campaigns. However, it is obviously not as simple as that and even more so in the case of social-media led advocacy. Any form of technology-led or technology-enabled advocacy sits side-by-side with tradition offline actions and it is far from easy to evaluate the effect that social media has had on a campaign. It would therefore seem an obvious area of research to empirically describe the effect of social media on advocacy campaigns and possibly establish a framework to measure this effectiveness.

Complexity theory, which is the study of dynamic living systems, can be applied to socio-political field where the reductionist approach is often taken especially with regards to policy development and implementation. Recognising that the issues faced by civil society and multidimensional and often interconnected it would be important to determine the effect of social media is generalising learning's gained from involvement in context-specific campaigns and actions.

The Structural Reorganisation of Civil Society Organisations

An obvious and important area of future research would be a deeper understanding of the structural changes brought about by the adoption of social media. Specifically, does the interactive nature of social media clash with traditional civil society mentalities and are CSOs flexible enough to accommodate a dialogue that supporters increasingly demand. To what extent are CSOs moving toward the new type of online CSOs, if at all, or even to what extent are new methods of online advocacy being adopted.

The adoption of social media influences the way organisations perceive themselves, and importantly the way they operate and campaign. Future research can examine how the adoption of technology, and social media in particular affects: organisational structures; strategy and tactics; and roles and responsibilities. Additionally, it would be instructive to understand how CSOs are attempting to formalise these changes.

The old adage of 'think global, act local' is being turned on its head and increasingly the call is for 'think local, act global' which of course is possible with a medium that has no regard for geographical or spatial boundaries. Increasingly social issues have a global perspective. Think climate change and the fight against apartheid, both of which has (or had) a global exposure and worldwide network of supporting organisations, activists and citizens. It is important to understand the role of emerging technologies in fostering these transnational actions.

Transnational Advocacy and Online Virtual Communities

More research is required in the formation and lifespan of online communities. Importantly the issue of strong and weak ties and the extent to which online groups gravitate towards communities that reinforce their points of view thereby further polarising the socio-political debate needs to be ascertained. Furthermore, to what extent do race and other demographics play a part, if any, in online communities?

Social movements and social actions are increasingly influenced by happenings in distant places with the revolution in communications transforming the world into the much-touted 'global village' which makes diffusion studies ideally suited to understanding mobilisation in a globalised world which would be an obvious area for research.

The growth in transnational advocacy organisations and campaigns, fuelled by an increase in resources necessitate involvement of people and organisations in structurally unequal positions. There is a very real possibility that tensions may surface around these inequalities further exacerbating the power dynamic that may already exist around the digital divide and issues of access. It is important to understand how the adoption of social media in transnational campaigning impact upon these inherent tensions.

IMPLICATIONS FOR FIRM'S GROWTH

Business growth is intimately linked with the firm's ability to launch and maintain successful marketing campaigns. Viewing social advocacy organisation as businesses in the traditional sense, albeit with the profit motive defined differently provides important insight into the use of social media in driving business value. As demonstrated by the Greenpeace campaigns, it is advisable for firms to consider a strategic blend of traditional and online initiatives when promoting their products or services. This allows firms to maximize their message reach to diverse audiences. The Greenpeace campaigns also show that the traditional and online campaigns are independent parallel campaigns, and do not rely on the audience being familiar with one campaign to understand the other. Often firms use integrated online and offline campaigns, thus excluding the majority of consumers who exist in either one or the other domain.

CONCLUSION

The adopting of emerging technologies and innovation, and the planning and management thereof, is almost always a complex and complicated exercise, with new sets of knowledge competencies having to merge with the organisations existing capabilities. In the case of civil society, add to this mix the emergence of new flexible and adaptable online CSOs all vying for the same set of supporters, and you have a situation that makes it incumbent for organisations to re-evaluate the very core of their values.

Social media has become a key ingredient of Greenpeace's campaigning strategy and has been embraced at both a strategic and operational level. The emergence of a collaborative communications paradigm has necessitated a level of organisational introspection. For example while many researchers point to the polarisation of the discourse in an online community, with people gravitating towards others who hold similar points of view, this research suggests that online communities have the ability to attract a diverse group of individuals and organisations, individual agendas and goals notwithstanding. Even arguments about the weakness of online ties have been addressed by firstly civil society's recognition of this argument, and secondly fundamental steps to counteract this i.e. adoption of specific strategies like the ladder of engagement.

At an operational level, long-standing traditional methods of organising and campaigning are being challenged and questioned. Social media give supporters an avenue to express themselves and they expect that organisations be receptive to their message. This has meant placing supporters at the center of campaigns, something that is at odds with Greenpeace's long-standing tradition of being the vanguard of the environmental justice movement. So too has the emergence of online virtual communities placed a new challenge for the organisation: how to harness the power of these communities, many of which have a short life-span, and are focused on a particular issue, and then disband just as rapidly. Social media also gives organisations an ability to creatively challenge the issues of state and corporate power, market forces, and cultural norms, which again necessitate a level of introspection at an organisational level. Finally, despite all theoretical deliberations Greenpeace needs to determine whether there is any contradiction between the street and cyberspace.

REFERENCES

Aaker, J., & Smith, A. (2010). *The Dragonfly Effect*. San Francisco: Jossey-Bass.

Anderson, K. (2011, December26). The Protester. *Time*, 38–68.

Appadurai, A. (2011). *Disjuncture and Difference in the Global Cultural Economy*. Retrieved October 15, 2011 from http://www.intcul.tohoku.ac.jp/~holden/MediatedSociety/Readings/2003_04/Appadurai.html

Arquilla, J., & Ronfeldt, D. (1998). Preparing for the Information-Age Conflict: Part 1 Conceptual and Organizational Dimensions. *Information Communication and Society*, *1*(1), 1–22. doi:10.1080/13691189809358951

Avaaz. (2014). Retrieved October 15, 2014 from Avaaz: http://www.avaaz.org/en/about.php

Benkler, Y. (2006). *The Wealth of Networks: How Social Production Transforms Markets and Freedom*. New Haven, CT: Yale Universty Press.

Benson, V., & Morgan, S. (2015). *Implications of Social Media Use in Personal and Professional Settings*. Hershey, PA: IGI Global; doi:10.4018/978-1-4666-7401-1

boyd, d. (2011). Social Network Sites as Networked Publics. In Z. Papacharissi (Ed.), *A Networked Self*. New York: Routledge.

Castells, M. (2000). *The Rise of the Network Society* (S. Edition, Ed.). Blackwell Publishing.

Dahlgren, P. (2005). The Internet, Public Spheres, and Political Communication: Dispersion and Deliberation. *Political Communication*, *22*(2), 147–162. doi:10.1080/10584600590933160

Deibert, R., & Rohozinski, R. (2008). Good for Liberty, Bad for Security? Global Civil Society and the Securitization of the Internet. In R. Deibert, J. Palfrey, R. Rohozinski, & J. Zittrain (Eds.), *Access Denied: The Paractice and Policy of Global Internet Filtering* (pp. 123–150). Cambridge, MI: The MIT Press.

della Porta, D., & Diani, M. (2006). *Social Movements: An Introduction*. New York: Blackwell Publishing.

DeMars, W. (2005). *NGOs and Transnational Networks*. London: Pluto Press.

DMC11. (2013). *DMCii imagery – Halting Deforestation in Argentina*. Retrieved October 15 from http://www.dmcii.com/?p=9215

Facebook. (2011, January 18). *Unfriend Coal*. Retrieved March 5, 2012 from http://www.facebook.com/unfriendcoal

Gilbert, E., Bergstrom, T., & Karahalios, K. (n.d.). Blogs Are Echo Chambers: Blogs Are Echo Chambers. *Proceedings of the 42nd Hawaii International Conference on System Sciences – 2009*. Retrieved October 15, 2014, from http://ieeexplore.ieee.org/stamp/stamp.jsp?tp=&arnumber=4755503

Gladwell, M. (2010, October 4). Small Change: Why the Revolution Will Not Be Tweeted. *The New Yorker*.

Glasius, M. (2002). *Global Civil Society Yearbook 2002*. London School of Economics.

Granovetter, M. (1983). The Strength of Weak Ties: A Network Theory Revisited. *Sociological Theory*, *1*, 201–233. doi:10.2307/202051

Greenpeace. (2014). *Green Gadgets: Designing the future The path to Greener electronice*. Retrieved October 15, 2014, from http://www.greenpeace.org/international/Global/international/publications/toxics/2014/Green%20Gadgets.pdf

Groundwire. (2012). *Home Page*. Retrieved March 1, 2012 from Groundwire: http://groundwire.org/

Jobs, S. (2007). Retrieved March 25, 2012, from http://www.apple.com/hotnews/agreenerapple/

Kaldor, M. (2003). Civil Society and Accountability. *Journal of Human Development*, *4*(1), 5–27. doi:10.1080/1464988032000051469

Kerbel, M., & Bloom, J. (2005). Blog for America and Civic Involvement. *The International Journal of Press/Politics*, *10*(4), 3–27. doi:10.1177/1081180X05281395

Kinkade, S., & Verclas, K. M. (2008). Text Messaging to Save Trees (Argentina). Wireless Technologies for Social Change: Trends in Mobile Use by NGOs, 45-47.

Mason, M., & Hacker, K. (2003). Applying Communication Theory to Digital Divide Research. *IT & Society*, *1*(5), 40–55.

Meikle, J. (2011). *Facebook 'Unfriends' Coal and 'Likes' Clean Power*. Retrieved from http://www.guardian.co.uk/environment/2011/dec/15/facebook-coal-clean-power-energy-greenpeace

Memmi, D. (2010). Sociology of Virtual Communities and Social Software Design. In S. Murugesan (Ed.), *Web 2.0, 3.0, and X.0: Technologies, Business, and Social Applications* (Vol. 2, pp. 790–803). New York: Information Science Reference. doi:10.4018/978-1-60566-384-5.ch045

Negroponte, N. (1995). *Being Digital*. London: Hodder and Stoughton.

Pew Research Center. (2012). *Why Most Facebook Users Get More Than They Give*. Pew Internet and American Life Project.

Poster, M. (1995). *CyberDemocracy: Internet and the Public Sphere*. Irvine, CA: From University of California. http://www.hnet.uci.edu/mposter/writings/democ.html

Rheingold, H. (2002). *Smart Mobs: The Next Social Revolution*. Cambridge, MA: Perseus Publishing.

Rigby, B. (2008). *Mobilizing Generation 2.0: A Practical Guide to Using Web 2.0*. San Francisco: Jossey-Bass.

Rogers, E. M. (2003). *Diffusion of Innovations*. New York: The Free Press, A Division of Simon&Schuster.

Ronfeldt, D., Arquilla, J., Fuller, G., & Fuller, M. (1999). *The Zapatista 'Social Netwar' in Mexico*. RAND.

Sayer. (2011). *Facebook Unfriends Coal, Friends Greenpeace in Clean Energy Campaign*. Retrieved from http://www.computerworld.com/s/article/9222721/Facebook_unfriends_coal_friends_Green-peace_in_clean_energy_campaign

Selva, S., Kuflik, T. & Gustavo, S. (2012). Changes in the discourse of online hate blogs: The effect of Barack Obama's election in 2008. *First Monday, 17*(11).

Shirky, C. (2008). *Here Comes Everybody*. Penguin Books.

Shirky, C. (2010a). *SXSW: South by SouthWest*. Retrieved March 15, 2011, from Why Would We Think Social Media Is Revolutionary?: http://schedule.sxsw.com/2011/events/event_IAP000246

Shirky, C. (2010b). *The Political Power of Social Media. Foreign Affairs*. Retrieved October 15 from https://www.foreignaffairs.com/articles/2010-12-20/political-power-social-media

Sigal, I. (2009). *Digital Media in Conflict-Prone Societies*. Center for International Media Assistance, National Endowerment for Democracy.

Stengel, R. (2011, December26). 2011 Person of the Year. *Time*, 36.

Sunstein, C. (2001). *Republic.com*. Princeton, NJ: Princeton University Press.

Surman, M., & Reilly, K. (2003). *Appropriating the Internet for Social Change: Towards the Strategic Use of Networked Technologies by Transnational Civil Society Organizations*. Social Sciences Research Council, Information Technology and International Cooperation Program.

The Argentina Independent. (2014). *Salta Governor closes Deforestation Loophole*. Retrieved October 15 from http://www.argentinaindependent.com/tag/forest-law/

The Climate Group. (2008). *SMART 2020: Enabling the Low Carbon Economy in the Information Age*. Global e-Sustainability Initiative.

The Guardian. (2014). *Google, Facebook and Apple lead on green data centers*. Retrieved October 15, 2014, from http://www.theguardian.com/sustainable-business/greenpeace-report-google-facebook-apple-green-data-centers

van de Donk, W., Loader, B., Nixon, P., & Rucht, D. (2004). Social Movements and ICTs. In W. van de Donk, B. Loader, P. Nixon, & D. Rucht (Eds.), *Cyberprotest: New Media, citizens and social movements* (pp. 1–25). London: Routledge.

Wellman, B. (2001). Physical Place and Cyberplace: The Rise of Personalized Networking. *International Journal of Urban and Regional Research*, 25(2), 227–252. doi:10.1111/1468-2427.00309

White, D., & Houseman, M. (2003). The Navigability of Strong Ties: Small Worlds, Tie Strength, and Network Topology. *WileyPeriodicals*, 8(1), 72–81.

White, M. (2010, August 12). *Clicktivism is ruining leftist activism*. Retrieved December 16, 2011, from http://www.guardian.co.uk/commentisfree/2010/aug/12/clicktivism-ruining-leftist-activism

Yang, G. (2009). *The Power of the Internet in China*. New York: Columbia University Press.

Yin, R. K. (2003). *Case Study Research Design and Methods*. London: Sage Publications.

KEY TERMS AND DEFINITIONS

Advocacy: The process of promoting an idea or policy through various means, including publicity campaigns, speeches, and other advertising.

Civil Society: The set of non-governmental and non-business organisations that champion the cause of the people. Synonymous with grassroots organisations.

Click Activism: This is a type of online activism that just requires the participant to click a mouse button to sign a petition, contribute funds, or support a cause. This is a type of armchair activism.

Network Effect: This describes the multiplier effect of many people using or responding to or sharing a resource. The more people use something the more valuable it becomes. A good example of the network effect is the growth of online social networks like Facebook.

Strong Ties: Within online social networks a strong tie may be defined as a link between two nodes (individuals) that are supported by other offline/online links, such as real-world friendships. That is, two nodes sharing strong ties share more than a single online friendship.

Virtual Communities: People and organisations that gather online (primarily through social networks) to promote a common cause.

Weak Ties: Within online social networks a weak tie may be defined as a link between two nodes (individuals) that are not supported by other offline/online links.

Chapter 5
Social Media, Participation, and Citizenship:
New Strategic Directions

Richard Bull
De Montfort University, UK

Monica Pianosi
De Montfort University, UK

ABSTRACT

Social media is a worldwide phenomenon with applications like Facebook and Twitter credited with everything from Obama's 2008 election victory to the Arab Spring. But alongside claims of a social media inspired 'revolution' lay more nuanced questions around the role and impact of digital tools, smartphones, and social media in 'every day' contexts. The chapter discusses the role and impact of social media in organisations through two case studies where social media and digital technologies were used to increase energy awareness and environmental citizenship within organisations. Encouraging findings are presented that show the potential of such tools to facilitate change within individuals and organisations yet a cautionary note is offered with regards implementing and measuring such campaigns. Results from the interviews are discussed revealing how claims of social media on participation can be tested, and recommendations offered on how to design interventions for future social media and environmental communication initiatives.

INTRODUCTION

Our electronic networks are enabling novel forms of collective action, enabling the creation of collaborative groups that are larger and more distributed than any other time. (Shirky, 2008, p. 48)

Social media has emerged as a worldwide phenomenon with applications like Facebook and Twitter credited with everything from Obama's 2008 election victory (Zhang, Johnson, Seltzer, & Bichard, 2009), to the Arab Spring (Ghonim, 2012). This chapter will explore the role and impact of social media

DOI: 10.4018/978-1-5225-0559-4.ch005

in wider society before considering the implications and opportunities for social media to be used in organizations for widening participation and improve their operation and performance.

Findings from two distinct but related cases are presented. The first is a social media campaign run buy the sustainability team of a city centre University in the United Kingdom. The second is a participatory approach to energy management in the energy services team of local authority in the same city. Both projects aimed to utilise and explore the same public participation principles afforded by new technologies. This chapter will first reflect on the literature surrounding social media, public participation and citizenship and introduce the two cases that illustrate the potential as well the barriers. Then findings are presented before critically reflecting on the challenges and opportunities for organisations using social media.

THE RISE OF SOCIAL MEDIA

This chapter is concerned with the concerned with the potential of social media to connect people. Clay Shirky (2008), one of the great proponents of the benefits of social media cites numerous examples of social media achieving this; such as the ability of people to self-organise photographs on Flickr, contribute their knowledge on shared documents on Wikipedia and engage in social activism. Groups like the American Red Cross (Briones, Kuch, Liu, & Jin, 2011), the UK based Forestry Commission (Stewart et al., 2012), and business leaders (Fischer & Reuber, 2011) are all using social media, especially Twitter. Through these interactions messages, information can spread – or go viral – in a matter of minutes to hundreds and thousands of users. Messages can be searched and identified using a #hashtag and enable messages to be aggregated and searched. Alongside the banal and gossip laden tweets, there are numerous examples of news storics breaking on Twitter before the formal news channels (Rheingold, 2002). So, what Ghonim (2012) referred to as 'Revolution 2.0' has cemented the argument for many that the dawn of the internet, and now the web-enabled capacity of smartphones, has changed the nature of how people connect and interact, share knowledge and act in a way that 'amplifies' individual actions.

Social media is not without its detractors though. Castells (2007), for example, argues that social media is a form of horizontal networked communication that is far from the democratic claims made by some. With only approximately 10% of users generating over 90% of the content there is understandable skepticism over the role and impact of Twitter and the limits of 'point and click' politics (van Dijck, 2012). Perceptions are not helped when commentators such as Van Djick argue that analysis of social media content shows that 40% of Tweets can be classified as 'pointless babble' (van Dijck, 2012) and Dahlberg (2001) argues participants simply huddle together in like-minded communities of interest.

Critics also argue that the notion that on-line spaces are neutral or uncontested is idealism (Castells, 2007; van Dijck, 2012). Mass self-communication spaces such as Twitter and Facebook are still subject to power relations and self-interest. Governments, corporate interests and the media are all influencing and affecting these on-line public spheres in ways that challenge the democratic and deliberative nature of the Internet. Critical theorist Jurgen Habermas' concepts of the public sphere and communicative competence have been explored as possible interpretive tools for the success or impact of social media (Dahlberg, 2001; van Dijck, 2012). Similarly, Habermasian ideals have been utilized to interesting effect within the risk communication literature where similar claims have been made around the power of discourse, participation and collaboration with increasing claims around social learning and behavior change (Bull, Petts, & Evans, 2008; Petts & Brooks, 2006; Webler, Tuler, & Krueger, 2001).

Social Media, Energy, and Buildings

One emerging area of research for the use of social media has been in the field of energy visualisation tools and 'dashboards' that provide feedback to the building user; these tools have been cautiously heralded as an opportunity for behaviour change (Darby, 2010; Hargreaves, Nye, & Burgess, 2013). Research has explored novel ways to re-connect people to energy through the use of systems that show the price, unit-cost or CO_2 consumption through a live feed or half-hourly metering, and the effects on building-users (Darby, 2010). But increasingly studies have been examining the potential of information technology and tools such as social media for behaviour change within energy and buildings (Burrows, Johnson, & Johnson, 2013; Crowley, Curry, & Breslin, 2014; Foster, Lawson, Wardman, Blythe, & Linehan, 2012; Lehrer & Vasudev, 2010). Crowley et al. (2014) for example linked up their building management system to Twitter to send building users targeted messages querying consumption. In their study this resulted in a 26% reduction in energy use. This is not quite living up to the 'social' dimension of social media though which sets out to draw on the wider knowledge of the community. Differences remain though between research that points to the potential of social media to have an impact (for example Lehrer & Vasudev 2010, Benson & Morgan 2015) and those that have actually attempted an intervention in the real world (Crowley et al, 2014). This aspect is explored by Foster et al. (2010) in which they explored workforces' perceptions of social media through a series of workshops. They note employees concerns around privacy and trust, two themes to which will be returned.

Concluding their research into providing individual energy feedback to University employees, Murtagh et al. (2013) offer a sobering reflection for behaviour change. Simply put, whilst the potential for significant savings are high, motivation is low. So, whilst many of these interventions to change behaviours are noble, well meaning and, sometimes, effective, they are based on a particular 'information-deficit' or rational approach to behaviour change – if 'they' have the right information 'they' will change behaviour. The need for increased user-feedback and engagement is noted but the prevailing tone of this literature and research errs towards the paternalistic with someone, the 'expert' or those in power, influencing other people (residents/employees/non-experts) to stop behaving one way and start behaving another. As earlier research into using the digital economy in buildings for energy behaviour change discovered, this is further complicated by the complex interplay of organisational culture and concerns over ethics and trust and their impact on behaviour (Coleman, Irvine, Lemon, & Shao, 2013, Benson, Saridaksis & Tenakoon, 2015).

Recent publications have highlighted this increasing complexity of energy behaviour change in the non-domestic setting. Research conducted into energy behaviours in a retail organization found that:

1. Employees' organizational roles and work objectives would often trump the energy efficiency imperative,
2. Employees had minimal control over energy consumption (Christina, Dainty, Daniels, & Waterson, 2013).

Chen & Knight (2014) note the importance of norms within the workplace and the effect of social context on behaviour. This was also seen to be the case in Dixon et al. (2015) research into energy behaviour in an American University where a sense of community had a 'small but significant direct effect on behavioural intention' (2015, p.125). Whilst these studies are instructive, they do not necessary fulfill some of the democratic ideals in which ordinary building users and non-experts are a source of knowledge rather than people who need to be corrected and act 'the right way', as Sovacool (2014) notes.

In response to this, Moezzi & Janda (2014) echo Owens & Driffill's (2008) argument by calling for greater understanding and recognizing the community and social potential of workplace cultures through organisations adopting a more participatory approach to energy management. Herein lies the potential for social media in organizational contexts – to engage a wider audience and to draw on the knowledge of all individuals enabling 'collective action' and, as we shall argue, a greater sense of environmental citizenship. Before presenting the two case studies these themes of participation are explored in a little more depth.

PUBLIC PARTICIPATION AND ENVIRONMENTAL CITIZENSHIP

Arnstein's (1969) 'ladder of participation' (see Figure 1) explored a set of steps to increased participation, and ultimately, empowerment. At the bottom was information provision, a predominantly one-way form of communication, and then moving to consultation, a relatively passive process asking for people's opinions but not necessarily engaging them in debate. Participation is normally used to refer to processes which allow people to participate in a decision by putting forward their views verbally whereas engagement goes further, suggesting an innovative and interactive, two-way process of discussion and dialogue (i.e. deliberation) to ensure that people's views inform a decision, alongside those of the expert and/or decision-maker. This is still one-step removed, however, from Arnstein's top step of her ladder that defines empowerment as people taking control of decisions and their implementation. In a parallel (e)ladder (Figure 2), Forrester Research (cited in Ferro & Molinari 2010) have mapped levels of (e)participation within society in the United States. In this new 'e-ladder' of participation, Ferro and Molinari (2010) note the key features of Web 2.0 and social media, notably the idea that people can move from being inactive (at the bottom of the ladder) to be creators (at the top). This maps across to Arnstein's ladder and the theme of increasing control.

Figure 1. Arnstein's (1969) ladder of participation

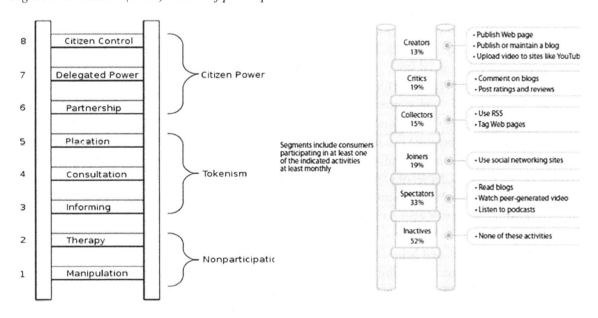

Figure 2. E-participation in the USA Ferro & Molinari (2010)

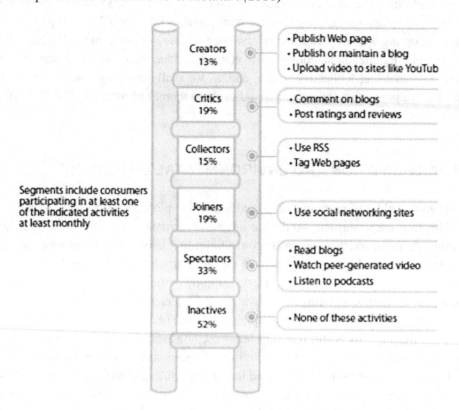

The principles of public engagement methods have been tried and tested in the siting of controversial facilities such as waste facilities (Bull et al., 2008) and transport planning (Bickerstaff & Walker, 2005). Sovacool (2014) notes three benefits of engaging 'non-experts,' first, democracy is increased as all citizens have a right to participate and be represented in environmental decision making, second, non-experts are often more attune to the ethical issues of a situation, and third, greater acceptance can often be achieved by involving those affected by the situation.

The theoretical underpinnings find their roots in Habermas' theory of communicative competence which was successfully mined in the early 1990s by Thomas Webler (1995). Webler (1995) explored how language functions to form key foundational principles for the management of deliberative practices within the school of risk communication. Working from the premise that participation is "interaction among individuals through the medium of language" (Webler, 1995, p. 40), Habermas (1979) argues that any communication between two individuals would fail without cooperation. An individual's ability to use language to create understanding and consensus is referred to as 'communicative competence'. (Habermas, 1979) outlined a set of ideal conditions in which communicative competence would be best served, known as his 'ideal speech situation'. (Webler, 1995) applied these principles of communication to the formulation of a set of criteria and rules that would transform democratic ideals of deliberative democracy into practice. Increasingly, links are made between public engagement and learning, increased environmental citizenship and behaviour change (Bull et al., 2008).

Environmental citizenship recognises the essential role of the ecosystem in providing individuals' basic needs and that humankind's survival depends on the physical environment (Dobson, 2010).

"Environmental citizenship is a personal commitment to learning more about the environment and to taking responsible environmental action. It encourages individuals, communities and organizations to think about the environmental rights and responsibilities we all have as residents of planet Earth. Environmental Citizenship means caring for the Earth" (Environment Canada 2004 quoted in Bell 2005). The concept of environmental citizenship involves looking beyond the satisfaction of immediate interests for the safety of the wider community, and being attentive of the needs of future generations. It can be considered as a way of promoting ecological sustainability and environmental justice (Dobson, 2010). In this way individuals are not solely consumers, but key players in the making of sustainable development. How this might apply in an organizational context, and what role social media may play in this is the subject of this chapter. The cases are now presented before discussing the opportunities and barriers.

CASE STUDY 1: USING SOCIAL MEDIA TO ENHANCE ENVIRONMENTAL CITIZENSHIP IN UNIVERSITIES

DMU is a city centre University with over 20,000 students. Their interest in sustainability started with its involvement in Leicester City Council's successful campaign to be the first environment city in 1991. This was followed by the establishment of the Institute of Energy and Sustainable Development in 1994. A commitment to sustainable development was embedded within DMU's Strategic Plan 2012-2015. A comprehensive range of activities have been undertaken to meet this strategic aim under the themes of research, teaching, management, community engagement, and health and well-being. As a result DMU has seen a rise in the People and Planet's Green League and been highlighted for its best practice in carbon management. In collaboration with the Sustainability Office at DMU, a Twitter account and a Facebook page were created (SustainableDMU). The accounts were launched prior to the intervention in order to create a significant number of followers and gain attention from DMU staff and students. In parallel the blog 'The Living Lab Iesd' was started to keep progress of research and to test different approaches.

The social media campaign was designed as a two-way process; Twitter and Facebook were used with the intention of providing information to DMU users (because without knowledge, actions cannot take place (Wolf, 2011)), but also of nurturing a participation process. In this way people would have a public, albeit virtual, place to talk about sustainability, exchange ideas, and to indicate to the sustainability office any concerns or inefficiencies around the university. To boost environmental citizenship, different messages were communicated. According to empirical studies (Jagers, 2009; Wolf, Brown, & Conway, 2009) environmental citizens:

1. Know about climate change and are positive about the role of human beings in causing it;
2. Feel a sense of responsibility to reduce their emissions, understand the impact that their actions have on the environment;
3. Are willing to act to respond to this sense of responsibility; and
4. Are active citizens, in the sense that they participate in their community or are part of humanitarian or environmental organisations.

Social media monitoring is a relatively young 'science', initially adopted by public relations and advertising agencies (Barker, Barker, Bormann, & Neher, 2012). It is defined as the activity of observing and tracking content on the social web. Each activity on social media has an outcome, or *effect,* which can be measured by observing and then quantifying specific behaviours on social media channels (ibid.). Effects can be: re-tweets, mentions, favourites, follows, likes, shares, comments, sentiment. However, what is central in the evaluation of the campaign is not only a quantitative analysis of the data downloaded during the campaign itself, but the qualitative analysis of the discussion created.

For this reason, thirty-two interviews were conducted at the end of the campaign with respondents being recruited via Twitter. The majority of the interviewees were recruited through this, others were found through a snowball sampling among online and offline friends and colleagues of recruited participants.

The aim of the interviews was to discover people's perceptions of the campaign and views on its effectiveness, to understand participants' use of social media and the impact on their lives, how they viewed sustainability at DMU and how important environmental issues were for them. In order to identify 'beyond the process' learning that can translate public engagement into environmental citizenship, the challenge was to inspect the words of 'ordinary' citizens and acquire an understanding of the impact that participation had on them.

Using a semi-structured qualitative interview process participants were asked whether the engagement process on social media led to an increased understanding of the performance of environmental sustainability in the institution and to a greater appreciation of participants' own responsibilities. Moreover, it was necessary to consider whether different factors can influence the outcome for the different participants; two key factors have been considered

Figure 3. Environmental attitudes and citizenship in e-participation

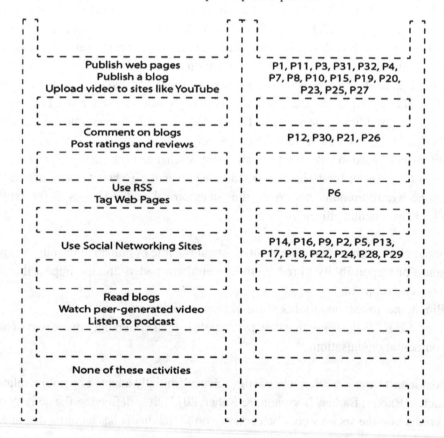

1. People's digital literacy, i.e. digital citizenship (presented in Figure 2) which could influence the way people see the digital tools;
2. People's environmental attitudes, i.e. environmental citizenship (presented in Figure 3), as to ascertain if people already very aware and active about the issue of environmental sustainability would learn differently to people with lower level of engagement.

It can be seen in Figure 3 that participants share high levels of e-participation; this is not surprising as the base level was the use of social networking sites and the process was happening on social media. People on this rung of the ladder are defined as 'joiners' and it is a very low level of engagement. However, the interviewees are, in the majority, higher consumers of content on the Internet and there are many cases in which they are creators of content as well-many of them fit in the highest rung of the ladder.

Figure 4 presents interviewees on a ladder of environmental citizenship. Only a few of them did not consider themselves to be environmental citizens. Their views however are highly relevant as they self-identify as active digital citizens; being on the top of the ladder they are the ones that are most likely to be influenced by information posted on social media. However, their environmental 'attitudes' might make them resistant to change in this context. As Figure 4 shows however, most of the interviewees fit in the top three rungs of the ladder, supporting the idea that the people most interested in interacting with SustainableDMU are like-minded people and already interested in the topic of sustainability. This

Figure 4. Interviewees on a ladder of environmental citizenship

Signs petitions and is active asking for change	P14, P11, P9, P17, P21
Sees the relatioship between himself and the ecosystem as a whole	P1, P16, P8, P13, P24, P28
Feels a sense of responsibility to minimise his environmental impact	P31, P4, P6 (no NGO), P2, P18, P19, P20, P22, P25, P29
Is willing to pay taxes for environmental purpose	P5, P10, P31
Is concerned by the effect of climate change	P12, P26
Is willing to participate in non-profit organisations	P32, P15
Believe climate change is happening and is human made	P3, P23
Do not qualify for any of these	P30, P7, P27, P32

reinforces Dahlberg's fear that it is small groups of people acting as 'echo-chambers'. It is easier to get their attention because they are very likely to be looking for that kind of information on social media; on the other hand, the information posted might have a lower impact on them, because they are already highly skilled environmental citizens. Nevertheless, these people still have the capacity to be influenced by others in the campaign.

When asked how the campaign helped them become more aware of their environmental impact and therefore in being better environmental citizens, participants reported different answers.

Some of them reported changing some behaviours as a consequence.

I wouldn't have bought a bike... you were tweeting about getting a free bike lock. So I thought I can actually have a bike to come on campus. So I bought a bike! If I have to be honest I would have never thought of getting a bike, if I haven't seen it on Twitter. (P3)

The same participant reported another occasion in which she changed her behaviour:

The same with the #lug-a-mug, the travel mug, I got one of them as well. I saw a picture, where there was a girl with it, and I thought I am so getting one of them. And now I am using it all the time. I have three of the big ones a day, and I didn't even use to go and recycle my cup. So I thought 'Oh my Gosh, how much waste I am creating.' So I got one of those. (P3)

What is even more interesting about this citation is that not only did she think of starting to use the reusable mug, but that she became aware of the amount of waste she was making, and that was the reason she decided to take responsibility. If we look at environmental citizenship level of P3 we can see that she sits on the very lower level of the ladder; therefore, the campaign did help her to change some behaviours, but did not change the way she prioritises sustainability. Another, and very different, participant mentioned the #lug-a-mug scheme as something that changed her behaviour:

I am thinking about taking your cup. That information it was something that I firstly see on Facebook and it did change me. Most of the things that came through that SustainableDMU were things that I did anyway, so I guess sometimes I am influenced by what I read. (P9)

P9 scores very high on the ladder of environmental citizenship; however, the information she found on Facebook helped her in being an even better environmental citizen; in this case she took advantage of the information she found on SustainableDMU Page. Again, the account did not change her mind about sustainability (fortunately), but helped her be a better environmental citizen. Another participant mentioned changing her behaviours because of the campaign; as presented in the quote below, P26 mentioned changing her eating behaviours because of the information posted on SustainableDMU:

Because I learned that by eating in a different way I could change my CO_2 emissions. What it changed is that I started buying more organic food and I started to look for seasonal food, and started thinking a bit more about what I eat, how I eat it and what I should do. (P26)

P26 is in the middle of the ladder of environmental citizenship. She stated that she started thinking about the implication of her behaviours related to the food she is eating; therefore, SustainableDMU did not only change a particular behaviour, but it made her re-consider her actions.

Other participants asserted that the campaign reinforced pro-environmental decisions they have already made. The first reported example relates again to behaviours connected with eating habits.

Mainly it was during the week you were tweeting about sustainable and local food, and I think it did made me think more about... and started to consider, and actually trying to buy local food and started eating less meat. I think following Facebook helped reminding me for that initial phase. I think it's very hard to change a habit for the first few weeks; after two or three weeks it became more a second nature. The conversation was reinforcing why I should change that behaviour. (P24)

P24 scores very high in the environmental citizenship ladder; however there is a place of improvement and he reported that the campaign helped him in finally making the step between the decision of eating less meat and the actual behaviour; another time, SustainableDMU did not help in changing his mind about it, but helped him in changing the behaviour. The same was reported by P28 regarding the issue of electricity:

That thing with trying to boil as much water as you need, no more in the kettle. I've done it before, but when I've seen that I said: 'Actually, I'll stick with that'. It was like... not a complete change, but that's a thing I'll remember because I've seen it there. (P28)

Hence social media can be useful in reminding people to be good environmental citizens, which might be difficult to individually do, particularly if we consider that it is easy and cost-effective to repeat messages.

In addition, P1 started to give an explanation for the reason he was influenced by SustainableDMU:

I guess I am open to be influenced by SustainableDMU. There might be a predisposition. If I am already thinking about 'Should I catch the bus or should I use the car?' and SustainableDMU says catching the bus is a good thing it might influence me but I've already made that decision. So I guess I am looking for what might be the next thing. (P1)

In the views of P1, he is open to be influenced because he is already an environmental citizen, hence he is already thinking about sustainability but wants to know what more he can do. And it is evident that Twitter and Facebook can help with this, through sending tweets and starting new conversations. This is reinforced by P22 that acknowledge how the information found on SustainableDMU "stays in the back of your mind after you read it" and P23 who stated "I think it's a great way of sort of learning about anything".

Other interviewees reported that the campaign did not make them change their behaviour, but made them 'think' about their actions and attitudes.

The discussion we had about diet I think there is probably some truth that might be worth look into. I don't think it's as extreme as the guy was posting, but I think there was a grain of truth in what they were saying, so I've learnt from that. I don't think I've changed behaviour because I think I am doing the behaviour that I believe to be correct and achievable. (P18)

In support of this, P4 reported the possibility that the information posted on social media made people think, as it does for him. In fact there is so much information that one is able to choose if ignoring it, or absorbing it:

Because it is on Twitter it's usually quite easy to absorb, ignore or take on board. There are so many things that are put out there. There are certainly been things that have got me thinking from them… (P4)

There are small but encouraging signs that social media can provide a platform for debate, deliberation and dissemination of ideas and move this type of sustainability campaign from communication to engagement. When these more participatory principles are adopted then the messages, in this instance, greater environmental citizenship, can be adopted more readily. The next case study delves deeper into the organizational and cultural complexities of using social media and digital tools for energy management within another public sector organization, a City Council.

CASE STUDY 2: A PARTICIPATORY APPROACH TO ENERGY MANAGEMENT

In 2013 a team of academics started working with the Energy Services team at Leicester City Council (LCC) in the East Midlands, England to explore a collaborative approach to energy management. The joint aims of the project were to explore a more participatory approach to energy management through the testing of digital tools such as smartphones and social media. A user-group was formed from representatives of a range of the council's non-domestic building stock. The purpose of the group was firstly to facilitate interactions and knowledge sharing about effective energy management between lay building users and experts. Second, the user-group would work with the research team to provide user-feedback on the development of an IT based application to foster interaction between building users across the city council and to test the potential for smartphones to help manage energy. The tool would go beyond the provision of energy 'feedback' to building users and would allow them (expert and non-expert) to provide real time comment on any problems and issues they identify in their buildings; they would be able to feedback into the system rather than simply receive feedback from it.

The user group was formed with help from the team leader of the Energy Services team who acted as 'gatekeeper' to the city council and included two members of the energy services team alongside staff members with no specific responsibilities for energy. The group met fortnightly for two months between May and July 2013. A series of 'expert' presentations were provided by the research team on the relationship between people and buildings, energy and buildings and social media and iPhones were provided to all members of the group who, during the initial meetings, were guided through the range of functions – texting, social media and the camera. On the fourth meeting participants reported on what form the application should take and this set the initial ground rules for the design of the app. The group decided that Twitter and Facebook had useful functionality (Twitter – the ability to share information, Facebook the ability to comment on posts) but that, due to concerns about the public nature of Twitter, would before a prefer a bespoke responsive web application. From September onwards the meetings switched from fortnightly to monthly until January 2014 as the development team began work on the design and functionality of the responsive web based application. At each monthly meeting the technical team and user-group would meet to review the progress and to decide on the key features of the app. These included being able to view the application on either webpages or smartphones, allow

Figure 5. Water usage in library

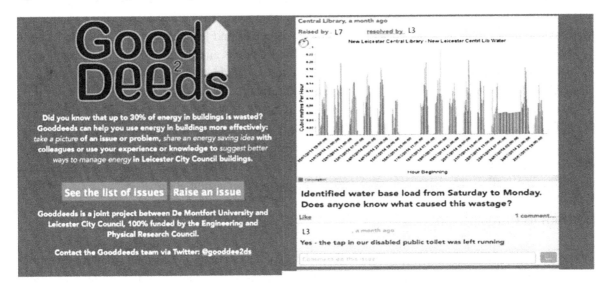

building users to raise an issue with a building and then comment on what needs to happen to resolve the issue (see Figure 5 for screenshots of the app). The energy team could post details of consumption and 'feedback' extracted from their building energy management system but the dashboard would allow building users to interact with it via posting comments. Crucially, this bespoke application allowed for the app to be only visible by employees of the Council through a secure log-in system.

The project evaluation was undertaken in two stages. A mid-point evaluation of the user-group process was undertaken before the app was launched in February 2014 via an independently chaired focus group. At the end of the project semi-structured interviews were conducted with members of the user-group as well as key stakeholders within the organisation, notably the head of energy services and staff responsible for communications and social media to review the use of the app.

Using the Gooddeeds App

The group was sceptical from the start about social media and this was evidenced by none of the group using social media accounts for commenting on energy use and the clear recommendation that the app was to have a secure log-in so that only local authority employees could use it, and that comments made would be unavailable for public view. Nonetheless, the group were encouraged to post issues of energy or wider environmental issues for others to comment on. A member of the energy team (L7) for example posted the chart presented in Figure 5 showing an unusual spike in water usage in the library over a weekend which did draw a response from the librarian (L3). On the whole though, members of the energy team were disappointed though by the poor response of the user-group to posting and responding to issues.

The energy services team leader (L1) noted, "I tried putting various things on at various stages but because there was no two-way communication . . . It just felt like we were putting things in but nothing was coming back." But he also went to admit that, "I did use it, not as frequently as I would've hoped to, I guess" (L1). Two members of the group did respond positively to using the tool though. One of the benefits of using a responsive web-app tool instead of a specific smartphone application was that users could use it either on their smartphones or from their personal computers. And it was here where there was actually more take-up of the tool, reflecting the working patterns and culture of the organization. Many participants were desk-bound with access to a computer and less need of smart phone technology. Three users did however note the ability to take photographs and then send and receive via email or social media was beneficial. For example, L3 who, having said he would not use his phone, added, "the only exception would be if I wanted to take a photograph."

One member of the group (L5) did inform us though that he had "put an icon on my desktop for Good Deeds . . . and I tend to look at [it] about once a week, usually after the weekend, because it's quite often if we're using too much water, someone's left something on over the weekend." So whilst the user-group saw the potential in the technology, this did not translate into universal acceptance and use of the application. The next section considers the barriers to participation.

Barriers to Participation

Two key barriers emerged to using social media and digital technologies in this particular context. First, fears over the privacy and trust at both the individual and organisational level; and secondly perceptions around notions of responsibility towards energy in the workplace.

Whilst the local authority was very supportive of the project, the reality of social media use and its very public dimension was something of concern both to the user group and those with wider responsibilities and was never fully reconciled. The head of energy services for example acknowledged these fears from the outset when he sought internal approval for the project. He (L8) said, "When I took the report to the directors' board…the comments were all about who's going to deal with all the complaints that will come through as a result of this?

The membership of the user-group was not pre-selected with any prior aptitude for technology and it was clear that for the majority of participants' social media and smartphones were quite novel; only two out of the six members of the focus group owned or had used a smartphone prior to the project, as opposed to the 60% ownership highlight by the UK communications regulator, Ofcom). Members of the group were all aware of social media tools, but none were overly active on it. In this group people seemed unhappy with both 'oversharing' their personal details on-line, preferring instead to follow newsfeeds rather than actually post information themselves. A member of the digital media team in Leicester City Council who stopped using social media because of an incident involving a colleague of hers from another local authority highlighted privacy issues though as a real concern. She (L10) remembered, "A colleague of mine used to post completely unprofessional things about her day…it was communicated to the powers that be that she was doing this, and even though it was personal, in her own free time and those managers hadn't seen it, she was told that it was inappropriate."

The user-group was also in agreement about the potentially negative effects of posting messages on other buildings and their users and customers (in the case of the library and leisure centre). People are "always trying to find faults or whatever" said L6 from the leisure centre, and the participant from the library echoed the difficulty of getting constructive customer feedback. "We welcome customer feedback as long as it's coherent customer feedback about things that we can actually do something about" (L3). This was noted as particularly evident given the financial situation of local authorities like Leicester who have to make difficult decisions around budget cuts and had in fact gone through a redundancy process whilst this project was ongoing.

At the wider organisational level (Leicester City Council as a whole) too, the project uncovered a cautious approach towards social media. The City Council uses social media as part of its marketing and communications strategy including its own Twitter feed with over ten thousand followers. The main City Council account is managed by the Social Media Lead who was interviewed for this project. He says that "it's very much geared around sort of headline corporate messaging really" (L9) and was very keen to declare himself a fan of Twitter due it being 'instant', especially for news. He goes on to say, "For finding out about breaking news Twitter is the place to be, and we're using that very much. We're even thinking about changing how we move our news provision media relations…to using social as the main output" (L9).

There is conflict both internally and externally. Internally employees are concerned about publicly highlighting areas of malpractice by other colleagues for fear there might be repercussions. Externally, colleagues are worried that if areas of wastefulness are highlighted then the public will seize on this information. One of the energy services team (L1) observed that, "Public funds are always scrutinised a lot more and therefore you have to be careful in terms of how you sort of say something. You know, if you put something like, oh yeah, your site has wasted, you know, £20,000 worth of water in the last six months, you know, that wouldn't go down well on a public domain."

Arnstein's ladder of participation moves all the way up to partnership to delegating power and control. This poses a challenge to the work place contract and is clearly an issue within a traditional organizational context such as a local authority? The head of energy services (L8) admitted that internal policies have "excluded people from using social media for quite a time", but he believed, "things are changing".

All those interviewed felt that there was something inherent in the nature of local authorities (not just Leicester) that affects innovation in this area. The head of energy services referred to them being "very conservative about these sort of things but I think a lot of them are seeing the advantages of using it for various things" (L8). This was noted for example with regards to IT policies and infrastructure, be it regarding using smartphones in the workplace, or simply being unable to get the latest web browser on their personal computers to wider approaches to change.

Of course in this case study the context is energy behaviours, and it is here, within the workplace that there is a central question, and barrier for using digital tools and social media for something like energy management in the workplace – who is responsible and who has control. Building users, and employees more widely, often feel they have limited opportunity to really change anything and as is seen below, a wider lack of responsibility for energy spend, and competing priorities in the workplace mean that energy management is not at the top of their 'to-do list'. For many it seems the pressure of simply doing their job well means that energy is the last thing on their mind. As the Admin and Business Support leader (L5) observed, staff have conflicting responsibilities and priorities, "they're more thinking about their day job and what we're doing and it's just tunnel, the vision's tunnelled into and the energy impacts are outside of that tunnel for me." This lack of engagement with energy may be due to ignorance and general busyness, for some though, members felt that a lack of engagement with energy, and wasting energy may be a result of tensions and 'animosity toward management' whereby leaving your computer on overnight is a way of asserting control by 'screwing the system'.

Many of these issues would be common to a range of both public and private sector organisations. Rarely in organisations, are there devolved energy budgets, and most would accept that they feel (even if they are not), bombarded with conflicting priorities, increased workloads and seemingly limitless email inboxes. A Local Authority context exhibits interesting features, not least in political and economic climates of reduced budgets; salary freezes and increased trade union activity. They are about delivering public services and value for money. It is against the backdrop of these competing organisational, institutional and political priorities that social media and digital tools reside, as we have seen with this case study on energy management.

CONCLUSION

Of course generalizations are limited and cautionary, given the scale of these two cases, but the findings do shed light on the potential of more participatory approaches to solving organizational problems such as reducing energy consumption in buildings and eliciting more sustainable attitudes in employees. Public engagement is today considered by many to be a tool capable of transitioning society toward a pro-environmental model. However, it is still uncertain the impact that participatory processes facilitated through social media can have on online contributors, especially in an organizational context. The key question in the present paper has been whether deliberative processes mediated through social media have the capacity of changing people's hearts and minds and of creating better environmental citizens.

In the first case study the results showed that participants learned new information and that in some cases this leads them to either reflect on their actions or to change their behaviours towards better environmental citizenship, even though in some instances the changes were relatively limited. Nevertheless, it is encouraging that the campaign helped people to think more about sustainability and is a tool able to reinforce behaviour and remind people what is expected from environmental citizens; in the words of one of the interviewees:

SustainableDMU put out little pulses of information, which do remind you 'Don't forget sustainability and here there is another way of looking at it.

The second case study encountered interesting challenges around financial cuts leading to job losses within the organisation and this created a challenging climate in which to conduct research. This will be a familiar context for many organisations across Europe and will no doubt affect further initiatives. Yet again it was seen that social media and smartphone technology have a clear technical potential to contribute to low-cost solutions to energy management by moving beyond the information-deficit model of feedback and signs of hope have been highlighted here.

ORGANISATIONAL IMPLICATIONS AND FUTURE RESEARCH DIRECTIONS

So what we can say to aspiring organisations wishing to utilize these benefits and researchers wishing to build on these exploratory studies? Firstly, attempting to 'climb' Arnstein's ladder of participation, be it a virtual one or not, poses challenges as well as opportunities to both individuals and organisations around notions of control, power and responsibility. For example, participation may require the 'non-expert' building users to take responsibility for switching appliances and lights off, where possible, but participation for the experts - those with designated responsibility for energy management - may result in a relinquishing of control which may be unsettling, especially in an uncertain organisational context. Both Arnstein's ladder and social media share a disruptive influence upon individual and organisational notions of control and responsibility. This is a key challenge for the future use of social media in organizational contexts and requires further understanding through larger scale field studies and ethnographic research. Second, there is an intriguing research challenge around how to actually conduct the research, where the power lies in terms of the intervention and the research team is located within the research. How to actually measure and isolate the influence and impact of the intervention also requires further research. Finally, greater understanding is required on the management, leadership and organizational cultures that would be naturally accommodating of these interventions. Both cases were public sector bodies, how would the findings have differed in a private sector organization such as a large multi-site transnational corporation or a family owned small to medium sized enterprise? Answers to these questions will help shed much needed light on these issues and enable organisations to fully realize the social potential of collective action that Shirky (2008) promises.

REFERENCES

Arnstein, S. R. (1969). A ladder of citizen participation. *Journal of the American Planning Association, 35*(4), 216. Retrieved from http://openurl.library.dmu.ac.uk/sfxlcl3?sid=google&auinit=SR&aulast=Arnstein&atitle=Aladderofcitizenparticipation&id=doi:10.1080/01944366908977225&title=JournaloftheAmericanInstituteofPlanners&volume=35&issue=4&date=1969&spage=216&issn=0002-8991

Barker, M., Barker, D., Bormann, N., & Neher, K. (2012). Social Media Marketing. A Strategic Approach. CENGAGE Learning South-Western.

Bell, D. R. (2005). Liberal Environmental Citizenship. *Environmental Politics, 14*(2), 179–194. doi:10.1080/09644010500054863

Benson, V., & Morgan, S. (2015). *Implications of Social Media Use in Personal and Professional Settings*. Hershey, PA: IGI Global; doi:10.4018/978-1-4666-7401-1

Benson, V., Saridakis, G., & Tennakoon, H. (2015). Information disclosure of social media users: Does control over personal information, user awareness and security notices matter? *Information Technology & People, 28*(Iss: 3), 426–441. doi:10.1108/ITP-10-2014-0232

Bickerstaff, K., & Walker, G. (2005). Shared Visions, Unholy Alliances: Power, Governance and Deliberative Processes in Local Transport Planning. *Urban Studies (Edinburgh, Scotland), 12*(42), 2123–2144. doi:10.1080/00420980500332098

Briones, R. L., Kuch, B., Liu, B. F., & Jin, Y. (2011). Keeping up with the digital age: How the American Red Cross uses social media to build relationships. *Public Relations Review, 37*(1), 37–43. doi:10.1016/j.pubrev.2010.12.006

Bull, R., Petts, J., & Evans, J. (2008). Social learning from public engagement: Dreaming the impossible? *Journal of Environmental Planning and Management, 51*(5), 701–716. doi:10.1080/09640560802208140

Burrows, R., Johnson, H., & Johnson, P. (2013). *Influencing Values, Attitudes and Behaviour via Interactive and Social-Media Technology: The Case of Energy Usage*. Unpublished. Bath, UK.

Canada, E. (2004). *An environmental citizen... who me?*. Academic Press.

Castells, M. (2007). Communication, power and counter-power in the network society. *International Journal of Communication, 1*(1), 29.

Chen, C., & Knight, K. (2014). Energy at work: Social psychological factors affecting energy conservation intentions within Chinese electric power companies. *Energy Research & Social Science, 4*, 23–31. doi:10.1016/j.erss.2014.08.004

Christina, S., Dainty, A., Daniels, K., & Waterson, P. (2013). How organisational behaviour and attitudes can impact building energy use in the UK retail environment: A theoretical framework. *Architectural Engineering and Design Management, 10*(1-2), 164–179. doi:10.1080/17452007.2013.837256

Coleman, M. J., Irvine, K. N., Lemon, M., & Shao, L. (2013). Promoting behaviour change through personalized energy feedback in offices. *Building Research and Information, 41*(6), 637–651. doi:10.1080/09613218.2013.808958

Crowley, D. N., Curry, E., & Breslin, J. G. (2014). Leveraging Social Media and IoT to Bootstrap Smart Environments. In N. Bessis & C. Dobre (Eds.), *Big Data and Internet of Things: A Roadmap for Smart Environments* (pp. 379–399). Spinger International Publishing Switzerland. doi:10.1007/978-3-319-05029-4_16

Dahlberg, L. (2001). The Internet and democratic discourse: Exploring the prospects of online deliberative forums extending the public sphere. *Information Communication and Society, 4*(4), 615–633. doi:10.1080/13691180110097030

Darby, S. (2010). Smart metering: What potential for householder engagement? *Building Research and Information, 38*(5), 442–457. doi:10.1080/09613218.2010.492660

Dixon, G. N., Deline, M. B., McComas, K., Chambliss, L., & Hoffmann, M. (2015). Saving energy at the workplace: The salience of behavioral antecedents and sense of community. *Energy Research & Social Science, 6*, 121–127. doi:10.1016/j.erss.2015.01.004

Dobson, A. (2010). Environmental citizenship and pro-environmental behaviour. Rapid research and evidence review. London: Academic Press.

Ferro, E., & Molinari, F. (2010). Framing Web 2.0 in the process of public sector innovation: Going down the participation ladder. *European Journal of ePractice, 9*, 1–15.

Fischer, E., & Reuber, A. R. (2011). Social interaction via new social media: (How) can interactions on Twitter affect effectual thinking and behavior? *Journal of Business Venturing, 26*(1), 1–18. doi:10.1016/j.jbusvent.2010.09.002

Foster, D., Lawson, S., Wardman, J., Blythe, M., & Linehan, C. (2012). "Watts in It for Me?": Design Implications for Implementing Effective Energy Interventions in Organisations. In *Proceedings of the SIGCHI Conference on Human Factors in Computing Systems* (pp. 2357–2366). New York: ACM. doi:10.1145/2207676.2208396

Foster, D., Linehan, C., Kirman, B., Lawson, S., & James, G. (2010). Motivating Physical Activity at Work: Using Persuasive Social Media for Competitive Step Counting. In *Proceedings of the 14th International Academic MindTrek Conference: Envisioning Future Media Environments* (pp. 111–116). New York: ACM. doi:10.1145/1930488.1930510

Ghonim, W. (2012). *Revolution 2.0*. Fourth Estate.

Habermas, J. (1979). *Communication and the Evolution of Society, translated by Thomas McCarthy*. Boston: Beacon Press.

Hargreaves, T., Nye, M., & Burgess, J. (2013). Keeping energy visible? Exploring how householders interact with feedback from smart energy monitors in the longer term. *Energy Policy*, *52*(0), 126–134. doi:10.1016/j.enpol.2012.03.027

Jagers, S. C. (2009). In search of the Ecological citizen. *Environmental Politics*, *18*(1), 18–26. doi:10.1080/09644010802624751

Lehrer, D., & Vasudev, J. (2010). *Visualizing Information to Improve Building Performance: A study of expert users*. Center for the Built Environment.

Moezzi, M., & Janda, K. B. (2014). From "if only" to "social potential" in schemes to reduce building energy use. *Energy Research & Social Science*, *1*(0), 30–40. doi:10.1016/j.erss.2014.03.014

Murtagh, N., Nati, M., Headley, W. R., Gatersleben, B., Gluhak, A., Imran, M. A., & Uzzell, D. (2013). Individual energy use and feedback in an office setting: A field trial. *Energy Policy*, *62*(0), 717–728. doi:10.1016/j.enpol.2013.07.090

Owens, S., & Driffill, L. (2008). How to change attitudes and behaviours in the context of energy. *Energy Policy*, *36*(12), 4412–4418. doi:10.1016/j.enpol.2008.09.031

Petts, J., & Brooks, C. (2006). Expert conceptualisations of the role of lay knowledge in environmental decisionmaking: Challenges for deliberative democracy. *Environment & Planning A*, *38*(6), 1045–1059. doi:10.1068/a37373

Rheingold, H. (2002). *Smart Mobs: The Next Social Revolution*. New York: Perseus Books.

Shirky, C. (2008). *Here Comes Everybody*. London: Penguin.

Sovacool, B. K. (2014). What are we doing here? Analyzing fifteen years of energy scholarship and proposing a social science research agenda. *Energy Research & Social Science*, *1*, 1–29. doi:10.1016/j.erss.2014.02.003

Stewart, A., Ambrose-Oji, B., & Morris, J. (2012). *Social Media and Forestry: A Scoping Report*. Academic Press.

Van Dijck, J. (2012). Facebook as a Tool for Producing Sociality and Connectivity. *Television & New Media*, *13*(2), 160–176. doi:10.1177/1527476411415291

Webler, T. (1995). `Right` discourse in citizen participation: an evaluative yard-stick. In O. Renn, T. Webler, & P. Wiedemann (Eds.), *Fairness and Competence in Citizen Participation: Evaluating Models for Environmental Discourse*. Dordrecht: Kluver Academic Press. doi:10.1007/978-94-011-0131-8_3

Webler, T., Tuler, S., & Krueger, R. (2001). What is a good public participation process? Five perspectives from the public. *Environmental Management*, 27(3), 435–450. doi:10.1007/s002670010160 PMID:11148768

Wolf, J. (2011). Ecological Citizenship as Public Engagement with Climate Change. In L. Whitmarsh, S. O'Neill, & I. Lorenzoni (Eds.), *Engaging the Public with Climate Change. Behaviour Change and Communication*. London: Earthscan.

Wolf, J., Brown, K., & Conway, D. (2009). Ecological citizenship and climate change: Perceptions and practice. *Environmental Politics*, 18(4), 503–521. doi:10.1080/09644010903007377

Zhang, W., Johnson, T., Seltzer, T., & Bichard, S. (2009). The revolution will be networked: The influence of social networking sites on political attitudes and behavior. *Social Science Computer Review*, 28(1), 75–92. doi:10.1177/0894439309335162

Chapter 6
Generation Y and Internet Privacy:
Implication for Commercialization of Social Networking Services

Zdenek Smutny
University of Economics, Czech Republic

Vaclav Janoscik
Academy of Fine Arts in Prague, Czech Republic

Radim Cermak
University of Economics, Czech Republic

ABSTRACT

This chapter addresses the issue of privacy settings with a focus on Generation Y from a technological, social, generational, cultural and philosophical point of view. After introducing the issue of Internet privacy and other relevant areas—generational and cultural differences, the philosophical framework, the postinternet condition, the possibilities of processing and (mis)using personal data, and privacy policy—the authors present their perspective on the issue, drawing implications for individuals and organizations based on their own research and other relevant studies. The authors discuss the possible implications in terms of a prospective use of personal data by companies (e.g. for marketing and management) and possibility of processing user data. Such perspective will allow them to formulate a critical basis for further assessment of social networking and Generation Y's attitudes to privacy. The chapter concludes by outlining several recommendations concerning the commercialization of social networking services with respect to the constantly changing conception of privacy.

DOI: 10.4018/978-1-5225-0559-4.ch006

INTRODUCTION

This chapter provides an interdisciplinary perspective on the attitude of today's young people from Generation Y towards self-disclosure and on the impact of such behaviour on the individual, as well as on the challenges for commercial exploitation of social networking services. A definition of Generation Y is given in the part *Cultural and generational differences*. From a firm's perspective, there are two reasons why it is important to focus on Generation Y:

- Generation Y has a positive attitude to information and communication technologies (ICT) (Valentine & Powers, 2013), which are already a common element in their lives (Benckendorff, Moscardo & Pendergast, 2010, p. 20; Lahtinen, 2012). This part of their life is reflected in social networking services and thus shared with other people. These (personal) data from various Internet-based services can be used in commercial and professional activity.
- Members of Generation Y are economically active. From a firm's perspective, this means that they can act as customers or as employees.

Internet privacy is viewed as the right of a subject (human) for the protection of their personal data and the way they are handled (Puddephatt et al., 2012) – i.e. stored, processed, used (including changes in their use), provided to third parties and displayed on the Internet. The information collected during an individual's interaction in a particular social networking service can be divided into personally identifying information (e.g. information that relates to a particular person or identifies them) and non-personally identifying information (e.g. anonymous information about an individual's behaviour on a web portal). (Cermak, Smutny & Janoscik, 2014)

A long-term trend in companies' activity is the collection of such data and its subsequent evaluation for various purposes of the companies (e.g. marketing). The sources of these data are the information and front-end systems of an organization (e.g. the collection of consumer data) (Roberts & Zahay, 2012, pp. 101-105), as well as freely accessible data on the Internet (e.g. the discussion of people on a particular web) (Sperkova & Skola, 2015). This also affects common users, who interact within various Internet-based services and thus create a large amount of personal data – this concerns mainly social networking services. The reason for such behaviour is today's information society, which unobtrusively prompts users to share their personal information on the Internet (e.g. people are positively motivated to share their personal information). This can also be described by the term self-disclosure (Benson, Saridakis & Tennakoon, 2015). Personal information accessible on the Internet can thus, on the one hand, help companies and their customers, from whom they can receive feedback or achieve personalisation to their customers based on individual data processing. On the other hand, it is a temptation for third parties to exploit these data.

A dual perspective (individual and firm) will be considered in this chapter. Companies should be aware of the challenges connected with individuals' Internet privacy, because those individuals may comprise customers and also their employees. Their personal information could be used for bullying or manipulating them to reveal a company secret or to become a serious security risk (Benson et al., 2015). This chapter focuses on the use of individual information disclosed on social networking services, primarily for marketing and management. Such systemic view on Internet privacy may be beneficial for organizations.

This chapter is organized as follows: Firstly, it introduces the theoretical foundations of technological, social, generational, cultural and philosophical issues of Internet privacy. It then discusses Generation Y's approach to self-disclosure on social networking services of users from France and the Czech Republic. The final two sections suggest future directions of research and highlight implications for policy and practice. This means particularly the possibilities of commercialization of available personal data.

BACKGROUND

In this section authors address various issues of privacy in the social web. After stressing the cultural and generational differences, the authors raise some questions stemming from the work of various thinkers in order to frame the problem of privacy in the postinternet condition. Postinternet is described as the 'moment in which the Internet is no longer a fascination or taboo, but rather a banal fact of daily living' (Arche, 2013). The postinternet condition is typical for the daily lives of Generation Y. The aim of the thematic sections is to expose essential standpoint in respect to Internet privacy connected with the needs of firms and other commercial activities online.

Cultural and Generational Differences

This chapter is focused on the representatives of the so-called Generation Y. The term Generation Y is nowadays assigned to young people who are newly economically active or will become economically active in the near future. Another important aspect is that this is the first generation that could in their childhood use ICT, especially computers and mobile devices. Its specificity can be defined using the time chronology.

Each generation overlaps, but we can, nevertheless, introduce at least an approximate chronological division: Baby Boomers (from the mid-1940s up to the early 1960s), Generation X (from the early 1960s to the early 1980s), Generation Y (from the early 1980s to the early 2000s), Generation Z (from the mid-1990s up to the early 2010s), Generation Alpha (after 2010). Representatives of Generation Y are the descendants of a significant generation called the baby boomers, who were born in the post-war period, and the oldest representatives of Generation X (Savage, 2011). Generation Y is also called the Next Generation, Millennials or the Net Generation and it is divided into three generation sub-units (Pendergast, 2010): Generation Why (born 1982-1985), Millennials (born 1985-1999) and iGeneration (born in 1999 -2002). In this chapter we focus on the first two sub-units. The reason for the focus on a selected group is the already mentioned fact that its members are gradually becoming fully economically active and are able to intuitively use modern Internet-based technologies (Benckendorff, Moscardo & Pendergast, 2010, p. 20; Valentine, Powers, 2013).

Along with the differences in generations, cultural differences should also be taken into account when discussing the differences in the approach to privacy. The term glocalization has been frequently discussed since the 1980s. It refers to the localization of a global product or service to a particular country or region. Web services are inherently ideal for global action and thus the issue of website localization for different cultures began to be researched intensively at the beginning of the millennium. The society of each country has its national traits, qualities, recognized values, habits, history and so on. All of this together creates a complex mix that forms the culture. It is therefore a complex concept that must be grasped somehow.

In this context, Hofstede's cultural dimensions are the most widely used tool. We can describe culture of each state by these dimensions. There are many studies showing a higher efficiency of culturally localized websites or Internet-based services – e.g. (Vyncke & Bergman, 2010; Cermak, 2015). This fact suggests that people from different countries have different expectations and behaviour, even when it concerns so global a medium as the Internet. For instance Li *et al.* (2009) supports this influence of cultural values on the approach to the use of ICT with a focus on online services. The results show that time orientation plays a significant role in the willingness to use new technology. Long-term oriented cultures are more compliant to use new technologies, because the features of long-term oriented users fit the nature of technology use. An important problem presents the dimension of individualism/collectivism. Users with higher values of individualism are more confident when working with technology in general and would find it less difficult.

Culture (as well as age, as mentioned above) is an important factor also in terms of the approach to the use of personal data. Miltgen and Peyrat-Guillard (2014), for example, provide interesting results within Europe. There is a difference in the north and the south of Europe concerning the importance of responsibility as opposed to trust. Another difference regards disclosure as a choice in Southern and as forced in Eastern Europe. Concerning the age, more positive attitudes toward data management, greater responsibility and greater confidence in the ability to prevent possible misuse of data can be found within the Generation Y.

Moreover, culture is stated as an important factor in a field of privacy also in the today's reflection about privacy in the information age (Dinev, 2014). The importance of culture show also previous articles of the author. Dinev *et al.* (2006) refer to the connection of cultural dimensions (especially Individualism-collectivism and Uncertainty Avoidance) and the concepts of trust and Internet privacy concerns and perceived risk, as the main variables for the use of services requiring personal data. Dinev *et al.* (2009) examined cross-cultural differences between South Korea and the United States in user behaviour towards protective information technologies and found that cultural factors are significant within the context of user attitudes and behaviour towards this type of technologies.

PHILOSOPHICAL ANCHORING OF SUBJECT PRIVACY

It is necessary not to lose sight of the theoretical and indeed the philosophical level. The reason is obvious: proceeding with the research of the issues concerning company growth or marketing would lead to a complete abandonment of the ethical or, more precisely, the normative and critical level, as illustrated by the relationship of ethical and economic behaviour of companies in (Sigmund, 2015). It is not possible only to propose how to target people within marketing; it is necessary to know what for and what social relations it affects or creates. It is impossible to simply describe what is being shared or kept in secret; it is necessary to know what concept of privacy it articulates. This attitude can prevent us from simply adhering to instrumental concepts of social media and privacy, for instance. More than ever before, it is important to realize that media, namely online social networks, are not mere means for our readymade identities and goals but that they involve their intrinsic rules of conduct deeply affecting our notions of identity, privacy or marketing communication. Therefore, the conclusion of this chapter is not simply deduced from research or the collected data itself, it rather springs from a deeper interest that is fuelled by critical thinking and philosophy.

These are inherently linked to art and its social imagination. Let us therefore begin with one artistic example – *Balconism* by Constant Dullaart (2014). It presents a text that is a kind of postinternet manifesto but also a gallery installation. On a general level, the balcony presents us with a spatial metaphor of the Internet itself. The basic, underlying condition of any conduct we take online is, that we are both in private and public. As on the balcony, we consider the space to be part of our private sphere. We excercize quite personal type of conduct here and that is why we actually talk about Internet privacy. But, on the other hand, we are visible. It does not matter whether someone actually watches us or uses our personal data; the important thing is that, potentially, we are being watched all the time, as if we were on a balcony. This brings us to the basic assumption concerning Internet privacy and its impact on our idea of the private sphere. Due to its inextricable connection with the public, we need on the one hand, to reflect its danger of abusing our private data (publically available), but on the other hand, we may address its mediatory potential, whether it is in political (the impact of social media in the Arab spring, for instance) or economic terms (tubers and bloggers).

On a theoretical level, we can summarize the historical development with Hannah Arendt's influential book *Human Condition* (*Vita Activa*) (Arendt, 1998). She argues that (1) in the ancient polis, the private sphere of a household (*oikos*) was strictly disengaged from and subordinate to the public sphere of the agora; everybody (except for slaves and women, of course) was equal within the public sphere, no matter what their private interests were. Nonetheless, this hierarchy is overturned in (2) the modern times, with individuals being determined by their profession, class or social position – i.e. by their private realm, which invades the public sphere. We seem to be entering yet another stage (3), in which it is increasingly difficult to disentangle these two spheres. Our privacy is constantly redefined and used within the public realm (of the Internet). Let us now connect this brief remark to our issue. Unlike common inquiries into the problem of Internet privacy, we tend not to take the very concept of privacy as predetermined, unequivocal or universal; it simply cannot be identified as a set of personal data (e.g. email address, pictures, consumption preference). Contrary to such implicit preconceptions, we believe that privacy is a deeply multifactorial and flexible concept that is being redefined along with its cultural, historical and even technological context.

As such, it cannot be separated from other underlying philosophical conditions, such as social order, economic system or media channelling. It is precisely (but of course not exclusively) through the notion of privacy that the phenomena of the Internet and social networking in particular transform our social communication and culture. And from the opposite direction, Internet environment not only poses new challenges for our privacy and its protection (Young & Quan-Haase, 2013), but our very notion of privacy is fundamentally transformed in an entirely new perspective. In a sense, the hypermedia reality is brought to its pinnacle. This means that the Internet environment as a medium absorbs all other media that are directed towards plurality and heterotopia of content and forms, thus creating a new logic of transparency of media content (Bolter & Grusin, 1999), along with setting a new dynamic of accessing one's private domain. Let us set the problem of privacy within a philosophical context with respect to its practices and human activities on three critical levels; namely in the context of (1) consumption, (2) freedom and (3) power.

Consumption

One of these lines is a critique of consumer culture. Perhaps the most radical formulation is provided by the so-called Frankfurt School and specifically Theodor Adorno. In his book *Minima Moralia* he states in the fragment *Asylum for the Homeless*: 'The predicament of private life today is shown by its arena. Dwelling, in proper sense, is now impossible. (...) It is part of morality not to be at home in one's home.' (Adorno, 2005, pp. 38-39) Throughout the entire book Adorno aims at an analysis of alienation, particularly in terms of consumerist culture. He concludes that, due to mass reproduction penetrating into all spheres of life, even our privacy is not the domain of individual freedom.

In 1951, when the book was first released, he provided an insight into the prospective development of reproductive technologies and their impact on privacy. Adorno is preoccupied mainly with radio and television. Nonetheless, it points again to the lack of division between private and public. For Adorno, it stems from the false identity of individual and general implied by modern media, including the Internet. Our identity and privacy falls prey to the public sphere ruled by uniformity and commercial exploitation. Uniformity of the private sphere is thus enforced as a means of identification with the community. Privacy in terms of mass media and especially social networking is not a sphere that would be only opposed to the threat of misuse, and thus driven by the dynamics of protection against the logic of the media. It also works in reverse dynamic through the pressure to publish the private content by the user himself. As users, we are motivated by a desire to identify ourselves with others on the basis of common or uniform private contents (holiday or celebration pictures, as well as information about school or hobbies).

Freedom and Its Media Logic

While on the first level we addressed the uniformity enforced within the medium, in the next stage we need to address the problem of new possibilities which the media provide us with. For it is true that new means create new forms of communication and action. In this respect we may turn to Michel de Certeau, who provides us with critique of these possibilities of media as they do not enlarge our freedom but on the contrary they entangle our action within their own logic. Media strive for a deeper penetration of their mechanisms into our lives and specifically our privacy.

In the words of De Certeau, as he writes in the chapter 'Reading as Poaching' in his book *The Practice of Everyday Life*: 'In any event, reader's increased autonomy does not protect him, for the media extend power over his imagination, that is, everything he lets emerge from himself into the nets of the text – his fears, his dreams, his fantasized and lacking authorities. This is what the powers work on that make out of "facts" and "figures" a rhetoric whose target is precisely this surrendered intimacy.' (De Certeau, 1984, p. 176) Though the text of 1980 was directed towards the medium of text and reading, we see its topicality in the perspective of social networking services. De Certeau shows here that the new options, such as the possibility to dispose of one's own personal data, may not be an increase of privacy protection. Because our will to limit this access to our personal data is based on the idea ('imagination') we have about our privacy, which is already incorporated in the logic of the social networking services. In addition, this phantasm of 'surrendered intimacy' allures through the promise of authentic human presence within otherwise highly impersonal communication in the Internet environment. Nonetheless, we can be cautious or even ironical; we can play along the lines of the medium and still keep our position safe. In one word, we can poach. This also resonates in the *Balconism* of Constant Dullaart who calls for self-awareness, coding and encryption that spring from the very nature of the (Internet) environment we entered.

Power

Both the preceding levels of critique of media direct our attention to the issues of power, surveillance or influence in shaping our personality. At this level, it is almost indispensable to take recourse in the analysis of Michel Foucault. In his work he dealt with the particular techniques of discipline in modern societies and institutions. He analysed the rise of modern hospitals (Foucault, 1963), psychopathology (Foucault, 1972), prisons (Foucault, 1975) or the history of sexuality (Foucault, 1976). Throughout his entire oeuvre Foucault warns against the reification or objectification of power as such. It cannot be simply seen as mere repression or a particular institution. Power is not only an invasion into the freedom of individuals. It is interplay of forces that have already shaped our concept of freedom. They are ubiquitous and inescapable. Not because they always surround us, but because power itself helps to shape our individuality, which seeks to resist the power (Foucault, 1976).

Foucault's analysis is even more appropriate in the perspective of Internet environment and the issue of privacy. He invites us not to define abuse on one side and, on the other, the protection of privacy on the Internet as two opposites. Undoubtedly, we enter a play of intersecting forces, which themselves constitute the entire sphere of privacy in the Internet environment. There is not only a counterweight or the result of our actions in the Internet environment, but rather its condition and constantly changing basis.

Summary of the Section

To conclude our philosophical exposition of the concept of privacy, we can note that (1) it naturally springs from our consumerist culture which defies any unproblematic notion of privacy ('to feel at home'), driving us constantly forward to look for means of identification with others or, more precisely, with their commoditized representations. (2) Nonetheless, this does not prevent us from developing our identity and Internet privacy. We just need to be self-aware and instead of relying on these commoditized forms we should critically appropriate them (therefore the concept of poaching). (3) Our privacy, just as our very subjectivity online (the condition of being an Internet user), is subjected to power and disciplination (of the medium). Therefore, we cannot disengage the protection and violation of one's privacy. We cannot divide our freedom and determination in the Internet environment; and last but not least, we do not have a shared preconception of privacy as it is constantly reshaped by our actual activities online. Like being on our balcony in slippers and housecoat – while being (potentially) visible to anybody.

Just as a person's cognitive abilities influence how he or she perceives and approaches the world, so the possibilities of processing personal data of (potential) customers create a broader view of firms on the environment in which they conduct their business and in which their activities take place. It is only at this basis that organizations can make decisions about their future activities, as is discussed in the following part.

THE POSSIBILITIES OF PROCESSING AND USING PERSONAL DATA ACCESSIBLE ON THE INTERNET

Personal data that can be accessed through various Internet-based services (blogs, forums, Facebook, Twitter) can be further processed and evaluated according to the objectives of a company. Personal data in particular are of a great help when analysing a large dataset and segmenting it. For example, the messages posted in discussion on forum are automatically processed and can be categorized by the sex or the hobbies of the users on the basis of acquired personal data. This way we can see the difference between opinions of women and men or categorize the posts by topic. In relation to the privacy of a subject on the Internet, it is appropriate to mention the basics of the acquisition, processing and evaluation of freely accessible personal data on the Internet, and the fundamental analytic approaches used in company and marketing management. Data can be acquired:

- Manually.
- **Automatically:** Data can be put in a database directly or by an artificial actor (softbot) programmed to acquire data on selected web pages or via selected Application Programming Interfaces (API).

In the case of manual data acquisition, an employee goes through each Internet-based service and creates his or her own database (e.g. in a spreadsheet application), which will be later interpreted and used for decision-making. For example, a marketing specialist can register data about the progression of marketing activities (e.g. the numbers of positive and negative feedbacks) which they will use later for the evaluation of marketing activities arranged through various tools (e.g. social media, forums, specialized web portals).

In the case of automatic data acquisition, it is necessary to select data sources and the way of acquiring data. With external data sources, it could be structured data acquired via API interface of a particular service, data acquired by front-end systems (e-shops), or non-structured data from web pages or documents – see the paper (Pavlicek & Novak, 2015) focused on external data sources. The application of a particular method of data acquisition relies on (besides the financial and technological state of a company) a specialist's conclusion – the resources and time needed to create a program for data acquisition vs. data volume, data processing, the extent of a campaign, future utilization of the data acquired, etc.

Data acquisition is followed by data processing – e.g. data conversion that enables their evaluation by methods used in knowledge discovery in databases (Witten, Frank & Hall, 2011; Rauch, 2013). Pre-processed data are further evaluated – e.g. by a reporting or analytic application (Kliegr et al., 2011), in most of cases with an objective to detect hidden correlations between variables (Pour, Maryska & Novotny, 2012). The results acquired this way must be put into context with other results and further interpreted. It should be considered that even in the case of automatically processed and evaluated data, the results are assessed by a specialist. When non-structured data (e.g. text on a web page without semantics for machine analysis) are processed, the pre-processing of these data is necessary to ensure a fundamental level of understanding of the content by a machine. Recently, the development of Web 3.0 technologies has started. These technologies are designated not only for human, but also for artificial actors, to whom they provide semantical information about the content of web pages. Possibilities of data processing and evaluation:

- **Manual:** An employee may use the tools of a selected office suite and put the acquired data into a table
- **Automatic:** Processing using selected technologies and approaches
  - **Structured Data:** Data available in the databases of particular systems, e.g. Customer Relationship Management (CRM) systems, e-shops or Enterprise Resource Planning (ERP) systems
  - **Non-Structured Data:** Data available mostly on the web or in documents, which need to be pre-processed by Natural Language Processing (NLP) approaches to ensure a fundamental level of understanding of the content by a machine

Among the necessary and the applied techniques for data acquisition and processing for companies are 'intelligence' approaches (particularly reporting and analytical applications). In the lead is business intelligence which is 'a set of processes, know-how, applications and technologies, which are targeted to support effectively and functionally the management activities in a company' (Pour, Maryska & Novotny, 2012, p. 16). These intelligence approaches amplify the ability of a company to use knowledge assets in action. Similar approaches were developed in other specific areas which affect management on a strategical and tactical level and related activities (e.g. competitive intelligence, marketing intelligence, customer intelligence, media intelligence). The term business intelligence has been used since the 1980s (Bartes, 2010), but similar intelligence systems used by big companies have been in use since the 1970s. As ICT was being developed, including the Internet, an emphasis was put on the acquisition and evaluation of internal and external data related not only to a company, but also to competitive subjects. Thus, Pranjic (2011) considers the two dimensions needed to make the right business decisions: business intelligence (to know yourself) and competitive intelligence (to know your environment, competitive subjects). It is competitive intelligence that allows companies and their brands to be integrated in a specific market environment and a socio-cultural context of particular phases of a company's or a product's life cycle. For example, it is very difficult to enter a new foreign market without a deeper understanding of the social, cultural and political environment. Thus, it is necessary to conduct a market survey on the level of competitive intelligence to understand its specifics and to use these pieces of knowledge for the strategic management of marketing activities (Tej Adidam, Gajre & Kejriwal, 2009).

Recent approaches have focused on the analysis of structured and non-structured data; non-structured data are pre-processed and converged to structured data using NPL dictionaries and are further analyzed (Baars & Kemper, 2008). Since we were evaluating non-structured data, we were not able to converge them to structured data absolutely correctly. Nevertheless, the available options are in most cases sufficient for the subsequent data processing. For example, in sentiment analysis (Liu, 2012) we are able to focus on the categories of sentiment, i.e. positive or negative feedback (Sperkova & Skola, 2015).

Some approaches and techniques used in business intelligence and other segments related to knowledge discovery in databases belong to the field of Data science, which is based on data-analytic thinking and data-managed decision-making across the organization (Provost & Fawcett, 2013). The roots of this scientific discipline go back to the 1960s. It is not a system or set of practices as in the case of business intelligence, but there are particular and generally applicable ways of knowledge discovery from acquired data which must be further integrated into specific models. One such example is data processing for predictive analysis. Data science also involves approaches dealing with datasets which are too large to be processed by common methods or systems – so-called big data (Provost & Fawcett, 2013). The processing and evaluation of big data is a current trend in many interdisciplinary informatics fields (e.g. community, humanistic, social or historical informatics) and also in the fields of the medial-communication cycle of science or marketing in relation to the evaluation of online communication or marketing activities.

Processing data available on the Internet is no longer just a challenge, but a reality. Both personal (consumer intelligence, marketing intelligence) and company (competitive intelligence) data is processed for commercial purposes. Apart from that, these data can be used in e-research and other activities which are in the public interest (e.g. security intelligence). We are witnessing a new dynamics and continuous changes in individuals' views on their privacy, which are influenced by the possibilities brought by ICT. Similarly, this dynamics affects the organizational context of firms (mainly security and communication) and their ability to process enormous sets of data, which has an impact mainly on their marketing and management.

The Limitations of Handling Private Data in Internet-Based Services

Information technology and the possibilities of Internet-based services constantly evolve. Almost every online service requires users' personal data for the possibility of its use. The safety and the handling of these data is a very important issue these days, both for the users and providers of online services – see also *Guide to data protection for public and organization* available at (ICO, 2015). Within the European Union – see (DLA Piper, 2014) – the default privacy principles are primarily governed by the European Directive 95/46/EC from 24 October 1995 on the protection of individuals with regard to the processing of personal data and on the free movement of such data. The year of its inception suggests that this directive is already quite old and therefore does not reflect the current situation. This directive needs to refine and thereby at least partially reflect current development.

Currently we can mention for example the act from 15 June 2015 when the EU Council approved a general approach to the general data protection regulation. It establishes rules adapted to the digital era and according to that cookies should be included in personal data. The current EU Directive 2002/58/EC on Privacy and Electronic Communications (known as the E-Privacy Directive) obliges member states to adopt legislation requiring a prior approval of the use of cookies. In practice, this means that when you use cookies, which are designed to collect users' personal data, you need to obtain the users' consent with the use of cookies on your website.

Besides the refinement and fragmentation of laws within the EU, there is a number of clarifications on the level of national laws – see (European Commission, 2015). This leads to each state having slightly different laws. When doing business in a foreign country, it is necessary to become familiar with the specific legislation of a particular state. The fragmentation of legislation worldwide is even greater. For example, the US laws vary across the individual states, but also with regard to the type of sector and media. In addition, there are often various exceptions.

If we are to summarize the basic principles, the following recommendations for practice can be drawn. User's consent must be obtained when collecting personal data (i.e. the opt-in principle) for a specific purpose. This purpose should be stated, for example in business conditions. Using personal data for subsequent marketing purposes makes it obligatory to give users the option of cancelling their agreement with the use of their personal data, and thus to 'unsubscribe' from a database of respondents. The user has the right to request a statement of his personal data stored by the data manager. He or she can also ask for their personal data to be deleted. The data manager must comply with the user's request.

THE NEGATIVE CONSEQUENCES RELATED TO THE ACCESSIBILITY OF PERSONAL DATA ON THE INTERNET

An important issue is the use and the possible misuse of the freely available personal data that can be manually or automatically harvested by bots (data-harvesting softbot) and further processed by third parties. As an example, It is presented information that can be obtained from the Facebook service, which can be used for human resource management (Bohmova & Malinova, 2013; Benson, Morgan & Filippaios, 2014), marketing (Jasek, 2015), or abused for various forms of (cyber)bullying in a workplace or used by malicious data miners to threaten the privacy of users (Al-Saggaf & Islam, 2015):

- **Personal Information:** Belief, orientation, references to family, political opinions, contact information, what the user likes, employment/school, partially also pictures and multimedia content.
- **Information on Location:** Address, current position.
- **Data on Interaction:** A post on the wall, partially pictures and multimedia content, comments.

These data can be (mis)used mainly for unfair marketing practices. On the one hand, these data are used by Facebook itself for targeted advertising. On the other hand, the publicly available data are misused by harvesting and subsequently selling them to third parties. These include e-mail, phone and instant messaging, which can be supplemented with additional information (e.g. physical location) of the subject that owns it and used for targeting in an unfair commercial communications campaign.

Equally important are the social consequences when these data are used by any person for the purpose of discrediting or damaging the reputation of a particular individual. It could be personal data, available posts, comments and pictures, which are a gate into his or her private activities. In the work environment the information can be used for cyberbullying a worker in a particular group. An example: an innocent photo from Facebook can be simply modified and send anonymously to group members. This conduct can have serious implications for team communication and working environment, which is negatively projected into the business activities of the organization. The following types of bullying are specific for a working team:

- **Mobbing:** Bullying by colleagues in a team.
- **Bossing:** Bullying by superiors.
- **Staffing:** Bullying by the subordinates of a superior, with the aim of unseating him or her.

The misuse of selected data (beliefs, political opinions, etc.) along with other forms of pressure – underestimation of work performance, constant criticism, assigning meaningless actions that have nothing to do with the working position or a person's real character – may amplify the negative effects. These are only some of the problems arising from the use of private information available about a person in the context of an organization and it is only one side of the coin. Concerning our topic, it is appropriate to refer to other resources where authors deal with the consequences associated with data available via social media – (Lashkari et al., 2010; Young & Quan-Haase, 2013; Ibrahim, Blandford & Bianchi-Berthouze, 2012).

Despite these potential dangers and possible negative consequences, today's young people leave in the Internet environment reflections of their daily activities, which together with other personal data present new possibilities for individual or personal online address. It is not only companies offering services to their customers, which can carry out a better segmentation of their customers and individually address them thanks to this information (Sperkova & Skola, 2015; Jasek, 2015). It is also for those who want to exploit a person – gaining control over their e-mails or identities and their potential future misuse, for example for botnet attacks (Boshmaf et al., 2013), gaining the trust and then manipulating a person in order to carry out certain actions, obtain certain information (e.g. credit card numbers) and disclose their secrets (Hadnagy, 2010). On the one hand, this provides greater comfort and thus better meets people's needs (connected with a better segmentation of customers), and on the other hand, there are risks that cannot be underestimated on the personal (gaining control over online identities, manipulation, etc.), organizational (disclosure of company secrets, cyberbullying in workplace) or societal level (ethics, different approach to privacy).

GENERATION Y'S PRIVACY SETTINGS IN SOCIAL NETWORKING SERVICES

After an overview of topics related to Internet privacy and the possibilities of the acquisition and processing of the data of the users of Internet-based services, we focus on the results of relevant research studies. We start with own research (Cermak, Smutny & Janoscik, 2014), in which we compare the approaches of young people (age 15-30) from France and the Czech Republic. In this survey, such differences in behaviour are accented that originate in the cultural specifics of each country. This section also includes other interesting results from relevant surveys focused on Internet privacy. The conclusions following from these studies will enable companies to create their own strategy for obtaining information about customers and their interactions – e.g. for the purposes of marketing and management. This concerns mainly the different tendencies of young people in different countries to publish certain types of personal data, which can then be automatically processed; and the elements that motivate a person to give away personal data of their own free will.

The survey (Cermak, Smutny & Janoscik, 2014) presents two perspectives on privacy in the social networking services, both from a theoretical and a philosophical point of view, as well as from the perspective of practical research on the social network Facebook. The aim is to synthesize those views and discuss the positives and negatives of the actual phenomena occurring in this environment during social interaction.

In total, we analysed 531 Facebook profiles of people aged 15-30 years. For each profile was gathered visible data in two cases. The first was the visibility of data from the perspective of a friend (i.e. we explored the account from a profile which was in the friends list). The second was the visibility from the perspective of a random user of Facebook, i.e. the user who was not included in the circle of friends in the monitored Facebook account. At first, we introduce the answers to the three main research questions of this study, which will be followed by a discussion:

- *What kind of information is most frequently freely available?* The most freely published data are name, gender, friends, liked pages, current location, school/university and posts on the wall related to personal experiences, posts containing entertaining content and comments on current events – i.e. the data of general character. In contrast, data containing contact information, such as address, phone number or e-mail and data relating to personal beliefs (religion, political beliefs) are published with the least frequency.

Interestingly, users from France do not publish their true name in more than a quarter of cases. They use a profile under a different name or nickname. But (unlike Czechs) the French frequently publish their e-mail address, date of birth and information about their current location and hometown. Czech users disclose more information about their current school/university, as well as about their friends and the pages they like.

- *What information is most often available to friends but hidden to other users?* When comparing the differences among public and private data available in each country, the most significant differences were found out in posts on the wall, date of birth and photos presented on Facebook. In the Czech Republic, there is a difference of about 70% (for example 96% of users from the Czech Republic make posts from personal life available to their friends, but only 23% to general public), in France it is about 50%. Approximately a 40% difference was found in data relating to family, employment position, e-mail, school and the pages that the user likes. For these data the differences are more or less the same for users from the Czech Republic and France. The most significant differences in data availability between France and the Czech Republic relate to the current employment position (33%), funny posts on the wall (28%), information about the user (25%) and published pictures (25%).

- *What is the most frequently shared information on the wall of Facebook in each country and is the information only visible to friends or to other users as well?* In the case of public posts, the French frequently publish posts about their personal life, work and past events. Czech people make more often available to public only the posts with funny character, compared to the French. In the case of posts published for a circle of friends, majority of Czechs and the French write on the wall posts from their personal life. The differences can be found in other types of posts. Czech people more often than the French publish on their wall posts commenting current events (news) and posts that are funny. On contrary, the French publish more posts associated with their employment. Overall, Czechs publish their posts frequently only in their circle of friends, while the French often leave their posts freely available.

Results from the evaluation of publishing pictures and information about friends and favourite websites show that in the case of friends, the information is more often published by Czech users in all cases. It is the same when publishing for the general public, except for pictures, which are more frequently published by the French.

With regard to the philosophical basis outlined in the background section, we can continue with a particular archaeology of subjectivity in the environment of social networks on the Internet. Based on our data collection, there is an obvious difference not only in the actual administration of users' personal data, but also in their relationship to the network as a whole. While French Facebook users show more effort to protect their information in general, in the case of the key items in relation to the profile on the network and their real lives, the opposite is true. Despite a greater tendency to publish a large number of surveyed items, Czech users very strictly protect information that makes them identifiable at other levels (phone number, email, location). For most of these items, the publishing rate by Czech users is around 1%, some items such as telephone number or zip code are not published at all. As opposed to a premature conclusion that could only quantitatively evaluate French privacy, we provide a more accurate insight. Differences in the data indicate rather a different role that the social networking services plays. In France, the network is more tightly linked to other layers of identity of the users. This naturally puts pressure on a better control of the published data. In the Czech Republic, social networks follow first the logic of remediation – rather than create a supplement to real identities, so they act as an alternative to real identities: social networking services is a space in which the users do not follow their identification data but rather generate new relationships on media basis. This can explain the lesser pressure on protecting the remaining items of personal data that are involved in the creation of an alternate reality (e.g. status, friends, favourite pages).

The survey results are therefore consistent with the philosophical basis. (1) At the level of criticism of consumer culture, we can use Adorno's conceptualization of the attack on privacy in data analysis. This happens not only through the threat of misuse, but from the opposite side by putting pressure on the publishing of personal information by a user. (2) At the level of media reflection along with De Certeau, we see that the media (in our case the social networks) extend the possibilities of user behaviour in relation to their data, but do not add autonomy of their users. Media logic penetrates the user's imagination, forms 'his fears, his dreams, his fantasized and lacking authorities' (De Certeau, 1984, p. 176) and thus also his or her idea of privacy. (3) We can expand together with Foucault these media penetration mechanisms into individual ideas. He tries to conceptualize the phenomenon of power not as a substance or a centre, which attacks our individuality, but as the fabric of the network which helps to create it, including our ideas about privacy and its protection. In the study of outlined power we cannot only monitor cases of penetration of privacy. It is necessary to describe and assess the acts of users themselves, who are always already shaped by that power relation.

In general, we can summarize that the social networks on the Internet are at a very specific level at which the individuality of the user interferes with the invasion of transpersonal structures, which are characterized here:

1. Their mass,
2. Media logic, and
3. Nature of power.

Naturally, this issue calls for a specialized interdisciplinary elaboration. It can not only provide the analysis, description and evaluation of the dangers that are hidden in the accessibility of personal data published by users, but it also develops some considerations (based on Adorno and Foucault) about the development of the human personality in today's dynamic environment. Although the survey is relatively limited and the comparison is only bilateral, the authors consolidated the general perspective on how to approach the issue of privacy on social networking services.

The afore-mentioned research will now be supplemented with the results of other relevant inquiries. Let us begin with (Syn & Oh, 2015), who confirm the diverse motivations for sharing private information within social networking services. These depend on demographic characteristics, experience with these services and Internet usage, as well as the characteristics and features of the services themselves. Users could be highly motivated by the learning and social engagement aspects of social networks.

Different attitudes can be found even among men and women. The latter are prone to a proactive privacy protection behaviour on social networking services and generally in a Web 2.0 environment than it was reported around the year 2000. Almost a half of both genders are not aware of how personal information is being used (Hoy & Milne, 2010). However, results from the research study (Benson, Saridakis & Tennakoon, 2015) show that control over personal information published in social networking services is negatively and statistically associated with information disclosure. Both user awareness and security notices have a positive statistical effect on information disclosure.

Another research (Cecere, Le Guel & Soulie, 2015) conducted in 26 European countries verifies that the conception and awareness of privacy is positively affected by national policies concerning personal data protection, which differs in individual countries. Similarly, it asserts that cultural and socio-demographical variables affect the level of concerns one has about his or her privacy online.

Although privacy is valued for many reasons, as was mentioned about Generation Y, who take the Internet as an integral part of their lives, this issue is still not taken seriously (Al-Saggaf & Islam, 2012). The educational programs currently implemented point towards information and security risks (Kolin, 2011), but this process started relatively late and it affects rather the Generations Z and Alpha, not the Generation Y, which currently becomes economically active. Another problem presents the relatively weak and fragmented support in the legislation of particular countries concerning possible misuse of personal data (Al-Saggaf & Islam, 2015). Nonetheless, we can consider the efforts taken by the social network providers themselves, in order to maintain the anonymity of their users using their particular services, as positive initiative (Wang et al., 2015; Rajaei, Haghjoo & Miyaneh, 2015). Despite that, the technological possibilities of misuse of available data has technologically advanced further than the options of both direct (technological) and indirect (awareness, proactive attitude of individuals) protection of user privacy.

On the other hand, social networking services make possible a leak of private information as observed by another study (Li et al., 2015) focused on Facebook, Google+ and Twitter services. This stems from the conflicts between privacy control and social networking services functionalities. Besides online social networking services themselves, we can observe the games played via social networking services. According to existing research (Chae & Lee, 2015), the attitude of users towards privacy in specific social networking service does affect their perception of advertisements within the games. Primarily, these games use the identity of a user to address his or her friends. Despite the fact that social networking services have been successful in limiting the risks of direct access to personal data, the danger resides in communication through the profile of a player, which can be seen as unfair marketing communication. These findings confirm our philosophical exposition of the problem of privacy in which we have argued against the extrapolated scheme (privacy versus intrusion) in favour of a more holistic view in which the privacy is not intruded but rather formed by the online social networks.

There is significant group of users who are aware of the potential dangers of personal data being accessible through various social media. Nonetheless, these negative aspects are in many cases outweighed by certain benefits. Existing research (Min & Kim, 2015) introduces three enticements: the motivation of relationship management through social networking services, the perceived usefulness of social networking services for self-presentation, and the subjective social norms of using social networking services. 'The results regarding the positive and negative effects of suggested benefit and cost factors on information disclosure show that only the combined positive effects of all three behaviour enticements exceed the negative effect of privacy concerns, suggesting that privacy concerns can be offset only by multiple benefit factors.' (Min & Kim, 2015) Possible threats connected to social networking services affecting users, including the means of their prevention, are listed here, for instance (Fogues et al., 2015).

SELECTED FUTURE RESEARCH DIRECTIONS AND ISSUES

Within the reflection on future paths of research and development approaches to Internet privacy it is necessary to offer once again the perspective of two levels – personal and organizational. If we begin with the personal level, we have to highlight the increasing global information and security literacy even among the representatives of Generation X and Y. On the other hand, new technologies still emerge. Consequently, these technologies bring new perspectives on privacy and also remake old approaches. We should mention mainly the services based on Web 3.0 and ubiquitous technologies.

In the case of Internet-based services built on the Web 3.0 technology, which focus mainly on the semantization of content on the Internet for artificial actors, there are new ways of influencing the subjectivity of the human user by the behaviour of artificial actors. Because of the fact that Internet-based services are not user-tailored only to people, but will also be readable for softbots, it can be expected that even the artificial actors will enter into relationships with human actors and will influence their subjectivity[1]. Artificial actors and their actions will thus affect human subjectivity more than now – see also the marketing concept of the management of subjectivity (Firat, 2014; Tadajewski & Jones, 2014).

For example, an artificial actor can seek and reach a human (at a similar level of communication as another human) who has a specific mix of interests, establish a relationship with him or her and influence them by its contributions. In the context of Internet privacy, this is an issue of the selective approach of artificial actors to personal information, primarily within a field of social networking services. In other words, we can distinguish between good softbots (e.g. indexing Googlebot) which increase attendance and bad softbots which abuse the personal data for the needs of their maker.

Ubiquitous technologies develop at the level of both physical and virtual environments (e.g. the terms as the Internet of Things, Internet of Services) as well as on the level of mixed reality. In the area of social networking, future development is associated with the development of ubiquitous social networking that will support the social wellbeing of people in their everyday lives. This means a diversion from the centralized web-based social networks and the transition to ad hoc social networks that are limited by certain physical areas, where they promote social interaction. Although there are not many real applications, an important aspect of these technologies is privacy – controlling the access to personal data (Sapuppo & Seet, 2015). A current trend is the development of general models that deal with specific problems associated with ubiquitous technologies – e.g. (Chikhaouia et al., 2014; Lopes et al., 2014; Pesout & Matustik, 2012).

From the perspective of organizations and the usefulness of freely available data on the Internet, mainly for marketing activities, current development focuses on the identification of customers through various Internet-based services. The aim is to identify the different identities (e.g. profiles on Facebook or Twitter) as one customer, which will contribute to a better monitoring of customer behavior (their web traffic), the individualization of services and enhancing marketing models working with customer data such as customer lifetime value or electronic word-of-mouth analytical models (Jasek, 2015; Sperkova & Skola, 2015; Cheunga & Thadani, 2012). First studies concerning this identification are currently available – see (Long & Jung, 2015) – which for this purpose process available (personal) data. Let us add that this task may become easier in the future if Web 3.0 technologies are fully enforced.

Although companies focus their attention mainly on the processing of internal and external data (of their customers), they are at the same time caught in a trap created by their problems (inability) with processing large amounts of data from a wide variety of structured and unstructured sources. For instance, according to a survey among Czech small and medium-sized companies (Smutny, 2015) the results show that the fundamental problems perceived in connection with the processing of data from the Internet for marketing purposes are in particular:

1. Increasing time demands associated with the use of a large number of tools and services (e.g. social media, advertising systems).
2. The inability to create a holistic view of the success of their marketing activities. Currently, they rely only on partial instruments providing individual statistics.

On the other hand, it should be noted that only a small proportion of companies from Central and Eastern Europe (contrary to Western Europe and the USA) is pressed by competition to increase their use of potential data sources, or rather to a synergistic use of online marketing tools (Janoscik, Smutny & Cermak, 2015; Smutny, 2015).

The issue of Internet privacy is closely associated with technological development as well as with information literacy of the users of Internet-based services – i.e. the awareness of the risks associated with the availability of personal data, especially within the group of users of social networking services.

As stated above, there is a large number of empirical studies dealing with the approach of Generation Y to self-disclosure, including the phenomena supporting this sometimes risky behaviour. From the perspective of firms, there is a trend to increase economic efficiency by supplying current marketing, data-driven and others models with qualitatively new data (Pavlou, 2011). However, this trend, in our opinion, is slowed down by a related problem, which is the lack of technological and expert resources within companies (Maryska & Doucek, 2012) that would enable carrying out the gathering and processing of available data at the required level.

CONCLUSION

This chapter brought up an array of topics directly attached to Internet privacy both from the perspective of a regular user and from that of commercial organizations. This view from both sides can provide companies with better understanding of various aspects of Internet privacy. Our main concerns with generational and cultural differentiations, philosophical scrutiny, possibilities of data acquisition and analysis, legal framework, and negative consequences of personal data availability, all these aspects do intersect and form a basis, on which we can articulate other ideas focused for instance on prospective usage of personal data available on the Internet with the emphasis on the needs of firms. On the other hand, it was addressed even the issues of their misuse in personal and organizational context (manipulation of users, security risks etc.).

In order to understand the contemporary behaviour of Generation Y and their attitudes towards self-disclosure through social networking services we have discussed our preceding comparative research[2] in its wider system-oriented framework and based on selected set of other studies. In concluding parts we have provided not only important findings of recent research concerned with young users of social networking services and their treatment of their personal data.

We discuss even some prospective technological trends, but also some problems involved in economic interests of companies. In this respect the chapter outlines basic directions for companies to set and realize their activities connected with usage of freely available (personal) data. These might be outlined as consolidating available means of data sources, using analytical approaches (e.g. business intelligence) and models (e.g. customer lifetime value, electronic word-of-mouth) and secondly clear set of ethical principles of work with personal data including legal integrity. These courses of action are essentially dependent on technically educated employees and technical possibilities of particular company.

The most important implication for company practice can be summarized in the following points:

1. In companies' effort to acquire data for their marketing and management activities through Internet-based services, it is necessary to motivate people to provide personal data of their own free will (e.g. special commercial offers, discounts, presents, promo actions, individual approach). Different generations (and target groups) have a different understanding of privacy and tendencies to self-disclosure. Privacy is not intruded but rather formed by social networking services. This way of acquiring personal data seems to be more fair, as opposed to e.g. harvesting personal data from selected websites without involving their owners.

2. Cultural and generational differences are reflected in social interactions via social networking services, but also in a preference for certain products or services and thus a demand for them. Every culture or country has a different set of values, which are reflected in the feedback or reactions

of people on media and marketing communication activities. Connected with that is the *Agenda-Setting Theory*, i.e. the ability of mass media to influence the audience and suggest topics which are then further dealt with via social networking services.

3. The *Glocalization* principle needs to be applied in the current Internet-mediated environment mainly for cultural and geographical reasons. This means adapting globally offered services and products on a defined local level (e.g. continent, country, language group), and their specific conditions (see *Hofstede's cultural dimensions theory*).

4. In the same spirit it is necessary to consider different aspects when targeting marketing activities (market segmentation). Those include generational (every generation has different needs, priorities, the ability to use modern technologies) and the above-mentioned cultural (the tradition of an established brand, established schemes and product types) specification of a particular group.

5. A problem connected with privacy is that of security and decreasing the danger of a leak of sensitive company data, which happens mainly via company employees. The basic solution is to limit access to individual data sources of potential information according to objective information requirements of a certain position.

6. When using social networking services on individual or company level, it is necessary to consider possible (mis)use of the published information, for example by business rivals (e.g. as part of competitive intelligence, targeted damage by unfair communication campaigns). Data can be automatically processed by softbots, which will increase further with the gradual supplication of Web 3.0 technologies.

Let us also mention two current technological trends with a great social impact that are connected with the continuous development of ICT and mainly social networking services, which will in the near future affect the majority of companies doing business over the Internet:

1. The development of Web 3.0 technologies and mainly the semantization of webs will lead to more effective use of artificial actors (softbots), which will no longer process only unstructured data, but more often rather structured data freely available on the Internet. Other artificial actors with their profiles on social networking services will then be able to affect human subjectivity – even now it is very difficult e.g. on Twitter to determine whether a profile belongs to a human, a softbot, or a human acting like a softbot. It can therefore be expected that there will be a massive use of various forms of artificial actors, for instance for marketing, communication or competitive activities of firms. This issue concerns not only collecting and processing available personal data, but mainly the direct effect on a person's subjectivity and thus also on their perception and understanding of certain topics (including their attitude to privacy).

2. The expected development of ubiquitous technologies brings also the so-called ubiquitous social networks. Ad hoc social connections will be established within a certain area, which again concerns the issue of privacy. This technology will affect mainly retailers in stores, who will have new possibilities for propagation thanks to localized social interaction. For a better idea, let us give an example: A person walking in a street will be notified via his or her mobile device (on the basis of their interests, age, recent social activity) about a relevant shop located nearby. If interested, this person will be able to see their current offer (e.g. he or she is motivated by some discount if he or she makes a purchase there during the following hour).

Nonetheless our excursus into the problem of Internet privacy has not been limited to exposing and discussing basic issues, risks and prospectives. Mainly due to our philosophical grounding we have critically reassessed the very notion of privacy after our massive experience with social networking services. We need to think about their impact on our private sphere neither in terms of intrusion nor with some preconceived understanding of what privacy actually is. By no doubts it is being rearticulated and not only distorted by new technological means. Moreover there is no unequivocal private sphere since the publicity on social networking services capitalizes precisely on exposing our personal data. Like being on our balcony; on one hand confined to our private household, and on the other hand being completely exposed (Arendt). Nonetheless even this irritating situation has its prospective courses of action. Firstly we need to be aware of this exposure (Adorno). But this does not prevent of from reaching into this metaphorical space of social networks. We just need to appropriate its consumerist background and turn it into more critical "alterconsumerist" approach (De Certeau) admitting our very privacy to be informed by the networking (Foucault).

REFERENCES

Adorno, T. W. (2005). *Minima Moralia: Reflections on a Damaged Life*. London: Verso.

Al-Saggaf, Y., & Islam, M. Z. (2012). Privacy in Social Network Sites (SNS): The threats from data mining. *Ethical Space: The International Journal of Communication Ethics*, 9(4), 32–40.

Al-Saggaf, Y., & Islam, M. Z. (2015). Data Mining and Privacy of Social Network Sites' Users: Implications of the Data Mining Problem. *Science and Engineering Ethics*, 21(4), 941–966. doi:10.1007/s11948-014-9564-6 PMID:24916538

Arche, K. (2013). *Postinternet Observations*. Retrieved November 20, 2015, from https://artaftertheinternet.files.wordpress.com/2013/10/eeadf-postinternetessay.pdf

Arendt, H. (1998). *The Human Condition*. Chicago: University of Chicago Press. doi:10.7208/chicago/9780226924571.001.0001

Baars, H., & Kemper, H.-G. (2008). Management Support with Structured and Unstructured Data — An Integrated Business Intelligence Framework. *Information Systems Management*, 25(2), 132–148. doi:10.1080/10580530801941058

Bartes, F. (2010). Competitive Intelligence. *Acta Universitatis Agriculturae et Silviculturae Mendelianae Brunensis*, 58(6), 43–50. doi:10.11118/actaun201058060043

Benckendorff, P., Moscardo, G., & Pendergast, D. (2010). *Tourism and Generation Y*. Cambridge: CAB International.

Benson, V., Morgan, S., & Filippaios, F. (2014). Social career management: Social media and employability skills gap. *Computers in Human Behavior*, 30, 519–525. doi:10.1016/j.chb.2013.06.015

Benson, V., Saridakis, G., & Tennakoon, H. (2015). Information disclosure of social media users: Does control over personal information, user awareness and security notices matter? *Information Technology & People*, 28(3), 426–441. doi:10.1108/ITP-10-2014-0232

Benson, V., Saridakisa, G., Tennakoonb, H., & Ezingeard, J. N. (2015). The role of security notices and online consumer behaviour: An empirical study of social networking users. *International Journal of Human-Computer Studies*, *80*, 36–44. doi:10.1016/j.ijhcs.2015.03.004

Bohmova, L., & Malinova, L. (2013). Facebook User's Privacy in Recruitment Process. In P. Doucek, G. Chroust, V. Oskrdal (Eds.), *Proceedings of the 21st Interdisciplinary Information Management Talks* (pp 159-168). Linz: Trauner Verlag.

Bolter, J. D., & Grusin, R. (1999). *Remediation: Understanding New Media*. Cambridge, MA: MIT Press.

Boshmaf, Y., Muslukhov, I., Beznosov, K., & Ripeanu, M. (2013). Design and analysis of a social botnet. *International Journal of Computer and Telecommunications Networking*, *57*(2), 556–578.

Cecere, G., Le Guel, F., & Soulie, N. (2015). Perceived Internet privacy concerns on social networks in Europe. *Technological Forecasting and Social Change*, *96*, 277–287. doi:10.1016/j.techfore.2015.01.021

Cermak, R. (2015). Multicultural Web Design: A Review. In P. Doucek, G. Chroust, V. Oskrdal (Eds.), *Proceedings of the 23nd Interdisciplinary Information Management Talks* (pp. 303–310), Linz: Trauner Verlag.

Cermak, R., Smutny, Z., & Janoscik, V. (2014). Analysis of the Facebook Privacy Settings of Young People with an Emphasis on the Czech Republic and France. In A. Rospigliosi & S. Greener (Eds.), *The Proceedings of the European Conference on Social Media ECSM 2014* (pp. 613-621). Reading: ACPI.

Chae, J. H., & Lee, Y. J. (2015). A Study on the Impact of Apprehension for Privacy concern and Attitude for Social Network Game Advertisement on the Use of Promotion Advertisement of SNG. *Journal of the Korean Society for Computer Game*, *28*(2), 151–157.

Cheunga, C. M. K., & Thadani, D. R. (2012). The impact of electronic word-of-mouth communication: A literature analysis and integrative model. *Decision Support Systems*, *54*(1), 461–470. doi:10.1016/j.dss.2012.06.008

Chikhaouia, B., Wanga, S., Xionga, T., & Pigot, H. (2014). Pattern-based causal relationships discovery from event sequences for modeling behavioral user profile in ubiquitous environments. *Information Sciences*, *285*, 204–222. doi:10.1016/j.ins.2014.06.026

De Certeau, M. (1984). *Practice of everyday life*. Berkeley: University of California Press.

Dinev, T. (2014). Why would we care about privacy? *European Journal of Information Systems*, *23*(2), 97–102. doi:10.1057/ejis.2014.1

Dinev, T., Bellotto, M., Hart, P., Russo, V., Serra, I., & Colautti, C. (2006). Privacy calculus model in e-commerce – A study of Italy and the United states. *European Journal of Information Systems*, *15*(4), 389–402. doi:10.1057/palgrave.ejis.3000590

Dinev, T., Goo, J., Hu, Q., & Nam, K. (2009). User behaviour towards protective information technologies: The role of national cultural differences. *Information Systems Journal*, *19*(4), 391–412. doi:10.1111/j.1365-2575.2007.00289.x

Dullaart, C. (2014). Balconism. *Art Papers*. Retrieved September 15, 2015, from http://artpapers.org/feature_articles/feature3_2014_0304.html

European Commission. (2015). *Fifteenth annual report of the Article 29 Working Party on Data Protection*. Luxembourg: Publications Office of the European Union.

Firat, A. F. (2014). Marketing challenges: A personal history. *Journal of Historical Research in Marketing*, *6*(3), 414–429. doi:10.1108/JHRM-11-2013-0062

Fogues, R., Such, J. M., Espinosa, A., & Garcia-Fornes, A. (2015). Open Challenges in Relationship-Based Privacy Mechanisms for Social Network Services. *International Journal of Human-Computer Interaction*, *31*(5), 350–370. doi:10.1080/10447318.2014.1001300

Foucault, M. (1963). *Naissance de la clinique*. Paris: Presses Universitaires de France.

Foucault, M. (1972). *L'histoire de la folie à l'âge classique*. Paris: Gallimard.

Foucault, M. (1975). *Surveiller et punir*. Paris: Gallimard.

Foucault, M. (1976). Histoire de la sexualité, 3 volumes: La volonté de savoir, L'usage des plaisirs, and Le souici de soi. Paris: Gallimard.

Hadnagy, C. (2010). *Social Engineering: The Art of Human Hacking*. New York: Wiley.

Hoy, G. M., & Milne, G. (2010). Gender Differences in Privacy-Related Measures for Young Adult Facebook Users. *Journal of Interactive Advertising*, *10*(2), 28–45. doi:10.1080/15252019.2010.10722168

Ibrahim, S. Z., Blandford, A., & Bianchi-Berthouze, N. (2012). Privacy Settings on Facebook: Their Roles and Importance. In *IEEE/ACM International Conference on Green Computing and Communications* (pp. 426-433). IEEE. doi:10.1109/GreenCom.2012.67

ICO. (2015). *Guide to data protection*. Information Commissioner's Office. Retrieved November 20, 2015, from https://ico.org.uk/for-organisations/

Janoscik, V., Smutny, Z., & Cermak, R. (2015). Integrated Online Marketing Communication of Companies: Survey in Central and Eastern Europe. In A. Kocourek (Ed.), *The Proceedings of the 12th International Conference Liberec Economic Forum* (pp. 376–383). Liberec: Technical University of Liberec.

Jasek, P. (2015). Impact of Customer Networks on Customer Lifetime Value Models. In R. P. Dameri, & L. Beltrametti (Eds.), *Proceedings of the 10th European Conference on Innovation and Entrepreneurship* (pp. 759-764). Reading: ACPI.

Kliegr, T., Svatek, V., Ralbovsky, M., & Simunek, M. (2011). SEWEBAR-CMS: Semantic analytical report authoring for data mining results. *Journal of Intelligent Information Systems*, *37*(3), 371–395. doi:10.1007/s10844-010-0137-0

Kolin, K. K. (2011). Social informatics today and tomorrow: Status, problems and prospects of development of complex lines in the field of science and education. *TripleC: Communication. Capitalism & Critique*, *9*(2), 460–465.

Lahtinen, H. J. (2012). Young people's ICT role at home – A descriptive study of young Finnish people's ICT views in the home context. *Quality & Quantity, 46*(2), 581–597. doi:10.1007/s11135-010-9409-6

Lashkari, A. H., Parhizkar, B., Ramachandran, A., & Navaratnam, S. (2010). Privacy and Vulnerability Issues of Social Networks (Facebook). In H. Xie (Ed.), *Proceedings of the International Conference on Internet Technology and Security* (pp. 157-163). New York: ASME. doi:10.1115/1.859681.paper31

Li, X., Hess, T. J., McNab, A. L., & Yu, Y. (2009). Culture and Acceptance of Global Web Sites: A Cross-Country Study of the Effects of National Cultural Values on Acceptance of a Personal Web Portal. *ACM SIGMIS Database, 40*(4), 62–87. doi:10.1145/1644953.1644959

Li, Y., Li, Y. J., Yan, Q., & Deng, R. H. (2015). Privacy leakage analysis in online social networks. *Computers & Security, 49*, 239–254. doi:10.1016/j.cose.2014.10.012

Liu, B. (2012). *Sentiment analysis and opinion mining*. San Rafael: Morgan.

Long, N. H., & Jung, J. J. (2015). Privacy-Aware Framework for Matching Online Social Identities in Multiple Social Networking Services. *Cybernetics and Systems, 46*(1-2), 69–83. doi:10.1080/0196972 2.2015.1007737

Lopes, J. L., Souza, R. S., Gadotti, G. I., Pernas, A. M., Yamin, A. C., & Geyer, C. F. (2014). An Architectural Model for Situation Awareness in Ubiquitous Computing. *IEEE Latin America Transactions, 12*(6), 1113–1119. doi:10.1109/TLA.2014.6894008

Maryska, M., & Doucek, P. (2012). ICT Specialists Skills and Knowledge – Business Requirements and Education. *Journal on Efficiency and Responsibility in Education and Science, 5*(3), 157–172. doi:10.7160/eriesj.2012.050305

Miltgen, C. L., & Peyrat-guillard, D. (2014). Cultural and generational influences on privacy concerns: A qualitative study in seven european countries. *European Journal of Information Systems, 23*(2), 103–125. doi:10.1057/ejis.2013.17

Min, J., & Kim, B. (2015). How Are People Enticed to Disclose Personal Information Despite Privacy Concerns in Social Network Sites? The Calculus Between Benefit and Cost. *Journal of the Association for Information Science and Technology, 66*(4), 839–857. doi:10.1002/asi.23206

Pavlicek, A., & Novak, R. (2015). Big data from the perspective of data sources. In R. Nemec, F. Zapletal (Eds.), *Proceedings of the 11th international conference on Strategic Management and its Support by Information Systems* (pp. 454–462). Ostrava: VSB-TU FE.

Pavlou, P. A. (2011). State of the information privacy literature: Where are we now and where should we go? *Management Information Systems Quarterly, 35*(4), 977–988.

Pendergast, D. (2010). Getting to know the Generation Y. In P. Benckendorff, G. Moscar, & D. Pendergast (Eds.), *Tourism and Generation Y* (pp. 1–15). Wallingford: CABI.

Pesout, P., & Matustik, O. (2012). On a Modeling of Online User Behavior Using Function Representation. *Mathematical Problems in Engineering, 784164*. doi:10.1155/2012/784164

Piper, D. L. A. (2014). *Laws of the World Handbook: Third Edition*. Retrieved September 15, 2015, from http://dlapiperdataprotection.com/#handbook/

Pour, J., Maryska, M., & Novotny, O. (2012). *Business intelligence v podnikové praxi*. Praha: Professional Publishing.

Pranjic, G. (2011). Influence of Business and Competitive Intelligence on Makong Right Business Decisions. *Economic Thought and Practice, 20*(1), 271–288.

Provost, F., & Fawcett, T. (2013). *Data science for business: What you need to know about data mining and data-analytic thinking*. Sebastopol, CA: O'Reilly.

Puddephatt, A., Mendel, T., Wagner, B., Hawtin, D., & Torres, N. (2012). *Global survey on Internet privacy and freedom of expression*. Paris: United Nations Educational, Scientific, and Cultural Organization.

Rajaei, M., Haghjoo, M. S., & Miyaneh, E. K. (2015). Ambiguity in Social Network Data for Presence, Sensitive – Attribute, Degree and Relationship Privacy Protection. *PLoS ONE, 10*(6), e0130693. doi:10.1371/journal.pone.0130693 PMID:26110762

Rauch, J. (2013). *Observational Calculi and Association Rules*. Berlin: Springer-Verlag. doi:10.1007/978-3-642-11737-4

Roberts, M. L., Zahay, D. L. (2012). *Internet Marketing: Integrating Online and Offline Strategies*. Mason, OH: South-Western Cengage Learning.

Sapuppo, A., & Seet, B. C. (2015). Privacy and technology challenges for ubiquitous social networking. *International Journal of Ad Hoc and Ubiquitous Computing, 18*(3), 121–138. doi:10.1504/IJAHUC.2015.068127

Savage, S. (2011). Making sense of Generation Y: The world view of 15-25 year olds. London: Church House Publishing.

Sigmund, T. (2015). The Relationship of Ethical and Economic Behaviour. *Politicka Ekonomie, 63*(2), 223–243. doi:10.18267/j.polek.998

Smutny, Z. (2015). Analysis of Online Marketing Management in Czech Republic. *Organizacija – Journal of Management. Informatics and Human Resources, 48*(2), 99–111. doi:10.1515/orga-2015-0010

Sperkova, L., & Skola, P. (2015). E-WoM Integration to the Decision-Making Process in Bank Based on Business Intelligence. In P. Doucek, G. Chroust, V. Oskrdal (Eds.), *Proceedings of the 23nd Interdisciplinary Information Management Talks* (pp. 207–216). Linz: Trauner Verlag.

Syn, S. Y., & Oh, S. (2015). Why do social network site users share information on Facebook and Twitter? *Journal of Information Science, 41*(5), 553–569. doi:10.1177/0165551515585717

Tadajewski, M., & Jones, D. G. (2014). Historical research in marketing theory and practice: A review essay. *Journal of Marketing Management, 30*(11-12), 1239–1291. doi:10.1080/0267257X.2014.929166

Tej Adidam, P., Gajre, S., & Kejriwal, S. (2009). Cross-cultural competitive intelligence strategies. *Marketing Intelligence, 27*(5), 666–680. doi:10.1108/02634500910977881

Valentine, D. B., & Powers, T. L. (2013). Generation Y values and lifestyle segments. *Journal of Consumer Marketing*, *30*(7), 597–606. doi:10.1108/JCM-07-2013-0650

Vyncke, F., & Bergman, M. (2010). Are culturally congruent websites more effective?: An overview of a decade of empirical evidence. *Journal of Electronic Commerce Research*, *11*(1), 14–29.

Wang, Y., Hou, J., Xia, Y., & Li, H. Z. (2015). Efficient privacy preserving matchmaking for mobile social networking. *Concurrency and Computation*, *27*(12), 2924–2937. doi:10.1002/cpe.3284

Witten, I. H., Frank, E., & Hall, M. A. (2011). *Data Mining: Practical Machine Learning Tools and Techniques*. Burlington, MA: Morgan Kaufmann.

Young, A. L., & Quan-Haase, A. (2013). Privacy protection strategies on Facebook: The Internet privacy paradox revisited. *Information Communication and Society*, *16*(4), 479–500. doi:10.1080/13691 18X.2013.777757

ADDITIONAL READING

Adorno, T. W. (2007). *Dialectics of Enlightenment*. Stanford: Stanford University Press.

Fromm, J., & Garton, C. (2013). *Marketing to Millennials: Reach the Largest and Most Influential Generation of Consumers Ever*. New York: AMACOM.

González-Fuster, G. (2014). *The emergence of personal data protection as a fundamental right of the EU*. New York: Springer. doi:10.1007/978-3-319-05023-2

Havens, J. (2015). *Hacking h(app)iness: Why your personal data counts and how tracking it can change the world*. New York: Penguin Group.

Luppicini, R. (2010). *Technoethics and the Evolving Knowledge Society: Ethical Issues in Technological Design, Research, Development, and Innovation*. PA: IGI Global. doi:10.4018/978-1-60566-952-6

Nissenbaum, H. (2010). *Privacy in Context: Technology, Policy, and the Integrity of Social Life*. Stanford: Stanford Law Books.

Patil, D. J., & Hilary Mason, H. (2015). *Data Driven: Creating a Data Culture*. Sebastopol: O'Reilly Media.

Quinn, M. J. (2014). *Ethics for the Information Age*. Boston: Pearson.

Sladek, S. (2014). *Knowing Y: Engage the Next Generation Now*. Lawrence: Association Management Press.

Sumner, S., & Rispoli, M. (2015). *You: For sale – Protecting your personal data and privacy online*. Waltham, Massachusetts: Elsevier.

Tanner, A. (2014). *What stays in Vegas: The world of personal data – lifeblood of big business – and the end of privacy as we know it*. New York: Public Affaires.

Ward, B. (2014). *Online Privacy: How to Remain Anonymous & Protect Yourself While Enjoying a Private Digital Life on The Internet*. Grand Reveur Publications.

Xu, Q., & Mocarski, R. (2014). A cross-cultural comparison of domestic american and international chinese students' social media usage. *Journal of International Students, 4*(4), 374–388.

Yang, K. C. C., & Kang, Y. (2015). Exploring big data and privacy in strategic communication campaigns: A cross-cultural study of mobile social media users' daily experiences. *International Journal of Strategic Communication, 9*(2), 87–101. doi:10.1080/1553118X.2015.1008635

Ziegeldorf, J. H., Morchon, O. G., & Wehrle, K. (2014). Privacy in the Internet of Things: Threats and challenges. *Security and Communication Networks, 7*(12), 2728–2742. doi:10.1002/sec.795

ENDNOTES

[1] Subjectivity can be understood as the condition of being an Internet user. Human subjectivity is individual experience, which is always unique and influenced by the environment and the actors in the environment (in the Internet environment, these could be human but also artificial actors) in which the subject resides.

[2] This chapter was prepared thanks to the same research project VSE IGS F4/18/2014 at the University of Economics, Prague.

Chapter 7
Social Media for Growing Collective Intelligence in Online Communities

Skaržauskienė Aelita
Mykolas Romeris University, Lithuania

Rūta Tamošiūnaitė
Mykolas Romeris University, Lithuania

ABSTRACT

Scientific society argues that human group demonstrates higher capabilities of information processing and problem solving than an individual does (Luo et al., 2009). Collective Intelligence (CI) is the general ability of a group to perform a wide variety of tasks (Woolley et al., 2010). With the growth and expansion of the Internet and social media technologies, "the way in which CI is utilized and leveraged has been fundamentally altered" (Wise, 2012). The new channels of social media enable new possibilities to be involved in collaborative activities for broader groups of people without limitations of time or geographical zones. The scientific problem in this chapter is defined is relationship between social media technologies and collective intelligence in networked society. The subject of the research are online community projects (collective intelligence ecosystems) which include social media tools allowing and encouraging individual and team creativity, collective decision making, on-line collaboration, entrepreneurship, etc.

INTRODUCTION

The growth of networked social media technologies, creative media industry, mobile telecommunications, emergence of web 2.0, 3.0 has contributed to "a thriving ecosystem of online social networks (OSN) serving various business models and personal interests for the citizens ranging from specialist interest groups to social meeting places" (Arniani, De Liddo, Georgi, Passani, Piccolo & Teli, 2014). The scientific and business communities are looking for possibilities to link social media to cloud services in order to maximise the network effect. "The explosion of user-generated content referred to as Web

DOI: 10.4018/978-1-5225-0559-4.ch007

2.0, including blogs, wikis, video blogs, podcasts, social networking sites, streaming, and other forms of interactive, computer to computer communication sets up a new system of global, horizontal communication networks" (Barahona, García, Gloor & Parraguez, 2012). The increasingly emerging new societal communication and relation forms claim to change essentially the traditional social practices. It`s important to understand how to exploit and to take advantages of the new ecosystem in order to serve more efficiently the society and economy. According Arniani et al (2014) the main characteristic of networked society is hyper-connectivity, which is the ability to network people, ideas and data across boundaries of any nature: geographical, cultural, disciplinary, linguistic, social, economic. "All of the most innovative game-changing ideas, from Skype to Wikipedia, from online cartography to app stores, had a very quick, viral spreading" (Arniani et al, 2014"). According to the MIT Centre for Collective Intelligence (USA) some of the most valuable results of collective intelligence include Google, Wikipedia, and InnoCentive. Some in the scientific community (e.g. Shneiderman, 2009; Vivacqua & Marcos, 2010; Furtado, Ayres, Oliveira, Vasconcelos & Caminha, 2010) argue that social participation using social technologies may be the only way to some of the biggest problems confronting the population (e.g. health care, climate change etc).

The chapter is focusing on the emergence of collective intelligence in digital enabled communities. The subject of the research are online community projects (collective intelligence ecosystems) which include social media tools allowing and encouraging individual and team creativity, collective decision making, online collaboration, entrepreneurship etc. The authors of this chapter maintain the position that the network structure (networked society) is one of the most prospective future societal organization forms. Although online communities are often criticized for the lack of direct contact, yet, in comparison with traditional communities the networked ones can operate more efficiently, due to technologies that make it possible not only exchange of large amounts of information, but also help to process the information more efficiently. New knowledge, ideas, found solutions, suggested problem solving methods, integrated public opinion, structured opinions and views, developed innovations, prototypes, generated added-value etc. are considered to be intellectual capacities of the community. The ability to recognize collective intelligence in virtual communities could contribute to solving other social problems of the networked society by multiplying the successful cooperation models and implementing them on the national or international scale through virtual means. The first research findings (Skaržauskienė et al, 2015) indicate a larger involvement of young people in virtual systems of collective cooperation as well as increasing civil power. What is more important, all this research is related to the common decision-making process, or what Bonabeu (2009) called "Decisions 2.0" in business context. This implies that the knowledge accumulated by researchers, the created models and recommendations can be relatively easily transformed in other spheres where:

1. It is necessary to make decisions;
2. People participate; and
3. There is a need to accelerate the decision making process or to solve problems of complexity through social technologies (Leichteris, 2011).

In the first part of the chapter, the concept of digital enabled collective intelligence is introduced. In order to answer the question what affect the growth and performance of online communities the defining principles for the emergence of CI were identified. The second part of the chapter presents the results and conclusions following the experimental evaluation of online communities in Lithuania using the new developed methodological framework.

DIGITAL ENABLED COLLECTIVE INTELLIGENCE

Approaches to studying collective intelligence (CI) have been diverse, from the purely theoretical (Szuba, 2002, Salminen, 2012) and conceptual (Luo et al., 2009) to simulations (Bosse et al., 2006), case studies (Gruber, 2008), experiments (Woolley et al., 2010) and system design (Vanderhaeghen &Fettke, 2010). Malone (2006) defines collective intelligence as groups of individuals acting collectively in ways that seem intelligent. According Woolley et al. (2010) "collective intelligence is the general ability of a group to perform a wide variety of tasks". Intelligence in groups emerges when each group member evaluates the overall situation and acts accordingly to achieve the overall goal (Leimester, 2010). Surowiecki (2005) made an extensive research on collective judgment and intuition of crowd. Based on empirical investigation author argues that "under the right circumstances, groups are remarkably intelligent, and are often smarter than the smartest people in them". In "The Wisdom of Crowds", Surowiecki (2004) identified the four basic criteria for emergence of collective intelligence: diversity, decentralization, independence and an appropriate mechanism for information aggregation. Diversity in groups of people usually refers to differences in demographic, educational and cultural backgrounds and differences in the ways that people represent and solve problems (Hong &Page, 2004). Wise et al (2010) proved empirically that groups leveraging CI could outperform individual experts in a controlled set. Both a simulation model by Hong and Page (2004) and an experiment with human groups by Krause et al (2011) have shown that under certain conditions groups of diverse problem solvers can outperform groups of high-ability problem solvers.

With the growth and expansion of the Internet, "the way in which CI is utilized and leveraged has been fundamentally altered" (Wise, Valliere &Miric, 2012). The new channels of communication and information flow enable new possibilities to be involved in collaborative activities for broader groups of people in shorter amounts of time. This behavior, which Preece &Shneiderman (2009) called Technology-Mediated Social Participation, "shows the ability of masses to achieve common goals through participation and collaboration on Web – goals that no single individual or organization could achieve alone" (Leimester, 2010). Social media tools have made it possible to develop new knowledge aggregation methods, such as information aggregation or prediction markets (Bothos, Apostolou &Mentzas, 2009), social tagging or folksonomies (Gruber 2007, Zettsu &Kiyoki, 2006), data visualization (Chen, 2007) etc. "The impact of gamification, competition, collaborative work are examples of strategies that have been evaluated to promote engagement and consequently bring about a change in behaviour" (Piccolo, Alani, De Liddo, &Baranauskas, 2013). The concept of collective intelligence is closely related with many other existing conceptualizations i.e. Open innovation (Chesbrough, 2003); Crowdsourcing (Howe, 2008); Wikinomics and Mass collaboration (Tapscott &Williams, 2006); Open collaborative innovation projects (Von Hippel et al, 2003); Transaction-free zones, Collaborative consumption, Electronic networks of practice or Online communities (Lewine &Prietula, 2015). Most discussed examples of Collective Intelligence applications are labelled as the Web 2.0 or Web 3.0 applications. "Exploitation of social media potential to leverage connectivity, responsiveness, creativity and innovation and co-creation of value with stakeholders is common for these paradigms" (Wise, 2012). Collective Intelligence may obtain different forms and developments from communities of interests, political parties to business enterprises collaborating or competing towards finding innovative solutions. Each attempt to systemize knowledge and conceptualize phenomenon of collective intelligence leads to promising future of CI purposeful application and effective employment in society life. Through extensive analysis of scientific literature, following areas of business activities were defined where emergence of the digital enabled collective intelligence could create additional social value (see Figure 1).

Figure 1. Value of digital enabled CI for business organizations

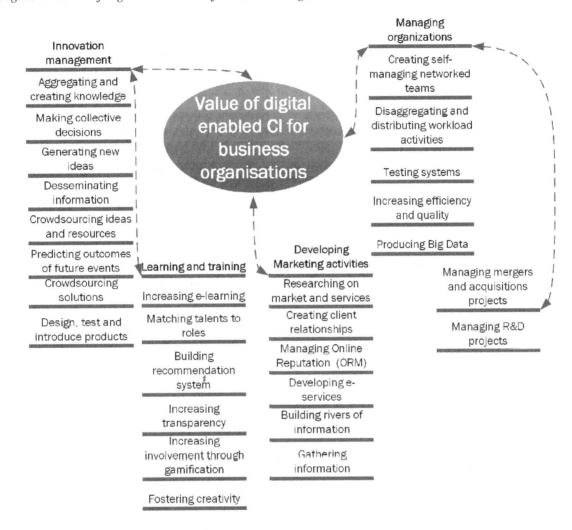

Investigation of literature related to innovation management lead to conclusion that there exist multiple of approaches, definitions and frameworks explaining emergence of innovative activities based on exploring CI. In general, the literature suggests following dimensions as a basis for successful innovation (Goyal & Akhilesh, 2007): "integration of talents; interdependence of roles; task complexity; interdepartmental collaboration; communication structures; diversity of knowledge, talents etc". The concept of CI systems is close related to the understanding of innovation: "to fuse the knowledge, experience and expertise of individuals, in order to elevate, through machine facilitation, the optimal information and decisions that will lead to the benefit of the whole community" (Kapetanios, 2008). Product innovation is considered a typical application of collective intelligence by Wang (2014). Ideation, concept development stages of product development require high richness in interaction and include different social media tools. "Product design, product testing and production introduction tools include mass customization of the product, web-based prototyping, virtual product testing and virtual market testing" (Wang, 2014). Product design by facilitating crowds provide few challenges i.e. multiple claims for ownership, complicated commissioning of participants, etc. but both organizations and especially participants always have opportunities to learn and grow intellectually by using the crowdsourcing model. The findings of several critical and extensive empirical studies suggest considerable benefits of collective decision making using social networking technologies to R&D project teams, and project teams (Cohen &Prusak, 2001; Cross &Parker, 2004). Research (Hulpia &Devos, 2010) determined a positive relation between team members' participation in collective decision-making processes and their organizational commitment. Getting knowledge from different companies involved in the process to design new high-performing teams can be highly valuable in mergers and acquisitions projects (Gloor, Paasivaara, Schoder &Willems, 2008). "A collective intelligence application is one that aggregates the knowledge and work of its users to provide the data for the application and to improve its usefulness" (Gregg, 2010). As Boder (2006) states, CI systems are a keystone in organizational knowledge generation by pooling and processing individual estimations to a collective estimation. Gloor et al. (2008) argues Collective Intelligence approaches could improve efficiency and productivity of sales and marketing. Changing technologies changed customer's role too hence "they are able not only to consume in new and diverse ways but also to influence organizations when developing and improving products, services and experiences of consumption" (Mačiulienė, Leichteris & Mačiulis, 2013). By Patel & Balakrishnan (2009) proposed recommendation system have to be based on the overall opinion of the user community and common patterns observed in the user behavior. Creation of collective intelligence systems is fostering learning. Properly constructed collective creativity environments can help build valuable expertise for participants. E-learning systems promote grow of human and computer capabilities by generating creative solutions to social and scientific problems (Wang, 2014). Beyond development of existing ideas and providing solution to existing ideas and solving contemporary issues, Collective Intelligence can be applied to predict the outcomes of future events (e.g. Microsoft project completion date prediction) (Malone et al., 2010). It facilitates making better, more informed predictions about the future, generation of potential solutions, predict outcomes of today's increasingly complex business challenges, and improve forecasting effectiveness (Bonabeau, 2009; Lesser Ransom, Shah & Pulver, 2012).

According Gregg (2010), most traditional applications have focused in improving the productivity or decision making of the individual user. Theoretical evaluation shows that Collective intelligence approach is "a fundamentally different way of viewing how applications can support human interaction and decision-making. Under the collective intelligence paradigm, the focus is "on harnessing the intelligence of groups to enable greater productivity and better decisions than are possible by individuals working in isolation" (Gregg, 2010).

COLLECTIVE INTELLIGENCE IN ONLINE COMMUNITIES

Many researchers have presented valuable results in exploring the potential of collective intelligence to solve various society problems or in modelling CI from a conceptual point of view (Luo, Xia, Yoshida, &Wang, 2009; Malone, 2006; Barahona et al, 2012; Salminen, 2012; Prpić, Taeihagh &Melton, 2014). This chapter is exploring CI system design and technological solutions, through "which collective intelligence could be able to emerge in a systemic manner" (Luo et al, 2009). Digital enabled Collective intelligence is becoming the subject of interdisciplinarity "since sociality is more and more something, that people create technically. Technology does not determine society it expresses it. But society does not determine technological innovation: it uses it" (Castells &Cardoso 2005). As discussed earlier, the information and communication technologies are critical for the formation of CI in modern society.

Online communities that use innovative instruments of collective decision making and social media tools to encourage collective collaboration, creativity and entrepreneurship were chosen as the research subject. The conducted study treated such indirect collaboration platforms as systems of collective intelligence. CI systems may differ in terms of users or purpose, but they all seem to share a number of common characteristics. Acting individually participants share common goals as a community. Community, according Luo et al (2009), "refers to any human group in which the members have some common characteristics, share same interests or views, have similar purposes." Collective Intelligence system can be conceptualized l"as knowledge network created by web-mediated (social technologies) interaction amongst individuals with personal knowledge" (Luo et al, 2010). Not only people, but also information communication technologies are involved in knowledge creation or aggregation in community network. The system is functioning effectively when the critical mass of system users is reached. As mentioned in the introduction, new knowledge, found solutions, suggested problem solving methods, shaped up public opinion, structured opinions and views, developed innovations, prototypes, generated added value, etc. are considered to be intellectual capacities of the community. The emergence of CI can be confirmed in the community, when community as whole system demonstrates higher intellectual capabilities than each individual member.

In order to answer the question what affect their performance the authors of this research project started with identifying some defining principles for emergence of CI in online communities (see Table 1). The defining principles, as well as the main challenges in the construction of the Collective intelligence ecosystem model were defined. According Luo et al (2009) the key feature of "community intelligence" (the authors use this definition for describing Collective Intelligence of online communities) is that it is self-organizing and "emergent." By developing individual cognitive processes and transmitting them to others, members' efforts lead to collective cognitive processes of communities (Lykourentzou, Vergados, Kapetanios &Loumos, 2011). The main difference of CI from team or organization intelligence is lack of "swarm effect" due to small number of individuals involved. Massive participants' inclusion into interactions ensure emergence of greater intellectual capabilities. Online communities tend to be more dynamic and open a feature that sets them apart from businesses, government bodies and other institutional organizations. Because of flexible and vague boundaries of online communities, people have more freedom of joining and leaving as opposed to fixed boundaries of institutional organizations. This results in easier recruitment of the new members and continual flow-in of new ideas and knowledge. In contrast to structured organizations, CI system are more dynamic. The Structural Model of Community Intelligence (Luo et al, 2009) explains how the community level intelligence may generate from the knowledge-related activities of the participants or the community members. First, the community should "contain a memory system that stores information and knowledge, analogous to the memory system in a human brain. Second, the community should have the capability of 'intelligent' problem-solving, i.e. the capability of utilizing the stored knowledge to solve problems; and the community should commonly exhibit higher-level intelligent capability than any community member" (Luo et al, 2009).

With the aim to evaluate technological readiness of online communities to generate collective intelligence, an instrument for measurement of social media tools has been developed on the basis of theoretical insights and tested during a scientific experiment.

Table 1. Defining principles of collective intelligence system

Defining Principles of CI System	Theoretical Insights
Diversity	• Describes "the differences in demographic, educational and cultural backgrounds and the ways that people represent and solve problems" (Hong &Page 2004). • "Fresh new source of ideas and knowledge may then be brought in together with the recruitment of the new members; and this continual flowing-in of new ideas and knowledge is beneficial for knowledge innovation inside the community" (Luo et al, 2009).
Dynamism, openness and flexibility	• "One critical difference between an online community and an institutional organization (e.g. a business company or a governmental agency) is that the community is more open and flexible" (Luo et al, 2009). • "The community boundary is vague and people have more freedom of joining and leaving the community" (Luo et al, 2009).
Knowledge aggregation, knowledge transmission and fusion	• Collective-level intelligence emerges from "in-group knowledge exchange activities such as collaborative learning and problem solving, which takes the form of opinion and expertise exchange" (Luo et al., 2009); "the distributed knowledge and expertise of individuals located inside and outside the formal boundaries of the enterprise, group, community" (Lesser et al., 2012). • According to O'Leary (2008) "knowledge management needs by capturing knowledge from those who have it, converting knowledge into an explicitly available format, connecting those who want knowledge with those who have it and linking knowledge to knowledge".
"Critical mass" of contributors within community to reach "swarm effect"	• "The critical mass may be at first roughly estimated for the specific problem e.g. through simulation modelling and then, after an initial period of system use it can be further fine-tuned to match the exact number of necessary users" (Lykourentzou, 2011). • "Research on prediction markets, virtual teams, and social networks suggests that the quality of aggregate information, number of ideas generated, and likelihood of a valuable answer increases with the number of participants. Having too many contributors can also be problematic. After a certain point, the marginal cost of adding new members exceeds its marginal value" (Foutz &Jank, 2010). • "As the number of contributors grows, the marginal value of additional contributors decreases while the cognitive and coordination costs associated with contributions increases" (Luo et al, 2009). "In particular, those involved in the co-creation of content are likely to suffer from information overload as they try to make sense of and respond to others contributions" (Ransbotham & Kane, 2011).
Independence	• Independence describes situation when the decision of an individual is not influenced by the decisions of other individuals. Bias is the tendency of individuals and groups to make systematically errors in decision-making situations. "Bias may arise in situations where early participants influence later ones or where the group of participants is not sufficiently diverse to include all relevant perspectives" (Malone, 2009). • "In order to eliminate negative social, psychological and other subjective impacts (subjectivity), we must guarantee anonymity of the participants` in online communities" (Norvaišas, 2011). • "Even a minor social influence can decrease the accuracy of a crowd" (Lorenz et al, 2011). • "Anonymity guarantees the better self-expression. On the other hand, it also creates an impression of absolute freedom of actions. Losing the control and feeling free to act without any responsibility often may drive towards violation of rights, which belongs to other people" (Skarzauskiene et al, 2013).
Transparency	• Transparency of information is necessary to create trust between community and society (Prahalad &Ramaswamy, 2004). • Empirical results of Dabbish et al (2014) inform that "imply a variety of ways that transparency can support innovation, knowledge sharing, and community building". However, Morozov (2013) is convinced, that "information should be distributed in full awareness of the social and cultural complexity of the institutional environment in which it is gathered".
Self-organization	• Describes "the emergence of order at the system level without central control, solely due to local interactions of the of the system's components" (Senge,1990). • "The organization process itself in online communities is autonomous, thus there is no central coordination that manages the organization" (Schut, 2010).

continued on following page

Table 1. Continued

Defining Principles of CI System	Theoretical Insights
Distributed memory system	• "The shared, often external, dynamic memory system that performs parts of "gents" cognitive processes" (Bosse et al 2006). Distributed memory facilitates communication and coordination between individuals. • "Community intelligence is generated upon the shared mental models. The community 'mental models' may embody as the shared understandings which basically reside in the community members' minds and which often attribute some degree of intangibility or tacitness; but they can also be exhibited in more tangible forms such as the written norms and regulations." (Luo et al, 2009). • "The community should contain a memory system that stores information and knowledge, analogous to the memory system in a human brain" (Luo et al, 2009).
"Wisdom of crowd" effect	• Describes "a rise of system level properties that are not present in its components: "the whole is more than the sum of its parts" (Surowiecki, 2005) • "The community should commonly exhibit higher-level intelligent capability than any community member" (Luo et al, 2012). • "Wisdom of crowds" is derived not from averaging solutions, but from aggregating them. For example, the average of several individuals" estimates can be accurate even if individual estimations are not" (Surowiecki, 2005).
Adaptivity	• Describes, "the ability of a system, or its components, to change themselves according to changes in the environment" (Schut 2010). • Schut (2010) distinguishes "enabling and defining properties of CI. The existence of enabling properties such as adaptivity, interaction and rules executed at a local level make it possible for collective intelligence to emerge from a system ("how do we build CI systems?")".

Experimental Evaluation of Social Media Tools in Online Communities

During the first stage of the scientific experiment (exploratory stage), the researchers used certain criteria to compile a list of online community projects. The researchers selected Lithuanian communities with specific business oriented goal and having capabilities to involve large number of members ("critical" mass of contributors to reach swarm effect). These criteria lead to selection of 8 innovation, business or entrepreneurship oriented communities (3 organization sponsored commercial communities and 5 organization-sponsored national and local governmental online community projects). The sample includes both member-initiated and organization-sponsored projects. At the onset of the exploratory stage, the researchers conducted a natural experiment with no direct interference into activities of the researched online communities. At final stage the evaluation of different social technological tools and platform`s designs was performed and conclusions based on qualitative analysis formulated. In addition, attempts were made to understand the impact tools and design of various social technologies have on results of network project activities. The social media tools were evaluated by following five indicators (see Table 2):

1. External and internal networking/collaboration tools;
2. Sharing/creating knowledge technologies;
3. Data aggregation and data access technologies;
4. Media/design quality;
5. Security and privacy enabling tools.

Table 2. Evaluation criteria for social media tools used by online communities

Indicator	Evaluation Criteria	Task
External and internal networking/ collaboration tools	• Existence of synchronous and asynchronous chat tools, open forums etc. • Provided access and integrated service to all devices (handhold, PCs etc.) • Existence of mechanism to create interests groups • Existence of "gamification" or other engagement increasing technologies • Technological and procedural accessibility • Network density (numeric value of the social network analysis) • Network amplitude (numeric value of the social network analysis).	Evaluation of possibilities for increasing diversity, dynamism, openness and flexibility and readiness to reach "Critical mass" of contributors
Sharing/creating knowledge technologies	• Existence of mechanism to add value to content or to generate feedback • Existence of mechanism for collective brainstorming • Existence of mechanism to vote/rank idea/solution and for idea/ solution classification • Existence of mechanism to make decision or conclusions • Existence of mechanism for mass argumentation.	• Evaluation of readiness for knowledge transmission and fusion, knowledge aggregation. • Evaluation of readiness to generate "wisdom of crowd" effect
Data aggregation and data access technologies	• Existence of mechanism to collect data • Existence of technological solutions for data visualization and organization • Existence of mechanism to share and re-use the data • Existence of mechanism to evaluate and analyze performance • Existence of mechanism to evaluate and analyze performance • Existence of memory function.	Evaluation of distributed memory of community
Media/design quality	• Quality of visualization • Level of development possibilities • The perpetual beta (updating possibilities) • Degree of user friendliness, speed and convenience • Description of the structure and procedures.	Evaluation of possibilities for adaptivity, self-organization and transparency
Security and privacy enabling tools	• Existence of mechanism for anonymous offering of ideas • Existence of mechanism for providing secure and legal activities, protection of personal data.	Evaluation of possibilities for independence

When analyzing the selected communities according to the level of their external and internal networking/collaboration technology, one can observe that, the best adapted technology is the technology for participating in the online activities using various devices (computers, smartphones, tablet devices, etc.). However, most of the communities` websites do not have sufficiently developed technological possibilities for discussion forums and more often members are redirected to register through social networks and to use the possibilities these networks offer. All observed projects had no restrictions on community member's gender or nationality. However, the vast majority of the communities use Lithuanian language - a limitation of diversity of national origin. Some communities are predominated by members of certain age groups although allow participation with no restrictions as to the age. One of the communities imposes limits upon professional occupation, job experience and extension of international experience of their participants granting full membership only to those who meet certain criteria in the aforementioned fields. The observation was made that the majority of virtual communities use standard modules that allow the spread of information through Facebook, Twitter, Google+, LinkedIn and email, however, very few communities use these platforms to the full extent. There are no elements of competition or elements of games in these communities either. The development level of knowledge aggregation and sharing technologies could be viewed as higher than average. The most popular technologies contribute to the visualization/organization of information and the formation of interest groups. Almost every community offers possibility for feedback or comments. Decision-making support mechanisms are directly related to the aims of communities to ensure or not ensure the decision-making process in their activity. About half of the virtual communities studied had installed technological solutions for collective brainstorming and conclusion or decision-making. However, only a few communities make use of voting and/or ranking mechanisms. For CI and innovations to occur, it is important that platforms allow collecting and storing knowledge, insights and expert evaluations of the groups that are vital for future decisions. In terms of data accessibility and aggregation, the communities studied have been best evaluated according to the existence of a data collection mechanism. The great part of the communities has applied more than one technological solution for collecting data. However, evaluations are less positive from the perspective of technology for analyzing and evaluating activity as well as sharing and organizing information. From a media and design quality perspective, the communities studied were generally evaluated as average, and just a few could be recognized as having created a user-friendly and convenient environment. It is also worth noting that, from a design perspective, the communities observed demonstrate high levels of consistency with their stated aims. Many of the communities present their work rather conservatively, thus their design solutions are accordingly spare. The evaluation of self-organization potential revealed that in many cases technical possibilities have been implemented, but there were no procedural explanations about how to use them. The evaluation revealed a low level of descriptiveness of general norms, procedures and activities. There are also a few exceptions that do present comprehensive information including the community values, history, terminology, a video, and all the technological possibilities about how to express views and aggregate solution from them. Communities that have figured out their ideological and procedural levels are distinctly better prepared technologically speaking and are better at engaging their members. The majority of communities installed technologies for ensuring security and privacy. The qualitative research has revealed that special attention has to be paid to gamification technologies for involvement of users, in particular young generation, into community activities.

Theoretical insights and empirical research results (Skaržauskienė, 2015) reveal that at the current knowledge level technological conditions in the online platforms are important features of the CI systems. Measuring them could be useful in predicting the performance of the system as a whole.

LIMITATIONS AND RECOMMENDATIONS

The experimental evaluation revealed the complexity of monitoring online community activities. Obviously, not all aspects of performance can be measured by qualitative criteria, but collecting data is extremely important for future communities` developments. Evaluating such data over a period could help diagnose and prevent reduction of community members' motivation or diminished activities. Testing demonstrated that some of criteria could be attributed to more than one element of the framework. However, the unique criteria could have different level of influence on different elements. In addition, different criteria for monitoring of the unique element could be of different importance. Therefore, it would be expedient to rank each criteria by its relevance. Therefore, the importance and correlations of diverse criteria were not analyzed yet and are planned for upcoming research stages. Moreover, the framework could be more sophisticated by demonstrating cause-effect links between criteria where applicable. However, for identification and validation of such relationships other research techniques are required ensuring collection and analysis of actual data and testing of hypotheses. The researchers notice, that possibility to gain independent access to the Google Analytics data of the community's website or collaboration with platform initiators by generating data reports increases validity of collected empirical data. Data mining and web scraping techniques could be suggested for comparative analysis of more homogenous communities in the future. These would improve the quality and reliability of such analysis, with small communities in particular, which use an individual domain for their activities.

In the future virtual scientific environment will be created for evaluation of potential of online communities with self-assessment questionnaires for community managers or initiators. The increased number of collected empirical data will increase the validity of the new developed instrument.

FUTURE RESEARCH DIRECTIONS

CI development field requires deeper research from academic and practical point of view. It would be important not only to identify the assumptions affecting development of CI, but also to predict possible development scenarios and to define risk areas. Future research directions should take the interdisciplinary nature of the phenomenon of CI into account. The proposed evaluation methodology could be combined with findings from social and cognitive sciences, informatics and biology. This kind of synergy is expected to broaden our understanding of CI and researchers could gain a more complex view on the subject. Relationship between collective intelligence and entrepreneurship could be an interesting research issue in the future. Participants of online platforms face such practical problems as big "noise" of social media, lack of innovative ideas, security of innovations, etc. A problem of mismatch between demand and offer, as technical development is faster than changes of socio-cultural development. Members of society without digital skills are not fully exploiting technological capabilities (Skaržauskienė, 2015).

CONCLUSION

The long term vision of CI systems is "to fuse the knowledge, experience and expertise residing in the minds of individuals, in order to elevate, through machine facilitation, the optimal information and decisions that will lead to the benefit of the whole community" (Kapetanios, 2008). To become smarter, organizations have to share power, knowledge and intelligence by involving customers and employees in strategic decision making. As a case in point, a recent Booz & Co. study found that "most of the top companies ranked by their peers as "innovative" weren't among the top five spenders on research and development" (Korn, 2011). Instead of spending on grow "the biggest innovators involve employees company-wide to help generate ideas" (Schreiber, 2015).

In network-type societies, whose specific feature is the impossibility of defining one clear power center, the need for understanding technological preconditions and characteristics is especially important. Speaking of Lithuania's online communities' potential for CI emergence, it is worth mentioning that the majority of Lithuania's online communities have already attained certain CI maturity level and tend to focus on social or business innovations. Online communities use social media technologies for increasing collaboration or creating competitive advantage, but without scientific reasoning they often choose not adequate tools or methods and don`t create expected value and sustainability.

REFERENCES

Armiani, M., Badii, A., De Liddo, A., Georgi, S., Passani, A., Piccolo, L. S. G., & Teli, M. (2014). Collective Awareness Platform for Sustainability and Social Innovation: An Introduction. France/Nice.

Barahona, M., García, C., Gloor, P., & Parraguez, P. (2012). *Tracking the 2011 Student-led Movement in Chile through Social Media Use*. MIT.

Boder, A. (2006). Collective Intelligence: A Keystone in Knowledge Management. *Journal of Knowledge Management, 10*(1), 81–93. doi:10.1108/13673270610650120

Bonabeau, E. (2009). Decisions 2.0: The Power of Collective Intelligence. *MIT Sloan Management Review, 50*(2), 45–52.

Bosse, T., Jonker, C. M., Schut, M. C., & Treur, J. (2006). Collective Representational Content for Shared Extended Mind. *Cognitive Systems Research, 7*(2-3), 151–174. doi:10.1016/j.cogsys.2005.11.007

Bothos, E., Apostolou, D., & Mentzas, G. (2009). Collective Intelligence for Idea Management with Internet-based Information Aggregation Markets. *Internet Research, 19*(1), 26–41. doi:10.1108/10662240910927803

Castells, M., & Cardoso, G. (2005). *The Networked Society: from Knowledge to Policy*. Washington, DC: Johns Hopkins Center for Transatlantic Relations.

Chen, C. (2007). Holistic Sense-making: Conflicting Opinions, Creative Ideas, and Collective Intelligence. *Library Hi Tech, 25*(3), 311–327. doi:10.1108/07378830710820907

Chesbrough, H. W. (2003). *Open Innovation, the New Imperative for Creating and Profiting from Technology*. Harvard Business School Press.

Cohen, D., & Prusak, N. (2001). *In Good Company: How Social Capital Makes Organizations Work*. Boston: Harvard Business School Press.

Cross, R., & Parker, A. (2004). *The Hidden Power of Social Networks*. Boston: Harvard Business School Press.

Dabbish, L., Stuart, C., Tsay, J., & Herbsleb, J. (2014). Social Coding in GitHub: Transparency and Collaboration in an Open Software Repository. *Collective Intelligence 2014*. Boston: MIT Center for Collective Intelligence.

Foutz, N. Z., & Jank, W. (2010). Research Note-Prerelease Demand Forecasting for Motion Pictures Using Functional Shape Analysis of Virtual Stock Markets. *Marketing Science, 29*(3), 568–579. doi:10.1287/mksc.1090.0542

Furtado, V., Ayres, L., Oliveira, M., Vasconcelos, E., & Caminha, C. (2010). Collective Intelligence in Law Enforcement – The WikiCrimes System. *Inf. Sci., 180*(1), 4–17. doi:10.1016/j.ins.2009.08.004

Gloor, P. A., Paasivaara, M., Schoder, D., & Willems, P. (2008). Finding Collaborative Innovation Networks through Correlating Performance with Social Network Structure. *International Journal of Production Research, 46*(5), 1357–1371. doi:10.1080/00207540701224582

Goyal, A., & Akhilesh, K. B. (2007). Interplay among Innovativeness, Cognitive Intelligence, Emotional Intelligence and Social Capital of Work Teams. *Team Performance Management, 13*(7/8), 206–226. doi:10.1108/13527590710842538

Gregg, D. G. (2010). Designing for Collective Intelligence. *Communications of the ACM, 53*(4), 134–138. doi:10.1145/1721654.1721691

Gruber, T. (2008). Collective Knowledge Systems: Where the Social Web Meets the Semantic Web. *Journal of Web Semantics, 6*(1), 4–13. doi:10.1016/j.websem.2007.11.011

Hong, L., & Page, S. (2004). Groups of Diverse Problem-solvers Can Outperform Groups of High-ability Problem-solvers. *Proceedings of the National Academy of Sciences of the United States of America, 101*(46), 16385–16389. doi:10.1073/pnas.0403723101 PMID:15534225

Howe, J. (2008). *Crowdsourcing: Why the Power of the Crowd Is Driving the Future of Business*. New York: Crown Business.

Hulpia, H., & Devos, G. (2010). How Distributed Leadership Can Make a Difference in Teachers' Organizational Commitment? *Teaching and Teacher Education, 26*(3), 565–575. doi:10.1016/j.tate.2009.08.006

Kapetanios, E. (2008). Quo Vadis Computer Science: From Turing to Personal Computer, Personal Content and Collective Intelligence. *Data & Knowledge Engineering, 67*(2), 286–292. doi:10.1016/j.datak.2008.05.003

Korn, M. (2011, October 24). Top 'Innovators' Rank Low in R&D Spending. *Wall Street Journal*.

Krause, S., James, R., Faria, J. J., Ruxton, G. D., & Krause, J. (2011). Swarm Intelligence in Humans: Diversity Can Trump Ability. *Animal Behaviour, 81*(5), 941–948. doi:10.1016/j.anbehav.2010.12.018

Leichteris, E. (2011). Mokslo ir technologijų parkai socialinių technologijų kontekste. *Social Technologies, 1*(1), 139–150.

Leimeister, J. M. (2010). Collective Intelligence. *Business & Information Systems Engineering, 4*(2), 245–248. doi:10.1007/s12599-010-0114-8

Lesser, E., Ransom, D., Shah, R., & Pulver, B. (2012). *Collective Intelligence. Capitalizing on the Crowd*. IBM Global Services.

Lewine, S. S., & Prietula, M. J. (2015). Open Collaboration for Innovation: Principles and Performance. Collective intelligence 2015.

Lorenz, J., Rauhut, H., Schweitzer, F., & Helbing, D. (2011). How Social Influence Can Undermine the Wisdom of Crowd Effect. *Proceedings of the National Academy of Sciences of the United States of America, 108*(22), 9020–9025. doi:10.1073/pnas.1008636108 PMID:21576485

Luo, S., Xia, H., Yoshida, T., & Wang, Z. (2009). Toward Collective Intelligence of Online Communities: A Primitive Conceptual Model. *Journal of Systems Science and Systems Engineering, 18*(2), 203–221. doi:10.1007/s11518-009-5095-0

Lykourentzou, I., Vergados, D. J., Kapetanios, E., & Loumos, V. (2011). Collective Intelligence Systems: Classification and Modelling. *Journal of Emerging Technologies in Web Intelligence, 3*(3), 217–226. doi:10.4304/jetwi.3.3.217-226

Mačiulienė, M., Leichteris, E., & Mačiulis, A. (2013). The perspectives of developments of virtual communities in Lithuania. In *Proceedings of Social Technologies'2013 conference*. Vilnius: MRU.

Malone, T. W. (2006). *What is Collective Intelligence and What Will We Do About it?* Edited transcript of remarks presented at the official launch of the MIT Center for Collective Intelligence, October 13, Cambridge, MA.

Morozov, E. (2013). *To Save Everything Click Here*. New York: Public Affairs.

Norvaišas, S., Mažeika, A., Paražinskaitė, G., Skaržauskienė, A., Šiugždaitė, R., & Tamošiūnaitė, R. (2011). Networked business informatics studies: methodical guidelines. Lithuania: Mykolo Romerio universiteto Leidybos centras.

O'Leary, D. E. (2008). Wikis: From Each According to His Knowledge. *Computer, 41*(2), 34–41.

Patel, A., & Balakrishnan, A. (2009). *Generic framework for recommendation system using collective intelligence*. Internet Technology and Secured Transactions, 2009. ICITST 2009. International Conference for, London, UK.

Piccolo, L., Alani, H., De Liddo, A. & Baranauskas, C. (2013). Motivating Online Engagement and Debates on Energy Consumption. In *Proceeding of WebSci 2014*.

Prahalad, C. K., & Ramaswamy, V. (2004). Co-creation Experiences: The Next Practice in Value Creation. *Journal of Interactive Marketing, 18*(3), 5–14. doi:10.1002/dir.20015

Preece, J., & Shneiderman, B. (2009). The Reader-to-leader Framework: Motivating Technology-mediated Social Participation. *AIS Transactions on Human-Computer Interaction, 1*(1), 13–32.

Prić, J., Taeihagh, A., & Melton, J. (2014). Crowdsourcing the Policy Cycle. *Collective Intelligence 2014*. Boston: MIT Center for Collective Intelligence.

Ransbotham, S., & Kane, G. C. (2011). Membership Turnover and Collaboration Success in Online Communities: Explaining Rises and Falls from Grace in Wikipedia. *MIS Quarterly-Management Information Systems, 35*(3), 613.

Salminen, J. (2012). Collective Intelligence in Humans: A Literature Review. *Collective Intelligence 2012*. Boston: MIT Center for Collective intelligence.

Schreiber, E. S. (2015). Intelligence is collective, Collective Innovation: The Known and the Unknown. Collective Intelligence 2015.

Schut, M. C. (2010). On Model Design for Simulation of Collective Intelligence. *Information Sciences, 180*(1), 132–155. doi:10.1016/j.ins.2009.08.006

Senge, P. (1990). *The Fifth Discipline*. New York: Currency Doubleday.

Shneiderman, B. A. (2009). National Initiative for Social Participation. *Science, 323*(5920), 1426–1427. doi:10.1126/science.323.5920.1426 PMID:19286535

Skarzauskiene, A., Ewart, J., Krzywosz-Rynkiewizc, B., Zalewska, A. M., Leichteris, E., Mačiulis, A., … Valys, T. (2015). *Social technologies and collective intelligence.* Vilnius: Baltijos kopija.

Skaržauskienė, A., Pitrėnaitė-Žilienė, B., & Leichteris, E. (2013). Following Traces of Collective Intelligence in Social Networks: Case of Lithuania. In *Proceedings of ICICKM 2013: the 10th international conference on intellectual capital knowledge management and organisational learning* (vol. 2, pp. 411-419). The George Washington University.

Surowiecki, J. (2005). *Wisdom of Crowds.* New York: Anchor Books.

Szuba, T. (2001). A Formal Definition of the Phenomenon of Collective Intelligence and its IQ Measure. *Future Generation Computer Systems, 17*(4), 489–500. doi:10.1016/S0167-739X(99)00136-3

Tapscott, D., & Williams, A. D. (2006). *Wikinomics: How Mass Collaboration Changes Everything.* New York: Portfolio.

Vivacqua, A. S. B., & Marcos, R. S. (2010). Collective Intelligence for the Design of Emerge ncy Response, In *Proceedings of 14th International Conference on Computer Supported Cooperative Work in Design (CSCWD)* (pp. 623–628).

Von Hippel, E., & Von Krogh, G. (2003). Open Source Software and the "Private-collective" Innovation Model: Issues for Organization Science. *Organization Science, 14*(2), 209–223. doi:10.1287/orsc.14.2.209.14992

Wang, K. (2014). Collective Innovation: The Known and the Unknown. *Collective Intelligence 2014.* Boston: MIT Center for Collective Intelligence.

Wise, S., Paton, R. A., & Gegenhuber, T. (2012). Value Co-creation through Collective Intelligence in the Public Sector: A Review of US and European Initiatives. *Vine, 42*(2), 251–276. doi:10.1108/03055721211227273

Wise, S., Valliere, D., & Miric, M. (2010). Testing the Effectiveness of Semi-predictive Markets: Are Fight Fans Smarter than Expert Bookies? *Procedia: Social and Behavioral Sciences, 2*(4), 6497–6502. doi:10.1016/j.sbspro.2010.04.059

Woolley, A. W., Chabris, C. F., Pentland, A., Hashmi, N., & Malone, T. W. (2010). Evidence for a Collective Intelligence Factor in the Performance of Human Groups. *Science, 330*(6004), 686–688. doi:10.1126/science.1193147 PMID:20929725

Zettsu, K., & Kiyoki, Y. (2006). Towards Knowledge Management Based on Harnessing Collective Intelligence on the Web. *Lecture Notes in Artificial Intelligence, 4248,* 350–357.

KEY TERMS AND DEFINITIONS

Adaptivity: "The ability of a system, or its components, to change themselves according to changes in the environment" (Schut 2010).

Collective Intelligence: The general ability of the group acting collectively to perform a wide variety of tasks.

Collective Intelligence System: The knowledge network created by web-mediated (social media) interaction amongst individuals with personal knowledge.

Community: The human group in which the members have some common characteristics, share same interests or views, have similar purposes.

Critical Mass: The minimum number of individuals that need to use the system, so that it will function effectively.

Self-Organization: "The emergence of order at the system level without central control, solely due to local interactions of the of the system's components" (Kauffman, 1993).

The "Wisdom of Crowds" Effect: Emergence of collective intelligence in crowd. The four basic criteria for groups to be smarter as individuals in them are: diversity, decentralization, independence and an appropriate mechanism for information aggregation (Surowiecki, 2004).

Chapter 8
A Tale of Two Banks:
Customer Services on Facebook

Nurdilek Dalziel
Staffordshire University, UK

Janet Hontoir
IFS University College, UK

ABSTRACT

By focusing on Facebook as an emerging Social Media (SM) customer services channel, this research provides an insight into social media service encounters. Data were collected from the Facebook pages of two British banks. Evidence is presented on the discrepancy between what customers expected of SM and what banks were prepared to offer, a discrepancy which resulted in customer frustration. The findings also demonstrate that, apart from banking regulation, a bank's own SM policies and the training and empowerment of its staff are likely to impact on the quality of firm-customer interactions on SM. It is challenging for financial institutions to develop strategies to address customer queries satisfactorily on their SM pages and at the same time to work within the rules of compliance regulations. Moreover, many customers who put up a complaint on SM are observed to have developed rather negative feelings about their banks and to have lost their trust, suggesting a lack of clarity about the limited role of banks' Facebook channel among customers.

1. INTRODUCTION

As "critical moments of truth" (Bitner et al, 2000), service encounters have attracted significant interest in the marketing literature. The conventional approach limits its scope to human interactions and views service encounters as: "the dyadic interaction between a customer and service provider" (Surprenant & Solomon, 1987, p.87). On the other hand, a broader view of the service encounter takes a holistic view of all aspects of this encounter, including human as well as virtual interactions, the service environment and other visible elements of a service, termed "the total customer experience" (Harris et al, 2003).

DOI: 10.4018/978-1-5225-0559-4.ch008

This chapter adopts the broader view of the service encounter. According to industry sources, 22 percent of US online adults used Twitter as customer service channels in 2014 while the ratio went up to 37 percent in 2015 (Jacobs, 2015). Consequently, we consider a broader view of the service encounter a better reflection of modern business circumstances.

The authors argue that social media service encounter (SMSE) is likely to reshape the provision of services between firms and their customers. However, service encounters research is still primarily focused on traditional channels. Hence this research aims to provide an insight into SMSE by addressing the following research questions:

1. Why do people post a customer services query on Facebook?
2. What is the quality of the interaction between firms and their customers on Facebook?
3. What are customers' expectations of service encounters on Facebook?

With these research objectives, we aim to bridge a gap in the literature by integrating service encounters and social media literature. We also aim to present an insight into how firms manage interactions with their customers on platforms that, unlike traditional delivery channels, are open to observation and the participation of other people. We discuss what opportunities social media customer services offer for firm growth,

This chapter will continue with a critical review of traditional and social media service encounters literature in Section 2, followed by the details of our research methodology in Section 3. In Section 4, empirical research data and findings are presented in relation to each of the research questions presented above. Section 5 discusses the implications of our research for policy and practice. In Section 6, the limitations of the research are outlined. The chapter ends with conclusions in Section 7.

2. LITERATURE REVIEW

2.1 Service Encounters

Due to the inseparability of the production and consumption processes, service encounters are reported to be "the service" from the customer perspective (Surprenant & Solomon, 1987; Bitner et al, 2000), highlighting the importance of service interactions in shaping customers' experiences. With the aim of investigating technology supported interactions, the literature review addresses human as well as virtual interactions in the sections below.

Human Interactions

In marketing literature, human interactions are considered during the service delivery and the service recovery. Human interactions during the service delivery play an important role in the relationship development process. When investigating why human interactions are essential in enhancing customer relationships, the social support which is likely to be delivered in a face-to-face setting is identified as a key aspect (Ford, 2001; (Adelman et al, 1994; Sharma & Patterson, 1999). Ford (2001) suggests that customers expect to engage in conversations of a social nature in their dealings with service providers. The social nature of human interactions is viewed as enhancing service relationships by reducing customers' perceived risks (Adelman et al, 1994; Sharma & Patterson, 1999) and, from a psychological perspective, by helping to create a sense of social connection (Adelman et al, 1994).

Dalziel (2007) argues that communications characteristics are not equally effective in all service provision situations. She identified a set of communication characteristics which were effective for service delivery and another set of characteristics for service recovery situations. Service recovery is defined as "the actions that a service provider takes to respond to service failures" (Lewis & Spyrakopoulos, 2001, p.37). Strikingly, it is not the initial failure to deliver the core service, but the response that causes dissatisfactory service encounters (Bitner et al, 1990).

A successful service recovery process is found to have three alternative outcomes on customer relationships:

1. No impact on the relationship development,
2. Threatening the relationship development and
3. Facilitating the relationship development.

Firstly, the success of the recovery process can prevent the relationship from deteriorating; i.e. customers experience minimal changes in their relationships when the service recovery has been to their satisfaction (Levesque & McDougall, 1996; Mattila, 2004). Secondly, customer satisfaction can decrease regardless of the success of the recovery process (McCollough et al, 2000). Thirdly, a successful recovery process can enhance the relationship development, in particular by reinforcing the relationship commitment (Hart et al, 1990; Jones & Farquhar, 2003).

According to Mattila (2004), these seemingly contrasting views on the impact of the recovery process on customer relationships can be explained by the type of the relationship. Mattila has demonstrated that a recovery process which is limited to an apology combined with a tangible compensation is adequate for customers with little emotional attachment to their organisations, while for emotionally-attached customers more customised service recovery strategies are needed.

Virtual Interactions

Virtual interactions involve no direct or indirect human communication, but take place electronically. In virtual interactions, customers use technology enabled channels such as the Internet, television or telephone (automated services) to interact with organisations. Although service encounters traditionally rely on human interactions, services are increasingly being delivered virtually with little personal communication between the parties (Long & McMellon, 2004).

Early research on the impact of virtual interactions on customer relationships argues that virtual interactions are likely to threaten the development of relationships due to their adverse impact on relationship building efforts (Warrington et al, 2000; Zineldin, 2000). Virtual interactions are viewed, by this group of researchers, as presenting challenges to organisations by removing human contact and visual cues (Patterson & Ward, 2000). When information technology is used as the only means of communication, it impersonalises relationships (Aladwani, 2001; Leek et al, 2003; Ryssel et al, 2004) and gradually reduces opportunities for social interactions (de Wulf et al, 2001). In situations where social interactions are limited, this may result in customers approaching organisations in a purely transactional manner (O'Loughlin et al, 2004). Moreover, virtual interactions are stated to be likely to threaten service differentiation efforts, therefore placing further challenges on organisations in terms of maintaining a committed customer base (Rexha et al, 2003). As a solution to these obstacles, Rexha et al (2003) suggest that only after having established a committed customer base should organisations consider shifting to virtual interactions.

Late research, on the other hand, presents more positive views on the impact of virtual interactions on customer relationships. For example, Patterson & Ward (2000) note that some customers may establish a type of relationship with their providers based on solely virtual interactions. Similarly, Tomiuk & Pinsonneault (2001) argue that electronic banking environment is not an impediment for the development of a loyal customer base. Despite reducing opportunities for social interaction, virtual interactions are believed to offer a number of alternative benefits to customers (de Wulf et al, 2001; Tomiuk & Pinsonneault, 2001; Yen & Gwinner, 2003). Today's customers have less time and subsequently desire convenience and increased accessibility (Solomon et al, 1985; Moutinho & Smith, 2000; Yen & Gwinner, 2003) as well as gaining control over their dealings with organisations (Yen & Gwinner, 2003). When an electronic delivery channel is being chosen by the customer as the primary interaction channel (as opposed to being forced by the service provider), virtual interactions are found to promote relationship development (Dalziel et al, 2011). Yet, none of these virtual interaction papers included social media platforms in their study design. In the context of bank-customer communications, virtual interactions are mostly researched in the context of telephone banking, Internet banking and recently mobile banking.

2.2 Social Media Service Encounters

There is no clear positioning of SMSE in terms of whether they should be considered a part of human or virtual interactions. If one differentiates the two types of interaction according to whether the interaction is a personal one, SMSE could be classified as part of human interactions. Unlike online banking and automated customer services, customer posts on social media are responded to by a member of customer services team, and hence SMSE have the potential of introducing a social element into firm-customer interactions, despite their virtual nature. The personal and social nature of interactions between the parties (which are attributed to human interactions) impacts on the development of customers' trust, satisfaction and commitment. Alternatively, if one differentiates service encounter according to the delivery channel used, SMSE does not take place face-to-face, but electronically; and hence could be classified as part of virtual interactions. SMSE customers expect a speedy service and convenience (which are attributed to virtual interactions). Consequently, it can be argued that service provision on social media presents a significant challenge to organisations due to its embracing the characteristics of both human and virtual interactions.

Investigating the utilisation of SM by financial institutions, retail banks are reported to be sceptical about the promises of Web 2.0 to revolutionize marketing. Concerns over the lack of control over content on SM, issues with regulatory compliance and information privacy, and the fear of dealing with customer criticism on SM are stated to discourage banks from embracing SM (Stone, 2009; Klimis, 2010; Pry, 2010). Furthermore, it is found that bank management views social media as "not reliable" or not a "serious" communication tool for banking institutions, and hence with possible negative implications on corporate image (Mitic & Kapoulas, 2012). Other issues on financial institutions' reluctance to participate in SM are documented as being more pragmatic such as lack of time, personnel, know-how and funding (Pry, 2010) and lack of evidence in turning SM investments into financial returns (Mitic & Kapoulas, 2012).

It should also be noted that demographics and personality are recognised to be key factors in determining people's behaviour on social media (Amichai-Hamburger, 2002; Ryan & Xenos, 2011). Focusing on Facebook users, Ryan & Xenos (2011) present evidence that Facebook is more likely to be used by people who have higher levels of extraversion, exhibitionism and leadership. Extraversion is also positively related to the use of the interaction features of Facebook, such as the Wall and Chat (Ryan & Xenos, 2011). Hence, it could be argued that e-service encounters are appealing to a particular group of bank customers.

3. RESEARCH METHODOLOGY

The context of this study is the banking industry. It aids understanding of SMSE since banks have started to include social media platforms in their multi-channel strategies. The focus of the study was the UK banking sector. Banks' involvement in social media platforms is monitored by regulatory authorities, but different banks operating under different regulations are likely to face varying restrictions. The study examined banks working under the same regulatory system in order to exclude the impact of such external forces on financial institutions' engagement with social media platforms.

By taking a qualitative approach, the study utilises textual data which is widely used in marketing (Rudolf et al, 2005) and social media research situations (Olkkonen et al, 2000; Jahn & Kunz, 2012; Bronstein, 2013). Since this study aimed to decode the meanings behind communication messages and how consumer experiences are reshaped as a result of those communications, a qualitative research approach has been adopted.

As a social media channel, Facebook was focused on since Facebook and Twitter are the most commonly used channels for customer service (Littleton, 2013). In this research we focused on Facebook customer services. Criteria are set to facilitate the inclusion of banks with an active Facebook page which allows consumers to post comments or queries on their page. In this chapter the analysis of two main banks with an active Facebook page is presented; these are labelled BankA and BankB.

The research data consisted of customers' initial banking queries, banks' replies to the initial inquiry and customer and bank follow-ups which took place on the two banks' Facebook pages. Due to the large number of consumer posts, it was decided to set a limit to the number of posts analysed. The data collection started on 15 May 2013 for BankA and ended when 100 customer posts had been accumulated. The last customer query in the data set was posted on 4 June 2013. It took 21 days for BankA to reach 100 customer posts. On the BankB Facebook page, the data collection took place between 24 June 2013 and 31 July 2013, which meant that it took BankB 38 days to reach 100 posts. The selection criteria for the sample of customer posts were:

- The post should be related to a service failure incident which was defined as "situations in which customers' perceptions of the service they receive fail to meet their expectations".
- The post should have been responded to by the BankA or BankB Facebook team (i.e. in each interaction there should be at least one customer query and one bank response).
- The post should be initiated by a BankA or BankB customer.

Following the identification of customer posts, the responses by the banks' Facebook team to these posts were analysed. Comments were tracked until there were no further posts on the particular issue. Since the focus of the study was on customer-firm dyadic interactions,

1. Posts which were not responded to by the banks, and
2. Comments from other Facebook users were excluded.

This data collection strategy resulted in the examination of a total of 451 posts for BankA, which consisted of 100 initial customer contacts, 100 BankA responses to the initial inquiry, and 251 customer and bank follow-ups. The average number of interaction per post was 4.51 while the mode and median was 2 and 4 respectively, indicating a negative skew in the data set. In comparison, BankB data consisted of a total of 492 posts consisting of 100 initial customer contacts, 100 BankB responses to the initial inquiry, and 292 customer and bank follow-ups. The average number of interactions per post was 4.90, which is slightly higher than BankA. Yet, similar to the BankA data set, BankB data had a negative skew: the mode and median values were 2 and 4 respectively.

The analysis of this textual data comprised technique used to obtain a systematic and objective description and explanation of textual data (Berelson, 1952; Kassarjian, 1977; Miles & Huberman, 1994). In this case, content analysis started with an a priori set of codes that emerged from the literature review and research objectives. Pre-structured coding is reported to facilitate the analysis by forcing the researcher to tie research questions or conceptual interests directly to the data (Miles & Huberman, 1994; de Wet & Erasmus, 2005). However, it is important to note that the initial code list is flexible and evolves along with the analysis. Consequently, in addition to the initial codes, new codes and sub-categories emerged while some codes were redefined, removed or merged with others as more data were analysed. Coding scheme is in Appendix 1.

NVivo10 qualitative data analysis computer software was used primarily to undertake such an analysis of data. First, transcripts were entered into NVivo10 using NCapture and were coded using individual posts as the unit of analysis. Through the concurrent processes of coding and comparative analysis, recurrent themes and patterns were identified, as well as discrepancies in those patterns (Miles & Huberman 1994).

4. RESEARCH FINDINGS

4.1 Why Do People Post a Customer Services Query on Facebook?

Starting with the profile of the sample of bank customers, only certain data can be provided since the data set was limited to the information people posted on their Facebook page. For this chapter, the authors analysed the gender of 200 customer posts. Overall, 40% post holders were female while 60% were male. For BankA data, the figures were 36% (females) and 64% (males). For BankB data, it was 45% (females) and 55% (males).

Contrary to the authors' initial expectations, both banks' Facebook pages were popular repositories for customer queries and comments. Since banking is associated with sensitive information and the need for customer privacy, it was unexpected to see a large number of banking queries openly posted on Facebook. The posts from bank customers provided an explanation to the question on why people wanted to contact their banks through Facebook. First, bank customers wanted a quick response. They had high expectations with regard to the speed of response on Facebook, which is supported by previous research (Murray et al, 2014). Second, it was due to the perceived inefficiency of other channels. The sample of bank customers did not feel they were being listened to on other channels. When they reached Facebook, they were already stressed, were feeling frustrated and had lost their trust in their bank. Hence, SM was viewed as a last resort when traditional channels have failed:

I am left with 1 Option 'Take it Public via the Media' as [BankA] don't give a toss about me as a customer! (BankA customer)

Hi there, I know this is perhaps not the best place to leave a message but you're not responding to me at all... I have still not heard thing and the line is constantly engaged!! Even at 11 at night it is, very very odd and suspicious... This is the worst ever customer service and if someone can look into this for me, this really needs sorting today now as next week is too late, and I will be even more angry with this situation and I didn't even think that was possible. Yours Hoping. (BankB customer)

4.2 What Is the Quality of the Interaction Between Firms and Their Customers on Facebook?

It is important that a service is delivered by competent staff in a polite, friendly and timely manner. Looking at the replies posted by the banks, the staff were competent in demonstrating such communication skills, in particular when a customer had a basic banking enquiry. A common theme emerging across the banks' Facebook pages was "we'd like to help". Both banks responded to customer posts in a polite and courteous fashion, even when a post was derogatory about the bank or the banking industry:

Hi there, thank you for taking the time to share your thoughts with us. Please let us know if you have any UK banking queries; we're here to help and offer assistance should you need any. (BankA Facebook team)

The tone of response was conversational, informal, jargon-free and even humorous:

Thanks for your comments ... [name] I hope you have a fab sunny weekend in the garden with a nice bottle of vino perhaps:o). (BankB Facebook team)

At the same time, the banks were happy to record and/or pass the customer feedback to a relevant department for action. Some BankA staff were even willing to ask the relevant department to get in touch with the customer directly. The banks responded with encouraging language for the customers to get in touch for further support if needed:

No problem ... [name], we're glad you've been able to get the issue resolved. If you ever do need any assistance you can contact us here on Facebook. (BankA Facebook team)

On the other hand, it is not sufficient to offer an efficient service. Going beyond basic communication skills, organisations should provide a service that is delivered in a personalised manner taking into account individual cases, i.e. customer-oriented (Sharma & Patterson, 1999, Dalziel et al, 2011). This

Figure 1. Interaction quality by BankA and BankB Facebook teams

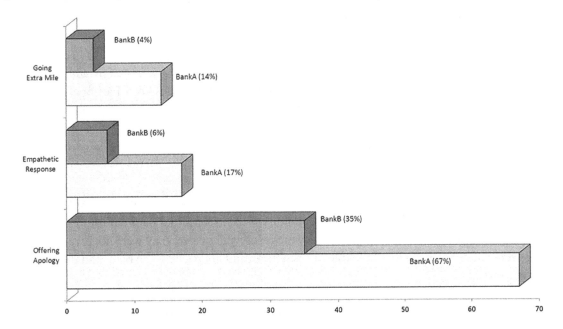

was an area where the banks' Facebook teams appeared to have weaknesses. As Figure 1 shows, the interaction quality by BankB staff was much lower than their BankA counterparts. Both banks were found to have weaknesses, in particular when it came to addressing customer complaints in an empathetic way.

Moreover, neither of the banks appeared to provide a service which promoted feelings of "going-extra-mile" which is defined in this chapter as "providing a type of service by a member of staff which goes beyond his/her duty that could be expected of him/her to please the customer". Examples of staff behaviour that were identified as going-extra-mile in the current research are:

1. Contacting the customer's branch or business manager on behalf of the customer to book an appointment.
2. Checking the image that the customer wanted to upload
3. Offering a local telephone number instead of a usual 084 number.
4. Posting a new card-reader to customer.
5. Offering a call back.

4.3 What Are Customers' Expectations of Service Encounters on Facebook?

There was little evidence that banks' Facebook team met the expectations of the sample of banking customers. Customer frustration was a common theme emerging from the data that was collected. It appeared that the frustrations of customers were often related to their misunderstanding of the role of their bank's Facebook page. Due to the perceived inefficiencies of other banking channels, customers wanted to post their queries and comment on their frustrations using Facebook; while banks wanted to deal only with more generalised banking queries on their Facebook pages:

If you ever have any general queries, we'll do our best to assist you over social media. However, any issues relating directly to your account will need to be discussed over the phone (or in a branch when a customer is in the UK). (BankA Facebook team)

Moreover, bank customers seemed to expect a more personalised service such as addressing them in person and solving their problems in a timely and empathetic manner. BankA Facebook staff signed each post with their name while BankB used just their initials, which was criticised by some customers:

Why is it [that] all [BankB] staff hide behind [their] initials and refuse to give names when asked on this site? (BankB customer)

Sincerity of interaction was another communication characteristic emerging from the research data. A script-read conversation and the sincerity of apology were aspects that bank customers commented upon. Customers appreciated that their problems were resolved; however they were not pleased that their problems were addressed because of the role of Facebook (and not because the bank had the customer's interests at heart):

I tried the usual route of phoning the fraud line, going into my bank branch. I finally got it sorted once I posted it on a social network site, not ideal. (BankA customer)

The sample of bank customers were also critical of the lack of service personalisation which resulted in banks' Facebook teams functioning like a reception desk – with a role restricted to directing customers to other communication channels including a call centre, website, bank branch, email or post. Most queries had complicated backgrounds such as a dispute about an online transaction, a declined mortgage application and the transfer of deeds from a bank to a house owner. The majority of customer posts were related to service failure incidents which were not resolved satisfactorily by other communication channels and there were also complaints about not being able to talk to the right person. Nonetheless, the Facebook team continued to direct customers back to other channels, and this caused frustration. Although there were a few occasions when Facebook staff tried themselves to help customers first, almost half of BankB customer queries were directed to other channels (46 percent); this was 14 percent for BankA customer queries.

4.4 Is Banking Regulation to Blame?

The social media literature emphasises the role of banking regulation as a restrictive force on banks' participation on social media platforms. However, the research data reveals considerable differences between the banks (Figure 1). BankA and BankB seemed to have different policies on whether to answer openly on Facebook or via a private message and whether to direct the customer to other channels. This was unexpected since both banks work under the same regulation. This implies that the way the Facebook team can respond to queries is not merely restricted by regulation. A bank's own social media policies, and the training and empowerment of its Facebook team are also likely to impact on its interactions with customers with the potential to influence the quality of interaction between the parties.

At the same time, the authors have identified inconsistencies across the Facebook teams within each bank. There were instances where the Facebook team responded satisfactorily but at other times did not respond in the same way to a similar type of query from another customer. There were also instances when the Facebook team openly answered a query on Facebook whereas a similar type of query was directed to another banking channel by another member of team.

5. IMPLICATIONS FOR POLICY AND PRACTICE

For basic banking queries such as queries about whether online / mobile banking was 'down', bank opening hours and how to open a bank account, social media teams were able to offer a satisfactory service. Nevertheless, for service failure related queries, Facebook teams appeared to have weaknesses which were related to their skills set as well as the level of training and empowerment that they had. It is documented in the literature that a service delivery team requires a different skills set from a service recovery team (Dalziel, 2007). The following service delivery characteristics are identified as having the potential to influence customer relationships:

1. Polite,
2. Helpful,
3. Competent,
4. Friendly,
5. Personalising the interaction,
6. Being fast
7. Efficient, and
8. Giving error-free service.

With relation to service recovery, different characteristics are identified: showing

1. Empathetic behaviour
2. Trust in the customer,
3. Apologising for mistakes,
4. Being proactive in dealing with mistakes,
5. Continuously communicating,
6. Adequate recovery speed, and
7. Whether the customer was refunded at the end of the recovery process (if relevant).

From the research data, it appeared that the two banks' Facebook teams mostly presented the skill set for an effective service delivery yet with a limited skill set for an effective service recovery. Hence, we argue that it is not sufficient simply to shift staff from traditional call centres to a social media team. In fact, it may be a better solution to have separate social media teams for service delivery and service recovery, and to train and empower each team accordingly.

The importance of customer orientation for a service organisation is well documented in marketing literature. According to Williams & Attaway (1996), customer orientation is "a philosophy and behaviour directed toward determining and understanding the needs of the target customer and adapting the selling organisation's response in order to satisfy those needs" (p.39). Customer care is a particularly important aspect of customer orientation, which is defined as "the customer's perception of the employee having genuine concern for the customer's well being" (Gremler et al, 2001, p.49). Another indicator of customer orientation is empathy which is about caring and paying individualised attention to the customer (Parasuraman et al, 1988). As part of effective communication skills, empathy allows the service provider to read customers' needs accurately. Empathy is reported as a critical aspect of service encounters, which eases the communication and facilitates the establishment of rapport and comfort between the relationship parties (Goodwin & Gremler, 1996). Despite its critical role, the service provided by the two banks' Facebook teams failed to provide a customer oriented service showing customer care and empathy. As highlighted in the literature "a successful service encounter is more than simply presenting the core product" (Dalziel, 2007, p.292). Questioning how a more customer oriented service can be provided by social media customer services, the following can be suggested for service providers:

- Using names to sign posts (not just initials).
- Showing empathy for the failure that customer is experiencing.
- Not script-read but sincere replies to customer queries.
- Offering a sincere apology.

For a customer oriented service, the staff should be supported by appropriate training programmes. Given that interpersonal skills along with technical capabilities result in service differentiation and customer retention, it is imperative that company staff who interact directly with customers are provided with intensive training. Likewise, giving the staff some degree of empowerment promotes trust in the service provider and relationship commitment. Empowerment means having the authority, responsibility and incentives to recognise, care about and respond to customer needs (Hart et al, 1990). Empowering staff by giving them authority, responsibility and incentives, which is fundamentally about giving the staff the ability to develop relationships, will enable the service provider to tailor their responses and actions. It is suggested that the ability of staff to make a proper response is largely a function of the staff's knowledge level and authority (Bitner et al, 1990; Lewis & Spyrakopoulos, 2001). Although standardised responses or actions can be desirable in some types of routine human interactions, interactions in most service failure incidents should be customised to the specific needs of the customer. Restrictive bank policies which are common in much of retailing are reported to hamper the development of customer relationships (O'Loughlin et al, 2004). All social media teams should have training and authority to enable them to answer customer queries satisfactorily. This is also important for a consistent provision of banking services across the banking channels and social media teams. If social media teams continue to act like a 'reception desk' (as outlined in previous sections), this is likely to have a negative impact on customer-bank relationships as the relationship marketing literature suggests. In this case, it may be a better option for a service provider not to offer a social media channel.

Training programmes are also likely to facilitate the provision of a consistent service across multichannels, which was one of the weaknesses emerging in our data set. When a customer with an existing service failure approaches their bank's Facebook page, they are likely to have raised their problem on other channels, such as their branch, call centre and the Internet team, with no satisfactory resolution. When the bank's social media team tries to direct the customer back to other channels, this causes more frustration for the customer. This highlights the important role of the social media team, who should work closely with service recovery teams.

However, solving an outstanding service failure on social media can be a double-edged sword. If an outstanding service failure is solved after being posted on a bank's social media channel, this may send the wrong message. Some customers may interpret this as the bank trying to save their reputation rather than keeping their customers' interest at heart; this is likely to have an impact on the level of trust toward the organisation and the quality of relationship between the parties.

Another important implication of our research is about whether highly regulated industries should offer services on social media. Clearly, banking regulation is a restrictive force for the effectiveness of banks' social media channels. However, as we have identified different levels of interaction quality from the two banks, we argue that it is possible to offer a customer oriented and effective service and at the same time stay within the requirements of banking regulation. Organisations should not use regulation as an excuse for a less effective or satisfactory customer service.

This research highlighted the role of Facebook customer service as a service delivery and recovery channel. We identified two groups of customers who preferred to contact their banks through Facebook instead of other traditional banking channels. This suggests, in combination with industry statistics about consumers' use of social media as a customer service channel (as presented in Section 1), that there is customer demand for the expansion of virtual customer services channels to include social media. Therefore, we recommend that firms should start considering social media platforms as a customer service channel in an effective way. Social media customer services are likely to become in the near future what an effective call centre means for customer services today.

Likewise, social media are increasing its popularity as a service failure & recovery channel. Yet, the evidence suggests that, in the case of service failure, traditional customer service channels are still the first point of contact by customers. Social media customer services teams are contacted when the service recovery is not managed to the customer's satisfaction. In this case, customers wanted to utilise the 'public space' nature of social media platforms to put pressure on firms to resolve their problem. This suggests, similar to our discussion on the role of social media as a service delivery channel, that SMSE play a crucial role as a service failure & recovery channel. When social media are designed to manage service failure situations, this requires a close co-ordination with other service failure & recovery teams. Firms should aim to resolve service failure situations by their traditional channels before customers post them on social media. When an outstanding service failure is posted on a platform it should be managed in a timely way and efficiently. The training and empowerment of social media customer services teams is likely to offer a competitive edge to those firms which can manage their customer interactions well. In contrast, if companies decide not to expand their customer services to social media or do not manage customer interactions and failure situations well, they are likely to fall behind the competition. This is because the demand for social media customer services will increase in parallel with the millennials' increasing use of social media in all aspects of their life.

6. STUDY LIMITATIONS AND FUTURE RESEARCH DIRECTIONS

The purpose of this research was to gain insight into service encounters on social media. This chapter looks at interactions on Facebook only, which is only one social media platform. Further research is needed to understand whether bank-customer interactions on other social media platforms are similar to Facebook customer services.

While the findings offer a good basis for an understanding of Facebook customer services, they cannot be generalised to a wider population. Banks' involvement on Facebook is monitored by regulatory authorities. Different banks operating under different regulations are likely to face different restrictions. The findings from this research can, therefore, not be generalised to financial services in other countries other than the UK. The extension of this study to other sectors or financial institutions operating in different regulatory and technological environments needs to be tested.

In this research the focus was on textual data available on banks' Facebook pages. It was not possible to identify whether the identified inconsistencies between the banks' Facebook teams were related to banks' own strategies or the issues in communicating those strategies to the Facebook team. Further qualitative research could be undertaken with members of staff to enhance the understanding of customer services on Facebook.

Many service providers offer live chats with their customers. It would be interesting to compare Facebook customer services with service provided through live chat in terms of customer expectations and the service performance.

Finally, posts on social media offer a good potential to provide insights into customer – firm discourse. There is extensive research on understanding the concepts such as the nature of apology, speed and the level of empathy, and their impact on relationship quality and customer satisfaction. However, those research heavily relies on either scenario-based research designs or collecting data from customers and / or firms after the interaction. In the case of scenario-based research design, it does not necessarily reflect customers' views, feelings and behaviour in the real situation. In the case of collecting data after the interaction, some important details may have been forgotten due to memory lapse. In comparison, when customer posts on social media are analysed, such limitations would not have been an issue since social media enables researchers to observe both parties interacting simultaneously.

7. CONCLUSION

In the service encounters literature, there is consensus that interpersonal communications characteristics are vital in customers' evaluations of service interactions. This research presents a valuable insight into service encounters on Facebook which is empirically an under-researched area. It examines why bank customers post a query on a public platform on issues which are considered sensitive and private, such as financial affairs. It is documented that banks fail to take a customer-oriented approach when they design their Facebook channel, which appeared to be a significant reason behind the sample of customers' frustration with their banks.

Service recovery is a particularly challenging area of service provision for any firm. The authors observed that in the majority of instances when a person posted on a bank's Facebook page they were already stressed and their relationships with their bank were under strain. This implies issues with the effectiveness of traditional customer services channels. If a service failure was successfully recovered when the customer initiated the contact with other channels, the banks' Facebook team would be able to offer a more efficient service. Banks' Facebook customer services were designed for generalised queries only; yet the bank staff were exposed to a large number of queries about personal accounts. This not only caused further frustration on bank customers, but also resulted in the Facebook team coming across with limited levels of competency and willingness to help their customers. The disconnection between customer expectations and staff responses could be related to the lack of clarity about the role of banks'

Facebook customer services. Checking the banks Facebook pages, the limited role of Facebook banking was not communicated clearly on the Facebook page, which may cause the identified gap between the customer expectations and service performance.

Moreover, some customers can still post a personal account query despite being knowledgeable about the limited role of their bank's Facebook team. The authors identified a temptation for customers to use Facebook. When they post a query on a social media platform or Facebook in particular, they expected their service provider to reply more quickly and in their favour in order not to attract negative publicity. Hence, Facebook customer services bring additional challenges to traditional service encounters because of being a public platform and because of its likely impact on customer expectations.

ACKNOWLEDGMENT

The authors wish to thank the Henry Grunfeld Foundation for the financial support provided for this research, and the reviewers of the European Conference on Social Media (ECSM2015) for their constructive feedback as well as our audience for their helpful comments when we presented our paper at ECSM2015.

REFERENCES

Adelman, M. B., Ahuvia, A., & Goodwin, C. (1994). Beyond Smiling: Social Support and Service Quality. In R. T. Rust & R. L. Oliver (Eds.), *Service Quality: New Directions in Theory and Practice* (pp. 139–171). London: Sage. doi:10.4135/9781452229102.n7

Amichai Hamburger, Y. (2002). Internet and Personality. *Computers in Human Behavior, 18*(1), 1–10. doi:10.1016/S0747-5632(01)00034-6

Beatson, A., Lee, N., & Coote, L. V. (2007). Self-Service Technology and the Service Encounter. *Service Industries Journal, 27*(1), 75–89. doi:10.1080/02642060601038700

Beatty, S. E., Coleman, J. E., Ellis Reynolds, K., & Lee, J. (1996). Customer-sales associate retail relationships. *Journal of Retailing, 72*(3), 223–247. doi:10.1016/S0022-4359(96)90028-7

Berelson, B. (1952). *Content analysis in communication research.* Glencoe, IL: The Free Press Publishers.

Bitner, M. J., Booms, B. H., & Tetreault, M. S. (1990). The service encounter: Diagnosing favourable and unfavourable incidents. *Journal of Marketing, 54*(1), 71–84. doi:10.2307/1252174

Bitner, M. J., Brown, S. W., & Meuter, M. L. (2000). Technology infusion in service encounters. *Journal of the Academy of Marketing Science, 28*(1), 138–149. doi:10.1177/0092070300281013

Bove, L. L., & Johnson, L. W. (2000). A customer-service worker relationship model. *International Journal of Service Industry Management, 11*(5), 491–511. doi:10.1108/09564230010360191

Bronstein, J. (2013). Like me! Analyzing the 2012 presidential candidates' Facebook pages. *Online Information Review, 37*(2), 173–192. doi:10.1108/OIR-01-2013-0002

Czepiel, J. A., Solomon, M. R., Surprenant, C. F., & Gutman, E. G. (1985). Service encounters: An overview. In J. A. Czepiel, M. R. Solomon, & C. F. Surprenant (Eds.), *The service encounter: Managing employee/customer interaction in service businesses* (pp. 3–15). Toronto: Lexington Books.

Dalziel, N. (2007). *The impact of marketing communications on customer relationships: an investigation into the UK banking sector.* (Unpublished doctoral dissertation). The Open University Business School.

Dalziel, N. (2014). Customer Complaints and Service Recovery on Social Media: An Investigation into Barclays Bank Facebook Page. In *Proceedings of European Conference on Social Media (ECSM2014)*, (pp. 111-119). University of Brighton.

Dalziel, N., Harris, F., & Laing, A. (2011). A multidimensional typology of customer relationships: From faltering to affective. *International Journal of Bank Marketing*, 29(4-5), 398–432. doi:10.1108/02652321111152918

de Wet, J., & Erasmus, Z. (2005). Towards rigour in qualitative analysis. *Qualitative Research Journal*, 5(1), 27–40.

de Wulf, K., Odekerken-Schröder, G., & Iacobucci, D. (2001). Investments in consumer relationships: A cross-country and cross-industry exploration. *Journal of Marketing*, 65(4), 33–50. doi:10.1509/jmkg.65.4.33.18386

Doney, P. M., & Cannon, J. P. (1997). An examination of the nature of trust in buyer-seller relationships. *Journal of Marketing*, 61(2), 35–51. doi:10.2307/1251829

Durkin, M., Howcroft, B., O'Donnell, A., & McCartan-Quinn, D. (2003). Retail bank customer preferences: Personal and remote interactions. *International Journal of Retail & Distribution Management*, 31(4), 177–189. doi:10.1108/09590550310469176

Ford, W. S. Z. (2001). Customer expectations for interactions with service providers: Relationships versus encounter orientation and personalised service communication. *Journal of Applied Communication Research*, 29(1), 1–29. doi:10.1080/00909880128098

Harris, R., Harris, K., & Baron, S. (2003). Theatrical service experiences: Dramatic script development with employees. *International Journal of Service Industry Management*, 14(2), 184–199. doi:10.1108/09564230310474156

Hart, C. W. L., Heskett, J. L., & Sasser, W. E. Jr. (1990). The profitable art of service recovery. *Harvard Business Review*, (July-August), 148–156. PMID:10106796

Howcroft, B., Hewer, P., & Durkin, M. (2003). Banker-Customer Interactions in Financial Services. *Journal of Marketing Management*, 19(9/10), 1001–1020. doi:10.1080/0267257X.2003.9728248

Jacobs, I. (2015). Take social customer service beyond your own walled garden. *Forrester Research Brief.* Retrieved 19 February 2015 from: https://www.forrester.com/Brief+Take+Social+Customer+Service+Beyond+Your+Own+Walled+Garden/fulltext/-/E-res119674

Jahn, B., & Kunz, W. (2012). How to transform consumers into fans of your brand. *Journal of Service Management*, 23(3), 344–361. doi:10.1108/09564231211248444

Jones, H., & Farquhar, J. D. (2003). Contact management and customer loyalty. *Journal of Financial Services Marketing, 8*(1), 71–78. doi:10.1057/palgrave.fsm.4770108

Kassarjian, H. H. (1977). Content analysis in consumer research. *The Journal of Consumer Research, 4*(June), 8–18. doi:10.1086/208674

Klimis, C. (2010). Digital marketing: the gradual integration in retail banking. *EFMA Journal,* (226), 16-19.

Leek, S., Turnbull, P., & Naudé, P. (2003). How is information technology affecting business relationships? Results from a UK survey. *Industrial Marketing Management, 32*(2), 119–126. doi:10.1016/S0019-8501(02)00226-2

Levesque, T., & McDougall, G. H. G. (1996). Determinants of customer satisfaction in retail banking. *International Journal of Bank Marketing, 14*(7), 12–20. doi:10.1108/02652329610151340

Lewis, B. R., & Spyrakopoulos, S. (2001). Service failures and recovery in retail banking: The customers' perspective. *International Journal of Bank Marketing, 19*(1), 37–47. doi:10.1108/02652320110366481

Littleton, T. (2013). Social media and customer service. *eModeration Report.* Retrieved May 2013 from: http://www.emoderation.com/social-media-publications/download-a-guide-to-social-media-and-customer-service

Long, M., & McMellon, C. (2004). Exploring the determinants of retail service quality on the Internet. *Journal of Services Marketing, 18*(1), 78–90. doi:10.1108/08876040410520726

Maclaran, P., & Catterall, M. (2002). Analysing qualitative data: Computer software and the market research practitioner. *Qualitative Market Research: An International Journal, 5*(1), 28–39. doi:10.1108/13522750210414490

Mattila, A. S. (2004). The impact of service failures on customer loyalty. *International Journal of Service Industry Management, 15*(2), 134–149. doi:10.1108/09564230410532475

McCollough, M. A., Berry, L. L., & Yadav, M. S. (2000). An empirical investigation of customer satisfaction after service failure and recovery. *Journal of Service Research, 32*(2), 121–137. doi:10.1177/109467050032002

Miles, M. B., & Huberman, A. M. (1994). *Qualitative data analysis: An expanded sourcebook.* London: Sage.

Mitic, M., & Kapoulas, A. (2012). Understanding the role of social media in bank marketing. *Marketing Intelligence & Planning, 30*(7), 668–686. doi:10.1108/02634501211273797

Moutinho, L., & Smith, A. (2000). Modelling bank customer satisfaction through mediation of attitudes towards human and automated banking. *International Journal of Bank Marketing, 18*(3), 124–134. doi:10.1108/02652320010339699

Murray, L., Durkin, M., Worthington, S., & Clark, V. (2014). On the potential for Twitter to add value in retail bank relationships. *Journal of Financial Services Marketing, 19*(4), 277–290. doi:10.1057/fsm.2014.27

O'Loughlin, D., Szmigin, I., & Turnbull, P. (2004). From relationships to experiences in retail financial services. *International Journal of Bank Marketing, 22*(7), 522–539. doi:10.1108/02652320410567935

Olkkonen, R., Tikkanen, H., & Alajoutsijärvi, K. (2000). The role of communication in business relationships and networks. *Management Decision, 38*(6), 403–409. doi:10.1108/EUM0000000005365

Parasuraman, A., Zeithaml, V. A., & Berry, L. L. (1988). SERVQUAL: A Multiple-Item Scale for Measuring Consumer Perceptions of Service Quality. *Journal of Retailing, 64*(1), 12–40.

Patterson, P. G., & Ward, T. (2000). Relationship marketing and management. In T. A. Swartz & D. Iacobucci (Eds.), *Handbook of Services Marketing and Management* (pp. 317–342). Sage. doi:10.4135/9781452231327.n22

Patton, M. Q. (2002). *Qualitative research & evaluation methods*. Thousand Oaks, CA: Sage.

Pry, C. G. (2010). Social Media: The Less-Noticed Risks. *ABA Bank Marketing, 42*(7), 22–27.

Rexha, N., Kingshott, R. P. J., & Aw, A. S. S. (2003). The impact of the relational plan on adoption of electronic banking. *Journal of Services Marketing, 17*(1), 53–67. doi:10.1108/08876040310461273

Rollason, H. (2012). *Why Social Media Makes Customer Service Better*. Retrieved 30 Sept 2013 from: http://mashable.com/2012/09/29/social-media-better-customer-service/

Rudolf, R. S., Elfriede, P., & Pervez, N. G. (2005). Analysing textual data in international marketing research. *Qualitative Market Research: An International Journal, 8*(1), 9–38. doi:10.1108/13522750510575426

Ryan, T., & Xenos, S. (2011). Who uses Facebook? An investigation into the relationship between the Big Five, shyness, narcissism, loneliness, and Facebook usage. *Computers in Human Behavior, 27*(5), 658–1664. doi:10.1016/j.chb.2011.02.004

Ryssel, R., Ritter, T., & Gemunden, H. G. (2004). The impact of information technology deployment on trust, commitment and value creation in business relationships. *Journal of Business and Industrial Marketing, 19*(3), 197–207. doi:10.1108/08858620410531333

Sharma, N., & Patterson, P. G. (1999). The impact of communication effectiveness and service quality on relationship commitment in consumer, professional services. *Journal of Services Marketing, 13*(2/3), 151–170. doi:10.1108/08876049910266059

Shostack, G. L. (1985). Planning the service encounter. In J. A. Czepiel, M. R. Solomon, & C. F. Surprenant (Eds.), *The service encounter: Managing employee/customer interaction in service businesses* (pp. 243–253). Toronto: Lexington Books.

Solomon, M. R., Surprenant, C. F., Czepiel, J. A., & Gutman, E. G. (1985). A role theory perspective on Dyadic interactions: The service encounter. *Journal of Marketing, 49*(1), 99–111. doi:10.2307/1251180

Stone, M. (2009). Staying customer-focused and trusted: Web 2.0 and Customer 2.0 in financial services. *Journal of Database Marketing & Customer Strategy Management, 16*(2), 101–131. doi:10.1057/dbm.2009.13

Surprenant, C. F., & Solomon, M. R. (1987). Predictability and Personalization in the Service Encounter. *Journal of Marketing, 51*(2), 86–96. doi:10.2307/1251131

Szmigin, I. (1997). *Cognitive style and the use of payment methods: An interpretative study of consumer initiator behaviour.* (Unpublished doctoral dissertation). University of Birmingham.

Tomiuk, D., & Pinsonneault, A. (2001). Customer Loyalty and Electronic-Banking: A Conceptual Framework. *Journal of Global Information Management, 9*(3), 4–14. doi:10.4018/jgim.2001070101

Warrington, T. B., Abgrab, N. J., & Caldwell, H. M. (2000). Building trust to develop competitive advantage in e-business relationships. *Competitiveness Review, 10*(2), 160–168. doi:10.1108/eb046409

Williams, M. R., & Attaway, J. S. (1996). Exploring salespersons' customer orientation as a mediator of organisational culture's influence on buyer-seller relationships. *Journal of Personal Selling & Sales Management, XVI*(4), 33–52.

Yen, H. J. R., & Gwinner, K. P. (2003). Internet retail customer loyalty: The mediating role of relational benefits. *International Journal of Service Industry Management, 14*(5), 483–500. doi:10.1108/09564230310500183

Zineldin, M. (2000). Beyond relationship marketing: Technologicalship marketing. *Marketing Intelligence & Planning, 18*(1), 9–23. doi:10.1108/02634500010308549

ADDITIONAL READING

Ballantyne, D., Christopher, M., & Payne, A. (1995). Improving the quality of services marketing: Service (re)design is the critical link. *Journal of Marketing Management., 11*(1-3), 7–24. doi:10.1080/0267257X.1995.9964326

Beuker, I. (2009). How digital brands can succeed and thrive in the engaged era. *Journal of Digital Asset Management, 5*(6), 375–382. doi:10.1057/dam.2009.28

Bitner, M. J. (1990). Evaluating service encounters: The effects of physical surroundings and employee responses. *Journal of Marketing, 54*(2), 69–82. doi:10.2307/1251871

Boshoff, C. (2007). Understanding service recovery satisfaction from a service encounter perspective: A pilot study. *South African Journal of Business Management, 38*(2), 41–51.

Chuang, S. C., Cheng, Y. H., Chang, C. J., & Yang, S. W. (2012). The effect of service failure types and service recovery on customer satisfaction: A mental accounting perspective. *Service Industries Journal, 32*(2), 257–271. doi:10.1080/02642069.2010.529435

Cocheo, S. (2009). Banks wade into new media stream. *ABA Banking Journal, 101*(5), 14–29.

Eriksson, K., & Soderberg, I. L. (2010). Customers' ways of making sense of a financial service relationship through intersubjective mirroring of others. *Journal of Financial Services Marketing, 15*(2), 99–111. doi:10.1057/fsm.2010.8

Fitzgibbon, C., & White, L. (2005). The role of attitudinal loyalty in the development of customer relationship management strategy within service firms. *Journal of Financial Services Marketing, 9*(3), 214–230. doi:10.1057/palgrave.fsm.4770155

Froehle, C. M. (2006). Service Personnel, Technology, and Their Interaction in Influencing Customer Satisfaction. *Decision Sciences*, *37*(1), 5–38. doi:10.1111/j.1540-5414.2006.00108.x

Gallaugher, J., & Ransbotham, S. (2010). Social Media and Customer Dialog Management at Starbucks. *MIS Quarterly Executive*, *9*(4), 197–212.

Goodwin, C., & Gremler, D. D. (1996). Friendship over the counter: How social aspects of service encounters influence consumer service loyalty? *Advances in Services Marketing and Management*, *5*, 247–282. doi:10.1016/S1067-5671(96)05059-7

Gremler, D. D., Gwinner, K. P., & Brown, S. W. (2001). Generating positive word-of-mouth communication through customer-employee relationships. *International Journal of Service Industry Management*, *12*(1), 44–59. doi:10.1108/09564230110382763

Hardey, M. (2009). The social context of online market research: An introduction to the sociability of social media. *International Journal of Market Research*, *51*(4), 562–564. doi:10.2501/S1470785309200785

Hoffman, K. D., Kelley, S. W., & Rotalsky, H. M. (1995). Tracking service failures and employee recovery efforts. *Journal of Services Marketing*, *9*(2), 49–61. doi:10.1108/08876049510086017

Johns, R., & Perrott, B. (2008). The impact of internet banking on business-customer relationships (are you being served?). *International Journal of Bank Marketing*, *26*(7), 465–482. doi:10.1108/02652320810913846

Keaveney, S. M. (1995). Customer switching behavior in service industries: An exploratory study. *Journal of Marketing*, *59*(2), 71–82. doi:10.2307/1252074

Mager, B. (2009). Service design as an emerging field. In S. Miettinen & M. Kivisto (Eds.), *Designing services with innovative methods*. Helsinki: Helsinki University of Art and Design.

Miller, J. L., Craighead, C. W., & Karwan, K. R. (2000). Service recovery: A framework and empirical investigation. *Journal of Operations Management*, *18*(4), 287–400. doi:10.1016/S0272-6963(00)00032-2

Moritz, S. (2005). *Service design: Practical access to an evolving field*. Cologne: Koln International School of Design.

Pannunzio, C. O. (2008). Leverage the Power of Social Media. *Journal of Financial Planning*, (September): 6–10.

Patricio, L., Fisk, R. P., Cunha, J. F., & Constantine, L. (2011). Multilevel service design: From customer value constellation to service experience blueprinting. *Journal of Service Research*, *14*(2), 180–200. doi:10.1177/1094670511401901

Roschk, H., & Kaiser, S. (2013). The nature of an apology: An experimental study on how to apologize after a service failure. *Marketing Letters*, *24*(3), 293–309. doi:10.1007/s11002-012-9218-x

Sashi, C. M. (2012). Customer engagement, buyer-seller relationships, and social media. *Management Decision*, *50*(2), 253–272. doi:10.1108/00251741211203551

Smith, A. K., & Bolton, R. N. (2002). The Effect of Customers' Emotional Responses to Service Failures on Their Recovery Effort Evaluations and Satisfaction Judgments. *Journal of the Academy of Marketing Science*, *30*(1), 5–23. doi:10.1177/03079450094298

Smith, A. K., Bolton, R. N., & Wagner, J. (1999). A Model of Customer Satisfaction with Service Encounters Involving Failure and Recovery. *JMR, Journal of Marketing Research, XXXVI*(August), 356–372. doi:10.2307/3152082

Vemuri, A. (2010). Getting Social: Bridging The Gap Between Banking And Social Media. *Global Finance, 24*(5), 20–21.

Zeithaml, V. A., Berry, L. L., & Parasuraman, A. (1990). *Delivering quality service: Balancing customer perceptions and expectations*. New York: Free Press.

KEY TERMS AND DEFINITIONS

Banking Channel: Related to delivery channel that banking services are provided which can be in the form of a branch (branch banking), a telephone (telephone banking), television (home banking), PC (internet banking), mobile telephone (mobile banking) and more recently social media (social media banking).

Facebook Customer Service: The provision of a service by a company to its customers with the purpose of addressing their queries and responding to their needs and wants through its Facebook page.

Human Interactions: Related to interactions between a service provider and its customers that may be in a direct form where the customer interacts with the staff in a face-to-face setting. The service also can be delivered indirectly, which involves verbal interactions between the parties in a non face-to-face setting using alternative delivery channels such as the telephone.

Relationship Marketing: The process of creating collaborative exchanges between organisations and their individual customers on a long-term basis, which are characterised with a level of customer confidence in their organisations, interdependence through some kind of bonds, and being beneficial to both parties involved.

Service Encounter: Related to interactions between a service provider and its customers through a range of channels from human interactions to virtual interactions. This broader aspect of service encounters is defined as "total customer experience".

Social Media Platform: A web-based technology tool that allows its users to create and exchange user-generated content that also promotes engagement and conversation among its users.

Social Media Service Encounter: Related to interactions between a service provider and its customers, which takes place through a social media platform.

Virtual Interactions: Involve no direct or indirect human communication between firms and their customers, but take place electronically. In virtual interactions, customers use delivery channels such as the Internet, television or telephone (automated services) to interact with their firms.

APPENDIX: CODING SCHEME

Customer posts:

1. Account opening related queries,
2. Badmouthing the bank,
3. Account management related queries,
4. Not able to contact bank,
5. Positive feedback,
6. Complaints about fraudulent use of account,
7. Mobile banking app related queries,
8. Complaints about waiting times in branches,
9. Not account management related queries,
10. Queries from overseas based customers,
11. Complaints about unavailable service,
12. Complaints about the service quality,
13. Threatening to close the account with bank,
14. Chasing social media team,
15. Queries already raised on other channels,
16. Posts with a potential for engagement,
17. Basic banking queries,
18. Commenting on bank products/product features,
19. Complaining about interest rates, fees and charges,
20. Threatening to contact baking ombudsman,
21. Leaving customer query unanswered.

Banks' responses:

1. Tone of response,
2. Proactive customer services,
3. Failed call back promises,
4. Censorship,
5. Engagement promoting responses,
6. Response time,
7. Who responded the query?,
8. Level of empathy,
9. Whether an apology is offered,
10. Directing the customer to other channels,
11. Asking to send the query by private messaging,
12. Promising to pass the feedback to relevant team,
13. SM team going extra mile to please the customer,
14. Offering an informative response,
15. Bank response to negative criticism from customers,
16. Service recovery related posts,
17. Not being able to help due to restrictive bank policies.

Chapter 9

With a Little Help from My Friends:
The Irish Radio Industry's Strategic Appropriation of Facebook for Commercial Growth

Daithi McMahon
Univeristy of Limerick, Ireland

ABSTRACT

Ireland has faced significant economic hardship since 2008, with the Irish radio industry suffering as advertising revenues evaporated. The difficult economic circumstances have forced radio station management to devise new and cost effective ways of generating much-needed income. The answer has come in the form of Facebook, the leading Social Network Site (SNS) in Ireland. Using Ireland as a case study, this chapter looks at how radio station management are utilising the social network strategically in a bid to enhance their audiences and revenues. Radio station management consider Facebook to be an invaluable promotional tool which is very easily integrated into radio programming and gives radio a digital online presence, reaching far greater audiences than possible through broadcasting. Some radio stations are showing ambition and are realising the marketing potential that Facebook and other SNSs hold. However, key changes in practice, technology and human resources are required to maximise the profit-making possibilities offered by Facebook.

INTRODUCTION

The Irish radio industry has undergone significant change in recent years due to the challenges posed by the economic recession and the pervasion of digital media. Irish radio stations are fighting for the attentions of modern audiences who have high demands placed on their time and attention from digital and social media. Through smartphones, individuals have the entire globe at their fingertips and this presents threats and opportunities to an older medium like radio.

DOI: 10.4018/978-1-5225-0559-4.ch009

This chapter explores how the radio industry in Ireland is incorporating the Facebook phenomenon into the traditional broadcasting business model. This ongoing development has involved modifications to radio production practices, an alteration of technology needs and additional human resources in the form of dedicated digital media managers. Management at some radio stations, particularly the youth oriented stations, are enjoying some success in using their significant social media followings to promote their commercial partners and gain revenue from these services. This chapter demonstrates that a dedicated and aggressive social media strategy can have a positive influence on audience ratings. Furthermore, the stations that are having the most success in exploiting social media for commercial gain are primarily the youth-targeted radio stations.

The main aim of this chapter is to assess the commercial impact of SNSs on Irish radio stations. First, it seeks to assess the importance of Facebook and other SNSs as conduits for communication between radio audiences and radio stations. Second, it attempts to assess how radio stations are using Facebook and other SNSs to engage with their audiences. The third objective is to gauge how SNSs are being used by radio stations for commercial gain. The hypotheses are two fold: first, that radio audiences and radio producers are spending increasing amounts of time interacting with one another on SNSs; and second that radio station management are successfully using SNSs to strategically build a strong online audience which can be sold to advertisers and sponsors, thus creating a new revenue stream to help grow their businesses.

BACKGROUND

The radio industry in Ireland has faced huge challenges since 2008 due to the economic recession that has gripped the country. The Independent Broadcasters of Ireland (IBI) is an organisation representing the interests of the thirty-four independently-owned commercial radio stations in Ireland. In 2013 IBI Chairman John Purcell revealed that revenue within the radio industry was down some forty percent compared to pre-recession figures (Purcell, 2013, np). It was in the context of these desperate economic times, that innovative minds within the industry spotted the potential to be gained from appropriating SNSs into the radio broadcaster's remit and set about exploiting the power of digital media for economic gain.

Independent commercial radio stations in Ireland are privately owned and operated enterprises which rely on commercial revenue via advertising, sponsorship and investment income. Although the four public service radio stations that are owned and operated by *Raidió Teilifís Éireann (RTÉ)* are largely supported by the television licence fee, independent stations do not receive any direct pecuniary input from the government and thus have been under severe financial pressure. *RTÉ*'s radio stations meanwhile have enjoyed the safety net provided by public funding, coupled with advertising and sponsorship revenue from the commercial market where they compete with independent radio stations.

Despite the initial threat to radio posed by digital media – namely that audiences would switch off radio in favour of online podcasts and digital streaming services – radio continues to survive, if not thrive, thanks to the emergence of one of the most pervasive of digital media, SNSs (colloquially known as social media). This is due to a number of factors. First, radio is a highly flexible and adaptable medium capable of adjusting to changes in the mediascape. Moreover, it faced down the arrival of television in the 1960s and the internet in the late 1990s, both of which, many predicted, would signal the end of radio. Instead of posing a threat to radio, SNSs have instead offered a significant opportunity, which the Irish radio industry has largely taken advantage of. This convergence of an old medium (radio) with new media (SNSs) is a significant phenomenon and has helped radio maintain its viability.

Despite having battled through over eight years of economic recession the industry has maintained its high standards of output and Irish audiences continue to listen in strong numbers with 83% of the adult population tuning in to live radio each day (Ipsos/MRBI, 2015a).

Social Network Sites (SNSs), also known as 'social networking media' or 'social media' are websites and web applications that allow users to connect and network with virtually millions of people around the world while also allowing individuals to participate in smaller networks of friends and online communities (Morris 2010, p. 13). SNSs continue to grow exponentially in popularity representing, "one of the fastest uptakes of a communication technology since the web was developed in the early 1990s" (Stefanone et al., 2010, p. 511). This makes the study of SNSs timely and relevant in modern media and communications academic studies.

Ellison et al. (2007) write, "Social network sites (SNSs)…allow individuals to present themselves, articulate their social networks, and establish or maintain connections with others" (Ellison et al., 2007, p. 1). This offers a clear and succinct description of what SNSs do, however one of the most comprehensive attempts to define and outline the phenomenon of SNSs was made by Boyd and Ellison (2007) who define them as:

Web-based services that allow individuals to (1) construct a public or semi-public profile within a bounded system, (2) articulate a list of other users with whom they share a connection, and (3) view and traverse their list of connections and those made by others within the system. The nature and nomenclature of these connections may vary from site to site (Boyd & Ellison, 2007, p. 211).

It is important to note that authors Boyd & Ellison (2007) make a key distinction between 'Social Network Sites' and 'Social Networking Sites', preferring the former to describe the computer-mediated movement in question, despite the latter existing commonly in public discourse and both terms being used interchangeably. The authors employ 'network' over 'networking' for two reasons:

… emphasis and scope. ''Networking'' emphasizes relationship initiation, often between strangers. While networking is possible on these sites, it is not the primary practice on many of them, nor is it what differentiates them from other forms of computer-mediated communication (CMC) (Boyd & Ellison, 2007, p. 211).

This is supported by evidence that suggests that SNSs are used to support existing offline friendships or connections rather than make new ones (Boyd & Ellison, 2007; Ellison et al., 2007; Dunbar, 2012). Dunbar argues that one of the reasons SNSs have flourished can be directly attributed to "the fact that they allow us to keep up with friends without seeing them face-to-face" (Dunbar, 2012, p. 3). Therefore, the fact that SNS users are not seeking out new connections but rather interacting with their existing network of contacts renders 'social network sites' a more apt term; this despite the prolific use of 'social networking sites' as a term in modern nomenclature. The author will thus adopt the term 'social network site' henceforth except when quoting other authors directly.

Methodology

Using the Irish radio industry as a case study, this research is based on qualitative interviews with N=10 radio industry professionals across four different radio stations. The radio stations were chosen for the diversity in programming and the geographic spread of the stations' broadcast areas. *RTÉ 2fm*, one of the four radio stations owned and operated by the state broadcaster RTÉ, broadcasts nationally to the 20-44 year old demographic. *Beat 102103* is one of three regional radio stations in Ireland targeting youth audiences and broadcasts to 15-35 year olds in the south-east of the country. *Spin South West* is also a regional station, which broadcasts to listeners aged 15-35 years in the south-west of Ireland. *Radio Kerry* is a regional radio station broadcasting to all adults in county Kerry, a rural county in the southwest corner of Ireland. Interviews were conducted during the month of July 2013.

Irish radio stations are engaging with audiences via a number of SNSs, and while this chapter discusses how Irish radio stations are using SNSs generally to promote growth, the research has focused on the use of Facebook primarily. Twitter is also commonly used by Irish radio stations but from an early stage the author decided to focus on Facebook for a number of reasons. First, preliminary research showed that Facebook offered the audience a much deeper participatory experience than Twitter. Second, the same preliminary research also showed that radio stations had significantly more audience members engaging through Facebook than Twitter. Third, Facebook is the most popular social network in Ireland with 59% of the population owning a Facebook account according to Ipsos/MRBI (2015b).

This research employed the inductive strategy of using newly sourced empirical data to develop original theory. This concept, known as grounded theory is the "discovery of theory from data systematically obtained from social research" (Glaser & Strauss, 1999, p. 2). Therefore the findings were used to inform the research and develop sound theory.

A multi-method approach was used to collect both quantitative and qualitative data for this research. The use of multiple methods allowed for a rich collection of information to be gathered and for the triangulation of data, which strengthened the veracity of the findings. The main source of qualitative data comprised of semi-structured interviews with industry professionals at the four Irish radio stations listed above. The working practices of the radio presenters and producers of three programmes were recorded by use of direct observation during the programmes' broadcast, namely *Kerry Today* on *Radio Kerry*, *Beat Breakfast* in *Beat 102103* and *Tubridy* on *RTÉ 2fm*. Finally, the content and activity on the Facebook pages of the stations in question were recorded and analysed. This textual analysis involved the recording by method of screen grabs, the entire content contained on one day of Facebook page posts from three of the radio stations involved (*Beat 102103*, *RTÉ 2fm* and *Radio Kerry*). This was repeated on four separate dates between July 2013 and August 2014. This material was then analysed and detailed records of the content made including types of posts, response from audience and number of likes, shares and comments made by the audience.

Three members of the *Tubridy* programme were interviewed: the programme presenter, the Producer-in-Charge and one of the researchers. Two staff members from *Beat 102013* were interviewed, the *Beat Breakfast* Producer and the station's Chief Executive Officer. At *Spin South West* the Assistant CEO/Programme Controller was interviewed. Four *Radio Kerry* staff members were interviewed: the General Manager, the Sales & Marketing Manager, the News/Current Affairs Editor and the Digital Media Manager. To protect the anonymities of those involved all names have been withheld and interviewees will be referred to by their respective job titles. The interviews were recorded, transcribed, and then analysed to identify consistent themes in their responses. These were then compared horizontally against field notes and observations to develop critical themes.

SOCIAL NETWORK SITES: A STRATEGY OF INTERACTION

This chapter investigates the use of Facebook as a conduit for communication and interaction between radio stations and their audiences. In order for this relationship to exist interaction is required from both parties. For their part audiences need to be active, meaning they need to visit radio station Facebook pages and engage with content through emoji reactions, shares or comments. Radio producers need to make efforts to draw the audience in by regularly posting stimulating or engaging material that will appeal to their target cohort.

Active/Interactive Audience

Before looking at how radio stations are using Facebook as a marketing tool, it is important to first understand how the radio audience comes to use Facebook to interact with radio stations. Recent research shows that the Irish public are using Facebook regularly and are spending significant portions of their days on the popular social medium (Ipsos/MRBI, 2015b). Furthermore, radio producers have noticed this shift and have established a presence for their brand on Facebook and are encouraging interaction by posting content that appeals to the audience's desire for information and entertainment (McMahon 2015).

McMahon's (2015) study found that audiences visit radio station Facebook pages seeking three main types of content

1. Additional information,
2. Entertainment, and
3. Opportunities to learn about and enter competitions.

These findings are in line with those of other authors analysing the motivations of Facebook use particularly the motives of seeking out information and entertainment (Park et al., 2009; Sheldon, 2008). McMahon (2015) found that audiences also want to exercise their agency by interacting and participating in the on-air and online discussions.

The evidence from the current research proposes that radio audiences operate in a cycle of broadcast and social media consumption which, if nurtured and encouraged, contributes to the building of their loyalty (Enli & Ihlebaek, 2011; McMahon, 2015). The cycle operates as follows. At the outset

1. The audience are regular listeners of a radio programme.
2. The audience visits the programme's Facebook page for an enhanced experience with more information, a wider variety of entertainment and the opportunities to enter competitions and win prizes.
3. At the third and final stage, the audience remains on the radio station's Facebook page for the opportunity to participate and contribute to the online discussions and debates.

As a result of an informative, entertaining and perhaps rewarding experience on-air and online, the audience returns to consume the on-air and online content again in the future, thus completing the cycle. As with any media product, the challenge for producers is to consistently stimulate and engage the audience, which is achieved by continually delivering quality content that is fresh and interesting, and that satiates the audience's wants.

Enli & Ihlebaek (2011) argue that audiences who are afforded the opportunities to participate in television programmes experience deeper engagement, which builds the audience's loyalty. This is precisely what the managers and producers at the commercial radio stations stated was their motivation behind using Facebook: to engage audiences in the expectation that they will return as radio listeners. Aside from the financial return achieved through improved ratings there are other ancillary benefits also. According to Chaputula et al. (2013), mass media organisations that use SNSs benefit not only through increased audiences but also constructive feedback that helps the organisation improve its product.

Social Media Strategies

The present research found that social media fits into an overall audience and revenue growth strategy for some of the radio stations involved. This strategy is made up of a four-step process which is orchestrated by radio station management and executed by presenters and producers. The process runs as follows: radio stations interact with their audience via Facebook to improve their online presence, which will create more opportunities. To promote the station, and to help increase audience interaction, which will ultimately increase listenership and create new revenue streams. Each step of the process is now discussed in detail.

Step 1: Increase Online Presence.

Digital media are a mainstay of modern society, becoming more and more prevalent as technology allows increased connectivity through mobile communication devices such as smartphones and tablets. "In the present-day radio landscape", argue Stark and Weichselbaum (2013), "one might not be wrong in declaring that a traditional radio station without a website of its own comes close to resembling radio without sound" (p. 186). This is an astute metaphor but could now be updated to read that a traditional radio station without a website and strong social media presence of its own comes close to resembling radio without sound. SNSs are the latest software to open new and exciting communication and connection opportunities, and the radio industry in Ireland has learned that it must have a strong online presence if it is to remain in the audience's daily consciousness. There are a host of new opportunities open to radio producers through simple-to-use online tools such as Facebook, which can enhance the overall entertainment package offered to the radio audience.

The CEO of *Spin South West* states that people are increasingly using Facebook to communicate and especially those within the station's key demographic, the 15-34 year old cohort. As CEO, she understands the importance of her station being present on Facebook, "we have to be there because that's where our listeners are". She further points out that being on Facebook is similar to her station being present at nightclubs and other places where young people gather in large numbers; it allows the station to get noticed and promotes the station's brand.

Beat 102103's CEO also posits that an online presence is absolutely essential "because we are a youth station and social media is so huge for our audience". She stresses the importance of all presenters and deejays being connected to the audience via social media, asserting that if the station is doing something on-air they have to be supplementing that item online, "we have to make sure it's part of what we do". Radio stations like *Beat 102103* have to embrace social media more than other companies, she believes, because the station has to be where their audience is and *Beat*'s audience is on Facebook: "they're all engaging with Facebook so it's really important that we're there" asserts the CEO.

Although *Radio Kerry*'s target audience is an older demographic than that of *Beat 102103* and *Spin South West*, the General Manager (GM) understands that her station needs to be online and active on Facebook if the station wants to reach listeners. "It's part of our listeners' world and if we want to engage with them then we have to be in their space, we have to be in their zone" according to the GM. She believes that any radio station would be foolish to ignore Facebook such is its prevalence in modern society and the strength of its relationship with modern audiences. Facebook is therefore a very useful way for stations to have a presence where audiences are spending increasing amounts of time.

The Producer-in-Charge of the *Tubridy* programme on *RTÉ 2fm* values the opportunities offered by Facebook as it provides a more vibrant, interactive and meaningful online presence compared to a radio station's website. He acknowledges that prior to the arrival of social media, a website was a radio station's only online platform and he believes the traditional website is becoming somewhat redundant today as a result of SNSs. According to the researcher on the *Tubridy* programme, having an online presence is also very useful for engaging those who cannot listen to the radio programme when it airs for whatever reason, but still want to follow the show and be involved. The *Tubridy* researcher goes on to explain how SNSs also allow her and her team to bring visual components into the radio show, thus enhancing the experience for the audience. In the case of the *Tubridy* programme, this usually comes in the form of photos or images often of the presenter in the office, in studio, with studio guests, or on an outside broadcast, thus giving the audience greater familiarity with the programme.

The presenter of the *Tubridy* programme agrees and certainly sees an advantage of being able to "bring a visual element to an aural product" by posting photos, videos and other audio visual multimedia on their Facebook page. Through such material, the production team are able to give listeners a better understanding of what the presenter is talking about on the programme or what the person he is interviewing actually looks like.

The increased online presence afforded by Facebook allows radio stations to reach new audiences and helps make the radio product more attractive. This raises the next function of Facebook for radio stations: its value as an effective promotional tool.

Step 2: Promote the Station.

According to marketing executives at *Beat 102103, Spin South West, RTÉ 2fm* and *Radio Kerry*, Facebook is an extremely useful tool for promoting the station online. The strategy being that Facebook content could drive online audiences back to the on-air product or the station's website, both of which are direct revenue generators for the stations.

Initially when radio stations started using SNSs in 2008, Facebook had imposed severe restrictions on radio stations running sponsored promotions on their Facebook pages. Recently however Facebook has softened their stance and at the time of writing (December 2015) management at *Beat 102103* had started selling integrated Facebook exposure as part of enhanced marketing packages for their clients.

This is a significant development in terms of the opportunities it presents for radio stations to exploit their massive followings on Facebook. In December 2015, *Beat 102103* had more than 470,000 followers on Facebook and growing by the day. When compared to the number of daily on-air listeners, which stood at 95,000 at the time of writing, it is clear just how much more pervasive Facebook can be, as five times more people are following *Beat 102103* on Facebook than are listening to the station's radio broadcasts (Ipsos/MRBI 2015a). This is further evidence that SNSs have significant potential as digital marketing tools, not only for radio stations, but for all commercial enterprises.

According to *Beat 102103*'s CEO, Facebook is an extension of the station's brand. "If we do something on-air, we always want to see how we can make more people aware of it". The CEO hopes that Facebook posts can be shared throughout their followers' social networks and make others aware of what *Beat 102103* do, thus courting new listeners to the station.

Building brand recognition was identified as an important factor by management at *Radio Kerry* and *Beat 102103*. Branding can be reinforced by a strong Facebook presence. A radio station's brand can be pushed to the forefront of people's minds if the content is engaging and achieves a strong reach via Facebook. A popular post that goes viral could result in a listener identifying *Radio Kerry* or *Beat 102103* as their preferred station at the time a listenership survey is being conducted, thus boosting the stations listenership figures.

Spin South West's Facebook page is highly reflective of their brand and is used very much as a promotional tool to encourage people to listen to the radio station or to visit the website. For example, if the station is running a competition to win concert tickets, they will always require that the audience listen on-air for instructions on how to enter. This allows the station to encourage more listeners to sample the station's on-air product and perhaps become regular listeners.

Step 3: Increase Interaction.

The third step of the social media strategy employed by radio stations is to generate increased interaction between the audience and station producers on Facebook. Modern Irish radio listeners want to engage in two-way communication with media producers and are demanding increased agency over the radio programmes they consume (McMahon 2013). This empowers the audience and makes them media users, rather than passive media consumers. Facebook fills this need by offering the audience increased interaction opportunities including the prospect of contributing content themselves.

Until only recently text messaging was the preferred method of audience interaction but Facebook offers a much more diverse range of options for the audience to communicate with a radio station. This includes audience members sharing photos, videos, images and links with a radio station and its followers. *Spin South West*'s CEO sees Facebook as,

… a way to connect with our audience, it's a way to gauge what our audience is doing, thinking about and how they feel about issues, music and what's going on in their lives and it's a direct communication with them.

Radio Kerry's News Editor believes that Facebook offers the audience more communication options and helps the producer to "get conversation from listeners" especially those who have outgrown the other forms of audience interaction such as telephone, text or email, or those who simply find it a less formal method of communication. *Radio Kerry* management feel that the more communication channels open to the audience, the better.

The *Tubridy* team feel that Facebook is an excellent resource that provides a wealth of information about the audience including their opinions on matters, what their likes and dislikes are, and what they want to talk about, which in turn informs the team as to what they should be covering in the show.

The Head of Music at *Beat 102013* argues that Facebook is another way of "attracting interaction from the audience" and agrees that the social network is a useful tool to gauge how people feel about what is going on. The creation of content for the *Beat Breakfast* programme forms an important part of the interactivity between station and audience. Facebook provides the audience with a platform to contribute that content, be that written text, an image, a video, a photo or any multi-media content they may want to share with others. According to Enli & Ihlebaek (2013), when an individual's material or contribution is included in a programme, they feel involved and this further engages them to continue to follow the programme to find out how they have influenced the outcome of the show, thus building loyalty. Engagement with audiences through Facebook is therefore viewed by industry management as part of a cohesive strategy to build listenership.

Step 4: Increase Listenership.

All independent radio stations in Ireland are commercial organisations and as such are focused on monetary profit. Traditionally this is achieved by growing a station's audience, which in turn allows a station to increase advertising and sponsorship rates. Therefore any tool or strategy that can increase listenership is naturally likely to be exploited for maximum return. From this perspective, radio stations see Facebook as an opportunity rather than a threat.

Spin South West has been consistently growing its Facebook audience and has one of the highest followings of all the radio stations in Ireland. The station has also experienced steady growth in listeners over the last number of years. The CEO uses Facebook because it makes people aware of the *Spin South West* brand in the hope that it may help recruit new listeners and maintain existing ones. However, she is hesitant to draw a direct correlation between the number of Facebook followers and listener ratings without evidence to support it and believes there are other factors at play. She describes Facebook as "a really important tool to drive people to listen to the radio and essentially sell advertising, because that's the basis of commercial radio".

The CEO of *Beat 102103* believes there is a correlation between Facebook engagement and listener numbers. She encourages the station's staff to use Facebook to engage the audience and "drive them back to listen on-air". She believes that Facebook has helped the station grow its listenership because of the staff's effective use of the social network. She points out that the station has seen consistent audience growth since 2004 and argues that the station would have become stagnant and probably lost listeners had they not embraced technology, including SNSs, from an early stage. Furthermore because of the rapid rate at which technology is evolving, she believes that some radio stations will fall behind if they choose not to keep up with technology and embrace SNSs. The CEO continues by stating that *Beat 102103* is growing its listener base primarily because the management are listening to what the audience want to hear on the radio; and the station is using Facebook to gather this information.

In addition to the assertion that Facebook helps grow listener ratings *Beat 102103*'s CEO has also realised the marketing potential of the popular SNS. By 2015 *Beat 102103* had employed three dedicated social media managers while the marketing department had not only incorporated social media exposure into sales and marketing strategies for clients on a larger scale but also developed dedicated social media sponsorship packages. These new sponsorship packages involve the integration of the client's branding and key messages into all social media output and on-air programming. The management of *Beat 102103* foresees significant financial opportunities in social media marketing due to the ability of SNSs to reach beyond the relatively limited on-air audience and communicate using a wider variety of multi-media messages. With the *Beat 102103* Facebook page boasting nearly half a million followers in late 2015, the station has the opportunity to reach one in nine adults in Ireland.

Radio Kerry's Marketing and Events Manager believes that a station has to reach out beyond the regular listeners if it wants to expand its listenership. If a station is promoting itself on the radio only, then the station is promoting itself to people who are already listening. The station is not reaching the non-listeners, and this is the advantage of using Facebook. It presents the opportunity to promote the station to those who might not necessarily be listening on a regular basis, but who are on Facebook and may come across a station's posts. Facebook offers the opportunity to be spontaneous and engaging to grab a user's attention and give them a reason to listen to *Radio Kerry*. Facebook therefore offers radio stations the opportunity to reach out to potential new listeners and draw them in.

Radio Kerry management are hesitant to state for certain that Facebook helps the station gain listeners due to the lack of evidence to support the theory but they do believe that Facebook is of benefit to the station because it is proven to engage Kerry people. Even if it only helps to maintain the existing audience, *Radio Kerry* management believe using Facebook is beneficial. The station's GM recognises that Facebook is more often used by younger audiences. However, she feels that connecting with younger audiences today will help establish their loyalty for the future when their tastes mature and *Radio Kerry*'s output is more inline with their preferred programming.

The *Radio Kerry* GM reiterates the point made above that a radio station's bottom line is "to keep your listenership up, so the more ways you can tell people about it and engage with them the better". The argument is that Facebook helps attract potential new listeners who would not normally interact with the station via traditional methods or be aware of what is available on-air. Therefore, in terms of promotion, the GM believes that by

… teasing people, hooking them, be it towards a programme piece or a competition, Facebook can be very useful for informing people of what is on- air and hopefully appealing to their tastes or interests.

The Producer-in-Charge of *RTE 2fm*'s *Tubridy* programme does not see increasing listenership as a primary function of Facebook for his programme. Nor does he believe that the social network can help increase listenership because there is no evidence to suggest it does. The *Tubridy* presenter agrees with his Producer-in-Charge declaring, "No, is the simple answer, I don't think it's actually going to garner more listeners". He believes the only way to gain more listeners is by having a quality radio show, not by having a good Facebook page. He argues that producers should "focus on the core product of broadcasting" as a means of increasing listeners.

The *RTÉ 2fm* staff members interviewed therefore have opposing viewpoints to their counterparts working in commercial radio and are reticent to draw any positive correlation between Facebook engagement and listenership figures. This may be due to the fact that *RTÉ* relies less on audience ratings to support its business model due to the public funding it receives through the television licence fee. This allows *RTÉ 2fm* to be less reliant on advertising revenue compared to commercial radio stations. It is clear from the interviews that Facebook and other SNSs hold significant present and future value for independent commercial radio stations but limited value for the state owned *RTÉ 2fm*.

Irish radio stations were found to be incorporating social media strategies into their wider marketing plans. The youth targeted radio station *Beat 102103* is the most dynamic and forward-thinking of the stations studied and is leading the way in terms of employing SNSs for maximum benefit. Further research is required to determine whether a direct correlation exists between increased Facebook interactions and increased radio listenership.

SOLUTIONS AND RECOMMENDATIONS

Changes in Radio Production

Along with the addition of Facebook to the radio producer's remit, there have also been a number of changes to how radio is produced. Producers now have to incorporate social media management into their daily routine meaning new practices have been incorporated, new technology has been introduced, and in some cases ancillary human resources have been added.

In radio production, the terms producer and presenter are often used interchangeably. In most instances a programme presenter is also the programme producer or co-producer. In some cases, when the budget allows, the roles of presenter and producer are separated and other positions may even exist in the team. Most often however, the presenter is also the producer and thus the term producer will be used hereafter to denote the role of the person primarily responsible for the programme's output.

Practice

Radio producers have had to alter their production practices to incorporate social media into their programmes. Producers have to constantly manage the station/programme Facebook page to ensure they are making the most of the technology. Because audiences interact with Facebook pages outside of programme transmission hours, management of social media content must continue before, during, and after each programme is aired.

Before a programme begins, the producer routinely checks the station Facebook page to review the posts other producers have published recently. This allows the producer to avoid duplication of information and bombardment of the audience with too many posts. The producer can also get an idea of what has proved popular or unpopular and generally get a feel for what is happening online at that time. Producers also regularly monitor their competitors' Facebook pages to see what content other stations are posting. The producer will often publish a post at the start of his/her programme to signal that a new programme is starting, to preview what is coming up on that programme and to encourage participation from the audience.

The *Beat Breakfast* producer will often post a *meme* (a humorous image with accompanying text) to incite a reaction from the audience. Common subject matter relates to being fatigued in the morning or a commentary regarding the general excitement felt on Fridays. These sorts of posts instil feelings of being part of an affective community of people who are all experiencing a similar feeling or emotion and thus makes the audience more engaged with the Facebook page and the radio station. Such content was found to be particularly popular amongst Facebook users as such posts would regularly receive high counts of emoji reactions, comments and shares.

A radio producer must manage a number of tasks that relate specifically to audience participation. During the programme's transmission the producer regularly monitors Facebook on one of the studio's computer monitors. S/he keeps the Facebook page open at all times to pick up on useful comments from the audience, react if something is proving popular and moderate any inappropriate comments that may be posted by the public.

The producer must also manage the flow of contributions from other communication channels including phone, text message, email and any other SNSs the station may use. These demands relate solely to the management of audience participation which is only a part of the producers remit. The producer must also continue to provide a quality on-air product to the audience, producing and presenting continuous content over several hours of broadcast. The remit of a radio producer is therefore ever-expanding due to the demands placed by SNSs. Producers often require further technological tools to carry out their duties effectively in the age of digital audience participation.

Technology

Radio stations and their producers have also had to make technological changes to adapt to social media use. Because Facebook is accessible via virtually any web browser, radio stations have not required upgrades in software or hardware to access and manage their Facebook accounts. Some producers however, have recognised that additional technology has been required in-studio to manage Facebook and other SNSs.

The most common in-studio set-up includes two computer monitors for the producer with one dedicated almost exclusively to the broadcast management system: the software used to arrange and play-out audio including ad breaks, music, sound clips, et cetera. The other computer monitor is used for researching and browsing the internet, monitoring and managing SNSs, sending/receiving email, managing incoming text messages, editing and reading word documents, communicating with colleagues via the intranet, and any other computer-based tasks the producer may need to carry out during the course of their broadcast.

This has put a great deal of pressure on the two monitors available to the producer and has led in some instances to the addition of a laptop into the studio. Such is the case at *Radio Kerry* where, during the *Kerry Today* programme, the producer now uses a laptop dedicated to Facebook and Twitter. This extra piece of hardware – only introduced into the studio in the spring of 2013 – allows the producer to constantly monitor the two social media accounts, publish posts, make comments, and read comments made by the audience.

Additional computers or monitors may not always be required, however, and some producers are finding that in fact mobile communication devices such as smartphones can be used to very good effect to manage social media. For example the *Beat Breakfast* Producer manages the station's Twitter account via his company-issued smartphone. Using a smartphone allows him more flexibility to supervise various communication channels without having a supplementary computer in studio. This is an example of a radio producer being adaptable and negates the need for additional computers, which can be costly and occupy valuable space in-studio.

In an effort to provide the audience with a deeper media experience beyond the aural radio broadcast, producers are increasingly using their mobile devices to capture images and videos and then post this content on Facebook. These images and videos provide in-studio and behind-the-scenes access to reveal to the audience more about the producers/presenters and their personalities.

Smartphones are also highly useful for producers when working on outside broadcasts. In such scenarios, producers are able to post images and other content relating to the outside broadcast in real time and offer an insight for the audience member who may be listening on-air or following online via social media.

Human Resources

The expansion of social media use by radio stations has saddled production personnel with added responsibilities and duties. Producers interviewed expressed their concerns at the time and energy required to manage numerous SNSs effectively. However they agree that it is a burden that must be adopted in order to maintain a competitive edge. This added workload, coupled with staff cut-backs during the economic downturn, has put considerable pressure or producers to do more with fewer resources.

Station managers appreciate the importance of Facebook but also accept that the SNS is a time-consuming and thus costly tool to manage. This raises an important dilemma for radio professionals: considering the value of Facebook, should stations be hiring dedicated social media managers to get the most out of SNSs or let existing staff manage it as best they can?

In some circumstances, notably *Spin South West, Beat 102103* and *Radio Kerry*, management have come to the realisation that bespoke staffing resources are required in order to maximise the potential of SNSs and vie with the competition in this fast-changing industry. These stations have hired dedicated social media/digital content managers, who are trained and experienced in their field, and are finding this to be a sound investment. Conversely at *RTÉ*, such a move has not been prioritised and the *Tubridy* programme's researcher has all social media responsibilities as part of her remit, despite the fact that her skills and training are in radio production. By hiring a social media/digital content manager, not only are the producers relieved of much of the burden of social media management, but those stations are now able to have a staff member apply dedicated time, energy and specific skills into improving the online content for the station. This represents a significant investment for struggling radio stations, but clearly station management are coming to appreciate that such recruitment and investment are necessary steps forward.

Spin South West's CEO affirms that she "could not afford not to employ someone" to manage the online content particularly social media as it is so important to the station's output and identity. At the time of interview (June 2013) *Spin South West* had just recently hired a Digital Media Manager. The individual is a university graduate with a master's degree in digital communications and is charged with driving content through SNSs and maintaining a vibrant and cutting edge presence across all of *Spin South West*'s online platforms.

This investment of scarce resources reiterates *Spin's South West* management's appreciation of the significance Facebook and other social media can have as a promotional tool for the station. The station's CEO sees digital marketing as the future and explains that advertising expenditure on digital media is growing significantly and is now higher in Ireland than on-air advertising. The management's strategy is to sell more website advertising because their research shows that 50% of *Spin South West*'s web traffic comes from Facebook.

The management at *Radio Kerry* feel that SNSs along with other online digital platforms such as the station's website is important enough that someone should be employed full-time to manage it but agrees that it comes down to resources. The main issue is that Facebook does not actually make any money directly for the station so it if difficult to justify the expenditure. At the time of interview (June 2013) *Radio*

Kerry had only recently hired an online content editor on a trial basis to assess the effectiveness of such an appointment. The Online Content Editor's role includes managing web content, uploading podcasts, running SNS analytics and managing social media content in conjunction with programme producers and marketing staff. The trial was a success and the editor continues to work at *Radio Kerry* in 2015, thus clearly justifying the cost of his salary through the effectiveness of his digital media management.

A further interview in 2015 with the *Beat 102103* CEO revealed that the station now has three dedicated Social Media Managers. In addition the marketing department was not only incorporating social media exposure into sales and marketing strategies for clients on a larger scale but also selling dedicated social media marketing packages to its clients. This represents another significant step forwards in terms of the use of SNSs for marketing purposes and is an example of *Beat 102103*'s innovation and aggressive strategy to exploit commercial opportunities.

FUTURE RESEARCH DIRECTIONS

As there is a clear dearth of research into the use of SNSs by radio stations – not only in Ireland but globally – more research is needed in this area. Several industry professionals interviewed as part of this project argue that an effective and sustained social media strategy can have a positive affect on listener ratings. Although there are some signs that suggest this may be true, further in-depth research on a much wider scale and over a sustained period of time is required to advance this argument. Expanding this research to examine the use of SNSs in the UK radio industry and other larger European media markets would also be beneficial.

CONCLUSION

The appropriation of SNSs by the radio industry in Ireland continues to expand rapidly with each station seeking an edge over the competition. These are changing times for radio as a medium that has changed relatively little over the last number of decades is quickly adapting to the digital age. As SNSs continue to become more pervasive, it is the responsibility of marketers to look at the opportunities rather than the threats provided by these digital phenomena. In some instances the commercial opportunities and potential presented by Facebook have been realised and some radio stations have formulated social media strategies to harness the power of the social network.

Radio has been able to converge almost seamlessly with SNSs because it is such a flexible and adaptable medium that has embraced the opportunities available. Radio stations have altered production practices, installed new technological hardware and invested in skilled staff to execute their social media strategies. Management at progressive, innovative radio stations have turned Facebook into a powerful marketing tool. Furthermore, because of the far superior reach of the Facebook pages compared to radio listenership, selling Facebook exposure could soon become more lucrative than selling airtime. What is not in question is the importance being placed on social media strategies, which involve investing in dedicated and skilled digital media staff. Ignoring the opportunities provided by SNSs may soon become detrimental to radio stations in Ireland.

REFERENCES

Boyd, D. M., & Ellison, N. B. (2007). Social Network Sites: Definition, History, and Scholarship. *Journal of Computer-Mediated Communication*, *13*(1), 210–230. doi:10.1111/j.1083-6101.2007.00393.x

Chaputula, A. H., & Majawa, F. P. (2013). Use of social network sites by mass media organisations in Malawi. *Aslib Proceedings*, *65*(5), 534–557. doi:10.1108/AP-06-2012-0055

Dunbar, R. (2012). *Social Networks*. Reed Business Info. Ltd. Available: http://search.ebscohost.com/login.aspx?direct=true&db=a9h&AN=74134004&site=ehost-live

Ellison, N., Steinfield, C., & Lampe, C. (2007). The benefits of Facebook "friends:" Social capital and college students' use of online social network sites. *Journal of Computer-Mediated Communication*, *12*(4), 12–25. doi:10.1111/j.1083-6101.2007.00367.x

Enli, G. S., & Ihlebaek, K. A. (2011). 'Dancing with the audience': Administrating vote-ins in public and commercial broadcasting. *Media Culture & Society*, *33*(6), 953–962. doi:10.1177/0163443711412299

Glaser, B. G., & Strauss, A. L. (1999). *The discovery of grounded theory: strategies for qualitative research*. New York: Aldine de Gruyter.

Ipsos/Mrbi. (2015a). *Joint National Listenership and Readership: Third Quarter 2015*. Dublin: Ipsos/Mrbi.

Ipsos/Mrbi. (2015b). *Social Media Quarterly: August 2015*. Dublin: Ipsos/Mrbi.

McMahon, D. (2013). *The Role of Social Media in Audience Engagement with Irish Radio*. Paper presented at the ECREA Radio Research Conference, London.

McMahon, D. (2015). *Old Dog, New Tricks: Can Social Media Help Youth Radio Stations Grow Their Audience?* Presented at the MeCCSA Conference, Newcastle.

Morris, T. (2010). *All a twitter: a personal and professional guide to social networking with Twitter*. Indianapolis, IN: Pearson Education.

Park, N., Kee, K. F., & Valenzuela, S. (2009). Being Immersed in Social Networking Environment: Facebook Groups, Uses and Gratifications, and Social Outcomes. *Cyberpsychology & Behavior*, *12*(6), 729–733. doi:10.1089/cpb.2009.0003 PMID:19619037

Purcell, J. (2013). Keynote Address. Paper presened at the IBI Radio: Future Shock Conference, Dublin, Ireland.

Sheldon, P. (2008). Student Favorite: Facebook and Motives for its Use. *Southwestern Mass Communication Journal*, *23*, 39–53.

Stark, B., & Weichselbaum, P. (2013). What attracts listeners to Web radio? A case study from Germany. *Radio Journal: International Studies in Broadcast & Audio Media*, *11*, 185–202.

Stefanone, M. A., Lackaff, D., & Rosen, D. (2010). The Relationship between Traditional Mass Media and "Social Media": Reality Television as a Model for Social Network Site Behavior. *Journal of Broadcasting & Electronic Media*, *54*(3), 508–525. doi:10.1080/08838151.2010.498851

Chapter 10
How Social Media Offers Opportunities for Growth in the Traditional Media Industry:
The Case of Travel Journalism

Andrew Duffy
Nanyang Technological University, Singapore

ABSTRACT

Under threat from social media and interactive Web 2.0, the traditional media industry seeks new models to maintain its viability. This chapter studies both consumers and prospective producers of one genre—travel journalism—to advocate a model that could help arrest the industry's decline and return to growth. It argues that one way forward for traditional media would be a new model of curatorship, in which a professional journalist collaborates with amateur contributors. It suggests that such a hybrid arrangement will be recognisable neither as professional newsroom nor as amateur social media, but a new model with features of both. This offers a way forward so that rather than contributing to the declining fortunes of the traditional media industry, as many journalists fear, social media can instead encourage progress.

INTRODUCTION

Journalism has worked hard to build and maintain professional values. It defines itself by norms such as objectivity, accuracy, independence and neutrality (Fredriksson & Johansson, 2014; Johnstone, Slawski & Bowman, 1972; Weaver, 1998). Such ideology is intended to distinguish between journalism and other writing to "self-legitimize their position in society" (Deuze, 2005: 446). Now other forms of writing are forming a credible opposition as information and opinions are provided by social media, which includes social networks such as Facebook, user-generated content (UGC), bloggers, and online user review sites (OURS). Given the resulting crisis in the Western news media industry since the turn of the millennium, there is little confidence or consensus about what journalism should be or do (Frank-

DOI: 10.4018/978-1-5225-0559-4.ch010

lin, 2012; Spyridou, Matsiola, Veglis, Kalliris & Dimoulas, 2013). While scholarly focus has been on citizen-centric hard news as a champion of democracy, this chapter considers consumer-centric lifestyle journalism—specifically about travel—and advocates a new model that could help arrest journalism's decline and return it to growth.

The media (in travel and tourism as in other areas) has been changed by Web 2.0, which "can be thought of as the technical infrastructure that enables the social phenomenon of collective media, and facilitates consumer-generated content" (Berthon, Pitt, Plangger & Shapiro, 2012: 262). The key word is 'consumer'. Travel journalism developed within a specific environment—newspapers, magazines and broadcast media directed at an audience of consumers. That environment has changed as the traditional media finds its economies, readership, professional relationships and status all undermined and altered by the rise of digital social media content distributed on the Internet (Benson & Morgan, 2015).

Crucially for this chapter, Web 2.0-enabled social media assumes some of the roles of journalism but follow different rules. It often abandons objectivity, accuracy and neutrality in favour of subjective opinion, dubious factuality and subliminal partisanship. Despite this, it has conspired to limit journalists' role as "new media technologies challenge one of the most fundamental 'truths' in journalism, namely: the professional journalist is the one who determines what publics see, hear and read about the world" (Deuze, 2005: 451). Yet it is possible that, far from challenging these professional values, social media can be integrated with them so that both are enhanced.

Journalism has its professional standards; Web 2.0 introduces social standards. This chapter argues for an integration of the two as a way forward for traditional media, suggesting that such a hybrid will be recognisable neither as professional newsroom nor as amateur social media, but a new species with features of both.

The argument is based on studies of two groups connected to travel journalism. The first study is of consumers, assessing the relative value they ascribe to professional versus amateur content, and what their attitudes towards social media might indicate for the practitioners who supply professional content. The second is of the next generation of travel journalists, and it assesses how social media influences them.

Both groups—consumers and prospective producers alike—share similar attitudes towards social media and traditional media, which offers a direction for the media to take. Yet, as it is unlikely that the practice of each can be reconciled with the values of the other, what is needed is a media model where they can merge. Looking at travel journalism, this chapter outlines how social media might be integrated with traditional media, the effect on the work practices of individuals within it, and some commercial implications.

I focus on travel journalists because they operate in a compromised area between the values of hard news reporting and the commercial values of softer, lifestyle writing. Their genre is one in which subjective experience is preferred over the expected journalistic standards of objectivity, offering a locus for an alternative to traditional professional practice.

I contend that one consequence of the changes wrought by social media and travel information freely available online will be to divide the roles of traveller and journalist, so that the traveller can deliver the subjective, credible reports-from-abroad, while the journalist packages (and sells) these under the auspices of the accepted, objectivity-based practice of the traditional media. This offers a way forward—for lifestyle and travel journalism, at least—so that rather than contributing to the declining fortunes of the industry, social media generates growth.

CHANGING JOURNALISM PRACTICES

Journalism has always been fluid. News values are shaped by a society to reflect its interests and concerns (Philips, 2005) and vary among countries (Weaver, 1998). Within the Western liberal model, time and technology have altered journalistic practice. Herbert (2004) observed a move from literary writing to the more direct style of modern news writing following the invention of the telegraph, when transmitting information became expensive so words had to be pared back. Today, too, the changing technological, social and economic environment is altering the practice of journalism (Tandoc, 2014). Four social media-led forces impact on travel journalism, and can demonstrate how the industry could adapt.

First, social media as a source of information and competition makes journalists both enthusiastic about and wary of this online newcomer (Hermida & Thurman, 2008; Nah & Chung, 2012; Paulussen & Ugille, 2008; Singer, 2003). The journalist as an observer and interpreter of society is under siege from bloggers (Carlson, 2007) and "the biggest challenge for travel journalists is the increasing number of amateur writers who generate travel information online" (Hanusch & Fürsich, 2014: 8). But as news organisations are playing catch-up with their technologically enabled audiences (Yaros, 2008), it is plausible to anticipate that social media which has precipitated a decline in the industry can equally contribute to a renaissance by supplying content which is then given the stamp of approval by media organisations.

Second, the democratic ideals of social media such as blogs and OURS—which represent the credible voice of the public untainted by commercial influence of travel companies, advertisers or the demands of a publication—alter the idea of what constitutes 'travel writing' (Volo, 2010; Xiang & Gretzel, 2010). The expert has been superseded by the amateur as the arbiter of travel information; for the former to regain lost ground, it must collaborate with the latter.

Third, the economics of commercial support for travel journalism have ebbed, which has coincided with advertisers shifting money off the printed page and onto bloggers' websites (Siles & Boczkowski, 2012). This led to less funding for travel, fewer positions for writers and a reliance on freelance contributions (Hanusch & Fürsich, 2014; Raman & Choudary, 2014). Continuing this same progression, the profession is now undermined by enthusiastic amateurs who provide content for free (Pirolli, 2014) making it harder to make a living as a travel journalist (Hanusch & Fürsich, 2014). Yet if traditional media co-opted those writers rather than being undermined by them, both could benefit. This impacts on the ideal of the travel writer as a member of a newsroom, however, and would mean delegating the time-consuming task of going overseas to outsiders—which questions the very essence of journalistic practice.

Fourth, much paid-for travel information previously supplied by traditional media has moved online for free and is increasingly used by travellers (Casaló, Flavián & Guinalíu, 2011; Hofstaetter & Egger, 2009), challenging paid travel journalists to maintain some form of value that differentiates them from the free competition. The question is, what form does that point of differentiation take? The worth of traditional media values such as expertise, accuracy and objectivity meet competition in the form of amateurs on social networking sites writing their own subjective, un-paid and unverifiable opinions un-moderated by editors (Pirolli, 2014). Travel journalism must face up to the new digital social media paradigm as it faces "an identity crisis as its gatekeeping role, much like that of travel agents, is slowly slipping into the hands of those it originally sought to serve" (Pirolli, 2014: 83). To do so requires maintaining its valuable, credible identity, but altering the work practice of the travel journalist in a media organisation. This chapter argues that one change that might be profitably made is to embrace and accept UGC and amateur travel writing as a benefit rather than a threat; and for traditional media organisations to develop ways to professionalise and monetise it as a resource.

(TRAVEL) JOURNALISTS' VALUES

This requires travel journalists to maintain their existing newsroom practice which is based on objectivity, accuracy, and reporting factual information as a detached observer rather than an active participant (Johnstone, Slawski & Bowman, 1972); and to adapt it to work with amateur UGC which may not follow any of these. This allows the credibility of both amateur and professional to flourish. To examine this, it is helpful to establish what values guide practice and how they are reflected in travel journalism. Deuze (2005) includes the following:

1. **Public Service:** Journalists provide a public service (as watchdogs or 'newshounds', active collectors and disseminators of information).
2. **Objectivity:** Journalists are impartial, neutral, objective, fair and (thus) credible.
3. **Immediacy:** Journalists have a sense of immediacy, actuality and speed (inherent in the concept of 'news').
4. **Autonomy:** Journalists must be autonomous, free and independent in their work.
5. **Ethics:** Journalists have a sense of ethics, validity and legitimacy (2005: 447).

Travel journalism conforms to some but not all of these, which raises the question of what travel journalists believe their roles are. What—if any—ideology of practice guides them? Travel journalism is distinct from both mainstream journalism and travel writing, being more subjective than the former and more factual than the latter. Compared to travel writing, which can be fictitious, "travel journalism is more closely connected to the professional notions around fact, accuracy, truthfulness and ethical conduct in journalism" (Hanusch & Fürsich, 2014: 7).

Hanusch and Fürsich offer a definition that travel journalism makes claims to be primarily factual, concerned with reporting travel and tourism from a consumer perspective, and while it operates within a broad journalism framework, it is subject to distinctive economic forces that constrain it. Practitioners may not adhere to standard journalistic norms that have grown up around hard news. Yet, if their commercially compromised standing makes them marginal in journalism scholarship, the breadth of their topic should edge them back into the limelight. Travel and tourism is by some counts the world's largest business sector, and there has been a growth in travel journalism alongside the growth in tourism figures (UNWTO, 2014).

Hanusch (2011) has done the only study of travel journalists' professional identities to date. Interviewing 85 Australian practitioners, he described their roles as entertainers first, then travellers, cultural mediators, information providers and critics last. High ethical standards common to other forms of journalism were evident. They believed it was important to declare if their trip had been sponsored, and that they should report accurately and truthfully even if it risked angering those sponsors; although Hanusch does note that self-reported ethical standards may not be reliable. Most significantly, the critic role, which is most associated with hard news, was the least valued. Additionally, subjects who had been trained as journalists were more likely to believe that sponsored travel would not affect their objectivity and neutrality; values instilled for one kind of journalism (news) seep into another (lifestyle). These can all be transferred into a new model in which the amateur and the professional collaborate.

SOCIAL MEDIA AND TRAVEL

Social media allows individuals to post and share information and opinions, pictures and videos, through blogs, virtual communities, shared endeavours such as wikis, and media sharing sites such as Flickr, Instagram and YouTube. Interactive Web 2.0 technologies which connect people (O'Reilly, 2005) include blogs, wikis, forums and online social networks (O'Connor, 2010).

Its effect on travel journalism has two components: on travel, and on journalism. To take the latter first, social media has been seen by journalists as both competition and collaboration. They have been slow to embrace it as a source of content, and while many have enthused about the democratic potential of citizen reporting, they have been more reluctant to actually engage with contributors from outside the newsroom, fearing that they would undermine journalistic norms and practices (Singer, 2010). Rebillard and Touboul (2010) found that contributions from the public were considered a 'play-ground' of news, rather than being taken seriously. Journalists have shown a desire to maintain a professional distance from social media contributions.

Second, interactive social media has become such a phenomenon in the travel industry that it has spawned the term Travel 2.0 (Xiang & Gretzel, 2010). Two effects are salient for this chapter: social media has changed the relationship between the public and the authorities, the consumer and the provider, the amateur and the expert; and it has changed the way people search for information and plan their travel. Both impact on travel journalism. Rather than turning to the experts for information, people can now use social media and aggregated knowledge from OURS (Lankes, 2008). In travel, this has led to easier planning by the individual rather than reliance on a tour operator or travel agent. Buhalis and Law (2008) suggest that the act of searching online has changed tourists' behaviour as they plan trips for themselves, making them more confident and more independent-minded travellers.

Other scholars have observed that "tourists now take a much more active and prominent role as image-formation agents than before the emergence of Web 2.0 tools, by publishing comments, advice and experiences on blogs, forums, social networks, etc" (Camprubí, Guia & Comas, 2014: 205). Much of the travel information for which readers once turned to journalists, they now turn to each other online. Amateur personal experience may have superseded the professional expert opinion as the common currency of the travel text (Author, 2014). But journalistic values are rarely in evidence. Blogs are usually written from a first-person viewpoint, reporting an individual's travels in emotional terms (Volo, 2012), while OURS report the subjective responses of individual people to a hotel: professional standards are superseded by amateur.

Historically, traditional media played a large role in travel planning. Hsu and Song (2013: 254) note that newspapers and magazines offer credible information which influences tourists: "The media, as one of the most important information sources for tourists... can affect people's cognitive and affective responses and influence their behavioral intentions." This has now been inverted by the arrival of interactive Web 2.0, so that now the tourists are considered a credible information source which may influence a journalist writing in traditional media.

To explore the distinctions between travel information based on professional journalism and that based on amateur social-media, two groups were interviewed. Taken together, they suggest that while professional travel journalism is respected, there is greater value to be found in social media travel information. For the traditional media industry to benefit from the social media revolution, therefore, it must integrate the two.

DATA GATHERING AND RESULTS

For the first study, 30 consumers who regularly use TripAdvisor were interviewed in 2012 to gauge the relative worth they ascribed to professional and amateur travel writing. They were selected for maximum variation sampling (Patton, 2002) with a broad array of professions and ages (22-60, M = 40), 16 female, 15 with/out children, and 17 Western (as distinct from Asian). Not all travellers would be expected to share their opinions, but as TripAdvisor (2015) claims 340 million unique monthly visitors, it is safe to say that these 30 users of the site are not alone. The study had two questions relevant to this chapter: Do users trust the site *because* it is an amateur source? And do they trust the site as much as friends and professionals?

They gave their opinions on the site as a shared resource with un-paid contributions by real people, and compared it with hotel reviews by professionals. Their views of the latter were dismissive, with 12 subjects offering reasons why they distrusted them, concerned that if professionals were sponsored, that would bias their reports: "It's very difficult to write a review when you've been given £800-worth of free hospitality and a bottle of champagne, to say this place is ghastly, the staff are grumpy and the food is overpriced." Others assumed that professionals would have different values from the average traveller, which made their reports less relevant: "A professional... has a specific set of criteria, probably they are taught to know what makes a five-star hotel, or a four-star hotel." In addition, six subjects said they preferred amateur hotel reviewers because they assumed there was no agenda and they could be honest so that "whatever you get is whatever the person has experienced."

Three said that professionals were suspect because they *were* paid: "The experts are being paid to write, and they are being fed rather large, lovely meals and given beer... so I am not sure if I can trust them". Three said amateurs were reliable because they *have* paid: "It's written by people who have put a value on their money." Nine subjects also noted that amateur writers were 'people like us', experiencing it as a genuine traveller. Equally commonly, amateur writers were valued above professionals by nine subjects for sharing knowledge for the common good: "we live in a society where we are trying to benefit from each other; you learn from your own mistakes but nowadays you can also learn from others' mistakes."

Nevertheless, there was not a clear division of professional-equals-bad and amateur-equals-good, as travel journalists were considered to be accurate, know what to look out for, and have skill in writing; while amateurs might not know what is good in a hotel, have different standards from the reader, and may lack the skill to report their experiences well. In addition to the reviewers themselves, the amateurs represented the 'wisdom of crowds' (Surowiecki, 2005) as their individually subjective reviews could be aggregated into a practicably objective review: "if a hotel has a reasonably large amount of reviews all saying the same thing, then of course you would have the law of large numbers which would support the same conclusion."

This implies that if travel journalists are not trusted, it is when they do *not* show professional norms of objectivity, independence and neutrality. If they accept paid hospitality, that undermines claims to impartiality. Amateurs, on the other hand, represent the public's interest rather than any commercial interest, and while their ability to accurately report on authentic experience was questioned, their intention to do so was not. The experiences of millions of amateurs replace the musings of a few experts (Jeacle & Carter, 2011). A media model that combined the amateur traveller experience with professional journalistic expertise would thus have the best of both worlds.

In a second study in early 2014, 19 university media students were interviewed and observed for one hour as they researched online for a travel-journalism trip to Istanbul. The aim was to see which websites the next generation of prospective producers of travel journalism considered valuable and why, for an insight into the relative value they ascribed to professional, traditional media, and that of amateur-generated social media. The research questions were what kind of sources do they use when planning their trip, and how do they value them? The subjects were aged between 19 and 25 ($M = 21.79$, $SD = 1.93$); 12 were female and seven male; 13 Asian and six Western.

Two initial genres of search were observed. First, they did a background search, often from two amateur UGC sites, Wikipedia or Wikitravel: "Quite often I'll go on Wikipedia or something like that just to get a general sense of what this is. But I won't spend long there… I'm trying to sum up what this place is all about." Wikipedia and Wikitravel offered two alternative routes for additional searches. On the one hand, subjects noted the attractions appearing frequently in their research, and wanted to know more about them "After that [Wikipedia], say something catches my eye such as the Grand Bazaar, I would just Google that specifically." Alternatively, they saw themselves as independent-minded post-tourists (Urry, 1990) and wanted to identify the more popular attractions in order to stay away from them: "So this article could tell me about the stock tourist attractions I should avoid."

Their attitudes towards amateur versus professional contributors were revealing. They commonly visited sites which represent the collective wisdom of amateurs: "I use the Internet because there's crowd-sourcing involved and usually crowd-sourced stuff is better." The value of amateur UGC lay in its independence; since the writers had paid for the travel themselves and were not beholden to any commercial organisations, they could report accurately on their travel experiences: "The power of it [UGC] is in the honesty of your opinion, because you're free to say whatever you want. In a magazine, you have the editor to answer to. For a blog, you just write what you think."

Blogs were also valued for going beyond traditional tourist fare: "Blogs give you access to things that you never get anywhere else." They were particularly respected when they gave the opinions of longer-term residents of the place: "they [two expatriate bloggers] can be trusted because two months in a place is reasonably long to know something about it… And they seem to want to experience Istanbul authentically." Much as Pirolli (2014) found, bloggers are judged as being able to engage with the destination at a level different from tourists: "I can trust what she is writing, like her experience was not with a profit motive or not too touristy… An experience that is probably similar to what someone who actually lives there would see every day."

The subjects also sought out amateurs on blogs and other social media because they invited interactivity. Social media is valued for being *social*:

I got in contact with the guy who writes the blog, and he's agreed to show me around Istanbul. That's going to be great, because of all the information he's got… This has an interaction element because you actually connect with somebody in Istanbul before you get there

and

If I see a hashtag for something, I would search it on Twitter because it puts you in touch with people, and it's a very easy way of sending out tweets to 10 different people, and someone might reply and say 'Oh that's cool, let's meet up in Istanbul'.

One key to valuable information on blogs was whether the subject identified with the blogger, once again placing a social rather than professional identity at the forefront:

I find that you can quickly work out within seconds whether the person writing the blog is in some way connected to how you think and feel. So I can tell by this, if I and this blogger would probably get along, if we have similar interests, that tells me it's worth my while to read on.

So not all bloggers and UGC contributors were valued, and subjects preferred to read contributions by people who were similar to them: "if you find someone who is on the same wavelength, I find it quite likely that he or she would appreciate the same things you would." They value a report specifically when there is an observable homophily (Lazarsfeld & Merton, 1954), or social identification between the writer and the reader. This was a repeated theme: "I think wherever you go in travel, you want to connect with like-minded people." This coincided with studies of the relative value given to travel information sources which found that people were likelier to trust friends than strangers to give travel recommendations, because friends were similar to them and knew their interests; while strangers on OURS were trusted when their demographics and travelling behaviour coincided with the individual's (Author, 2015).

And yet, blogs lacked the professionalism and credibility of branded sites: "I guess when it comes to travel research, Lonely Planet is one of those places which are always at the top of your head. It's like Google for travelling." Subjects also clicked on news journalism sites, including AP and AFP, the *Huffington Post* and CNN, and *The Guardian* and the *Daily Mail*: "The *Daily Mail* is quite reputable. I'll see what they have to say." Journalists were trustworthy, possibly because the subjects themselves identified with journalism: "A journalist who has lived in Istanbul… For me, journalists are more credible writers… And she's married to a Turk. It makes the whole thing even more credible for me." Once again, a combination of amateur travelling adjudicated by professional standards offers a new media model.

DISCUSSION

Based on these two studies, I contend that readers' expectations of what constitutes valid, valuable travel writing (journalism, blogs, UGC, OURS) does not follow professional journalistic norms. As a result, traditional media organisations with a travel element should evolve to work with rather than against these new, web-influenced expectations. One implication of the suggested new model is that the role of the professional journalist is more that of an editor—'curator' is a current buzz word (Howarth, 2015)—who assesses and judges UGC for inclusion. The amateur is the traveller; the professional is the gatekeeper.

This coincides with the 'curatorial turn' in journalism studies since 2010, which some have seen as an opportunity for the industry to throw off existing practices—or fail (Picard, 2014). The institutional logics of organisation (Thornton, Ocasio & Lounsbury, 2012) must be recreated to accommodate the digital revolution, and curation is one option. It has been described in terms of "harvesting and managing contributions… finding, gathering, cleaning and formatting" and is already becoming a standard task for journalists and editors, as well as for bloggers and other collectives (Bakker, 2014: 597). It relies on a network of suppliers offering content; whereas previously the travel desk's role was to liaise with public relations for tour operators and government tourist organisations, their role would now be to grow and maintain a network of travellers. These may not be journalists; indeed, some bloggers maintain a nomadic lifestyle supported by payment for their writing.

Another expectation expressed by the interview subjects was the opportunity to identify with the writer. Both studies suggested that one benefit of social media and travel UGC is to enable the reader to interact with the writer, to some extent based on similarity of interests and purpose. This is what is valued, and it is a long way from the distant, detached and objective values of the traditional journalist (Singer, 2007). Pirolli (2014: 94) noted that the social element of Web 2.0 is powerful and that "readers connect to the bloggers like old friends". And one interview subject said, "if I and this blogger would probably get along, if we have similar interests, that tells me it's worth my while to read on." Blogs and OURS often give cues, such as descriptions of the blogger, or whether the reviewer is travelling on business, with a family, or as part of a couple, for example. These are more directly assessable than the less precise cues implicit in a newspaper, for example, which might be judged to have broadly the same values as the reader rather than a demonstrable similarity between writer and reader (Kramer, 2004).

Thus an additional task for a travel journalist as curator would be to encourage and monitor online conversations among contributors and consumers. This dramatically alters the role of the travel journalist, from one who travels to one who maintains a community of travellers (Bakker, 2014). As well as becoming a curator of travel UGC, polishing it according to professional standards and presenting it for public consumption, the travel journalist also becomes a moderator of online conversation. The idea of the audience interacting with a writer has not been considered important in traditional media. But the change has already started, and scholars have noted that journalists already anticipate greater interactivity being the future of their profession (Ramirez de la Piscina, Zablondo, Aisteran & Agirre, 2015), and interaction may be significant.

These changes have implications for growth in the industry. First, media organisations will benefit if they embrace UGC and citizen contributions, placing the reader at the centre as 'prosumers' or 'produsers' (Toffler, 1980; Bruns, 2006) who actively contribute to the information distributed through the media. Media organisations which place the reader at the forefront often make more long-term changes (Lowrey, 2011). Utterback (2003) talks in terms of symbiosis, with old and new forms of journalisms (a new term is surely called for) collaborating. One inevitable effect if this, ironically, is that travel journalists would travel less. Travel becomes a domain expertise rather than an activity; just as wine writers rarely own vineyards, music writers rarely headline at rock festivals, and science writers hardly ever take out their own patents, travel journalists would rely on someone else to do the actual travelling.

This links to the second change, which concerns the relationship between travel journalism and commerce. The traditional media model saw a close relationship between practising travel journalists and commerce before and after travel. The trip was usually sponsored by a tour operator or destination tourism office, and the pages devoted to travel were there to attract advertising revenue. The financial reward to the media organisation came at the expense of journalistic credibility; and now that the reward element is gone, the issue of credibility is once more open to negotiation.

This model of networked travel contributors and centralised editorial curators benefits consumers who get the credibility and honesty of the amateur writer, coupled with the expertise and professional standards of the curator. But the influence of commerce is still present; it just changes. In the traditional model, the professional felt beholden to the company that sponsored the trip, and wrote accordingly; in the new model, the curator is likely to leverage on the travel UGC they are delivering to readers to grow advertising revenue. Even so, the glory days of the late 20th century when advertising revenue flowed into media organisations' coffers (and onwards into the pockets of journalists) are gone; but they were, in any case, a temporary phenomenon, and journalism has historically struggled with profit (Picard, 2014). Today, commercial expectation should be more modest, particularly as any new business model is as yet not established and will take time to develop.

To observe how this division of amateur and professional may take place, it is instructive to return to Deuze's (2005) five values which make up journalists' identities, and compare them with the practice of travel bloggers, UGC and social media. This reveals competing forces that must be reconciled for the new model to emerge.

First, Deuze observed that journalism is a public service, whether treating the audience as consumers or citizens. Bloggers and travel UGC are seen as more of a public service, as the contributions are un-paid and consequently credible: "there is a sense of altruistic benefit to society" as one subject said. Commercial influence, however, brings uncertainty as to whether the interests of the tourism board or the public are central.

Second, journalistic credibility is predicated on objectivity and neutrality. Yet precisely the opposite is true for travel UGC, where a subjective report on authentic experience and engagement with the destination are the watchwords. Zelizer (2004) has observed that facts, truth, and the reality of journalism are called into question by modern conceptualisations of subjectivity. Singer (2007: 85) saw the difference between journalists and bloggers with regard to truth thus: Journalists see the providence of truth to be their duty in order to enable citizens to be free and self-govern, while bloggers "see truth as emerging from shared, collective knowledge—from an electronically enabled market place of ideas". Offline, objectivity trumps subjectivity; online, mass subjectivity yields a form of objectivity. Journalists cannot claim the 'expert' last word on any subject; instead, they are credible contributors to and directors of an online conversation.

Third, while news reports benefit from immediacy, travel journalism may not, and professional guide books even less so given the long production process. Travel UGC, on the other hand, can describe the previous night's stay in a hotel rather than one from months ago: "we can immediately know if there is a change between someone who went there five years ago, someone who went there five months ago, and someone who went there now and just came back from there," said one subject. Traditional media which set themselves up as a central (travel) information source can benefit from fast turnaround of UGC so that they become the go-to sites for travel planning. Alternative (non-traditional) media sources such as Lonely Planet, TripAdvisor and blogging collectives such as Urban Travel Blog and A Luxury Travel Blog already do this, with searchable databases so that readers can customise their searches by destination and by how recent reports are.

Fourth and fifth, ethical behaviour, editorial autonomy, freedom from censorship and the independence to write what they like are central tenets of traditional journalism. Yet these qualities are exactly what are *not* enjoyed by travel journalists whose travel is sponsored by commercial entities leading to at best a suspicion that they are not free to write what they want: "The experts are being paid to write… so I am not sure if I can trust them," reported one subject. And these qualities are exactly what *are* valued in travel bloggers and UGC, who are considered free to write independent accounts of their experiences: "In a magazine, you have the editor to answer to. For a blog, you just write what you think," said one student.

CONCLUSION

This proposed hybrid form of media combining the best of amateur subjectivity and credibility with the best of journalistic professionalism and standards has potential to create new forms of employment, opens up new commercial opportunities and build stronger (and hence more marketable) relationships between media and reader. In addition, as a model it offers potential for further academic research, such as a comparative study of blogs which are already pursuing this model such as Wanderlust and Lipstick, and traditional media which rely heavily on UGC for their travel content, such as the *Times of India*. A 'distributed newsroom' (Cokley & Eeles, 2003) with a few curators and a massive network of weak-tie contributors also invites research into how such an organisational structure would work. Most studies of journalistic roles are based on the traditional, Western model of newsrooms; new research is needed into how curators and contributors see their identity, role and values (Bakker, 2014).

Further research could also counter the limitations evident in this chapter. Any study which predicts a future route for an industry stands on uncertain ground. Such exploratory research, particularly using students rather than practitioners, cannot confirm any shift in professional practice, even if it demonstrates that it is plausible. Yet, taken together, the evidence that the media industry is undergoing profound changes and the parallels between the attitudes towards social media content of the two groups studied here does suggest that the professional practice of journalists could do well to adapt to the new environment alongside and within which they must now operate. Ethnographies of the 'new' digital newsrooms would enhance the picture.

This chapter can also be critiqued for proposing a direction for traditional media by examining associated industries rather than the media itself. The counterpoint would be that while there is an argument for studying an industry itself for new directions, there is a stronger one for studying allied industries. Organisations which look to similar others for guidance can become caught in existing structures and path dependencies, and be less able to adapt to new ecosystems triggered by changing technology (Ouchi, 1998; Preston, 2008). By contrast, those which look to tangentially connected industries for innovation are likelier to thrive. Exploiting weak ties is more advantageous than relying on strong ties (Granovetter, 1973), so examining associated areas may yield ideas that consulting peers in the same area does not.

Equally, this chapter does not detail mechanisms by which the new model would ease traditional media's commercial travails. This is for two reasons: first, it is wearisome for professionals in any field to be advised by scholars on how to do business; and second, any scholar who knew a means of monetise UGC would likely be in the more lucrative field of consultancy than in impecunious academia. Traditional media are fully engaged in this task, and have suggested and tried many business models (Franklin, 2014; Kaye & Quinn, 2010). It seems likely that a combination of all of them offers the best hope. Just as the industry itself becomes disjointed and complicated by the digital revolution, so the business model solutions are similarly fragmented (Picard, 2014).

There are also other possibilities which have not been detailed here. Alongside curation as an innovative work practice in traditional media newsrooms, fragmentation of journalistic output is also emerging as a phenomenon of the post-digital shakeout as organisations service a niche area of readers, or specialise in delivering one form of content to a larger organisation (Sirkkunen & Cook, 2012), a significant move away from the industrialised, one-size-fits-all, one-price-for-all agglomeration of multiple content streams into the average daily newspaper. Pirolli (2014) has suggested that online travel information sources such as blogs might evolve more professional, standards to meet audience demands. One example would be Wanderlust and Lipstick which is helmed by a professional travel journalist, and aims to attract advertisers. While traditional media may add social media credibility to its mix, social media can equally perform the obverse by adding professional editing to its own offerings. Either way, the integration of amateur and professional credibilities and values offers a new model for existing and emerging media organisations. Travel journalists may find that, in the absence of a way to beat bloggers and social media, the future growth of their profession might be best secured by joining them.

REFERENCES

Bakker, P. (2014). Mr Gates returns: Curation, community management and new roles for journalists. *Journalism Studies*, *15*(5), 596–606. doi:10.1080/1461670X.2014.901783

Benson, V., & Morgan, S. (2015). *Implications of Social Media Use in Personal and Professional Settings*. Hershey, PA: IGI Global; doi:10.4018/978-1-4666-7401-1

Berthon, P., Pitt, L. F., Plangger, K., & Shapiro, D. (2012). Marketing meets Web 2.0, social media, and creative consumers: Implications for international marketing strategy. *Business Horizons*, *55*(3), 261–271. doi:10.1016/j.bushor.2012.01.007

Bruns, A. (2008). *Blogs, Wikipedia, Second Life, and Beyond: From Production to Produsage*. New York: Peter Lang.

Buhalis, D., & Law, R. (2008). Progress in information technology and tourism management: 20 years on and 10 years after the Internet – the state of etourism research. *Tourism Management*, *29*(4), 609–623. doi:10.1016/j.tourman.2008.01.005

Camprubí, R., Guia, J., & Comas, J. (2013). The new role of tourists in destination image formation. *Current Issues in Tourism*, *16*(2), 203–209. doi:10.1080/13683500.2012.733358

Carlson, M. (2007). Blogs and journalistic authority: The role of blogs in US Election Day 2004 coverage. *Journalism Studies*, *8*(2), 264–279. doi:10.1080/14616700601148861

Casaló, L. V., Flavián, C., & Guinalíu, M. (2011). Understanding the intention to follow the advice obtained in an online travel community. *Computers in Human Behavior*, *27*(2), 622–633. doi:10.1016/j.chb.2010.04.013

Cokley, J., & Eeles, S. (2003). The origin of a species: 'The distributed newsroom'. *Australian Studies in Journalism*, *12*, 240–261.

Deuze, M. (2005). What is journalism? Professional identity and ideology of journalists reconsidered. *Journalism*, *6*(4), 442–464. doi:10.1177/1464884905056815

Franklin, B. (2012). The future of journalism. Developments and debates. *Journalism Studies*, *13*(5-6), 663–681. doi:10.1080/1461670X.2012.712301

Franklin, B. (2014). The future of journalism in an age of digital media and economic uncertainty. *Digital Journalism*, *2*(3), 254–272. doi:10.1080/21670811.2014.930253

Fredriksson, M., & Johansson, B. (2014). The dynamics of professional identity. *Journalism Practice*, *8*(5), 585–595. doi:10.1080/17512786.2014.884746

Granovetter, M. (1973). The strength of weak ties. *American Journal of Sociology*, *78*(6), 1360–1380. doi:10.1086/225469

Hanusch, F. (2011). A profile of Australian travel journalists' professional views and ethical standards. *Journalism*, *13*(5), 668–686. doi:10.1177/1464884911398338

Hanusch, F., & Fürsich, E. (2014). On the relevance of travel journalism: An introduction. In F. Hanusch & E. Fürsich (Eds.), *Travel Journalism: Exploring Production, Impact and Culture* (pp. 1–17). Basingstoke, UK: Palgrave Macmillan. doi:10.1057/9781137325983.0005

Herbert, J. (2004). *Journalism in the Digital Age: Theory and Practice for Broadcast, Print and On-Line Media*. Oxford, UK: Focal Press.

Hermida, A., & Thurman, N. (2008). A clash of cultures: The integration of user-generated content within professional journalistic frameworks at British newspaper websites. *Journalism Practice*, 2(3), 343–356. doi:10.1080/17512780802054538

Hofstaetter, C., & Egger, R. (2009). The importance and use of weblogs for backpackers. In Information and Communication Technologies in Tourism. New York: Springer-Verlag.

Howarth, A. (2015). Exploring a curatorial turn in journalism. *Media/Culture Journal, 18*(4).

Hsu, C. H. C., & Song, H. (2013). Destination image in travel magazines: A textual and pictorial analysis of Hong Kong and Macau. *Journal of Vacation Marketing, 19*(3), 253–268. doi:10.1177/1356766712473469

Jeacle, I., & Carter, C. (2011). In TripAdvisor we trust: Rankings, calculative regimes and abstract systems. *Accounting, Organizations and Society, 36*(4–5), 293–309. doi:10.1016/j.aos.2011.04.002

Johnstone, J. W. C., Slawski, E. J., & Bowman, W. B. (1972). The professional values of American newsmen. *Public Opinion Quarterly, 36*(4), 522–540. doi:10.1086/268036

Kaye, J., & Quinn, S. (2010). *Funding Journalism in the Digital Age: Business Models, Strategies, Issues and Trends*. New York: Peter Lang.

Kramer, S. D. (2004). CBS scandal highlights tension between bloggers and news media. *Online Journalism Review*. Retrieved from http://www.ojr.org/ojr/workplace/1096589178.php

Lankes, R. D. (2008). Trusting the Internet: New approaches to credibility tools. In M. J. Metzger & A. J. Flanagin (Eds.), *Digital Media, Youth and Credibility* (pp. 101–122). Cambridge, MA: MIT Press.

Lazarsfeld, P., & Merton, R. (1954). Friendship as a social process: a substantive and methodological analysis. In M. Berger, T. Abel, & C. H. Page (Eds.), *Freedom and Control in Modern Society* (pp. 18–66). New York: Van Nostrand.

Lowrey, W. (2011). Institutionalism, news organizations and innovation. *Journalism Studies, 12*(1), 64–79. doi:10.1080/1461670X.2010.511954

Nah, S., & Chung, D. S. (2012). When citizens meet both professional and citizen journalists: Social trust, media credibility, and perceived journalistic roles among online community news readers. *Journalism, 13*(6), 714–730. doi:10.1177/1464884911431381

O'Connor, D. (2010). Apomediation and ancillary care: Researchers' responsibilities in health-related online communities. *International Journal of Internet Research Ethics, 12*, 87–103.

O'Reilly, T. (2005). *What is Web 2.0? Design patterns and business models for the next generation of software*. Retrieved 25 February 2014 from: http://oreilly.com/web2/archive/what-is-web-20.html

Ouchi, W. (1980). Markets, bureaucracies and clans. *Administrative Science Quarterly, 25*(1), 129–141. doi:10.2307/2392231

Patton, M. Q. (2002). *Qualitative Research and Evaluation Methods*. Thousand Oaks, CA: Sage.

Paulussen, S., & Ugille, P. (2008). User generated content in the newsroom: Professional and organisational constraints on participatory journalism. *Westminster Papers in Communication and Culture, 5*(2), 24–41.

Philips, A. (2005). Who's to make journalists? In H. de Burgh (Ed.), *Making Journalists* (pp. 227–244). Abingdon: Routledge.

Picard, R. G. (2014). Twilight or new dawn of journalism? *Digital Journalism, 2*(3), 1–11. doi:10.108 0/21670811.2014.895531

Pirolli, B. (2014). Travel journalism in flux: New practices in the blogosphere. In F. Hanusch & E. Für-sich (Eds.), *Travel Journalism: Exploring Production, Impact and Culture* (pp. 83–98). Basingstoke, UK: Palgrave Macmillan. doi:10.1057/9781137325983.0011

Preston, P. (2008). The curse of introversion. *Journalism Studies, 9*(5), 642–649. doi:10.1080/14616700802207516

Raman, U., & Choudary, D. (2014). Have travelled, will write: User-generated content and new travel journalism. In F. Hanusch & E. Fürsich (Eds.), *Travel Journalism: Exploring Production, Impact and Culture* (pp. 116–133). Basingstoke, UK: Palgrave Macmillan.

Ramirez de la Piscina, T., Zabalondo, B., Aisteran, A., & Agirre, A. (2015). *The future of journalism—who to believe? Different perceptions among European professionals and internet users*. Journalism Practice.

Rebillard, F., & Touboul, A. (2010). Promises unfulfilled? Journalism 2.0, user participation and editorial policy on newspaper websites. *Media Culture & Society, 32*(2), 323–334. doi:10.1177/0163443709356142

Siles, I., & Boczkowski, P. J. (2012). Making sense of the newspaper crisis: A critical assessment of existing research and an agenda for future work. *New Media & Society, 14*(8), 1375–1394. doi:10.1177/1461444812455148

Singer, J. B. (2003). Who are these guys? The online challenge to the notion of journalistic professionalism. *Journalism, 4*(2), 139–163.

Singer, J. B. (2007). Contested autonomy: Professional and popular claims on journalistic norms. *Journalism Studies, 8*(1), 79–95. doi:10.1080/14616700601056866

Singer, J. B. (2010). Quality control: Perceived effects of user-generated content on newsroom norms, values and routines. *Journalism Practice, 4*(2), 127–142. doi:10.1080/17512780903391979

Sirkkunen, E., & Cook, C. (Eds.). (2012). *Chasing Sustainability on the Net: International Research on 69 Journalistic Pure Players and Their Business Models*. Tampere, Finland: Tampere Research Centre for Journalism, Media and Communication, University of Tampere.

Spyridou, L.-P., Matsiola, M., Veglis, A., Kalliris, G., & Dimoulas, C. (2013). Journalism in a state of flux: Journalists as agents of technology innovation and emerging news practices. *The International Communication Gazette, 75*(1), 76–98. doi:10.1177/1748048512461763

Surowiecki, J. (2005). *The Wisdom of Crowds*. New York: Random House.

Tandoc, E. (2014). The roles of the game: The influence of news consumption patterns on the role conceptions of journalism students. *Journalism and Mass Communication Educator*, *69*(3), 256–270. doi:10.1177/1077695813520314

Thornton, P. H., Ocasio, W., & Lounsbury, M. (2012). *The Institutional Logics Perspective: A New Approach to Culture, Structure and Process*. Oxford: OUP. doi:10.1093/acprof:oso/9780199601936.001.0001

Toffler, A. (1980). *The Third Wave*. New York: Morrow.

TripAdvisor. (2015). Accessed at http://www.tripadvisor.com.sg/PressCenter-c6-About_Us.html

UNWTO. (2014). *Tourism Highlights*. Retrieved 30 September 2015 from: www.unwto.org/pub

Urry, J. (1990). *The Tourist Gaze: Leisure and Travel in Contemporary Societies*. London: Sage.

Utterback, J. (2003). The Dynamics of Innovation. In *The Internet and the University* (pp. 81-103). Aspen Institute Forum, Educause.

Volo, S. (2010). Bloggers' reported tourist experiences: Their utility as a tourism data source and their effect on prospective tourists. *Journal of Vacation Marketing*, *16*(4), 297–311. doi:10.1177/1356766710380884

Weaver, D. H. (Ed.). (1998). *The Global Journalist*. Hampton Press.

Xiang, Z., & Gretzel, U. (2010). Role of social media in online travel information search. *Tourism Management*, *31*(2), 179–188. doi:10.1016/j.tourman.2009.02.016

Yaros, R. A. (2008). Digital natives: following their lead on a path to a new journalism, *Nieman Reports*, 13–15.

Zelizer, B. (2004). When facts, truth and reality are God-terms: On journalism's uneasy place in cultural studies. *Communication and Critical Cultural Studies*, *1*(1), 100–119.

KEY TERMS AND DEFINITIONS

Blogs: Online personal diaries written in reverse chronological order, often reporting on an individual's life or area of specialist interest.

Curating: A new role for journalists, similar to editing, which sees them gathering, checking, validating and presenting content provided by non-professional contributors.

Homophily: The tendency of individuals to seek out, associate and make connection with similar others.

Objective: Not biased by personal feelings or external influences, and based on verifiable facts rather than personal feelings.

OURS: Online User Review Sites in which consumers share their experiences of a product or service. Examples include TripAdvisor, Epinions, RateMyTeachers, and Zagat.

Professional Identity: An individual's self-concept in the workplace, based on their beliefs, their motives, their experiences and various attributes.

Social Identity: An individual's self-concept based on their interaction with their peers, and their desire for inclusion within a social group.

Social Media: Online tools that allow individuals to create and share content, information, images and text across virtual networks and communities. Examples include Facebook, YouTube, Youku, Wikipedia, Cyworld, Twitter, blogs, OURS, Sina Weibo, Yelp, and Flickr.

Subjective: Based on personal feelings, activities and reactions rather than verifiable facts.

Travel Journalism: Content created in relation to a trip to a destination, often foreign, which purports to be a representation of reality, and which is aimed at consumers and tourists as inspiration for future travels.

Chapter 11
Social Media in Micro SME Documentary Production

Friedrich H. Kohle
University of Applied Sciences, Germany

ABSTRACT

Micro SME documentary producers are challenged to understand, adapt and apply social media technology in the creative economies. This paper examines the technological premise of social media, applications and limitations in documentary filmmaking. Drawing from other fields such as psychology, the author proposes a Real- and Virtual World Networking Model (RVNM), theorizing on how documentary producers can connect via social media networking to generate strong system support for their documentary project. RVNM helps documentary filmmaker make sense of the complexity of social media from development to distribution in order to further stimulate significant growth within the creative industries.

INTRODUCTION

Why Social Media Counts: More than 1 Billion Users Use Facebook Regularly

According to Joshua Oppenheimer, 'The Act of Killing' was made available to more than 1400 community screenings via an underground distribution network and social media (Oppenheimer, 2014), (Bjerregaard, 2014). Brian Knappenberger and his team successfully raised $ 93,724 for 'The Story of Aaron Swartz' (Kickstarter, 2014). On January 18 John Pilger's War Documentary closed its crowd funding campaign exceeding the £ 60,000 funding goal by £ 11,830 (Pilger, 2015). Kartemquin films raised $153,875 exceeding the original funding goal by 3,875 to produce 'Life Itself – A feature documentary based on Roger Ebert's memoir' (Kartemquin Films, 2015). A quick search on crowd-funding platforms will produce a number of similar successes. Still, as we will discover, social media and connected crowd-funding campaigns are perceived as a 'waste of time', even as begging: 'chatting on Facebook does not produce films' (Denis Vaslin, Personal Communication, 2014). This perspective very much represents the old paradigm in a swiftly changing global media landscape. On the other hand, micro SME documentary producers embracing this new technology experience and define social media as value enhancing, as

DOI: 10.4018/978-1-5225-0559-4.ch011

we will see later. Social media provides new opportunities to micro SME documentary producers as traditional power structures in broadcasting significantly shift away from traditional broadcasting models: game changing OTT streaming services serving for example Netflix, dominated much of IBC's theme in Amsterdam (IBC Content Everywhere, 2015). Chaired by Publisher Andrew Neil (Preston, 2002), Bruce Tuchman of the AMC and Sundance Channel (AMC Networks, 2015), Michael Harrit of Sony (Sony UK, 2015), Rhys Noelke of RTL Group (RTL Group, 2015) discussed how traditional broadcasters need to adapt to OTT services at the IBC keynote forum (ibTV, 2015): more bandwidth, more video streaming, more network intelligence applications analysing user behaviour and preferences, continue to challenge traditional broadcasters. There is no reason to assume that this trend is going to reverse any time soon. Reacting to this trend, traditional broadcasters are developing and implementing social media strategies to remain competitive, contracting OTT service providers in order to set up their own VOD brand. HBO for example launched its OTT service in 2014 (Littleton, 2014). Joram ten Brink, Co-Producer of 'The Act of Killing' rightly points out that broadcast commissions continue to shrink, budgets are not getting bigger and competition for these funds is increasing (Joram ten Brink, Personal Communication, 2014). Social media is being discussed at micro SME level, broadcasters such as HBO, Channel 4, BBC, ARD – all are adapting to this new challenge by setting up their own OTT video streaming services involving social media. But what exactly is social media? How did it evolve and why is it important to documentary filmmakers? To understand how social media is influencing documentary production we examine social media in documentary production from an economic, technological, ethnographic, psychological and marketing perspective. Social media is a multi-faceted phenomenon and cannot be sufficiently explored from a single perspective. What technological developments took place giving rise to and social media? How did the participatory culture in social media evolve? What is needed for a credible and authentic virtual presence? And why is all of this important to documentary filmmakers?

BACKGROUND

The Technological Evolution of Social Media

Social media is intrinsically linked with 'cloud' based binary technology. The cloud allows users to run applications and store information on server farms run for example by Google or Facebook, accessing and contributing information globally in digital form. Dropbox (2009) and Google Drive (2015) are examples of data sharing cloud services; social networking sites such as Facebook, Twitter and Linked-in store user information in the cloud. Social network giant Facebook, established in 2004 (Philips, 2007), features of all social media networking site the most user subscriptions: 1.49 billion in the first quarter of 2015 (Statista, 2015). One in every five people on Earth has a Facebook account and more users are joining Facebook by the hour. 800 million users worldwide (Statista, 2015) subscribed to mobile messaging service WhatsApp, founded in 2009 (Satariano, 2014). Twitter came online in 2006 (Liedtke, 2013) counting 304 million subscriptions (Statista, 2015). Linked-in began developing its social networking services in 2002 (Linked in, 2015) with 354 million users worldwide (Statista, 2015). Video streaming experienced strong growth with the arrival of digital networking technology and sufficient bandwidth. YouTube, established in 2005 (Monica, 2006), streamed its first video on April 23, 2005 (Karim, 2005) and features globally over one billion users (Youtube, 2015). Mobile devices have reached 6,9 billion subscriptions worldwide. 9,5 billion users are projected to have a mobile device by 2020 with access to social media networking sites (Ericson Mobility Report, 2014), or in other words: by 2020 there will be more mobile devices online compared to the estimated 7,7 billion humans living on Earth. (Geo-hive, 2015) Google's Loon project aims to provide Internet access anywhere via balloons in the earth's stratosphere (Google, 2013). Social media and networking monoliths Facebook, Twitter, WhatsApp and Linked-in are all sites used by documentary producers embracing this technology during any stage of production. Social media is needed to tap into or create communities, run a successful crowd-funding campaign on sites such as Kickstarter (Kickstarter, 2008) and Indiegogo (Indiegogo, 2008). Distribution of documentaries increasingly relies on cloud-based services such as Without-a-box (2011), Filmfreeway (2011) and broadcasting OTT-operators (Ooyala, 2015) such as Netflix (2015), which added another 4,9 million subscribers to its streaming service in the first quarter of 2015 (Spangler, 2015), bringing the total number of subscribers up to 62.3 million. The arrival of sufficient bandwidth and digital cloud services during the 2000s laid the foundation making global social media and networking sites possible. Millions of people participate, access, and contribute information and knowledge as individuals or part of a community to the cloud every hour of the day. Billions of mobile devices ensure that users have access to the social networking sites anywhere and anytime. To understand these phenomena we need to examine the evolution of social media technology, how users act and connect in large networks and establish how SME documentary producers, digital natives and immigrants (Prensky, 2001), (Benson, Saridakis, & Tennakoon, 2015) perceive the phenomena.

1971 was the year that saw what arguably could be called real social human-to-human interaction via the Internet: email. Computer systems programmer Ray Tomlinson created a feature called 'electronic mail', passing messages between computers via ARPANET (The First Network Email, 2015). Email took off instantly and within a few years 75% of all ARPANET traffic was email. ARPANET now featured the technological foundation needed to share information via email across large networks. The term INTERNET was coined (Kleinrock, 2010) as the ARPANET began to include networks not associated with ARPA. The idea of free sharing of information in education was strongly influenced by the counterculture of the 60-ties in the US and UK. Roy Rosenzweig describes how system programmer Richard Stallman conducted a guerilla war at MIT's artificial intelligence lab against the introduction of passwords. (Wizards, Beureaucrats, Warriors, and Hackers: Writing the History of the Internet, 1998), (Levy, 2001). Rosenzweig's account on the history of the Internet confirms Leonard Kleinrock's perspective (An Early History of the Internet, 2010), (Appendix), but is a great deal more critical and features more detail on what happened after the ARPANET became the Internet, examining clashing ideologies as to the purpose of the internet: free sharing of information or secrecy required by the military. It is this difference in approach, education versus military, still visible today; surveillance and abuse of the internet by secret service agencies limiting the full potential of an invention ironically explored and implemented by the military in conjunction with knowledge created in the educational sector. This conflict is central to the nature of the Internet: it was initially not conceived to be a commercial venture, to create new markets and generate profits. Technologists working in education and for the military conceived the technology needed for the Internet, both fields featured opposing visions of what the Internet should be. With ARPANET these pioneers laid the technological foundation of what became the Internet. Craig Partridge provides a detailed account regarding the development of Email, highlighting for example how Abhay Bhushan was involved in the development of the email header (Partridge, 2008). In 1971 Abhay Bhushan was instrumental in the design and development of the file transfer protocol (FTP), allowing users to transfer files across large networks. This by no means was sufficient to make this technology available to ordinary citizens. In 1983 Sandra Emerson described a Unix based network system termed USENET, allowing users to 'send and receive mail, transfer files, and discuss the delights and frustrations of using the Bell Laboratories' operating system' (Usenet: A Bulletin Board for Unix Users, 1983). USENET was developed and established in 1980 by Duke University, connected to ARPANET and in the two years preceding her article, USENET had grown from 50 to more than 500 sites. USENET quickly became a network connecting users across universities, featuring many of the interactive qualities we take for granted: discussion threads, file-sharing, email and newsgroups provided a platform administered by enthusiastic volunteers. Sandra Emerson states that the 'initial social contract among Usenet members –to forward news, respond to requests for information and participate in network maintenance- will continue to be a vital part of USENET'. The history of the Internet is the history of educational and military research intertwined. Free sharing of information and in the spirit of the 60-ties, administered and practiced by volunteers and educational researchers, took place on a technological platform maintained by reactionary military and defense authorities. By 1988 USENET featured 11,000 sites, a decade earlier the Department of Defense was hoping to sell off ARPANET: ironically the big telecommunications companies such as IBM and AT&T showed little interest. Instead they began to develop their own network technologies such as SNA and DECNET with the intent to bind their customers to their 'closed' network. The US administrations decision to make open standards a requirement put an end to those plans. Nevertheless, for the many volunteers and netizens at the time, increased privatization and monetization of the Internet came as a disappointment.

In 1989 another key milestone was reached when Tim Berner-Lee developed the world-wide-web at CERN (World Wide Consortium, 2015). His contribution was the development of the hyper-text-transfer-protocol (HTTP) allowing for the transmission of hyper-text-marked-up-language (HTML) pages. FTP was too slow and not user friendly to most users, HTTP and HTML provided a solution to set up and establish web-pages and blogs. On August 6, 1991, Tim Berners-Lee published the very first html web-page on the alt.hypertyext newsgroup, marking the third key moment in the rise of the Internet: the debut of HTML via HTTP (CERN, 2015). WYSIWYG –what you see is what you get- hypertext editors helped establish web-pages placed online by an increasingly less tech-savvy user base. Email and Usenet contributions featured a common way of keeping track of communications: threads. With HTML it became possible to take threads and establish them not only via email or in UseNet posts, but make them available to any user on the World Wide Web able to decode HTML pages. Retrospectively the term Web1 was created to describe a period in the 90-ties where bandwidth was still growing, yet the technological foundation for electronic and digital interaction was established. Since then the Internet has been growing and from a few hundred html pages in 1991, billions of pages have been recorded by search engines such as Google. Increased bandwidth, improved programming and better standards such as HTML5 have ensured that the original vision Leonard Kleinrock described in 1969 has become a global reality: today computer networks are servicing almost all individual homes and offices across the Western World, with growth continuing on a global scale.

From Web 1 to Web 3

With the hardware, efficient transfer protocols and HTML in place, users began to populate the infant virtual space. Webpages were uploaded and by 1993 14,161,570 users were active worldwide (Internet Live Stats, 2015), by 2014 this grew to 2,925,249,355. At the time of writing 3 billion recorded users were registered worldwide, or more than 40% of the worlds population. There is no reason to assume growth will slow down any time soon. With the arrival of social media networking sites such as MySpace and Facebook, the period preceding SNS's was termed Web 1: users gathered and consumed information via websites and blogs, content creators were still relatively few (Krishnamurthy & Cormode, 2008).

The arrival of Web 2 technologies changed the nature of the Internet significantly. No longer were users merely browsing for information, users began to actively create and contribute content. Increasing bandwidth and improved connectivity enabled the rise of sites such as video streaming sites YouTube and social networking sites (SNS) such as Facebook. Strong social and user generated content such as photos, video featuring comments and ratings allowed vivid interaction between users and communities. Nevertheless, it can be difficult to distinguish exactly when a particular site is Web 1 or Web 2 as Krishnamurthy and Cormode realized (Key differences between Web 1.0 and Web 2.0, 2008): as Web 1 evolved into Web 2 the transition and implementation to more dynamic pages gradually evolved over a period of time, when owners of the site deemed it necessary. Nevertheless, the arrival of SNS sites such as Facebook is considered Web 2 sites. Social content usually entails users establishing an online profile, and once established in the virtual world in this way, they begin to form and participate in various network activities. Combining social content was further encouraged with new technologies such as API's enabling third party developers to contribute plug-in's to 'mash-up' content. An API is an application programming interface to between different application modules, making it possible to share data (Random House Dictionary, 2015): users are able to integrate and link to YouTube video on their Facebook or Web-page, cross linking content from other SNS's in this way. Facebook turned out to be extremely successful in providing strong incentives –or stickiness- for users to stay on the SNS, creating more opportunities for commercial content to be delivered. Nevertheless, Facebook too finds its roots not in the commercial world, but initially was established to provide a platform among university students. Upon launch in 2004 more than 1,200 Harvard students subscribed to the service (Phillips, 2007). It then quickly spread first to other Universities and US High-schools, and in 2006 Facebook opened its virtual gateways to the greater public. More than a billion users worldwide have subscribed to Facebook since 2004, contributing to the growing global collective consciousness.

John Markoff of the New York Times describes the arrival of Web 3 technologies in his article "Entrepeneurs See a Web Guided by Common Sense" (2006). By then billions of documents and websites were populating the internet, Web 2 social network technologies made the arrival of SNS's such as MySpace and Facebook possible, and scientists as well as start-ups continue to investigate ways to data mine the staggering amount of data available in the virtual world. The World Wide Web Consortium (W3C) also calls Web 3 the semantic web (W3C, 2015) because of its capacity to link data in a meaningful intelligent way. Data mining and the introduction of 'intelligent' algorithms provide another level of user experience predicting trends based on user preferences. SNS', Google, YouTube – all are employing network intelligence technologies to anticipate which advert users should see in their browser, based on user data collected. While Web 2 technologies continue to be an important part of the web, i.e. mash-ups, cross-linking of content, Web 3 technologies are delivering smart system responses to users, analyzing available data of the user and matching it with relevant online content. But interconnectivity does not stop with Web 3 technologies. The Internet of Things is a term coined by Kevin Ashton in 1999 (Ashton, 2009). RFID technology is crucial for the Internet of Things: RFID's are tags transmitting properties of the object –or thing- they are attached to via the Internet to systems analyzing that data. The purpose of the Internet of Things is to connect the physical world to the virtual online world. Companies such as Cisco realize the benefit of this technology: objects that are near the end of their lifespan can be replaced in time, resources can be managed more efficiently and more importantly, according to Kevin Ashton, this technology will allow computers to 'observe, identify and understand the world –without the limitations of human-entered data'. Combined with intelligent algorithms, artificial intelligence RFID technology is in the process of creating a virtual 'mirror' image of the real world. It is foreseeable that once 'every thing' has been recorded and analysed by an online virtual intelligence exceeding the human capacity for doing the same, the Internet will reach yet again another key milestone in its evolutionary history. Futurist Ray Kurzweil is the expert at Google, developing projects bringing 'natural language understanding' to the search engine (Jenkins, 2013): due to the exponential speed of technological development he describes the moment in human history when artificial intelligence will surpass that of a human, with humans and technology merging from that point forward as 'The Singularity' (Kurzweil, 2009). We established how social media technology developed, discussed future trends and next we need explore how the participation and user interaction evolved via social media. How do users connect and interact with each other? And how is this relevant for documentary producers?

NETWORK INTELLIGENCE AND BUILDING AN EFFECTIVE SOCIAL MEDIA STRATEGY

The Rise of Participatory Social Media in Documentary Production

Before the arrival of the Internet, social media producers relied on old-fashioned methods: engaging and meeting with others at festivals, conferences and screenings. Networking in the real world was and still is key to successful completion of a documentary project. Paco de Onis account regarding the production of a Quechua-Language version of 'State of Fear' in Peru (Onis P. D., 2009) demonstrates the importance of real-world networking for documentary producers. The International Center of Transitional Justice (ICTJ) suggested to Skylight Pictures, a company producing films on human rights and social issues for more than 25 years, to produce the Film 'State of Fear: The Truth About Terrorism" (Yates, 2005) including a social media strategy. ICTJ helped secure initial funding, and Producer Paco de Onis approached the Ford Foundation in Santiago, Chile for further funding. With the help of Peru's National Human Rights Coordinator Skylight Pictures gained access to 67 human rights NGO's operating in Peru to distribute DVD's of the completed film. Lima based Tornonja communications assisted by assigning a project manager for the Quechua language version of the film. In addition a social media platform was set up serving as an archive to engage human rights activists, victims and educators (Onis P. d., 2006). Twitter, Flickr, Google Maps, blogs– all of these social media tools were applied. Local NGO activists were given FLIP cameras to record and upload clips to the project site, further enhancing to the overall trans-media narrative of the project. This example highlights how important real world contacts are, how they contribute and lead to a virtual world and social media strategy. Participation in real-world events such as festival, screenings and industry conferences are essential networking fore for SME producers. Key contacts are established, which at a later stage become crucial for the implementation of an effective social media strategy. Contacts may include key stakeholders such as funders and production staff and as we will discover later, without these an effective real-world support network, a social media campaign less likely to be successful.

How Do Users Connect and Participate in Large Networks?

Web 1, 2, 3 and the Internet of Things continue to drive the expansion of the World Wide Web. But how do users connect with each other? What are the cultural and participatory exchanges taking place online? The arrival of the internet allows humans to connect in a new virtual world though scholarship during the 80-ties was critical towards the Internet and did not consider large networks a 'social' place at all: it lacked the depth for needed for real human interaction (Daft & Lengel, 1986). Despite the criticism, users found ways to participate and express themselves in rich and unexpected ways via websites, blogs and SNS'. Communities formed with the arrival of USENET and expanded onto other platforms such as the World Wide Web, Web 2 and now Web 3 technologies. Community building systems such as Nationbuilder (Nationbuilder, 2015) analyse available user data, providing sophisticated network intelligence to match the needs of a user with the purposes of the Nationbuilder operator, thus assisting intelligently in the creation of online communities. Psychologist Westaby at al undertook the task to analyse how users connect and what kind of connections they have between each other (Westaby, Pfaff, & Redding, 2014). The Dynamic Network Theory (DNT) postulated explains how users position and connect with each other in large networks. By means of a sociogram (Burt, Kilduff, & Tasselli, 2013) Westaby's team propose a perspective illuminating density of a connection and how users connect. We transposed the DNT model into a the possible sociogram setting Micro SME documentary producer Tom might find himself in (Figure 1).

Micro SME Producer Tom represents a social media user and connections made to friends and colleagues. Density describes in this case 6 existing out of 10 possible connections and is calculated as follows: 10 possible divided by 6 existing connections result in a density of 0.6. Existing connections approaching the number of possible connections increase density to a maximum of 1, signifying that everyone is connected and interdependent. A density of 0 means no connections exist and each node or user is independent. In this way it is possible to determine how dense a user is connected to others on a network.

Figure 1. Virtual world network
Based on Sociogram by Westaby, Pfaff & Redding, 2014.

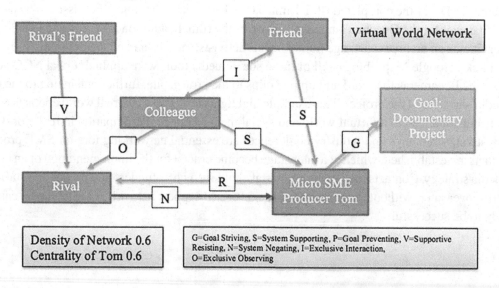

Centrality is another criteria used by Westaby to determine the degree of information flow. For example, a documentary producer socially active in the virtual world, occupies a central position in social networking as team-members pass on information to him or her. In turn s/he may distribute to others information accordingly. Real-world power structures are reflected in this way in social networks, including all the risks: for example, the potential abuse of the central position by controlling the flow of information. Linton Freeman provides a mathematical model illustrating how centrality in large networks approaching a value of 1 suggests that information is channelled via key entities or nodes in a network (Freeman, 1978/9). With centrality approaching 0 no single node or user is more central than the other nodes or users in the network. Web 3 technologies increasingly develops the capability to analyse and act on density and centrality data, and conclusions can be made as to the nature of the user or node. Westaby quotes research drawing from disciplines such as Applied Psychology and Management Sciences illustrating how centrality relates to power, performance, charismatic leadership and perceived status in an organisation. (Kameda, Ohtsubo, & Takezawa, 1997), (Ahuja, Galletta, & Carley, 2003), (Borgatti, Brass, & Labianca, 2009), (Balkundi, Kilduff, & Harrison, 2011) (Venkataramani, Green, & Schleicher, 2010). DNT illustrates how users connect, but it says little about the quality of connections made.

In his book Netnography (2015) Robert Kozinets adds to Westaby by discussing the quality of the social experience in large networks, highlighting how Netnography applies social science research methods to 'present a new approach to conducting ethical and thorough ethnographic research that combines archival and online communications work, participation and observation, with new forms of digital and network data collection, analysis and research representation'. More useful to ethnographers, Netnography nevertheless provides relevant insight into how users connect to each other in the virtual online world: Kozinet theorises on the nature of an 'intensely personal and deeply meanginful' community or Gemeinschaft-relations, and those more superficial, short-lasting and more market-and-transaction or Gesellschaft- orientated online exchanges. His ideas of Gemeinschaft and Gesellschaft are based on Ferdinand Tönnies theories describing communities –or Gemeinschaft- as deeper and more social circles, whereas market and corporate –or Gesellschaft- exchanges are considered superficial and short-lived (Tönnies, 1887). Kozinet illuminates how users experience social interaction online but neither Kozinet, nor Westaby make a connection to the ideas of C.G. Jung. While Kozinet refers to McLuhan, McLuhan's investigation and references to Jung and the collective unconscious remain undiscussed. Astonishingly the idea that the Persona and Shadow of the user-self extending itself virtually via Web 1, 2 & 3 technologies is not part of the discussion. Perhaps this is less surprising for social-media marketing expert Kozinet, though Westaby, a psychologist, could have considered a link to Jung as his ideas illuminate how multiple inventions, synchronicity, not only assisted in the establishment of the internet simultaneously in the educational but also military field of interest.

Leaning on Jung's idea of the Shadow and Persona (Jung C., 1928), the dichotomy of the internet, the education-persona versus the military-shadow, intertwines social media and the internet as a whole: education with its philosophy of openness and sharing opposed to the military requiring secrecy and application of passwords. This conflict is at the heart of the Internet, and remains unresolved to this day. Neither IBM nor AT&T (Kleinrock, An Early History of the Internet, 2010) considered the internet's predecessor ARPANET a profitable investment. Both turned down an offer by the Department of Defence to further develop its infrastructure and monetisation of the internet and social media occurred relatively late after its original conception. The world wide web originally was not designed to be commercial: in education scientists such as Kleinrock perceived it more as a public commodity such as roads are an integral part of a countries transportation infrastructure. Roads by themselves hardly produce profit, it is the traffic on them that does. The same is true for the internet: the internet itself does not generate profit, it is the digital traffic channelled via nodes, switches and computers that does.

But how is this traffic defined? How do users connect with each other? Westaby's DNT approach sheds more light on user's online behaviour, yet it lacks depth when it comes to a deeper understanding of the extension of the users self and the evolving global consciousness discussed earlier. The taxonomy presented by Westaby et al, provides insight into online roles users adopt in their online world. In order to understand the relevance for documentary filmmaking better, those roles are briefly summarised below:

1. **Goal Striving Role (G):** This role is characteristic for individuals motivated to reach or pursue a goal. For example, this could be a documentary producer whose goal it is to obtain crowd-funding for project. Goals such as this often trigger sub goals and other social network roles as well.

2. **System Supporting Role (S):** This role is adopted by individuals with the intend to support others in their goal striving activity, i.e. by liking the goal striving users Facebook page, financial support via crowd-funding, moral support on a blog or by sharing a link. For documentary film-makers in pursuit of realising their production goal, gaining as much System Support as possible is crucial regarding the build-up of social capital, establishing or tapping into online communities and obtaining financial resources. Software solutions such as Nationbuilder, originally developed and designed for election campaigners, specialise in managing and growing system support accordingly. Especially SNS' are crucial in securing and maintaining system support.

3. **Goal Preventing Role (P):** Users acting as goal preventers attempt to hinder and stop goals pursued by others. As a result they create a competitive and conflicted social environment. For example documentary producers with the intent to prevent the construction of a fracking facility on native Indian territory may adopt a goal preventing role online. Perspective is relevant here because it is possible to reframe the perspective of goal prevention also as a goal itself. More importantly is to note the relative motivation of the goal pursuer and goal preventer in the context of the issue at hand.

4. **Support Resisting Role (V):** Individuals engaging in this role support others in their online resistance. For example in the example given above, the lawyer of the native Indian group may receive support from individuals or organisations supporting their goal prevention. Users featuring strong centrality are also more likely to be more influential in supportive resistance networks. To make this example more relevant to documentary film-making, documentary film-makers might consider approaching central support resistors who can significantly amplify the online presence of the documentary project.

5. **System Negating Role (N):** Online bullies fall into that category, for example by negatively responding to goal pursuers and their goals. System negators often need extensive moderation in SNS'. Documentary producers tasked with SNS and blog moderation need to apply strict guidelines to system negators in order to avoid demotivation of the goal pursuer.

6. **System Reacting Role (R):** This occurs as a result of system negating. For example the victim of online bullying may respond with emotional distress. Or a documentary producer may become irritated and even cancel an otherwise viable documentary project. System negation can also have a positive outcome, for example when a system negator highlights serious flaws in the way a goal is pursued: as a result the goal pursuer may revise and improve on his goal.

7. **Interacting Role (I):** This role implies that the individual has no intention of supporting or preventing goals, but is merely occupied in navigation his or her interactions with others online. This can slow down a goal pursuer.

8. **Observing Role (O):** These are individuals who are engaged in observation alone. To illustrate, this could be observing the Arab Spring unfold online via YouTube. Users in this role are not supporting or negating the revolutionaries' goal to topple the Libyan administration. Experienced goal strivers might be motivated by the traffic generated by observers, yet inexperienced goal strivers may be distracted and anxious when attracting large numbers of observers.

Figure 1 demonstrates that documentary producer Tom may have a crowd-funding campaign as a goal and thus as the producer adopts a goal-pursuing role. Friends and colleagues in this model may act in system supporting roles while merely interacting between themselves. The producers rival may negate and resist the goal of the producer, thus provoking the producer to adopt a system reaction role. Friends of the rival may get involved as support resistors. DNT provides a practical model describing how users act online and why they adopt one of the eight roles described in the theory. Density and centrality help to understand the influence and position users have in a network. This way we understand how emotions are transmitted via large networks in relation to goal striving. If for instance goal striver Tom succeeds to obtain his goal, perhaps crowd-funding for his documentary project, not only Tom, but system supporters, i.e. friends and colleagues, are also experiencing positive emotional reactions. Network contagion is not restricted to system supporters, though users exclusively observing or interacting are not expected to experience the same level of emotions. As a result Tom will feel more confident about his goal pursuit and establish a stronger relationship with his system supporters.

Goal success does not imply positive emotions throughout – Tom's rival may become even more encouraged to resist Tom's future goals as a result of his success. According to Westaby, cognitive network accuracy plays an important to determine if a user is centrally positioned in a large network. Network Intelligence is crucial in obtaining qualified system support. Dynamic Network Intelligence or DNI, explores the degree of awareness users have regarding others in a large network and their goal striving or system resisting processes. Awareness of how others act and position themselves in large networks is thought to increase the likelihood of a goal striver to position him or herself with a strategic advantage. Building on Westaby's ideas we now formulate our idea of the Real and Virtual- Network Model (Figure 2, RVNM).

Figure 2 illustrates how documentary producer Tom can be enabled to gain stronger system support for his project if he also activates positive system support in the real world (R), based on accurate network intelligence. Broadcasters, distributors, funders and NGO's need to receive a qualified system support request from Tom, this maximising potential system support for Tom's project. Strong network intelligence is essential to ensure that system support requests made by Tom are not only targeted at real- and virtual world system supporters with high centrality, but also with the capacity to minimise any possible system negation by, for example, not exclusively interacting or observing, but also by taking on the role of mediator if necessary. The more real world system support with high centrality Tom receives, the more likely will his project grow and maintain a sizable community. RVWNM explains how documentary producers can maximise their system support requests in the real and virtual world. But it does not explain the exceptions, i.e. users so successful in posting content that their clips go viral without real-world support, i.e. Miranda sings (Ballinger, 2015), or the epic rap battle YouTube channel (Ahlquist & Shukoff, 2015). To understand these exceptions we turn next to the topic of authenticity and the role the 'real' plays in the virtual world.

Figure 2. Real and virtual network model

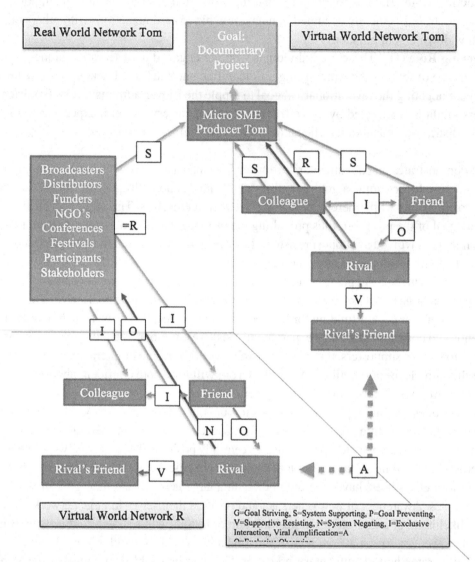

THE PSYCHOLOGY OF C.G. JUNG: AUTHENTICITY AND THE YIN & YANG OF SOCIAL MEDIA

'A corporation cannot laugh or cry,' said David Loy of Tokyo's Bonkyo University. 'It cannot enjoy the world or suffer with it. Most of all, a corporation cannot love.' David Boyle, Authenticity (2003).

We briefly explore C.G. Jung's ideas on the human psyche relevant to Social media, in particular the 'Persona' (Jung C., 1928) in order to better understand what makes the social media phenomena more authentic. The participatory culture of social media technology is particularly notable in the examples of Lloyd Ahlquist and Peter Shukoff and their YouTube channel Epic Rap Battles of history: 12 million subscribers and 100 million views propelled them to YouTube stardom. On Vine, the 6-second maximum length video platform, Andrew Bachelor, aka 'King Bach', has more than 13 million followers for his narrative clips (Bachelor, 2015). Variety reports that Andrew has signed for a movie with Martin Lawrence (Jarvey & Svetkey, 2015). Colleen Ballinger aka as Miranda Sings on YouTube, has a total of 7 million followers across her YT-channels: sings, gossips with an extra amount of lipstick painted on her lips. Just these three examples alone are among of the top social media phenomena raking in millions of subscriptions and views in a new market. None of the three represent large companies or organisation, all of them produce content in small team or even by themselves. New Realists explored by David Boyle are expecting the real, authentic thing. And the more fakeness we encounter online, the more authentic content is in demand to maintain the overall balance: the World Wide Web too is subject to the Yin & Yang of life. We will call this phenomena new realistic authenticity. What makes something real and authentic? When does content speak to us?

Jung's ideas of the self, the persona and shadow, can help provide insight into the matter of authenticity. Hundreds of millions of views for the above examples and none are corporations, illustrate how users are able to distinguish between fake versus real, complete versus incomplete. The one-sided short-lived corporate product offered to us by marketers lacks depth because the shadow part does not exist or is kept secret: it lacks character and imperfection. To be human means to be imperfect. And this is reflected in the Yin and Yang, or the Persona and Shadow of an individual's self. Those unafraid to show their whole and true self, but within the rules set by the collective consciousness, are more likely to be perceived as authentic.

Millions of users have created and are in the process of creating a virtual online extension of their Persona. The Persona is not the same as a person's personality: it is the part of our ego presented to the public, designed to impress and conceal the true nature of an individual. Only after becoming aware of that mask is the individual empowered to discover his or her true self: authenticity requires a good, deep look into the mirror asking, "What am I seeing? Who is this? Why am I using social media?' Social Media invites users to project their Persona online, serving as a reminder that social media cannot be defined from a business and marketing perspective alone. It provides a virtual mirror reflection of ourselves. Ironically companies such as IBM understand this; their AI Watson offers services such 'Personality Insights' to analyse and describe a user's Persona. (IBM, 2015) AI's such as Watson are considered accurate enough by Human Resources departments to pre-select and screen potential candidates (Broersma, 2014): the data trail users leave behind in social media is creating a 'digital Persona', open to dataveillance techniques. (Clarke, 1994) Social Media is not and has never been just a marketing and distribution platform providing interactive services to users and communities, as claimed by Kaplan and Haenlein. It is an extension of a user's Persona; millions of users are testament to this every minute of the day.

The Darker Shadow-Side of Social Media

Social Media has a darker side: it can provide transparency and encourage discussion online, but it can also obscure and confuse. Users project their Persona, the acceptable public 'mask' of their personality, via social media. As in real life, individuals have a darker side, which Jung calls the 'Shadow' (Jung C., 1928). The 'Shadow' is all that the Persona is not: the Shadow contains repressed items of our ego and is closer to our collective unconscious. The darker side of a users 'Shadow' notably occurs in anonymous or trolling online content. Censorship, propaganda and clandestine online surveillance can be interpreted as the 'Shadow' side of a society or culture; it can be difficult to distinguish authentic from propaganda content. Recent revelations regarding secret services activities (Macaskill & Dance, 2013) and involvement of secret services funding Google Earth (Shachtman, 2010) are hindering the development of the true potential of social media. Unless appropriate legislation establishes and enforces better protection of privacy, these issues will continue to hold social media back. Dr. Petra Grimm of the 'Hochschule der Medien', Stuttgart, even suggested that Facebook has become so important that it should no longer be a privately owned company. Instead, a license-based system should be considered, as is the case with public broadcasters such as the BBC or ARD, offering a social media network that is independent, secure and trustworthy. (ZDF, 2015) Educators and parents are often overwhelmed with the challenges social media presents them with and health professionals are concerned about children and teenagers being addicted to online services (Kohle & Raj, Implications of Social Media Use in Personal and Professional Settings, 2015).

The history of media is one of war, whether we like it or not. Without conflict media technology would not have developed the way it did. Beginning with the arrival of language, followed by cave art, pictograms, hieroglyphs, the invention of the alphabet, the print press, radio, Film & TV: media is used to tell stories of battles lost and won, document the power of rulers, and influence entire populations to support totalitarian regimes (Kohle F. H., 2015). The Internet too is no exception: developed in the field of education and military, ARPANET was funded by the US Department of Defense. What became known as the Internet was never conceived as a commercial venture. IBM and AT&T declined to invest into the Internet as they did not realize its commercial potential. And to this day the dichotomy at the heart of the world wide web also hinders its potential growth: openness and free information sharing are deeply rooted in the philosophy applied by those researchers who developed the internet in the field of education. Password protection, security and surveillance are measures implemented by researchers working for the military. Recent revelations by whistleblowers such as Edward Snowden (Greenwald, 2014) highlight how government agencies operate in clandestine fashion to obtain and analyse user data.

Ray Rosenzweig provides more intricate detail of the effects the 60-ties counterculture had on the early Internet: some 'radicals wanted to smash technology rather than liberate it' (Rosenzweig, 1998), though a network of volunteers enthusiastically administered USENET in the spirit of free information sharing. He makes a compelling argument demonstrating that many of the 'open impulses' find their roots in relevant counterculture. On the other hand, the cold war dominated military thinking during that time and the need for a 'closed' network philosophy to secure and protect military assets. This contradiction is not the product of neo-liberalism, but a balance of two opposing perspectives in education and military –or the Persona and Shadow of the Internet- at the time. Without this contradiction and balance of opposing positions, the Internet and social media would not exist.

Despite the downsides, producers and users continue to engage in social media, social networking sites keep growing and digital natives perceive themselves as participants in a worldwide global social media culture. Documentary Producers need to be aware of the evolving virtual Persona and Shadow side of social media to successfully develop a social media strategy. Colleen Ballinger extending her Miranda-persona is a good example of how this can work. As we will learn later, Filmmakers such as Koen Suidgeest (IMDB, 2015a) are successful in projecting their own Persona to build and maintain a community surrounding their projects. A credible and authentic virtual Persona adds significant value to a documentary project. As a result, documentary producers need to have awareness of their own Persona and Shadow if they are considering extending their self into the virtual world. Individuals too adapted to society and the public, or if they identify their ego with the Persona projected, are likely to create an exaggerated presence (Huang, 2014) or even experience psychological difficulties (Schoen, 2009). This then raises the question as to how micro SME documentary producers see themselves online and how they perceive social media.

RECOMMENDATIONS FOR MICRO SME DOCUMENTARY PRODUCERS

Drawing from an Experiential Account

From media theory to user expectations: the experiential part of this research involved the production of documentaries seeks to apply new knowledge gained and explore what it is like to go through the process. Three documentaries were produced; all of them featured social media applications. Limitations were that all three documentaries were produced part-time, outside the authors working hours as a teacher at NHTV: projects needed to fit the authors existing workload. The expected outcome illuminates what it is like to use social media in documentary filmmaking practice, based on knowledge gained via qualitative research methods.

'God, Church, Pills & Condoms' is a documentary about a new controversial health care reform in the Philippines, providing families on low income, young men and women, access to free contraception methods such as condoms and anti-baby pills. The Catholic Church still plays an important role in Philippine culture politics: the church strongly opposes any other form of contraception other than natural methods. This law has been proposed almost 20 years ago and because of lobbying by the Catholic Church and affiliated organizations such as Pro-Life Philippines, passing and implementation of the law was successfully delayed. Social media played a crucial role in the development of this film. It would not have been possible to research the topic without the many leads available via social media. News headlines, blogs, Facebook posts – all helped identify potential real and virtual-world system supporters for the film before production began in Manila. Soon a small community formed around the projects Facebook page 'Tiny Little Doclab' (Kohle F., Tiny Little Doclab, 2009) which in turn provided new leads to help target specific groups regarding the distribution of the film. A small crowd funding campaign raised a modest amount of money towards the production and distribution costs of the film, (Tiny Little Doclab, 2011). Social media had a significant influence regarding festival distribution via online platforms (Film Freeway, 2011), (Without a Box, 2011). In addition to traditional festival submissions, the film was successfully released and accepted into a number of international festivals resulting in formal invitations for the director of the film to Cinemalaya 2012, Manila (Cinemalaya, 2012), and the Hanoi International Film Festival (Hanoi International Film Festival, 2012). The film was made available online via Vimeo (Vimeo, 2012) for festival promotion. Real-world support requests were made from politicians, clerics, medical professionals and educators. Young man and women were made aware in this way in the real- and virtual world. The aim was not to generate profits but to raise awareness about the topic and encourage participants and the audience to form their own opinion based on the arguments presented in the film. Facebook, Vimeo and YouTube statistics show that a sizeable community discussed the film, relevant virtual system supporters with high centrality such as Elisabeth Angsioco (Democratic Socialist Women of the Philippines, 2010) further enhanced the value of the film by ensuring the film was promoted to relevant target groups in the Philippines. The results speak for themselves, bearing in mind that this film was produced part-time, during holiday breaks, weekends and while teaching at NHTV, the results speak for themselves.

'5 to 12' is a documentary about elderly athletes. The goal was to produce a documentary about aging and sports as well as to explore how the largest growing demographic group in developed countries, namely people above 50 and older, are engaging with social media.'5 to 12' tells the story of two friends, Kees and Rinus, both of whom are in their late 70-ties and active athletes. Learning from Ben Kempas example, i.e. social media applied for 'I am breathing', real-world supporters with high centrality with an interest in the film were identified via social media. Eventually an online discussion with interested individuals emerged, which then led to our first meetings with the participants of the film during development. Short behind the scene video clips were uploaded regularly, which in turn created interest in this age group to participate via social media. '5 to 12' was submitted to various film festivals via sites such as Freeway and Without-a-box and achieved international releases in festivals such as Docfeed in Eindhoven, the 21st International Sedona Film Festival and the Films-by-the-Sea Festival in Zeeland; a formally invitation was extended to the director of the film to attend the festivals. '5 to 12' was made available online via Vimeo to participants of the film and a community screening was organized at the AV56 athletes association in Goes.

Both of these examples highlight how documentaries produced in a micro SME production environment can draw valuable system support and accurate network intelligence during all stages of production. Combined with real-world support, social media strategies regarding development, production and distribution can be amplified. Micro SME Producers without the resources needed initially to adhere to the traditional funding procedure are able to attract relevant system support to 'get the ball rolling': the likelihood to obtain more funding becomes larger with a well thought out social media strategy in place.

Micro SME Documentary Producers benefit from the RVWNM; it helps them identify highly central network users in real- and virtual world settings with high density to generate strong real- and virtual system support for their documentary project. RVWNM combined with accurate network intelligence and an authentic extension of the Producers Persona maximises the documentary projects social media strategy. Micro SME producers are better positioned to extend an authentic online Persona compared to large corporations, which lack a Persona and rely branding instead.

CONCLUSION

Why Is Social Media Important to Micro SME Documentary Producers?

We investigated how social media technology developed and gained insight into how users connect in large networks, drawing from network theories in other fields such as netnographer Kozinet, and Psychologist Westaby. Marketing experts Haenlaein's and Kaplan's definition of social media describes potential business applications (Kaplan & Haenlein, 2010) and Vladica (Vladica, 2009) offers useful insight into social media applications in filmmaking from a marketing perspective; but neither ontology, epistemology and role of the online Persona as an extension of the user personality are addressed and discussed in detail. Social media is multi-faceted and needs to be examined from more than one perspective. Marketing on its own does not explain the success of social media in non-commercial applications, such as the Occupy movement. The real and virtual world model (RVNM) helps explain the success of non-commercial projects. Social Media is not just a collection of statistics, interactive blogs, social media networking sites and communities. The real strength of social media lays in the extension of the users virtual Persona and his or her contribution towards the formation of a collective global consciousness, as anticipated by McLuhan.

We also learned how abuse of this technology, for example anonymous online bullying (Juvonen & Gross, 2008) and unauthorized mass surveillance (Macaskill & Dance, 2013), continues to destroy trust in social media. Surveillance is becoming a real problem, and as the nation state will become less important in the future, representatives of the nation state idea are expected to use social media for propaganda and surveillance purposes (Greenwald, 2014). As a reaction to this, it will become increasingly difficult for those in power to ignore the growing number of voices, spy on or manipulate users. Documentary filmmakers need to be part of that process; they cannot afford to stand on the sidelines, especially if their goal is to contribute towards this new global collective consciousness by raising awareness on a given topic of their choice. Paul Mason (Post Capitalism: A Guide to Our Future, 2015) argues that the Internet and Social Media is the product of Neo-liberal policies, carrying with it the technological seeds of the destruction of capitalism. Our position is different: we have shown that the Internet was not conceived as a commercial and neo-liberal venture, but as a collaborative project in education and the military during the 1960-ties. Researchers in education exposed to and participating in the US and UK counterculture during that time strongly opposed the establishment and the military perspective.

We learned that when given the opportunity to invest into the Internet early in its development, corporate giants such as IBM declined to take advantage. Finally, in 1985 an angry young Bill Gates wrote a letter addressing the 'Hobbyists' freely sharing and hacking a computer programme in the Hobby-community (Gates, 2015). In the letter Bill Gates asks if it is fair to steal software from others in this way. During the 90-ties commerce became a viable option as Internet giants such as Amazon and e-bay established themselves. Today, the Internet is threefold: open and free information sharing opposed by clandestine military surveillance, and thirdly commercialised by capital. All three positions have created the Internet and social media we see today; all three elements, education, military and commerce, were necessary to develop, implement and advance technology. At the same time, all three of them are threatened by the emerging participatory culture the technology enables: education and information sharing is available to any one participating in the virtual world challenging traditional education structures, clandestine surveillance is increasingly uncovered by whistle-blowers sharing information freely online challenging power structures in government and commerce is under pressure to develop new concepts outside their corporate identity and branding strategy.

We explored how real world support requests based on strong network intelligence are crucial in obtaining virtual world system support in large networks. Applying RVNM in an experiential setting, we examined how documentaries such as 'God, Church, Pills and Condoms' (IMDB, 2012) benefitted from social media practices. Producers embracing this technology experience social media as value enhancing, creating new opportunities for SME producers to target niche and censored markets, as 'The Act of Killing' demonstrates (IMDB, 2013). Documentaries produced as part of the experiential research confirm the importance of an effective social media strategy during all stages of a project. 'God, Church, Pills & Condoms' highlights how socials media raises awareness regarding teenage pregnancies and implementation of controversial family planning laws in the Philippines. '5 to 12' illustrates how real and virtual network support can be generated in the fastest growing population segment in the western world: citizens above 65 years of age. Social media is a tool that helps increase awareness on a given topic, a grass-roots platform providing an open discourse between the documentary filmmaker and communities, audiences and stakeholders.

We theorised on the importance of an authentic extension of the documentary filmmaker's self in social media, exploring how Jung's ideas of the Persona and Shadow are reflected in the virtual world: people have a real identity, a real self. Corporations do not, they extend a corporate image and brand, lacking personality and depth. (Boyle, 2003) New Realists want more than just a faceless one-sided short-term and superficial online experience. As David Boyle puts it, they want 'the real thing' (Athenticity, 2003). Micro SME's are ideally positioned to develop an online identity that is engaging and highly likely to provide an authentic experience. We discovered that most micro SME documentary production companies have an advantage due to their size over corporations that are struggling to extend a credible online identity. The playing field has become a great deal more equal for micro SME Producers in the field of documentary production.

FUTURE RESEARCH

We illustrated how and why social media matters. We established RVWNM to help micro SME Producers make sense of the way users connect in the virtual world, how real world support can amplify a social media strategy, identify users with high centrality and network density and how to use accurate network intelligence to maximise a social media campaign. Implications of this research indicate that producers willing to engage with social media are more likely to develop a constructive and meaningful relationship with their audiences online as well as via traditional broadcasts. Implementing a viable social media strategy can be cost effective when applying the RVWN-model, which is especially useful to micro SME Producers operating on a small budget. Future research should not only address how social media influences traditional production, funding and distribution, but also explore how social media shapes growth areas within the creative industries, such as Video-on-Demand (VDO) and OT-operators like Netflix.

REFERENCES

W3C. (2015, September 23). *W3C*. Retrieved September 23, 2015, from Semantic Web: http://www.w3.org/standards/semanticweb/

Ahlquist, L., & Shukoff, P. (2015). *YouTube*. Retrieved from Epic Rap Battles of history: https://www.youtube.com/user/ERB

Ahuja, K., Galletta, D., & Carley, D. (2003). Individual centrality and performance in virtual R&D groups: An empirical study. *Management Science*, *49*(1), 21–38. doi:10.1287/mnsc.49.1.21.12756

Ashton, K. (2009, June 22). The Internet of Things Thing. *RFID Journal*.

Bachelor, A. (2015). *Vine*. Retrieved from King Bach: https://vine.co/u/934940633704046592

Balkundi, P., Kilduff, M., & Harrison, D. (2011). Centrality and charisma: Comparing how leader networks and attribution affect team performance. *The Journal of Applied Psychology*, *96*(6), 1209–1222. doi:10.1037/a0024890 PMID:21895351

Ballinger, C. (2015, September 23). *You Tube*. Retrieved September 23, 2015, from Miranda Sings: https://www.youtube.com/user/mirandasings08

Baran, P. (1962). *On Distributed Communications Networks*. Rand.

Berners-Lee, T. (2015, September 14). *World Wide Consortium*. Retrieved September 14, 2015, from Berners-Lee: https://www.w3.org/People/Berners-Lee/

Bjerregaard, M. (2014, March 5). What Indonesians really think about The Act of Killing. *The Guardian*.

Bolt, Beranek, & Newman. (1981). *A History of the ARPANET*. Arlington, VA: BNN, Inc.

Borgatti, S., Brass, A., & Labianca, D. (2009). Network Analysis in Social Sciences. *Science, 323*(5916), 892–895. doi:10.1126/science.1165821 PMID:19213908

Boyle, D. (2003). *Athenticity*. Hammersmith: Harper Collins.

Broersma, M. (2014). *Techweek Europe*. Retrieved from IBM Watson Powers Natural-Language Analytics: http://www.techweekeurope.co.uk/workspace/ibm-watson-analytics-152450

Burt, R., Kilduff, M., & Tasselli, S. (2013). Social networks Analysis: Foundations and frontiers of advantage. *Annual Review of Psychology, 64*(1), 527–547. doi:10.1146/annurev-psych-113011-143828 PMID:23282056

CERN. (2015, September 14). *Berners-Lee posts a summary of the project on alt.hypertext*. Retrieved September 14, 2015, from CERN: http://timeline.web.cern.ch/berners-lee-posts-a-summary-of-the-project-on-althypertext

Cinemalaya. (2012). *Cinemalaya*. (F. Kohle, Producer, & Tiny Little Doclab). Retrieved from Screening Schedule: http://cinemalaya.org/schedules_calendar.htm

Clarke, R. (1994). The digital persona and its application to data surveillance. *The Information Society: An International Journal, 10*(2).

Daft, R., & Lengel, R. (1986). Organisational Information requirements, Media Richness and Structural Design'. *Management Science, 32*(5), 554–571. doi:10.1287/mnsc.32.5.554

Davies, D. W. (1966). *Proposal for a Digital Communication Network*. Retrieved from NPL: www.archive.org/details/NationalPhysicalLaboratoryProposalForADigitalCommunicationNetwork

Democratic Socialist Women of the Philippines. (2010). *Democratic Socialist Women of the Philippines*. (F. Angsioco, Producer). Retrieved from Democratic Socialist Women of the Philippines: https://vimeo.com/105547859

Dropbox. (2009). *Dropbox*. Retrieved from Dropbox: www.dropbox.com

Durkheim, E. (1893). *De la division du travail social: étude sur l'organisation des sociétés supérieures*. Paris: ALCAN.

Emerson, S. L. (1983). Usenet: A Bulletin Board for Unix Users. *Byte Magazine, 8*(10).

Films, K. (2015, Sept. 30). *Indiegogo*. Retrieved Sept. 30, 2015, from Life Itself - A feature documentary based on Roger Ebert's memoir: https://www.indiegogo.com/projects/life-itself-a-feature-documentary-based-on-roger-ebert-s-memoir#/

Freeman, L. C. (1978, January). Centrality in Social Networks Conceptual Clarification. *Social Networks, 1*(3), 215–239. doi:10.1016/0378-8733(78)90021-7

Freeway, F. (2011). *Film Freeway*. Retrieved from Film Freeway: https://filmfreeway.com

Gates, B. (2015, Sept 28). *Digibarn*. Retrieved Sept 28, 2015, from Digibarn - Bill Gates' letter to Hobbyists: http://www.digibarn.com/collections/newsletters/homebrew/V2_01/homebrew_V2_01_p2.jpg

Geohive. (2015). *Geohive.* Retrieved from Geohive - Projected World Population by year 1950-2100: http://www.geohive.com/earth/his_history3.aspx

Google. (2015). *Cloud Storage.* Retrieved from Google: https://cloud.google.com/storage/docs/overview

Google. (2013). *Project Loon.* Retrieved from Google: http://www.google.com/loon/

Greenwald, G. (2014). *The Intercept.* Retrieved from How Covert Agents Infiltrate the Internet to Manipulate, Deceive, and Destroy Reputations: https://firstlook.org/theintercept/2014/02/24/jtrig-manipulation/

Hanoi International Film Festival. (2012). *Hanoi International Film Festival.* (F. Kohle, Producer, & Tiny Little Doclab). Retrieved from Short Documentary & Animation: http://www.haniff.vn/en/giai-thuong-va-ban-giam-khao/ban-giam-khao-phim-truyen/9-main-news/88-short-documentary-animation.html

Huang, H.-Y. (2014). *Self-presentation Tactics in Social Media.* Xiamen University, School of Journalism and Communication. doi:10.2991/icss-14.2014.76

IBC. (2015, Sept 30). *IBC Content Everywhere.* Retrieved Sept 30, 2015, from IBC Content Everywhere Hub Programme: http://www.ibc.org/

IBM. (2015). *Watson Developer Cloud.* Retrieved from Personality Insights: https://watson-pi-demo.mybluemix.net/

IMDB. (2015a). *IMDB.* Retrieved from Koen Suidgeest: http://www.imdb.com/name/nm0837639/

IMDB. (2012). *IMDB.* (F. Kohle, Producer). Retrieved from God, Church, Pills & Condoms: http://www.imdb.com/title/tt2170682

IMDB. (2013). *IMDB.* (J. Oppenheimer, Producer). Retrieved from The Act of Killing: http://www.imdb.com/title/tt2375605/

Indiegogo. (2008). *Indiegogo.* Retrieved from Indiegogo: www.indiegogo.com

Internet Live Stats. (2015, September 15). *Internet Live Stats.* Retrieved September 15, 2015, from Internet Users: http://www.internetlivestats.com/internet-users/#trend

Jarvey, N., & Svetkey, B. (2015). Yes, Hollywood this is your future. Variety, p. 88.

Jenkins, H. W. (2013, April 12). Will Google's Ray Kurzweil Live Forever? *The Wall Street Journal.*

Jonsson, P. (2014). *Ericson Mobility Report.* Ericsson. Ericsson.

Jung, C. (1928). *Two Essays on Analytical Psychology.* London: Baillière, Tindall and Cox.

Jung, C. G. (2011). Die Archetypen und das kollektive Unbewusste. London: Patmos.

Juvonen, J., & Gross, E. F. (2008). Extending the School Grounds?—Bullying Experiences in Cyberspace. *The Journal of School Health, 78*(9), 496–505. doi:10.1111/j.1746-1561.2008.00335.x PMID:18786042

Kameda, T., Ohtsubo, Y., & Takezawa, M. (1997). Centrality in sociocognitive networks and social influence: An illustration in a group decision-making context. *Journal of Personality and Social Psychology, 73*(2), 296–309. doi:10.1037/0022-3514.73.2.296

Kaplan, & Haenlein. (2010). Users of the world, unite! The challenges and opportunities of Social Media. *Science Direct, 53*, 59-68.

Kapp, E. (1877). *Grundlinien einer Philosophie der Technik*. Braunschweig: Westermann.

Karim, J. (2005). *Me at the Zoo*. Retrieved from Youtube: https://www.youtube.com/watch?v=jNQXAC9IVRw

Kickstarter. (2008). *Kickstarter*. Retrieved from Kickstarter: www.kickstarter.com

Kleinrock, L. (2010). *An Early History of the Internet. IEEE Communications Magazine.*

Kleinrock, L. (2011, April 6). *The Day the Infant Internet Uttered its First Words*. Retrieved September 14, 2015, from UCLA: http://www.lk.cs.ucla.edu/internet_first_words.html

Knappenberger, B. (2014, December 30). *Kickstarter*. Retrieved September 17, 2015, from Aaron Swartz Documentary - The Internet's Own Boy: https://www.kickstarter.com/projects/26788492/aaron-swartz-documentary-the-internets-own-boy-0

Kohle, F. (2009). *Tiny Little Doclab*. Retrieved 7 16, 2015, from Facebook: https://www.facebook.com/tinylittledoclab

Kohle, F., & Raj, S. (2015). Implications of Social Media Use in Personal and Professional Settings. In S. M. Vladlena Benson (Ed.), Abuse of the social media brain: Implications for media producers and educators (pp. 102-117)). IGI-Global.

Kohle, F. H. (2015). The Social Media "Information Explosion" Spectacle: Perspectives for Documentary Producers. In J. Sahlin (Eds.), Social Media and the Transformation of Interaction in Society (pp. 173-187). London: Academic Press.

Kozinets, R. (2015). *Netnography: Redefined*. London: SAGE. doi:10.1002/9781118767771.wbiedcs067

Krishnamurthy, B., & Cormode, G. (2008). Key differences between Web 1.0 and Web 2.0. *First Monday, 13*(6).

Kurzweil, R. (2009, April 28). *Youtube*. Retrieved September 15, 2015, from Big Think - Ray Kurzweil: The Coming Singularity: https://www.youtube.com/watch?v=1uIzS1uCOcE

Leibnitz, M. (1703). Essai d'une nouvelle science des nombres. Paris: Académie royale des sciences.

Levy, S. (2001). *Hackers: Heroes of the Computer Revolution*. Penguin.

Licklider, J. (1960). Man-Computer Symbiosis. *IRE Trans. Human Factors in Electronics*, 4-11.

Licklider, J., & Clarke, W. (1962, May). On-line Man `computer Communication.*Spring Joint Comp. Conf.*, 21, 113-28.

Liedtke, M. (2013). *Twitter's Founders Differ On The Creation Of The Social Network*. Retrieved from Huffington Post: http://www.huffingtonpost.com/2013/11/06/twitter-creation-founders_n_4228473.html

Linkedin. (2015). *A brief history of Linkedin*. Retrieved from Linkedin: https://ourstory.linkedin.com/

Littleton, C. (2014, October 15). *Variety*. Retrieved September 23, 2015, from HBO to Launch Standalone Over-the-Top Service in U.S. Next Year: http://variety.com/2014/tv/news/hbo-to-launch-over-the-top-service-in-u-s-next-year-1201330592/

Macaskill, E., & Dance, G. (2013). *The Guardian*. Retrieved from NSA Files decoded: What the revelations mean for you.: http://www.theguardian.com/world/interactive/2013/nov/01/snowden-nsa-files-surveillance-revelations-decoded#section/1

Markoff, J. (2006, November 12). Entrepreneurs See a Web Guided by Common Sense. *New York Times*.

Mason, P. (2015). *Post Capitalism: A Guide to Our Future*. London: Penguin.

Massie, W., & Underhill, C. (1908). The Future of the Wireless Art. *Wireless Telegrpahy and Telephony*, 67-71.

McLuhan, M. (1962). *The Gutenberg Galaxy: The Making of Typographic Man*. Toronto: University of Toronto Press.

Merton, R. (1961). *Phenomenon of independent scientific discoveries*. Academic Press.

Monica, P. L. (2006). *Google to buy YouTube for $1.65 billion*. Retrieved from CNN Money: http://money.cnn.com/2006/10/09/technology/googleyoutube_deal/index.htm?cnn=yes

Nationbuilder. (2015). *Nationbuilder*. Retrieved from Jeff Dunne: http://nationbuilder.com/jeffdunne

Neil, A. (2015, September 23). *ibTV*. (IBC, Producer). Retrieved September 23, 2015, from Facing the Internet Era keynote forum: http://site-73.bcvp0rtal.com/detail/videos/2015-keynotes/video/4501428165001/thursday-facing-the-internet-era-keynote?autoStart=true

Netflix. (2015). *Netflix*. Retrieved from A brief history of Netflix: https://pr.netflix.com/WebClient/loginPageSalesNetWorksAction.do?contentGroupId=10477

Networks, A. M. C. (2015, September 23). *AMZ Networks*. Retrieved September 23, 2015, from Bruce Tucman, President, AMC Global and Sundance Channel Global: http://www.amcnetworks.com/about-us/leadership/bruce-tuchman

Nyce, J., & Kahn, P. (1991). *From Memex to Hypertext - Vannevar Bush and the Mind's Machine*. Academic Press Inc.

Onis, P. d. (2006, September 9). *Skylight Pictures*. Retrieved September 18, 2015, from Quechua 2.0 - A Film Reborn: http://skylight.is/2008/09/quechua-2-0-a-film-reborn/

Onis, P. D. (2009). Documentary Film and Social Networking in Human Rights: Producing and Distributing a Quechua-Language Version of 'State of Fear' in Pero. *Journal of Human Rights Practice, 1*(2), 308–314. doi:10.1093/jhuman/hup010

Ooyala. (2015). *Ooyala*. Retrieved from Ooyala: http://www.ooyala.com/ott-tv

Oppenheimer, J. (2014, February 28). The Act of Killing. (R. Salam, Interviewer). *Vice*.

Partridge, C. (2008, April). The Technical Development of Internet Email. *IEEE Annals of the History of Computing*, 9.

Patienkin, D. (1983). Multiple Discoveries and the Central Message. *American Journal of Sociology*, *89*(2), 306–323. doi:10.1086/227867

Philips, S. (2007). *A brief history of Facebook*. Retrieved from The Guardian: http://www.theguardian.com/technology/2007/jul/25/media.newmedia

Phillips, S. (2007, July 25). A brief History of Facebook. *The Guardian*.

Pilger, J. (2015, Sept. 30). *Indiegogo*. Retrieved Sept. 30, 2015, from John Pilger - The Coming War documentary: https://www.indiegogo.com/projects/john-pilger-the-coming-war-documentary#/

Prensky, M. (2001). Digital Natives, Digital Immigrants Part 1. *On the Horizon*, *9*(5), 1–6. doi:10.1108/10748120110424816

Preston, P. (2002, January 6). Sic transit Andre Neil. *The Observer*.

Random House Dictionary. (2015, September 30). *Dictionary.com*. Retrieved September 30, 2015, from Random House Dictionary: http://dictionary.reference.com/browse/application programming interface

Rosenzweig, R. (1998, December). Wizards, Beureaucrats, Warriors, and Hackers: Writing the History of the Internet. *The American Historical Review*, *103*(5), 1530–1552. doi:10.2307/2649970

RTL Group. (2015, April 9). *RTL Group*. Retrieved September 23, 2015, from RTL Group invests in Clypd: http://www.rtlgroup.com/en/news/2015/15/rtl_group_invests_in_clypd.cfm

Satariano, A. (2014). *WhatsApp's Founder Goes From Food Stamps to Billionaire*. Retrieved from Bloomberg Business: http://www.bloomberg.com/news/articles/2014-02-20/whatsapp-s-founder-goes-from-food-stamps-to-billionaire

Schoen, P. M. (2009). *Der Mensch auf dem Weg der Individuation*. Muenchen: Herbert Utz Verlag.

Shachtman, N. (2010). Exclusive: Google, CIA invest in 'Future' of Web Monitoring. *Wired*.

Sony,U. K. (2015, March 2). *Sony UK*. Retrieved September 23, 2015, from Sony appoints strategic media industry expert to lead European Professional AV & Media solutions marketing team: http://www.sony.co.uk/pro/press/sony-michael-harrit-appointment

Spangler, T. (2015). *Netflix Adds Record 4.9 Million Subscribers in Q1*. Retrieved 7 31, 2015, from Variety: http://variety.com/2015/digital/news/netflix-adds-record-4-9-million-subscribers-in-q1-1201473151/

Statista. (2015a). *Number of monthly active Facebook users worldwide as of 2nd quarter 2015 (in millions)*. Retrieved from Statista: http://www.statista.com/statistics/264810/number-of-monthly-active-facebook-users-worldwide/

Statista. (2015b). *Number of monthly active Twitter users worldwide from 1st quarter 2010 to 2nd quarter 2015 (in millions)*. Retrieved from Statista: http://www.statista.com/statistics/282087/number-of-monthly-active-twitter-users/

Statista. (2015c). *Number of monthly active WhatsApp users worldwide from April 2013 to April 2015 (in millions)*. Retrieved from Statista: http://www.statista.com/statistics/260819/number-of-monthly-active-whatsapp-users/

Statista. (2015d). *Numbers of LinkedIn members from 1st quarter 2009 to 1st quarter 2015 (in millions)*. Retrieved from Statista: http://www.statista.com/statistics/274050/quarterly-numbers-of-linkedin-members/

ten Brink, J. (2014). Joram ten Brink, Personal Communication. *Breda.*

Tiny Little Doclab. (2011). *God, Church, Pills & Condoms*. Retrieved from Indiegogo.com: https://www.indiegogo.com/projects/go-forth-and-multiply-a-documentary/x/243560#/story

Tiny Little Doclab. (2012). *Vimeo*. (A. Cuevas, Producer, & Tiny LIttle Doclab). Retrieved from God, Pills, Church & COndoms: https://vimeo.com/105547859

Tomlinson, R. (2015, September 14). *The First Network Email*. Retrieved September 14, 2015, from Raytheon / BBN: http://www.raytheon.com/news/rtnwcm/groups/public/documents/content/rtn12_tomlinson_email.pdf

Tönnies, F. (1887). Gemeinschaft und Gesellschaft. Leipzig: Fues' Verlag.

Tugend, T. (1969). *UCLA*. Retrieved from UCLA Press: www.lk.cs.ucla.edu/LK/Bib/REPORT/press.html

Venkataramani, V., Green, S., & Schleicher, D. (2010). Well-connected leaders: The impact of leaders' social network ties on LM and members' work attitude. *The Journal of Applied Psychology, 95*(6), 1071–1084. doi:10.1037/a0020214 PMID:20718519

Vladica, F. (2009). *Business Innovation and New Media Practices in Documentary Film Production and Distribution: Conceptual Framework and Review of Evidence*. Retrieved 7 21, 2015, from Digital Value Lab, Rogers Communications Centre: http://www.ryerson.ca/~c5davis/publications/Vladica-Davis%20business%20innovation%20and%20new%20media%20pracitices%20in%20documentaries%20FINAL%2013%20October%2008.pdf

Wells, H. (1938). *World Brain*. Methuen & Co.

Westaby, J., Pfaff, D., & Redding, N. (2014, April). A Dynamic Network Theory Perspective. *The American Psychologist, 69*(3), 269–284. doi:10.1037/a0036106 PMID:24750076

Without a Box. (2011). *Without a box*. Retrieved from Without a box: http://withoutabox.com

Yates, P. (Director). (2005). *Stae of Fear* [Motion Picture].

Youtube. (2015). *Statistics*. Retrieved from Youtube: https://www.youtube.com/yt/press/statistics.html

ZDF. (2015). *Schoene digitale Welt*. Retrieved 7 17, 2015, from Diskussionsveranstaltung Evangelischer Kirchentag 2015: http://www.zdf.de/ZDF/zdfportal/programdata/3c6207e5-5373-4524-870d-7e7c80b6e84f/20443602?generateCanonicalUrl=true

Zuse, D.-I. H. (2015, September 14). *Konrad Zuse*. Retrieved September 14, 2015, from Z1: http://www.konrad-zuse.de/

APPENDIX: WHO MADE THE INTERNET AND WHY? A BRIEF HISTORY

To understand the nature of social media, we need to examine how the technology evolved: for example, without a digital computer, a digital network had nothing to connect to: in 1938 German scientist Konrad Zuse privately funded the development of the Z1: the first digital computer. (Zuse, 2015). Leonard Kleinrock's was the first human to transmit the letters L and O digitally via a network: his account describes how the internet developed and which technological advances had to take place (An Early History of the Internet, 2010) On October 29, 1969, at 10:30pm, Kleinrock transmitted the letters 'log' at a 'blazing speed of 50 kb/s' for the first time via what was then know as Arpanet. After the letters l and o were transmitted the system crashed. This was a key moment in the history of the internet, the only official document of that moment are Kleinrock's hand-written notes (Figure 3).

Kleinrock explains how the Internet was the created by research conducted in education and military domain. Though Ernst Kapp (Grundlinien einer Philosophie der Technik, 1877) already theorised about a global nervous network system originating from the telegraph, and while McLuhan (McLuhan, 1962) speculated on the rise of a global consciousness during the 60-ties, Kleinrock engaged in the practicalities of creating such a network at UCLA. Researching system control in large networks he described in a July 3, 1969 UCLA press release (Tugend, 1969) that as networks continue to grow we will 'see the spread of computer utilities which, like present electric and telephone utilities, will service individual homes and offices across the country'. Preceding Kleinrock, J.C.R Licklider at BNN (Bolt, Beranek, & Newman) established that 'time-sharing' computers were needed to efficiently share computer resources across a network (Man-Computer Symbiosis, 1960). The Defense Advanced Research Projects Agency (DARPA) recognised the importance of large, decentralised networks as a reaction to the threat posed by the then Soviet Union during the cold war period. In 1981 BNN published a report on the first ten years of ARPANET (Bolt, Beranek, & Newman, 1981). The report acknowledges that ARPANET was one of the most successful projects ever undertaken by DARPA, changing how computers were used by the military, education and in public: "Just as the telephone, the telegraph and the printing press had far reaching effects on human intercommunication, the widespread utilization of computer networks which has been catalysed by the ARPENT projects represents a similarly far-reaching change in the of computers by mankind." BNN was not developing ideas on the implementation of large networks alone,

Figure 3. Kleinrock's hand-written note
Source: The Day the Infant Internet Uttered its First Words, 2011.

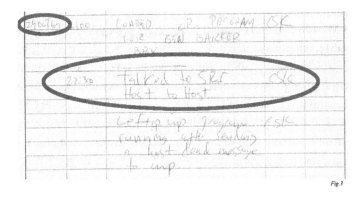

UCLA was developing similar ideas, for example Leonard Kleinrock's Phd thesis focused on transmission protocols for time-sharing networks: Ideas for the then 'future Internet' surfaced at the same time with a number of researchers and organisations, highlighting how ideas surface simultaneously in science. While Kleinrock was busy investigating how to effectively switch in large networks at MIT, Paul Baran at the RAND Corporation was working on the idea to establish a large, decentralised network for military purposes during the cold war (On Distributed Communications Networks, 1962). In 1962 Licklider joined the Advanced Research Projects Agency (ARPA) and predecessor to DARPA, and established a team of technologists nicknamed 'The Intergalactic Network' to develop advanced networks supporting social interactions online (Licklider & Clarke, 1962). Baran and Kleinrock understood the importance of a digital network but the mathematical foundations were laid by Leibniz (Essai d'une nouvelle science des nombres, 1703) almost 250 years preceding Barans publication in 1962: we notice that the invention and establishment of the internet is not a single event that can be described from a single perspective. Technologists such as Kleinrock and Baran describe the scientific advances in detail, but the evolution and epistemology of the internet, or the idea of it, can be traced back to Kapp, with Leibniz providing a mathematical model enabling Kleinrock and Baran to develop and implement programming languages for a digital network.

Kleinrock opens his paper 'History of Communications' describing how Nikola Tesla foresaw a technology that would allow 'a business man in New York to dictate instructions, and have them instantly appear in type at his office in London or elsewhere'. (Massie & Underhill, 1908) He refers to H.G. Wells who described a 'world-brain' (1938), and Vannevar Bush' conception of the Memex, a form of online encyclopaedia. (Nyce & Kahn, 1991). To illustrate further how ideas of a large, global network developed simultaneously and independent from each other is illustrated by the work of Donald Davies at the National Physics Laboratory (NPL) in the UK. Davis was working on the question of information distribution via networks and earns the credit to have coined the term 'packet' for small amounts of information transmitted via large networks in 1965. (Proposal for a Digital Communication Network, 1966). Licklider, Baran, Kleinrock, Davies and The Intergalactic Network-team: all developed ideas at a similar moment in time, exchanging and building on each other's ideas at conferences and via various publications. Kleinrock points out in the opening of his paper 'An Early History of the Internet' that we do not know 'why the specific events, people, and circumstances that formed the internet when they did'. Jung's idea on the collective unconscious explains how ideas form in this way: synchronicity makes plausible how events, which are not connected by cause and effect, occur at the same time (Jung C. G., 2011 edition). Working empirically, Jung established what he termed the collective unconscious (Jung C. G., 2011 edition), theorising that civilisations and cultures develop similar ideas when reaching a certain level of development. History is littered with inventions and discoveries evolving independently from each other. Robert Merton contends that all discoveries are multiple (Phenomenon of independent scientific discoveries, 1961), whereas Don Patinkin argues that not all are multiple discoveries (Multiple Discoveries and the Central Message, 1983). Jung provides a reasonable explanation regarding these phenomena from a psychological perspective, a framework that is not discussed by technologists or ethnographers exploring this topic. The idea of the collective unconscious is very relevant to our research into social media, as the establishment of ARPANET and the Internet is resulting in the formation of a global consciousness. Groups, Tribes, Nations not only require culture, but also ethical guidelines determined by a collective consciousness (Durkheim, 1893). French sociologist Emile Durkheim developed the idea that societies share a set of shared beliefs, ideas and moral attitudes. The Internet and social media are, for the first time in the history of mankind, establishing a digital technology platform making possible a collective global consciousness, with the potential to connect to everyone and everything on earth at unprecedented speed.

Chapter 12
The Role of Social Media in Shaping Marketing Strategies in the Airline Industry

Deniz Akçay
İstanbul Gelişim University, Turkey

ABSTRACT

Tourism is one of the leading sectors based on other people's views and comments found on the Internet. Prior to deciding where they would like to go, individuals obtain information about the travel agencies they will use, the hotels they will stay at and the regions they would like to visit, plus the views and experiences of others in terms of these issues, which are largely shared via social media environments. Accordingly, it has become a necessity for establishments to follow the main social media platforms, such as Facebook, Twitter, Instagram and so on, and develop their goods and services in line with the comments shared on these platforms. In this study, how national and international airline companies implement the 4Ps of marketing (product, price, place, promotion) in social media environments is investigated through examples and analysed through data obtained via interviews.

INTRODUCTION

With the adaptation of the Internet to mobile devices, social media applications have become a part of smart phones and tablets. Today, social media has come to be positioned as a separate marketing tool from the Internet. Blackshaw and Nazzaro (2004) stated that social media is consumer-gererated and that various online information sources, which are created, are employed by users to educate one another on other brands, services and various issues (as cited in Mangold & Faulds, 2009)

Kane, Alavi, Labianca and Borgatti (2004) stated that although social media has adapted to the majority of users, social media applications have organizational purposes that take priority, such as marketing and information management.

DOI: 10.4018/978-1-5225-0559-4.ch012

Leonardi and Et al. define social media as external parties that enable communication with customers, salespeople and the public through various platforms, such as Facebook, Twitter and MySpace (Leonardi, Huysman, & Steinfeld, 2013). In the digital world, users follow brands they like and are interested in, and that the groups formed by these brands come together on a common platform in support of the brands. For instance, there are groups that are interested in certain brands and brand communities, such as Harley Davidson or Volkswagen, which have been created on the Internet environment. Kucuk (2009) stated that these new customer groups, defined as brand communities, put pressure on the brand to re-evaluate brand management, which has been grounded in basic disciplines for years (as cited in Quinton, 2013). Jevons et al. (2005) stated that brands are no longer passive agents, and that through consumers who provide input via online brand communities, in particular, brands exist as a partially independent from the market (as cited in Quinton, 2013).

According to a study conducted by Tomoson Research Institute (2015), consumers are increasingly using the Internet and social media to inform their preferences and purchases because of the influencers. In light of these results, it can be stated that the importance of social media in the service sector will gradually increase. Establishments within the service sector are able to reach more people through social media. Customers make great use of the Internet and social media in order to conduct research, evaluate alternatives, select/purchase products and broadcast behaviours displayed after purchasing in the area of airline transportation, which constitutes an important part in the service sector.

In this study, social media will be investigated through the lens of the historical development of marketing, and then evaluated in its use in airline marketing. In the section entitled Main Focus of the Chapter, we will evaluate how Turkish Airlines and Emirates use social media; their social media accounts and websites will be analysed and compared to the interviews conducted with the social media managers of both airline companies. Based on our analysis, we will evaluate how Emirates and Turkish Airlines use the 4P elements of marketing (*product, price, place, promotion*) in their social media marketing. According to our analysis, both airline firms use all product elements in order to improve their services. In addition, they use the *place* element to make sales through the Internet and the *price* element to give information about ticket prices. These airline firms also use another 4P component, *promotion*, to effectively advertise and promote products on social media platforms.

BACKGROUND

For establishments in competitive environments, which are shaped by information communication technologies, marketing is as important as the quality of goods and services. Today, with developments in the areas of industry, science and technology, the competition environment has increased even more. It has become a necessity to analyse the target groups and understand rivals in this competition environment. This entails the planning of marketing that uses new scientific methods. McCarthy created the concept of the 4Ps in order to show how to begin marketing during this process of change and within the overbearing competition environment; and through which stages it should move and be promoted (as cited inAnderson &Taylor, 1995:5) McCarthy defined the 4Ps as price, product, place and promotion.

Constantinides (2006) stated that the original marketing mix is based on the 12 controllable marketing elements (goods, pricing, branding, distribution channels, individual sales, advertising, promotion, packaging, exhibition, service, physical distribution, data collection and analysis), which have been defined by Neil Borden as result of "profitable business operation." Constantinides (2006) stated that McCarthy later on condensed these factors developed by Borden into four elements (product, price, promotion, place) and conceptualized these four elements into a marketing model (Constantinides, 2006: 408)

"Philip Kotler (1986) suggested an expansion of 4Ps to include 'power' and 'public relations', so he emphasized the growing importance of the exercise of 'power' and 'public relations', with traditional targets (i.e., consumer and the trade) and others with whom the typical marketer might have less experience (i.e., labor unions, government agencies, special interest groups, etc.)" (as cited in Anderson & Taylor, 1995, p. 5). Anderson and Taylor stated that Kotler's power and public relations argument is particularly important in the international market. Kotler (1994) defined his marketing management as analysis, planning, implementation and control and emphasized how important public relations is in marketing management (as cited in Anderson & Taylor, 1995, p. 5). Kotler argued, "[a] more basic criticism has been that the 4Ps represent the seller's mind-set, not the buyer's mind-set" (2003, p. 109). "The inclusion of product policy and channel policy, as well as market research, as part of the 'plan behind the campaign' was essential in the 4Ps type of idea and distinguished it from sales management or sales force management" (Usui, 2008, p. 16). Dann (2011) argued, "4P represents those elements of marketing that are controllable and can be manipulated by marketing managers to ensure the maximum appeal of their campaign" (as cited in Wasan & Tripathi, 2014, p. 128).

The purpose in the *goods* part is to develop goods or services that are marketable. Within this framework, the elements that should be considered in terms of goods or services are branding, functionality, shape, variety, name, packaging, guarantee, quality and reliability. Within the scope of *pricing*, aspects include how the goods are to be marketed with suitable prices (e.g., pricing strategies, price reductions, loans). In the *promotion* section, activities include brand positioning, advertising and public relations in order to encourage the target group to purchase the goods or services. In the area of *distribution*, companies need to decide through which channels goods or services will be transported to the target groups.

In the Internet environment, it is possible for target groups to perceive or feel the characteristics of goods or services as if in real life. Companies are able to share quality visuals of their goods or services with their customers through technology. Talpau (2014) stated that the Internet environment presents opportunities for establishments to sell their goods or services, and separated these goods and services into three basic categories:

1. Physical or tangible products, such as clothing, books, electronics, and furniture.
2. Intangible products/services, such as tickets, travel insurance, and holidays.
3. Digitized products, such as electronic books and software products.

AIRLINE MARKETING AND SOCIAL MEDIA

Today, creating technical solutions to the problems faced by customers and achieving superiority in terms of competition are not sufficient for establishments to increase their market share and achieve continuity. In order to be competitive and increase customer loyalty, establishments must provide the service during the process and afterwards. Within this framework, service marketing plays a significant role for establishments to prove themselves on the international platform. There are certain criterion that are used in defining services, as outlined below (Murdick, Render, & Russell, 1990):

- Services are intangible and provide benefits to those who purchase them.
- Customers also participate in the production of services.
- Services provide variable benefits that are not standard.
- There is a great amount of communication between the producer and customers during the service process.
- Services cannot be stored; they are consumed the moment they are produced.
- Pricing options are more detailed.
- The measuring of service quality is subjective.
- Service production is labour intensive.
- Mass production cannot be performed for services.
- Quality control is basically limited with process control.
- Service production and consumption take place at the same time.
- Services cannot be protected with patents.

Marketing plans are generally constructed around the traditional 4Ps (price, product, place, promotion). However, when services begin to position themselves as a marketing tool, an additional 3Ps (personnel, physical facilities, process management) are added to the process (Magrath, 1986). *Personnel* is about the external appearance of the people providing the service; for instance, whether they are cheerful. *Process management* is how the service is provided (i.e., its speed, quality, cleanliness) and *physical facilities* is everything about the physical place, such as the ambiance of the decoration, and the premises' cleanliness and lighting. "The sub-discipline of service(s) marketing is recognized as having a mid–late-20th-century origin" (Baron,and et al. 2014, p. 150).Service marketing cannot be seen, tasted or touched, unlike other tangible goods and other types of marketing. "The rationale for a separate treatment of services marketing centers on the existence of a number of characteristics of services which are consistently cited in the literature: intangibility, inseparability of production and consumption, heterogeneity, and perishability" (Zeithaml, et al. 1985, p. 33).

According to the *process* aspect of the 3P characteristics of service marketing, the quality, layover and cleanliness of airlines, food, beverages, accommodation, finance, health, etc., which are services that can benefit from service marketing, influence the perception of target groups about them. For instance, the 90-second service time at McDonald's for all its customers in cars is a determining factor of its service performance (Lund & Marinova, 2014).

The main purpose of airline services, as mentioned earlier, is to provide passengers with safe and comfortable flights and allow them to reach their desired destination on time. Additionally, passengers expect to receive quality service, be greeted by cheerful personnel and travel in a safe and comfortable manner, in return for the price they pay. Regarding airline services, passengers assess the quality of the service in accordance with how the service is provided. Therefore, airline companies can obtain information about the quality of the services they provide through feedback from passengers. Airline companies that give priority to service quality make changes to their service in line with the expectations of customers. Sickert (2010) stated that airline marketing teams' primary strategy is the immediate operational readiness in their relationship with customers and that service facilities, such as check-in counters, ticket offices, lounge spaces and back offices, are all assessed by customers. Therefore, airline customers will give certain advantages to airline companies that meet their expectations. Shaw (2007) stated that the segmentation of the airline passenger market is based on three traditional variables, and defined these as the purpose of the passenger's journey, the length of their journey and their country or culture of origin. More specifically, Shaw stated the following:

- The purpose of airline passengers' journey can be classified as business or leisure, where the ticket fees of those who go on business journeys are paid by the companies they work for, whereas those who go on leisure journeys either work in smaller companies or freelance.
- Journeys that take place within continents and those that are intercontinental differ. While services, such as the comfort of the seats or quality of the food, are more important in airline experiences within continents, flight experience is more important for intercontinental flights. The number of international passengers must be taken into consideration when assessing the quality of intercontinental flights. As Petrevska stated, "international tourist arrivals reached 1,138 million in 2014 (a 4.7% increase over 2013), while the number of overnight visitors reached 1,138 million in 2014 (51 million more than in 2013)" (Petrevska, 2015, p. 263).
- Passengers from different cultures have different needs. For example, most people in northwest Europe or North America would recognize a stereotypical 'business traveller' as someone who is middle-aged, soberly dressed and carrying only a small amount of baggage.

Lovelock and Wright (1999) stated that although services involve elements such as seats, food or repair of damaged equipment, service performance is essentially intangible, and the perceived value is derived from the performance. For instance, Lovelock and Wright (1999) stated that Southwest Airlines follows a low-priced airline ticket strategy and has established a culture in which employees try to perform their roles at as low cost to the airline as possible. According to Southwest Airlines' Annual Reports from 1996–1999, the airline company has used only Boeing 737 and 350 vehicle fleets, thus simplifying their operations and reducing costs (as cited in Lovelock and Wright, 1999). The reports also revealed that Southwest Airlines provides transportation for the basic needs of passengers. The reports stated that the passengers had not encountered any surprises concerning unreserved seats, flights not having menus, and a lack of baggage transfer service to other airlines. It is also stated that Southwest is characterised by safe flights and cheerful employees, and creates value in this manner.

Today, many companies determine and implement strategies through social media, in terms of public relations, customer relationship management, customer loyalty, marketing, and so on. While social media environments, which play an important role in increasing brand recognition and allowing brands to connect with large audiences, they also allow brands to connect with the correct target group. Social media platforms, which are among the most important marketing strategies of brands today, are important in creating a quality brand perception. When brands are joined with the contexts they create, social media and other communication channels become more effective in connecting with the target groups. "Social media should be serving a company's previously established strategic marketing plan as a successful channel integrated among other communications channels ranging from radio and print advertising to the customer service person answering the phone" (Reid, 2015, p. 27). In terms of how companies use social media, Deutsch stated that the problem with the use of social media is that companies treat it as a marketing tool; what is important in social media is understanding what people are saying, and instead of selling them something, communicating with them should be the main purpose (as cited in Reid, 2015). Brands that interact with target groups and answer their questions and views create a positive perception among those groups. Social media environments play an effective role in transmitting the voice of brands to the correct target groups in the most efficient manner. Therefore, it is important for brands to analyse their social media performance and determine their strategies in line with certain criteria by evaluating the results they achieve. Schlinke and Crain (2013) listed the following priorities of companies in their use of social media:

- To establish a reputation as thought leaders in their subject area,
- To be the source of current, relevant news around a topic,
- To make the members of the organization more accessible and create more robust relationships with existing clients, and/or
- To extend the current brand as one serving a specific demographic.

The greatest advantage social media provides, in terms of brand recognition, is that it allows for word-of-mouth (wom) communication. "The brands have realized that, by establishing a close and long-term relationship between their brands and consumers, and by converting the latter into brand ambassadors willing to support the brand in obtaining new clients through WOM, they would be able to achieve economical advantages" (Blackstone, 2000; Dowling, 2002; Reichheld, 1996; Winer, 2001, as cited in Barreto, 2013, p. 632).

Kates (2004) and Muñiz-O'Guinn (2001) argued that social media communities of which consumers are a part of during the postmodern process of production can be seen as tribes; through the sharing views, organizations and promotions by these tribes, the value of communities increases and a contribution is made to their existence (as cited in Csordas & Gati, 2014). Piskorski (2011) posited that a social media strategy differs largely from a digital marketing communications strategy (as cited in Csordas & Gati, 2014). The use of social media is increasing throughout the world. For instance, according to the Pew Research Center, 71% of adults used Facebook and 23% used Twitter in 2014. It is stated that "[c]hances are, your potential customers are on one or both of these sites" (as cited in Reid, 2015, p. 28).

Due to the rapid access to information afforded by the Internet, consumers can shape their travel plans using social media. In this aspect, the Internet and, in particular, social media have become platforms from which users obtain references on tourism. "Generally, travelers place a high degree of trust in their social media networks – information is gathered and synthesized from other travelers" (Popesku, 2014, p. 717). Toh and Raven (2003) stated that as the Internet has begun to be used in the airline sector passengers have been able to purchase flight tickets on the Internet, and that customers who purchase their tickets using the Internet are usually cost-conscious and non-business passengers.

Social media plays a special role in the activities of destination marketing organizations. Destinations marketers can use social media before (e.g., to inspire, inform, engage), during (e.g., to facilitate at the destination) and after travel (e.g., to remember, share and engage) (Popesku, 2014). Nick Smith, investment director at Scottish Widows Investment Partnership woe deals with logistics warehouses at major UK airports, including London Heathrow, has stated that he can only see social media use – such as Facebook, Twitter and LinkedIn – growing in the airfreight industry (Solomon, 2014). However, VanAuken (2015) stated that social media is not extensive or supplementary in marketing strategies and that it is an effective tool in the recognition of airline companies' brands and promotion of key services. With the expansion of information communication technologies, airline companies have begun using these technologies in an effective manner. Peterson stated that "[w]hile many airports still use cameras solely for security purposes, video analytics and other technologies, e.g., bar coded boarding pass tracking, Bluetooth, thermal sensors, and Wi-Fi are being introduced in airports across the globe to monitor customer habits and use that data to improve their overall experience" (2012, p. 1).

According to the 12th annual SITA/Airline Business IT Trends Survey (2015), 129 airline companies stated that 25.8% of 40.8% of tickets they sold were purchased on the Internet, 10.7% were bought through call centres and 4.3% were sold interlining tickets (Eye for Travel, 2015). Additionally, the SITA/Airline Business IT Trend Survey announced that 86% of airline companies provide service through social media and, by the end of 2017, 86% will be using social media for their promotions. The report also stated that as of 2017, 80% of airline companies will make their announcements via social media and 73% will provide customer service in the same manner, while 61% of airline companies will provide the opportunity for their passengers to check in over Facebook and 65% will be providing ticket sales and services over social media (SITA, 2015).

MAIN FOCUS OF THE CHAPTER

Airline companies currently, and will continue, to use social media effectively. A general look at the use of social media by airline companies reveals that they communicate with customers by answering the latter's questions and suggestions via social media. In addition, airline companies have reservation buttons on their social media accounts with the purpose of facilitating their customers' purchase activities via social media environments, in particular through their Facebook pages. It is also observed that airline companies follow the positive or negative comments made via social media and develop their goods or services accordingly, using the *product* characteristic of the 4Ps. In addition, while using the *place* characteristic of the 4Ps to sell tickets on the Internet and using the Internet as a distribution channel of their services, they use the *price* characteristic to broadcast information via social media about the prices of flight tickets. The other aspect of the 4Ps, *promotion*, which is the activity of advertising and public relations for the promotion of goods/services, is used actively on social media by airline companies. Additionally, as mentioned earlier, the 3Ps (personnel, physical facilities and process management) were developed as a complement to the 4Ps for the service sector and is added to this chaos as well. The *personnel* characteristic is about the external appearance of the people providing the service, such as whether they are cheerful; *process management* is about how the service is presented (e.g. its speed, quality, cleanliness); and *physical facilities* is everything about the physical place, such as its decoration, ambiance, cleanliness and lighting. Within the 3Ps, it is observed that airline companies reflect in particular the characteristics of *process management* and *personnel* through the videos and photographs they share on social media regarding the quality and speed of service and photographs that display the cheerfulness of their personnel.

In this study, the social media representatives of international airline companies such as Air France, Qatar, Virgin Atlantic, Swiss Airlines, Aeroflot Russia, Emirates and Turkish Airlines were sent questions regarding how they use social media. John Saydam, the social media representative of Emirates Airlines, and İnanç Emre Albayrak, the social media representative of Turkish Airlines, Turkey's national airline company, answered the questions.

The questions sent to the airline company representatives included whether they follow the comments posted on social media, share all of the comments they see regarding their organisation, and communicate with their customers over social media, and whether they have developed any goods or services within the framework of the comments on social media. In this study, we analysed the Facebook, Twitter and Instagram accounts of Emirates and Turkish Airlines to determine how they use social media. In addition, we analysed the official websites of both airline companies and evaluated the policies they implemented over social media in terms of service marketing.

Emirates Airlines, which is based in Dubai, UAE (United Arab Emirates), was founded in 1985. It assets include 229 planes, and it offers two service types, First Class and Business Class. It flies to over 140 points in six continents, informs its customers of discount flights through a "special offers" button on its website, and rewards customers with flight points through its Emirates Skyward and Business Rewards cards.

Emirates operates an exclusively wide-bodied aircraft fleet, consisting of three aircraft families: A330/340, A380 and Boeing 777. Reflecting the nature of Emirates operations with no real short haul network, it is one of only nine airlines to operate an all wide-body aircraft fleet, and it is now the largest in the World in terms of scheduled international passenger-kilometres flown (http://www.airreview. com/Emirates/Fleet.htm). Emirates keeps its customers informed through special buttons such as *online check-in, baggage status, check flight status, planning and reservation* and *special offers* on its corporate website. The airline uses Facebook, Twitter and Instagram, as well as other social media environments.

While Emirates provides information about its flight routes and planes in general on Facebook, it also informs customers about activities using this medium. Emirates, which has received 4,828,170 likes on Facebook, shares videos and photographs about its planes, flight schedules, activities and countries with users. Using its *book a flight* button on its Facebook page, users are able to make a reservation with the click of a button without having to go to the Emirates website. The company has 560,000 followers on its Twitter account, through which it again shares information, videos and photographs about its sponsored activities, flight schedules, planes and countries, similar to its Facebook page. Emirate's Instagram account has 645,000 followers. Through Instagram, Emirates shares various visuals about its planes, flight schedules, activities and countries, similar to its Facebook and Twitter accounts.

In general, Emirates' social media shows that the airline company provides information about its A380 and Boeing 777 planes and cabin crew; through sharing context about its investments, it shows its customers that it is one of the leading international airline companies. Emirates approaches consumers candidly, as can be seen from its social media promotion activities. Similar to how social media users share their experiences in the form of videos and photographs, Emirates allows its customers to get to know its brand through a fictionalized story presented through videos and photographs (http://bethere. emirates.com/globalista/jeremy-christine). In the fictional story, titled Culture & Vultures, as seen in Figure 2, two members of the cabin crew named Jeremy and Christine share their cultural experiences regarding the destinations they have been to through videos and photographs on Emirates' social media pages (see Figure 1). Jeremy and Christine's sharing of images in the Culture&Vultures applications is similar to the Periscope and Swarm applications. In the Periscope application, users share videos recorded from their own point of view with other users around the world. Swarm is a mobile app which allow to users share their locations in social media platforms. People who watch these videos can share them in other social media environments. In a similar manner, Jeremy and Christine share videos of countries they go to with users via social media. The Foursquare application allows users to check in at places they go to and are awarded with titles, such as "mayor" or "being adventurous", in line with the number of check-ins.

For the last 19 years, Emirates has shared with its customers information about its investments in the Boeing 777 programme; it supports business and innovation in the USA, as illustrated through the information it provides over Facebook and Twitter (see Figure 3). Similarly, the airline company gives information on the A380, thus informing its customers about the safety of its planes, as seen in Figures 4, 5, 6.

Emirates sponsors sports events and announces these sponsorships via social media. Its most important sponsorship has been the Rugby World Cup, which it has continually sponsored since 2007. The purpose of the Rugby World Cup sponsorship, which Emirates first sponsored in 2007 in France, is to

Figure 1. Jeremy and Christine adventures on Emirates Facebook page

preserve the basic values of the sport; the airline company expends efforts to enrich the experiences of rugby fans throughout the world (http://www.emirates.com/ac/english/about/emirates-sponsorships/rugby/rugby.aspx).

Emirates aims to increase the experiences of fans by interacting with them on social media through various activities, as seen Figure 7; the company has shared clues with its users on social media outlets, such as Facebook, Twitter and Instagram, in order for the flag of Cardiff, a city in Wales, to be included in the Rugby World Cup organization with the rugby star James Hook (Griffiths, 2015).

Figure 2. Emirates website

Figure 3. Information about Boeing 777 on Emirates Facebook page

Figure 4. Information about A380 on Emirates Facebook page

Figure 5. Information about A380 on Emirates Twitter page

Figure 6. Information about A380 on Emirates Instagram account

Figure 7. #emiratesflag hashtag search on Twitter

Emirates announced through the #BringingRugbyHome hashtag, created on its Facebook page for the Rugby World Cup organization, that it would be giving away various prizes to users through a competition; users were able to participate by posting photographs taken during the organization (2015).

Through the activity "Share Your Passion", Emirates asked its followers on Instagram to take selfies with the Cardiff flag, which the company placed in various parts of the world, similar to how James Hook had done with his own flag, as seen Figure 8, and send these to the company between the 9:00AM–9:00 PM timeframe. The person with the best photograph won the opportunity to be the team captain in the Rugby World Cup.

In the interview with John Saydam, Emirates Group's Social Media Department official, he stated that Emirates actively uses both its own websites and social media accounts. Saydam, who stated that Emirates actively communicates with its customers on social media platforms, said the company follows all comments made about Emirates on social media and tries to develop its services accordingly. For instance, he stated that the company has developed services such as *delay notification, exact notifications for customers about ticket reservation, selling, cancellation and refund, lost and damaged baggage, customer relationship management, special day offers and discounts (e.g., honeymoon, birthday, festival, the New Year)* and *VIP service on the plane,* in accordance with comments made on social media. Saydam also stated that the company obtains the views of its customers about Emirates through social media. Saydam stated that Emirates interacts with customers on its website through initiatives such as *games, special day offers, contact forms,* etc. and that the website is updated every 15 days.

Figure 8. Cardiff flag selfies on Instagram

As a result, Emirates develops its own services in the *product* 4P area using comments shared on social media. In addition, its customers' purchasing of tickets and making reservations via its website shows that the airline company uses the Internet, the 4P characteristic area, *place,* for the distribution of goods and services and that its customers save time in such processes as purchasing tickets and following up on baggage. Emirates also underlines how high quality its *goods* are through the videos and photographs it shares about its planes' characteristics.

Turkish Airlines, which is the first national airline company of Turkey, was founded in 1933. Turkish Airlines has 267 planes. With its Miles & Smiles card, customers can gain flight points, and the airline presents three types of flights: Economy, Comfort and Business Class. Turkish Airlines shares its flight information and menu information with customers prior to, during and after flights. Through the online services menu of its website, Turkish Airlines' passengers can manage and view missing luggage, flight reservations, online check-ins, take-off and landing hours, the reservations; additionally, they can learn about the reward points they have earned with their Miles & Smiles cards. Through the Turkish Airlines corporate menu, customers can retrieve information on the company's vision and mission, history, business partners and investor relationships.

On its corporate website, Turkish Airlines defines the strategy it follows in terms of being a global brand as a worldwide sponsorship activity and states that it sponsors sports, which attract the most attention, in order to increase its brand recognition Turkish Airlines generally sponsors world-famous football teams, such as Barcelona and Manchester United. According to a news article published on September 22, 2015 in the Economy section of *Milliyet*, one Turkey's national newspapers, Turkish Airlines will be sponsoring Rome at a cost of 7 million euros annually (*Milliyet*, 22.09.2015).

Turkish Airlines has received 7,103,888 likes on its Facebook page. The airline generally provides information about ticket prices of flight destinations (as seen in Figures 9 and 10), various social activities (Figure 11), countries, favourite cities in Turkey (as seen in Figure 12) and various foods that belong to the Turkish culture (as seen in Figures 13 and 14). The Turkish Airlines Facebook page has a *make a reservation* button; however, there is no reservation button on the airline's English Facebook page.

Figure 9. Information about ticket prices on Turkish Airlines Facebook page

Figure 10. Information about ticket prices on Turkish Airlines Twitter page

Figure 11. Information about Venice Film Festival on Turkish Airlines Facebook page

Figure 12. Information about Cappadocia on Turkish Airlines Facebook page

Figure 13. Information about mooncake on Turkish Airlines Twitter page

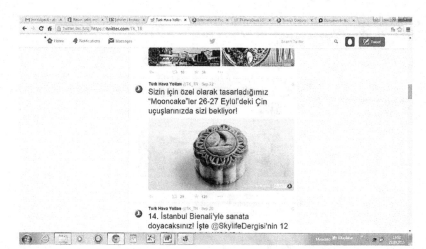

Figure 14. Information about cheese stuffed pastry on Turkish Airlines Facebook page

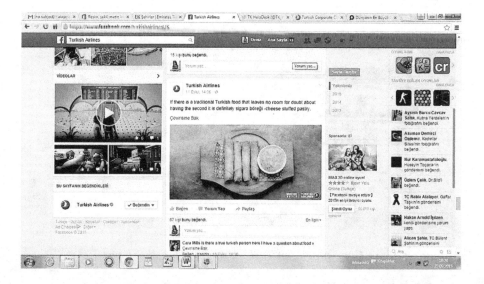

Turkish Airlines has 894,000 followers on its official Twitter account. On this account, the airline provides information about ticket prices of flight destinations, various social activities, countries, favourite cities in Turkey and various foods that belong to Turkish culture, similar to its Facebook page. However, the use of its Twitter account in English, as well, will allow Turkish Airlines to reach more users. Additionally, the airline has a total of 10,800 followers on its "TK Help Support" twitter account. Turkish Airlines generally provides information about cancelled flights to its customers via this Twitter account.

Turkish Airlines does not have an Instagram account that is actively used. However, in 2014, Turkish Airlines sponsored five foreign Instagram photographers with the purpose of sharing their Istanbul-themed photographs on social media to increase recognition of Istanbul worldwide. Within the #InstaMeetTK0001 project, photographers took photographs of Istanbul from 11 different points.

In the interview carried out with Turkish Airlines social media manager, İnanç Emre Albayrak, he stated that the company constantly interacts with its customers regarding different topics, such as games or offers about special days, via social media.

Albayrak stated that the company has an official who answers the comments made on social media, and that it shares all positive/negative comments regarding interactions with the Turkish Airlines personnel on social media. He stated that the company constantly interacts with its customers through its corporate website in different contexts (e.g., games, offers on special days, communication forms) and that it also communicates with customers through e-mail. Albayrak also explained that Turkish Airlines obtains the views of its customers through telephone calls, surveys, observation and social media.

Thus, Turkish Airlines, in general, *places* importance on its sponsorship and promotional activities with leading sports teams throughout the world. Additionally, the airline does not use social media to develop its good or services, as Emirates does. Turkish Airlines uses the 4P *price* aspect through the information it provides on flight prices. In addition, Turkish Airlines does not actively use social media to reach target groups/customers, as it does not have an active Instagram account and its twitter accounts are only in Turkish.

SOLUTIONS AND RECOMMENDATIONS

Companies in the service sector, particularly airline companies, can earn more in the future by following developing technology trends and especially using these as a marketing tool, which lowers information communication technology costs. However, there are certain points that airline companies need to take into consideration, in terms of being more productive in their use of the Internet and social media.

Firstly, airline companies should make social media icons visible on their websites and allow these icons to give users direct access to their social media accounts. In addition, messages transmitted through social media should be translated into English, which will create an opportunity to interact with tourists. Incentivising airline companies' customers with various prizes for sharing photographs, videos or information from their social media accounts will allow companies to reach other customers as well. Additionally, airline companies should make the necessary updates to keep their social media accounts active at all times. Providing options, such as allowing customers to purchase flight tickets, make reservations via social media accounts and carry out other processes without accessing the airline companies' official sites, will positively affect the companies' sales. Lastly, airline companies can increase their number of followers through special offers announced via social media.

FUTURE RESEARCH DIRECTIONS

In order for customers to benefit from social media and mobile applications, in terms of airline service marketing, customers need to use both their mobile applications and social media in a much simpler manner. Within this framework, creation of related applications in accordance with users' perceptions of users will allow service marketing to benefit much more effectively from the Internet. Accordingly, future research should evaluate how airline companies use their websites, social media platforms and mobile applications through experimental observation of a selected focus group. The data obtained can be evaluated in line with the ISO 9241 principles, which are international standards developed with the purpose of facilitating the use of computers. According to Bevan (2006), these standards, especially parts 10 through 17, include requirements and recommendations for creating the most ergonomic features for users. (as cited in Akçay, 2013:51-52). Below are examples of such ISO 9241 principles:

Part 10 - ISO 9241-10 (1996) Dialogue Principles: This part deals with general ergonomic principles, which apply to the design of dialogues between humans and information systems: suitability for the task, suitability for learning, suitability for individualization, conformity with the user expectations, self-descriptiveness, controllability, and error tolerance.

Part 12 - ISO 9241-12 (1998) Presentation of Information: This part contains specific recommendations for presenting and representing information on visual displays. It includes guidance on ways of representing complex information by using alphanumeric and graphical/symbolic codes, screen layout, and design, as well as windows.

Part 13 - ISO 9241-13 (1998) User Guidance: This part provides recommendations for the design and evaluation of user guidance attributes of software user interfaces, including prompts, feedback, status, on-line help and error management.

Part 14 - ISO 9241-14 (1997) Menu Dialogues: This part provides recommendations for the ergonomic design of menus used in user–computer dialogues. The recommendations cover menu structure, navigation, option selection and execution, as well as menu presentation (e.g., by various techniques including windowing, panels, buttons, fields).

Part 15 - ISO 9241-15 (1997) Command Dialogues: This part provides recommendations for the ergonomic design of command languages used in user–computer dialogues. The recommendations cover command language structure and syntax, command representations, input and output considerations, as well as feedback and help.

Part 16 - ISO 9241-16 (1999) Direct Manipulation Dialogues: This part provides recommendations for the ergonomic design of direct manipulation dialogues and includes manipulation of objects, and design of metaphors, objects and attributes. It covers those aspects of graphical user interfaces that are directly manipulated and not covered by other parts of ISO 9241.

CONCLUSION

Today, the Internet and, in particular, social media has become an inevitable part of marketing. Some aspects that make social media the strongest in marketing include: its low cost, the speed at which information is expanded and updated, its honest environment, the ability to understand target groups and the reliability of information provided by references.

The development of Web 2.0 technology and users being able to comment on all types of news has allowed companies to follow comments on social media; thus, listening to and analysing the target groups/users is quite important for establishments, in terms of creating their strategies and implementing them. As mentioned earlier, consumers decide how to shape their travel plans over social media using the Internet. The Internet and, in particular, social media have become platforms through which users can obtain information in the area of tourism. Among the most basic reasons for this are that online communities have an efficient role in the lives of their members and give an important "reference group" service for the participants of these communities. In addition, the numerous personal spaces and profiles created by users in the Internet environment constitute a large database and establishments can measure and evaluate their marketing strategies in this manner. As a result, companies, in terms of the airlines' marketing, can easily collect information on customers through the Internet and social media and can evaluate their expectations, satisfaction and dissatisfaction. Thus, they get a chance to create their marketing strategies in a much more effective manner.

REFERENCES

Akçay, D. (2013). *The effects of interaction design in mobile publishing: Research on newspaper web pages compatibility to mobile devices.* (Unpublished doctoral dissertation). Yeditepe University's Graduate Institute Of Social Sciences, Istanbul.

Anderson, L., & Taylor, R. (1995). McCarthy's 4PS: Timeworn or time-tested? *Journal of Marketing Theory and Practice, 3*(3), 1–9. doi:10.1080/10696679.1995.11501691

Baron, S., Warnaby, G., & Hunter-Jones, P. (2014). Service(s) marketing research: Developments and directions. *International Journal of Management Reviews, 16*(2), 150–171. doi:10.1111/ijmr.12014

Barreto, A. (2013). The word-of-mouth phenomenon in the social media era. *International Journal of Market Research, 56*(5), 632.

Constantinides, K. (2006). The marketing mix revisited: Towards the 21st century marketing. *Journal of Marketing Management, 22*(3-4), 407–438. doi:10.1362/026725706776861190

Cornelissen, J. (2004). *Corporate communications: Theory and practice.* London: Sage Publications.

Csordas, T., & Gati, M. (2014). The new (marketing) role of firms as media content providers: The case of SME's strategic social media presence. *Budapest Management Review, 45*(2), 22–32.

Emirates Fleet & Seats. (n.d.). Retrieved from http://www.airreview.com/Emirates/Fleet.htm,15.09.2015

Eye for Travel. (2015, September 12). *Airlines to sell the majority of tickets direct to passengers by 2013: Survey.* Retrieved from http://www.eyefortravel.com/mobile-and-technology/airlines-sell-majority-tickets-direct-passengers-2013-survey

Fauld, D., & Mangold, W. (2014). Developing a Social Media and Marketing Course. *Marketing Education Review, 24*(2), 127–144. doi:10.2753/MER1052-8008240204

Griffiths, G. (2015, June 19). *Rugby World Cup 2015: James Hook launches Emirates hunt to find official tournament flag bearers.* Retrieved from http://www.walesonline.co.uk/sport/rugby/rugby-news/rugby-world-cup-2015-james-9482006

Gundclach, G., & Wilkie, W. (2009). The American Marketing Association's new definition of marketing: Perspective and commentary on the 2007 revision. *Journal of Public Policy & Marketing, 28*(2), 259–264. doi:10.1509/jppm.28.2.259

Kane, G. C., Alavi, M., Lacianca, G., & Borgatti, S. P. (2014). What's different about social media networks? A framework and research agenda. *Management Information Systems Quarterly, 38*(1), 275–304.

Kotler, P. (2003). *Marketing mix.* Hoboken, NJ: John Wiley & Sons, Inc.

Leonardi, P. M., Huysman, M., & Steinfeld, C. (2013). Enterprise social media: Definition, history, and prospects for the study of social technologies in organizations. *Journal of Computer-Mediated Communication, 19*(1), 1–19. doi:10.1111/jcc4.12029

Lovelock, C., & Wright, L. (1999). *Principles of Service Marketing and Management* (2nd ed.). Prentice Hall.

Lund, D., & Marinova, D. (2014). Managing revenue across retail channels: The interplay of service performance and direct marketing. *Journal of Marketing, 78*(5), 99–118. doi:10.1509/jm.13.0220

Magrath, A. (1986). When marketing services, 4Ps are not enough. *Business Horizons, 29*(3), 44–50. doi:10.1016/0007-6813(86)90007-8

Milliyet. (2015, September 22). *Thy which fly to Roma*, Retrieved from http://www.milliyet.com.tr/roma-ya-ucan-thy-/ekonomi/detay/2105730/default.htm

Murdick, R. G., Render, B., & Russell, R. S. (1990). *Service operations management*. Allyn and Bacon.

Peterson, K. (2012). How social media and emerging technologies influence passenger flow. *Airport Business*. Retrieved from. http://www.aviationpros.com/article/10815625/how-social-media-and-emerging-technologies-influence-passenger-flow,29.08.2015

Petrevska, B. (2015). Assessing tourism development: The case of Krusevo, Macedonia. *Economic Development, 17*(1–2), 261–275.

Popesku, S. (2014). *Social media as a tool of destination marketing organizations*. E-Business in Tourism and Hospitality Industry.

Quinton, K. (2013). The community brand paradigm: A response to brand management's dilemma in the digital era. *Journal of Marketing Management, 29*(7–8), 912–932. doi:10.1080/0267257X.2012.729072

Reid, K. (2015). *Social media and your business: How to approach this marketing channel with balance and control.* Retrieved from https://www.highbeam.com/doc/1G1-413779851.html, 02.09.2015

Schlinke, J., & Crain, S. (2013). Social media from an integrated marketing and compliance perspective. *Journal of Financial Service Professionals, 67*(2), 85–92.

Shaw, S. (2007). *Airline Marketing and Management*. Ashgate Publishing Limited.

Sickert, A. (2011). Airline marketing and service quality: Foundations for growing nonaeronautical revenue — An Indian perspective. *Journal of Airport Management, 5*(3), 213–225.

SITA. (2015, September 10). *The social journey.* Retrieved from http://www.sita.aero/resources/air-transport-it-review/air-transport-it-review,issue-3-2014/the-social-journeya-bigger-role-for-social-media

Solomon, A. (2014). *The question of social media and air cargo.* Retrieved from http://aircargoworld.com/the-question-of-social-media-and-air-cargo-9822/

Talpau, A. (2014). The marketing mix in the online environment. *Bulletin of the Transylvania University of Braşov. Series V. Economic Sciences, 7*(56), 53–58.

Toh, R., & Raven, P. (2003). Perishable asset revenue management: Integrated internet marketing strategies for the airlines. *Transportation Journal Press*, *42*(4), 30–43.

Tomoson Research Institute. (2015). *Influencer marketing study.* Retrieved from http://blog.tomoson. com/influencer-marketing-study/,02.12.2015

Turkish Airlines. (2010, September 15). *Turkish Airlines annual report2010.* Retrieved from http://investor.turkishairlines.com/documents/ThyInvestorRelations/kurumsal/faaliyet-raporu/2010/tr/m-6-8-1.html

Usui, K. (2008). *The development of marketing management: The case of U.S.A 1910–1940.* Ashgate Publishing Limited.

VanAuken, K. (2015). Using social media to improve customer engagement and promote products and services. *Journal of Airport Management*, *9*(2), 109–117.

Wasan, P., & Tripathi, G. (2014). Revisiting social marketing mix: A socio-cultural perspective. *Journal of Service Research*, *14*(2), 128.

Zeithaml, V. A., Parasuraman, A., & Berry, L. L. (1985). Problems and strategies in services marketing. *Journal of Marketing*, *49*, 33–46.

KEY TERMS AND DEFINITIONS

3P: Personnel, physical facilities and process management.

4P: Price, product, place, promotion.

CRM: Customer Relation Management.

Periscope: An application that allows users to do live broadcasts on Twitter on the Internet.

Swarm: An application that allows users to share their place, city and other kinds of locations with their friends.

Web 2.0: Both writeable and readable web.

WOM: Word-of-Mouth.

Chapter 13
Can the Use of Social Media be Useful in Universities' Career Services?
An Overview of Five European Countries

Ginevra Gravili
University of Salento, Italy

ABSTRACT

Social media tools are becoming an important presence in recruitment processes, transforming them. They allow an instant sharing of ideas, opinions, knowledge and experiences, creating a new "space-time" dimension that could be translated in a new way (additional) to "recruit" workers. Although there are many benefits and promises from social media, however several risks are associated with their use. The ambiguity related to legal and ethical issues of social media, at the same time, contains the enthusiasm related to the potentialities that social media offer. In particular, this chapter aims at analysing the perceived risks and benefits of social media by students to understand if it can be useful for University Career Services (referred to UCS) to use these tools in job placement. The analysis is conducted in five countries: Netherlands, Sweden, Lithuania, Bulgaria and Croatia. It can be useful for managers of universities and firms to understand whether the presence of Universities on social media by students and firms is positive or not.

INTRODUCTION

The ability of social media to create and disseminate information is playing a supporting role in social change (Lenhart, 2009; Madden, 2009), increasing propagation of messages in an easier time and reducing the costs of coordination. As consequence, the enterprises are progressively changing their recruitment processes abandoning more and more the traditional forms in favor of new processes that guarantee a quality workers profile that measure up to the challenges dictated by globalization and technology. In

DOI: 10.4018/978-1-5225-0559-4.ch013

this context also Universities are making rapid change into organizational communication and public relations, emphasizing concepts such as participation, connectivity, user-generation, information sharing, and collaboration, to fit to characteristics of students that have a "digital identity".

Whereas the University's main goal, apart from training, is that of encouraging its graduates to enter the job market, guaranteeing their placement also with the support of innovative communication tools, Universities are transforming the static practices of placement of University Career Services (referred to UCS) in interactive and collaborative processes, creating new opportunities for interaction among students, business, and public organizations.

In this way students' larger groups can take on some kinds of coordinated actions, such as participation to job placement's meeting with firms that were previously reserved for few students. The use of social media in the placement processes is an opportunity that can develop a fruitful collaboration and a positive synergy of resources in a working space within which knowledge can be co-constructed, negotiated, and revised over time; where disparate students from different backgrounds, even internationally, can not only understand the working opportunity at hand but understand that everyone else does, too.

Although it is clear that social media is a very powerful recruitment tool, many executives and rectors are reluctant to develop strategies and allocated resources to engage effectively with social media.

BACKGROUND

The Job placement service in athenaeums aim at facilitating contacts between graduates and working world. Today, working world is changing. New lifestyles, values, language, and behaviour require universities investments in new efficient communication processes. In this scenario, the HRM are progressively changing their recruitment processes abandoning more and more the traditional forms in favour of new processes, such as social recruitment, that guarantee a quality workers profile that measure up to the challenges dictated by globalization and technology. Recruitment "has been, substantially, influenced by social media" (Schramm, 2007, Kaplan and Haenlein, 2010), which allow companies to look for not only the "active candidates" (Furness, 2008; Doherty 2010) but also "passive candidates" (Williams and Verhoeven, 2008; Jackson, 2010), through the construction of a relationship based on mutual interest and understanding (Davison, Maraist and Bing, 2011). The use of social media also allows potential candidates to get to know the brand of the company (Schramm 2007; Dickson and Hollet, 2010), which can show "the human aspect of society" and "an idea about daily activities" (Richards, 2007, Madia, 2010). In this way the job seeker can choose an appropriate employer (Peluchette and Karl, 2010).

As consequence, recruitment process takes place in a "market sphere" constituted of two sub- worlds: a physical world in which it is necessary to use a traditional form of recruitment and in which managers can see and meet job seekers, and a virtual world made of information.

For this reason, many athenaeums have decided to be present and active on social networks, allowing their graduates to be more easily identified or introduced for recruitment to managers from enterprises found all over the world. The benefit that can be obtained from this communication and recruitment tool is greatly above its cost and it is superior to traditional methods. In fact, messages sent through social media, besides being more plausible, have a relatively low transmission cost and possess increased applications. The time that enterprises spend in developing relationships that lead to the recruitment of successful candidates can also help in collecting reference information and improving selection. Thanks to the job placement office's simple registration as "fan" on the employer page of an enterprise, all students are signalled within the flow of the enterprise's activity and are visible to the friends on the web.

There is a dual benefit: the "employed" enterprise will directly improve its visibility and image, and there will be an effect on the sale of products. In fact, the methods, the tools and the approaches developed by using social networks for recruitment can be transferred directly to other entrepreneurial functions like marketing, customer services, product development, etc.

The "employer" enterprise, that is, the Athenaeum, improves its visibility by using social networks and it significantly improves, on the one hand, its perception and, on the other hand, the employment of the most qualified graduates. Thanks to the high visibility of social networks, a high number of qualified candidates can be published who, otherwise, would not have been able to be employed using other sources. Besides, if the high rate of utilities are to be considered as well as the quick answers from enterprises on online social communication channels, the key posts could be filled more quickly, resulting in a reduced number of unemployment of its graduates.

Facebook, today, deeply penetrates users' everyday life and it becomes invisible once it is widely adopted, everywhere, and taken for granted (Luedtke, 2003), so that users do not see its risks. Smith and Kidder (2010) explain how students in universities do not realise that the information they are posting on their profiles and the pictures they are uploading of their experiences can be used by employers as a means of checking up on possible recruitments. Therefore, the main risks are related to privacy and changes in the relationship between public and private spheres, such as inadvertent disclosure of personal information, damaged reputation due to rumours and gossip, unwanted contact and harassment or stalking, use of personal data by third-parties, and hacking and identity theft (Boyd & Ellison, 2008).

MAIN FOCUS OF THE CHAPTER

The use of social media in the recruitment/placement processes allows the selection of active and passive candidates, reducing costs and supporting the University Career Services (referred to UCS) to the placement of graduates in the labour market, but, for this to occur, it's necessary that students are aware of the benefits that may result from their use. This study is a cross-sectional study and we use a revisited benefit-cost analysis to compare the benefits (opportunities) perceived by students associated with the use of Facebook in the placement process of the Athenaeums with costs (risks) of this policy. In its broadest form, benefit-cost analysis can be used as a framework for social analysis, where any benefit or cost that can be measured is weighed against all other benefits or costs. However, benefit-cost analysis often assumes a limited scope of review due to limits on available information of all analysed consequences. So, the purpose of our study is not to resolve all such disputes, or eliminate uncertainty, but rather to provide a rich body of information assembled in a disciplined manner that can aid decision-makers faced with difficult choices or policy decisions. As consequence, in this chapter, we explore the perception of social media's use for students of public universities in five European countries through an Internet search, to understand their tendency to use social media in placement process. It's useless, in fact, for UCS to offer a service if it is not perceived positively by the users.

The research includes the following countries: Netherlands, Sweden, Lithuania, Bulgaria and Croatia. The sample survey of this study has been divided in two parts.

Figure 1. Number of public universities and UCS in five European countries

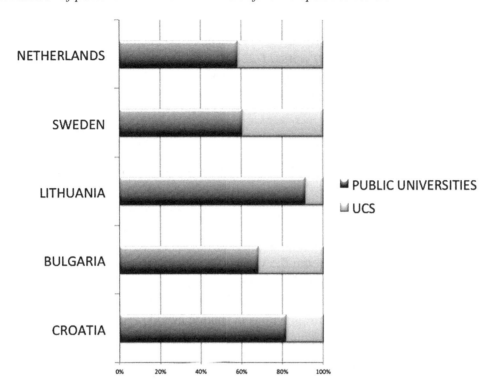

In the first, we identify all public Universities present in analysed European Countries in 2014, searching for lists of universities on Wikipedia (Figure 1). Our research shows that, in Netherlands there are 21 Universities with 15 Career Services; in Sweden there are 29 Universities that include 19 Career Offices; in Lithuania there are 42 Public Universities with only 4 UCS; in Bulgaria there are 28 Universities, only 13 of them have a Career Service Office and in Croatia there are 27 Universities and 6 Career Services. Consequently, we contacted only students of these universities.

The second part of the research was administered to students to evaluate the perception of the potential benefits or risks of the use of social media in the placement process. In particular, it explores Facebook users' awareness of the perceived benefits and if these will outweigh the observed risks.

The research was developed directly on the Internet by distributing a questionnaire among students, randomly selected from the list of public Universities. We have divided them in two categories: students with a Facebook profile and students without Facebook profile. So, in order to facilitate the accurate and consistent acquisition of information we have posted the questionnaire in the message form on Facebook page for students with a Facebook profile and we have sent the questionnaire with e-mail for all the others.

The questionnaire has been initially tested on a limited number of users (400 students) in order to understand at which point the questions were correct and the presentation form was accepted. Then it has been posted to the entire sample.

Sample

Originally, the sample of study has consisted of 10.000 members, constituted by 2.000 students for each country. They were divided among 18-20 years; 21-22 years; 23-24 years; over 24 years while there were 55% of men and 45% of women. Of these only 4% are married or engaged.

The sample at last was composed of N=8.225 students.

The Data Analysis

The data on opportunities and risks of the social media's use in UCS has been obtained by comparing the analysis of students' perceptions.

We have used 16 items to analyse their perceptions, to which interviewees were given a rating from 1 to 5. It has used a Likert scale, in which there are 5 elements: 5=Strongly Agree, 4=Agree, 3=Neutral, 2=Disagree 1=Strongly Disagree.

To report on a Likert scale we have sum the values of each selected option and we have created a score for each respondent. This score has been used to represent and evaluating a respondents' opinions. The scores have been used to create a chart of the distribution of opinion across all population. At the end we have crossed tabulate the score mean with contributing factors.

We catalogued, then, the answers in a range between α and β, where α is the minimum value of the score attributable to the evaluation (1 = Strongly Disagree) and β the maximum value attributable (5 = strongly agree). Relative advantage (definited Opportunities/Benefits, O) refers to the degree to which students' adopter perceives the Facebook's use as an improvement of communication system in comparison to traditional methods. Relative disadvantage (definited Risks/Costs, R) refers to a deterioration.

Relative advantage ($O => [(\alpha+\beta)/2; \beta]$) refers to the degree to which the adopter perceives the innovation to represent an improvement in either efficiency or effectiveness in comparison to traditional methods. Relative disadvantage ($R => [\alpha; (\alpha+\beta)/2]$) refers to a deterioration.

The sum of the benefits perceived represent the total Utility deriving from the use of Fb of single country as means of placement's communication.

Therefore, in order to obtain this value, we have analysed the values of each item selected and we have created a score for each respondent of a country. In order to create such utility functions that may represent perceptions for each single item, the average value of the answers was calculated. By so doing, a matrix was created which simply highlighted the resulting evaluations: Total utility (Utility by all sample) is positive each time the result of the algebra sum of the Utility by each country becomes positive, while it will be negative when the algebra sum becomes negative.

Each item falls into one of the five categories. The first category is Influence. It concerns the ability of Facebook to influence the choice of job seekers or firms in placement/recruitment process. The second category is Connection. It includes metrics that measure the ability to connect job seekers with the firms or job seekers (students) with UCS to each other. The third category is Access. It examines all the items that minimize barriers between job seekers, firms and UCS. The fourth category is Sharing. It analyses the capability of Facebook to support hiring process. The last category is Coordination. It includes items that improve job seekers-job seekers, job seekers-firms and firms-UCS coordination. In each categories we have identified a single item as an opportunity, when the values Ut are positive and higher than 3,5; as a risk, when Ut is negative and lower than 2,5; as an opportunity/risk, when values range from 3,5 and 2,5 it is necessary that the item is used with competence and caution. For example,

Comment about recruitment process experiences, reviews online of firm's information, information on job seeker and Information on firm, depend on the accuracy of information. This is true for all the items in which we recognize opportunity/risk.

SOLUTIONS AND RECOMMENDATIONS

The majority of students, both those contacted with Fb that those contacted traditionally, (80,5% approximately) have been using social media platforms for at least two years and the most used social network is Facebook. This result is similar for all the 5 countries analysed: Netherlands 82% Sweden 79%, Lithuania, Bulgaria 78% and Croatia 81%.

Once got this information, we built five "utility functions" that compare the perceptions of the Facebook 'use in UCS (Appendix). The graphs (Figure 2, Figure 3, Figure 4, Figure 5 and Figure 6) highlight the perceptions that students of five countries have of the 16 items tested, divided in categories. In principle, the perceptions regarding the items that fall into all categories are similar in Croatia and Bulgaria; in Sweden and Netherland while it's quite different for Lithuania students.

Of particular importance is then the graph (Figure 7) that analyses the average evaluation deriving from the algebraic sum of the all partial Utilities. This analysis indicates that the UCS of all countries have a neutral or positive perception of the use of Fb.

However, we have to highlight that most of the problems for all students about the possible use of Fb is linked to the Information on job seekers and on firms, as well as to the reviews online of firms and to following some friend's placement experience

Also, a lot of uncertainty arouses, among all students, the possibility that in Fb comments about recruitment process experiences, video or photos of recruitment processes (except Sweden students for minimal value) and sharing of iter of recruitment process (except Sweden and Netherlands students) could be misleading.

Figure 2. Perception of utility of Fb by Croatia's students

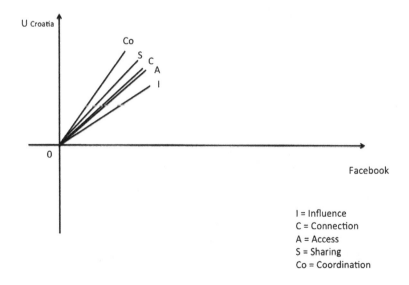

Figure 3. Perception of utility of Fb by Bulgaria's students

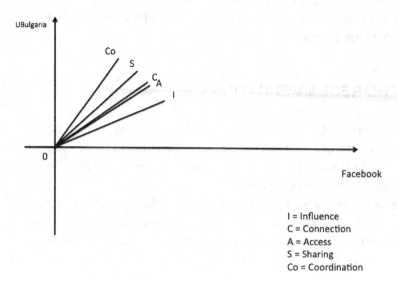

Figure 4. Perception of utility of Fb by Lithuania's students

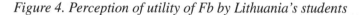
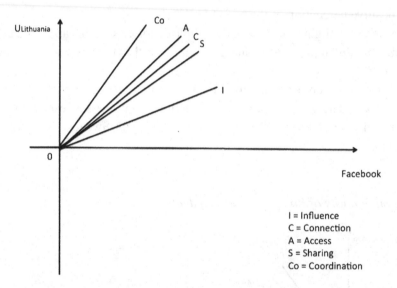

FUTURE RESEARCH DIRECTIONS

The I.T. challenges force the organizations to use sophisticated technological tools to communicate but the difference is in its use, that is, the way in which man manages to adapt it to his own needs.

This study could be essential and valuable for both Universities and practitioners for a number of important reasons. From the academic community point of view, it is generally established that service quality assessment depends on the consumers' evaluation of the service (Tih, 2004). Therefore, Internet service providers need to be aware of the key determinants used by consumers in evaluating Internet service quality in order to improve the overall performance of Internet service quality (Tih, 2004). From

Figure 5. Perception of utility of Fb by Netherland's students

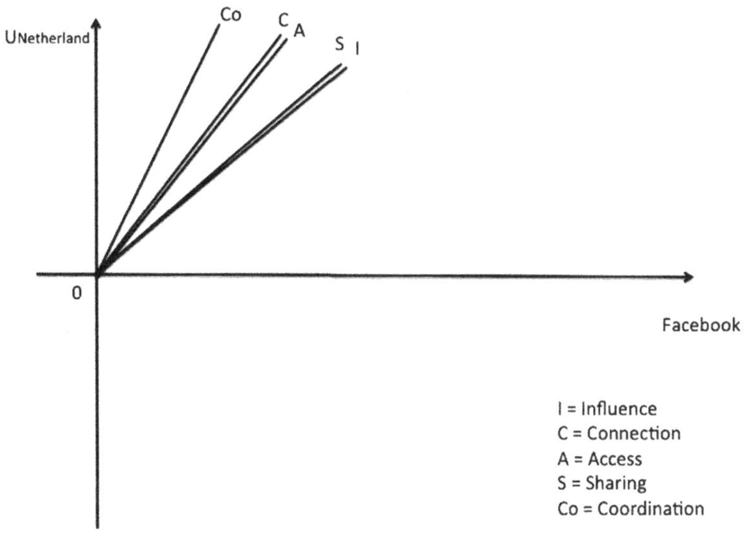

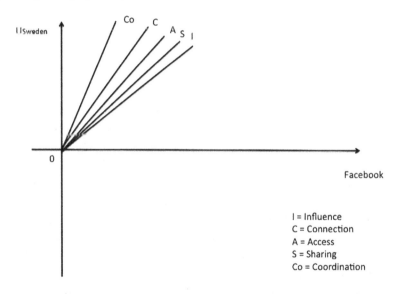

Figure 6. Perception of utility of Fb by Sweden's students

the practitioner's point of view, the survival of any company in a highly competitive environment depends on its ability to provide the best service quality to its existing customers as the quality of service is a key factor in the success of any organisation (Tih, 2004). In business practice, measurement of service quality is considered as an important process for improving the quality of the service (Jayawardhena et al., 2004). For the purpose of services delivered electronically, this is can be accomplished by developing a comprehensive conceptual model for customer service quality perceptions in the web-based services. So the findings of this study will be significant for both scholars and practitioners in this area.

Figure 7. Perception of utility of Fb of five countries

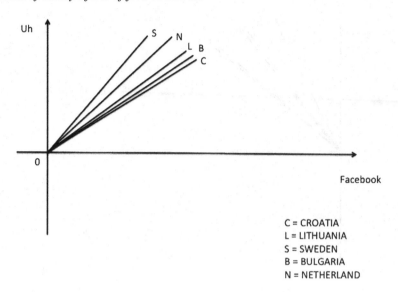

C = CROATIA
L = LITHUANIA
S = SWEDEN
B = BULGARIA
N = NETHERLAND

The use of social networks within athenaeums raises a few issues regarding legal matters. Privacy is a right, which must definitely not be harmed but it is necessary not to emphasize the idea, interfering with the quality of the services that a public structure can offer its students. In actual fact, the present laws should be modified in the administration of social networks. An inappropriate use of Facebook may create serious problems also in the relationship between students and universities or between career offices and firms. Provocative and inappropriate photos, comments on drinking and the use of drugs, negative judgments on firms where one has worked in the past or on colleagues, scarce communication capacity, discriminatory comments, sharing confidential information, inadequate qualifications can have a negative influence (Lorenz, 2009), persuading a student to choose a specific firm or a university rather than others.

What is more alarming, however, is not only the legal issue but rather the ethical-moral aspects. The information published could be the same as "nosing" into other people's lives, even if you don't want allow others to get to know specific things, these very same things should not be published. In the long-run, the truth is that even when we are sure that information on a profile is visible only by specific users, there is the risk that a simple technical error or, a premeditated violation could be published.

To overcome such ethical-social issues in using social networks, it would be advantageous for universities to use clear procedures informing the student on his/her concern and committing himself not to use confidential information. From their perspective, students should learn to be more cautious and diligently control his/her profile intervening with the administrator should one of the above-mentioned inconveniences occur.

CONCLUSION

The use of social media in recruitment process is growing and there is not no signs of slowing down. The purpose of this study is to measure the perception of the use of Facebook among students of five European countries. The list of opportunities and risks for students included in this paper is no exhaustive, but it represents a good point to start.

Research demonstrates that there are many potential benefits for students from the use of social media in UCS. They can access recruitment information. They can share their fears, opinions, moods. Thanks to social networks as Facebook, they can exchange experiences, impressions and opinions, maintaining discussions on different topics regarding recruitment processes. With use of social media, they can streamline recruitment procedures, they can connect to experts and colleagues, they can communicate quickly.

This proves that when communicative relationships have taken place among people with the same interest or problem, it is possible a harmony in terms of social and empathic competences and, at times, cognitive and technical.

The choice of social media as tool for communication could contrast with the values, traditions and uses of local culture of a country changing, for example, the relationships between two users: instead of respecting the status relative to each other (high power distance), it treats everyone as a "friend" (low power distance). So, in the last years, numerous researchers have applied the analysis of cultural dimensions to the studies of Internet-related communication (Rosen et. al, 2010; Marcus and Gould, 2000; Lee, 2000; Zahir, Dobingand and Hunter, 2002; Brown et al, 2006; Srite and Karahanna, 2006), but few studies contain specific and explicit reference to each cultural dimension and to social media. In a previous study (Gravili, 2015) we have demonstrated that there is a relationship between Hofstede's cultural dimensions and social media penetration. In particular Individualism and Indulgence are positively correlated to social communication' use, while Masculinity is negatively related to the use of social media communication. So, considering that, in Hofstede research:

- **Netherlands has values equal to:** Individualism=80; Masculinity=14; Indulgence=68;
- **Sweden has values equal to:** Individualism=71; Masculinity=5; Indulgence=78
- **Lithuania has values equal to:** Individualism=60; Masculinity=19; Indulgence=16
- **Bulgaria has values equal to:** Individualism=30; Masculinity=40; Indulgence=16;
- **Croatia has values equal to:** Individualism=33; Masculinity=40; Indulgence=33.

It's evident that although not sharing a physical space share a mental (or digital) one, students like to give information on their recruitment processes, to cooperate, to interact, to share and to act through a continuous sharing of information. All participants would like found answers to their specific informational needs in a less conventional way than in the real world, using simple language and within limited time. In Bulgaria and in Croatia students don't like Facebook (Facebook penetration is of 43% and 40% respectively) and for this reason they have doubts on its use. Probability it's due to the cultural values still very anchored in mentality of the population. In Netherland and Sweden (Fb penetration is of 52% and 57% respectively) there is a positive perception of Fb' use and in fact, in these countries, there is a good presence of UCS that use Fb.

While a particular analysis it's required for Lithuania (35% of Fb penetration) where the study of cultural factors of Hofstede and their relationship with social media penetration shows that can be achieved different results.

Probability it's due to the fact that explosion of digital media in Lithuania coincided with the country's second decade of independence and with the economic crisis of 2009-2010. In 2010 began a dynamic growth in ownership of PCs, laptops, mobile phones, and later smart phones. So the Internet diffusion increased especially among younger audiences.

However, there are no separate regulations or legal liability provisions concerning Internet content that differ from those, which apply to other media. There is a big dispersion among several public organizations which don't always coordinate among themselves. This fragmentary protection explains because Lithuanians are still sceptical on the use.

Our research, therefore, demonstrates that it's required a deep reflection on the part of managers and institutions. Only with investments and laws that clearly define the roles, duties and responsibilities of Facebook users (students, rectors and Universities), the possible risks can be transformed into enormous opportunities for all users. Only by encouraging a correct social media communication, UCS can implement their support students and their families.

REFERENCES

Amichai-Hamburger, Y., & Vinitzky, G. (2010). Social network use and personality. *Computers in Human Behavior*, *26*(6), 1289–1295.

Arboledas, J. R., Ferrero, M. L., & Vidal-Ribas, I. S. (2001). *Internet recruiting power: opportunities and effectiveness*. University of Navarra.

Bartram, D. (2000). Internet recruitment and selection: Kissing frogs to find princes. *International Journal of Selection and Assessment*, *8*(4), 261–274. doi:10.1111/1468-2389.00155

Berry, B. (2004). Recruiting and retaining 'highly qualified teachers' for hard-to-staff schools. *NASSP Bulletin*, *88*(638), 5–27. doi:10.1177/019263650408863802

Boyd, D., & Ellison, N. (2007). Social network sites: Definition, history, and scholarship. *Journal of Computer-Mediated Communication*, *13*(1), 210–230. doi:10.1111/j.1083-6101.2007.00393.x

Boyd, D. M., & Ellison, N. B. (2007). Social network sites: Definition, history, and scholarship. *Journal of Computer-Mediated Communication*, 13.

Cappelli, P. (2001). On-line recruiting. *Harvard Business Review*, *79*(3). PMID:11246921

Catone, J. (2010), *Should Employers Use Social Network Profiles in the Hiring Process?* Retrieved May 7, from http://www.readwriteweb.com/archives/should_employers_use_social_netowrking_when_hiring.php

Davidson, M. M. (2001). The computerization of career services: Critical issues to consider. *Journal of Career Development*, *27*(3), 217–228. doi:10.1177/089484530102700308

Ellison, N., Steinfield, C., & Lampe, C. (2000). Ensuring service quality for campus career services centers: A modified SERVQUAL scale. *Journal of Marketing Education*, *22*(3), 236–245. doi:10.1177/0273475300223007

Furnes V., (2007, January). The new frontier. *Personnel Today*.

Galanaki, E. (2002). The decision to recruit online: A descritive study. *Career Development International*, *17*(4).

Gravili, G. (2008). *La cooperazione conveniente: I virtual social networks*. Bari, Italy: Cacucci Editore.

Gravili, G. (2011). *Il social recruitment.* Bari, Italy: Cacucci Editore.

Gravili, G. (2015). Social communication in management: implications in recruitment processes of Latin American countries. In *ECMLG Proceeding*.

Hammond, M. S. (2001). Career centers and needs assessments: Getting the information you need to increase your success. *Journal of Career Development, 27*(3), 187–197. doi:10.1177/089484530102700305

Hofstede, G. (1991). *Cutures and Organizations: Software of the Mind*. New York, NY: McGraw-Hill.

Kaplan, A. M., & Haenlein, M. (2010). *Users of the world, unite! The challenges and opportunities of Social Media*. Elsevier.

Lampe, C., Ellison, N., & Steinfield, C. (2007). A familiar Face(book): Profile elements as signals in an online social network. In *Proceedings of the SIGCHI Conference on Human Factors in Computing Systems* (pp. 435-444). New York: ACM Press.

Minkov, M., & Hofstede, G. (2011). The evolution of Hofstede's doctrine. *Cross Cultural Management: An International Journal, 18*(1), 10–20. doi:10.1108/13527601111104269

Peluchette, J., & Karl, K. (2010). Examining Students' Intended Image on Facebook: "What Were They Thinking?! *Journal of Education for Business, 85*(1), 30–37. doi:10.1080/08832320903217606

Richards, J. (2007). *Workers are doing it for themselves: Examining creative employee application of Web 2.0 communication technology*. Paper presented at the Work, Employment and Society (WES), Aberdeen, UK. Retrieved from http://www.scribd.com/doc/6873217/JRichardsWES2007

Schramm, J. (2007). Internet connection. *HRMagazine, 52*(9).

Valenzuela, S., Park, N., & Kee, K. F. (2009). Is there social capital in a social network site?: Facebook use and college students' life satisfaction, trust, and participation. *Journal of Computer-Mediated Communication, 14*(4), 875–901. doi:10.1111/j.1083-6101.2009.01474.x

Weigley, S. (2011, August 5). Employers recruiting off-campus. *Wall Street Journal*.

KEY TERMS AND DEFINITIONS

Hofstede Dimensions of Culture: They are represented by six cultural dimensions - four identified in Hofstede's classic model (1991) and two in the advanced model (2010).

Individualism: Measures the degree of how much people are integrated into groups. That means is there a feeling of "we" or "I".

Indulgence: A society with a high level of indulgence it is very easy to gratify the natural human drives and basic needs and desires as well as to have fun. In restraint countries the society tries to control every part of human life and restricts the gratification of the mentioned needs by rules and norms.

Masculinity: Expresses the society's preference for achievement, heroism, success on the masculine side – or the preference for cooperation, taking care for others and quality of life on the feminine side.

Social Media: Web based technologies to create, share or exchange information, career interests, ideas, and pictures/videos. Example: social networks, wiki, pod cast, second life, RSS Feed, blogs, email, file sharing tool, text messaging.

Social Recruitment: Recruitment processes with the use of social media.

UCS: Office of Universities is dedicated to educating, advising, and connecting students to job opportunities.

APPENDIX

Table 1. Risks and opportunities values of five European countries

Categories	Items	Utot.	O or R	UCroatia	USweden	ULithuania	UBulgaria	U Netherlands
Influence	Information on job seeker	Uneg.	R	2,3	3	2,3	2	2,9
	Information on firm	Uneg.	R	2,2	3,5	2	2,1	3,5
Connection	Video or photos of recruitment processes	Uneu.	O/R	2	3,7	2,4	2	3,4
	Video or photos of firms	Upos.	O	2,7	4,6	3,4	3	4,5
	Support to confirm the date and the place of recruitment process	Upos.	O	2,6	4	3	2,9	3,9
	Improve diffusion of information	Upos.	O	3,2	4,5	4	3,8	4,2
	Comment about recruitment process experiences	Uneu.	O/R	2,7	3,4	3,2	3	3,2
Access	Communication = use of simple language to explain the professional figure to be selected	Upos.	O	3,2	4	3,6	3,5	4
	Communication = use of simple language to explain the hiring process	Upos.	O	3,1	4,6	4,3	3,4	4,5
	Reviews on line of firms	Uneg.	R	1,5	3	2,7	1,7	3
Sharing	Sharing of CV	Upos.	O	3,7	4,5	4,25	4	4,3
	Sharing of iter of recruitment processes	Uneu.	O/R	3	4	3,1	3	3,8
	Follow some friend's personal placement experience	Uneg.	R	1,8	2,1	1,9	1,9	2
Coordination	Coordination	Upos.	O	3,4	4,1	3,7	3,5	4
	Transfer of information fastly and quickly	Upos.	O	3,8	4,6	4,4	4	4,4
	Ask an appointment	Upos.	O	3,2	4,5	4	3,6	4,1

Chapter 14
Strategic Role of Social Networking and Personal Knowledge Management Competencies for Future Entrepreneurs

Oliana Sula
Estonian Business School, Estonia

Tiit Elenurm
Estonian Business School, Estonia

ABSTRACT

The mission of this chapter is to explore the role of social networking and knowledge management competencies combined with social networking strategies as an essential component and support for the development of co-innovation and business co-creation processes for future and potential entrepreneurs enrolled in higher education programs. Business students are active users of social networks but usually do not have clear business-focus priorities when devoting their time to social networking. Social networks enable virtual communities which allow knowledge sharing and collaborative learning a different stages of new business development. These networks have the potential to create ties for cross-border business initiatives that cannot be created in face-to-face networks. Innovative ideas often emerge from combining different sources of knowledge. Social networks can be used for action learning and cross-border knowledge sharing in the academic context in order to enhance cross-border entrepreneurship.

INTRODUCTION

Social networking sites are known to facilitate socializing and networking. Entrepreneurial literacy, learning skills and innovation skills are considered important soft skills (Benson et al., 2010). Social media can be used to enhance these skills. Business students from former command economies, including

DOI: 10.4018/978-1-5225-0559-4.ch014

Albanian and Estonian business students, are part of this globalization's generation Y that is familiar with online communication (Valentine & Powers, 2013). Their networking priorities for business development remain unclear (Bolton et al., 2013). Economic development increasingly depends on knowledge-based entrepreneurship. Co-creative orientation and co-innovation are intertwined with networking readiness and knowledge sharing. Stakeholders are the basis of co-creative thinking (Ramaswamy & Ozcan, 2013). The objective of this chapter is to explore the role of social networking competencies in developing networking strategies for co-creative entrepreneurship.

The concept of social networks as entrepreneurial knowledge networks is discussed. Integration of networking competencies, entrepreneurial business development process and entrepreneurial orientations are presented; the strategic role of social networking for different types of entrepreneur focusing on co-innovation and business co-creation is described. Competencies for social networking, innovative learning barriers in social networks and e-mentoring as a tool that contributes to overcoming those barriers are discussed. Chapter presents empirical evidence from a comparative study of Albanian and Estonian business students that combined the analysis of 180 questionnaires and 8 in-depth interviews. Experience of action learning applications that prepare students for cross-border virtual networking is analysed. This chapter concludes with some recommendations for educational policy, business education practice and its implications for economic growth.

APPLYING SOCIAL NETWORKS TO ENTREPRENEURSHIP

Social networking, learning communities and collaborative innovation networks are essential business development tools (Gloor, 2006) that help in overcoming distance and time obstacles. Academic impact of online social networking is however still an issue for debate among educators in developed and in developing countries (Ahmed & Qazi, 2011). Networks are a distinct organizational form, they are hybrid form composed by independent actors operating at a market and stable organizational structures which imply exchange of knowledge that is difficult to codify (Powel, 1990). Exchange of knowledge in networks is determined by relational social mechanisms. Networks are characterized by an open nature, consequently they may provide new business opportunities influencing the development of knowledge through dynamic processes and through bringing to networks new competencies (Powel et al., 1996).

Earlier research showed that the start-up success depends on the personal networks hypothesis (Birley, 1985; Aldrich et al., 1987; Johannisson, 1987). This approach is justified by the fact that through networks entrepreneurs can gain access to new resources more effectively compared to market transactions and more flexibly than in hierarchical forms of organizations (Dubini & Aldrich 1991). According Von Krogh and Kahne (1998) networking can occur at different contexts: physical, virtual (virtual teams) or cognitive (common values, ideas, ideals) "places". Networks can be formal or informal. They link knowledge to work processes and facilitate integration of different concepts and ideas. Knowledge transfers inside networks can be efficient and effective. Online social networking have radically increased knowledge sharing opportunities of early-stage entrepreneurs in cross-border networks (Elenurm, 2008).

Social Networks as Entrepreneurial Knowledge Networks

Latour (1987) defines network as an interlinked web of "knot and nodes". In a knowledge network these "knot and nodes" are loaded with knowledge. Knowledge networks are not a new concept, they came together with the development of the history of the humanity. Many formal or informal networks existed between artists, tradesmen and artisans already centuries ago. Knowledge network's members share a common goal, their relationship is not contractually determined enabled by the existence of a formal hierarchy of the firm. Knowledge dimension of networks influences innovative perspectives in business (Nahapiet & Ghoshal, 1998). New knowledge emerging from networks is crucial in a context where innovation expectations are high. Knowledge and networks are related through two dimensions: structural dimension and relationship dimension (Granovetter 1973; Nahapiet & Ghoshal 1998). The structural dimension defines network as a system of interconnected relationships that are not isolated from the external environment (Håkansson & Snehota 1989). Every relationship reflects a connected structure.

Networking behaviour can be perceived as opportunistic, but it means primarily a long-term relationship building. Trust is essential in networking for knowledge sharing, it strengths the ties of the network. Trust implies also that the relationship is predicted to be long term (Blau, 1964). Networking is a social skill, people interconnect with each other. Social skills approach is applied mostly in political sciences that focus on social astuteness (the ability to identify and understand social interactions), interpersonal influence (how powerful are you in order to influence others), apparent sincerity (appear to others as having high levels of integrity) and networking ability.

In social networking websites individuals can construct public or semi-public profile within a bounded system, a list of other users with whom they share a connection and view and traverse their list of connections and those made by others within the system can be articulated (Boyd and Ellison, 2007). In social networks different actors give different contribution to knowledge: "the communicator" serves as "a gatekeeper" that links to external networks, "the collaborator" is a task organizer, "the creator" has a vision of a "salesman" and "knowledge expert" serving as source of explicit knowledge. These contributions can be transformed to corresponding roles in entrepreneurial start-up teams.

Knowledge networks are important in knowledge management because they link different areas of current and present knowledge. It is necessary to mobilize different types of knowledge through networking (explicit, implicit) and networking between different levels (individual, group networking, and organizational networking) (King, 2008).

Online social networking tools include: blogs, social networking sites including Facebook, Google+, LinkedIn, Instagram and other specialized social networks. Social networks imply user-generated content that is co-created by users through comments, evaluations, editing in the online social networks (Boyd and Ellison, 2007). O'Reilly (2007) defines content generation in social networks as the principle of "harnessing collective intelligence". It is easier to share superficial situational feelings but more difficult to share deep knowledge through social networks. Social networks are generally user-friendly as their use does not require high technological proficiency. They are generally open and cost-effective. Users can benefit from a variety of dynamic creative and practical features that benefit knowledge sharing (Zheng et al., 2009).

Pugh and Prusak (2013) estimate that due to technological evolution we experience the presence of virtual networks that help to share codified knowledge for lower cost. Four dimensions of a knowledge network according to their view are: coordination, learning/innovation, translation/local adaptation and the support of individual. It can be combined with Parsons' (1991) definition about networks that adds to these four dimensions; interactions between the members of the networks and to feed to common goals. Networking among young people and especially among students is intensified by interpersonal and personal relationships that students have.

Entrepreneurship is defined as a "learning process" (Minitti & Bygrave, 2001). Individual learning skills determine entrepreneurial behaviour. Entrepreneurial learning is a life-long process but universities have crucial role in introducing to potential entrepreneurs learning skills that they need in order to identify business opportunities in social networks (Benson et al., 2014). Business school students are familiar with some social networks and they use social network tools in their everyday lives outside university (Baird & Fisher, 2005). Ho et al. (2013) used action research, where they instructed students to use knowledge sharing through blogs and Facebook. They coded online knowledge management processes (knowledge capture- knowledge sharing and dissemination and knowledge acquisition and application) and also socio-emotional expressions such as emotional expressions and social support). Facebook was found more common in sharing knowledge and information because of student interaction. Blogs were considered diaries.

Social media supports the bottom up building of new networks. New online social networks are continuously emerging but Facebook remains the most popular (Wright and Hinson, 2012). The results of a survey about the use of social media by US college students conducted by Ezumah (2013) demonstrated the dominant position of Facebook, raising popularity of Twitter and low popularity of LinkedIn. 32% of respondents answered that they had never heard of LinkedIn. 98% of respondents mentioned keeping in touch with friends as the number one reason for using social media networking sites. Making professional and business contacts were mentioned only by 27% and learning by 26% of respondents.

Benson et al. (2013) in their research on UK business graduates' usage of professional networks give evidence that undergraduate students are mostly engaged in Facebook and postgraduate students, while also using Facebook, are significantly more active users of LinkedIn. According to this study, peer pressure from friends appears to be the least influencing factor for joining a professional online network in order to explore new career opportunities and to build social capital. Benson et al. (2013) recommend that students develop their skills for assessing and updating profiles online but also for researching information about organizations and jobs online and critically analysing information that is available in social networks.

In the context of entrepreneurship opportunities, students should do more than simply create a personal profile to be accessed by employers. They should monitor information about new business opportunities based on technology and market trends and increase their social capital by finding new friends that could in future be their business partners or investors addressing to the empirical evidence of this domain.

Social Networking Competencies in Co-Creative Processes

Professional network building is influenced by social structures and by the holistic perception of networks (Hakansson and Snehota, 1995). Human action is a key factor for the development of networks. Networks and especially innovative networks add an original dimension to business and to entrepreneurship. Business networks are a particular conceptualization of entrepreneurship, where different actors can participate and exchange information and services. These networks that incorporate formal and informal relationships are socialization and business-transaction oriented. Entrepreneurship in one hand is characterized by independence and individualism but on the other hand when it comes to networks, entrepreneurs should deal with non-individualist notions such as dependent ties of trust and cooperation.

Entrepreneurs with collaborative goals tend to be more successful than those who do not have coopera-tive goals, assuming that they manage to use such benefits from networks as resources, equipment and competencies (Burt, 2003).

Finding business opportunities, business partners, making contacts, exchanging knowledge can be handled virtually. When compared to using physical networking facilities, online social networking for business purposes enables knowledge exchange between distant locations and trust building with new co-operation partners. It helps to manage long-term online co-operation even if partners do not have regular opportunities for face-to-face meetings (Kaplan et al., 2010).

Networking among students is influenced by their enrolment in higher education institutions or other formal networks that enable learning communities. Culture plays an important role in networking that is not limited to university's campus. In some cultures, students are more attached and they still live with their families, in some other cultures students are more independent (Benson et al., 2014). More independent students have to search already during their studies contacts for finding employment of entrepreneurship opportunities in order to have personal income.

Networking competencies are important for entrepreneurs as entrepreneurship is by its nature network-oriented, assuming at least contact network with customers, even if an entrepreneur prefers individual action. The main benefits of using online social networks for increasing the customer base are information sharing and knowledge exchange (Bell 2011), providing real time Facebook feedback from consumers as customers are looking for personal attention; they want to feel valued, taken care of and, most importantly, heard and to belong to a community that shares similar consumer preferences. In order to do this, a company must understand the needs of its customers and provide them with what they are looking for. Social networking can be an amazing tool in the accomplishment of this challenging task (Sannino, 2010). Many companies use online business networking for marketing but that is only one of networking functions for entrepreneurs.

In order to assess networking needs of acting or potential entrepreneurs, networkers should understand different implications of imitative, individually innovative and co-creative entrepreneurial orientations.

The imitative orientation can be successful in a business environment, where empty market niches can be filled by introducing business ideas that have proved their effectiveness and efficiency in simi-lar conditions in other markets (Elenurm et al., 2007). This orientation should not be seen simply as copying the ideas of other entrepreneurs, but also as a readiness to monitor and introduce existing best practices efficiently without losing time for inventing new "bicycles" if exiting best practices of other entrepreneurs can meet the needs of customers in the home market of the entrepreneur (Elenurm et al., 2007). Entrepreneurs that follow imitative orientation can also benefit from social networks in order to collect information about best practices and to discuss which products to import or which franchises to buy. This orientation at the same time limits their capability and readiness to contribute to knowledge sharing for developing new business ideas in online communities.

An individual innovation orientation strategy is good for entrepreneurs operating in markets where production differentiation is the main competitive advantage. This orientation seems working for long-term research and development but if the entrepreneur is not active in co-operating with other stakeholders in the innovation ecosystem, he/she should personally afford financing, infrastructural, marketing and internationalisation for innovation (Adner, 2012). Networking needs of individual innovators are mainly focused on monitoring information about new technology and market trends. Innovative entrepreneurship is a challenge in developing countries, where low production cost are the main competitive advantage but it is difficult to establish international credibility of a locally developed innovative product.

The co-creative orientation is the most evident reflection of the emerging network economy, where new innovative business models are created and commercialized in co-operation between several business partners and contributors. Software development projects that are based on open source code and voluntary communities of practice are examples of co-creative environments that may generate synergetic entrepreneurial ideas. The co-creative entrepreneurial orientation uses knowledge sharing in social and business networks and open innovation for developing new business ideas. Open innovation assumes the use of purposive inflows and outflows of knowledge to accelerate internal innovation and simultaneously to expand markets for external use of innovation (Chesbrough et al., 2006). Co-creative orientation assumes competencies for applying knowledge received from other networking partners but also competencies for sharing entrepreneur's knowledge in order to create value for other network members. Co-creation and co-innovation are intertwined to networking readiness and knowledge sharing that assume networking competencies.

Networking competencies include knowledge, skills and attributes of an individual to fulfil a role through networking. A challenge is to find the right combination of face-to-face and online networking competencies and to enhance skills of students for finding these online networking tools that support them as independent professionals and entrepreneurs.

Benjamin Bloom (1956), an educational psychologist working at the University of Chicago, developed the taxonomy of educational objectives. His taxonomy of learning objectives has become a key tool in structuring and understanding the learning process. Bloom's Taxonomy in its revised form has been used by Churches (2008) in developing digital taxonomy of educational objectives. Focusing on the cognitive domain, the digital taxonomy provides a comparison of old and new versions of Bloom's taxonomy as well as an extensive, though certainly not exhaustive, list of Web 2.0 resources that could be incorporated into educational settings to help meet the objectives set out in the course and for the students. The revised taxonomy begins with the word "remembering" before moving to "understanding, "applying, "analysing, "evaluating" and "creating". There has been a general consensus of a change at level five and six, with "evaluating" being seen as a lower level to that of "creating". Result of creating can be a new business model that will be implemented and proven in practice after the course but it can be also social capital, including involvement in entrepreneurial networks, created during academic studies but more fully used during student's later business activities. Bloom's taxonomy revised later by Churches helped to identify networking competencies for Albanian and Estonian Students.

Knowledge entrepreneur is an individual that has the ability to create an economic activity that is based on creating and using new knowledge and will be able to contribute to economic and social development. Collaborative competencies are essential in co-creative processes that imply knowledge sharing and learning in social networks. Technical networking competencies are influenced by the operational configuration of the network and by its infrastructure. Students should be able to develop some basic technical skills that specific for social media and online social networks such where to use different elements and where to use them such as links, tags or hashtags. They should be able to understand the difference between different platforms for example: Facebook and LinkedIn.

Creative competencies are required to personalize business or entrepreneurial profiles. Some basic technical creative skills mostly in graphic design are sometimes needed. Students should be able to balance creativity with ethical concerns and optimize between transparency and privacy. Online storytelling competencies are useful in social networks in order to be attractive has to be short and catchy without being victims of the blogging's style. In order to be attractive, storytelling in an online social network has to be short and catchy without being victims of the blogging's style. Effective communication competencies in online social networks involve immediate reaction through responding quickly and in the way that avoids misunderstandings.

Relationship building competencies are needed for long-term contact building process based on trusting online social networks. Too many contacts can at first seem to be a good thing, but students should be able to filter them periodically and constantly, taking into consideration their self-development and business development priorities. It is not only important to have contacts but also to know and be willing to discover what opportunities are associated with them. You cannot build business relationships or identify business or entrepreneurial opportunities online without taking risks and without willing to learn and exchange information.

Empathy will determine the impact of interpersonal competencies in building business relationships based on trust but will also allow to build networker's own networking capability. The first step of building interpersonal skills is the identification of the personal behavioural style. Monitoring competencies are needed for monitoring and filtering contacts and information on a regular basis. Students should learn how to apply critical thinking in order deal with myths and misconceptions about online social networks.

DEVELOPING NETWORKING COMPETENCIES FOR OVERCOMING BARRERS IN KNOWLEDGE SHARING FOR ENTREPRENEURSHIP

The main disadvantages of using social media for business purposes is the fact that a lot of valuable time is consumed in social networks without real business development outcome. Potential entrepreneurs would need to prioritize their social networking activities depending on their business development needs and taking into consideration features of the network, where they are involved. Users can experience barriers to the learning process. Castells (2009) argues that knowledge network groups should be integrated also to face-to-face meetings if there is possible. In the global business landscape it is however often impossible or too expensive to bring all relevant new business stakeholders to face-to-face meeting in order to jump-start their co-operation.

Entrepreneurship educators have to support individual drive for discovering business opportunities but also the co-creation of business opportunities in an innovation ecosystem. Sharing in online social networks involves two types of individuals, knowledge seekers, individuals who seek for knowledge and knowledge source who shares knowledge. Effective knowledge sharing occurs, when individuals know each other and understand when to turn to each other. They do not only get information from this interaction but mainly they are able to solve problems through knowledge sharing, individuals have timely access to each other and the whole process includes learning and creativity.

Lesser and Fontaine (2004) suggest that the main barriers to effective knowledge sharing are that the seeker and the source of knowledge are not aware and cannot access all the time to the kind of the knowledge that they respectively dispose. There is also often perception that knowledge cannot be applied and knowledge sharing behaviours are not respected and evaluated.

E-Mentoring as Social Networking Strategy in Overcoming Learning Barriers in Online Social Networks

Personal knowledge management has a central role for new entrepreneurs. Collaborative learning and knowledge sharing through providing assistance and building on existing knowledge of stakeholders facilitates the learning process. There is a link between new and earlier knowledge in the process of opportunity identification (Davidsson & Honig, 2003). Entrepreneurial opportunities in the domain of knowledge management differ from codified to tacit depending on uniqueness of the business field and innovativeness of the business idea. Codified opportunities are discovered through systematic research, tacit opportunities are based on previous knowledge and personal contacts.

Business students need to gain real world experience involving the utilization of online social networks. The main strategic dimensions of a network are objectives, goals, purposes of the network, student's inclusion and participation and understanding the roles of coaches, mentors and experts. Linking business owners and managers with university students helps to overcome their respective barriers while providing real world contexts for student learning. Action learning and learning from experience, where individualized mentoring intervention are enabled, seems to be preferred by entrepreneurs (Laister, 2012).

Mentoring is a complex process that does not only offer guidance but also development of skills, judgements, professional expertise, attitudes and competencies that are transferred from a member of the organization or an external person with more experience called mentor to a newcomer or to a less experienced individual called mentee (Johnson and Ridley, 2008). It facilitates knowledge transfer and learning process. Hamburg (2012) proposes two typologies of mentoring. Formal mentoring which is facilitated by formal organizational structure, the transferred knowledge is known at the beginning, mentors and mentees are paired based on compatibility and the objectives of the mentoring process are predetermined. Informal mentoring is considered a spontaneous mentoring support that a mentee can ask from a mentor.

Mentoring has traditionally included primarily one-to-one and face-to-face confidential relationships between mentors and mentees (Collin, 1979). With the evolution of the digital technology accentuated by the apparition of online social networks, e-mentoring has appeared as new opportunity in mentoring strategies.

E-mentoring can be defined as a form of mentoring that is mediated through web based technologies (Headlam-Wells, 2004). It provides very flexible communication between mentors and mentees. Mentors and mentees in different locations of the world can exchange knowledge. Less experienced mentees are provided with new skills acquired from the mentors in informal context (Hunt & Michael, 1983). E-mentoring is usually considered to be a supplement of mentoring, not a substitute (Stokes et al., 2003). Starwood (2010) would admit that most people prefer e-mentoring to mentoring because they do not have real contact with the mentor. The key success of any form of mentoring is relationship building and the key success for e-mentoring is managing relationships online (Bierema & Merman, 2002). For Homitz and Berge (2008) mentor's skills are crucial in building and maintaining the e-mentoring relationship in the network.

Entrepreneurship is an ongoing process that requires knowledge and skills that can be offered by education institutions in interactive learning arrangements (Fayolle et al., 2006). E-mentoring can contribute to knowledge sharing and knowledge exchange. A few empirical evidence is available on the impact of e-mentoring on the entrepreneurial process.

Some studies focus specifically on coaching for SMEs (Gray, et al., 2011). A mentor's functions in the entrepreneurial context can be defined through four psychological functions: reflector, reassurance, motivation and confidant those can be combined with four career related functions such as integration, confrontation, guide and information support (St Jean, 2011). Entrepreneurs require flexible learning environment but they need to be guided, e-mentoring is compatible with entrepreneurship and learning in entrepreneurial networks (Gibb, 1997).

Applying academic faculty as mentors in e-learning is an established e-mentoring approach but social networks broaden networking approach by involving students, entrepreneurs and other resources outside a specific higher education institution as learning community members; e-mentoring as e-learning tool has advantages compared to other forms of traditional education, it can provide access to a wider and more diverse network of potential mentors (Smith-Jentsch & Scielzo, 2007).

Young people are supposed to be more technically experienced and active users of social media than older generation. They are able to be mentors for older colleagues in capacity building for online social networking competencies (Tapscott, 2008). Younger generation's focus can be short-term, but learning and working are not perceived as separated processes in a social media environment. In order to build cross-border entrepreneurial networking skills and to specify needs for competency development and mentoring in this context, pre-knowledge and experience of students as social networkers in different countries has to be studied.

Comparing Estonian and Albanian Entrepreneurship Students as Social Networkers

Research on networking behaviour and experience of Estonian and Albanian business students combined quantitative data collected from questionnaires that were analysed through frequency analysis and content analysis of answers to open questions and qualitative data collected through semi-structured interviews. Two parallel research sessions were carried out in Estonia and Albania from October 2013 until October 2014 in order to assess social networking competencies and possible social networking strategies based on e-mentoring.

The first phase of research included parallel distribution of 90 questionnaires to Albanian and Estonian bachelor and MBA students during the classes of entrepreneurship in October 2013 and March 2014.50 pilot questionnaires were distributed respectively to Bachelor students in both countries and 40 pilot questionnaires were distributed to MBA students in each country. These questionnaires were developed based on the discussion with the participants in order to collect qualitative and quantitative data with perspective of a future action research. Students answered Likert scaled questions about their involvement in face-to-face and online social networks and with whom they discuss their business ideas. In the questionnaire there were also two open questions about student's perception about online social networking as business tool and their real involvement in online social business networks.

The size of the groups was small. It allowed discussing survey results at the end of the classes and getting student's feedback and interpretations of survey summaries. Results of comparing networking priorities and knowledge gaps were presented. Discussion sessions focused on online networking priorities, learning in online social networks, related barriers and on the need of capacity building in online networking competencies.

In the second phase of research 8 semi-structured interviews were carried out with student entrepreneurs in Albania during August 2014, their main orientation was online networking mentoring in the innovative entrepreneurial learning process and in online networking capacity building.

Comparing Knowledge Sharing Barriers between Albanian and Estonian Students

Questionnaire analysis from 90 pilot questionnaires collected in Estonia and 90 pilot questionnaires collected in Albania follow up discussion revealing barriers for students in both countries.

- **Lack of Control during the Knowledge Sharing Process:** In both countries students affirm that sharing knowledge through social media and especially through social networks is beneficial because it allows sharing knowledge quickly. Informal learning in social networks allows to students to be independent learners and to share the kind of knowledge that they want. The main problem for 60% of students in Albania and 70% of Estonia is the lack of control and supervision during learning activities for entrepreneurial and business purposes. Students need orientation in filtering, scanning and classifying the right knowledge in the process of identifying of the business opportunities.
- **Isolated Learning during the Knowledge Sharing Process:** Bachelor students in both countries perceive that sharing knowledge in social networks, even if it is considered as dynamic process because it involves working in virtual teams for different projects and assignments, remains still an isolated process because it is not as effective as face-to-face communication and feedback is perceived differently. One student in Estonia stated that when sharing knowledge online, he felt more belonging to the online social network rather than to his own local knowledge network.
- **Lack of Learning Motivation during the Knowledge Sharing Process:** For master's students in both countries sharing knowledge in social networks is inhibited by lack of discipline by other online networkers. Students are not very motivated to learn in such environment. When sharing knowledge for innovation and business purposes, they prefer face-to-face networks in order to have efficient time management in projects.
- **Cost Barriers:** Sharing knowledge in social networks is perceived as time consuming by 40% of Albanian students and 30% of Estonian students. Students feel that they lose a lot of time in order to get the right knowledge from social networks. For master's students in Estonia premium paying versions of LinkedIn do not still allow them to get the knowledge they need in specific moments. In Albania students feel that there is lack of support from higher education institutions in giving the right environment to student to work and learn in knowledge networks.
- **Social Interaction and Communication Barriers:** There is absence of emotionally rewarding interaction in such networks, students do not feel participating emotionally. This is due also to the physical distance barrier. Students are willing for more interaction while sharing knowledge in online social networks, greater honesty and a sense of community which provides inclusion for everyone and allows a greater sharing. Students mention that sometimes online networking can work better than face-to-face networks especially while exchanging routine information and numerical data. Technical problems which are frequent in online social networks can however block communication and interaction between students.

- **Cultural Barriers:** Are translated through different knowledge sharing cultures and are accentuated through intercultural communication problems. 65.3% of Students in Albania prefer to discuss business opportunities with family members and students from their university, but at the same time they would prefer to have a foreign business partner due to the instability of business environment in Albania. Students in Estonia consider that looking for foreign opportunities should be the main aim of a business. Language barrier can cause communication problems.

- **Mentors and Social Networking Competencies:** Were considered as essential in over overcoming knowledge sharing barriers and in constructing a profile of personal knowledge management for future potential student entrepreneurs. In order to develop their social and business networking competencies, students in follow-up discussions recognized the role of both classical and collaborative mentoring strategies.

- **Classic Mentoring Strategy:** Mentors help students to overcome lack of control barriers and communication barriers through helping students to develop their online networking skills such as monitoring skills, technical skills and communication skills. A classic mentor can be also a young entrepreneur experienced in social networking and having some information technology background. Classic mentors can do inverse mentoring to adult people if you suppose that younger generations are more at ease with online social networking tools.

- **Collaborative Mentoring Strategy:** Collaborative mentors are usually young people who mentor young people or adults who mentor young. They help students in overcoming isolation barriers, cost barriers, motivation barriers and cost barriers. Online social networks should push students to think in a creative and co-creative way while sharing knowledge. They should be able to apply critical reasoning while solving cost barriers. Students should be motivated internally and externally from the networks making them clear what leverage they can get from the networks. Students should develop relationship building competencies and narrative competencies in order to overcome these learning barriers.

Action Learning for Developing Cross-Border Social Networking Readiness

Social and business networking tools can prepare students for entrepreneurship initiatives at the global scale. Estonian Business School has applied different tools that enhance cross-border networking readiness. Cross-border online teams for assisting enterprises in their internationalization efforts bring together Erasmus exchange students and local students. During the period from 2006 to 2012, international student teams of the Estonian Business School conducted field projects for 61 Estonian SMEs in order to support their internationalization efforts. Each team consisted of 4-6 students representing different nationalities. Among the business sectors represented in these team projects, the most active were innovative entrepreneurs involved in start-ups in ICT, design, and tourism. During several years these teams mainly worked in face-to-face communication mode, both inside classroom and visiting their project enterprises, although Moodle e-learning was applied to train students for online teamwork.

In 2013 and 2014, cross-border online teams were created that involved students studying at the Haaga-Helia School of Applied Sciences and at the Estonian Business School. Experience of these two years demonstrated challenges of online teamwork, where student teams could independently choose their project work and online communication tools. These teams that devoted more time to face-to-face meetings with enterprise representatives have attained better results compared to teams that have mainly used online communication or have not visited the enterprise at all due to travel costs. The projects have also demonstrated that students representing Nordic low context cultures are better prepared for the use of online tools than Erasmus exchange students representing Southern European more high context cultures. These online tools included various web sources and social media for acquiring pre-knowledge about the business context of the client entrepreneur before asking additional information from the project entrepreneur and online communication tools for efficient team collaboration. A challenge has been to agree on timing to use Skype conferences, Google Hangouts or other synchronous communication tools. Master's students are working for their employers during office hours and prefer to have such meetings in the evening while students involved in bachelor studies prefer to have study-related online communication in such a way that their evenings are left for spare time activities. It has been difficult to match preferences and habits of using different networking tools. This action learning experience has demonstrated the need for more active involvement of faculty members as online mentors of cross-border project teams and devoting more time during class activities to reflecting and overcoming barriers in cross-border online co-operation.

X-Culture online project work was implemented at the Estonian Business School in 2013 as a pilot project in order to assess the suitability of this online co-operation tool for the international business course or for a special free elective. In 2015 it was used during the international business course for the whole 39-student group. The global X-Culture consortium connects approximately 2,500 students from 80 universities in 40 countries each semester (http://www.x-culture.org/ 2014). X-culture creates multicultural teams in order to enable action learning for overcoming cultural difference in online networking. Team members cannot choose other team members. X-Culture organizers allocate students to virtual teams following the principle of geographical and cultural diversity of each team. They have to build their team consensus on the international business opportunity example they develop together online over a period of two months. Students have to pass pre-test in order to demonstrate their knowledge about online communication and knowledge sharing tools and X-Culture rules. During the project work weeks students are involved in regular peer-review assessments in order to understand their pluses and minuses in online co-operation from the point of view of other online team members. Participation in X-Culture has demonstrated challenges of aligning knowledge sharing styles and online tool user experiences, including social media applications, in situations where team members never meet each other in the same location and have no direct contact with the client enterprise in their project work.

In order to train such networking modes that will lead to generating and assessing new ideas, Tricider www.trcider.com for online brainstorming has been used in the change management course since 2012. Tricider specifies clearly structured spaces for describing the idea, for highlighting its advantages and disadvantages and for voting in order to select the best ideas. That enabled a structured assessment of ideas. In 2013, two Italian Erasmus exchange students asked students from their Italian *alma mater* and their friends to check their ideas in Tricider and to vote for these ideas. That game changing initiative was a new lesson learnt for the course leader (Elenurm, 2014). He had to accept the highest rating of ideas gained by these two students as there were no regulations that ruled out the involvement of outsiders. In new creativity-focused courses we consider explicitly allowing and encouraging all course participants to encourage their social network friends to rally in favour of their ideas in Tricider.

Action learning in online co-operation of business students that has been directly focused on business projects has given evidence that in order to increase student readiness for such cross-border teamwork, broader social networking competencies are useful. Estonian Business School has for two years conducted courses *Business opportunities in social networks* both in its main Tallinn campus and in its subsidiary in Helsinki. During these courses students discuss the strategic role of social networking for their future career and business opportunities. Estonian and Finnish students and Erasmus exchange students from different countries have to create new online networking tools for cross-border student co-operation. Students have to choose and involve team members for their new network development task from another country based on online information in Facebook, LinkedIn and Tricider without meeting other team members in any physical location. This process has demonstrated that students have unequal readiness for using online tools in order to broaden their network for further business activities. Students are interested in creating new networking tools for sharing information about future employment opportunities or for bringing together start-up entrepreneurs and business angels. Majority of students have regular activity in mainstream social networks such as Facebook or Instagram but they often lack pre-knowledge about existing more specialized social networks that already have similar functions to these that they intend to create. At the same time some teams have managed to develop new social networking applications that can be used in further joint entrepreneurial initiatives.

IMPLICATIONS FOR POLICY AND PRACTICE

Educational policies in the field of developing competencies for entrepreneurship should take into consideration that social networking and business networking processes have become more integrated than some decades ago. Entrepreneurship education is not limited to individual skills for developing a business idea, compiling a business plan and creating an enterprise. In order to succeed in commercializing business models that depend on communications with communities or early users and on interaction with stakeholders in innovation ecosystems, social networking competencies should be essential objectives when developing skills of acting and potential entrepreneurs.

Knowledge-based networking of entrepreneurs is essential in developing economies where entrepreneurship has to become more innovative and export is essential for business growth. Both in Albania and in Estonia social media is a powerful knowledge sharing tool for cross-border business initiatives that can help students who use the right networking competencies to overcome learning barriers and to be part of cross-border collaborative social media networks. Capacity building in online networking skills is necessary in both countries and evidently in other small open economies.

Support systems for early-stage entrepreneurs will enhance networking in the business development process in more focused way if differences between networking needs of imitative, individually innovative and co-creative entrepreneurs are taken into consideration. These entrepreneurs have different readiness to share their business ideas online and to use social networks for open innovation.

Degree programs at universities will improve cross-border entrepreneurship opportunities by developing social networking and personal knowledge management competencies of students in order to link student involvement in social networking to their self-development priorities and to creating social capital for entrepreneurial initiatives. Academic staff should increase its own awareness of new social networking trends in order to act as e-mentors. Learning barriers in online social networks such as lack of control over the knowledge sharing process, cultural, cost and other barriers can be confronted in joint efforts, where both academic staff and more experienced students act as mentors for other networkers.

Students can benefit from action learning experiences that apply both more supervised and less supervised networking in business development projects. Less structured approaches allow students to understand self-regulative features of social networking and related needs to align their priorities with other networkers and project stakeholders such as busy entrepreneurs that are less active online. More supervised and structured approaches give students regular feedback from other online team members and mentors in order to understand their strengths and weaknesses in social and business networking.

FUTURE RESEARCH DIRECTIONS

Empirical evidence discussed in this chapter is limited to business students but entrepreneurship and related social networking processes involve also many other specialities, including technology and arts. Social networking patterns and barriers of students and young people that have different educational background is a future research direction. There is a need to study deeper cultural learning barriers in perspective as a further research step for creating international virtual communities of practice by involving entrepreneurial students interested in business co-operation between Albania and Estonia. More qualitative and quantitative international data from different developing and advanced economies have to be collected in order to compare networking barriers and competence gaps internationally. Interviews can be extended also to adult mentors who have mentored young people online and to young people who mentored adults in social networking.

A future research path can be action research of cross-border learning teams or international learning teams in the open innovation context. The perspective of future research is to focus on innovative cultural learning dynamics through virtual student teams.

CONCLUSION

The chapter highlights that to harness the full potential of social networks for business development, young people have to experience learning processes, where they face cross-border co-creation challenges and link international entrepreneurship opportunities to their personal knowledge management and social capital development strategy. There are differences in the networking competencies of bachelor and MBA students. Bachelor students lack knowledge for the effective use of business online networking competencies and business relationships. MBA students are older and because of their family and work obligations less active in online social networking but at the same time more clear in their self-development priorities. Even if they have experience in online network relationship building and interpersonal competencies, they prefer networking at some physical space because of the absence of time and trust. There is a need for developing effective communication skills than combine online and face-to-face networking opportunities. Bachelor students, who are part of this young generation evolving, use effectively technical competencies and creative competencies but they lack information monitoring competencies and relationship building competencies. General understanding of social networking trends and challenges is a prerequisite for successful business networking applications.

Developing online social networking and knowledge sharing competencies of business students has practical implications for improving the cross-border entrepreneurship readiness of young people. They will be more prepared to create entrepreneurial teams that use synergy between market opportunities, knowledge, financial, natural and other resources of distant countries. Enabling cross-border entrepreneurship in such modes, where online business networking is used for overcoming distance and time zone barriers has strategic role both for advanced and developing market economies. Entrepreneurs in high cost countries can increase their international competitiveness if they outsource some work online to low labour cost countries. Entrepreneurs from low-cost developing economies will be able to use international online crowdfunding tools to raise money for their ventures and social networks for accessing markets in advanced economies. At present, when Europe faces massive immigration pressure, focus on online business networking can for many talented young people outside Europe create an alternative to becoming an economic refugee in Europe. Strategic approach to cross-border online networking and knowledge sharing offers to them and option to implement their entrepreneurial ideas without moving permanently away from heir motherland.

REFERENCES

Adner, R. (2012). *The wide lens. A new strategy for innovation*. London: Penguin Group.

Ahmed, I., & Qazi, T. F. (2011). Deciphering the social costs of Social Networking Sites (SNSs) for university students. *African Journal of Business Management*, *5*(14), 5664–5674. Retrieved from http://www.academicjournals.org/article/article1380721081_Ahmed%20and%20Qazi.pdf

Aldrich, H. E., Rosen, B., & Woodward, W. (1987). The impact of social networks on business foundings and profit: a longitudinal study. In Frontiers of Entrepreneur-ship Research. Wellesley, MA: Babson College.

Benson, V., Morgan, S., & Filippaios, F. (2010). Online Social Networks: Changing the Face of Business Education and Career Planning. *International Journal of Business and Management*, *40*(1), 20–33.

Benson, V., Morgan, S., & Filippaios, F. (2014). Social career management: Social media and employability skills gap. *Computers in Human Behavior*, *30*, 519–525. doi:10.1016/j.chb.2013.06.015

Bierema, L. L., & Merriam, S. B. (2002). E-mentoring: Using Computer Mediated Communication to Enhance the Mentoring Process. *Innovative Higher Education*, *26*(3), 211–227. doi:10.1023/A:1017921023103

Birley, S. (1985). The Role of Networks in the Entrepreneurial Process. *Journal of Business Venturing*, *1*(1), 107–117. doi:10.1016/0883-9026(85)90010-2

Blau, P. (1964). *Power and exchange in social life*. John Wiley & Sons. Retrieved September 2, 2015, from http://garfield.library.upenn.edu/classics1989/A1989CA26300001.pdf

Bloom, B., Englehart, M., Furst, E., Hill, W., & Krathwohl, D. (1956). *Taxonomy of educational objectives: The classification of educational goals. In Handbook I: Cognitive domain*. New York: Longmans, Green.

Bolton, R. N., Hoefnagels, A., Migchels, N., Kabadayi, S., Gruber, T., Loyreiro, Y. K., & Solnet, D. (2013). Understanding generation Y and their use of social media: A review of research agenda. *Journal of Service Management*, *24*(3), 245–267. doi:10.1108/09564231311326987

Boyd, D. M., & Ellison, N. (2007). Social network sites: Definition, history, and scholarship. *Journal of Computer-Mediated Communication*, *13*(1), 210–230. doi:10.1111/j.1083-6101.2007.00393.x

Burt, R. (2003). The social capital of structural holes. In *The new economic sociology: developments in an emerging field* (pp. 148-189). New York, NY: Russell Sage Foundation. Retrieved September 2, 2015, from http://www.arschile.cl/moodledata/2/Mod3/Propiedades/SocialCapitalStructureHole-Burt.pdf

Castells, M., Fernandez-Ardevol, M., Qiu, J. L., & Sey, A. (2009). *Mobile communication and society: A global perspective*. University of Southern California. Retrieved September 28, 2015, from http://hack.tion.free.fr/textes/MobileCommunicationSociety.pdf

Chesbrough, H. W., & Crowther, A. K. (2006). Beyond high-tech: Early adopters of Open Innovation in other industries. *R & D Management, 36*(3), 229–236. doi:10.1111/j.1467-9310.2006.00428.x

Churches, A. (2008). Bloom's taxonomy blooms digitally. *Tech & Learning, 1*, 1-6. Retrieved September 13,2015 https://edorigami.wikispaces.com/file/view/bloom's+Digital+taxonomy+v3.01.pdf

Collin, A. (1979). Notes on some typologies of management development and the role of the mentor in the proof of adaption of the individual to the organization. *Personnel Review, 8*(4), 10–14. RetrievedSeptember262015. doi:10.1108/eb055392

Davidsson, P., & Honig, B. (2003). The role of social and human capital among nascent entrepreneurs. *Journal of Business Venturing, 18*(3), 301–331. doi:10.1016/S0883-9026(02)00097-6

Dubini, P., & Aldrich, H. (1991). Personal and Extended Networks are Central to the Entrepreneurial Process. *Journal of Business Venturing, 6*(5), 305–313. doi:10.1016/0883-9026(91)90021-5

Elenurm, T. (2008). Applying cross-cultural student teams for supporting international networking of Estonian enterprises'. *Baltic Journal of Management, 3*(2), 145–158. doi:10.1108/17465260810875488

Elenurm, T. (2014). Combining social media and collaborative e-learning for developing personal knowledge management. In *Proceedings of the European Conference of Social Media; ECSM 2104* (pp. 185-192). Reading, UK: Academic Conferences and Publishing International.

Elenurm, T., Ennulo, J., & Laar, J. (2007). Structures of Motivation and Entrepreneurial Orientation in Students as the Basis for Differentiated Approaches in Developing Human Resources for Future Business Initiatives. *EBS Review, 23*(2), 50–61.

Ezumah, B. A. (2013). College students' use of social media: Site preferences, uses and gratifications theory revisited. *International Journal of Business and Social Science, 4*(5), 27-34. Retrieved November, 30, 2015, from http://ijbssnet.com/journals/Vol_4_No_5_May_2013/3.pdf

Fayolle, A., Gailly, B. T., & Lassas-Clerc, N. (2006). Assessing the impact of entrepreneurship education programmes: A new methodology. *Journal of European Industrial Training, 30*(8/9), 701–720. doi:10.1108/03090590610715022

Fisher, M., & Baird, D. (2005). Online Learning Design that Fosters Student Support, Self-Regulation, and Retention. Campus Wide Information Systems. *International Journal on E-Learning, 22*. Retrieved from https://pantherfile.uwm.edu/simonec/public/Motivation%20retention%20articles/Articles/Fisher_OnlineLearningDesign.pdf

Gibb, A. A. (1997). Small firms training and competitiveness: Building upon the small business as a learning organisation. *International Small Business Journal, 15*(3), 13–30. doi:10.1177/0266242697153001

Gloor, P. (2006). *Swarm Creativity, Competitive advantage through collaborative innovation networks.* Oxford, UK: Oxford University Press. doi:10.1093/acprof:oso/9780195304121.001.0001

Granovetter, M. S. (1973). The Strength of Weak Ties. *American Journal of Sociology, 78*(6), 1360–1380. doi:10.1086/225469

Gray, D., Ekinci, Y., & Goregaokar, H. (2011). Coaching SME Managers: Business development or personal therapy? A mixed methods approach. *International Journal of Human Resource Management, 22*(4), 862–881. doi:10.1080/09585192.2011.555129

Hakansson, H., & Snehota, I. (1989). No Business is an Island: The Network Concept of Business Strategy. *Scandinavian Journal of Management, 4*(3), 187–200. doi:10.1016/0956-5221(89)90026-2

Hamburg, I. (2012). eLearning and social networking in mentoring processes to support active ageing. *eLearning Papers, 29*(4). Retrieved December 1, 2015, from http://portal.sio.si/uploads/media/e-Learning_in__druzbeno_mrezenje_FromField_29_1.pdf

Heallam-Wells, J. (2004). Mentoring for aspiring women managers. *Gender in Management, 19*(4), 212-218. Retrieved September 27, 2015, from http://www.emeraldinsight.com/doi/full/10.1108/09649420410541281

Homitz, D. J., & Berge, Z. L. (2008). Using e-mentoring to sustain distance training and education. *The Learning Organization, 15*(4), 326–335. doi:10.1108/09696470810879574

Hunt, D. M., & Michael, C. (1983). Mentorship: A career training and development tool. *Academy of Management Review, 8*, 475–485.

Johannisson, B. (1987). Anarchists and Organizers: Entrepreneurs in a Network Perspective. *International Studies of Management & Organization, 17*(1), 49–63. doi:10.1080/00208825.1987.11656445

Johnson, W. B., & Ridley, C. R. (2008). *The elements of mentoring.* New York, NY: Palgrave Macmillan.

Kaplan, A. M., & Haenlein, M. (2010). Users of the world, unite! The challenges and opportunities of Social Media. *Business Horizons, 53*(1), 59–68. doi:10.1016/j.bushor.2009.09.003

King, W. R. (2008). An integrated architecture for the effective knowledge organization. *Journal of Knowledge Management, 12*(2), 29–41. doi:10.1108/13673270810859497

Laister, J. (2012). *Creativity & Innovation Training in SME I-Create.* Paper presented at the International Conference The Future of Education, Florence, Italy.

Latour, B. (1987). *Science in Action. How to follow Scientists and Engineers through Society.* Milton Keynes, UK: Open University Press.

Lesser, E. L., & Fontaine, M. A. (2004). Overcoming knowledge barriers with communities of practice: Lessons learned through practical experience. *Knowledge networks: Innovation through communities of practice,* 14-23.

Minniti, M., & Bygrave, W. (2001). A dynamic model of entrepreneurial learning. *Entrepreneurship: Theory and Practice, 23*(4), 41–52.

Nahapiet, J., & Ghoshal, S. (1998). Social Capital, Intellectual Capital, and the Organizational Advantage. *Academy of Management Review*, *23*(2), 242–266. Retrieved from https://www.uzh.ch/iou/orga/ ssl-dir/wiki/uploads/Main/v26.pdf

O'Reilly, T. (2007). What Is Web 2.0 - Design Patterns and Business Models for the Next Generation of Software. *Communications & Stratégies*, *1*. Retrieved from https://mpra.ub.uni-muenchen.de/4578/1/ MPRA_paper_4578.pdf

Parsons, S. (1991). *Qualitative Methods for Reasoning under Uncertainty*. Cambridge, MA: The MIT Press.

Powell, W. W. (1990). Neither market nor hierarchy: Network forms of organization. *Research in Organizational Behavior*, *12*, 295–336. Retrieved from http://www.uvm.edu/~pdodds/files/papers/others/1990/ powell1990a.pdf

Powell, W. W., Kenneth, W. K., & Smith-Doerr, L. (1996). Interorganizational Collaboration and the Locus of Innovation: Networks of Learning in Biotechnology. *Administrative Science Quarterly*, *41*(1), 116–145. doi:10.2307/2393988

Pugh, K., & Prusak, L. (2013). Designing effective knowledge networks. *MIT*. *Sloan Management Review*, *55*(1), 79–88. Retrieved from http://web.stanford.edu/~woodyp/Rso1.pdf

Ramaswamy, V., & Ozcan, K. (2013). Strategy and co-creation thinking. *Strategy and Leadership*, *41*(6), 5–10. doi:10.1108/SL-07-2013-0053

Smith-Jentsch, K. A., & Scielzo, S. A. (2007). *Exploring gender-based differences in e-mentoring. In Refining familiar constructs: Alternative views in OB, HR, and I/O, research in organizational science* (Vol. 2). Greenwich, CT: Information Age Publishing.

St-Jean, E. (2011). Mentor functions for novice entrepreneurs. *Academy of Entrepreneurship Journal*, *17*(2), 65-84. Retrieved December 3, 2015, from http://crawl.prod.proquest.com.s3.amazonaws.com/fp cache/8d9db01cfd5e3c33cc93a5c3fef393d3.pdf?AWSAccessKeyId=AKIAJF7V7KNV2KKY2NUQ& Expires=1449270707&Signature=%2Be79k4vrQ7gzYZ%2Bv4sin5F%2BoR%2BA%3D

Starwood, H. (2010). Starwood Hotels pilots e-mentoring: Success depends on mutual trust. *Human Resource Management International Digest*, *18*(7), 29–31. doi:10.1108/09670731011083798

Stokes, A. (2001). Using tele-mentoring to deliver training to SMEs: A pilot study. *Education + Training*, *43*(6), 317–324. doi:10.1108/00400910110406833

Tapscott, D. (2008). *Grown Up Digital: How the Net Generation is Changing Your World*. New York, NY: McGraw-Hill.

Valentine, T. B., & Powers, T. L. (2013). Generation Y values and lifestyle segments. *Journal of Consumer Marketing*, *30*(7), 597–606. doi:10.1108/JCM-07-2013-0650

Von Krogh, G. (1998). Care in knowledge creation. *California Management Review*, *40*(3), 133–154. doi:10.2307/41165947

Wright, D. K., & Hinson, M. D. (2012). *A four-year longitudinal analysis measuring social and emerging media use in public relations practice.* Paper presented to the 15th Annual International Public Relations Research Conference, Coral Gables, FL.

Zheng, Y., Zhang, L., Xie, X., & Ma, W. (2009). Mining interesting locations and travel sequences from gps trajectories. In *Proceedings of the 18th International Conference on World Wide Web* (pp. 791-800). New York, NY: ACM. doi:10.1145/1526709.1526816

Chapter 15
Key Success Factors of Using Social Media as a Learning Tool

Alexander K. Kofinas
University of Bedfordshire, UK

Abdallah Al-Shawakbeh
University of Greenwich, UK

Andriew S. Lim
Hotelschool The Hague, The Netherlands

ABSTRACT

Students are dedicated and innovative users of Social Media; in the context of Higher Education they use such media in a pragmatic fashion to enhance their learning. Higher Education institutions are thus in a position to facilitate their students' learning by embedding Social Media in their teaching and learning pedagogy. This chapter will discuss the Key Success Factors of using Social Media as a coordinating, managing, and learning tool to enhance students' education in the context of Higher Education. The Key Success Factors are mapped along the communication and activity flows of the student's study enterprise as viewed from an Actor-Network Theory lenses.

INTRODUCTION

This research conducts a meta-analytical review to investigate the effect of social media (hereinafter SM) on the way people organise their work (Biasutti & El-Deghaidy, 2015; Dery, Tansley, & Hafermalz, 2014; Hanna, Rohm, & Crittenden, 2011; Maloney, Moss, & Ilic, 2014). In the context of Higher Education the SM revolution has had a profound effect on the way students think and process data, making it a challenge for them to succeed academically in the traditional teaching environment (Al-Shawabkeh & Lim, 2014; Dickie & Meier, 2015; Garcia, Elbeltagi, Brown, & Dungay, 2015; Karahan & Roehrig, 2014; Page & Reynolds, 2015; Prensky, 2001). According to literature these Digital Natives are native speakers of the virtual world as experienced via video games, mobiles, tablets and other conduits of the Internet (Donlan, 2014; Oeberst, Halatchliyski, Kimmerle, & Cress, 2014; Prensky, 2001; Schlicht, 2013).

DOI: 10.4018/978-1-5225-0559-4.ch015

This new generation of students has provoked the proliferation of technology resources that could be used by academic staff to facilitate the students' learning experience (Benson, 2014). According to Shang et al. (2011) since the arrival of these tools, the processes of learning developed by students have changed as there are now opportunities for students to socialise, externalise, combine and internalise knowledge in novel ways. Traditional methods of teaching would fail to engage them, a truism that has been discussed at length in the literature (Dickie & Meier, 2015; Donnelly & Hume, 2015; Guerin, Carter, & Aitchison, 2015). These changes have had an impact on the Higher Education sector as well as the workplace graduates later enter.

To identify the characteristics of these digital natives, a number of typologies have been suggested; typologies that map the different types of internet and SM users. User typologies are typically based on distinct user behaviour instead of their goals or motivations (Brandtzaeg & Heim, 2011). The main aim of expanding into user typology in this chapter is to classify diverse SM usage behaviour into meaningful categories.

The typology presented in Table 1 represents different modes of social engagement and would be applicable in an online SM space. As SM is becoming increasingly important in the learning process, students can use the various SM platforms in order to enhance their academic activities, share their learning experience and interact with other students (users and peers) freely. SM technologies have both audio and visual functionality offered via various technology platforms, such as blogs, wikis, social bookmarking, media sharing space, Rich Site Summary feeds, micro-blogging sites, Facebook, and LinkedIn, all of which offer a support for social interactions and communication. With the help of information technologies, students are now able to socially interact within their peers while they are able to gain more knowledge and improve on their weaknesses as well as create, share or exchange information and ideas in virtual communities and networks (De Wever, Hämäläinen, Voet, & Gielen, 2015; Ha & Shin, 2014; Zheng, Niiya, & Warschauer, 2015). Higher level of interaction is the main link between SM, information technology, and learning.

However, translating students' online social activities into an opportunity for increasing the learning and teaching effectiveness can be a challenge and there are pros and cons with any such approach (Al-Rahmi, Othman, & Musa, 2014; Al-Shawabkeh & Lim, 2014; Buzzetto-More, 2012). Examining how different types of SM can facilitate the engagement, coordination and learning of these digital natives is invaluable in the higher education context as well as the practitioner context that these students will

Table 1. SM user typology

User Type	Frequency of Use	Typical Activity
Sporadic	Low use	No particular activity. The internet is rarely used for private purposes. Low interest, and less experienced.
Lurker	Medium use	Lurking, time killing
Socialiser	Medium use	Socialising, keeping in touch with friends and family, and connecting with new acquaintances.
Debater	Medium use	Discussion and information acquisition and exchange. Purposeful action.
Actives	High use	All (gaming, homepage design, shopping, programming, video, etc.)

Brandtzaeg & Heim, 2011.

enter upon graduation. In examining the empirical stories of SM usage, this chapter utilises a systematic review of the empirical literature within the HE sector in order to highlight the key success factors that guide the successful implementation of SM as a coordination, management, and learning tool. The review results are mapped against the learning enterprise that would emerge against each of the four types of SM (adapted from Latour, 1999). This conceptual mapping is focusing on the Key Success Factors that enable a successful learning experience at the centre of the learning enterprise.

The structure of the chapter is as follows:

- Introduction,
- Background,
- Methodology,
- Activity Analysis,
- Discussion,
- Managerial Implications,
- Future Research Directions,
- Conclusion.

BACKGROUND

SM allows people to create, share content and interact with others and can be defined as a group of internet applications that allows the creation and exchange of user-generated content. SM can be divided into different types: collaboration, community, creativity, convergence and communication highlighting their importance in supporting students to publish, share images or useful resources, audio and even videos. The typology advocated by Kaplan and Haenlein (2010) has influenced a number of subsequent authors, for example Hew and Cheung (2013) and Taylor, King, and Nelson (2012), the framework suggested has been adapted in Table 2.

These types of SM functions can become the basis for learning tools that allow students to work in a team and be able to reflect, communicate, discuss, and share knowledge regardless of their physical location. SM functionalities include knowledge seeking, knowledge storing, writing reflections, contributing to discussion boards, engaging in asynchronous & synchronous discussions, developing collaborative documentation, and sharing efforts (Benson, Morgan, & Tennakoon, 2012). The study of these functionalities is relevant for any kind of work and in any context; however, this chapter will illustrate their effect in the particular context of Higher Education.

Table 2. Examples of technologies used by students

Functionality	Example	Synchronicity
Self-Expression and Online Reflection Spaces	Blogger, Tumblr, other blogs	Asynchronous
Online Collaboration Communities	PB wiki, Wetpaint, Wimba voice, Voicethread	Asynchronous
Social spaces	Facebook, Twitter	Synchronous
Content Communities	YouTube, Houndbite, Chirbit	Asynchronous

Adapted from Hew & Cheung, 2013; Kaplan & Haenlein, 2010.

The literature provides ample examples of the usage of SM in Higher Education (Arnold & Paulus, 2010; Bennett, Bishop, Dalgarno, Waycott, & Kennedy, 2012; Cole, 2009; Lederer, 2012). These studies show that incorporating SM, which is user-driven and easy to use into higher education, could potentially provide an extra edge in enhancing students' learning and employability. As an example, students create information, re-create and then publish for others to see, which can be in the form of the video or audio on SM. They can also record their lectures and then post them on SM. Thus, SM can be used as a web-based system that supports students-lecturers and student-student connections (Duarte, 2015; Maloney et al., 2014; O'Boyle, 2014; Page & Reynolds, 2015).

METHODOLOGY

The heuristic classification propounded in the earlier section becomes the basis of the structured literature review in this chapter. In order to explore each of these functionalities, the authors have focused and reviewed in-depth an example from each. For Online Reflection Spaces, the literature search focused on the word "blog" while with regards to Online Collaboration Communities the emphasis was on "wiki" as the dominant collaboration platform. For Social Spaces, the platform of choice was the most popular i.e., Facebook, and for content communities the research team opted for YouTube. That does not imply that each of the particular examples focuses on a sole function of SM. El Ouirdi et al. (2014) in their typology clearly demonstrate how most SM include more than one function, for example a wiki may contain much contents, may also have a social space where contributors and other visitors interact as well as a blog function. However, the logic in using specific platforms as examples for each type of SM is that each platform is an exemplar of that particular SM type. A structured literate review on each SM platform was conducted. The criteria applied are shown in Table 3.

Table 3. Process of structure literature review

Platform	Blog	Wiki	Facebook	YouTube
Time Period	2004-Present	2004-Present	2004-Present	2004-Present
Key Search Words	Blog Higher Education Learning	Wiki Higher Education Learning	Facebook Higher Education Learning	YouTube Higher Education Learning
Type	Article or Review	Article or Review	Article or Review	Article or Review
Search Fields	Title, Abstract, Key Words	Title, Abstract, Key Words	Title, Abstract, Key Words	Title, Abstract, Key Words
Quality	Not limited by Journal Quality	Not limited by Journal Quality	Not limited by Journal Quality	Not limited by Journal Quality
Databases	Scopus	Scopus	Scopus	Scopus
# of Articles	88	76	56	27
Exclusion Criteria:	• Non-English • Conceptual Papers • Duplicates • Conference Papers • Irrelevant Articles	• Non-English • Conceptual Papers • Duplicates • Conference Papers Irrelevant Articles	• Non-English • Conceptual Papers • Duplicates • Conference Papers Irrelevant Articles	• Non-English • Conceptual Papers • Duplicates • Conference Papers Irrelevant Articles
Total # of articles	70	70	42	17

Table 4. Chronological spread of identified articles

Technology/ Functionality	2006	2007	2008	2009	2010	2011	2012	2013	2014	2015	Total
YouTube					3	1	1	4	5	3	17
FaceBook					4	4	12	6	13	3	42
Blog			4	2	6	12	14	13	13	6	70
Wiki	1		3	3	10	7	14	14	11	7	70
Total (Total excluding duplicates)	1	0	7	5	23	24	41	37	41	24	**199 (177)**

With regards to the exclusion criteria, the articles that were deemed irrelevant were articles that focused on virtual learning environments or on teaching and learning with only a passing reference to the social tools. Also the authors excluded as irrelevant articles those that did not focus specifically on a platform and considered SM as a single unit of analysis. Perceived quality of the journal article itself was not used as an exclusion criterion, as long as they were peer-reviewed. The reason for this is the fact that the SM field is a relatively new and emerging field and the likelihood of finding very relevant material in non-ABS ranked publications can be high. The articles that were kept for this analysis were only empirical and provided an account and/or evaluation of how the particular platform was used to facilitate learning in an educational context. The chronological spread of the articles for the four media types is shown in Table 4.

This chronological spread immediately highlights that research in the potential of SM as tools for meaningful learning activity started relatively late; with the exception of a single article in 2006 (Yukawa, 2006) extensive empirical research started 7 years ago (from 2008). Interestingly, research started in 2008 mainly focused on blogs and wikis, a logical outcome as both SM platforms are older than social spaces and content communities. Facebook enters the table in 2010 when it becomes popular and has a peak in 2012. In general, the studies identified were spread relatively equally among Blogs (n=70), wikis (n=70), and Facebook (n=42). However, YouTube (n=17) yielded far fewer empirical studies. An analysis of the articles identified indicated that either YouTube is not deemed as relevant to Higher Education pedagogy or that the functionality of YouTube is not salient or distinct enough to offer a real alternative to the other three SM types. At this point a decision was made to exclude YouTube (even though it is the most popular content provider) from this literature review, although some of the findings of the relevant papers will be presented in the discussion section.

The authors then proceeded to review these articles in order to identify, extract and integrate the Key Success Factors as identified when using any of the three different types of SM as a learning tool in Higher Education. In order to map out these Key Success Factors in a dynamic fashion, the analytical framework utilised was based on an Actor-network theoretical conceptualisation. In Latour's (1999) original understanding, any human enterprise is composed of five flows of human activity that encompass all the actors involved in a particular enterprise. The incorporation of SM in HE learning can be seen as such a human activity and its five socio-technical flows of activity are intermeshed with each other and at the same time integrated; in this case integrated around the learning experience of a student. These five activity flows are not in a hierarchical relationship to each other, nor epistemologically significant

Figure 1. The activity flows of a student's teaching and learning enterprise
Adapted from Latour, 1999.

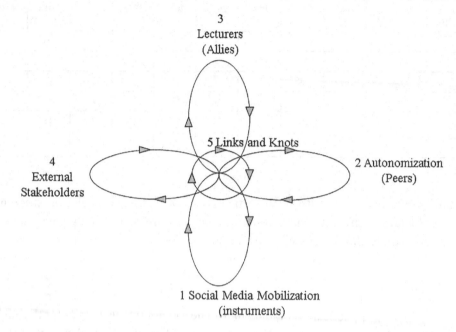

but they are functionally and pragmatically helpful in delineating what makes a successful student engagement with a particular SM type. Figure 1 is an adaptation of Latour's (1999) original conception from the vantage point of a student.

The first loop refers in this case to the mobilization of the world (all actants loaded in a particular activity) with a particular focus for this empirically-based literature review on SM types. The second loop is that of Autonomization whereupon the students engage with their peers aiming to interact in a meaningful attempt of capturing learning. According to Latour (1999) this drive for Autonomization is the force behind the formation of communities of practice (or learning in this particular case), a conception that resembles the scientific communities, as exemplified by Kuhn (1996). The third loop concerns the formation of alliances, and in this particular review the focus will be on the lecturer as a shaper and potentially powerful ally in this activity. The fourth loop represents the wider society, other stakeholders and actors that are loosely connected to the student's activity but are not directly involved or affected by the activity. The fifth and final loop is the students themselves forging the cognitive links and constructing the conceptual knots of their particular learning engagement out of these disparate engagements thus enabling the plucky act of making sense out of the online chaos they face during their learning engagements.

The visualisation of these communication and activity loops enables the actor-network theoretical lens to become a convenient map of the dynamic context of the learning enterprise. It is the final loop, the one that represents the students and their work to make sense of the complex nexus they create and are created by, that encapsulates the learning experience at its core. Latour (1999) in his seminal work invites us to think of it as the sense-making centre which for this review represents the flexible network of ideas, concepts and connections that permeate the deeper learning that the students may achieve when engaged with SM.

Figure 2. The key success factors in the blog-enabled learning activity

+ Instructors are instrumental for adopting Blogs and their involvement key in students' perception of usefulness
+ The interactions have to be dialogic, and geared towards peer reviews, and reflection for Blogs to be successful.

- Staff should be well-trained in utilising the technology
- Proper design of the assessment by lecturers that fits the medium

3
Lecturers
(Allies)

+ Must facilitate the interactions among students and design activities promoting reflexivity and developing a learning community
+ Encourage the user population to engage
+ Important to have buy-in (use of FB should be student-driven)

- Blogs can be difficult to engage with; there is a certain approach and interactive patterns in blogging communities that may not fit all students.

5 Links and Knots

4
External
Stakeholders

2 Autonomization
(Peers)

+ Blogging is perceived as helpful in synthesis of content
+ Evaluating and using Blog content is challenging; students find it difficult to understand how to process these new resources
+ The Learning activity should take advantage of the opportunities Blogs offer to provide a voice to quieter and introvert students

- The reflective and creative construction of knowledge can be side-tracked by the blogging activity itself

1 Social Media Mobilization
(instruments)

+ Support from institution and Lecturers
+ Appropriate use of blog as communication tool rather than a social tool (it is not FB)
+ Quality of system
+ Format and content (short titles; intelligent and controversial topics)

- Excessive Time Demands
- Complex copyrights

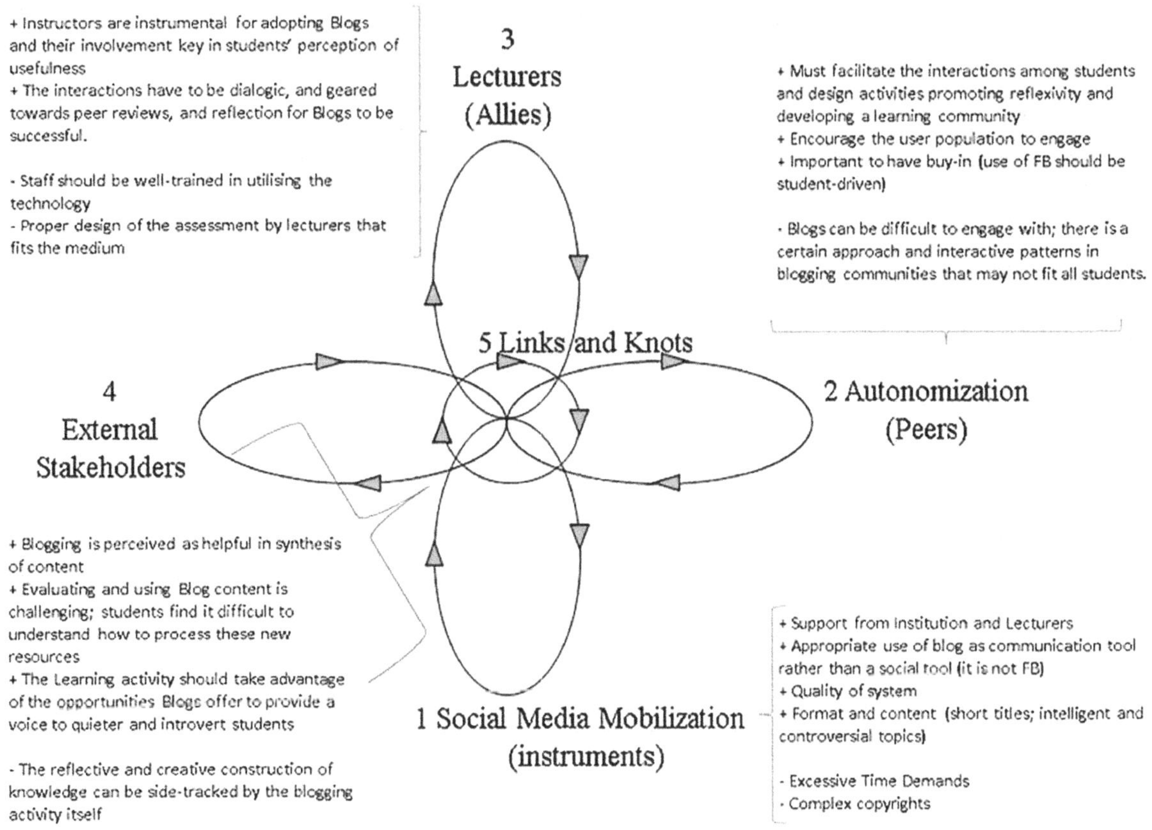

The activity analysis that follows, utilises the five communication and activity loops in order to map the key factors for each of the three SM investigated. The discussion indicates each of the loops under investigation using parentheses and relevant number.

ACTIVITY ANALYSIS

The Blog-Enabled Learning Activity

The research papers identified in relation to blogs were mapped against the activity flow map in order to demonstrate the key issues for each. For each of the activity flows key success and failure factors were identified. The use of blogs in learning mirrors the perceived functionality of the blogs as personal reflection spaces as can be seen from Figure 2.

There is a strong tendency when using blogs as an educational medium for teaching and learning in Higher Education to emphasise dialogue and participation (3). Interestingly, when it comes to the students' interaction with the tool reflexivity, and communication are the foremost issues rather than social interactions (1). It appears that students find it difficult to engage with peers via blogs as the interactive patterns enabled seem not to fit all learners. Actually, to enable contributions in blogs there is a high

Figure 3. The key success factors in the Wiki-enabled learning activity

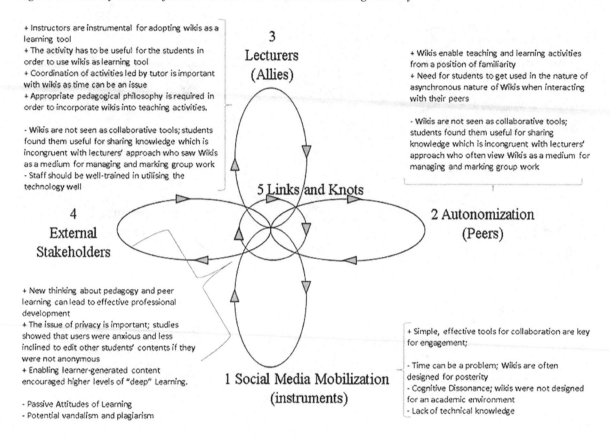

+ Instructors are instrumental for adopting wikis as a learning tool
+ The activity has to be useful for the students in order to use wikis as learning tool
+ Coordination of activities led by tutor is important with wikis as time can be an issue
+ Appropriate pedagogical philosophy is required in order to incorporate wikis into teaching activities.

- Wikis are not seen as collaborative tools; students found them useful for sharing knowledge which is incongruent with lecturers' approach who saw Wikis as a medium for managing and marking group work
- Staff should be well-trained in utilising the technology well

3
Lecturers
(Allies)

+ Wikis enable teaching and learning activities from a position of familiarity
+ Need for students to get used in the nature of asynchronous nature of Wikis when interacting with their peers

- Wikis are not seen as collaborative tools; students found them useful for sharing knowledge which is incongruent with lecturers' approach who often view Wikis as a medium for managing and marking group work

5 Links and Knots

4
External
Stakeholders

2 Autonomization
(Peers)

+ New thinking about pedagogy and peer learning can lead to effective professional development
+ The issue of privacy is important; studies showed that users were anxious and less inclined to edit other students' contents if they were not anonymous
+ Enabling learner-generated content encouraged higher levels of "deep" Learning.

- Passive Attitudes of Learning
- Potential vandalism and plagiarism

1 Social Media Mobilization
(instruments)

+ Simple, effective tools for collaboration are key for engagement;

- Time can be a problem; Wikis are often designed for posterity
- Cognitive Dissonance; wikis were not designed for an academic environment
- Lack of technical knowledge

need for staff that are well versed and effectively engaged with blogging technology (3). Once the initial resistance is overcome, blogs have the distinct advantage of enfranchising groups of students who are usually quiet in the normal classroom setting (2). Another unique aspect of Blogs is the role they may be able to play in the broadcasting and subsequent synthesis of content via trial and error. That can only be facilitated though if the students do not get side-tracked by the blogging activity itself (5). It seems that even though blogs may enable the publication of content, blogs are not equivalent to YouTube; the content is linked to the personal and reflexive processes encouraged by blog technology.

The Wiki-Enabled Learning Activity

The use of wikis in learning mirrors the perceived functionality of the wikis as online collaboration communities. The asynchronous nature of wikis and the ability for multiple users to edit the material makes wikis unique as can be seen from Figure 3.

The use of Wiki as an educational medium for teaching and learning in Higher Education offers some very interesting challenges with the technical challenge being probably the most prominent (1). Students find it difficult to engage with the tool unless it is relatively straightforward to use (1). The other cognitive dissonance to overcome is the idea that wikis are only collaborative tools and they are not meant for learning (5). The other rather unique aspect of wiki is that its advantage (i.e., many users working on the

Figure 4. The key success factors in the Facebook-enabled learning activity

+ Instructors are instrumental for adopting FB as a learning tool
+ The activity has to be meaningful for the students in order to use FB as learning tool
+ A Course interaction Strategy is paramount
+ The academics should ensure that the environment is safe and the behaviour of participants appropriate

- Staff should be well-trained in utilising the technology well

3
Lecturers
(Allies)

+ Complementary pedagogical philosophy (instead of substitution)
+ Safety has to be of primary importance
+ Important to have buy-in (use of FB should be student-driven)

- FB is in the sphere of personal life
- FB is used for student-led activities (often assessment-related); needs a change of mind-set to embrace FB as learning tool

5 Links and Knots

4
External
Stakeholders

2 Autonomization
(Peers)

+ Perceived usefulness of the activity and clarity of instructions
+ Relaxation of academic authority; student-centred pedagogy
+ Communications, Social Relationships and level of Participation are key

- Preference for face-to-face interactions in some disciplines
- Tackling the attitude towards FB is the largest obstacle

1 Social Media Mobilization
(instruments)

+ Design of the Activity;
+ Course delivery should be adjusted to the FB medium

- Cynicism with regards to FB as learning Tool.
- FB as a casual, peer-based environment
- Demands on Time
- Issues of Privacy
- Lack of technological understanding

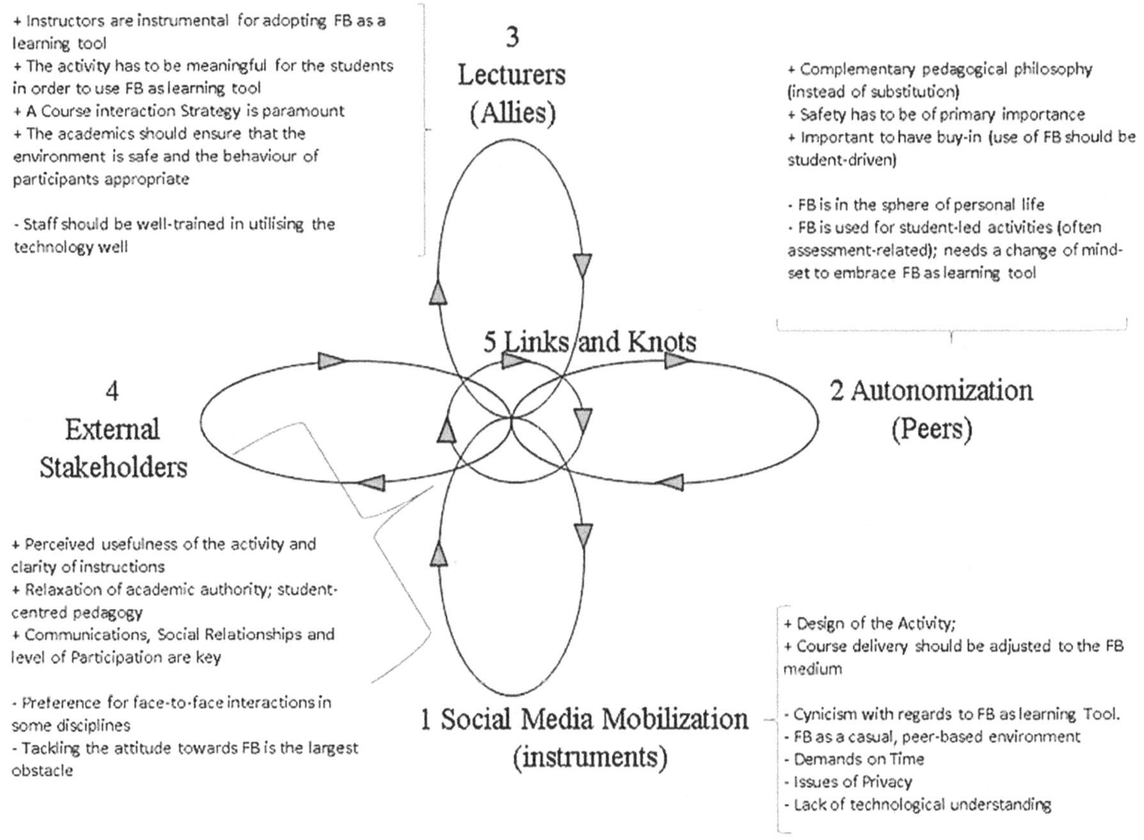

same material at different times) in the Higher Education context also became a disadvantage as many students were reluctant to edit other students' comments and content (2). The flip-side of this was the perception that wiki allowed for bullying, vandalism and potential plagiarism and thus could generate conflict within the learning community (4). Once again, the design of the wiki-based learning activity and the educator's approach in using it were paramount anchors for a positive learning experience (3).

The Facebook-Enabled Learning Activity

The review clearly indicated that Facebook was the most challenging social medium in the context of learning. When used for learning it was seen as a confusing platform. It could enable most of the functionality of blogs and content communities. However, the biggest obstacle is users' perception as can be seen from Figure 4.

The issue of privacy was front and centre in the interactions between students and the medium (1) as well as in the interactions among students (2) and in the interactions of students with their lecturers (3). In contrast to blogs and wikis, Facebook was perceived by the majority of students as the province and extension of students' personal life. Thus, there was considerable resistance in converting this medium into a learning tool (5). More than other tools, in Facebook the educator needs to tread carefully when utilising it in teaching and learning (3). Most research concurs that there is a place for learning through Facebook, but the design of the course has to allow for seamless integration, the educator has to provide an environment for secure and appropriate conduct among students (3) and, probably most important, there is a need for buy-in, most easily achieved if the requirement to use Facebook is generated by the students themselves rather than the lecturers (2).

DISCUSSION

Students in institutes of Higher Education are particularly savvy users of SM and they do use such media in a pragmatic useful fashion to enable their learning (Al-Rahmi et al., 2014; Donlan, 2014; Donnelly & Hume, 2015; Guerin et al., 2015). The review of the literature revealed a plethora of studies, which attempt to integrate SM enabled activities with the learning activities that occur within the context of Higher Education. This places the onus on Higher Education practitioners to identify what makes the use of such SM effective in teaching and learning. This chapter outlines a number of the key success factors when utilising any of the three main types of SM.

The first important realisation when dwelling into the literature is that there are different types of SM and thus by necessity the Key Success Factors that would apply to one type of SM may not necessarily apply to the other types of SM. Four distinct types of SM were originally identified: Self-Expression and Online reflection spaces, Online collaboration Communities, Social spaces, and Content communities. An example of each was used as the basis for this literature review, and a total of 199 case studies were identified, reviewed and analysed. The articles were categorised in each of the four types revealing that content communities do not tend to be used heavily as tools to facilitate learning. YouTube that tends to be the main content community example yielded only 17 articles and the manual analysis of those articles indicated that YouTube is often utilised as a platform to publish student-generated material. The functionality of YouTube does not appear to be distinct enough to offer a real alternative to the other three SM types. Thus at the end, YouTube as a SM tool was excluded from this study. The remaining three types of SM were mapped out against Latour's activity flows in order to identify relevant key success factors along the main communication flows of the student's learning enterprise. This conceptual mapping focused on the key factors that enable a flow of activities and communications via each loop thus facilitating a successful learning experience.

The second very important finding was that there were a number of key success factors that were identical for all three SM types:

1. The instructor and their knowledge of the medium were paramount for the successful use of that medium in the learning activity.
2. User's engagement was paramount for its success. This engagement was contingent of the:
    a. Relevance of the activity to the student's learning,
    b. The robust design of the learning activity,
    c. The care for privacy and appropriate behaviour online, and
    d. The overcoming of the cognitive dissonance that users had for each of the SM types.

However, the particular cognitive dissonance users had for each social medium was probably the one important differentiating factor among the various SM and their usage in teaching and learning. Each of the SM types was perceived in a different way by the students, and that had serious consequences in the utilisation of the tool in the Higher Education Context which are examined below in turn:

- **Blogs:** Were seen as useful to provide contextualisation of the information which is vital to the process of peer support. Through dialogues initiated by authors and followed by readers, blog platforms build a viable base of shared experiences and mutual relationships. Therefore, the learning activity should take advantage of the opportunities Blogs offer to provide a voice to quieter and introverted students. The analysis indicates that learners' level of engagement with the task is a salient parameter for learning to take place. There are also particular complexities with blogs, one being the issue of copyrights and the demand in time. Institutions may need to provide the required support to lecturers and students in order to encourage them to use this media in the learning activities.

- **Wikis:** Has been found very useful in creating constructivist learning environments that challenge students to participate more actively in their own education. Also, Wiki has been viewed as an enabling tool for knowledge construction and sharing. It is a less introspective tool than Blogs and is seen as a collaborative tool, while blogs are seen as self-expression tools. Time is seen differently in the development of a wiki; wikis are always work in-progress and are built forever; they never finish. With Blogs, each entry has a beginning, middle and end, but the wikis are different. Correspondingly, the activity has to be useful and meaningful in that conceptual frame of mind for students to encourage them to use Wikis as a learning platform.

- **Facebook:** Is currently considered as the most popular platform for online social networking among university students (Kabilan, Ahmad, & Abidin, 2010), and yet, it probably poses the highest resistance in any attempts to use it as a learning and teaching tool as it is often seen as an intrusion to the personal space of the student. Facebook can be useful if the instructor is able to change the particular conception. The issue of privacy has been front and centre in the analysis. In Facebook, even more than other SM types, the instructors have to provide an environment for secure and appropriate conduct among students and should pursue a buy-in from the student population.

Finally, an important observation can be made with regards to the loop of communications with external stakeholders: the results did not acknowledge the wider context and the external stakeholders in their analysis, which tended to be very topical and focused on the triad of lecturer-student-SM tool. This highlights a potential gap in the literature that should be explored further.

MANAGERIAL IMPLICATIONS

The results of this research warrant two managerial implications for businesses and practitioners. The first important implication is the issue of engagement; a reason why the Higher Education sector is experimenting with SM has been the difficulty of engaging students with the process of learning. Business has found it equally challenging to engage with employees in the workplace (Kreutzer & Land, 2015; Parry, Professor Stefan Strohmeier, Guillot-Soulez, & Soulez, 2014) and customers in the virtual marketplace (Chu & Kim, 2011; Sashi, 2012). The identified Key Success Factors are relevant with both constituents of the business, and the way the companies choose to design their SM activities should take the specificity of communication and activity enabled by each of the SM available. The suggested analysis makes it clear that different SM types enable different types of work and practitioners must be mindful of the implications when using a particular SM type.

The second serious implication arises when the Higher Education sector is eventually successful in implementing SM in the teaching curriculum. That would lead to the creation of a new generation of graduates who will have a very different skillset from the previous generations, and thus would have expectations from the workplace, which may not always be met by the employer. Thus, the employers should prepare for this eventuality and be aware of the consequences of these coming generations of future graduates.

FUTURE RESEARCH DIRECTIONS

This chapter has highlighted the key success factors when engaging SM in students' learning process. The structured literature review revealed a number of gaps that future research could investigate further. The first and most obvious gap relates to the relative dearth of empirical articles focusing on content communities such as YouTube. There is a need to explore this relative silence and unearth the potential of online content communities in the context of Higher Education. Another surprising gap related to the lack of research on the impact of the external social environment to the learning activity. Loop number 4, which was related to external stakeholders, was not investigated by the population of articles this research considered, and it seems to be a silent partner in the learning activities of students. It is not in the remit of this work to speculate about the reasons, though suggestions spring readily in mind, for example, lack of interest on external stakeholders from the researchers' point of view. However, this gap needs to be explored. Social media, when used for educational purposes, straddle two important spheres of influence in a student's life: the personal social world with the academic knowledge-based world.

Finally, it is very important to expand this research and investigate to what extent the context of organisations and businesses gives rise to the same modes of activity among employees as the Higher Education context. A starting point could be a similar kind of research repeated for employees within the private sector.

CONCLUSION

This chapter has utilised a structured literature review to identify the key success factors that determine the successful use for teaching and learning purposes of each of the three main types of SM in the context of Higher Education. The SM types include Self-Expression and Online reflection spaces, Online collaboration Communities, and Social spaces. A fourth SM type was considered: Content communities. However, the early research indicated that there was a dearth of critical mass in research literature to warrant its inclusion.

When examining the key success factors for each SM type, there was substantial commonality across all three types: the instructor's ability with the media, the engagement level of students with the activity, an appropriate and meaningful course design to name a few. Overall, the different technological platforms did not appear to be the issue; the main point of concern was the fit of the chosen social medium to the learning activity in question. What became apparent from the findings is that different types of SM are perceived differently by students who consequently have different expectations and demands with regards to its use. For example, Blogs are seen as quite personalised, reflective and geared towards asynchronous communication, while wikis are seen as collaborative tools requiring a higher level of technical expertise. In contrast to both types of media, Facebook is conceived as a very personal platform, which offers the highest cognitive barrier for users who may be utilising it as a learning tool.

In conclusion, social media can be used in Higher Education for teaching and learning. The key success factors that are important for each type were successfully identified, but the most influential factor related to users' perception of each social media type highlighting the need for the educator to adopt carefully designed assessments to overcome this user-centred cognitive dissonance.

REFERENCES

Al-Rahmi, W. M., Othman, M. S., & Musa, M. A. (2014). The improvement of students' academic performance by using social media through collaborative learning in Malaysian higher education. *Asian Social Science*, *10*(8), 210–221.

Al-Shawabkeh, A., & Lim, A. (2014). The Use of Social Media In Higher Education Learning: SWOT Analysis of Using Social Media for Learning. In *Proceedings of the European Conference on Social Media (ECSM)*. University of Brighton.

Arnold, N., & Paulus, T. (2010). Using a social networking site for experiential learning: Appropriating, lurking, modeling and community building. *The Internet and Higher Education*, *13*(4), 188–196. doi:10.1016/j.iheduc.2010.04.002

Bennett, S., Bishop, A., Dalgarno, B., Waycott, J., & Kennedy, G. (2012). Implementing Web 2.0 technologies in higher education: A collective case study. *Computers & Education*, *59*(2), 524–534. doi:10.1016/j.compedu.2011.12.022

Benson, V. (2014). *Cutting-edge technologies and social media use in higher education*. IGI Global. doi:10.4018/978-1-4666-5174-6

Benson, V., Morgan, S., & Tennakoon, H. (2012). A framework for knowledge management in higher education using social networking. *International Journal of Knowledge Society Research*, *3*(2), 44–54. doi:10.4018/jksr.2012040104

Biasutti, M., & El-Deghaidy, H. (2015). Interdisciplinary project-based learning: An online wiki experience in teacher education. *Technology, Pedagogy and Education*, *24*(3), 339–355. doi:10.1080/1475939X.2014.899510

Brandtzaeg, P. B., & Heim, J. (2011). A typology of social networking sites users. *International Journal of Web Based Communities*, *7*(1), 28–51. doi:10.1504/IJWBC.2011.038124

Buzzetto-More, N. A. (2012). Social networking in undergraduate education. *Interdisciplinary Journal of Information, Knowledge, and Management*, *7*, 63–90.

Chu, S., & Kim, Y. (2011). Determinants of consumer engagement in electronic word-of-mouth (eWOM) in social networking sites. *International Journal of Advertising, 30*(1), 47–75. doi:10.2501/IJA-30-1-047-075

Cole, M. (2009). Using Wiki technology to support student engagement: Lessons from the trenches. *Computers & Education, 52*(1), 141–146. doi:10.1016/j.compedu.2008.07.003

De Wever, B., Hämäläinen, R., Voet, M., & Gielen, M. (2015). A wiki task for first-year university students: The effect of scripting students' collaboration. *The Internet and Higher Education, 25,* 37–44. doi:10.1016/j.iheduc.2014.12.002

Dery, K., Tansley, C., & Hafermalz, E. (2014). Games people play: social media and recruitment. *Proceedings of the 25th Australasian Conference on Information Systems*. ACIS.

Dickie, V. A., & Meier, H. (2015). The facebook tutor: Networking education. *Ubiquitous Learning, 8*(2), 1–12.

Donlan, L. (2014). Exploring the views of students on the use of Facebook in university teaching and learning. *Journal of Further and Higher Education, 38*(4), 572–588. doi:10.1080/0309877X.2012.726973

Donnelly, D. F., & Hume, A. (2015). Using collaborative technology to enhance pre-service teachers' pedagogical content knowledge in Science. *Research in Science & Technological Education, 33*(1), 61–87. doi:10.1080/02635143.2014.977782

Duarte, P. (2015). The use of a group blog to actively support learning activities. *Active Learning in Higher Education, 16*(2), 103–117. doi:10.1177/1469787415574051

El Ouirdi, M., (2014). Social Media Conceptualization and Taxonomy: A Lasswellian Framework. *Journal of Creative Communications, 9*(2), 107–126. doi:10.1177/0973258614528608

Garcia, E., Elbeltagi, I., Brown, M., & Dungay, K. (2015). The implications of a connectivist learning blog model and the changing role of teaching and learning. *British Journal of Educational Technology, 46*(4), 877–894. doi:10.1111/bjet.12184

Guerin, C., Carter, S., & Aitchison, C. (2015). Blogging as community of practice: Lessons for academic development? *The International Journal for Academic Development, 20*(3), 212–223. doi:10.1080/1360144X.2015.1042480

Ha, J., & Shin, D. H. (2014). Facebook in a standard college class: An alternative conduit for promoting teacher-student interaction. *American Communication Journal, 16*(1), 36–52.

Hanna, R., Rohm, A., & Crittenden, V. L. (2011). We're all connected: The power of the social media ecosystem. *Business Horizons, 54*(3), 265–273. doi:10.1016/j.bushor.2011.01.007

Hew, K. F., & Cheung, W. S. (2013). Use of Web 2.0 technologies in K-12 and higher education: The search for evidence-based practice. *Educational Research Review, 9,* 47–64. doi:10.1016/j.edurev.2012.08.001

Kabilan, M. K., Ahmad, N., & Abidin, M. J. Z. (2010). Facebook: An online environment for learning of English in institutions of higher education? *The Internet and Higher Education, 13*(4), 179–187. doi:10.1016/j.iheduc.2010.07.003

Kaplan, A. M., & Haenlein, M. (2010). Users of the world, unite! The challenges and opportunities of social media. *Business Horizons, 53*(1), 59–68. doi:10.1016/j.bushor.2009.09.003

Karahan, E., & Roehrig, G. (2014). Constructing Media Artifacts in a Social Constructivist Environment to Enhance Students' Environmental Awareness and Activism. *Journal of Science Education and Technology, 24*(1), 103–118. doi:10.1007/s10956-014-9525-5

Kreutzer, R. T., & Land, K.-H. (2015). *The Necessity of Change Management: Why Our Traditional Communication and Organizational Structures Are Becoming Obsolete. In Digital Darwinism* (pp. 209–248). Springer.

Kuhn, T. S. (1996). *The Structure of Scientific Revolutions* (3rd ed.). The University of Chicago Press. doi:10.7208/chicago/9780226458106.001.0001

Latour, B. (1999). *Science's Blood Flow; An Example from Joliot's Scientific Intelligence. In Pandora's Hope: Essays on the Reality of Science Studies* (pp. 80–112). Cambridge, MA: Harvard University Press.

Lederer, K. (2012). Pros and cons of social media in the classroom. *Campus Technology, 25*(5), 1–2.

Maloney, S., Moss, A., & Ilic, D. (2014). Social media in health professional education: A student perspective on user levels and prospective applications. *Advances in Health Sciences Education: Theory and Practice, 19*(5), 687–697. doi:10.1007/s10459-014-9495-7 PMID:24566977

O'Boyle, I. (2014). Mobilising social media in sport management education. *Journal of Hospitality, Leisure, Sport and Tourism Education, 15*(1), 58–60. doi:10.1016/j.jhlste.2014.05.002

Oeberst, A., Halatchliyski, I., Kimmerle, J., & Cress, U. (2014). Knowledge Construction in Wikipedia: A Systemic-Constructivist Analysis. *Journal of the Learning Sciences, 23*(2), 149–176. doi:10.1080/10508406.2014.888352

Page, K. L., & Reynolds, N. (2015). Learning from a wiki way of learning. *Studies in Higher Education, 40*(6), 988–1013. doi:10.1080/03075079.2013.865158

Parry, E., Professor Stefan Strohmeier, D., Guillot-Soulez, C., & Soulez, S. (2014). On the heterogeneity of Generation Y job preferences. *Employee Relations, 36*(4), 319–332. doi:10.1108/ER-07-2013-0073

Prensky, M. (2001). Digital natives, digital immigrants part 1. *On the horizon, 9*(5), 1–6. doi:10.1108/10748120110424816

Sashi, C. M. (2012). Customer engagement, buyer-seller relationships, and social media. *Management Decision, 50*(2), 253–272. doi:10.1108/00251741211203551

Schlicht, P. (2013). Turning the digital divide into digital dividends through free content and open networks: Wikieducator learning4content (l4c) initiative. *Journal of Asynchronous Learning Networks, 17*(2), 87–100.

Taylor, R., King, F., & Nelson, G. (2012). Student learning through social media. *Journal of Sociological Research, 3*(2), 29–35. doi:10.5296/jsr.v3i2.2136

Yukawa, J. (2006). Co-reflection in online learning: Collaborative critical thinking as narrative. *International Journal of Computer-Supported Collaborative Learning*, *1*(2), 203–228. doi:10.1007/s11412-006-8994-9

Zheng, B., Niiya, M., & Warschauer, M. (2015). Wikis and collaborative learning in higher education. *Technology, Pedagogy and Education*, *24*(3), 357–374. doi:10.1080/1475939X.2014.948041

KEY TERMS AND DEFINITIONS

Actor-Network Theory: A theoretical approach is used in the field of science studies which treats objects part of a social network.

Blogs: A regularly updated discussion published on a website or web page, typically run by an individual or small group and written in an informal or conversational style.

Digital Natives: Native speakers of the digital language of computers, video games and the Internet.

Facebook: A free social networking website that allows registered users to create profiles, upload photos and video, send messages and communicate with other users.

Information Technologies: A field concerned with the use of technology in managing and processing information.

Social Networks: A network of social interactions and personal relationships.

User Typology: A typology is based on distinct user behaviour, instead of their goals or motivations.

Wikis: A collaborative website or database developed by a community of users, allowing any user to add and edit content.

Chapter 16

Desperately Seeking Customer Engagement:
The Five-Sources Model of Brand Value on Social Media

Inna P Piven
Unitec Institute of Technology, New Zealand

Michael Breazeale
Mississippi State University, USA

ABSTRACT

Since 2004 when Myspace was converted from a file storage service to a social networking site, social media has become an integral part of people's everyday experiences. Social media has also come to play an influential role in business. The purpose of this chapter is to introduce the Five-Sources Model of Brand Value that illustrates the importance of functional, emotional, self-oriented, social, and relational brand consumption experiences helping different organisations get a clear sense of where they can add value to their marketing communication strategies on social media. The model is consumer-centered and is grounded in consumers' experiences collected through interviews and Facebook focus group. This chapter is based on an on-going project that first started as a Masters research in 2011. It has continued with conferences and academic papers, in conjunction with consulting and lecturing on social media applications in New Zealand business and education context.

INTRODUCTION

It has become clear in the past few years that the most noticeable changes in all aspects of our collective, private and public lives are connected to the emergence of social media. In practice, this means that new media has "transformed consumers from silent, isolated and invisible individuals, into noisy, public, and even more unmanageable than usual, collective" (Patterson, 2011, p. 2). Millions of ordinary social media users now have the ability to discuss and share their ideas and opinions publicly, influence

DOI: 10.4018/978-1-5225-0559-4.ch016

service or product development (even building design), create a brand community and communicate with brands on Facebook and Twitter (Benson & Morgan, 2015). The practical consequence of this is perfectly illustrated by Marc Kushner, whose architecture firm proposed a community building, by sharing photorealistic renderings of the building on Facebook and Instagram "to let people do what they do: share it, comment, like it, hate it…two years before the building was complete, it was already a part of the community" (Kushner, 2015). This example shows why many businesses nowadays accept the need to shift their traditional marketing into social media marketing. However, some doubts have also been raised as to the benefits of social media ventures. It is, therefore, not surprising that both academic and market research put a great deal of time and energy into understanding the meanings and functions of social media in business. It is crucial for companies and organizations to translate the abstract descriptions of emerging concepts and ideas into concrete applications and strategies to be used. Therefore, the following research question is posed: *How are brands conceptualised in the consumption of a social media community?*

To answer that question, this chapter introduces the Five-Sources Model of Brand Value creation, which describes the specific social media practices for effective collaboration between firms and consumers. This model is grounded in the reality of consumers' experiences, and evaluated against existing marketing concepts. The chapter is first concerned with a number of ways in which social media may impact the relationships between brands, consumers, and, all in all, the process of brand value creation. Secondly, this chapter offers a practically tested foundation for branding via social media, paying attention to consumers' role in the production and consumption of brand experiences. Finally, the chapter aims to provide marketing practitioners with a new way to examine proposed social media tactics.

The first part of the chapter introduces a theoretical background within which to think about the changed relationship between organisations and individuals. It then goes on to present the Five-Sources Model of Brand Value, offering five new perspectives to discern how consumers experience brands in social media settings. The model is supported by figures and examples illustrating the nature of consumer-brand interactions, and how brand value can be activated via social media. This includes functional, emotional, self-oriented, social, and relational aspects of brand consumption. With a strong focus on the research data, this chapter will present solutions and recommendations, concluding by discussing future research directions and making suggestions for additional reading.

BACKGROUND

The idea of community has a long history in sociological, cultural and communication research. The term is often applied, regardless of online or offline context, where a specific type of bond between people defines the community. The idea of a consumption community arose as marketers recognised that consumers often have shared emotions and habits in the consumption of common objects (Friedman *et al.*, 1992), for example, of beloved brands such as Macintosh, Harley-Davidson and *Star Trek*. Muñiz and O'Guinn (2001) define these communities as a human consumption experience in which members are not necessarily physically close and their social relationships are defined by shared morality, consciousness, rituals and traditions. Further, Schouten and McAlexander (1995) argue that these relationships help to form consumption subcultures that meet some specialised needs of those consumers (Fournier & Lee, 2009).

Consumption communities typically revolve around a brand in a human affiliation in which a shared passion or interest toward a particular product, service or consumption activity unites the members. The brand becomes the basis of the specific interrelationships (Davis, Buchanan-Oliver & Brodie, 2000). Therefore, consumers in brand communities are 'psychically' connected. It is a union that helps members gratify functional or emotional needs (Bagozzi & Dholakia, 2002; Murray, 1991).

But what do we know specifically about the enactment of brand communities within the context of social media? In recent years, social media have made possible a more instant and personal interaction between the brand and its community (Nambisan & Watt, 2011). The ease of participating in online social communities removes many of the barriers to interaction, increasing the likelihood of participation by consumers who may not have been able or inclined to do so before. Further, access such as this is no longer limited to those that are willing to sit in front of a computer screen while they interact. Indeed, the constant availability of Internet-enabled mobile devices has made possible not only instant consumption, but almost continual interactivity between the brand and its consumers (Davis & Sajtos, 2008).

This enhanced interaction capability is an efficient way for users to share their experiences and opinions of the brand. In so doing, community members have the potential to shape the brand offering and to impact other users' opinions of and experience with the brand.

Besides the ability of consumers to shape the brand, social-media-enabled brand communities also allow consumers to define their own identities individually and collectively, with an emphasis on the brand's personality (Avis, 2012; Seimiene, 2012; Aaker, 1997). Aaker (1997) suggests that consumption is often motivated by consumers' perceptions of a brand's human characteristics. Interacting around the brand with other interested consumers creates valued experiences for consumers as well. Not only does it help the consumer and marketers make the brand interaction more meaningful in the mind of the consumer, it also enhances consumers' abilities to shape and display their actual, ideal, social and virtual selves.

With brand personality-based consumption, the ease of participating in an online community typically increases the diversity of community members. Bagozzi and Dholakia (2002) suggest that virtual communities lower the importance of members' social characteristics, physical appearance and nonverbal expressions, but elevate the importance of that which is communicated and freedom of expression. Cova and Pace (2006) conclude that consumption is actually the personal self-exhibition of brand rituals in front of other consumers.

Also, some consumers may be avid users who would take part in the community even if the barriers to participation were higher, but others may be less interested in the brand and want other benefits from their participation. It could also be the case that the responsibilities and social intimacies that often characterize face-to-face communities may decrease in an online community (Bagozzi & Dholakia, 2002). In these cases, social media brand consumption may only be devoted to specific commercial or informational objectives rather than social responsibility and mutual support.

Finally, social media brand consumption places emphasis on the interactive experience (Yoo *et al.* 2010; Downes & McMillan, 2000; Rafaeli, 1998). Consumption is two-way, and in social media consumption, the roles between consumer, brand, and community converge (Davis & Sajtos, 2008). As consumers co-create the experience, they seek personalisation (Yoon *et al.*, 2008; Vlasic & Kesic, 2007; McMillan & Hwang, 2002) and the immediate experience of their interactions (Haeckel, 1998; Hoffman & Novak, 1996). It is a codependent process that is fuelled by both the consumer's needs and the marketer's need for the benefits that arise from the interactivity (Yoo *et al.*, 2010; Park & Park, 2009; Trappey & Woodside, 2005). It is important to note that the responsiveness allowed by this type of interactivity actually represents more than just a dialogue between consumer and brand. It represents a consumer's commitment to the brand, his or her role in an active relationship (Mollen & Wilson, 2010).

Despite the importance of the early work on brand consumption in social media communities that has been discussed here, no research has focused solely on social media communities and brand consumption. The Five-Sources Model presented in this chapter represents the first attempt to specifically describe the nature of the consumer's experience of consumption, paying close attention to the benefits that consumers derive from their participation in a social media community. The model also examines the way that brand meaning is created and adapted by community members. In discussing the benefits sought and achieved by consumers, the authors are also able to present meaningful suggestions for marketers who wish to capitalize on social media marketing to create stronger relationships with their customers.

MAIN FOCUS OF THE CHAPTER

Before social media, marketing communications was a relatively stable and predictable business; the traditional approaches generally worked, keeping advertisers and PR strategists sufficiently satisfied. Social media created an entirely different marketing landscape characterised by "real time information exchange" (Hennig-Thurau *et al.*, 2010, p. 311), "excessive information flow", "an emphasis on techno-logical innovation" (Morgan-Thomas & Veloutsou, 2011, p. 2), and "higher-order goals: connect, create, consume and control" (Hoffman & Novak, 2011, p. 4). Users seem to have welcomed the emerging media, motivated by almost endless opportunities for creating and consuming content. One of the most obvious signs of this is the steady growth of the social media population – "one billion tweets are now sent every two and a half days, making it hard to deal with in retrospect, never mind in real time" (Vis, 2013, p. 2). In this respect, marketers' basic concerns are whether social networking sites are the best medium, as so many suggest, to reach their consumers.

The core idea of the Five-Sources Model of Brand Value is to create a tool that might help different organisations and businesses effectively adapt social media practices their consumers can engage with. Ideally, this model offers peace of mind to companies and organizations in regards to their interactions with consumers on social media. How does it happen, what does it mean, and what outcomes might it have for all parties involved? In a sense, the Five-Sources Model represents strategic directions for branding via social media that focus on the relationships among a brand, individual consumers, and a social media community.

Implementing netnography in the form of an asynchronous Facebook focus group and face-to-face non-directive interviews, researchers identified five core sources of brand value creation that include functional, emotional, self-oriented, social, and relational. The next five sections draw on these novel insights into brand value creation through consumption scenarios. Collectively, the five sources described herein constitute the Five-Sources Model. The model is presented in conjunction with research data and examples of New Zealand companies that interview and focus group participants often referred to during data collection.

Functional Source of Brand Value

It [social media] is the quickest way to say something, be heard and responded to. – Facebook focus group participant

In general terms, prior research has investigated the scenarios in which consumers may engage with brands on social media, on Facebook and Twitter in particular. Among the many reasons given, the most common is problem solving, as "consumers consider social media to be a platform for addressing problems when other communication channels are unavailable or unsatisfying" (Davis, Piven & Breazeale, 2014, p. 130). From the consumers' perspective, there are a number of ways to fix problems when a brand is not responsive via traditional channels – a forty-minute wait on the phone has transformed into 140 characters on Twitter, or a short status update on Facebook. Moreover, the research has also shown that consumers' most memorable experiences often relate to problem solving:

I remember we were after tennis tickets; I think it was the Auckland Open. It was last minute tickets available, and my friend was after those tickets for us. He communicated with that person from Auckland Open on Twitter. He got replies straight away, which was quite spectacular. We ended up actually getting tickets for another day; we didn't get what we wanted. But just the fact that they got back to us very quickly via Twitter, it was quite good. (Piven, 2012, p. 173)

In this respect, it should be noted that consumers might never contact a business on social media until certain problems occur. Being asked to comment on people's willingness to engage with business on Facebook, one participant noted the following:

I'm almost prepared to bet that a lot of the companies that people follow, they did so 6 months, a year, 2 years ago. They've never looked at that Facebook site since...unless they have a problem...

What appears to take place is that consumers are looking for money and timesaving solutions when it comes to their communications with a brand, and meeting in person seems to be gradually becoming an archaic option:

I've bought five or six cars from the same people, and they'll always remind me when I need to get a service. I would prefer they communicate that electronically rather than picking up the phone or actually speaking to me. It just allows me to sort of respond in the way in which I want to respond, and I feel it's not encroaching on my time.

When almost everyone has their own mobile devices and multiple profiles on social media, it is surprising that some organisations and businesses still rely primarily on traditional marketing communications. This is unfortunate because from the consumers' perspective, there is a real value in connecting on social media:

A lot of my business information is coming in and updates about companies through LinkedIn. I have 10 or 20 different sources I find myself going back to repeatedly, and it's simply because they have all of the information I need.

Consistent with the sentiments above, Brodie *et al.* (2011) suggest that "the triggers prompting the onset of specific consumer engagement states occur when the consumer recognises a need to solve a specific problem or satisfy a want, performs a search..." (p. 7). Referring to Grönroos (2001, p. 150), it can be said that business profiles on social media serve as the "quality-generated resources", which may determine consumers' attitude towards the brand. In other words, customers view brands on social media as a "membership club", "information desk" or "showroom" that enables them to gain exclusive insight into the brands' offers, rewards and specials, or a "brand lounge" that allows people to come to

Figure 1. Functional source of brand values on social media (value-creation process through brand functionality)

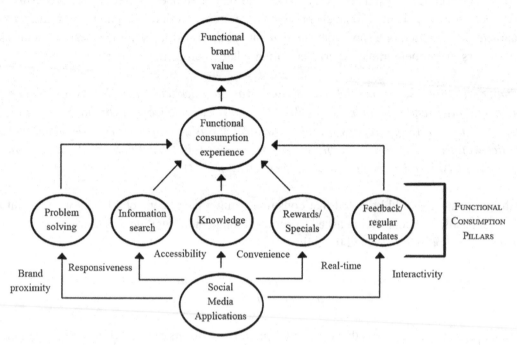

a common place to find an answer, or have a conversation with the brand and other followers (Davis, Piven, & Breazeale, 2014). To put it differently, a brand acts as a source of functional benefits related to consumers' needs such as; information availability, access to rewards and specials, real-time communication, prompt response to urgent matters, and a channel for providing feedback (Piven, 2012). In this respect, brand value on social media can be created through consumers' functional brand experiences. Figure 1 emphasises the role of different functional pillars in this value-creation process.

The research evidence led to a conclusion that brands perform various functional roles on social media, ranging from simple to complex, but all are anchored in the consumer's needs and specific situations. In some cases, consumers' engagement with brands on social media can be motivated less by personal needs and more by professional interests or duties:

Out of duty, I follow quite a lot. I follow all of my competition. For instance, Neat Meat is my competition, and I go through everyone they like and see who they like, what are their new products? Also my background is sales, but it's always been advertising, print and media. Now I'm in a whole new industry, so you need to educate yourself.

Consumers' interest in brands on social media can also be explained by the drive to get access to brand's specials. Although some participants report that possible rewards are the only reason they engage with a brand via social media, it should be said that "such reward-focused communications with brands can actually lead to the beginning of a new relationship" (Davis, Piven, & Breazeale, 2014, p. 130):

If I'm making my own purchasing decisions, I do look at whether or not they've got a social media presence, and my preference is probably to go with someone who does.

A theme that emerged through the data analysis is that social media allow consumers to implement "higher-order tasks" such as:

1. Providing cost and time saving solutions,
2. Reducing stress caused by problems associated with a brand failure, and
3. Giving consumers more control over a situation due to a brand's proximity (Piven, 2012). Table 1 shows the most common situations, both positive and negative from consumers' experiences with New Zealand brands.

Table 1. Functional consumption scenarios

Functional Pillars	Functional Consumption Scenarios
Problem Solving A need to solve emerging problems when other communication channels are unavailable, time or money consuming (Piven, 2012, p. 80).	Telecom (currently Spark), https://twitter.com/SparkNZ "I was looking for some new mobile phones for work. I sent out a tweet to Telecom and GNI, because we deal with both of them at work. And said, you know I'm looking for some new phones what can you recommend? Within an hour I had replies from both companies saying, you know here's a link off to our web site with all the new handsets. That was great; it was like "whoa, okay, here's all the information". So I was able to just fire off an email and say "right I'll get 10 of those please". They took all the pain off me having to go in and research them all." Telecom (currently Spark), https://twitter.com/SparkNZ "This afternoon we had a woman that sent a tweet to us, Vodafone and 2Degrees, and said "I'm looking to buy an iPhone today, who can do me a deal?" I can't do her a deal, but I just simply tweeted back and said that this is where you can go and get an iPhone, and we were the only ones that replied to her. And she said "Thanks, I'm going to go and buy one from Telecom". So that's a bread and butter kind of example. Just by being there, by being available and helpful it looks like we might have sold a phone."
Information Search/ Regular Updates A need to get required information about brand, available alternatives, expert's advice or updates (Piven, 2012, p. 83).	Kiwi Bank, https://twitter.com/KiwibankNZ "I'm with Kiwi Bank and I follow them on Twitter. I have had a couple of brief interactions with them around some banking services. That was a really positive experience. Within a couple of hours, they replied with a link to their website to a specific part that I was interested in." New World, a shopping centre, https://www.facebook.com/newworld "If I follow New World and they don't have a post at least once a week, I'm going to get really bored very quickly with them. Then if they do end up putting up a post - and it's something that I find completely boring, or irrelevant to me-, chances are I'll go off and get rid of them. I've done that a few times with companies."
Rewards/Specials A need to have access to a brand's deals, specials, giveaways and gifts (Piven, 2012, p. 89)	Essenze, home décor https://www.facebook.com/essenzedesign/ "Seven days before the event we wanted to go to, I checked out their Twitter page, what people said about it and their Facebook page, as Dee (*wife) said to me, "a contest is going on there". So I wrote a slogan and won a double pass to the event. That's the whole deal – you go there for a reason. They actually engaged me for participating in the contest, giving me a double pass."
Convenience/ Responsiveness A need for instant and convenient access to a brand's information and services, and for real-time communication	ASB Bank, https://www.facebook.com/ASBBank "My bank is ASB. The reason I bank with ASB is that they provide me with very easy to use, very easy to look at, it's functional, it's pretty, they're clear – for both, Android and iPad. And you feel secure. I think you can like a bank on what they can offer you." Countdown, shopping mall https://www.facebook.com/countdown "It's interesting with Countdown. Over the Easter people were asking "Are you open on Easter Monday?" and there were no responses. I'm not sure if they tweeted…You expect them to be online."
Providing Feedback A need to provide a brand with feedback on product/ service quality and operations	Urbis Magazine, https://www.facebook.com/UrbisMagazine/info/ "Yesterday we went to Urbis design day. I was not happy with the fact that we had to wait for a long time in a queue. What I would do now is to go to the Urbis design page and comment to make sure that next year they do something about it. If none of us say something, then they probably will not look at it. And usually they are looking for us to provide feedback."

Emotional Source of Brand Value

I'm not interested in a brand if it doesn't do something spectacular on social media; I just don't see a reason to follow. – Interview participant

When a business wants to stimulate discussion on social media, it is important to keep in mind that consumers' interests in brands are often motivated by emotional drivers. Knowing, for example, that "information-seeking is curiosity's most basic behavioral manifestation" brands can create multiple scenarios to activate consumers' curiosity (Loewenstein, 1994, p. 84). It seems fair to say that the brand's curiosity value goes well with human nature – the desire to "uncover" what is behind a quiz or an interesting image on Facebook may encourage consumers' interaction with a brand (Davis & Piven, 2013):

It's just curiosity. You never know what that link might give you. It might give you a piece of information of business that I need for myself.

I've got a nut allergy and a beautiful Anzac recipe was posted up on one of the chefs I follow. And I asked a question, do I need to substitute it with more flour to make it more balanced, and she [the chef] got back straight away and said: "No, it's fine you don't have to". I was genuinely interested, and I was curious to see also how quick they'd respond, what their response would be.

It can be suggested that social media helps brands supply the ingredient that seems to be missing in traditional marketing communications – curiosity keeps the conversation going, stimulates and encourages participation, and creates a conversation that potentially may get good press down the line. The recent and much publicised white/gold/blue/black dress mystery illustrates how social media use curiosity as a hook. The story started on Tumblr and took Twitter and Facebook by storm – everyone felt a need to discover what was going on. The debate surrounding the dress – whether the stripes were white and gold, or blue and black – attracted much attention from journalists, scientists, and celebrities like Ellen DeGeneres, who tweeted "the dress is gonna start world war 3" (Udland, 2015). The role of fantasy and curiosity in brand consumptions is supported by Poulsson and Kale's (2004) idea that, for example, service experiences "should be perceived as personally relevant" and include elements of "novelty, surprise, learning, and engagement" (p. 267):

… yesterday I joined Esprit. I like this brand. I did it just because I wanted to state my preferences, and now I would like to see how it would benefit me in the future.

I wouldn't join a "dead" page just because someone sent me an invitation. It should be in my areas of interest, but it also should post daily updates, create discussions, upload pictures, offer to take part in competitions…

The most interesting insight into emotional consumption is that consumers have much more personal feelings towards brands on social media than was expected. For example, some research participants tend to believe their fellowship in a brand community gives a feeling of being privileged and recognised by a brand:

A couple of weeks ago I was approached by an ice cream brand, which is starting up. Delicious stuff. And they said, 'We would love you to try and if you like it, talk about it'. They didn't say you must tweet about it... I didn't really feel obligated to blog about it or anything like that. But I tried their stuff and because I genuinely liked it, I tweeted about it.

Consumers value the brand's proximity on social media as it helps them with a variety of needs including "emotional support and encouragement" (Fournier & Lee, 2009, p. 106):

I was afraid of becoming a part of a community; I was not interactive – but not any more. I decided to start interacting to become a part of it and I'm stepping out of my comfort zone, because I'm confident about our business, I'm happy I can be a part of a community. (Piven, 2012, p. 175)

It is interesting to note that consumers are more likely to feel emotionally connected to a brand if elements of humor and entertainment are incorporated into their brand experiences (Piven, 2012). This is supported by Holt's (1995) remark that consumers "use consumption objects as resources to interact with fellow consumers...to entertain each other" (p. 9):

I try to identify which group I belong to. Whether I am among majority or minority? Maybe it sounds weird, but I keep the score just for my own curiosity. (about reading comments on a business page)

Figure 2 reflects the process of emotional value creation. Based on research results, it can be noted that brands are assigned a specific role in the fulfillment of consumers' needs "for emotional end-states, e.g. security, happiness, or social acceptance" (Sandström *et. al.*, 2008, p. 119). In this regard, the study argues that a brand's emotional value on social media is created through consumption experiences that embody entertainment, enjoyment, problem alleviation, privilege, recognition, fantasy and curiosity (Piven, 2012).

In closing, social media offers an excellent environment and resources to tap into consumers' emotions. The result is consistent with Fournier's (1998) relationship theory, in which the quality of relationships between brands and consumers is characterised by the degree to which customers feel emotionally attached to a brand. In this sense, it is important to look across opportunities presented by social media to understand how to bring them together to ensure that a brand community on Facebook, Twitter or Instagram is alive and engaging (Table 2).

Self-Oriented Source of Brand Value

It [social media] enables us to feel like we are 'making a difference' in some way, interacting with our communities. – Facebook focus group participant

When the question is how to integrate social media into marketing communication strategies, an understanding of self-oriented brand consumption is a must. It should come as no surprise that consumers express their interest in brand experiences that resonate with their lifestyle, personal or professional goals, or help to facilitate their daily activities (research labels this as the "life arrangement" pillar). What becomes clear through research is that a brand on social media plays the role of a facilitator by helping consumers to:

Figure 2. Emotional source of brand value on social media (value-creation process through emotional consumption)

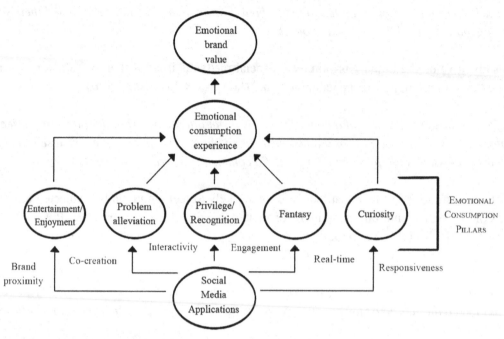

Table 2. Emotional consumption scenarios

Emotional Pillars	Emotional Consumption Scenarios
Entertainment/Enjoyment A need for experiences that include elements of entertainment and enjoyment (Piven, 2012).	House of Travel, https://www.facebook.com/houseoftravelNZ & Flight Centre, https://www.facebook.com/FlightCentreNZ "I was following House of Travel and Flight Centre, and Flight Centre kept putting up "these are all our sales". Whereas House of Travel would put up, occasionally "these are our sales", but then they'd actually put up information about a lot of their destinations, so I could actually click through and learn about the destination… So, Flight Centre I unliked, because they kept pushing…. but I've kept with House of Travel. Instead of saying "give us 3 thousand dollars and you can go to Samoa for 10 days", it was more "here's Samoa, isn't it nice, these are all the relaxing things you can do, and things like that"…I'm going to go talk to them [House of Travel], because they've tried to a develop relationship with me, instead of just forcing stuff on me."
Problem Alleviation A need for experiences that help to alleviate personal problems (Piven, 2012)	New Zealand Herald, https://www.facebook.com/nzherald.co.nz "The very reason I subscribe to NZ Herald is to help alleviate the homesickness. This pic [fish and chips on the beach] epitomises my former life in many ways, and is vastly different to the life I live now."
Privilege/Recognition A need for experiences that make consumers feel privileged and recognised by a brand (Piven, 2012)	Tasti, muesli bars and baking bits, https://twitter.com/TastiNZ "I'm an official Tasti tester, Tasti is a brand of seeds, nuts and muesli bars. They actually have been in New Zealand for years. I tweeted them the other day saying: "I just realized that I actually use one of your products at least once a day, but I just didn't know…" I engage with them over Twitter because I love to bake. It turned out the day of their new product launch, I was just tweeting excitedly about their new stuff, …some looked really yummy, and so I just tweeted back and forth. And then they started the Tasti Tester competition, "Tell us, why you should be a Tasti tester", …anyway she [company's community manager on Twitter] made me a tester, so I'll get a box from them to try next week."
Fantasy/Curiosity A need for curiosity-driven brand experiences or experiences that include elements of fantasy	Pinterest, https://www.pinterest.com "11 million people on it [2012 data], it's the fastest growing network ever. But if someone asks me "Hey, do you really need to use Pinterest? – No. I don't think so". I don't have a business there, I don't make money of it, it's curiosity and knowledge, and I want to know what this is. That's what keeps me going back...there might be something about it, and the only way is to go and find out."

1. Have brand experiences that suit their personal schedules and
2. Effectively manage various tasks.

This could be anything from getting news from *The New Zealand Herald,* to becoming familiar with a new country. The evidence is particularly apparent in consumers' interactions with media, sports, telecommunication, travel, and leisure companies (Piven, 2012):

I'm following the Expedia travel business page for discounts and promotions. I used to read the Air New Zealand page, but I unsubscribed a year ago. It always depends on where I'm in the world now; it dictates which business pages I follow.

It's a nice constant or concreteness of having your regular updates, having a sale or product launch, this kind of thing. Telecom or banks and things like that, serious creditable businesses. Now you're able to tweet them and get an answer in a second.

The scope of self-oriented brand consumption, to a certain extent, replicates some of the functional and emotional elements. The difference, however, lies in an emphasis on the consumer's lifestyle and the goals that drive that lifestyle (Davis, Piven & Breazeale, 2014). Having looked at the core scenarios of self-oriented consumption, the research suggests that social media offer numerous opportunities for consumers to express themselves through brand-related activities, and therefore make the whole experience more valuable. Some findings report that consumers are willing not just to engage with a brand, but to become a brand ambassador, as long as the brand's symbolic meanings are congruent with their sense of self (Schouten, 1991):

Sometimes you just like the page because you want people to see that you like that brand, because you want to be associated with a brand, and with the values or image they project.

I would divide all companies I follow on Facebook into three groups. First group consists of companies I joined by chance, who offered a good deal/price. Second one represents businesses I like. I joined companies from the third group, because I had an intention to be identified with those businesses.

In fact, many self-oriented consumption practices are inhabited by a variety of consumers' social roles – from being a responsible employee to a devoted fan of the Twilight Saga (Piven, 2012). For example, the research recognises that some consumers believe their career prospects might be advanced through their brand interactions on social media:

I like a lot of European pages, so that what I'm bringing through is something a little different. A different perspective, different culture, different ideas, different chefs...I think it's a unique selling point as well. I have to, I work for a company, but also I might not work for them in two or three year's time. I think it's very important as a person to brand myself.

From an employment point of view, let's say if you are searching for a company, you want go to Facebook and like their page. When you go for an interview, you want to show that you're interested in that company.

The central focus of self-oriented brand consumption is the consumers themselves. Through interacting with a brand on social media, consumers may satisfy their need for self-branding or self-actualisation. The conclusion is consistent with Cova's (1997) prediction that with the development of online reality, consumers are likely to embrace multiple possibilities for self-expression through brand consumption (as cited in Piven, 2012):

I cover a lot of territory... I have to do this. It's about self-actualization. You recognize the gaps, keep your mind open of course, because you are always learning some little new things and filling out these gaps. It's just the way to get the knowledge out there. It's important for me to be there on a maturity continuum. It's a huge part of my life, but it's never about me. It opens up the world... (Piven, 2012, p. 177)

Many businesses have already found that supporting consumers' desire for self-presentation has certain benefits for branding. For example, KiwiYo, a fast-growing chain of frozen desserts in New Zealand, blurs the line between its offline and online presence: photos taken by consumers in the cafe go to the company's social media profiles in KiwiYo's colorful promotional picture frames. KISS, an iconic American rock band, is famous for allowing their fans to display their photos on the stage jumbo screens, as well as on social media during the band's performance. According to KISS' website, they were the first band to experiment with "interactive concert photo experiences" (KISS debuts "KISS Liveshare", 2010). It seems that some consumption practices take on new meaning in the context of social media – without being broadcast, they are pointless:

It's just like being a guru; it keeps me in touch with the universe. [I can] be in ten places at once.

What is fascinating is that in response to a brand's social media presence, some consumers are willing to compromise the fact that they have nothing in common with the brand they follow. Thus, the brand "may fail in the self-relevancy dimension, but can still create a connection with consumers through interactivity" (Davis, Piven & Breazeale, 2014, p. 131). A good example is Giapo ice cream, a small boutique shop in Auckland famous for its "ice community" on social media (McDonald, 2010):

It's a tiny, tiny little ice cream shop. I have never even been to his ice cream shop, but I know him; I know about his specials; I know when he is making new flavors; never met him [Giapo, the shop owner], but he creates a feeling of, like a little club, like Giapo Club. And I don't even like ice cream. (Piven, 2012, p. 178)

The study assumes that self-oriented experiences on social media are often formed by and associated with consumers' actions undertaken to fulfill the needs for self-expression, self-actualisation, and self-branding (Piven, 2012). From Salomon's (1983) point of view, "the consumer often relies upon the social information inherent in products to shape self-image, and to maximize the quality of role performance" (p. 320). At this point, the pillars of self-oriented consumption outlined in Figure 3 represent an important direction for marketers. If brands do not offer their consumers an opportunity for self-expression through brand endorsement, brand conversations, or brand affiliations, then it might be wasting time on social media.

Figure 3. Self-oriented source of brand value on social media (value-creation process through self-oriented consumption)

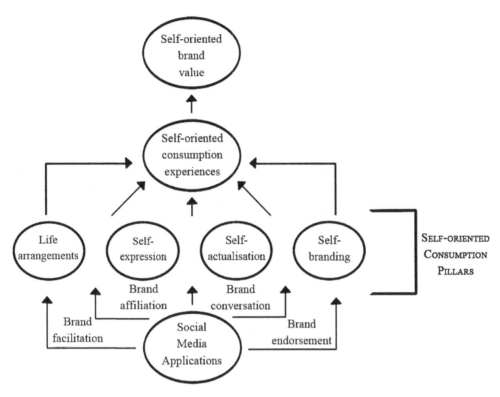

In summary, the research indicates that brand value can be created through reassuring consumers' personal objectives. By mobilising all pillars of self-oriented consumption, a brand can build a solid infrastructure on social media and deliver the best experiences for consumers (Table 3).

Social Source of Brand Value

People want to be a part of a community, to feel involved. You feel like you have authority. – Interview participant

Social media is the shared (communal) environment that provides consumers with multiple scenarios for information sharing, experience exchange, interactions with others, community involvement, and link building. It is well known that brand communities play a critical role within marketing communications. However, there is no agreement between scholars regarding whether brand communities emerging on social media should be seen and treated in the same way as traditional (face-to-face) ones. Debates surrounding this issue have been well-substantiated with dictionary definitions of community developed centuries ago - "the word seemed to connote a specific group of people, from a particular patch of earth, who knew and judged and kept an eye on one another, who shared habits and history and memories, and could at times be persuaded to act as a whole on behalf of a part" (Giridharadas, 2013).

Table 3. Self-oriented consumption scenarios

Self-Oriented Pillars	Self-Oriented Consumption Scenarios
Life Arrangements A need for brand experiences that help to facilitate, optimize and manage different tasks (Piven, 2012, p. 106).	Tuihana Café, https://twitter.com/tuihanacafe "Well, the coffee shop down the road says you tweet them and they will have the coffee ready when you arrive, instead of going in the queue." Remuera district, https://www.facebook.com/remueracommunity "I've liked that page because I want to be aware of what is happening in this area, on the weekend, to know what we should do..."
Self-Expression/Self-Actualisation A need to achieve personal goals and potential through brand-related activities (Piven, 2012, p. 101).	Blind Foundation, NGO, https://www.facebook.com/RNZFB "I guess, for me that's a part of the power and attraction of social media, it does break down the international barriers. We're not locked into just listening to what the New Zealand Blind Foundation has to say. But we can see what their counterparts in the US, and Canada, and Australia, all have to say about different issues, and how they approach them, and things like that...it's a part of my personality. And, you know, New Zealand is a very small country...for a lot of things getting an external perspective... can deliver a lot of value I think...I could take that and apply it in a slightly different way for my own purpose...but with a lot of the ideas and things that come up from international sites, brands..." Vodafone, telecommunication https://www.facebook.com/vodafoneNZ "I like the fact that I can express my side as well. Like recently, Vodafone did a poll on "if you were given extra broadband, what would you use it for?" It makes you feel like you're engaging in a business decision" (Piven, 2012, p. 183).
Self-Branding A need to build social self-identity through brand endorsement and brand affiliations (Piven, 2012, p. 104)	WWF, New Zealand https://www.facebook.com/wwfnewzealand "...I belong to different groups, which is WWF, different animal groups based in Singapore, of course I follow Cesar Millan. What I intend to do is to pick up information because I think this is relevant to what is going on in the world, and disseminate that on my wall. I put it on my wall to let people see that. I am also in a 21st-century education business group, on the Entrepreneurs page. People follow my wall a lot. As a social entrepreneur I like to make a difference for people."
Self-Relevance A need in experiences that are congruent with consumers' life style, professional or personal interests (Piven, 2012, p.102)	BNZ bank, https://twitter.com/BNZ "I follow the BNZ bank on Twitter...I'm interested in web stock, I'm interested in entrepreneurship and start-ups so there might have been something in there. The stuff they do with the literary awards, I think that might have been the first time I noticed BNZ on Twitter last year ... So when brands do things like that, when they become trending topics ...I will tend to follow."

Much criticism of online brand communities has come from Fournier and Lee (2009) who view them as "nothing more than far-flung focus groups established in the hope that consumers will bond around the virtual suggestion box" (p.109).

Other scholars believe that an online community is a social phenomenon (Toral, Martınez-Torres, Barrero & Cortes, 2009) that unites people with common consumption interests (Piven, 2012). Nambisan and Watt (2011) compare online brand community with a "lounge" area for customers to hang out and talk to one another" (p. 894). Regardless of how contemporary research defines an online brand community, it is important to understand that brands are capable of delivering a social value to consumers by serving as a meeting or networking platform. In this respect, the study identified that consumers' involvement with brand communities on social media is often activated by a need for social interaction and link building:

We interact with other individuals and businesses whose physical location may inhibit such communication; we obtain news quickly; and can exchange videos and images rapidly. I like Facebook; it is a bit like 'going home'. We also interact with individuals and businesses who might be right next door too!

At the level of education, there will be people who lead forums, boards, this sort of information they bring in, this information I would share with my community because it's about your personal development – raising your performance, your work, your life. It's very cool.

I'm certainly following some brands on both Facebook and Twitter, and through various dialogues, I started talking with some people ... So it certainly adds value... I've met this person who's also interested in these things, plus some other things that I didn't know I might have been interested in.

It is interesting to note, however, that consumers' engagement with a brand community does not necessarily imply an attachment to the brand community (Davis, Piven & Breazeale, 2014). The notion that people are attentive to friends' recommendations also found insignificant support from research data:

To be honest, I don't actually see a lot of people from my Facebook friends recommending companies, I don't think it happens; it might be different for other people. (Piven, 2012, p. 178)

I just follow the page. I just get the news and not get connected to anyone.

While the importance of friends' recommendations in social media settings seems debatable, some evidence suggests that consumers trust communal experiences in general. In this case, the process of social consumption is characterised by consumers' readiness to publicly display their personal, brand-related activities regardless of its outcomes - which can be both negative and positive. Experience exchange seems to be one of the most common practices consumers engage with, not only for their own benefits (like self-branding), but also for the benefits of others (Piven, 2012). Throughout the short history of social media, brands have always been challenged by consumers' proficiency in practicing their social agency. One of the most recent examples is when TV3 quickly came under fire from the audience of X Factor New Zealand, after two judges humiliated one of the contestants. Both judges were fired within 24 hours after the viewers/social media users launched a petition on Facebook. What also stood out in data analysis is research participants are willing to act not only as brand prosecutors, but as brand advocates as well:

I have to say people were extraordinarily nice on the day all the payment stuff fell over (BNZ bank). The community on Facebook decided to self-regulate it a little bit, so there were people saying, "hey, this isn't their fault...They're working on Anzac Day". There were a lot of people on Twitter saying "you should totally go and have a cup of tea and a lie down now, or a beer or whatever", so there was quite a lot of genuine understanding.

This evidence is consistent with Murphy's (2000) idea that people may engage with online communities "to make better decisions and to influence the decisions made by others" (p.107), but it is opposed to Bagozzi and Dholakia's (2002) concerns that online communities are lacking social ties as well as "feeling of social responsibility for performing extra contributions" (p.17).

Figure 4 illustrates the drivers behind social brand consumption and demonstrates how a collaborative environment can be created to deliver meaningful social experiences for consumers.

Figure 4. Social source of brand value on social media (value-creation process through social consumption)

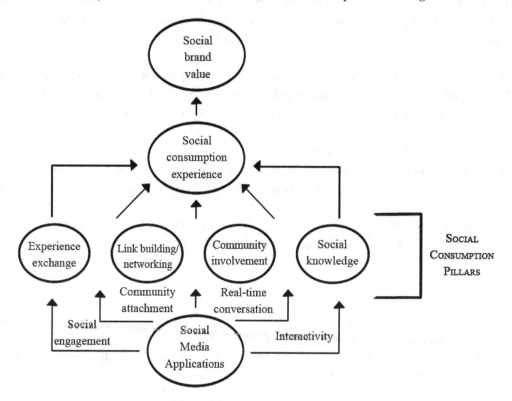

The idea of community is essential for a brand's creation of social values. However, the question of whether brands are capable of building a community and bringing people together on social media remains unanswered. In a recent *Harvard Business Review*, Henry Mintzberg advised, "If you want to understand the difference between a network and a community, ask your Facebook friends to help paint your house" (2015). Contrary to Mintzberg's (2015) belief that all electronic devices can do is to put people in touch with a keyboard, Giapo ice cream shop and Mr. Vintage t-shirt company testified to the possibility to develop a highly participative and collaborative environment that can be called a community:

He [Giapo] has created this following, and the other day he is like 'ok, I need feijoa leaves; who's got feijoa leaves?' and everybody offered feijoa leaves, and he got them for free. This way he has made Twitter feel like they are a part of his endeavor. He has made contact with people, they are all now talking about this new ice cream he is making with these feijoas and leaves, which were donated.

Mr. Vintage, I think they do a good job. Most of their marketing is online, and they've done a really good job building a brand around themselves as an irreverent, cheeky kind of company that uses the community they've created really well... they're always producing t-shirts that people have suggested to them, it's just a really neat, simple way of building their own brand and building their community.

Interestingly enough, some research data pointed to the fact that while a full understanding of community in the social media domain has not developed yet, research participants tend to define social

Table 4. Social consumption scenarios

Social Pillars	Social Consumption Scenarios
Experience Exchange A need to share personal brand experiences to the benefit of others (Piven, 2012, p. 109).	Mashable, digital media/news, https://www.facebook.com/mashable "Mashable is probably the best example because they are always posting the latest information. I like to share this information as well. I like to add value by sharing information to people who follow me. I build my followership on Twitter, I also use LinkedIn as my network to join the discussions…all the different groups I follow, I would like to know what people are talking about – what is happening in social media today."
Link Building/Networking A need of link building and networking for professional or personal purposes (Piven, 2012, p. 113).	Glengarry Wines, https://www.facebook.com/glengarrywines "I've just done a Facebook competition for Glengarry's, the wine company. I want to build an alliance with Glengarry's because I believe they've got a very big database, I believe there's a certain section of their customers who can afford my product."
Community Involvement A need for a community and communal brand experiences (Piven, 2012).	Wattie's food/beverages, https://www.facebook.com/WattiesNZ "It feels like you're a part of something. Like you're a part of a club. Like Wattie's, that is a very New Zealand thing. We belong to that, that's ours." Lululemon, https://www.facebook.com/lululemonathleticaAusNZ "I think Lululemon does particularly well. They are growing very fast in New Zealand. They are a part of a massive growing company. They don't have Twitter, but have a Facebook page. They are really into community and really focus on it." IHC New Zealand, disability services https://www.facebook.com/IHC.New.Zealand "Blind Foundation that I follow, and IHC, both of those companies will post up a topical item. So, you know it could be an issue with the unions, or something that has happened overseas. Then straightaway, you see hundreds of comments from people engaging and saying, "yeah, I know what you mean by this", and somebody else will chip in and say, "well I actually disagree", and some other people are coming in saying "well, you know we respect your point of view, but this is my experience with them" and things like that. So particularly for those type of brands (NGOs), I see a lot of engagement and healthy debate around topics."
Social Knowledge A need for social power and knowledge in the decision making	Cadbury, chocolate https://www.facebook.com/Cadbury "…Everybody realised Cadbury's was just all about getting the price of the chocolate down and substituting our products, and all the pictures of Burma came up in front of it. Now what happened to Cadbury, when in the course of months, I think, their sales dropped 25% in New Zealand alone. So you can now take an iconic brand that had been around for 100 years and they could be wiped out in months by social media…So okay now that's how social media can be used for destructive and constructive purposes depending on how the company handles it, that's what you can learn."

media profiles of some nonprofit organisations as communities. Unfortunately, the study did not produce enough evidence to support that definitively. In the future, research into the applicability of the Five-Sources Model to nonprofits' PR strategies on social media would be beneficial (Table 4).

Relational Source of Brand Value

It's all about making people feel like they are involved. – Interview participant

Blake Morgan, a Forbes contributor on social media, recently wrote "today social media still remains a constant battle for both marketers and consumers. Unless personalisation improves, consumers do not want their content and streams interrupted with advertising" (2015). The conclusion points to the fact that while brands demonstrate their growing reliance on social media marketing, "the interaction rates are not much better…, and they are only getting worse" (Griffith, 2015). Early academic studies also criticise a lack of personal touch in brand experiences that are "limited and planned…" and "too coherent and pre-determined and have therefore met with resistance from a number of consumers" (as cited in Bonnemaizon, Cova & Louyot, 2006, p.55).

What is personalisation in the context of social media? Whether the brand's primary intention is to communicate a meaningful message, or to introduce a new product or service, or to build a fellowship, in all cases a focus should be on consumers' experiences "at an individual or collective level" embedded in their values and goals (Bonnemaizon *et al.*, 2006, p. 55). In line with this assumption, research identified that social media platforms are capable of making brand communications close and personal. "Regardless of the consumption type, consumers do not want to interact with a faceless organisation, preferring instead to know the real people behind the brand. Moreover, consumers want to establish a close contact with brand representatives or experts on social media, even if that contact is utilitarian and brief" (Davis, Piven & Breazeale, 2014, p. 133):

Facebook – it's like a secret doorway to their shop, a little bit of knowledge on what they [the brand] are doing, latest deals... their customers feel privileged, it gives a feeling that you're friends.

I'm actually off to the Gold Coast in a couple of weeks for an international conference. And they're already promoting it via Twitter, and getting anybody with a Twitter account to engage with the hash tag. And now they're organizing offline meetings once we get to the conference. And all that's been done through Twitter. It's not just for the sake of saying 'we're all gonna catch up and talk about something' ...everybody's following this hash tag. We'll be catching up at 5 o'clock after drinks. We'll be catching up over breakfast for another topic. That's really useful for me...it needs to have some value to me, not to the brand.

From participants' perspectives, brands on social platforms should be working towards one big idea –shared values and goals with their consumers. This process, however, is complex and should not be seen as an algorithm with a definite answer. To create a responsive and peronalised brand on social media, it is important to understand determinants of consumer-brand relations such as 1) brand relevance, 2) the consumption purpose, 3) consumes' experiences with brand inquiry and brand responses, 4) frequency of communication, 5) situational dependency, and 6) the nature of the product/service (Piven, 2012). Ideally, these factors are assumed to enable brands to avoid communication failures on social media. Bombarding consumers with sales and promotions is not human interaction, but engaging them in a conversation, being genuinely interested in their opinions, and making them feel valued overall – definitely is:

I follow a couple of restaurants online, and I find now if I go to a restaurant, I normally Facebook them beforehand. 'On our menu this month we have this type of dish from Italy'. And then they'll post some information about that particular region in Italy – how that particular wine was produced, for instance. So when I actually go to the restaurant, it helps me enjoy it a bit more, knowing other than this is a bowl of pasta. This recipe's been around for generations and things like that ...It's about a bit more of the fluffy stuff around the edges that can add value... By having this extra information provided, it helps me develop a stronger relationship with that restaurant.

The recent changes in marketing communications driven by social media have resulted in the types of relationships consumers form with brands. Prior research has developed a number of typologies of consumer-brand relationships (Fournier, 1998; Hennig-Thurau *et al.*, 2004), however, due to the dynamic nature of social media, they are not necessarily applicable in this context. For example, research demonstrates that social media can produce "fickle" consumers, whose "behavior...is difficult to predict and manage because of the situational dependency of their consumption practices" (Piven, 2012, p. 147):

Once you like something, it doesn't mean you are married to the brand...I don't think that I would go and check business pages on a regular basis until I have a reason to.

I'm following Expedia travel business page for discounts and promotions. I used to be reading the Air New Zealand page, but I've unsubscribed a year ago. It always depends on where I'm in the world now; it dictates which business pages I follow.

The question to explore further is whether such one-off contacts with a brand create value for consumers. Cova's (1997) message is clear in this respect – "if the consumer is fickle and unpredictable, it is not so important to predict their behavior as to be able to react immediately to their new aspirations through the maintenance of a continuous relation" (p. 309). Because almost everyone is on Facebook, it is not surprising that a number of typical stories from research participants pointed to another type of consumer-brand relationships marked as "emerged", i.e. occurred for the first time on social media and shaped by online experiences only (Piven, 2012). In these circumstances, it is important not to take these newborn and fragile relationships for granted:

So what you've got to do is to build the relationship up with me...Credibility takes a long time, contrary to what they think.

Businesses and organisations attempting to go social should understand that they are dealing not with abstract users, but with real people, and many of them became loyal consumers long before social media. In this regard, research identified that consumers' relationships, particularly with a service brand, are often driven by pre-existing brand experiences (Piven, 2012):

I started following a brand that I used to like first; example would be brands like Nike or Skechers. I appreciate when businesses tweet back, but I don't tweet for a reaction necessarily... I'm using Twitter on a different level; the way I use it is very personal.

So because we have built up relationships with people previously, they weren't the ones that were abusing us (about Spark's broadband failure). If it was our own community turning on us, then I would have found that a lot harder to take.

The importance of having long-time consumers in a brand fellowship is difficult to overestimate – the earlier comment on BNZ's bank services failure and their customers' willingness to overlook that failure illustrates the advantages of pre-existing relationships. Figure 5 introduces the forms of relational value and its determinants that became evident through data analysis.

In summary, consumers value personalised communications with a brand. The benefits of having a chat with a bank broker on Twitter after hours or receiving a complement from a local airline on Facebook should be viewed as positive outcomes of a brand's interactivity and co-creation, which in a social media context "signify practices...consumers participate in as brand co-producers, reviewers or marketers" (Table 5) (Piven, 2012, p. 146).

Figure 5. Relational source of brand value on social media (value-creation process through relational consumption)

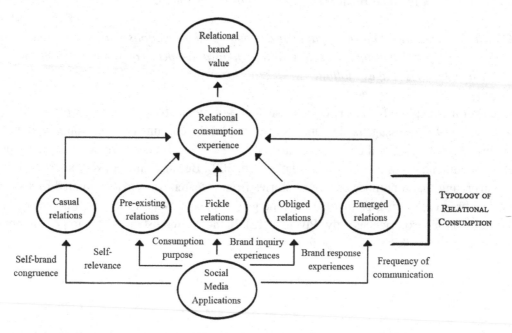

SOLUTIONS AND RECOMMENDATIONS

As should be clear after reading these accounts, social media are challenging many accepted norms in marketing communications. At the same time, this new reality gives brands the chance to build fellowship and create interesting and relevant experiences for consumers. This study has described the Five-Sources Model of Brand Value, which can be used as a starting place for branding on social media (figure 6).

The first takeaway from the model is that brand value creation on social media is dependent on consumers' functional, emotional, self-oriented, social and relational consumption experiences. The second concept is that all of these experiences are shaped, communicated and shared within and by a social media community through interactivity, co-creation, brand conversations, brand affiliation, and experience exchange (Piven, 2012). And the third idea is that all consumption practices presented in the model are mutually dependent. Now, armed with the Five-Sources Model, how can brands practically create value for consumers?

There are many functional consumption scenarios in which consumers play an active role by taking advantage of a brand' proximity on social media. The goal then is to enhance brand functionality through creating an environment in which meeting consumers' needs through social media resources becomes the standard. This can be accomplished in several ways:

- **Undertaking Problem Solving Issues:** Focus on real-time communication, responsiveness and willingness to solve consumers' problems as soon as they occur. There is no need to redirect customers to a website or ask them to phone a company's representative.

Table 5. Relational consumption scenarios

Relational Pillars	Relational Consumption Scenarios
Personalised Communication	Air New Zealand, https://www.facebook.com/AirNewZealand "I hated their campaign and expressed my displeasure! They responded quickly assuring me that I would never be seated beside the offensive mascot [puppet Rico, a character promoting AirNZ 777 planes in 2010). I liked their style and it certainly kept me loyal to them…I received bouquets and brickbats for my opinions."
Casual Relations Result of accidental or irregular experiences regardless of online or offline context (Piven, 2012)	Essenze, home décor https://www.facebook.com/essenzedesign/ "I would not go to this design page on a regular basis, it's not that sort of things that you would buy every day."
Pre-Existing Relations Result of customers' prior brand knowledge and experiences (Piven, 2012)	Vodafone, telecommunication https://www.facebook.com/vodafoneNZ "I've been a customer of Vodafone since my arriving in New Zealand. Obviously I'm with them for a long time, 7 years now. They provided me with my first Internet, my first cell phone and once they went to Facebook, I started following them because yeep, I'm with Vodafone."
Fickle Relations Result of temporary contacts often dictated by the present situation (Piven, 2012)	Farmers, retail https://www.facebook.com/FarmersNZ "I follow not too many companies on FB. Most of them I "liked" once in the past, but don't really keep an eye on them…For example, I'm not a big fan of Farmers. I "liked" this business because they had a kind of Christmas promotion - to get into the draw to win $15,000 just by clicking "Like" button. I realized that chance to win is one in a million though."
Obliged Relations Result of statutory obligations, not because they are wanted or desirable (Piven, 2012)	BNZ bank, https://twitter.com/BNZ "I think it's very difficult for a bank to build a community around banking. It's kind of a necessary evil in a lot of ways." Telecom (Spark) https://www.facebook.com/spark & Vodafone https://www.facebook.com/vodafoneNZ "Power companies, telephone companies, banks… people will never like them. There is no way. And that is because at the end of the day people have the conscious level of believing they are forced to deal with them. You have to have a bank, and you have to have a Telco. I'm never going to like them."
Emerged Relations Occurred for the first time on social media (Piven, 2012)	Mishka, fashion https://www.facebook.com/MishkaBoutique "I was looking through Indian clothes design pages, because I love their clothing and their culture and one lady friend - requested me there, Mishka. And she was just beginning her business. So I said: "Let's see how I may help you". My friends they are quite active; they follow my wall for some reasons. I would make a genuine comment on clothing she was designing, I supported her on a first three months and she has become a really good friend."

- **Indulging the Desire for Two-Way Communication:** It is important to ask and answer questions, invite consumers' opinions and feedback, and be conversational as consumers tend to ignore brand-centered conversations that ignore their participation.
- **Regular Updating:** Consumers are very attentive, and they quickly notice when a brand's engagement is falling off.
- **Offering Different Social Media Platforms and Mobile Applications:** Brand mobility and flexibility is a must as consumers are looking for communication options that suit them best.

Unfortunately, the study indicated that from a variety of functionality-related activities, "businesses tend to employ mostly specials and giveaways, still considering social media as an additional channel for sales and advertising" (Piven, 2012, p. 167). It might explain why "despite [the] increasing…volume of posting on just about every social media platform, the percentage of posts that garnered interactions with users fell" (Griffith, 2015).

The research indicated that the idea of entertaining and curiosity-driven experiences is essential in the construction of emotional consumption. How can this be enacted in practice?

Figure 6. The five-sources model of brand value on social media (value-creation process through functional, emotional, self-oriented, social, and relational consumption)

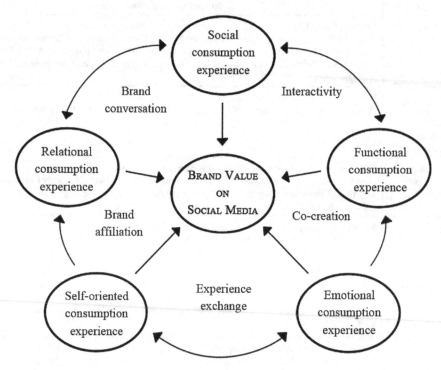

- **Avoid Dry Communication:** A lack of emotions and/or self-contained conversations lead to consumers' disengagement.
- **Include Quizzes, Games, Polls in Social Media Posts:** They may help to activate consumers' interaction with brands.
- **Share Stories:** This makes consumers feel close and personal with the brand (Piven, 2012, p. 169).
- **Acknowledge Consumers for Their Contributions:** Air New Zealand sends them bouquets.
- **Make a Brand's Social Media Presence Visually Appealing:** Like much marketing communication, social media still tend to be visual media.
- **Make Consumers Feel Welcome:** The focus is on consumers' individual and collective interests.

One group of consumption experiences that was identified as particularly valuable was the one we deemed self-oriented. This kind of value is responsible for delivering connections between "a consumer's personal goals, values, and interests" and "brand meanings" (Piven, 2012, p. 172). How can brands ensure that their social media presence is in line with consumers' personal needs?

- Provide consumers with content they can relate to and may be inclined to publically share.
- Recognise consumers that lead brand conversations, rewarding them and assigning them the role of an expert in a brand community (Piven, 2012).

- Learn what makes consumers engage with a brand. There are numerous personal and professional reasons. Use this knowledge to change approaches to social media content and conversations (Piven, 2012).
- Turn consumer-brand interactions into "red carpet" or "award ceremony" experiences by taking advantage of modern technologies in conjunction with social media.

While looking at the flow of information on social media, brand managers likely feel that they have an understanding of where the direct links to consumers' individual and collective needs are. The following represents the core value opportunities in relation to consumers' social experiences:

- Allow consumers to share their stories within a community, and be a part of that conversation.
- Focus on local context – this makes a brand relevant to consumers (Piven, 2012, p. 173).
- Organise community events with support from a social media community; it is important to keep consumers engaged by sharing pre- and post-event updates.
- Inform consumers about different community-oriented events, even those not necessarily related to the brand.
- Provide a safe place for consumers to interact and collaborate with a brand and a social media community where they do not feel they are being actively sold to.

The final source of the brand value creation on social media was described as relational. In this respect, the ultimate goal for any brand, regardless of industry, is to provide consumers with personalised experiences. Considering the steady decline in consumers' interactions with brands during the past two years, attention should be paid to ways to improve relationships, not sales. To accomplish this:

- Let consumers know the people behind the brand on social media.
- Regularly provide consumers with the opportunity to talk directly to company management or experts (Piven, 2012).
- Be honest during brand failures; consumers appreciate the fact that a brand can openly talk about its issues in front of thousands of social media users. It has the potential to turn consumers into brand advocates (Piven, 2012).
- Use social media for relationships; selling and advertising are for websites (Piven, 2012).

CONCLUSION

This chapter has presented the Five-Sources Model of Brand Value on social media, the outcome of a long-term study that explored:

1. How social media, specifically Facebook and Twitter, enable brands to enhance consumers' consumption experiences, and
2. Whether these consumption experiences lead to brand value creation.

The study identified five sources of brand value in relation to consumers' functional, emotional, self-oriented, social and relational consumption patterns.

Emerging from the experiences of actual consumers, the model's purpose is to help different businesses and organisations link their social media communication tactics with consumers' values and personal goals. The importance of the Five-Sources Model lies in its capacity to go beyond traditional marketing communications. The study has concluded that by being an active part of community-oriented media, through consumers' co-creation and visible interaction, brands have become increasingly meaningful to customers (Piven, 2012). This finding is in line with Reyneke *et al.*'s (2011) statement that social media "support the democratisation of knowledge and information, transforming individuals from mere content consumers into content producers" (p. 22).

This chapter has specifically looked at the drivers, processes, themes, and outcomes of the five types of consumption, which lead to brand value creation. Although research has confirmed the importance of the five sources of brand value for social media marketing in relationship formation, the study did not produce enough data to suggest a direct link between a brand's functional, emotional, self-oriented, social, and relational value and consumers' intention to purchase.

FUTURE RESEARCH DIRECTIONS

Future research should most likely begin with an exploration and confirmation of the role of brand personality and its human characteristics in brand consumption via social media. How does the manner in which brands enact their personalities impact consumers' expression of their actual, ideal, social and virtual selves? If brand personality is truly as important as we believe, how can it increase, in individual as well as cross-cultural settings, the consumer's brand preference, loyalty and usage (Malar, Krohmer, Hoyer & Nyffenegger, 2011)? Does brand personality impact both utilitarian consumption values as well as the more hedonic consumption that research informants typically described? In either context, the congruity of self-image with brand personality could play a valuable function for the consumer (Aguirre-Rodriguez, Bosnjak, & Sirgy, 2012; Helgeson & Supphellen, 2004; Sirgy, 1982).

Future work also could focus on defining the difference between the various components of consumption. For instance, is social brand consumption more about interaction between consumers themselves, and relational consumption more about interaction between the consumer and the brand?

Further research might also focus on drawing distinctions between product and brand consumption in social media, as this type of knowledge would be very useful for both researchers and practitioners (Danaher, Wilson & Davis, 2003). Comparing a non-branded product model to the Five-Sources

Model would be very interesting. Additionally, research might also focus on a service brand in particular to explore how online brand consumption varies depending on the nature of the service. For instance, will consumers' drivers be different for a service that is consumed out of perceived necessity (such as a physician or attorney) as opposed to one that is consumed for more personally satisfying reasons (such as a personal trainer or music instructor)? It is also critical to expand social media research into nonprofit domains to identify the type of knowledge required and the research agenda.

Because theory on brand relationships in social media is still in its infancy, further exploratory research is appropriate. Case studies could yield further insights into consumers' brand-related behaviors and also some interesting nuances in consumer-brand interactions in social media communities. The growth of social media is related to the rapid growth of smart mobile devices and the resultant shortening of the distance between brands and consumers (Davis, Lang & San Diego, 2014; Hoffman & Novak, 2012). Ongoing research should further conceptualise consumer-brand interaction in a social media context in light of the ubiquitous nature of connected mobile devices and their role in retailing and consumer-to-consumer interactions (Sands, Harper, & Ferraro, 2011). Future work might also examine the fit between brand and social skills on and offline (Hurrell & Scholarios, 2013).

As social consumption continues to evolve as an important economic consideration, the Five-Sources Model should prove valuable to both researchers and practitioners as they attempt to better understand the value that consumers receive from and help to create for brands in the social media context.

REFERENCES

Aaker, L. J. (1997). Dimensions of brand personality. *JMR, Journal of Marketing Research, 14*(1), 347–356. doi:10.2307/3151897

Aguirre-Rodriguez, A., Bosnjak, M., & Sirgy, J. (2012). Moderators of the self-congruity effect on consumer decision-making: A meta-analysis. *Journal of Business Research, 65*(8), 1179–1188. doi:10.1016/j.jbusres.2011.07.031

Avis, M. (2012). Brand personality factor based models: A critical review. *Australasian Marketing Journal, 20*(1), 89–96. doi:10.1016/j.ausmj.2011.08.003

Bagozzi, R. P., & Dholakia, U. M. (2002). Intentional social action on virtual communities. *Journal of Interactive Marketing, 16*(2), 2–21. doi:10.1002/dir.10006

Benson, V., & Morgan, S. (2015). *Implications of social media use in personal and professional settings.* Hershey, PA: IGI Global; doi:10.4018/978-1-4666-7401-1

Bonnemaizon, A., Cova, B., & Louyot, M. (2007). Relationship marketing in 2015: A Delphi approach. *European Management Journal, 25*(1), 50–59. doi:10.1016/j.emj.2006.12.002

Brodie, R. J., Ilic, A., Juric, B., & Hollebeek, L. (2011). Consumer engagement in a virtual brand community: An exploratory analysis. *Journal of Business Research, 66*(1), 105–114. doi:10.1016/j.jbusres.2011.07.029

Brogan, R. J., & Smith, J. (2009). *Trust agents: Using the Web to build influence, improve reputation, and earn trust.* Hoboken, NJ: John Wiley & Sons.

Cova, B. (1997). Community and consumption: Towards a definition of the linking value of product or services. *European Journal of Marketing, 31*(3/4), 297–316. doi:10.1108/03090569710162380

Danaher, P. J., Wilson, I. W., & Davis, R. A. (2003). A comparison of online and offline consumer brand loyalty. *Marketing Science, 22*(4), 461–476. doi:10.1287/mksc.22.4.461.24907

Davis, R., & Piven, I. (2013). *Social media branding: Manifesto for the branding revolution* (1st ed.). Available from https://books.google.co.nz/

Davis, R., Piven, I., & Breazeale, M. (2014). Conceptualising brand consumption in social media community. In *Proceedings of the European Conference on Social Media* (pp.128-135). Reading, UK: Academic Conferences and Publishing.

Davis, R., & Sajtos, L. (2008). Measuring consumer interactivity in response to campaigns coupling mobile and television media. *Journal of Advertising Research, 48*(3), 2008–2391. doi:10.2501/S0021849908080409

Downes, E. J., & McMillan, S. J. (2000). Defining interactivity: A qualitative identification of key dimensions. *New Media & Society, 2*(2), 157–179. doi:10.1177/14614440022225751

Fournier, S. (1998). Consumers and their brands: Developing relationship theory in consumer research. *The Journal of Consumer Research, 24*(4), 343–373. doi:10.1086/209515

Fournier, S., & Lee, L. (2009, April). Getting brand communities right. *Harvard Business Review, 87*(4), 105–111. PMID:19736854

Giridharadas, A. (2013, September 20). Draining the life from 'community'. *The New York Times*. Retrieved from http://www.nytimes.com/2013/09/21/us/draining-the-life-from-community.html?_r=0

Griffith, E. (2015 August 25). Brands are using social media more than ever, and users are ignoring them more than ever. *Fortune*. Retrieved from http://fortune.com/2015/08/25/social-media-brands-ignore/

Grönroos, C. (2001). The perceived service quality concept - a mistake? *Managing Service Quality, 11*(3), 150–152. doi:10.1108/09604520110393386

Haeckel, S. H. (1998). About the nature and future of interactive marketing. *Journal of Interactive Marketing, 12*(1), 63–71. doi:10.1002/(SICI)1520-6653(199824)12:1<63::AID-DIR8>3.0.CO;2-C

Helgeson, J. M., & Supphellen, M. (2004). A conceptual and measurement comparison of self-congruity and brand personality: The impact of socially desirable responding. *International Journal of Market Research, 46*(2), 205–233.

Hennig-Thurau, T., Malthouse, E. C., Friege, C., Gensler, S., Lobschat, L., Rangaswamy, A., & Skiera, B. (2010). The impact of new media on customer relationships. *Journal of Service Research, 13*(3), 311–330. doi:10.1177/1094670510375460

Hoffman, D. L., & Novak, T. P. (1996). Marketing in hypermedia computer-mediated environments: Conceptual foundations. *Journal of Marketing, 60*(3), 50–68. doi:10.2307/1251841

Hoffman, D. L., & Novak, T. P. (2012). *Why do people use social media? Empirical findings and a new theoretical framework for social media goal pursuit*. Retrieved From Social Science Research Network: http://Papers.Ssrn.Com/Sol3/Papers.Cfm?Abstract_Id=1989586

Hurrell, S., & Scholarios, A. D. (2013). The people make the brand: Reducing social skills gaps through person-brand fit and human resource management practices. *Journal of Service Research, 17*(1), 54–67. doi:10.1177/1094670513484508

KISS debuts "KISS Liveshare ". (2010). Retrieved from http://www.kissonline.com/news?n_id=51273

Kushner, M. (2015, May 18). *Why the buildings of the future will be shaped by ... you* [Video]. Retrieved from https://www.ted.com/talks/marc_kushner_why_the_buildings_of_the_future_will_be_shaped_by_you

Loewenstein, G. (1994). The Psychology of curiosity: A review and reinterpretation. *Psychological Bulletin, 116*(1), 75–98. doi:10.1037/0033-2909.116.1.75

Malär, L., Krohmer, H., Hoyer, W. D., & Nyffenegger, B. (2011). Emotional brand attachment and brand personality: The relative importance of the actual and the ideal self. *Journal of Marketing, 75*(4), 35–52. doi:10.1509/jmkg.75.4.35

McDonald, G. (2010). Networking in an icy community. *Stuff.* Retrieved from http://www.stuff.co.nz/business/small-business/3501543/Networking-in-an-icy-community

McMillan, S. J., & Hwang, J. (2002). Measure of perceived interactivity: An exploration of the role of direction of communication, user control, and time in shaping perceptions of interactivity. *Journal of Advertising, 31*(3), 29–42. doi:10.1080/00913367.2002.10673674

Mintzberg, H. (2015, October 5). Networking and communities. *Harvard Business Review*. Retrieved from https://hbr.org/2015/10/we-need-both-networks-and-communities

Mollen, A., & Wilson, H. (2010). Engagement, telepresence and interactivity in online consumer experience: Reconciling scholastic and managerial perspectives. *Journal of Business Research, 63*(9/10), 919–925. doi:10.1016/j.jbusres.2009.05.014

Morgan, B. (2015, August 31). When brands try too hard on social media. *Forbes*. Retrieved from http://www.forbes.com/sites/blakemorgan/2015/08/31/when-brands-try-too-hard-on-social-media/

Morgan-Thomas, A., & Veloutsou, C. (2013). Beyond technology acceptance: Brand relationships and online brand experience. *Journal of Business Research, 66*(1), 21–27. doi:10.1016/j.jbusres.2011.07.019

Muniz, J. A. Jr, & O'Guinn, T. C. (2001). Brand community. *The Journal of Consumer Research, 27*(4), 412–432. doi:10.1086/319618

Murphy, T. (2000). *Web rules: How the Internet is changing the way consumers make choices.* Chicago: Dearborn Financial Publishing, Inc.

Murray, K. (1991). A test of services marketing theory: Consumer information acquisition activities. *Journal of Marketing, 55*(1), 10–25. doi:10.2307/1252200

Nambisan, P., & Watt, J. H. (2011). Managing customer experiences in online product communities. *Journal of Business Research, 64*(8), 889–895. doi:10.1016/j.jbusres.2010.09.006

Orsman, B. (2005, March 18). Readers nominate Auckland's ugliest buildings. *New Zealand Herald.* Retrieved from http://www.nzherald.co.nz/nz/news/article.cfm?c_id=1&objectid=10116020

Park, M., & Park, J. (2009). Exploring the influences of perceived interactivity on consumers' e-shopping effectiveness. *Journal of Customer Behaviour, 8*(4), 361–379. doi:10.1362/147539209X480990

Patterson, A. (2011). Social-networkers of the world, unite and take over: A meta-introspective perspective on the Facebook brand. *Journal of Business Research, 65*(4), 527–534. doi:10.1016/j.jbusres.2011.02.032

Piven, I. (2012). *Conceptual model of consumer service brand consumption in a social media community.* (Masters dissertation). Unitec Institute of Technology, Auckland, New Zealand.

Rafaeli, S. (1988). Interactivity from new media to communication. In R. P. Hawkins, J. M. Wiemann, & S. Pingree (Eds.), *Advancing Communication Science: Merging Mass and Interpersonal Processes* (pp. 110–134). Beverly Hills, CA: Sage.

Reyneke, M., Pitt, L., & Berthon, P. R. (2011). Luxury wine brand visibility in social media: An exploratory study. *International Journal of Wine Business Research, 23*(1), 21–35. doi:10.1108/17511061111121380

Sands, S., Harper, E., & Ferraro, C. (2011). Customer-to-noncustomer interactions: Extending the 'social' dimension of the store environment. *Journal of Retailing and Consumer Services, 18*(5), 438–447. doi:10.1016/j.jretconser.2011.06.007

Sandström, S., Edvardsson, B., Kristensson, P., & Magnusson, P. (2008). Value in use through service experience. *Managing Service Quality, 18*(2), 112–126. doi:10.1108/09604520810859184

Schouten, J. W. (1991). Selves in transition: Symbolic consumption in personal rites of passage and identity reconstruction. *The Journal of Consumer Research, 17*(4), 412–425. doi:10.1086/208567

Schouten, J. W., & Mcalexander, J. H. (1995). Subcultures of consumption: An ethnography of the New Bikers. *The Journal of Consumer Research, 22*(1), 43–61. doi:10.1086/209434

Seimiene, E. (2012). Emotional connection of consumer personality traits with brand personality traits: Theoretical considerations. *Economics and Management, 17*(4), 1477–1478. doi:10.5755/j01.em.17.4.3016

Sirgy, J. M. (1982). Self-concept in consumer behaviour: A critical review. *The Journal of Consumer Research, 9*(3), 287–300. doi:10.1086/208924

Solomon, M. R. (1983). The role of products as social stimuli: A symbolic interactionism perspective. *The Journal of Consumer Research, 10*(3), 319–329. doi:10.1086/208971

Thompson, C. J. (1997). Interpreting consumers: A hermeneutical framework for deriving marketing insights from the texts of consumers' consumption stories. *JMR, Journal of Marketing Research, 34*(4), 438–455. doi:10.2307/3151963

Toral, S. L., Martinez-Torres, M. R., Barrero, F., & Cortes, F. (2009). An empirical study of the driving forces behind online communities. *Internet Research, 19*(4), 378–392. doi:10.1108/10662240910981353

Trappey, R. J., & Woodside, A. (2005). Consumer responses to interactive advertising campaigns coupling short-message-service direct marketing and TV commercials. *Journal of Advertising Research, 45*(4), 382–401.

Udland, M. (2015, February 27). The internet is losing its composure over this dress that might be white and gold or black and blue". *Business Insider*. Retrieved from http://www.businessinsider.com.au/white-and-gold-black-and-blue-dress-2015-2

Vis, F. (2013). A critical reflection on Big Data: Considering APIs, researches and tools as data makers. *First Monday, 18*(10), 1–14. doi:10.5210/fm.v18i10.4878

Vlasic, G., & Kesic, T. (2007). Analysis of consumers' attitudes toward interactivity and relationship personalization as contemporary developments in interactive marketing communication. *Journal of Marketing Communications, 13*(2), 109–129. doi:10.1080/13527260601070417

Wilson, S. (2015, January 22). The city's shame: Why is Auckland's urban design so bad? *The Metro*. Retrieved from http://www.metromag.co.nz/metro-archive/citys-shame-aucklands-urban-design-bad/

Yoo, W., Lee, Y., & Park, J. (2010). The role of interactivity in E-tailing: Creating value and increasing satisfaction. *Journal of Retailing and Consumer Services, 17*(2), 89–96. doi:10.1016/j.jretconser.2009.10.003

Yoon, D., Choi, S. M., & Sohn, D. (2008). Building customer relationships in an electronic age: The role of interactivity of E-commerce web sites. *Psychology and Marketing, 25*(7), 602–618. doi:10.1002/mar.20227

ADDITIONAL READING

Albert, N., Merunka, D., & Valette-Florence, P. (2013). Brand passion: Antecedents and consequences. *Journal of Business Research, 66*(7), 904–909. doi:10.1016/j.jbusres.2011.12.009

Atkinson, L. (2008). Commodifying the Self: Online Social Networking Profiles as Brand Communities. *Advances in Consumer Research. Association for Consumer Research (U. S.), 35*, 936–937.

Breazeale, M., & Ponder, N. (2013). Get the picture? Visual servicescapes and self-image congruity. *Journal of Business Research, 66*(7), 839–846. doi:10.1016/j.jbusres.2011.06.009

Cooke, P. (2013). *Unique: Telling Your Story in the Age of Brands and Social Media*. Ada, MI: Baker Publishing.

Dessart, L., Veloutsou, C., & Morgan-Thomas, A. (2015). Consumer engagement in online brand communities: A social media perspective. *Journal of Product and Brand Management, 24*(1), 28–42. doi:10.1108/JPBM-06-2014-0635

Dwyer, P. (2007). Measuring the value of electronic word of mouth and its impact in consumer communities. *Journal of Interactive Marketing (John Wiley & Sons), 21*(2), 63-79.

Fournier, S., Breazeale, M., & Avery, J. (Eds.). (2015). *Strong Brands, Strong Relationships*. London: Routledge.

Fournier, S., Breazeale, M., & Fetscherin, M. (Eds.). (2012). *Consumer-Brand Relationships: Theory and Practice*. London: Routledge.

Habibi, M. R., Laroche, M., & Richard, M. (2014). Brand communities based in social media: How unique are they? Evidence from two exemplary brand communities. *International Journal of Information Management, 34*(2), 123–132. doi:10.1016/j.ijinfomgt.2013.11.010

He, H., Li, Y., & Harris, L. (2012). Social identity perspective on brand loyalty. *Journal of Business Research, 65*(5), 648–657. doi:10.1016/j.jbusres.2011.03.007

Hildebrand, C., Häubl, G., Herrmann, A., & Landwehr, J. R. (2013). When Social Media Can Be Bad for You: Community Feedback Stifles Consumer Creativity and Reduces Satisfaction with Self-Designed Products. *Information Systems Research, 24*(1), 14–29. doi:10.1287/isre.1120.0455

Holt, D. B. (1995). How consumers consume: A typology of consumption practices. *The Journal of Consumer Research, 22*(1), 1–17. doi:10.1086/209431

Hwang, J., & Kandampully, J. (2012). The role of emotional aspects in younger consumer-brand relationships. *Journal of Product and Brand Management, 21*(2), 98–108. doi:10.1108/10610421211215517

Johnson, A. R., Matear, M., & Thomson, M. (2011). A Coal in the Heart: Self-Relevance as a Post-Exit Predictor of Consumer Anti-Brand Actions. *The Journal of Consumer Research, 38*(1), 108–125. doi:10.1086/657924

Kazuhiro, K. (2014). Brand Communities in Social Networking Services: Two Types of Interaction and Self-Construals. *AMA Winter Educators' Conference Proceedings, 25*E-44-E-48.

Khim-Yong, G., Cheng-Suang, H., & Zhijie, L. (2013). Social Media Brand Community and Consumer Behavior: Quantifying the Relative Impact of User- and Marketer-Generated Content. *Information Systems Research, 24*(1), 88–107. doi:10.1287/isre.1120.0469

Kim, M., & Thompson, S. A. (2014). Customer-to-Customer Relationship Management (CCRM): CCRM Strategies and Customer Responses. *AMA Winter Educators' Conference Proceedings, 25*E-17.

Laroche, M., Habibi, M. R., & Richard, M. (2013). To be or not to be in social media: How brand loyalty is affected by social media? *International Journal of Information Management, 33*(1), 76–82. doi:10.1016/j.ijinfomgt.2012.07.003

Morgan-Thomas, A., & Veloutsou, C. (2013). Beyond technology acceptance: Brand relationships and online brand experience. *Journal of Business Research, 66*(1), 21–27. doi:10.1016/j.jbusres.2011.07.019

Muñiz, A. M. Jr, & Schau, H. J. (2007). Vigilante marketing and consumer-created communications. *Journal of Advertising, 36*(3), 35–50. doi:10.2753/JOA0091-3367360303

Noble, C. H., Noble, S. M., & Adjei, M. T. (2012). Let them talk! Managing primary and extended online brand communities for success. *Business Horizons, 55*(5), 475–483. doi:10.1016/j.bushor.2012.05.001

Park, H., & Kim, Y. (2014). The role of social network websites in the consumer–brand relationship. *Journal of Retailing and Consumer Services, 21*(4), 460–467. doi:10.1016/j.jretconser.2014.03.011

Plangger, K. (2012). The power of popularity: how the size of a virtual community adds to firm value. *Journal of Public Affairs (14723891), 12*(2), 145-153.

Poulsson, S. H. G., & Kale, H. (2004). The experience economy and commercial experiences. *The Marketing Review, 4*(3), 267–277. doi:10.1362/1469347042223445

Safko, L. (2013). *The Social Media Bible: Tactics, Tools, and Strategies for Business Success* (3rd ed.). Hoboken, NJ: Wiley & Sons.

Sloan, S., Bodey, K., & Gyrd-Jones, R. (2015). Knowledge sharing in online brand communities. *Qualitative Market Research: An International Journal, 18*(3), 320–345. doi:10.1108/QMR-11-2013-0078

Steinmann, S., Mau, G., & Schramm-Klein, H. (2015). Brand Communication Success in Online Consumption Communities: An Experimental Analysis of the Effects of Communication Style and Brand Pictorial Representation. *Psychology and Marketing, 32*(3), 356–371. doi:10.1002/mar.20784

Târnovan, A. M. (2011). The Social Capital of Brand Communities. *Proceedings of The European Conference On Management, Leadership & Governance*, 402-409.

Willi, C. H., Melewar, T. C., & Broderick, A. J. (2013). Virtual brand-communities using blogs as communication platforms and their impact on the two-step communication process: A research agenda. *Marketing Review, 13*(2), 103–123. doi:10.1362/146934713X13699019904560

Wirtz, J., den Ambtman, A., Bloemer, J., Horváth, C., Ramaseshan, B., van de Klundert, J., & Kandam-pully, J. et al. (2013). Managing brands and customer engagement in online brand communities. *Journal of Service Management, 24*(3), 223–244. doi:10.1108/09564231311326978

Zaglia, M. E. (2013). Brand communities embedded in social networks. *Journal of Business Research, 66*(2), 216–223. doi:10.1016/j.jbusres.2012.07.015 PMID:23564989

Zhou, Z., Zhang, Q., Su, C., & Zhou, N. (2012). How do brand communities generate brand relationships? Intermediate mechanisms. *Journal of Business Research, 65*(7), 890–895. doi:10.1016/j.jbusres.2011.06.034

KEY TERMS AND DEFINITIONS

Brand Community on Social Media: A brand affiliation initiated and established by a company for marketing purposes. It is characterised as a) non-geographically and voluntary bonded affiliations with no barriers for entry and exit, b) an online consumption community, c) a place for information exchange and interaction between consumers and brands. The communication content is typically produced and updated by the company. Members' social status and physical appearance are unimportant (Piven, 2012).

Social Media: A shared collaborative ubiquitous environment that allows users to produce, consume, and exchange content, publically express opinions, align with other online platforms and unite for influence.

Chapter 17
The Emergence of Social Media as a Contemporary Marketing Practice

T. Solomon
Massey University, New Zealand

R. Peter
Massey University, New Zealand

ABSTRACT

In this era of rapid technological change, Social Media has emerged as a key marketing practice in the ICT sector in India. In this chapter, the authors examine the emergence of Social Media as a marketing practice, its application in Relationship Marketing and Market Research and the influence of these on Customer Satisfaction in a B2B market. This research integrates Social Media with the widely prevalent Marketing Management and Relationship Marketing paradigms. A web based survey was used to collect data from a sampling frame of ICT firms in India. Factor analysis evidenced the emergence of Social Media as a unique and distinct factor. It also clearly shows the use of Social Media for Relationship Marketing and Market Research purposes by these ICT firms. Multiple regression analysis showed a significant positive relationship between the independent variables - Social Media, Relationship Marketing and Market Research and the dependent variable Customer Satisfaction.

INTRODUCTION

There has been a revolutionary growth in the Information and Communication Technology (ICT) sector in India since 2001. According to a report prepared by the trade council of India (2014), the revenue of the country's ICT sector was valued at USD 108 billion and is expected to reach USD 220 billion by 2020. As of 2014 this sector had the highest relative share of 9.5% in the national gross domestic product (National Association of Software and Services Companies, 2015). ICT also contributes to economic growth, globalization, foreign exchange earnings, market diversification, employment generation and socio-cultural developments of the country (Ministry of Statistics & Programme Implementation, 2010).

DOI: 10.4018/978-1-5225-0559-4.ch017

The marketing of high technology products, such as the ICT products, differs significantly from the marketing of other low technology products (Mohr, Sengupta & Slater, 2010; Yadav, Swami & Pal, 2006; Traynor & Traynor, 2004). This difference is attributed to the volatile marketing environment of the high technology firms which is characterised by market uncertainty, technological uncertainty and competitive volatility (Mohr et al, 2010).

In spite of the widely acknowledged differences in marketing practices of the technology intensive firms, very little research has been undertaken to identify the strategic marketing practices that are adopted by these firms (Hills & Sarin, 2003). The gap in literature for the general theory development related to the marketing for HT firms has also been identified by Uslay, Malhotra and Citrin (2004). Their study noted the need for both conceptual and empirical research regarding the marketing practices of HT firms. This paper explores some of the marketing practices of ICT firms.

The use of social media in the B2B market clients is a relatively a new phenomenon and remains largely unexplored in literature (Järvinen, Tollinen, Karjaluoto & Jayawardhena, 2012; Schultz, Schwepker & Good, 2012). ICT firms have the technological competency to use online networks and their customers are proficient in internet use. These firms rely on the internet more than any other firms in the business sector. Hence engagement in social media platforms has become a strategic choice for the success of these firms. Because of the importance of the ICT firms to the Indian economy, Sarin (2012) also addressed the need for more research into the strategic marketing practices of these technology intensive firms.

The objective of this paper is to enhance the understanding of Social Media as a contemporary marketing practice. Further it also explores the link between Social Media, Relationship Marketing and Market Research and their influence on Customer Satisfaction in the Information and Communication Technology (ICT) firms in India. This is a part of a larger study in which the authors investigated the marketing practices of the ICT firms in India and their influence on Customer Satisfaction and Firm Performance. The specific research questions of this paper are:

1.   Is there evidence to support that Social Media is a contemporary marketing practice?
2.   Is there a nexus between Social Media, Relationship Marketing and Market Research practices of these ICT firms?
3.   What is the influence of Social Media, Relationship Marketing and Market Research practices on Customer Satisfaction in these ICT firms?

THEORETICAL BACKGROUND

Lehtinen (2011) proposes that an integrated approach to marketing must be used to understand the strategic marketing practices of firms as most empirical research in marketing emphasize the combined use of transactional and relationship marketing approaches by firms. The two approaches were found to complement each other and it is difficult to separate them both in theory and in marketing practice. Coviello and Brodie (2000) concluded that in order to capture the scope of what is being practiced in firms the theoretical framework should include the full spectrum of marketing practices which include the elements of both transactional and relationship marketing practices. Further, Fruchter and Sigue (2005) also contend that marketing is about both exchange transactions and exchange relationships. Hence an integrated approach was used to develop the conceptual framework for this research study. A combination of the Marketing Management perspective and Relationship Marketing perspective were used to identify the marketing practices of the ICT firms in India and to understand the influence of these practices on Customer Satisfaction and Firm Performance. A brief note of the two different perspectives of marketing is discussed below.

Marketing Management Perspective

The Marketing Management school of thought evolved in the late 1950s and the 1960s was characterized by a decision-making approach to manage the marketing functions with an extended focus on customers. Drucker (1954) characterised marketing as a decision-making activity directed at satisfying customers at a profit by targeting a market and then making optimal decisions on the marketing mix or the 4ps. The focus of the firm is on managing the marketing mix decision variables– Product, Price, Promotion and Place (distribution) in order to attract customers. Segmentation and targeting, differentiation and positioning were also introduced in the marketing literature, during this period. Marketing Research also gained significance in marketing management practice as an instrument for aligning the firms' productive capabilities with the needs of the market place (Webster, 1992). Thus, the marketing management school formed a union between the "marketing concept" that firms exist to satisfy customer wants with the perspective of optimizing profit through the management of the marketing mix (Pels & Saren, 2009). The practices relating to the Marketing Management components lead to Customer Satisfaction resulting in higher firm performance (Slater, Hult & Olson, 2007). It is also acknowledged that application of strategic marketing management practices in high technology firms increased Customer Satisfaction (Mohr et al., 2010).

Relationship Marketing Theory

The services marketing discipline acquired a distinct position in the early 1970s, as more researchers began to emphasise the unique characteristics of the services (for example, see Shostack, 1977; Bessom & Jackson, 1975). Increasingly services became a part of the physical products and were mentioned as an important element of the augmented product dimension as noted by Kotler, Armstrong, Saunders and Wong (2000). Two major elements contributed to the development of the services marketing literature: firstly, services became an important source of corporate revenue and a major instrument of all economic activities. Secondly, service was introduced as a significant dimension of product differentiation and also as an important basis of competitive advantage (Constantinides, 2006). The advent of the services marketing perspective raised questions about the relevance and application of the traditional marketing management perspective to services marketing. The primary concern of such researchers was that that the marketing-mix approach did not include the modelling and the managing of the relationships between the service provider and the customers (Möller & Hallinen, 2000). The emphasis on the importance of the development and the maintenance of buyer-seller relationships led to the emergence of relationship marketing.

Also, since early 1980's there has been a significant increase of interest in theory, research and practice focusing on the buyer-seller relationships in marketing (Dwyer, Schurr & Oh, 1987; Lewin & Johnston, 1997). During these decades companies competing in both consumer and industrial markets sought the help of their suppliers to support them to achieve stronger competitive advantage by supplying them with higher quality products, improved services, and efficient distribution systems. Thus, they began to embrace co-operative buyer-seller relationships. Accordingly, the parties involved in the exchange attained and settled for lower total costs by working together to ensure efficient management of inventories, to share risks and to eliminate unnecessary tasks and procedures (Lewin & Johnston, 1997). These "discrete" market relationships were progressively displaced by closer, long-term relationships between the buyers and the sellers. (Lewin & Johnston, 1997).

The term "Relationship marketing" was first alluded to by Thomas in 1976 (cited by Harker & Egan, 2006). This term was explicitly used by Berry (1983) in the context of services marketing. Relationship marketing is described as attracting, maintaining and enhancing customer relationships. Servicing existing customers and selling to them is viewed to be just as important to long-term marketing success as acquiring new customers (Berry, 2002).

Although research identifies numerous factors associated with relationship marketing constructs the factors that were most cited are trust, commitment and communication. These three factors are consistently identified as significant for relationship marketing practice to be successful. Trust is recognised as the central component in all relational exchanges (Dwyer, Schurr & Oh, 1987; Lewin & Johnston, 1997). Trust exists when one party in the exchange process has confidence in an exchange partner's reliability and integrity. Also Dwyer et al. (1987) argue that trust provides a basis for future collaborations, which results in long term relationships among the partner firms. It is proposed that trust is the extent to which the customer believes that the vendor has intentions and motives beneficial to the customer and is concerned with creating positive outcomes for the customer

Commitment is the other major component of relational exchanges (Anderson & Weitz, 1992; Moorman, Zaltman & Deshpande, 1992). It is defined by Moorman, Zaltman and Deshpande, (1992) "as an enduring desire to maintain a valued relationship" (p. 316). Studies propose that relationship commitment is the crux of all successful working relationships and is also commended as an essential ingredient in successful long term relationships. It is posited that commitment increases with the ability of the exchange partners providing positive outcomes to one another in their relationship.

Communication is also an important aspect of successful relationships and a major antecedent to trust and commitment (Anderson & Narus, 1984; Mohr, Fisher & Nevin, 1996). Anderson and Narus describe communication as "formal and informal sharing of meaningful and timely information

between firms' (1990, p.44). Empirical research from literature suggests that communication increases the level of trust between firms (Anderson & Narus, 1984; Anderson & Weitz, 1992). Along with the partners' ability to align their expectations and perceptions communication also helps build trust among partners by providing a mechanism that could be used to resolve conflicts (Arnett & Badrinarayanan, 2005).

Social Media

In the recent years, the radical technological advancements have a profound impact on the marketing practices that are adopted by firms (Ramaswamy & Namakumari, 2012). Developments in marketing are closely intertwined with the technological developments in the information and communication sector. Brady, Saren and Tzokas (2002) argued that marketing is context dependent and when one of the contextual element like the technological environment changes, it has a significant impact on the nature and scope of the marketing discipline. Hence the developments in technology were expected to have a radical impact on how marketing is being practiced in firms.

Among the various internet-based technologies, social media has dramatically influenced businesses and industries. Social connectivity through this online platform has become a key to marketing in firms (Geho & Dangelo, 2012). Firms have adapted themselves to harness this web technology and have adopted strategic approaches to use this online tool for the benefit of the firm.

Social media includes a variety of online information sharing platforms covering all social networking sites (for example, Facebook, LinkedIn and Myspace), creativity work-sharing sites (for example, YouTube and Flickr), collaborative websites such as Wikipedia and microblogging sites (for example, Twitter) (Mangold & Faulds, 2009). These platforms have revolutionised the ways firms relate to market place thus creating a new world of possibilities in all management practices in firms (Aral, Dellarocas & Godes, 2013; Schultz, Schwepker & Good, 2012).

In literature, there are numerous definitions for social media. In a broader sense, social media has been defined as the digital content and the network based interactions which are developed and maintained by and between people (Cohen, 2011). Two primary themes of social media use are highlighted in literature. They are digital content creation and network-based interactions. Many authors see the technologies relating to social media as a paradigm shift that have facilitated a culture of participation through users interacting and collectively creating and sharing knowledge over the internet (for e.g. Benson & Morgan, 2015; Vuori, 2012; Schneckenberg, 2009).

Being present in these online platforms provides significant benefits for firms. They acquire privileged access to customers, discover customer needs early and get increased customer referrals which results in generating revenue. It also provides close proximity to customers which helps to coordinate value co-creation and to deliver superior value through customer relationships, especially in the business-to-business market place (Agnihotri, Kothandaraman, kashyap & Singh, 2012; Vargo & Lusch, 2011; Plouffe & Barclay, 2007). Marketers are increasingly aware of the potential use of this online platform is becoming and have embraced the ability of these tools to assist in marketing practices in firms (Andzulis, Panagopoulos & Rapp, 2012). In this research, all those aspects of social media that are increasingly recognised to provide potential value to the firms in the business context are included in the study.

A steady increase in references in literature about the potential use of social media for marketing purposes in firms signals that social media is becoming a mainstream marketing strategy of the practitioners in firms. Agnihotri, Kothandaraman, Kashyap and Singh (2012) conceded that a practical understanding of how social media is deployed in firms for maximum benefits is still in its infancy, despite a large body of emerging literature in social media marketing. It has also been indicated that social media practioners seek best practices for contexts in which it is widely applicable.

According to Brennan and Croft (2012) and Naude and Holland (2004) the most successful marketing organisations in this era will be those that make the most effective use of information technology tools in developing their marketing strategy. As discussed, the latest tool to emerge that has a huge impact on the marketing practices of firms is social media. Hence social media was integrated into the theoretical framework along with the Marketing Management and the Relationship Marketing perspectives.

Social media not only facilitates firms to interact with their customers directly but also helps the firms to listen to what their customers say about them and their products and services, thereby enhancing the relationship between them. Because social media helps to know the pulse of the customer and deepens the relationship with customers, it is proposed in this study that it would influence customer satisfaction.

Market Research

Market research is posited as the heart of any marketing program in business-to-business markets (Zimmerman & Blythe, 2013). It includes the set of processes that are employed to obtain information about customer needs and market conditions (Vorhies, Harker & Rao, 1999). It is often used in firms for forecasting, developing trends, finding market potential and competitor analysis. Research related to product attributes and product acceptance also comes under the scope of market research in firms. Malhotra (2012) defined market research as "the systematic and objective identification, collection, analysis, dissemination and use of information that is undertaken to improve decision making related to identifying and solving problems in marketing" (p.5).

Market research is widely recognised as a major source of information for marketing decision making, as it serves as the link between the customers and the marketer (Hart & Diamantopoulos, 1993). It provides information that is necessary to identify and define marketing opportunities and problems and helps to develop, evaluate and refine marketing actions so that they can be made more effective (Malhotra, 2010). In high tech markets market research is consistently used to gather information from the marketplace, to incorporate customer needs into the product development and for the marketing process (Mohr et al., 2012).

In regards to market research it is necessary to understand: 1) whether any market research activity was conducted by the firms, 2) how market research information was generated by these firms and 3) what type of information was sought after by the ICT firms. Hart and Diamantopoulos (1993) suggested that primarily, it must be established as to whether market research is done by firms internally, by an in-house department and/or externally, through specialist agencies or external contractors. Relevant information can be collected by firms either by meeting customers formally or gathering the needed information through informal networks (Vorhies, Harker & Rao, 1999). Market research databases that are published online by large firms can also be sources of information (Brooksbank, 1991).

Market research is identified as a quality marketing practice in firms. It helps to identify customer needs. As firms meet these needs, the level of customer satisfaction increases, providing firms with the competitive advantage which is vital for their operations (Kuratko, Goodale & Hornsby 2001). Firms that lead in identifying customer needs have a superior understanding of the factors that affects customer purchase decisions and have strong marketing capability (Dutta, Narasimhan & Rajiv, 1999). These firms achieve better targeting and positioning of its products and services relative to the competitor's.

Customer Satisfaction

According to Gupta and Zeithaml (2006) customer satisfaction is defined essentially as the consumer's judgement that a product or service meets or fall short of expectations. Firms seek to improve and increase customer satisfaction, as satisfied customers ultimately lead to financial benefits to the firms who serve them (Ranaweera & Prabhu, 2003).

There is significant evidence in the marketing literature that customer satisfaction is an important driver of a firm's profitability. For example, Rust, Moorman, and Dickson (2002) report a positive impact of customer satisfaction on financial performance, such as return on investment and return on assets. A study on the personal computers industry by Smith and Wright (2004) suggests that the firm's ability to satisfy its customers provides a sustainable competitive advantage that allows higher average prices, higher sales growth and higher return on assets. Customer satisfaction is also recognised as one of the market assets that can be leveraged to produce superior financial performance (Clark, 1999).

In response to the competitive market place managers seek to improve organisational effectiveness by identifying organisational metrics which contribute to long term success (Sui-Hua, 2007). Sui-Hua contend that organisations are touting for continuous improvement strategies to stay ahead of the competition. In order to drive continuous improvement researchers are placing more importance on measuring organisational performance from the customer's perspective. A growing number of organisations are using customer satisfaction measures in developing, monitoring and evaluating product and service offerings (Anderson, Fornell & Lehmann, 1994). This is because the firm's ability to satisfy customers provides a sustainable competitive advantage which is necessary to operate in today's competitive global environment (Smith & Wright, 2004).

Customer satisfaction is a more fundamental indicator of firm's performance due to its link to behavioural and economic consequences that are beneficial to the firm. According to Gupta and Zeithaml (2006) customer satisfaction is expected to lead to repurchase behaviour (behavioural consequence), which translates into increased sales and profits (economic consequence). Also, customer satisfaction is the central element in the marketing exchange process (Martin-Consuegra, 2007). The marketing concept starts with a well-defined market, focuses on customer needs, coordinates all the activities that affect customers, and produces profit by satisfying customers (Kotler & Keller, 2009). In this study, Customer Satisfaction is measured from the firms' perspective (Hung & Wong, 2007).

METHODOLOGY

This section discusses the research design, data collection and sampling methods employed in this research. Sub-sections which describe the questionnaire design, sampling design, instrumentation and survey implementation are included in the discussion.

Exploratory research design was used in this research to obtain insights into the different marketing practices of the ICT firms in the Indian context. To achieve this, survey method of data collection was used for the study (Malhotra, 2010; McDaniel & Gates, 2010). The choice of the suitable survey method depends on the context of the specific research and the advantages of the chosen method over the other options. This study includes ICT firms and so the sample population has access to the internet. Hence web survey method was adopted for the study as it facilitates speedy data collection, geographical flexibility, less cost and there is less interviewer interference (Zikmund & Babin, 2012).

The sampling frame for this research comes from the list of registered online panel members of a reputed market research agency who provided the data collection services for this research. Managers were used as proxies for firms and the managers in all the 2983 firms were invited to participate in an online survey. A number of these ICT firms have offices in multiple locations in the country. In order to avoid duplication of data from the same company, respondents were required to specify the name of their firm. Only 187 respondents had provided this information yielding a response rate of 6.3%. Hence only these were considered in the data analysis. MacCallum, Widaman, Zhang and Hong (1999) and Tabachnick and Fidell (2013) indicated that a sample size in the range of 100-200 is acceptable with well determined factors. The sample used for the current study is 187, and is within this guideline.

A formal, well-structured questionnaire was used to obtain specific information. Structured questions were used in the questionnaire. Fixed alternative questions were used because it was easier for the respondents to answer and it enabled comparability of answers, facilitated coding, tabulation and interpretation of data (McDaniel & Gates, 2010; Hair, Black, Babin, Anderson & Tatham, 2006). To minimize the risk of comprehension and misinterpretation problems, definitions of key question concepts were made available to the web survey respondents (Peytchev, Conrad, Couper & Tourangeau, 2010). This helped the researcher to communicate the intended meaning of the key concepts in the questionnaire to the survey respondents, thereby increasing the accuracy of the responses. All key concepts were clearly defined in the questionnaire to improve the accuracy of the survey results.

In the web survey questionnaire, all the items for a construct were presented in the same page. This facilitated easy referencing to the definitions of the construct and to effectively lead the respondents through, to complete the questionnaire. All the questions and the definitions for the constructs were highlighted. A "progress bar" to indicate the percentage completion of the questionnaire was included in each page of the questionnaire. The "back button" option was added to assist respondents, if they want to go back and change the answers. The respondents were required to access a uniform resource locator (URL) to take the survey. Because of the save and continue option in the questionnaire, they also had the possibility of completing the survey at their convenience within the stipulated time frame of two weeks.

Likert scales were used in this study to evaluate the items. Accordingly a series of statements that expressed either a favourable or an unfavourable attitude were employed to assess the concept under study. The respondents were asked to indicate their level of disagreement or agreement with each statement. The anchor points were, 1=strongly disagree and 7 = strongly agree with 4 being the neutral point. Even though the assumption of equal intervals between the anchor points in Likert scales are debated in literature, the averages derived from these scales are found to be meaningful, thus rendering this type of scale closer to interval scale than to ordinal scale measurement (Meyers, Gamst & Guarino, 2013). Also multivariate analysis techniques like regression analysis are robust to deviations from equivalency of intervals between scale units and are not overly susceptible to relaxing interval data requirement. All the constructs were measured with a number of items and therefore a multi-item scale was used in this study. Using different items to measure the same concept provides a more accurate cumulative measure than single-item estimates. The respondents were asked to select from a limited number of ordered categories for each of the statements that measured the various constructs. A review of relevant literature and a series of informal discussions with the academic staff and experts in ICT firms guided the development of the survey instrument of this study.

The ten items identified for the relationship marketing construct were specifically aimed at measuring the different dimensions of relationships that exist between the exchange partners in the given context. In the literature four major dimensions of relationship marketing are identified - trust, commitment, communication and customer relationship orientation in firms. The scale items that were adapted to measure Relationship Marketing practices are —

RM1: In our organisation, retaining customers is considered to be a top priority (Jayachandran, Sharma, Kaufman & Raman, 2005);

RM2: In our organisation, customer relationships are considered to be a valuable asset (Jayachandran et al., 2005);

RM3: Our senior management emphasizes the importance of customer relationships (Jayachandran et al., 2005);

RM4: In our organisation, employees receive incentives based on customer satisfaction measures (Jayachandran et al., 2005);

RM5: We can rely on our firm to keep the promises that it makes to the customers (Lawson-Body, Willoughby & Logossah, 2010);

RM6: In our relationship with customers, our firm can be trusted at all times (Lawson-Body et al., 2010);

RM7: Our firm rewards employees who do their very best to solve customer problems (Lawson-Body et al., 2010);

RM8: We fulfil all obligations and promises we make to customers (Negi & Ketema, 2010);

RM9: We nmake significant investments (in terms of time and resources) in building relationship with our customers (Palmatier, Gopalakrishna & Houston, 2006); and

RM10: We are committed to establishing long term relationship with our customers (Sin, Yau, Chow, Lee & Lau, 2005).

Respondents were asked to indicate how market research information was gathered in their firm and what kinds of information were obtained. The following seven items were used to assess the Market Research practices of the ICT firms in India:

MR1: In our firm, we do a lot of in-house marketing research (Hart & Diamantopoulos, 1993; Jaworski & Kohli, 1993);

MR2: In our firm, we use external contractors to do market research for us (Hart & Diamantopoulos, 1993; Jaworski & Kohli, 1993);

MR3: In our firm, we meet our customers formally to find out their future requirements (Vorhies et al., 1999);

MR4: In our firm, we use the marketing research database that is published online by large firms (Vorhies et al., 1999);

MR5: In our firm, we collect relevant industry information through informal networks (Vorhies et al., 1999);

MR6: In our firm, we gather data to understand the market perception of our new products and services (Hart & Diamantopoulos, 1993); and

MR7: In our firm, we gather data regarding the customer acceptance of our products and services (Hart & Diamantopoulos, 1993).

The scale items for Social Media were drawn from literature and were not from previously established or published scales. All the eleven items captured the potential purposes of the use of social media by the ICT firms in India. The items are:

SM1: Managers in our firm actively participate in professional social networks (like Linked In) (Smith, 2009);

SM2: Our firm actively searches for market opportunities in user generated blogs in online communities (Smith, 2009; Moen, Madsen & Aspelund, 2008);

SM3: our firm constantly monitors social network sites for reviews of our products and services (Fisher, 2009; Moen, Endresen & Gavlen, 2003);

SM4: In our firm, we constantly check online networks to know about competitor's products and services (Moen, Madsen, & Aspelund, 2008);

SM5: We encourage our customers to participate in live and interactive discussion forums in our website (Moen et al., 2008; Deans, Gray, Ibbotson, Osborne & Knightbridge, 2003);

SM6: Our firm has increased efficiency in developing products due to online customer interaction at various stages of product development (Fisher, 2009; Moen et al., 2008; Deans et al., 2003);

SM7: Our constant interaction with customers through online networks has improved our customer relations (Moen et al., 2008; Deans et al., 2003);

SM8: There is a reduction in online customer support because of the information we provide through our online discussion forums (Fisher, 2009; Deans et al., 2003);

SM9: We use our online networks to explain our products/services to customers (Deans et al., 2003);

SM10: We use our online networks to facilitate endorsement of our product/services by customers (Pfeiffer & Zinnbauer, 2010); and

SM11: Our engagement in the online social networks help build our firm's reputation (Pfeiffer & Zinnbauer, 2010; Fisher, 2009; Moen et al., 2003).

In this study Customer Satisfaction was measured from the firm's perspective. The items include both the firm's assessment of Customer Satisfaction and the practices that they use to enhance Customer Satisfaction. The nine items are:

CS1: We get more clients/business through positive word of mouth from our existing customers (Szymanski & Henard, 2001);

CS2: Our customers frequently return for additional business to our firm (Makarem, Mudambi & Podoshen, 2009);

CS3: All departments are responsive to, and are integrated in serving customers (Hung & Wong, 2007);

CS4: We deliver the offering in the time frame that the customer desires or needs (Boyd, 2002);

CS5: We respond to customer complaints and suggestions without delay (Hung & Wong, 2007);

CS6: We have a system of conflict resolution that is fair to the customer and to us (Boyd, 2002);

CS7: Our firm responds quickly to changing customer requirements (Hung & Wong, 2007);

CS8: Our firm obtains feedback from our customers through formal review meetings (Makarem et al., 2007); and

CS9: We often rely on informal networks to assess the satisfaction of our customers with our products and services (Makarem et al., 2007).

Once the questionnaire was developed, it was pre-tested with a small group of respondents as suggested by Zikmund and Babin (2007). This facilitated pre-testing the questionnaire for clarity of questions, relevance and completeness which improved the face validity of the survey questionnaire. Further modifications to the questionnaire content, format, wording and response alternatives were

made based on the results of the pretest. Also, every effort was undertaken to develop the final questionnaire more respondent friendly.

The authors employed Exploratory Factor Analysis (EFA) and Multiple Regression analysis to test the proposed conceptual model. However, only the results pertaining to the marketing practices relating to Social Media, Relationship Marketing and Market Research are presented in this paper, since it brings out the nexus between these constructs.

RESULTS

EFA was used in this study to identify the underlying structure among the independent variables (IVs) in the analysis and to reduce their number to include only the most parsimonious sets of variables in the subsequent multiple regression analysis (Hair, Black, Babin & Anderson,2010). A significant score of .904 for the KMO measure of sampling adequacy and a Chi-square value of 5135.122 (significant at .000) rendered the data suitable for EFA. As recommended by de Winter and Dodou, (2012) principal axis factoring with oblique rotation (promax) was employed in this research study.

Eigen values were used to determine the number of factors to be extracted. Items with factor loadings less than .30 were deleted from the analysis. Single item factors were also excluded from the analysis from the standpoint of parsimony (Lawson-Body, Willoughby & Logossah, 2010). Items with squared multiple correlations less than .4 were excluded from the analysis (Anna & Osbourne, 2005). EFA resulted in a final instrument of 43 items representing 10 distinct factors. These 10 factors explained 72.36% of the variance. The tables below (Table 1, Table 2 and Table 3 present the EFA results for the three factors of interest, viz, Relationship Marketing practices, Market Research practices and Social Media practices, together with the squared multiple correlations (communalities) and the Cronbach's Alpha (coefficient of reliability).

Factor 1, 'Relationship Marketing Practices' explained 39% of the total variance and consisted of 10 items with factor loadings ranging from .513 to .821. It is interesting to note from the above table that some of the items that were used to assess the Social Media practices (SM5, SM6 & SM7) loaded under this factor. It appears therefore, that social media is effectively used by the ICT firms in India to improve relationship with customers by constant interaction with customers through online networks (SM7), to encourage customers to participate in live and interactive discussion forums (SM5) and to increase efficiency in developing products due to online customer interaction at various stages of product development (SM7). The results show that social media practices are prevalent in the ICT firms in India and are efficiently used by these firms to build relationships through effective communication.

Table 1. Factor 1: relationship marketing practices

Items	Factor Loadings	SMC*
RM10: We are committed to establish long term relationship with our customers	.821	.764
RM2: In our organization, customer relationships are considered to be a valuable asset	.750	.779
RM8: We fulfill all obligations and promises we make with customers.	.692	.689
SM7: Our constant interaction with customers through online networks has improved our customer relations.	.666	.635
SM5: We encourage our customers to participate in live and interactive discussion forums in our website.	.656	.642
RM5: We can rely on our firm to keep the promises that it makes to the customers	.646	.692
RM3: Our senior management emphasizes the importance of customer relationships	.633	.609
SM6: Our firm has increased efficiency in developing products due to online customer interaction at various stages of product development.	.602	.610
RM6: In our relationship with customers, our firm can be trusted at all times	.587	.685
RM9: We make significant investments (in terms of time and resources) in building relationship with our customers	.513	.638

*Squared Multiple Correlations; Cronbach's α: .920.

Table 2. Factor 2: market research practices

Items	Factor Loadings	SMC*
SM3: Our firm constantly monitors social network sites for reviews of our products and services.	.793	.662
SM2: Our firm actively searches for market opportunities in user generated blogs in online communities.	.644	.656
MR2: Use external contractors to do market research for us	.513	.515
SM4: In our firm, we constantly check online networks to know about competitor's products and services.	.387	.545

*Squared Multiple Correlations; Cronbach's α: .806.

Table 3. Factor 3: social media practices

Items	Factor Loadings	SMC*
SM10: We use our online networks to facilitate endorsement of our product/services by customers	.813	.728
SM9: We use our online networks to explain our products/services to customers.	.666	.629
SM11: Our engagement in the online social networks helps build our firm's reputation.	.566	.660

*Squared Multiple Correlations; Cronbach's α: .825.

Table 2 includes the four items that describe the Market Research practices that loaded under this factor. Once again it can be seen that the ICT firms tend to use social media for market research purposes. Along with using external contractors for market research, firms are found to use social media to know about the reviews of their firm's products and services (SM3) and to know about competitor's products and services (SM4). Also market opportunities are actively searched for in user generated blogs in online communities (SM2). Hence this factor is assigned the name 'Market Research Practices'.

Three items that pertain to Social Media loaded on to the third factor. These items explain the purposes of using social media by the ICT firms, for reasons other than for relationship marketing and marketing research. Social media is found to be used by the firms to facilitate endorsement of the firm's products (SM10), to explain the products and services to customers (SM9), and services by customers and to build firm's reputation (SM11).

As the next step, the summated scales for these three factors, viz, Relationship Marketing practices, Market Research practices and Social Media practices were computed. As recommended by Hair, Black, Babin & Anderson (2010), these summated scales were formed by combining the individual variables loading into a factor to compute the composite measure. The composite measure for Customer Satisfaction practices was also computed. These composite measures represent the new composite latent variables that were used in the subsequent regression analysis. The results of the regression analysis are presented below

A standard multiple regression was performed using the composite measures of the latent variables. The Dependent Variable – Customer Satisfaction was regressed against the Independent Variables (IVs) - Relationship Marketing practices, Market research practices and Social Media practices. Regression results presented here follow the pattern adopted by Tabachnick and Fidell (2013). The analysis yielded a statistically significant result. R (the multiple correlation coefficient) for regression was significantly different from zero, F (3,183) = 96.228, p<.001. The adjusted value of R^2 = .606 indicated that approximately 61% of the variability in Customer Satisfaction is influenced by the IVs chosen for this analysis. Relationship Marketing practices has the highest β value of .547 indicating that it has a strong positive influence on Customer Satisfaction. This is also supported by a highly significant t-value (t = 8.483, p = .000). Social Media practices has the next highest influence on Customer Satisfaction with β = .185, t = 3.134 and p = .002. This is followed by Market Research practices with β = .155; t = 2.572 and p = .011. The influence of Social Media and Market Research are also significant at p < .01.

FINDINGS AND IMPLICATIONS

Empirical evidence supports the emergence of Social Media as a unique and distinct marketing practice. Besides Social Media is also used by these firms for Relationship Marketing and Market Research purposes. Further, this study clearly indicates that the three marketing practices, viz, Relationship Marketing practices, Social Media practices and Market Research practices significantly influences Customer Satisfaction in these firms. Customer Satisfaction is widely accepted in literature as one of the major outcomes of all marketing activities. However, most of the empirical research supporting this proposition was conducted in the context of other countries and other industries. The current research extends the existing body of knowledge to include the ICT firms in the Indian context by providing incremental evidence in understanding how these three marketing practices enhances Customer Satisfaction in these firms.

The findings pertaining to the individual constructs are discussed below.

Relationship Marketing Practices

The three important elements of Relationship Marketing - trust, commitment and communication between the exchange partners were assessed in this research together with the customer relationship orientation in these firms. All three elements emerged as components of Relationship Marketing practices. Existing Relationship Marketing literature points out that retaining existing customer is more profitable, especially in the B2B sector. Hence managers and practitioners must put their efforts on being customer relationship orientated and to build trust and commitment with their customers through constant and consistent communication.

The importance of communicating and interacting with business-to-business customers to develop and maintain relationships through the use of Social Media is established in this research. Relationship Marketing literature posits communication as an integral element to enhance and maintain relationships with customers, especially in B2B firms. This research empirically establishes Social Media as an integral part of the firms' Relationship Marketing strategy. Managers need to use Social Media effectively to build and maintain relationships with customers. This can be accomplished through constant communication and interaction with customers.

Market Research Practices

The EFA results show that three items pertaining to Social Media loaded on to Market Research practices. The items clearly indicate the use of social media for market research purposes by the ICT firms in India. Firms use social media: to know about the reviews of their firm's products and services; to know about competitor's products and services, and to actively search for market

opportunities in user generated blogs in online communities. It is evident that the information available through Social Media is used by the ICT firms for market research purposes

Social networking capabilities enable firms to generate market knowledge which facilitates firms to develop and deploy information (Heirati, O'Cass & Ngo, 2013). The use of Social Media is a cost effective means to reach a wider audience in the market. Further an online presence creates and enhances product and/or brand awareness and builds brand reputation. Social Media needs to be leveraged for Market Research purposes by the ICT firms in India. Social Media tools need to be strategically used by practicing managers of these ICT firms to enhance their market research practices and to complement the objectives of strategic marketing in these firms.

Social Media Practices

The ICT firms in India employ distinctive Social Media practices. Social media is found to be used by the firms to facilitate endorsement of the firm's products, to explain the products and services to customers, and services by customers and to build firm's reputation. Managers of the ICT firms in India should diligently seek to establish these practices in their firms.

This research makes a distinct contribution to Social Media literature. It addresses the gap in literature by providing an understanding of the actual use of Social Media for commercial purposes by the B2B firms in the ICT sector in India. It provides empirical evidence to support that Social Media is effectively utilised for marketing purposes in these firms. Social Media technologies have been found to support other marketing practices such as Relationship Marketing and Market Research.

Practitioners need to encourage their firms to engage diligently in Social Media given the findings that it supports marketing practices in firms. Firms in this sector should leverage Social Media to facilitate Relationship Marketing and Market Research practices. Social Media practices were found to significantly influence Customer Satisfaction in the ICT firms in India. Therefore marketing practitioners should increasingly advocate the use of Social Media technologies to improve Customer Satisfaction in their firms. In this digital era the unparalleled speed of information diffusion through Social Media undoubtedly improves and enhances the success of firms that take advantage of Social Media technologies. Hence it would be advisable for managers in ICT firms to prioritise and use various Social Media platforms along with other Strategic Marketing Practices to enhance and increase Customer Satisfaction.

CONCLUSION

The results of EFA show that each construct was well defined by multiple indicator variables. This is further confirmed by the measures of reliability with Cronbach's α ranging from .806 to .902. The contribution of this study to theory development emerges from the valid operationalisation of Social Media as a construct that has hitherto not been considered. Social Media has emerged as a distinct and unique marketing practice in itself in B2B marketing. There is also evidence to support the use of Social Media for Relationship Marketing and Market Research purposes by the ICT firms in India. The nexus between Social Media, Relationship Marketing and Market Research can be clearly seen by the loading of items pertaining to Social Media in Relationship Marketing and Market Research. Finally all three latent variables have a significant positive influence on Customer Satisfaction. The present study draws its conclusions from the empirical testing of data from the ICT sector in India, which contributes significantly to the economic growth in India. In order to bring in Social Media into mainstream theory it will be necessary to undertake this research in other countries. We welcome researchers to undertake similar studies in other cultural and economic contexts.

REFERENCES

Agnihotri, R., Kothandaraman, P., Kashyap, R., & Singh, R. (2012). Bringing "Social" into Sales: The Impact of Salespeople's Social Media Use on Service Behaviors and Value Creation. *Journal of Personal Selling & Sales Management, 32*(3), 333–348. doi:10.2753/PSS0885-3134320304

Anderson, E., & Weitz, B. (1992). The Use of Pledges to build and Sustain Commitment in Distribution Channels. *JMR, Journal of Marketing Research, 29*(1), 18–34. doi:10.2307/3172490

Anderson, E. W., Fornell, C., & Lehmann, D. R. (1994). Customer Satisfaction, Market Share, and Profitability: Findings from Sweden. *Journal of Marketing, 58*(3), 53–66. doi:10.2307/1252310

Anderson, J. C., & Narus, J. A. (1984). A Model of the Distributor's Perspective of Distributor- Manufacturer Working Relationships. *Journal of Marketing, 48*(4), 62–74. doi:10.2307/1251511

Andzulis, J. M., Panagopoulos, N. G., & Rapp, A. (2012). A Review of Social Media and Implications for the Sales Process. *Journal of Personal Selling & Sales Management, 32*(3), 305–316. doi:10.2753/PSS0885-3134320302

Aral, S., Dellarocas, C., & Godes, D. (2013). Social Media and Business Transformation: A Framework for Research. *Information Systems Research, 24*(1), 3–14. doi:10.1287/isre.1120.0470

Arnett, D. B., & Badrinarayanan, V. (2005). Enhancing Customer-Needs--Driven CRM Strategies: Core Selling Teams, Knowledge Management Competence, and Relationship Marketing Competence. *Journal of Personal Selling & Sales Management, 25*(4), 329–343.

Benson, V., & Morgan, S. (2015). *Implications of Social Media Use in Personal and Professional Settings*. Hershey, PA: IGI Global; doi:10.4018/978-1-4666-7401-1

Berry, L. L. (1983). *Relationship Marketing*. Paper presented at the Emerging Perspectives on Services Marketing, Chicago, IL.

Berry, L. L. (1995). Relationship Marketing of Services-Growing Interest, Emerging Perspectives. *Journal of the Academy of Marketing Science, 23*(4), 236–245. doi:10.1177/009207039502300402

Bessom, R. M., & Jackson, D. W. Jr. (1975). Service Retailing: A Strategic Marketing Approach. *Journal of Retailing, 51*(2), 75–85.

Boyd, A. (2002). The Goals, Questions, Indicators, Measures (GQIM) Approach to the Measurement of Customer Satisfaction with e-commerce Web sites. *Aslib Proceedings*, *54*(3), 177–187. doi:10.1108/00012530210441728

Brady, M., Saren, M., & Tzokas, N. (2002). *Integrating information technology into marketing practice - the IT reality of contemporary marketing practice*. Academic Press.

Brennan, R., & Croft, R. (2012). The use of social media in B2B marketing and branding: An Exploratory Study. *Journal of Customer Behaviour*, *11*(2), 101–115. doi:10.1362/147539212X13420906144552

Brooksbank, R. W. (1991). Successful Marketing Practice: A Literature Review and Checklist for Marketing Practitioners. *European Journal of Marketing*, *25*(5), 20–29. doi:10.1108/EUM0000000000619

Clark, B. H. (1999). Marketing Performance Measures: History and Interrelationships. *Journal of Marketing Management*, *15*(8), 711–732. doi:10.1362/026725799784772594

Cohen, C. (2011). Interconnections: Brand Reputation And Free Online Monitoring Tools. *Franchising World*, *43*(7), 18.

Constantinides, E. (2006). The Marketing Mix Revisited: Towards the 21st Century Marketing. *Journal of Marketing Management*, *22*(3/4), 407–438. doi:10.1362/026725706776861190

Coviello, N. E., & Brodie, R. J. (2001). Contemporary marketing practices of consumer and business-to-business firms: How different are they? *Journal of Business and Industrial Marketing*, *16*(5), 382–400. doi:10.1108/08858620110400223

Deans, K. R., Gray, B. J., Ibbotson, P., Osborne, P., & Knightbridge, K. (2003). Web Marketing Practices of Service Providers. *Service Industries Journal*, *23*(3), 82–102. doi:10.1080/714005119

Drucker, P. F. (1954). *The Practice of Management*. New York: Harper and Row.

Dutta, S., Narasimhan, O., & Rajiv, S. (1999). *Success in High-Technology Markets: Is Marketing Capability Critical?*. Academic Press.

Dwyer, F. R., Schurr, P. H., & Oh, S. (1987). Developing Buyer-Seller Relationships. *Journal of Marketing*, *51*(2), 11–27. doi:10.2307/1251126

Fisher, T. (2009). ROI in Social Media: A look at the Arguments. *Journal of Database Marketing & Customer Strategy Management*, *16*(3), 189–195. doi:10.1057/dbm.2009.16

Fruchter, G. E., & Sigué, S. P. (2005). Transactions vs. Relationships: What Should the Company Emphasize? *Journal of Service Research*, *8*(1), 18–36. doi:10.1177/1094670505276629

Geho, P. R., & Dangelo, J. (2012). The Evolution of Social Media as a Marketing Tool for Entrepreneurs. *Entrepreneurial Executive*, *17*, 61–68.

Gupta, S., & Zeithaml, V. (2006). Customer Metrics and Their Impact on Financial Performance. *Marketing Science*, *25*(6), 718–739. doi:10.1287/mksc.1060.0221

Hair, J. F., Black, W. C., Babin, B. J., & Anderson, R. E. (2010). *Multivariate data analysis* (7th ed.). Upper Saddle River, NJ: Pearson Prentice Hall.

Harker, M. J., & Egan, J. (2006). The Past, Present and Future of Relationship Marketing. *Journal of Marketing Management, 22*(1/2), 215–242. doi:10.1362/026725706776022326

Hart, S., & Diamantopoulos, A. (1993). Marketing Research Activity and Company Performance: Evidence from Manufacturing Industry. *European Journal of Marketing, 27*(5), 54–72. doi:10.1108/03090569310039723

Heirati, N., O'Cass, A., & Ngo, L. V. (2013). The Contingent Value of Marketing and Social Networking Capabilities in Firm Performance. *Journal of Strategic Marketing, 21*(1), 82–98. doi:10.1080/0965254X.2012.742130

Hills, S. B., & Sarin, S. (2003). From Market Driven to Market Driving: An Alternate Paradigm for Marketing in High Technology Industries. *Journal of Marketing Theory and Practice, 11*(3), 13–24. doi:10.1080/10696679.2003.11658498

Hung, H., & Wong, Y. H. (2007). Organisational Perception of Customer Satisfaction: Theories and Evidence. *Service Industries Journal, 27*(4), 495–507. doi:10.1080/02642060701346540

Jaworski, B. J., & Kohli, A. K. (1993). Market Orientation - Antecedents and Consequences. *Journal of Marketing, 57*(3), 53–70.

Jayachandran, S., Sharma, S., Kaufman, P., & Raman, P. (2005). The role of relational information processes and technology use in customer relationship management. *Journal of Marketing, 69*(4), 177–192.

Kotler, P., Armstrong, G., Saunders, J., & Wong, V. (2000). *Principles of Marketing* (2d Russian Ed). Moscow: Williams Publishing House.

Kotler, P., & Keller, K. L. (2007). *Marketing Management*. Praha: Grada Publishing.

Kuratko, D. F., Goodale, J. C., & Hornsby, J. S. (2001). Quality Practices for a Competitive Advantage in Smaller Firms. *Journal of Small Business Management, 39*(4), 293–311.

Lawson-Body, A., Willoughby, L., & Logossah, K. (2010). Developing an Instrument for Measuring E-Commerce Dimensions. *Journal of Computer Information Systems, 51*(2), 2–13.

Lehtinen, U. (2011). Combining Mix and Relationship marketing. *Marketing Review, 11*(2), 117–136.

Lewin, J. E., & Johnston, W. J. (1997). Relationship Marketing Theory in Practice: A Case Study. *Journal of Business Research, 39*(1), 23–31.

Makarem, S. C., Mudambi, S. M., & Podoshen, J. S. (2009). Satisfaction in Technology-enabled Service Encounters. *Journal of Services Marketing, 23*(2-3), 134–143. doi:10.1108/08876040910955143

Malhotra, N. K. (2010). *Marketing Research: An Applied Orientation* (6th ed.). Upper Saddle River, NJ: Pearson Education. doi:10.1108/S1548-6435(2010)6

Mangold, W. G., & Faulds, D. J. (2009). Social Media: The New Hybrid Element of the Promotion Mix. *Business Horizons, 52*(4), 357–365. doi:10.1016/j.bushor.2009.03.002

McDaniel, C. D., & Gates, R. H. (2010). *Marketing Research Essentials* (7th ed.). Hoboken, NJ: John Wiley & Sons.

Meyers, L. S., Gamst, G., & Guarino, A. J. (n.d.). Applied multivariate Research: Design and Interpretation (2nd ed.). Thousand Oaks, CA: SAGE Publications.

Ministry of Statistics & Programme Implementation. India. (2011). *Value Addition and Employment Generation in the ICT Sector in India.* Retrieved from http://mospi.nic.in/mospi_new/upload/val_add_ict_21june11.pdf

Moen, O., Endresen, I., & Gavlen, M. (2003). Executive insights: Use of the Internet in International Marketing: A Case Study of Small Computer Software Firms. *Journal of International Marketing, 11*(4), 129–149. doi:10.1509/jimk.11.4.129.20146

Moen, O., Madsen, T. K., & Aspelund, A. (2008). The Importance of the Internet in International Business-to-Business Markets. *International Marketing Review, 25*(5), 487–503. doi:10.1108/02651330810904053

Mohr, J., Slater, S., & Sengupta, S. (2010). *Marketing of High-Technology Products and Innovations* (3rd ed.). Upper Saddle River, Prentice Hall.

Mohr, J. J., Fisher, R. J., & Nevin, J. R. (1996). Collaborative communication in interfirm relationships: Moderating effects of integration and. *Journal of Marketing, 60*(3), 103. doi:10.2307/1251844

Möller, K., & Halinen, A. (2000). Relationship Marketing Theory: Its Roots and Direction. *Journal of Marketing Management, 16*(1-3), 29–54. doi:10.1362/026725700785100460

Moorman, C., Zaltman, G., & Deshpande, R. (1992). Relationships Between Providers and Users of Market Research: The Dynamics of Trust Within and Between Organizations. *JMR, Journal of Marketing Research, 29*(3), 314–328. doi:10.2307/3172742

National Association of Software and Services Companies. India. (2013). *Indian IT-BPO Industry.* Retrieved from http://www.nasscom.in/impact-indias-growth

Naudé, P., & Holland, C. P. (2004). The Role of Information and Communications Technology in Transforming Marketing Theory and Practice. *Journal of Business and Industrial Marketing, 19*(3), 165–166. doi:10.1108/08858620410531298

Negi, R., & Ketema, E. (2010). Relationship Marketing and Customer Loyalty: The Ethiopian Mobile Communications Perspective. *International Journal of Mobile Marketing, 5*(1), 113–124.

Palmatier, R. W., Gopalkrishna, S., & Houston, M. B. (2006). Returns on Business-To-Business Relationship Marketing Investments: Strategies For Leveraging Profits. *Marketing Science, 25*(5), 477–493. doi:10.1287/mksc.1060.0209

Pels, J., Möller, K., & Saren, M. (2009). Do we really understand business marketing? Getting beyond the RM and BM matrimony. *Journal of Business and Industrial Marketing, 24*(5/6), 322–336. doi:10.1108/08858620910966219

Peytchev, A., Conrad, F. G., Couper, M. P., & Tourangeau, R. (2010). Increasing Respondents' Use of Definitions in Web Surveys. *Journal of Official Statistics, 26*(4), 633–650. PMID:23411499

Pfeiffer, M., & Zinnbauer, M. (2010). Can Old Media Enhance New Media?: How Traditional Advertising Pays off for an Online Social Network. *Journal of Advertising Research, 50*(1), 42–49. doi:10.2501/S0021849910091166

Plouffe, C. R., & Barclay, D. W. (2007). Salesperson navigation: The Intraorganizational Dimension of the Sales Role. *Industrial Marketing Management, 36*(4), 528–539. doi:10.1016/j.indmarman.2006.02.002

Ramaswamy, & Namakumari. (2013). *Marketing Management: Indian Context* (5th ed.). McGraw Hill Education (India) Private Limited.

Ranaweera, C., & Prabhu, J. (2003). On the relative importance of Customer Satisfaction and Trust as Determinants of Customer Retention and Positive Word Of Mouth. *Journal of Targeting. Measurement & Analysis for Marketing, 12*(1), 82–90. doi:10.1057/palgrave.jt.5740100

Rust, R. T., Moorman, C., & Dickson, P. R. (2002). Getting Return on Quality: Revenue Expansion, Cost Reduction, or Both? *Journal of Marketing, 66*(4), 7–24. doi:10.1509/jmkg.66.4.7.18515

Sarin, S. (2012). My Years with B2B Marketing in India: Reflections and Learnings from a Journey of 40 years. *Journal of Business and Industrial Marketing, 27*(3), 160–168. doi:10.1108/08858621211207199

Schultz, R. J., Schwepker, C. H., & Good, D. J. (2012). An Exploratory Study of Social Media in Business-To-Business Selling: Salesperson Characteristics, Activities and Performance. *Marketing Management Journal, 22*(2), 76–89.

Shostack, G. L. (1977). Breaking Free from Product Marketing. *Journal of Marketing, 41*(2), 73–80.

Sin, L. Y. M., Tse, A. C. B., Yau, O. H. M., Chow, R. P. M., Lee, J. S. Y., & Lau, L. B. Y. (2005). Relationship Marketing Orientation: Scale Development and Cross-Cultural Validation. *Journal of Business Research, 58*(2), 185–194.

Slater, S. F., Hult, G. T. M., & Olson, E. M. (2007). On the Importance of Matching Strategic Behavior and Target Market Selection to Business Strategy in High-Tech Markets. *Journal of the Academy of Marketing Science, 35*(1), 5–17. doi:10.1007/s11747-006-0002-4

Smith, R. E., & Wright, W. F. (2004). Determinants of Customer Loyalty and Financial Performance. *Journal of Management Accounting Research, 16*(1), 183–205. doi:10.2308/jmar.2004.16.1.183

Smith, T. (2009). The social Media Revolution. *International Journal of Market Research, 51*(4), 559–561. doi:10.2501/S1470785309200773

Sui-Hua, Y. (2007). An Empirical Investigation on the Economic Consequences of Customer Satisfaction. *Total Quality Management & Business Excellence, 18*(5), 555–569. doi:10.1080/14783360701240493

Szymanski, D. M., & Henard, D. H. (2001). Customer Satisfaction: A Meta-analysis of the Empirical Evidence. *Journal of the Academy of Marketing Science, 29*(1), 16–35. doi:10.1177/0092070301291002

Tabachnick, B. G., & Fidel, L. S. (2013). *Using Multivariate Statistics* (6th ed.). Boston: Pearson Education.

Traynor, K., & Traynor, S. (2004). A Comparison of Marketing Approaches used by High-tech Firms: 1985 versus 2001. *Industrial Marketing Management, 33*(5), 457–461. doi:10.1016/j.indmarman.2003.08.013

Uslay, C., Malhotra, N. K., & Citrin, A. V. (2004). Unique Marketing Challenges at the Frontiers of Technology: An Integrated Perspective. *International Journal of Technology Management, 28*(1), 8–30. doi:10.1504/IJTM.2004.005050

Vargo, S. L., & Lusch, R. F. (2004). Evolving to a New Dominant Logic for Marketing. *Journal of Marketing, 68*(1), 1–17. doi:10.1509/jmkg.68.1.1.24036

Vorhies, D. W., Harker, M., & Rao, C. P. (1999). The Capabilities and Performance Advantages of Market-driven Firms. *European Journal of Marketing, 33*(11/12), 1171–1202. doi:10.1108/03090569910292339

Vuori, M. (2012). Exploring Uses of Social Media in a Global Corporation. *Journal of Systems and Information Technology, 14*(2), 155–170. doi:10.1108/13287261211232171

Webster, J. F. E. (1992). The Changing role of Marketing in the Corporation. *Journal of Marketing, 56*(4), 1. doi:10.2307/1251983

Yadav, N., Swami, S., & Pal, P. (2006). High Technology Marketing: Conceptualization and Case Study. *Vikalpa: The Journal for Decision Makers, 31*(2), 57–74.

Zikmund, W. G., & Babin, B. J. (2012). Marketing Research (10th ed.). South-Western/Cengage Learning.

Zikmund, W. G., Babin, B. J., Carr, J. C., & Griffin, M. (2010). *Business Research Methods*. South-Western Cengage Learning.

Zimmerman, A. S., & Blythe, J. (2013). *Business to business marketing management: a global perspective* (2nd ed.). New York: Routledge.

Chapter 18

Getting New Business Contacts in Foreign Markets through Social Networking Sites:
Perspectives from Professionals of Basque Region in SPAIN

Aitziber Nunez-Zabaleta
University of the Basque Country UPV/EHU, Spain

Elena Olabarri
University of the Basque Country UPV/EHU, Spain

Sergio Monge-Benito
University of the Basque Country UPV/EHU, Spain

ABSTRACT

Being able to find information, people and expertise helps business to grow and remain competitive. Professional networking using the web 2.0 is providing entry opportunities into international markets, allowing professional workers to interact with both workers and companies in markets worldwide. For that reason our research seeks identify the Social Networking Sites (SNSs) used with business purposes by professional workers, as well as to test the importance given by workers of the Basque Country region in Spain, to the use of social networks, particularly SNSs, to find new professionals around the world and help the workers network. Business Networking is a valuable way to expand knowledge, learn from the success of others, attain new clients and tell others about the business.

INTRODUCTION

The need for a cross-border collaboration and information sharing has never been greater, given the trend towards remote control and the rise in the number of companies spread across different territories. Web 2.0 tools, particularly social networking sites (SNSs), make it possible to bring together thoughts and ideas from professional workers scattered across a country, or even around the world.

DOI: 10.4018/978-1-5225-0559-4.ch018

In the midst of Web 2.0, we find SNSs, which include professional networking sites (SNSs for business purposes). One key reason behind the growth experienced by business networking sites recent years is the ability of Internet to connect people globally and cost effectively on the professional networking aspect (Benson & Morgan, 2015). Individuals and businesses need to explore all possible avenues of professional and corporate growth (Lloyd, 2009). On the one hand the environment in which small and medium enterprises (SME) are set up, move and develop has radically changed in the last decade (Ruzzier, Hisrich & Antoncic, 2006). On the other hand the creation of business networks a decade ago started to became increasingly important (Holmlund & kock 1998) as a tool that facilitated internationalization process (Coviello & McAuley 1999).

The penetration of social networking sites in all areas is reaching its mature stage: Eight out of ten internet user aged between 18 and 55 use SNSs with general-purpose, with as many purposes as it offers possibilities (IAB, 2013, p.10). At the professional level, tools provided by Web 2.0 in general and professional SNSs in particular, give a new boost to establish and maintain relationships and new ways of making things. It is in this area where we wanted to know the level of SNSs use among professional workers.

There are few studies focused on how workers use web 2.0 as highlighted in (Benson & Morgan, 2015) and most of those that do exist consider companies mainly in Marketing. For that reason our research seeks to test the importance given by workers of the Basque Country region in Spain, to the use of social networks, particularly SNSs, to find new professionals not only in domestic markets but also in foreign ones. A field study therefore conducted involving a web based survey among professional workers of the Basque Country. A descriptive analysis was then applied to their responses.

This chapter offers two fundamental contributions:

1. To identify the SNSs professional workers are actually using for business purposes, and
2. To find out what these professionals think about the usefulness and the perceived potential of Web 2.0 tools, in order to contact professionals of interest businesswise all around the world.

In both cases, we consider the differences in terms of certain socio-demographic variables such as age, gender, type of worker (self-employed or salaried employee) and also of the features of their companies, such as size of the company (measured in number of workers), operating economic sector and type of target consumer (other business or final consumer).

BACKGROUND

Business Networks in International Trade

As a consequence of SME environment conditions, many enterprises considered export as an easier option than continuing operating in the intensely competitive domestic market (Chetty & Campbell-hunt, 2004). With regard to SMEs, we can state that they were forced to begin or accelerate their internationalization processes and that the main driver pushing them beyond country boundaries was the need to overcome the aggressive local competitiveness in search of new markets for their products, new opportunities and enterprise profitability growth in an economic environment that had been dramatically open to the world

(Cedrola, 2005). For many SMEs, establishing and/or reinforcing relationships with local counterparts is a fundamental key for creating an international network: relationships are developed as bridges into foreign markets (Meyer & Skak, 2002).

Numerous types of SME internationalization processes have been identified (Freeman, 2002) and review of the literature seems to propose nine schools of thought (Leonidou & katsikeas, 1996; Laine & Kock, 2000). One of these groups includes the network approach, which focuses on the relationships between companies, involved in production, distribution and use of goods and services within an industrial system. According to this view, enterprises internationalize by establishing and cultivating relationships with partners in foreign networks. Many authors agree with the idea that the creation of business networks is becoming increasingly important (Holmlund & Kock 1998) and facilitating internationalization process (Coviello & McAuley 1999). Networks can assist SMEs regarding scarcity of resources and enable early and fast internationalization (Coviello & Munro, 1997; Oviatt, 1994). Firms seldom survive and prosper solely through their individual efforts. Each firm's performance depends upon the activities and performance of others and hence upon the nature and quality of the direct and indirect relationships a firm develops with its counterparts (Wilkinson & Young, 2002).

Networks can be used to transmit information about current opportunities for profitable international trade or investment. Within a given foreign market, transnational networks can also help producers of consumer goods to find appropriate distributors, assemblers to find the right component suppliers, and investors to find joint-venture partners (Weiden-baum & Hughes, 1996).

A network is a set of items, which we will call vertices or, at times, nodes, that are interconnected by edges (Newman, 2003). If a social network is a set of people or groups of people with a pattern of contacts or interactions between them, we can conclude a business or professional network is a group of people with business interactions between them (Benson & Fillipaous, 2015).

The network model of internationalization was developed in the 1980s when it became evident that most firms used various networks to facilitate their internationalization activities (Johanson & Mattsson 1987). Johnsen & Johnsen (1999) relate a network to a collection of "actors" that can include people, departments, or businesses and their strategic links to others such as family, community as well as financial or business alliances.

Networks expose SMEs to international markets through an accumulation of institutional, business, and internationalization knowledge, which provide the necessary intelligence in support of the process (Eriksson et al., 2000; Mejri & Katsuhiro, 2010). Some of the benefits Networks provide:

- They can help businesses gain knowledge about foreign institutions so that they are aware of current rules and regulations.
- They also provide links to the conduct of business and market intelligence that help them decide when and how to internationalize (Johanson & Mattsson 1987).
- Networking offers SMEs a reduced risk when entering into other markets (Coviello & McAuley 1999).
- Networking can help overcome size inconveniences as it allows organizations to build relationships with established firms and so lessen the risk (Madhok 1997).
- Connections with others allow SMEs to gain knowledge on foreign markets, access to required resources and capabilities, and assist them to reduce entry barriers (Chen 2003; Coviello & Munro 1995; Johanson & Mattsson 1987).

On a review of the internationalization process of companies carried out by Cano and Rodenes (2009), they observed several variables, such us Information Technology and Web 2.0 that were connected with that process. They concluded that the most use of Web 2.0 tools by a company, the better results they get at their exporting efforts. This happens even the companies belong to the secondary industrial sector, where the information technologies are taken on later than in other sectors.

A survey commissioned by Fundación Banesto (2011) among SMEs, show that there is a direct relationship between companies operating in foreign markets (exporting or with physical presence abroad) and the use of Web 2.0 tools, concluding that SNSs can be an instrument that facilitate the international process. In the same way MillwardBrown together with Google state that people working in SME with an international reach, are more enthusiastic about potential social tools have to improve the way they work (MillwardBrown, 2012).

Gaining Knowledge through Social Networks

Knowledge has been recognized as a strategic asset and a source of competitive advantage especially in multinational enterprises (Nonaka & Takeuchi, 1995). Business networks are forming around knowledge bases such that the maximization of this knowledge is obtained through network collaboration rather than through individual business unit (Benson & Filipaious, 2015). As a result, connections with others allow SMEs to gain knowledge in foreign markets, access to required resources and capabilities, and assist them to reduce entry barriers (Chen 2003; Coviello & Munro 1995; Johanson & Mattsson 1987). This knowledge about foreign marketplaces not only creates opportunities for the firm to internationalize but also allows firms to formulate strategic plans to accelerate their internationalization process, engage with born-global pattern, and ensure survival in the long run (Dib et al. 2010; Korhonen et al. 1996; Liesch & Knight 1999; Moen & Sevaisg 2002; Wincent 2005). Moreover, having the knowledge and appraising them against their organizational capabilities allows SMEs to assess their abilities to venture out (Blomstermo & Sharma, 2003). Networking can also influence strategic decisions through the exchange of resources among different members or by bringing in new ideas from within or outside the SME networks (Fuller-Love & Thomas 2004; Wincent 2005). Utilizing networks also helps to build international contacts and find suitable agents and this affects market and product development selections and foreign entry mode choice (Coviello & Munro 1995; Johanson & Mattsson 1987). Accessing networks allows products to be integrated through affiliation with global brands, enabling firms to gain familiarity with the global business environment, including about their competitors and awareness of international standards, requirements, and quality (de Wit & Meyer 1998; Yakhlef & Maubourguet 2004).

Social Networking Sites

We argue that digital SNSs and other types of social software (Web 2.0) create a unique opportunity to establish new business contacts with people from unexplored markets to gain new customers or other business partners. Harris & Rae (2009) predicted that internet social networks would play a key role in the future of marketing; externally they can replace customer annoyance with engagement, and internally they help to transform the traditional focus on control with an open and collaborative approach that is more conducive to success in the modern business environment.

Some SNS have specific orientation, for example they can serve as professional networking sites, focused mainly on business purpose interaction. A professional business network is used for the business to business marketplace. This type of professional service enables business professionals to network and collaborate by title, industry and business interests so that they can discuss common themes, stay informed and share knowledge (Benson & Morgan, 2015). By creating informative and interactive meeting places, professional networks attract, aggregate and assemble large business-focused audiences. These networks also improve the ability for people to advance professionally and are often used to identify career opportunities. Business professionals can share experiences with others who have a need to learn from similar experiences (Lloyd, 2009).

The core of these online networks (SNSs) consists of profiles of its users, which are combinations of personal data, lists of interests, and connections with different levels of privacy in terms of information revealed, depending on the type of network (Benson, Saridakis & Tennakoon, 2015). By creating and disseminating their profile, participants establish connections with other network participants, share contents of different nature, and the network will be getting consolidated (Mislove *et al.*, 2007).

Business Networking through SNSs

Recent IMP literature uses the term business networking to refer to the conscious attempts of an actor to change or develop the process of interaction or the structure of relationships in which it is directly or indirectly involved and has suggested that networking is at the core of management in the business landscape (Ford, Gadde, Håkansson, & Snehota, 2002; Ford & Mouzas, 2010; Håkansson et al., 2009; Henneberg, Naudé, & Mouzas, 2010). But the concept of business networking is not yet well developed, there is no coherent theoretical structure that could form a basis for the empirical investigation of business networking or that could express the concept in a form of value to practitioners or explain how it relates to the conventionally defined tasks of marketing and purchasing (Ford & Mouzas, 2013).

Networking is progressively gaining in importance and assuming an ever-larger role in the companies: professionals with wide-ranging network of contacts are highly valued (greatly appreciated), because they are considered to have de capability to generate business for the companies they work for. The activities covered by networking pursue different objectives depending on the work area: to introduce the company or a business idea to stakeholders, strengthening relationships with current customers, better understand customers and their expectations, made known to other professionals, introduce new products and services, find business opportunities, get to know customers and commercial partners, get back in touch with known people (López, 2008).

Web 2.0 tools in general, and professional social networking sites in particular, provide tools that enable to find professionals, develop an extensive network of contacts, and create their own network that facilitate to share information and knowledge, That is to say, "do networking" (Alcázar, 2010).

According to Fuero and García (2008), business SNSs are develop in order to support networking in a corporative environment and as a management tool in work tasks. These type of SNSs are meant to share information between partners, to get new business contacts in order to establish new commercial relationships (Uned, 2011).

In a research study conducted through an online survey among the group "Business & Jobs Portugal" of the social network LinkedIn (Cruz *et al.*, 2012), was conclude that mentioned business networking site presents itself as a facilitator for the expansion of new professional opportunities and that although

Facebook and Twitter are known as networking tools with great potential, LinkedIn is the network that best suits the needs of those who seek professional contacts and promotion of business, which corroborates the findings of other studies (Fretzin, 2009; Donath, 2008).

In another study commissioned by Google (MillwardBrown, 2012), the use and impact of social tools by 2,700 executives in seven countries in Europe was assessed. The objective was to review current relevance and perceived importance of social tools in business. The following are some of their views regarding to business issues: professionals are primarily using social tools to find information, people, or expertise more quickly (41%), followed by improving cooperation, collaboration and knowledge sharing (37%), widening personal networks, building professional relationships, raising profiles and creating communities (34%) and bringing together ideas and thoughts from a geographically dispersed team. At the same time, 76% of senior managers believed businesses that embrace social tools would grow faster than those who ignored the technology, meanwhile 53% believed that businesses will not survive unless they embrace social media.

McKinsey Global Institute analyzed the potential value that could be obtained through the use of social technologies and found that social technologies, when used within and across enterprises, have the potential to raise the productivity of the high skill knowledge workers that are critical to performance and growth in the 21st century by 20 to 25 percent (Bughin, Chui, M. &Miller, 2009).

According to HubSpot.com (2012), LinkedIn 277% more effective for lead generation than Facebook and Twitter, and so LinkedIn is considered to be most efficient social network for lead generation.

METHODOLOGY

Industrial activities in the Basque Country were traditionally centered on steel and shipbuilding, mainly due to the rich resources found during the 19th century. These activities fell into decline during the economic crisis of the 1970s and 1980s, making room for the development of the services sector and new technologies. Even so, the industrial sector is still highly important in the Basque economy, and this is one reason why the Basque government has an established network of support services for the industrial sectors. The drivers of this network are the various Basque Country cluster associations, providing essential support for over 1,000 member companies in terms of promotion, incentives and intermediary activities.

This research study has been conducted based on a survey of 283 Basque professional workers, and complemented by six face-to-face interviews. Data was collected from a sample of 25,000 professional workers (in non-manual but office-based roles) in companies of the Basque Country, in the north-east in Spain. The targeted companies were from various economic sectors (manufacturing, services and knowledge) and ranged in terms of employee numbers from 1 to 500 (See Appendix 1 for the distribution of the sample). The database belongs to Euskadi+innova, a Basque government institution in charge of economic and competitive development, whose main goal is to drive change toward an innovative culture by fostering the implementation and use of ICTs in companies.

In addition, we undertook in-depth interviews with six of the employees. A total of six employees (employed and salaried employees, in large and small companies) were interviewed. The interviews were recorded and lasted 40 minutes on average.

We specially focus on small and medium enterprises (SME) operating on business-to-business (B2B) markets- We do not only consider organizations belonging to industrial sector, but also the ones operating in tertiary and quaternary sector.

The questions covered some of the existing SNSs and other Web 2.0 tools they were using for business purposes, as well as their opinions regarding the potential role of these tools in helping to make new contacts in foreign countries.

Almost 80% of professionals in the sample (see Appendix 1) work for small and medium-sized companies (SME), and 85% of these companies sell to other businesses (B2B)

RESULTS OF THE SURVEY

Type of Social Networking Sites Used by Professional Workers

Respondents from the survey were asked about some of the existing SNSs and other Web 2.0 tools they were using with business purposes and related to work tasks such as LinkedIn, Xing, Viadeo, Twitter, Facebook, Google+, Blog and corporate Website. They were then asked about some points related to the use of these tools.

Our research results show that the average number of Web 2.0 tools used for business purposes by professional workers is 4.81. Regarding the type of these tools, LinkedIn is the most used, and also the most efficient when it comes to making new professional contacts.

Respondents from the survey were asked about some of the existing SNSs and other Web 2.0 (Figure 1)

Results were statistically analyzed using the Chi Square test for independence and statistically significant differences were found for several variables regarding both worker and company features, which are summarized below:

- **Gender:** LinkedIn, Twitter and Google+ are more used by men than by women.
- **Age:** Twitter is more used among younger people (age 24-30), while Google+ is more used among older ages (41-50).

Figure 1. Use of SNSs and other Web 2.0 tools by professional in their work tasks

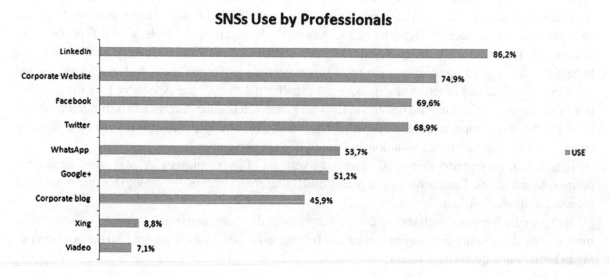

- **Type of Worker:** Self-employed people, make greater use of Twitter, Google+ and corporate blogs in comparison with salaried employee workers.
- **Size of the Company:** Facebook is less widely used in large companies (more than 250 employees) than in SMEs.
- **Type of Consumer (B2B, B2C):** LinkedIn is more used in companies operating in B2B markets.

It should be noted that self-employed people use a wider range of SNSs to accomplish their work tasks than compared to salaried employees. Apart from the professional networks, they use other SNSs such as Twitter, Google+ and LinkedIn.

As regards the corporate blog, it should be noted that the blog is one of the Web 2.0 tools that prove to be a showcase for professionals to write in a personal capacity, as is the case of self-employed workers of our survey, although an increasing number of companies are opting to do so.

Another of the results obtained is that Facebook is used less by large companies than by SMEs. There are several reasons behind that. On the one hand, Facebook is perceived as a site for having a presence without a defined strategy, and is mostly used by companies selling to the final consumer (Banesto, 2012). On the other hand, some of large companies could be blocking access (partly or completely) to certain websites such as Facebook and Twitter. According to a survey commissioned by Robert Half Technology (2009), 54 percent of U.S. companies say they have banned workers from using social networking sites like Twitter, Facebook, LinkedIn and MySpace, while at work. The study, released today, also found that 19 percent of companies allow social networking use only for business purposes, while 16 percent allow limited personal use.

The results we obtain regarding the use of Twitter are similar to the ones for Facebook, and we therefore have reasons to believe that the management of large corporations is blocking access to both Facebook and Twitter, but grants access to LinkedIn, given its professional features. LinkedIn was developed exclusively for professional use and for companies dealing with other companies (B2B). Professionals and businesses consider LinkedIn to be of great importance to develop their business activity, they have a vast contact portfolio of clients' suppliers, potential customers and distributors among others. In our opinion B2B companies should establish more intensive relationships with each of their clients in comparison with B2C ones, as each of these clients has a greater value in terms of turnover. Turnover and strengthening bonds is therefore fundamental in order to establish possible future relationships.

Professionals Working in Export Companies

The results of our research highlight the greater importance given to the usefulness of SNSs by professional workers in export companies (see Figure 2). 30% of the companies in our sample do export or do have a subsidiary in a foreign country.

We have analyzed the relation of four variables:

1. First point "the SNSs have helped me to get in touch with foreign professionals",
2. Second point "the contacts of my community in the SNSs have helped me to get in touch with companies/professionals from foreign markets",
3. The fact of being an exporter company,
4. The economic sector which the workers belong.

Figure 2. The average assessment the workers give to first and second points respectively, depending on whether or not they are exporters

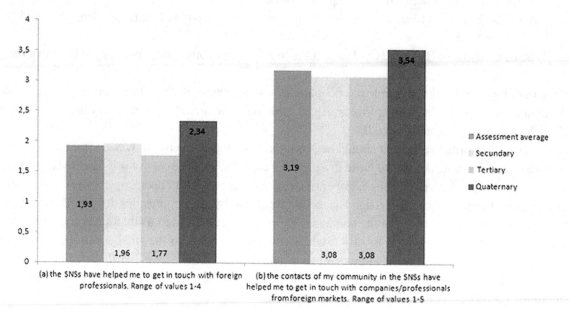

The assessment average of the first two points (the two opinions) is 1.93 and 3.19 respectively (Both opinions show a positive correlation with a level of significance of 0.01. If the respondents rated one highly, their assessment of the other was also high (see Appendix 2)).

Statistically significant differences were observed: The fact that the company exports its products to a foreign market influences both the first opinion (1) "the SNSs have helped me to get in touch with foreign professionals" and second opinion (2) "the contacts of my community in the SNSs have helped me to get in touch with companies/professionals from foreign markets" (see Appendix 2).

Figure 2 illustrates the average assessment of points (two opinions), as well as the score given by workers in both export and non-export companies (Figure 3).

Figure 3 shows the average assessment of both points are higher in export companies (2.35 and 3.54), and rated lower in non-export companies (1.7 and 2.95). It could be argued that people working for export companies are more likely to endeavor to get in touch with people, not only from their current export markets, but also from potential markets to which they could export if a business opportunity appeared. The low assessment of these points by people from export companies could be due to their position not being related to sales or public relations, where meeting people and building a business network becomes crucial, and therefore the use of SNSs for these purposes would not be appreciated.

This is the case regardless of the economic sector. Most of SMEs with an international presence belong to the industrial sector, with a smaller natural presence in SNSs; industry, construction and logistics. It is thus conceivable to think that industrial companies make use of these tools to a lesser extent than those in the service and knowledge sectors, but the results of this research show that the average assessment of industrial exporting companies is high, which leads us to believe that Web 2.0 is being more utilized in export companies, dealing with foreign markets.

Figure 3. The average assessment the workers give to first and second points respectively, depending on the economic sector in question

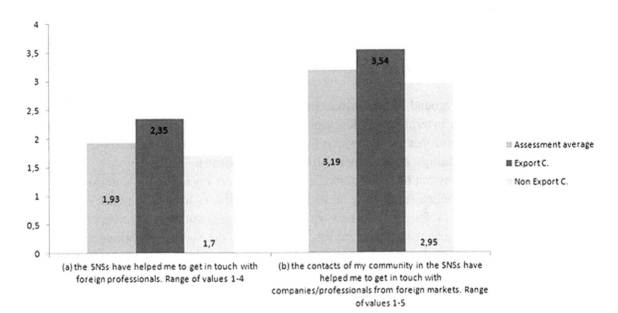

Workers from Industrial and Knowledge Economic Sector

Statistically significant differences were also observed for the economic sector in which the company operates: The economic sector where the worker belongs to, has influence in the average assessment in both the first point (1) "the SNSs have helped me to get in touch with foreign professionals" and second point (2) "the contacts of my community in the SNSs have helped me to get in touch with companies/ professionals from foreign markets (see Appendix 2).

Figure 3 shows the higher score given to both points by the quaternary sector workers (2.34 and 3.54) compared to tertiary sector workers (1.77 and 3.08). This result could be explained by the fact that only 21.5% from the tertiary sector do export, while half of the quaternary do, and knowing that being an export company influences both points. The above results show that further reason could be the actual tasks carried out by the workers. Yet, when the companies from two sectors are analyzed in depth, the roles of the companies in the quaternary sector can be seen to be related to the ICTs, research and education, whereas the companies in the tertiary sector are not. We believe that the workers in different departments carrying out different tasks in the quaternary sector are involved in sharing information and ideas, not only inside the company but also with people from other companies, where territorial barriers are broken in the search for new business opportunities.

Regarding the results of our study, companies from the quaternary economic sector, the sector of the knowledge, can be said to be using several Web 2.0 tolls, along with the networks provided by the government as complementary tools, to broaden the net and to thus be able to span a wider area and to benefit from contacting professionals of interest. Quaternary industries emerge from breakthroughs in science and the outcome is social transformation. Novel solutions to human problems are developed, and choice in the marketplace expands. With new markets, new business practices come into being and the dynamics of human relationships change as the new technology is taken into households, (Anderson D.G., 2002).

DISCUSSION OF RESULTS

The fact that workers from around the world share professional information using Web 2.0 tools makes companies more productive in terms of efficiency, as they are creating knowledge while saving on travel costs. Numerous studies show that social media is helping companies to grow and promote (Bughin, *et al.*, 2009; Kiron, Palmer, Phillips, & Kruschwitz, 2012; MillwardBrown, 2012).

A wide range of opinions can be found among economic sectors regarding the statement that "the contacts belonging to my online community on social networking sites have been useful in getting to know other companies and professional workers with similar business purposes in foreign countries".

Professionals from the quaternary sector are successfully using the Social Networking Sites (SNSs) to get in touch with people with business interests in foreign markets. In the knowledge based sector, the staff carrying out different tasks are involved in sharing information and ideas, not only inside the company but also with people from other companies all around the world, where territorial barriers are broken in the search for new business opportunities. Sharing information with other firms makes it possible to get to know prospective clients and to take advantage of the business opportunities the international market offers. Everybody becomes the public relation officer of the firm in knowledge based companies.

Business Networking is a valuable way to expand knowledge, learn from the success of others, get in touch new clients and tell others about your business.

Now more than ever, professionals and enterprises need to explore new horizons and take advantage of all the opportunities for professional and corporate growth. The ability of the Internet in general, and the set of tools provided by Web 2.0 in particular, to get in touch and communicate with anybody anywhere in the world, are key for a possible market expansion at geographical level. It is for this reason that we have considered to be of great interest to establish what professional workers think about the usefulness of using SNSs to contact other professionals abroad.

The SNSs facilitate the task of getting in touch with people we do not know, we never have seen and we have never heard of, and in the Basque Country not only companies from the quaternary sector but also export companies are embracing the opportunity the SNSs, and particularly the professional networks provide. Professionals belonging to export companies particularly in the industrial sector (exporting products, services and knowledge) rate SNSs highly regarding help provided by the sites to get in touch with other workers and firms with business interests in foreign markets. These people working for export companies are using SNSs to contact people not only from the markets they export to, but also potential markets where they could export if a business opportunity appeared. Most workers now appreciate the need to embrace Web 2.0 tools as a way of communicating, marketing and selling.

Developing policy guidelines on the use of Web 2.0 tools with business purposes would be recommended, in order to make correct and appropriate use of these tools, while taking advantage of social networking channel.

CONCLUSION AND FUTURE RESEARCH DIRECTIONS

While *Facebook* remains the *most popular social media site* for general purposes, LinkedIn is the preferred site by professionals using the social media for business purposes: LinkedIn is the preferred tool for professional workers to network, 87% make used of it. Besides LinkedIn they are using the Corporate Website, Facebook and Twitter for business tasks.

Regarding the usefulness and the perceived potential of SNSs, the main results are, on the one hand, that workers belonging to the quaternary economic sector (knowledge sector) give greater importance to the use of SNSs to find professional contacts in unexplored business markets than that given by workers in other sectors. On the other hand, professionals working for export companies, even those belonging to industrial sectors, also give great importance to using SNSs to find new business contacts around the world.

This study opens up several areas for further research. First of all, a more in-depth study should be conducted to discover the goals professional pursued on SNSs, the topics and matters they like to discuss, the protocols they use for the first contact and the specific Web 2.0 used for each particular matter. Secondly, we should consider how Management is informed about the use employees make of these tools, what they think about it, and see if they are supporting this activity or conversely, they are setting up barriers.

REFERENCES

Alcázar, P. (2010). *Estrategias de marketing en las redes sociales*. Retrieved from http://www.emprendedores.es/gestion/marketing-en-redes-sociales/sumario

Anderson, D. G. (2002). Biotechnology and the quaternary industrial sector. *Australasian Biotechnology*, *12*(1), 21–21.

Banesto Fundación. (2011). Observatorio sobre el uso de las redes sociales en las PYMEs españolas (F. Banesto, Ed.). Author.

Banesto Fundación. (2013). Observatorio sobre el uso de las redes sociales en las PYMEs españolas (F. Banesto, Ed.). Author.

Benson, V., & Filippaios, F. (2015). Collaborative competencies in professional social networking: Are students short changed by curriculum in business education?. *Computers in Human Behavior*, *51*(B), 1331-1339.

Benson, V., & Morgan, S. (2015). *Implications of Social Media Use in Personal and Professional Settings*. Hershey, PA: IGI Global; doi:10.4018/978-1-4666-7401-1

Benson, V., Saridakis, G., & Tennakoon, H. (2015). Information disclosure of social media users: does control over personal information, user awareness and security notices matter? *Information Technology & People*.

Bughin, J., Chui, M., & Miller, A. (2009). *How companies are benefiting from web 2.0: McKinsey global survey results*. Retrieved from: www.mckinsey.com

Cedrola, E. (2005). *Il marketing internazionale per le piccole e medie imprese*. Milano: McGraw-Hill.

Chen, T. J. (2003). Network resources for internationalization: The case of Taiwan's electronics firms*. *Journal of Management Studies*, *40*(5), 1107–1130. doi:10.1111/1467-6486.t01-1-00373

Chetty, S., & Campbell-Hunt, C. (2004). A strategic approach to internationalisation: A traditional versus a born-global approach. *Journal of International Marketing*, *12*(1), 57–81. doi:10.1509/jimk.12.1.57.25651

Chui, M., Manyika, J., Bughin, J., & Dobbs, R. (2012). *The social economy: Unlocking value and productivity through social technologies*. McKinsey Global Institute.

Coviello, N. E., & McAuley, A. (1999). Internationalization of smaller firm: A review of contemporary empirical research. *Management International Review*, *39*, 223–256.

Coviello, N. E., & Munro, H. J. (1997). Network relationships and the internationalisation process of small software firms. *International Business Review*, *6*(4), 361–386. doi:10.1016/S0969-5931(97)00010-3

Cruz, M., Varajao, J., & Goncalves, P. (2012). The perceived potential of business social networking sites. *International Journal of Web Portals*, *4*(1), 1–15. doi:10.4018/jwp.2012010101

De Wit, B., & Meyer, R. (1998). *Strategy: Process, content, context*. London: Thomson Business Press.

Donath, J. (2008). Signals in social supernets. *Journal of Computer-Mediated Communication*, *13*(1), 231–251. doi:10.1111/j.1083-6101.2007.00394.x

Ellison, N. B. (2007). Social network sites: Definition, history, and scholarship. *Journal of Computer-Mediated Communication*, *13*(1), 210–230. doi:10.1111/j.1083-6101.2007.00393.x

Eriksson, K., Johanson, J., Majkgård, A., & Sharma, D. D. (2000). Effect of variation on knowledge accumulation in the internationalization process. *International Studies of Management & Organization*, *30*(1), 26–44. doi:10.1080/00208825.2000.11656781

Ford, D., Gadde, L. E., Håkansson, H., & Snehota, I. (2002). Managing networks. In *18th IMP Conference*, Perth, Australia.

Ford, D., & Mouzas, S. (2013). The theory and practice of business networking. *Industrial Marketing Management*, *42*(3), 433–442. doi:10.1016/j.indmarman.2013.02.012

Freeman, S. (2002). *A comprehensive model of the process of small firm internationalisation: A network perspective*. Competitive Paper for IMO Conference, Dijon, Francia.

Fretzin, S. (2009). Get terworking. *Benefits Canada*, *33*(10), 7–10.

Fuero, A., & García, J. M. (2008). Redes sociales. contextualización de un fenómeno "dos-punto-cero" [Social Networks. Contextualizing the Phenomenon of Web 2.0]. *TELOS Cuadernos De Innvación y Comunicación, 76*.

Fuller-Love, N., & Thomas, E. (2004). Networks in small manufacturing firms. *Journal of Small Business and Enterprise Development*, *11*(2), 244–253. doi:10.1108/14626000410537182

Harris, L., & Rae, A. (2009). Social networks: The future of marketing for small business. *The Journal of Business Strategy*, *30*(5), 24–31. doi:10.1108/02756660910987581

Holmlund, M., & Kock, S. (1998). Relationships and the internationalization of finnish small and medium-sized companies. *International Small Business Journal, 16*(4), 46–63. doi:10.1177/0266242698164003

Hubspot. (2012). *LinkedIn 277% more effective for lead generation than facebook & twitter*. Retrieved from http://blog.hubspot.com/blog/tabid/6307/bid/30030/LinkedIn-277-More-Effective-for-Lead-Generation-Than-Facebook-Twitter-New-Data.aspx

IAB. (2013). IV estudio anual de redes sociales. IAB.

Johanson, J., & Mattsson, L. G. (1987). Interorganizational relations in industrial systems: A network approach compared with the transaction-cost approach. *International Studies of Management & Organization, 17*(1), 34–48. doi:10.1080/00208825.1987.11656444

Johnsen, R. E., & Johnsen, T. E. (1999). International market development through networks: The case of the ayrshire knitwear sector. *International Journal of Entrepreneurial Behavior & Research, 5*(6), 297–312. doi:10.1108/13552559910306114

Kiron, D., Palmer, D., Phillips, A. N., & Kruschwitz, N. (2012). *Social business: What are companies really doing*. MIT Sloan Management Review.

Korhonen, H., Luostarinen, R., & Welch, L. (1996). Internationalization of SMEs: Inward-outward patterns and government policy. *Management International Review*, 315–329.

Laine, A., & Kock, S. (2000). *A process model of internationalization-new times demands new patterns*. 16th IMP-Conference, Bath, UK.

Leonidou, L. C., & Katsikeas, C. S. (1996). The export development process: An integrative review of empirical models. *Journal of International Business Studies, 27*(3), 517–551. doi:10.1057/palgrave.jibs.8490846

Levitt, T. (1983). The globalization of markets. *Harvard Business Review, 26*(3), 92–102.

Liesch, P. W., & Knight, G. A. (1999). Information internalization and hurdle rates in small and medium enterprise internationalization. *Journal of International Business Studies, 30*(2), 383–394. doi:10.1057/palgrave.jibs.8490075

Lloyd, B. A. (2009). Profesional networking on the internet.*IEEE Conference Record of 2009 Anual Pulp and Paper Industry*, Birmingham, AL. doi:10.1109/PAPCON.2009.5185427

López, F. (2008). *El poder del networking. trabaja tu red de contactos. España: NETBIBLO S.L.*

Madhok, A. (1997). Cost, value and foreign market entry mode: The transaction and the firm. *Strategic Management Journal, 18*(1), 39–61. doi:10.1002/(SICI)1097-0266(199701)18:1<39::AID-SMJ841>3.0.CO;2-J

Mejri, K., & Umemoto, K. (2010). Small-and medium-sized enterprise internationalization: Towards the knowledge-based model. *Journal of International Entrepreneurship, 8*(2), 156–167. doi:10.1007/s10843-010-0058-6

Meyer, K., & Skak, A. (2002). Networks, serendipity and SME entry into eastern Europe. *European Management Journal, 20*(2), 179–188. doi:10.1016/S0263-2373(02)00028-2

MillwardBrown. (2012). *How social technologies drive business success. European survey results.* Retrieved from http://www.millwardbrown.com/docs/default-source/insight-documents/articles-and-reports/Googe_MillwardBrown_How-Social-Technologies-Drive-Business-Success_201205.pdf

Mislove, A., Marcon, M., Gummadi, K. P., Druschel, P., & Bhattacharjee, B. (2007). Measurement and analysis of online social networks. *IMC '07 Proceedings of the 7th ACM SIGCOMM Conference on Internet Measurement.*

Moen, Ø., & Servais, P. (2002). Born global or gradual global? examining the export behavior of small and medium-sized enterprises. *Journal of International Marketing, 10*(3), 49–72. doi:10.1509/jimk.10.3.49.19540

Newman, M. (2003). The structure and function of complex networks. *SIAM Review, 45*(2), 167–256. doi:10.1137/S003614450342480

Nonaka, I., & Takeuchi, H. (1995). *The knowledge-creating company: How japanese companies create the dynamics of innovation.* Oxford University Press.

Oviatt, B. M., & McDougall, P. P. (1994). Towards a theory of international new ventures. *Journal of International Business Studies, 25*(1), 45–64. doi:10.1057/palgrave.jibs.8490193

Peláez, M., & Rodenes, M. (2009). La internacionalización de empresas: Relación entre el capital social, las tecnologías de la información relacional y la innovación. *Redalyc, 12*(25), 111–138.

Robert Half -Technology. (2009). *Whistle-but-don't tweet-while you work.* Retrieved from http://rht.mediaroom.com/index.php?s=131&item=790

Ruzzier, M., Hisrich, R. D., & Antoncic, B. (2006). SME internationalization research: Past, present, and future. *Journal of Small Business and Enterprise Development, 13*(4), 476–497. doi:10.1108/14626000610705705

Sharma, D. D., & Blomstermo, A. (2003). *The internationalization process of born globals: A network view.* Academic Press.

UNED. (2011). *Un community manager: ¿Qué son las redes sociales profesionales?* Retrieved from http://www.uncommunitymanager.es/redes-profesionales/

Wilkinson, I., & Young, L. (2002). On cooperating: Firms, relationships, networks. *Journal of Business Research, 55*(2), 123–132. doi:10.1016/S0148-2963(00)00147-8

Wincent, J. (2005). Does size matter? A study of firm behavior and outcomes in strategic SME networks. *Journal of Small Business and Enterprise Development, 12*(3), 437–453. doi:10.1108/14626000510612330

KEY TERMS AND DEFINITIONS

Business-to-Business (B2B): This term refers to a situation where one business makes a commercial transaction with another business. Business-to Consumer (B2C) refers to companies that sell its products or services to the final consumer.

Euskadi+Innova: The strategy shared by the individuals and entities that work to promote Innovation in order to turn the Basque Country into a European point of reference for Innovation.

IMP: IMP Group International Inc. is focused on global, sustainable growth, with over 4,500 experienced people delivering service, quality and value to customers across diverse sectors such as aerospace and defense, aviation, airline, healthcare, information technology, hospitality and property development.

Lead Generation: Lead generation is the process of making contacts which may lead to a sale or other favorable outcome. The leads may come from various sources or activities, one of which is digitally via the Web 2.0.

Professional Worker: We consider a professional, a worker with non-manual but office-based roles, either self-employed or salaried employee, and with some qualification to accomplish tasks in their works.

APPENDIX 1: METHOD AND COMPOSITION OF THE SAMPLE

Data was collected from a sample of 25,000 professional workers (in non-manual but office-based roles) in companies of the Basque country, in the north-east in Spain. These professionals mostly work for small and medium enterprises (SME) operating in a B2B market. The database belongs to the Basque government institution in charge of economic and competitive development. The targeted companies were from various economic sectors (manufacturing, services and knowledge) and varied in terms of employee numbers from 1 to 500. 320 questionnaires were returned with 283 being fully completed. The questionnaire was created and published using *Encuestafacil* (http://www.encuestafacil.com) and was made sent out to be answered between 6 May and 13 May. The results were processed using a statistical software, Statistical Package for the Social Sciences (SPSS®) version 19.

Table 1 provide the composition of the sample, according to both variables related to the characteristics of professionals (gender, age, type of worker), and variables related to the characteristics of the companies for which professionals work (company size measured by number of workers, operating economic sector, type of consumer where it sells: final consumer, other company, both).

Table 1. Composition and distribution of the sample

Gender	Male Female	48.8% 51.2%
Age	24-30 31-40 41-50 51-64	12.4% 40.6% 38.9% 8.1%
Type of Worker	Salaried employee Self-employed	70% 30%
Company Size	<10 10-49 50-250 >250	43.1% 19.1% 14.1% 23.7%
Sector	Primary Secondary Tertiary Quaternary	1.1% 9.2% 65.7% 24%
Type of Company	B2B B2C B2B2C	50.2% 14.8% 35%

APPENDIX 2: STATISTICAL SIGNIFICANCE

Relation between both opinions (1), (2) and the fact of being an export company (3)
The fact that the company exports its products to a foreign market influences both the first opinion (1) and second opinion (2) in the average assessment as confirmed with Mann-Whitney U test (see Table 2 and Table 3)
Relation between both opinions (1), (2) and the economic sector in which the company operates (4). The economic sector where the worker belongs to has influence in the average assessment on both first point (1) and second point (2) as confirmed with a Kruskal-Wallis Test (Table 4 and Table 5).
Both opinions show a positive correlation with a level of significance of 0.01. If the respondents rated one highly, their assessment of the other was also high.

Table 2. Statistical significance between (1) and (3) variables

	(1) The SNSs have helped me to get in touch with foreign professionals	Grouping variable: (3) Does the company export its products to any foreign market?
Mann-Whitney U	5,013.000	
Z	-5.003	
Asymp. Sig. (2-tailed)	.000	

Table 3. Statistical significance between (2) and (3) variables

	(2) The contacts of my community in the SNSs have helped me to get in touch with companies/professionals from foreign markets	Grouping variable: (3) Does the company export its products to any foreign market?
Mann-Whitney U	5,686.500	
Z	-3.697	
Asymp. Sig. (2-tailed)	.000	

Table 4. Statistical significance between (1) and (4) variables

	(1) the SNSs have helped me to get in touch with foreign professionals
Chi-Square	14.693
gl	3
Asymp Sig	.002
Grouping variable: (4) Economic sector	

Table 5. Statistical significance between (2) and (4) variables

	(2) The contacts of my community in the SNSs have helped me to get in touch with companies/professionals from foreign markets
Chi-Square	9.631
gl	3
Asymp. Sig.	.022
Grouping variable: (4) Economic sector	

Chapter 19

Manually Profiling Egos and Entities across Social Media Platforms:
Evaluating Shared Messaging and Contents, User Networks, and Metadata

Shalin Hai-Jew
Kansas State University, USA

ABSTRACT

Social media accounts on various social media platforms represent the public-facing Web presences of egos (individuals) and entities (groups). On the surface, these may be understood based on their profiles, their shared contents and postings, and their interactions with other user accounts online. A number of software tools and analytical techniques enable further analyses of these accounts through network analysis, content analysis, machine-based text summarization, and other approaches. This chapter describes some of the capabilities of "manual" or semi-automated (vs. fully automated) remote profiling of social media accounts for insights that would not generally be attainable by other means.

INTRODUCTION

Social media platforms are considered to be interactive spaces where individuals and groups congregate, socialize, share, intercommunicate, interact, and otherwise engage. An "ego" is understood as a person, a persona, or some type of agent with awareness, perspective, and will. An ego is understood to have preferences or "biases." An "entity" is understood as a group, with an identity, purpose, impetus, resources, and will. When people want to "check out" each other online, they will visit their respective social media accounts online, peruse shared contents, explore messaging and images, see how others interact with that individual online, and often call it good. In some cases, the curious may have to create an account in order to check out others' identities on a particular closed social media platform (and often inadvertently leave a signature on an online guestbook to record the visit). Some may actually engage with their target, by posting messages and eliciting responses.

DOI: 10.4018/978-1-5225-0559-4.ch019

In general, they pursue information that is readily available, maybe with links appearing in the top few pages of a Google search. Beyond the Surface Web, they may tap some portals to the Deep Web (websites not easily trawled using classic web browsers built to access http-based web pages) to check out people's government records, legal records, property records, marital status, pay information, and other data. They may look up property records and map those to a location. The exploratory actions may be an expression of social, professional, personal, or other interest(s); such explorations may be an extension of their own social performances in engaging with others—by building up an online network that demonstrates clout or attractiveness or wealth or some other socially desirable feature. In general, people pursue information that is readily available. They pursue information that is generally processed (vs. raw). What they are leaving untapped is latent (hidden, non-obvious) information that is not so directly readily available. They are often not exploiting data leakage from unintended revelations. They are not exploiting structural trace data (created from people's interactions with a system). They are not using metadata or information about information.

A more technologically-based approach, which enables the collection of a wider range of open-source intelligence (OSINT), involves applying a semi-automated way of remote profiling egos and entities across social media platforms. This is considered a semi-automated approach because this is a human-supervised data extraction, a "manual" vs. a "fully-automated" (and "unsupervised" machine learning) approach. This approach involves analysis of three main areas of information:

1. Messaging and shared (multimedia) contents (for content analysis),
2. Trace data (for link analysis), and
3. Metadata (for network analysis, for categorical analysis, for spatiality analysis).

"Content data" on social media sites may include a variety of textual messages (such as "short message service" or "SMS" texts, microblogging messages, emails, and others), images, memes, audio files, video files, slideshows, and other contents. "Trace data" generally refers to "log data" or records of interactions (the interacting user accounts, the times of interactions, and other data). "Metadata," broadly speaking, is labeling data about information. The applied analytical approaches for (1) content data involves content analysis (writ large), and machine-based text summarization; for (2) or trace data, it involves electronic social network analysis (e-SNA); and (3) for metadata, it involves related tags network analysis.

All three types of data analyses methods include extracted data visualizations (the mapping of the extracted data to graphs, maps, and other visuals). A fourth data type is human- and machine-coding, which may aid in the extraction of themes and other insights from the collected data. (This fourth type is beyond the purview of this chapter but is understood as an important element in data analysis.)

The intuition behind this chapter is that being aware of how an ego or entity manifests across social media platforms offers a deeper and more holistic understanding of the target at three main levels: the target node, its ego neighborhood, and its broader standing in a social media context. This is not to suggest that this approach reveals all, but a social media analysis approach is complementary to other ways of on-ground knowing. Another general insight is that social media platforms involve digital files in a variety of file format types. While textual communications are basic to virtual communities of all stripes and seminal in their "evolution, growth, and sustenance" (Bagozzi & Dholakia, 2002, p. 4), there is a lot of social media data that is heterogeneous and multimedia-based, which requires some additional work to enable information extraction (such as transcription and coding).

An early data run to test this approach was conducted on IGI-Global, the publisher, and appeared in the *C2C Digital Magazine* (Hai-Jew, Nov. 12, 2015). This early experience was successful and showed how applying a number of analytical approaches surfaced some insights about the target publishing company. To surface insights about how to profile egos and entities across social media platforms, an exemplar case was chosen: the entity of Reddit as it instantiates on social media platforms at this particular moment-in-time. Reddit was selected as an exemplar case because it is a highly public entity with presences across both mainstream and social media. It commands a large space on the Web and Internet. It has high name recognition and is disambiguated. As a topic, it offers up a rich amount of social media data extraction approaches. The author does not have any prior experience with Reddit, so she is parachuting into the topic, with little in the way of pre-conceptions but also with little in the way of previous experience. "Reddit" and related terms were used to "seed" data extractions (act as the source term for types of data extractions).

What follows is a review of the literature. Then, there is an introduction of remote profiling (in theory) and the types of available latent information from social media platforms. This analytical approach then is applied using Reddit as the target, with various social media data extractions and light analyses that follow.

REVIEW OF THE LITERATURE

People have a variety of purposes when investing their time and effort in building up social media profiles, sharing digital contents, interacting with others, and otherwise engaging on social media platforms. For many, their purposes are better served by engaging across a number of social media platforms because each may attract a different demographic slice of the population, and each enables a broader range of socio-technical affordances. To create powerful interaction effects between platforms, individuals (egos, also "actors" and "agents") and groups (entities) will use their various actions on various sites to drive traffic, raise awareness (and sensitize others to particular issues), and spark individual and mass behaviors. For example, Twitter has long been a driver of consumption of digital objects on other platforms like YouTube and Flickr, albeit without necessarily a reciprocal effect from the content-based social media platforms back to the microblogging Twitter service (Jain, Rodrigues, Magno, Kumaraguru, & Almeida, 2011). Researchers have found that there is influential cross-pollination across online social media (OSM) in order to find audiences for digital contents.

Twitter users might have access to the content of a source OSM without having an account on it. Around 65% of the Twitter users who shared YouTube videos have an account on YouTube; while only 10% of the Twitter users who shared Flickr photos have an account on Flickr...Interestingly, only 4.2% of YouTube users, creators of videos, have an account on Twitter, while 20.1% of owners of photos on Flickr have an account on Twitter as well. On manual inspection, we found that most YouTube videos are of general interest, like comedies and music clips, while most part of Flickr photos are of personal interest. So, theoretically, YouTube videos attract interest of a higher number of users, who watch and share them on Twitter most frequently than Flickr photos, which are mostly shared by their own creators to a limited number of their friends. (Jain, Rodrigues, Magno, Kumaraguru, & Almeida, 2011, p. 481)

Online social spaces evolve partially based on individual aspirations and group intentions about how to cooperate and what will be collaboratively achieved. Several works suggest an underlying rational agent model of participation in social media environments. Based on the assumptions of expectancy theory, people decide whether or not they want to engage and how-so and how-much. Researchers suggest that individual characteristics (like *"attitudes, perceived behavioral control, desires, and anticipated emotions"*) are at play as well as social influences on the individual (like *"compliance, identification, and social identity"*) in affecting individuals' intentions to participate in a virtual community (Bagozzi & Dholakia, 2002, p. 4). People go online to share emotions on social media spaces, and to meet their needs; those who design and develop such platforms need to find ways to help people receive responses for their shared emotions:

People often share emotions with others in order to manage their emotional experiences. We investigate how social media properties such as visibility and directedness affect how people share emotions in Facebook, and their satisfaction after doing so. 141 participants rated 1,628 of their own recent status updates, posts they made on others' timelines, and private messages they sent for intensity, valence, personal relevance, and overall satisfaction felt after sharing each message. For network-visible channels—status updates and posts on others' timelines—they also rated their satisfaction with replies they received. People shared differently between channels, with more intense and negative emotions in private messages. People felt more satisfied after sharing more positive emotions in all channels and after sharing more personally relevant emotions in network-visible channels. Finally, people's overall satisfaction after sharing emotions in network visible channels is strongly tied to their reply satisfaction. (Bazarova, Choi, Sosik, Cosley, &Whitlock, 2015, p. 154)

To encourage long-term participation on socially mediated spaces, community members need to receive desirable feedback.

Users spend more time in communities where they have received social-psychological feedback, and in communities where they have previously invested more time. While behavior is stochastic, an analogy to humans playing mixed strategies in matrix games provides a simple and effective learning model in this setting. Our quantitative model gives insight into individual user behavior in social media, and provides a solid foundation for studying the dynamics of communities of agents with mutual feedback and complex collective learning. (Das & Lavoie, 2014, p. 660)

On social media platforms, the narratives about its members and their identities are part of the appeal for the use of the site; over time, these narratives become built into the culture. Researchers found the following:

Specifically, it was found that narratives play two roles: first, as an amplifier of membership and shared values in the effects each of these have in participation; and second, as a mediator between both needs fulfillment and influence and shared emotional connection, and participation. (Escobar, Kommers, & Beldad, 2014, n.p.)

Other researchers have posited that people evaluate social media sites based on its usefulness and ease-of-use, and their attitudes towards the platform results in their evaluation of the site along dimensions of "loyalty, trust-benevolence, competence, and integrity" (Kumar & Benbasat, 2002, p. 5). There is a sense of connectivity between writers (content producers) and readers (content consumers) on social media, with a sharing of emotions and mutual influence (Yang, Lin, & Chen, 2009).

Certainly, the way individual and group identities manifest on various platforms may vary widely because of platform affordances, personal and social objectives, the social contexts and norms, and other factors. In more recent research, users tend to continue to participate if they feel affirmed and their contributions are acknowledged. There are a rich variety of interaction effects among individuals and groups on social media platforms.

What are the implications of millions of users providing and receiving feedback, influencing and being influenced? We liken social media to a game, where a user's strategy helps to determine the social feedback received by others, and the choices made by other users influence a user's own utility. As users learn and adapt their strategies, they create and abandon groups, communities, and whole venues. Understanding the complex social dynamics governing the evolution of these communities is a key challenge for those who study multiagent systems and collective intelligence. (Das & Lavoie, 2014, p. 653)

In other words, a systems view of a social media environment enables a deeper understanding of the social and technical dynamics. Researchers have been working on fully automated systems to collect distributed information about users based on their shared data on the social web (in order to personalize services across systems and platforms); one research team has developed an algorithm to uniquely identify users in different online social systems, and with varying degrees of estimated accuracy (Carmagnola, Osborne, & Torre, 2010).

REDDIT: THE TARGET ENTITY

So what is Reddit? In a four-quadrant social media matrix typology, Reddit is labeled as a type of Collaboration site (Zhu & Chen, 2015, p. 337). Others have termed it an online forum, a digital news bulletin board, an open-source online community bulletin board, a social blogging site, a user-curated social news feed recommender, a social news website, and an affinity space (where people find like-minded others)

The website www.reddit.com is the 10th most trafficked website in the U.S., according to Internet tracker Alexa, and it is said to have 7 billion page views by its 164 million users in June 2015 (Vella, July 20, 2015, p. 48). Reddit's own traffic statistics suggest that it has some 15 – over 20 million unique visitors per months and approximately 150 million pageviews per month ("traffic statistics for /r/AskReddit," Aug. 27, 2015) or "202 million unique visitors" based on company statistics (Hempel, Oct. 6, 2015). It is said to have "more than 112 million unique visitors from over 195 countries each month" (Singer, Flöck, Meinhart, Zeitfogel, & Strohmaier, 2014, p. 517). As such, it is considered one of the largest online communities in the world.

Its start was quite humble. Reddit, a phonetic contraction of the past tense "read it," (Vella, July 20, 2015, p. 48), was launched in June 23, 2005, by two University of Virginia students, Alexis Ohanian and Steve Huffman. It bills itself as "the front page of the internet." Early on, to encourage site visitors to participate, Reddit was seeded with contents from "sybils or paid participants" (Das & Lavoie, 2014,

p. 659). How information flows through social networks affect the network structure, and the network structure affects information propagation (Mayande & Weber, 2012). Whether a website makes or not depends in part on its ability to attain critical mass, with visitors attracted by contents; researchers have found that rising levels of contents brings more visitors and registrants but does not necessarily increase user participation (Moniz & Yuan, 2015). Ten years in, with years of leadership changes and tensions between Reddit management and its rambunctious users, both original founders Ohanian and Huffman are back at Reddit and trying to rework it for the next stages of its evolution (Hempel, Oct. 6, 2015).

The Reddit interface, which has not changed much since its launch, looks haphazard, fairly simple, and text heavy, almost retro mid-1990s in terms of design. It has its iconic alien mascot nicknamed Snoo (from "what's new") designed by Mohamed A. Elgharabawy. It has an open application programming interface, enabling access to its data. There are also automated agents used to help provide a wide range of functionalities on the site:

In Reddit, bots have recently emerged to provide new functionalities to the news aggregation and discussion site. These include bots that scan for new submissions, perform automated tasks such as transcribing image macros or scanning for reposts, and then post this information as a comment to the associated discussion thread. (Geiger, 2013, p. 51)

The basic concept for the site is simple. Members share links and comments on those links, and registered members vote the links up or down. Uplinks push a link higher on the site to promote it for others' attention, and they include promotion of the individual who submitted the link or comments (and who acquires "link karma" and "comment karma" points for their respective link and comment popularity); downvotes mean that a submission is not much seen because it is not promoted forward.

The way the system is designed has occasionally been an issue of contention. Does the karma points system tend to benefit older contents more than new contents, given that there is more time for contents to accrue votes? Are provocative contents ["sexuality, humor, violence and nudity" (Porter & Golan, 2006), as cited in Haralabopoulos, Anagnostopoulos, & Zeadally, 2015, p. 89]—which tend towards virality—more likely to be selected by the broad masses? A research study of information flows and diffusion on Reddit and its lifespan shows that positive contents tend to be more viral than negative but also that viral contents are rare, and popular links and messaging occur usually within the first few hours of posting (Haralabopoulos, Anagnostopoulos, & Zeadally, 2015, p. 97). A one-degree skim of controversial Reddit communities shows a 56-vertice graph (in Figure 1) with a wide range of topics and deep connections with mainstream media:

If controversy is one dimension of virality, Reddit, on that count, is very much viral, and that observation is borne out in this site's word-of-mouth. The sharing of information connects social networks, and the flow of information has been found to have "micro and macro effects across the traversed networks" (Haralabopoulos, Anagnostopoulos, & Zeadally, 2015, p. 97). The authors write:

More specifically, a single post (microeffect) in the parent domain connected with a post in Reddit, starts to accumulate views (macroeffect) up to a point where the information hops to OSNs (first in Twitter and then in Facebook) flowing through individuals and eventually the interest dies off. (Haralabopoulos, Anagnostopoulos, & Zeadally, 2015, p. 95)

Figure 1. Controversial Reddit communities article network on Wikipedia (1 deg.)

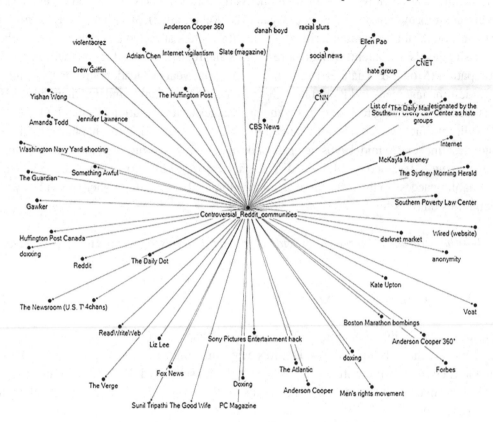

Karma points are calculated in a fairly straightforward way as…

… the sum of all the upvotes minus the sum of all the downvotes a user receives. Posts that acquire a high vote ratio (positive to negative) in a short time period after their submission are moved to the front page. (Haralabopoulos, Anagnostopoulos, & Zeadally, 2015, p. 89)

The tendency to go to Reddit for popular contents lessens the likelihood that lesser popular contents will be brought up on the site (Burke & Wagner, 2015, p. 146). This same insight about the "popular get more popular" dynamic on Reddit was observed by another research team:

The filtering algorithms services use when distributing activity to network members often have a "rich get richer" effect around attention. Content that receives initial positive responses is promoted both in public lists (as with upvotes in reddit) and by filtering algorithms, while content that doesn't receive early attention may languish. This would lead to worse outcomes from sharing emotions with others, especially to the extent that negatively valenced items receive fewer responses. (Bazarova, Choi, Sosik, Cosley, &Whitlock, 2015, p. 161)

There are also ways to "hide spam, flames, or comments that do not add to the overall discussion from view" (Bergstrom, 2011, p. 4), and collapsed comments have to be clicked to be viewed. Both Reddit leadership and Redditors (Reddit + editors) have communicated the need for authenticity and avoidance of "karma/whoring" or vote manipulation. There is a sense of awareness of others' credibility and their effect on the virtual community, with members calling out others whom they see as fraudulent. The idea is to avoid getting taken or powned (or "pwned" or "player owned").

Karma numbers are listed next to a user's name, and apparently, they may have some bitcoin value through the Reddit Bitcoin Faucet (r/bitcoin, 2015) as well as social capital value. Competition for karma points is seen as counterproductive to the community and takes away from intrinsic motivations to interact (Richterich, 2014, p. 12). One meme on Reddit reads, "upvote everything make karma worthless" (Richterich, 2014, p. 9). Another concern with the use of karma, a gamification feature, is that there may be widespread under-provisioning of human attention to rank stories (Gilbert, 2013); users are relying on others' crowd-sourcing work that is not necessarily forthcoming.

The Pew Research Center's Internet & American Life Project found that "6% of online adults" are Reddit users. Of these, there are twice as many males as females using Reddit. The user demographics trend young, with some 11% surveyed from the 18 – 29 age category, 7% in the 30-49 category, 2% each in the 50 – 64 age category and then those 65+. Nine percent of the Reddit users surveyed had no high school diploma, 4% were high school graduates, 6% had some college, and 7% were college graduates. Six percent of Reddit users earned less than $30,000 annually, 6% earned between $30 - $49,999, 7% earned between $50,000 - $74,999, and 6% earned more than $75,000. Seven percent live in urban areas, 6% in suburban areas, and 2% in rural ones (Duggan & Smith, July 3, 2013). There is also a low cost-of-entry on Reddit:

A registered Reddit account is not required to access the majority of the site's content. Anyone who ventures on to the site will have the same read–only access as anyone who has registered for an account. It is when one wishes to upvote (or downvote) a submission, submit a link, or make a comment that you are prompted to register. Upon attempting to do so without an account, you will be redirected to the account creation screen. The only information required for an account is a username, password, and passing a captcha test. Providing your e–mail is not required (but necessary if you lose your password at a later date). Underneath the "create account" button it reads "is it really that easy? only one way to find out". (Bergstrom, 2011, p. 4)

Most can participate as they generally wish unless they are seen as spamming or not following the global rules for the space. In those cases, individuals may be banned, which is a rare occurrence, according to Reddit Help. Others may experience "shadow banning," which renders their contributions to the site invisible to other users ("What can a Reddit user do about a Reddit-wide shadowban?" 2015)

Reddit enables one-time use accounts by requiring only a new user name, password, and CAPTCHA verification that the signer is not a robot (Leavitt, 2015, p. 320). There are no limits to the numbers of accounts that people can make, and the ease of creating multiple and unverified identities has resulted in the creation of throwaway accounts that people can use to engage on different topics (on the various "subreddits"). It is thought that female participants take on temporary and provisional pseudonymous identities to engage on the male-dominant Reddit in order to negotiate their own identity boundaries and to avoid harassment. One researcher found that women were 154% more likely than men to use a throwaway account on Reddit, controlling for all other variables (Leavitt, 2015, p. 323). The phenomenon of "multiple profile maintenance" (MPM) involve the creation of alternate identity profiles as a form of privacy management (Leavitt, 2015, p. 318). There is no private messaging on the Reddit site.

The research literature includes insights on how Redditors interact around mental health issues, which may be socially stigmatized. Self-disclosures regarding mental health on Reddit tended to rank as "high" levels of self-disclosure in terms of shared information (Balani & De Choudhury, 2015). Many who engage in such discussions tend to use throwaway accounts, according to one empirical study:

We observe that mental health discourse from throwaways is considerably disinhibiting and exhibits increased negativity, cognitive bias and self-attentional focus, and lowered self-esteem. Throwaways also seem to be six times more prevalent as an identity choice on mental health forums, compared to other reddit communities. We discuss the implications of our work in guiding mental health interventions, and in the design of online communities that can better cater to the needs of vulnerable populations. We conclude with thoughts on the role of identity manifestation on social media in behavioral therapy. (Pavalanathan & De Choudhury, 2015, p. 315)

Subreddits

Within Reddit, there are 9,000 single-topic communities or subreddits (https://www.reddit.com/reddits/), which deal with a wide range of topics. In these subreddits, communities form around shared interests. The formal categories of subreddits are as follows: educational, entertainment, discussion-based, humor/light-hearted, image sharing, self-improvement, technology, and meta (announcements) ("Reddit," Aug. 18, 2015). During a recent visit, there were subreddits on politics, "shower thoughts" (thoughts during people's showers), World of Warcraft, funny insights, and "Today I Learned" (TIL), among others. The structure of Reddit discussions have been empirically found to generally represent topical hierarchies; if a thread's topic diverges too much from the original root, new ones are created to accommodate the discussion; further, top-level comments tend to be created "during the early stages of the post's life cycle" (Weninger, Zhu, & Han, 2013, p. 583).

Empirical research has found that "expert crowds" on social media sites to persist longer than non-expert or typical crowds, which may come together only for short-lived real-time interests (Kamath & Caverlee, 2012, p. 195). Similarly, in electronic social media analysis, larger clusters or groups tend to endure longer whereas smaller groups, pendants, and isolates tend to either recombine with a larger group or disappear over time.

A network analysis of four subreddits was done to compare how effectively karma aligns with network analysis metrics for influence or "centrality".

We created scatter plots of compiled datasets from ten different submission networks for four subreddits in which centrality measures are compared to karma. Our script produced networks which illustrate a positive correlation of karma in relation to closeness and clustering coefficient. The relationship between karma and the other two measures (eigenvector and betweenness) is negative. We can assume the negative correlation is due to the abundance of low karma nodes in the network which skew the influence that popular nodes have on the network. The nature of Reddit's popular content decreases the likelihood that it is connected to unpopular content. (Burke & Wagner, 2015, p. 146)

It is said that a majority of the site's users tend to trend young and male, and the culture is one of "ironic irreverence" (Mori, Gibbs, Arnold, Nansen, & Kohn, 2012, p. 401). A *Time Magazine* cover story termed it "the most interesting unruly website on the Internet" (Vella, July 20, 2015, p. 47). Reddit's edgy and freewheeling atmosphere may be a result of its users' sense of disinhibition (Gagnon, 2013), which may be exacerbated by the lack of non-verbal and paralinguistic cues. While some may self-disclose with their actual personally identifiable information (PII), others compartment their participation on Reddit from their real social lives.

Not only are disclosures involving reddit infrequent, but some users actively separate their life on reddit from their social life beyond the website—a practice we call compartmentalization. While not all users engage in compartmentalizing their disclosures, many users have a strong reasons to do so. Separating social life on anonymous media sites from external social spaces helps people react to disparate social norms and expectations. (Shelton, Lo, & Nardi, 2015, p. 7)

While social media users may let loose, so to speak, on "carnival" spaces online with "ethical situationalism" in play (per Bakhtin, 1984), many do seem to take the approach that what happens in online confessionals stays online, and they will be careful when selecting their audience for shared personal information (Shelton, Lo, & Nardi, 2015, pp. 10 - 11).

Based on some of the more popular forums, many go to Reddit to be entertained, others to be informed, with news being vetted through others' personalities and interests. Some visit Reddit to fact-check information and identify sources for further information (Kim, Ko, Jung, Lee, Kim, & Kim, 2015). For this case, some Reddit users will post questions and try to activate the network to do some of the research legwork for them. An interest in having an impact on others and the world may be a major motivating factor for those in Reddit:

A sense of "safe space" focus the motivational framework for the social news domain, the recreational value of the information posted to Reddit, along with the powerful possibilities for customization appear to be the most powerful incentives for using Reddit. Perhaps surprisingly, the social aspect of social news sites is not a motivating factor for the majority of Reddit users. Influencing the placement and reception of news stories in their niche communities of interest is what draws people to sites such as Reddit. (Bogers & Wernersen, 2014, p. 329)

Reddit's shared contents are not only occasionally "NSFW" (not safe for workplace viewing), but Reddit has a reputation for having a dark side. As a back alley of the Internet, Reddit has had a reputation for the sharing of offensive images, videos, and messaging; some of its members have used anonymized accounts to engage in trollish or victimizing behavior—behavior that breaks trust, harms others, harasses, misinforms, or otherwise disrupts the social order. ["To be trolled is to be made a victim, to be caught along in the undertow and be the butt of someone else's joke" (Bergstrom, 2011, p. 3).] There are various discussion threads, with topics such as "self-harm pics" and "cute female corpses" (Vella, July 20, 2015, p. 48). Subreddits about white supremacy, child porn, and other topics have also been offensive and earned the site a reputation as "a platform for racist, anti-Semitic, misogynistic and other hateful conversations" (Hempel, Oct. 6, 2015). One researcher conducted a study of two Reddit communities based around pornography: "r/PornVids, a board for mainstream porn, and r/ChickFlixxx, a board for woman-friendly or feminist porn" and found insights about pornographic consumption patterns and "distinctly gendered preferences" (Smith, 2014, p. 17). In this study, the researcher found over 2,000 subreddits focused on pornographic content.

For years, Reddit has dealt with issues of distributed community management, balancing between near-absolute free speech rights and the respect for larger community sensitivities. In Reddit's content policy, unwelcome contents include anything illegal, threatening, misleading or fraudulent, spamming, or violence-inciting; further, "involuntary pornography" is prohibited ("reddit content policy," 2015). A more recent point of anxiety-producing notoriety has been the work of online sleuths on Reddit who shared the photo of an innocent bystander who was mistakenly identified as a suspect in the Boston Marathon bombings (April 15, 2013). Sometimes, in the fog of crisis events, a heightened sense of fast-moving events results in unvetted, inaccurate, and incomplete information dissemination. Online messaging becomes "bursty" (typified by sharp spikes and dips in episodic activity) both on mainstream media and social media. Sometimes, mainstream and social media feed the hyper-speed dynamics in the other--not always to positive effect.

Crowd opinion is a core part of Reddit's organizational DNA and branding, but that is not an absolute value but affected by other considerations; indeed, competition over the future of the site has resulted in a restive user base overthrowing multiple leaders based on decisions that the membership disagreed with (Graham, 2015). When leadership (particularly by "the makers and maintainers of the system") contravenes the values and practices of particular subcultures, those groups may become reactive (Potts & Harrison, 2013, p. 143). A research team created a parsimonious model based on Reddit depicting an online society comprised of two "species": ordinary users and behavior enforcers (moderators). Moderators choose whether to be positive or negative ("harsh"), and the players choose whether to cooperate or defect. Using their model, built with two differential equations, the authors can show the evolutionary dynamics of the proposed system. Moderators can affect the limiting behavior of the system, and these combined dynamics often result in self-regulating (stable) systems (Griffin, Mercer, Fan, & Squicciarini, 2012, p. 39). As a decade-old organization, Reddit is continuing to work to achieve the right balance of decentralization and hands-off-ness and oversight.

A popular feature on the site is the "IAmA" forum (https://www.reddit.com/r/IAmA/) through which people self-identify with certain skill sets and respond to questions ("ask us anything!") from the broader public about their area of expertise. There are Ask Me Anything (AMA) and Ask Us Anything (AUA) events on Reddit. Various luminaries in a variety of backgrounds have taken on the "answer-person role" on Reddit.

Reddit is a social and cultural phenom onto itself. The members of Reddit are not just about sharing digital contents and ideas and upvoting and downvoting them. They engage in crowd-funding endeavors; distribute electronic petitions; and promote social organization and social activism. Online chatter often starts at Reddit, but even if it doesn't start there, it passes through that site. Some suggest that the Reddit community "is changing the methods of discourse online" (Weninger, Zhu, & Han, 2013, p. 579).

Reddit has a lot of street credibility, cachet, and power, online and offline; it has had a history of "breaking" the Internet with attention-getting contents. A lesser known fact is that Reddit is part of Advance Publications of Conde Nast, which also owns *Ars Technica* and *Wired*. Reddit brought in $8.6 million in ads in 2014 (Vella, July 20, 2015, p. 50.) Its offices are in San Francisco, California. Reddit's coarse street credibility and its text-heavy messy look give it a sense that someone's tech-savvy cousin created the site; it does not give off a sense of mainstream media with millions in revenues.

REMOTE PROFILING IN 360 DEGREES (IN THEORY AND MAYBE PRACTICE)

What is remote profiling through social media platforms? To elaborate further, the idea of remote profiling egos and entities on social media platforms is to understand information on a few basic tracks.

How does the ego or entity self-portray? Self-depictions in text, images, videos, messaging, and shared digital contents may be understood on multiple tracks—what the target thinks is being shared and what is actually shared. There is in virtually every messaging situation the intended messaging and also unintended messaging (a form of data leakage). How people hide and what they hide can be revealing. What people share and what they choose not to share are potentially revealing. One common issue is that people share information on public (or what they think is private) platforms in a narrow- or microcasting way; they are conceptualizing their own objectives and their own target audiences. However, when that information is widely available (broadcast), there are many other applications of that same information. It takes sophisticated communications skills to simultaneously message to multiple audiences with clarity, while controlling for unintended messaging, and that approach is fairly rare even with special professional training. The complexities of social media in a global environment only make the challenges of clear communications more acute.

A remote profile, in the 360-degree sense, involves those with affinities with the target ego or entity. In other words, to understand the target, it helps to know what those around the target say about the target, and how they interact with the target. This analysis involves examining those in the close-in network for the target. Even further out, this may also include the broader societal chatter. Some common headlines allude to the idea of understanding something of the collective consciousness (broad public opinion), with headlines asserting responses by "The Internet." Research assumptions are also that more non-obvious information may be capturable using this method to tap the collective subconscious and the collective unconscious (latent public opinion or meta-perspective) about the target. This is then a rigorous and full-field remote profiling exercise. The idea is that there are some ego or entity reflectances of identity in the two outer circles in Figure 2.

A remote profile could begin with some exploratory questions:

Figure 2. A full-field remote profiling exercise: target ego or entity, ego neighborhood, and larger online environment

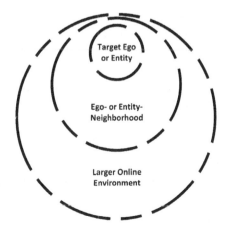

Ego and Entity-Level Questions

- What is the apparent messaging stream of the user account (in the profile, in the shared textual/image/video/other contents, in the planned interactivity, in the *ad hoc* interactivity)? What is the latent messaging (the subtext)? Are there themes in the shared messaging and contents?
- What are the apparent objectives of the ego? The entity?
- How active is the ego? The entity? Where are the ego's or entity's energies and resources apparently applied on the social media platform?
- What is the cognitive capability of the ego? The intelligence capabilities of the entity?
- What are the personal characteristics of the ego? The entity (or the membership in the entity)?
- What are the social characteristics of the ego? The entity?
- What is the apparent skill set of the ego? The entity?
- What are the resources of the ego? The entity?
- What facets of the ego or entity are apparent on the respective social media platforms?
- Is the ego (entity) apparently consistent or inconsistent? Is the messaging created by "one hand" or multiple hands? How aligned are the respective findings? If there are apparent discrepancies or conflicts, what are they, and what might these mean? In groups (entities), what are the dominant personalities and voices and calls-to-action? What are some ways to differentiate the different membership of that entity and also the different authorship of that entity?
- What does the formally or socially declared networks look like vs. the *ad hoc* ones? Who are the other "alters" in a direct network? What do the formal communications look like compared to the off-the-cuff ones?
- What is (are) the spatial location(s) of the ego or entity? What insights may be understood from the location—its social context, culture, languages, and other features?

Ego and Entity Neighborhood-Level Questions

- Who are the egos and entities in the 1-degree ego neighborhood of the target? Who are the egos and entities in the 1.5-degree graph of the target? What may be seen by the "company" that the target ego or entity keeps?
- What sorts of messaging (and multimedia content) is shared among those in the ego neighborhood?
- What sorts of messaging (and multimedia content) is shared at 1.5 degrees? 2 degrees?

Larger Online Environment-Level Questions

- What is the reputation of the ego or entity? Are there themes emerging from potentially diverse opinions? How valid do the opinions seem to be, and what are they apparently based on?
- What sorts of messages are being received from the ego or entity, and how are these messages received by the broader public?

Additional customized top-level questions and sub-questions may be added to develop this approach more effectively. Particularly, questions may be tailored to particular contexts, targets, and social media platforms.

This approach involves capabilities based on selecting from amongst available functionalities of publicly available and known software tools. Data extraction tools used include NodeXL Basic (Network Overview, Discovery, and Exploration in Excel), Maltego Chlorine v. 3.6.0 and v. 3.6.1, NCapture on NVivo 10, and various browser add-ons. Data processing was done in NodeXL 1.0.1.341, Maltego Chlorine 3.6.0 and 3.6.1, NVivo 10, and other tools. The types of social media platforms explored include the following: microblogging sites, social networking sites, crowd-sourced online encyclopedias, image- and video-sharing sites, image-sharing sites, video-sharing sites, and the World Wide Web (WWW) and Internet. Other types of social media, not analyzed here, include social bookmarking sites, Web communities, virtual immersive worlds, game sites, podcasts, life streams, online forums, and blogs. Social media enable people to create parasocial relationships through mediated sociality to inter-communicate, share, and engage as "valid social actors" (Kumar & Benbasat, 2002, p. 1). The social media platforms used in this work, based on their Web-based application programming interfaces (APIs) and the middleware enabling access to those APIs, include (in the broad order of presentation) Twitter, Facebook, Wikipedia, Flickr, Instagram, YouTube, and the WWW and Internet. All these platforms are broad- and multi-purpose ones, without a locked-in or dedicated approach (as compared to game-based virtual worlds) (Benson, Saridakis, Tennakoon, & Ezingeard, 2015). As such, these platforms are used in a wide variety of ways and for various purposes. A survey instrument was used to understand the purposes of social media usage among young Americans, and this included a variety of motivations: to learn more about something or someone, to "find places to eat or services to use," to improve a skill, to give updates, to have fun, to laugh, to "see/hear something entertaining," to teach others about new knowledge, to collaborate around a shared goal, and others (Luchman, Bergstrom, & Krulikowski, 2014, p. 139); to achieve these various aims, they went to a number of different social media platforms and online spaces.

In this chapter, the various social media platforms are exemplars in their classes, and the reasonable size limits of this chapter means that each category actually only contains one example. This chapter describes some of the capabilities of "manual" or semi-automated (vs. fully automated) profiling of social media accounts for insights that would not generally be attainable by other means.

Some Research Assumptions

This research approach assumes that there is some inextricable linkage of online digital presences to individual's real lives. People express something of their public and private interests in their online sharing and communications. Their reputations are built over time and across social media platforms, and this reputation may be seen based on their own behaviors and those of their acquaintances and friends. Even with all the social posturing, social media analysis will result in some useful insights.

It is possible that those who have active accounts across multiple platforms are a minority of a minority based on the intuition of the 1% rule on the Internet. [In Internet culture, there is a version of the Pareto principle (albeit with different numbers). The idea is that of those online, 1% are direct new-content contributors while 99% are lurkers who consume what is created. A variant is the 1-9-90 rule which posits that 1% create contents, 9% edit those contents (as on a wiki), and 90% only view or consume the contents.] This concept is explained:

That is, without incentives for users to participate in multiple communities, only a small fraction of the already small fraction of significant users are likely to exhibit this behavior. In non-voluntary networks that develop in organizations with boundaries between units or departments, however, this behavior may

Table 1. Types of extractable information about egos and entities across social media platforms and the Web and Internet

Types of Extractable Information about Egos and Entities	Microblogging Sites	Social Networking Sites	Crowd-Sourced and Open-Access Online Encyclopedia Sites (and Wiki Sites)	Image- and Video-Sharing Sites	Image-Sharing Sites	Video-Sharing Sites	WWW and Internet
Messaging and Shared Contents (for Content Analysis)							
Profile-based Self-Descriptions	x	x	x	x	x	x	x
Extracted Account Messaging	x	x	x	x	x	x	x
Topic Messaging, Commenting	x	x	x	x	x	x	x
Scraped Images, Thumbnail Images	x	x	x	x	x	x	x
Trace Data (for Link Analysis)							
Declared User Networks	x	x	x	x	x	x	x
Ad Hoc User Networks (built around contents)	x	x	x	x	x	x	x
Metadata (for Network Analysis, for Categorical Analysis, for Spatiality Analysis)							
Related Tags Networks				x			
Geolocation Data	x	x	x	x	x	x	x

differ significantly. For instance, networks in which a participant has responsibility in multiple segments of the community (as with a manager and her interactions with subordinates and upper management) might require multi-community interaction. (Buntain & Golbeck, 2014, p. 620)

If the 1 percent rule about Internet culture is true, then a cross-social media platform approach to understand identity may be applicable only to a small target group, a percent of a percent of egos and entities online. This approach may help profile larger-scale elite social media targets, but these techniques may also be applied to smaller scale ones as long as they may identifiably be seen to manifest across social media platforms.

To provide an overview of the types of social data that may be extracted and processed, Table 1 offers a summary of the types of information generally extractable from each of the site types.

Table 1 is not a complete table by any means. Quite a few types of social media platforms have not been included (in part because they are not accessible by the software tools deployed here). The respective approaches result in different data patterns and different types of knowability.

Delimitations

To accurately set the stage for the following findings about Reddit, it is helpful to summarize some of the limits to the assertions. These limits likely apply well beyond the findings of this work, so they are potentially relevant beyond this exemplar case. These delimitations are numbered for easier reference. There are six main delimitations:

1. Strategic targeting through seeding terms,
2. Private or hidden accounts,
3. Partial data extractions (due to incomplete data extractions, time-limited extractions, and single-role limited extractions),
4. Unsuccessful data extractions, and
5. Inherent ambiguity in symbolic systems (specifically messaging and contents).

Figure 3 provides a sense of limitations to the data capture and analysis in a somewhat process-linear form.

1. **Strategic Targeting through Seeding (Source) Terms:** Research has never been a costless effort. To enhance the value of research from social media, it is important to strategically seed data extractions from the respective platforms. For example, which egos and entities should be explored, and what should be explored? What #hashtags and keywords should be used for capturing *ad hoc* microblogging discussions, related tags networks, and video networks? How should eventgraphs (in-world events captured as networks of data) be captured?

Figure 3. Some delimitations to extracted social media data and their analysis

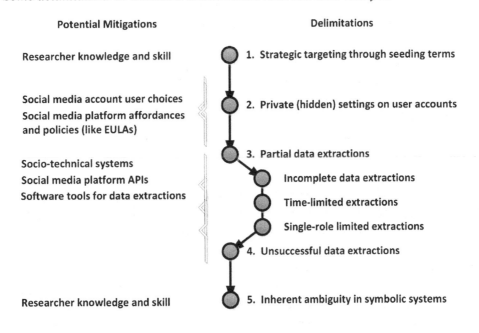

Most text-seeded data extractions are ambiguous because of the variant uses of language. Also, particularly for trending events, there are often multiple "starts" with differing #hashtags and keywords addressing the same issue or event. Also, there may be misspellings that may draw off a part of the momentum of shared discussions into other "threads." A more complete extraction of data would entail multiple seeding hashtags, keywords, and possibly languages.

People's social media accounts may be named around elusive word combinations or maybe have no discernable direct meaning; as part of anti-forensics efforts, many create throwaway accounts (with many identities built on faux information) (McDermid, 2014, pp. 230 – 231); users build fake footprints to throw off others in a surveillance-heavy electronic environment. In part, the anti-forensics efforts have come about as part of a self-protection mechanism. Researchers have identified "what information may be captured and exploited from social media" and online social networks in a data reachability matrix (Creese, Goldsmith, Nurse, & Phillips, 2012, p. 1124), especially in the hands of a savvy and determined malicious individual or group. Some hackers and "trolls" use others' private data in unintended ways, in a phenomenon known as "the secondary use problem" (Krishnamurthy, 2013, p. 15). One potent example is the widespread re-distribution of people's private hacked intimate images or personally identifiable health data, and even sensitive background checks of those working in government. Self-disclosure of information—on any electronic platform—carries with it some risk of mis-use.

On the other hand, particularly among law enforcement and system administrators, there are efforts to try to identify individuals running multiple accounts under alias on social media platforms. Several approaches involves string-based analysis, "time profiling," stylometric analyses of messaging, and social network-based matching (Johansson, Kaati, & Shrestha, 2013). Another approach matched user accounts likely to belong to similar individuals across online social networks based on name-based features, user profile details, and social network features (such as shared mutual friends between two accounts) (Peled, Fire, Rokach, & Elovici, 2013, p. 339). If egos and entities that are duplicated may be identified, the quality of the social networks may be better understood.

Temporary identities may be created to engage with a particular event or topic. Pseudonyms are consistent artificial identities used over time (in a disambiguated way) and are often exclusive to the respective user. Anonymous names are those that people take on that do not directly reflect themselves per se and may not directly be linked to one person; for example, "Anonymous" is used broadly and is taken on by a broad number of individuals. There are many who use their own names or emails or initials in a uniquely identifiable way. People's online identities can be quite meaningful. Online, interacting with others as a way of exploring individual identity (Turkle, 1998). Some will use the social networks of others to assess a human source of information in order to know how much trust to put in it (Sohn, 2013).

2. **Private (Hidden) Settings on User Accounts, Suspended Accounts:** There are social media accounts and groups which are set to private and are invitation-only. They are not generally visible to regular users, and information cannot generally be extracted or scraped from them. It is hard to collect information on what is not publicly seeable except for the moments or the aspects that the egos and entities choose to share. (It is said that an ego or entity may be understood by "the company it keeps," or the members of its close-in and more extended social network, but if the company is also discreet and invisible, it is much less possible to infer presence based on the surrounding nodes and others' commentaries.) For trending issues, accounts may be suspended by the

service provider, which also renders the information inaccessible. When social media platforms work effectively and when they actually protect their data against hacking, there is no smoke and no fire apparent—in true hiddenness.

3. **Partial Data Extractions:** The "big data" premise does not apply here. Virtually all data extractions are necessarily partial because of incomplete data extractions, time-limited extractions, and single-role limited extractions.

    a. **Incomplete Data Extractions:** For a majority of the social media platforms, data extractions are rate-limited, which means that access to the data is often time-interrupted (to enable fairer distributed access). All datasets are also generally limited, so there is no full set or N = all, unless researchers either go through a commercial entity that access the full set or the company behind the social media platform. (Some MediaWiki extractions—such as article-article networks and user networks may be complete, but this is anomalous.) Limitations may occur based on the capturing tool. For example, tools used to extract data for network analyses often include top limits because networks that tend to be too large or dense tend to be visually ambiguous and difficult to analyze (and require access to the underlying data). There are also further limiting parameters to data extraction tools based on decision-making by the researcher. Data extractions may be accomplished at various sizes in terms of the numbers of vertices and relationships (and relationship types).

The challenge is that it is not possible to know what part of data was "skimmed" and what was left out. It is highly possible that the skim was a convenience one and not actually a random sample, which may suggest that conclusions drawn from the dataset may be biased or misleading. Sometimes, there may not be a way to "proof" the findings through other means of data extraction. Or, two data extractions using different software tools may result in such variant and disjoint datasets that trying to bring them together for comparison and summarization may be impossible because of the overlap; rather, in such cases, each set is adding fresh insights.

    b. **Time-Limited Extractions:** Another limitation revolves around time. After all individuals and groups manifest in time; they have pasts, presents, and futures. They have prior histories, current actions, and aspirations. To fully profile egos and entities, it is helpful to have a sense of the target "agent" and its networks and other information in a time context.

Some social media platforms may have fairly high turnover of users, with limited active lifespans and weak social ties among their members. Twitter, the microblogging site, shows a lot of change over time and dynamism, seen as a reflection of the need for people to be adaptive in a highly competitive society (Arnaboldi, Conti, Passarella, & Dunbar, 2013). Intuitively, Twitter accounts that have a reciprocal following dyadic relationship tend to be more resilient than those that do not: "(In the raw data, the break rate for reciprocated ties was 16.4%, while as many as 44.5% of unreciprocated ties broke by Time 2" (Kivran-Swaine, Govindan, & Naaman, 2011, p. 3). The denser the network, the less likelihood of tie breaks, and further, the greater the number of the dyad's common neighbors (at a 1.5 degree network), the lower the weaknesses of the ties (Kivran-Swaine, Govindan, & Naaman, 2011, p. 3).

Those who tend to leave the Twitter site altogether tended to do so within a little over two months on average. One research team found that the average on-site lifespan of users who left Twitter was 73.21 days:

As a first contribution of our analysis, we studied the behaviour of users that abandoned Twitter. We say that a user has abandoned Twitter if her active lifespan is followed by a period of at least six months of inactivity. In the data set, the average active lifespan of users that abandoned Twitter is 73.21 days, indicating that most of them are occasional users. In fact, over a total of 159, 069 accounts that abandoned Twitter (i.e., 24.7% of our data set), 88.27% are occasional users, whilst only 11.6% are regular users and 0.13% are aficionados. From the distribution of the active lifespan of occasional users...we can notice that there is a small number of accounts with duration between 50 and 365 days. Yet, there is a non-negligible number of occasional users with a very short lifespan (i.e., < 50d). These accounts represent people that joined Twitter more than one year before the download, but that abandoned it after a short period of activity. This class of users can be seen as a sub-class of occasional users, who subscribed to Twitter only to "give it a try", but abandoned it very soon. (Arnaboldi, Conti, Passarella, & Dunbar, 2013, p. 22)

Most of the social media data extractions described here involve slice-in-time or cross-sectional data. In other words, they were collected from a clearly defined period, with a clear start and end time. Messaging on social media platforms has been mapped to particular periods of activities in the day, with highly active periods and those of relative silence (Atig, Cassel, Kaati, & Shreshtha, 2014).

Such time-series data requires continuous- or fairly frequent interval- captures of user interaction information over time. Those who can go directly to their computers (without mediating software programs) and use command line requests for information from social media APIs may capture data more continuously and for longer periods and archive the information on databases, enabling a more complete and continuous sense of evolving social networks and dynamic data.

Another limitation is the fact that extracted data may be highly time-sensitive, particularly *ad hoc* and trending microblogging conversations. Video networks, related tags networks, article-article networks, and so on, may be less dynamic or more static. Another challenge is that many social media platforms do not enable access to their historical data past a certain point. Those who may want to profile an ego or entity from the beginning of his / her / their history will often not be able to access information from the inception of the accounts, without paying a commercial service (which have protected access to the near-complete or complete data repositories). On a side note, if laws and policies enabling people to have the so-called "right to be forgotten" are passed, then historical data may be less practically available.

Another time limitation may occur from happenstance; for example, there may be a delay in capturing available information from a researcher lack of awareness of an important target ego or target entity. For those using these described methods, the inability to tap data completely and retroactively may be highly limiting.

c.   **Single-Role Limited Extractions:** A third limitation involves the fact that these tools currently show individual nodes and individual groups in single networks. In the real, individual nodes and groups are often multi-faceted: individuals are members in a number of groups (e.g. an individual as a member of families, teams, work-groups, hobby groups, religious groups, and others); groups themselves may belong to multiple communities and play multiple roles (e.g. a neighborhood organization is a member of the local community, a liaison group for businesses and government, a planning group for neighborhood changes, a member of the bank as a customer, and so on). The cyber equivalencies would be an individual node on an image and video-sharing social media platform who is a member of multiple interest groups—such as photo groups representing various personal, hobbies, and work interests, and *ad hoc* groups that share overlapping and cross-over interests (such as political action groups that engage within multiple smaller communities). Current widely-available network analysis tools show single-facet relationships in most cases even though there are now early mentions in the research literature about methods for depicting multi-faceted egos and entities in networked relationships. More accurate depictions would show individual nodes with maybe percentages of time spent in various groups on a social media platform or *ad hoc* groups as those with overlapping linkages with other communities of interest. In the real, egos and entities do have multiple affiliations (Wang, Tang, Gao, & Liu, 2010); they engage in a wide range of activities and events. Current data extraction systems do not yet capture that mixed engagement complexity. One research team describes this limitation and a strategy to allow nodes to "vote" for the communities that they belong to based on non-obvious or latent features:

Community discovery in complex networks is the task of organizing a network's structure by grouping together nodes related to each other. Traditional approaches are based on the assumption that there is a global-level organization in the network. However, in many scenarios, each node is the bearer of complex information and cannot be classified in disjoint clusters. The top-down global view of the partition approach is not designed for this. Here, we represent this complex information as multiple latent labels, and we postulate that edges in the networks are created among nodes carrying similar labels. The latent labels are the communities a node belongs to and we discover them with a simple local-first approach to community discovery. This is achieved by democratically letting each node vote for the communities it sees surrounding it in its limited view of the global system, its ego neighborhood, using a label propagation algorithm, assuming that each node is aware of the label it shares with each of its connections. The local communities are merged hierarchically, unveiling the modular organization of the network at the global level and identifying overlapping groups and groups of groups. (Coscia, Rossetti, Giannotti, & Pedreschi, 2014, p. 6)

While the algorithm for mapping multi-membership features of nodes has apparently been developed and has been shown to be effective, it is not yet publicly available (to the best knowledge of the author).

5. **Outright Fails: Unsuccessful Data Extractions:** While a number of data extractions were attempted for this chapter, not all were successful. For those that failed, a failure was reported only when multiple attempts had been tried under multiple conditions and with multiple software tools (where relevant) and on multiple machines and at multiple times. In other words, reporting out on failures is not done lightly.

6. **Inherent Ambiguity in Symbolic Systems: Polysemic Language and Speech, Multiple Languages, and Multimedia Contents:** Once data have been collected, the challenges are only then beginning. There are challenges with both human- and machine-based analytics. Much of human conduct depends on exchanged information—through language (spoken and written). Language, by nature of its adaptivity, is polysemic or multi-meaninged, with different understandings based on context, culture, speakers, tones, and other features. In the online context, the multi-meaninged aspects of language are multiplied manifold because a number of global languages are in play and a multitude of cultural contexts. Further, people interact around images, audio files, slideshows, videos, games, simulations, and other multimedia contents; they share URLs, tags, comments, and

metadata. Besides the inherent ambiguity, there is also the challenge of purposeful noise and image management, social performance, and reputation building, in people's public-facing communications. There are often discrepancies between private and public lives, and various discrepancies between private and public information. Online, people interact with others as a way of exploring their highly mutable individual identities (Turkle, 1998). Pseudonyms may be revelatory as well (Dennen, 2009, p. 27), by deduction and inference. Online identities are "constructions that develop over time" (Dennen, 2009, p. 23), sometimes to the point that anonymous posts are automatically recognized by others based on voice and context alone (p. 29). Identities are socially constructed and influenced by the online and social environment and others responses.

In most research contexts, the information captured is limited and presented in a qualified way. There are varying confidence levels for any particular assertion, ranging from a minimal hunch to certitude or a probability of one (1). The point of mentioning the delimitations is that in any research question, there will be some degree of obscurity, masking, and opacity. In many cases, some information is better than no information, and occasionally, sometimes a hint is enough (if that hint is presented accurately).

This following section summarizes some initial findings about Reddit on a number of social media platforms. The treatment here is not a full one but is done in a way to highlight social media extraction tool capabilities and applied methods.

REMOTE PROFILING EGOS AND ENTITIES ACROSS SOCIAL MEDIA PLATFORMS...BASED ON REDDIT

Microblogging Sites

A microblogging site enables people to share short text messages (with embedded URLs, images, audio files, and video files). Users may often re-share others' messages. They may select others' messages to favorite.

On Twitter

Twitter is the foremost microblogging platform in the U.S. and other parts of the world. One way to explore an ego or entity on Twitter is to examine its text-based messaging (Tweets) and its multimedia contents.

- **NCapture in NVivo 10:** There were several attempts to capture the @reddit Tweetstream from Twitter, using NCapture of NVivo 10 on Windows. The idea was to capture the Tweets (including re-tweets) as a dataset. The account apparently blocks such data sharing because the attempts were not successful, per Figure 4. There were multiple different types of failure messages though, with one suggesting that there had been other accesses to Twitter in the past 15 minutes (not true) or a simple 404 error message, so the ultimate reason for the failure was not clear. The @ Science_Reddit was not capturable either.

Figure 4. Multiple unsuccessful attempts to download the @reddit Tweetstream from Twitter using NCapture of NVivo 10

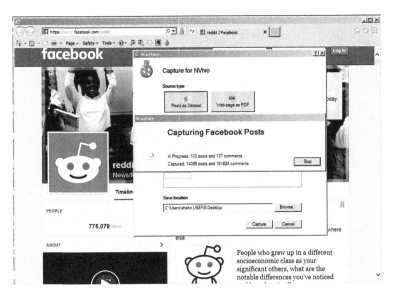

The @reddit_AMA (available at https://twitter.com/reddit_AMA) was available for a Tweetstream extraction. At the time of the data extraction, that account had 5,192 Tweets, 43 following, 54,3K (54,300) followers, and 185 favorites. This account focuses on the Ask Me Anything (AMA) feature. The capture resulted in 3,201 Tweets. Figure 5 shows the information.

Figure 5. Table view of the extracted @reddit_AMA Tweetstream (in NVivo 10)

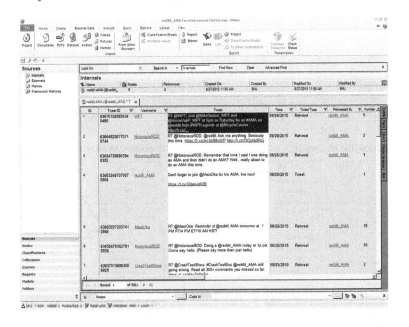

Figure 6. Word Cloud from the @reddit_AMA Tweetstream (in NVivo 10)

A word cloud was created from the extracted Tweetstream dataset with the "http" and "https" removed in the customized stopwords list, used in addition to the built-in stopwords list. In Figure 6, the word cloud indicates which words were most used in the messaging and gives a rough summary sense of the emphasized topics.

In NVivo, a word tree was created for "AMA" to understand how "AMA" is used. There were 2,926 references to "AMA". The word tree may be viewed in Figure 7.

Figure 7. "AMA" word tree from the @reddit_AMA Tweetstream (in NVivo 10)

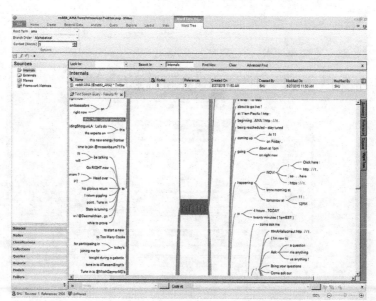

Figure 8. @reddit user network on Twitter (with friends and followers) (1 deg.)

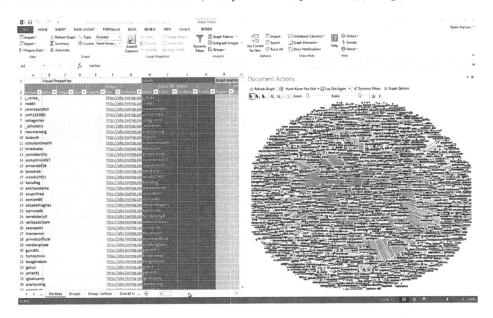

A more in-depth content analysis of Reddit-linked Twitter accounts would include explorations of all extracted uniform resource locators (URLs), images, audio, and video. It would involve follow-up analyses on major topics of conversation, and so on.

- **NodeXL:** Network Overview, Discovery, and Exploration for Excel (NodeXL) is a freeware tool (with a commercial Pro version) that enables the extraction of social media data from various social media platforms and through the use of third-party data importers. It is a strong tool for graphing relationships and for link analysis. The Twitter User Search feature was used to capture the @reddit account on Twitter—to show its friends and followers in Figure 8. At the left is a data table with some of the ego neighborhood "alters" (nodes with direct ties to the target node, altogether comprising the ego neighborhood around the focal node) visible; to the right is the graph pane with the data graphed.

NodeXL enables the output of a graph metrics table for all extracted networks as seen in Table 2. The @reddit network has over 2,294 friends and followers in its ego neighborhood (at 1 degree).

Another type of data extraction is the #hashtag search, which captures all those who have recently used a particular #hashtag to label their conversations. A hashtag search for #redditor was recently conducted and found a network of 85 vertices with 87 unique edges, and 65 groups based on the Clauset-Newman-Moore clustering algorithm. This means a variety of small groups or individual nodes in the #redditor network on Twitter about a week before the data extraction. (Twitter's API does not allow going much further back in time for this type of query.) This #redditor hashtag network is shown in Figure 9. Sometimes, people are just sharing information into the electronic universe without necessarily engaging directly in conversations with others; in the vernacular, they are "just putting it out there" or "sending a message out to the universe." In cases when individuals are just labeling a message with a hashtag, but no one else directly interacts with them around that message, that account and message will be depicted as an isolate (unattached, unrelated) node.

Table 2. Graph metrics for the @reddit user network on Twitter (with friends and followers) (1 deg.)

Graph Metric	Value
Vertices	2294
Unique Edges	2284
Edges With Duplicates	181
Total Edges	2465
Self-Loops	143
Reciprocated Vertex Pair Ratio	0.00130833
Reciprocated Edge Ratio	0.00261324
Connected Components	1
Single-Vertex Connected Components	0
Maximum Vertices in a Connected Component	2294
Maximum Edges in a Connected Component	2465
Maximum Geodesic Distance (Diameter)	2
Average Geodesic Distance	1.998257
Graph Density	0.00043649
Modularity	Not Applicable
NodeXL Version	1.0.1.341

Figure 9. #redditor hashtag search on Twitter (basic network)

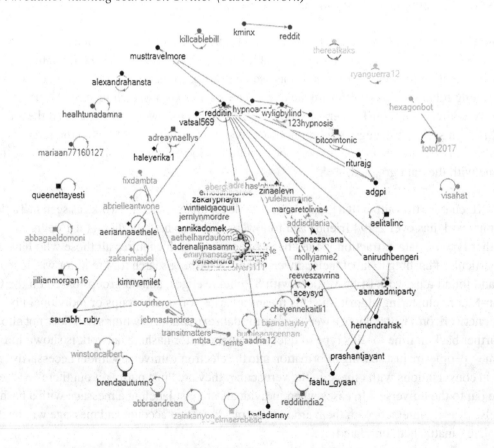

Figure 10. The sentiment analysis setup to analyze the results of a #reddit hashtag search on Twitter (basic network)

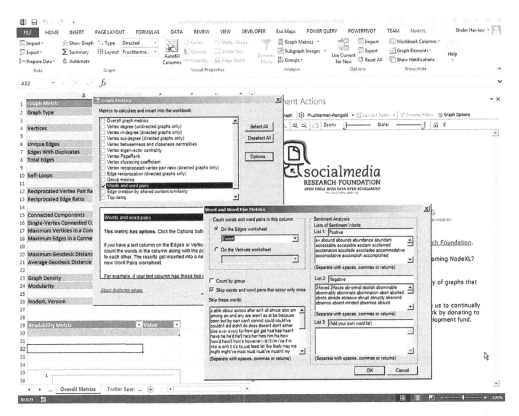

It is possible to conduct analyses of the extracted network on measures of centrality to try to ascertain the most influential conversationalist in the extracted network around the particular topic. This is often done to understand some of the power and communications dynamics. In more complex *ad hoc* #hashtag networks, denser substructures (clusters within clusters) may be captured to reveal the social network topology, and to understand the various subgroups communicating using the particular hashtag on Twitter.

NodeXL has a new feature that was in beta at the time that this chapter was written. This feature enables a sentiment analysis of extracted networks. In this case, Tweets from a #reddit hashtag search were analyzed for sentiment, generally, positive or negative, based on built-in word lists (Figure 10).

In Figure 11, the screenshot shows the sentiment analysis data on the datasheet to the left and the resulting graph from an overall treemap box layout algorithm and the Harel-Koren Fast Multiscale layout algorithm for each cluster.

This network extraction resulted in a graph with 451 vertices and 288 unique edges. The largest connected component had 217 vertices. The graph's geodesic distance (graph diameter) was four, and the average geodesic distance between nodes was 1.66.

A keyword search of "reddit" was also conducted. Oftentimes, a keyword search will result in a larger graph because this search is not limited to those with the hashtag label. Indeed, a keyword search for "reddit" on Twitter found a network with 5,301 vertices and 4,130 unique edges. The maximum geodesic distance (graph diameter) was 21, and the average geodesic distance between nodes was 4.912. There were 2,400 groups or clusters in this network. This graph is viewable in Figure 12.

Figure 11. #reddit hashtag search on Twitter (basic network) with sentiment analysis

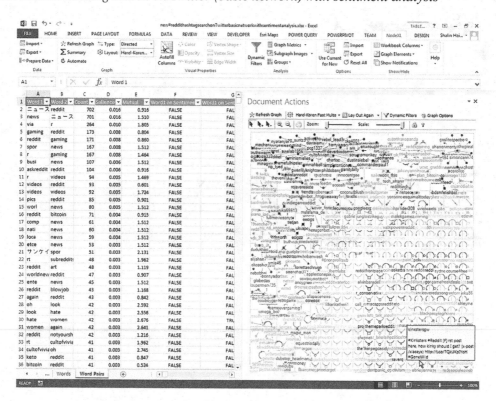

- **The Tweet Analyzer (in Maltego Chlorine 3.6.0 and 3.6.1):** Another tool enables sentiment analysis of messaging from Twitter based on the AlchemyAPI. A "reddit" keyword search using the Maltego Chlorine "Tweet Analyzer" Machine (over a number of iterations) shows the term trending positive over all but with some messages trending negative and some neutral. The initial parameters set for the data extraction was at 10,000 messages (the graph size options on the slider are 12, 50, 255, and 10K). For each node, there is a Twit (Twitter identity) and part of the message, and other metadata about the message, in addition to other information. See more on Figure 13.

This listing of first the NodeXL sentiment analysis findings and then the one from Maltego Chlorine begs the question of how easy it may be to compare findings. Assuming that the initial parameters are comparable (such as both extracting hashtags vs. keywords, or vice versa) and the data extractions were done at the same time, it is possible that there may be some overlap in information. However, given that both extractions are rate-limited by the Twitter API and the fact that the amount of information available is just a few percent of what is available, the actual comparability of such sets are in question.

Finally, metadata may also be collected from Twitter. These include various types of data labels. These also include geolocational data, which may be linked to the user profiles, particular Tweets, EXIF (exchangeable image file format) data on imagery, and app-linked check-ins. Within NodeXL, it is possible to view locational data in a location column in the extracted data. Within NVivo, it is possible to coarsely map locations of where accounts are that participate in a particular Twitter user's network. Because geolocational data is often sparse or folksonomically described, geolocational data is often incomplete and sometimes inaccurate.

Figure 12. "reddit" keyword search using Twitter search feature in NodeXL

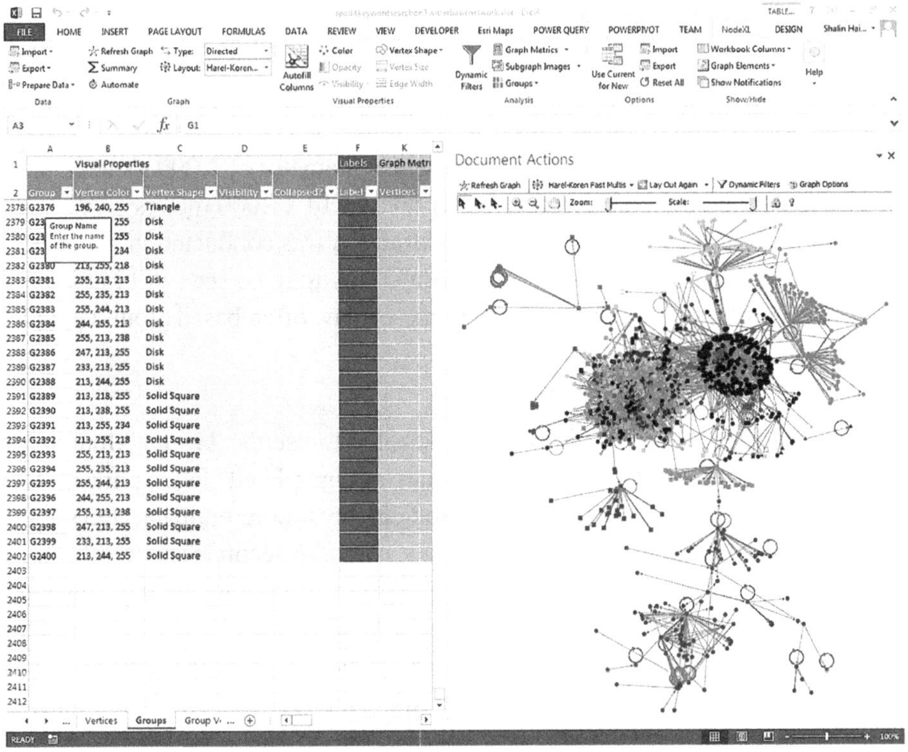

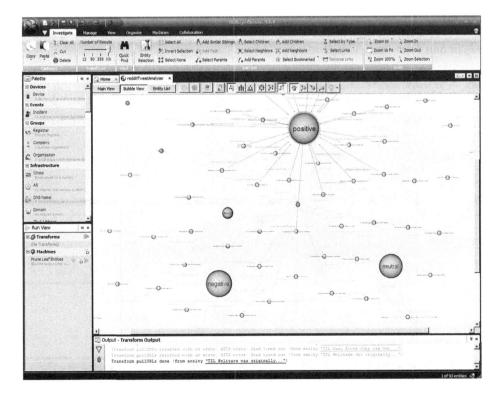

Figure 13. "reddit" keyword search using the tweet analyzer in Maltego Chlorine 3.6.0

Circular Area

A refreshing way to benefit from physical spatiality is to choose a physical location on a map—defined by latitude and longitude—and extract proxemics Tweets to that location. Reddit's HQ is widely publicized to be located at 530 3rd Street, San Francisco, CA 94107. On Google Maps, its latitude and longitude is 37.780980, -122.395442. Using Maltego Chlorine 3.6.0 and 3.6.1, Tweets were collected in a circular area around this defined spot to a radius of 1,000 meters, a diameter of 2,000 meters, and a circumference of 6,283.19 meters, or a 3,141,590 square meter area (3.14 x 2000 meters^2). A screenshot of this "machine" in action may be seen in Figure 14. This extraction was conducted in the evening.

Another was conducted the morning of the next day. This may be seen in Figure 15. The gists of Tweets and Twitter discourses change based on the time-of-day, often based around people's activities.

The Twitter Monitor (in Maltego Chlorine 3.6.0)

For a more continuous extraction from Twitter, it is possible to use the Twitter Monitor "machine" on Maltego Chlorine. This captures text-seeded Twitter messaging, related URLs, phrases, locations, Twit identities, and other data. In some ways, this extraction captures more multi-faceted data than a Tweet Analyzer. The data extractions occur at regular intervals, every 76 seconds apparently, according to the built-in timer on the Twitter Monitor tool. This tool also offers a running count of the nodes or entities captured. In the corresponding data table, there are additional details. If there are particular nodes or clusters (or branches) of interest, Maltego Chlorine enables the capturing of additional related information. A "reddit" search on the Twitter Monitor captured a wide range of topics and links to #news, for example, as may be seen in Figure 16.

Figure 14. Near real-time evening tweets from a 1000 meter circular area around Reddit HQ (37.780980, -122.395442) in San Francisco, California

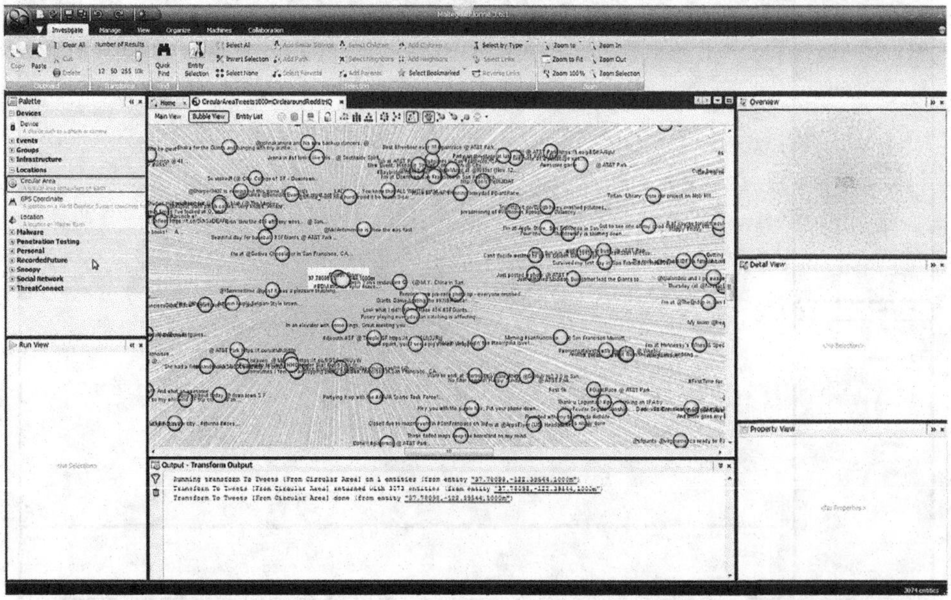

Figure 15. Near real-time morning tweets from a 1000 meter circular area around Reddit HQ (37.780980, -122.395442) in San Francisco, California

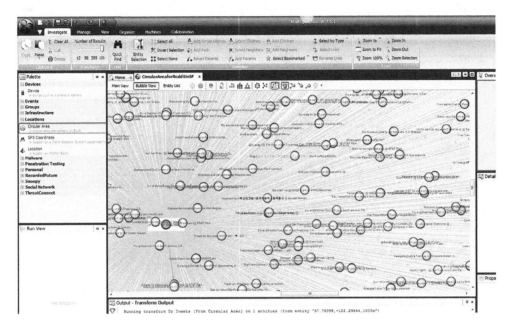

Figure 16. "reddit" as represented by the Twitter monitor in Maltego Chlorine 3.6.0

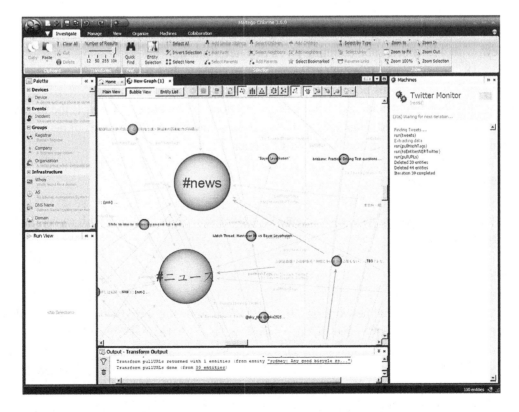

Figure 17. An exploding "bubble view" of "reddit" in the Twitter monitor in Maltego Chlorine 3.6.0

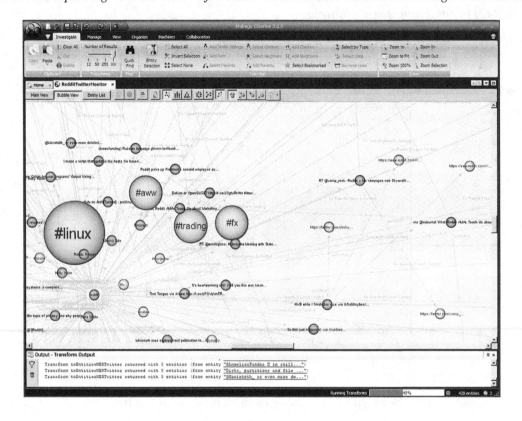

In Figure 17, the same "reddit" data extraction on the Twitter Monitor may be seen in an exploding bubble view, with 428 entities and counting just a few iterations in.

In Figure 18, the same "reddit" graph in the Twitter Monitor is shown in a Main View, which enables zoomed-in close-ups of various nodes in the structured network.

The closest thing to an official and explicit social network for Reddit on Twitter is the formal @reddit user network, with declared relationships; however, there are clearly other types of networks such as those around the reddit keyword and the #reddit hashtag.

Social Networking Sites

Social networking sites enable its users to create virtual presences and interact with each other along a number of dimensions.

On Facebook

Facebook is the foremost social networking site in the West, with a reported 1.5 billion monthly active users ("Number of monthly active Facebook users worldwide…" 2015) and 700 million unique accesses daily. Reddit's Facebook page (located at https://www.facebook.com/reddit) has the site self-identifying as a "News/Media Website." It had 769,382 likes at the time of the visit. The extractable messaging and shared contents include profile information, posts, images, and other data. To use Facebook's API, a researcher has to have an actual account.

Figure 18. A zoomed out and zoomed-in (inset) "main view" of the "reddit" twitter monitor

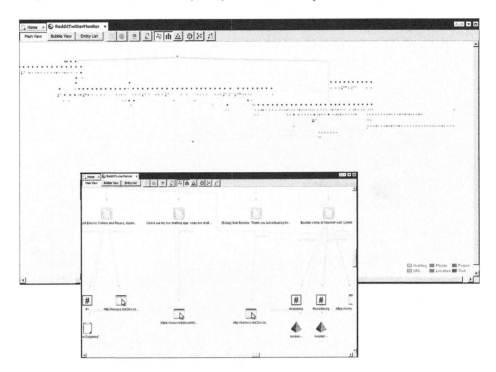

In Figure 19, "An Attempt to Map the Reddit Facebook Fan Page with NodeXL," the window shows some of the available data dimensions. This screenshot also shows an account with 772,484 likes and 34,380 "talking about this" and a NameID: 7177913734. Multiple attempts to extract both unimodal networks based on user-user ties (based on co-likes and co-commenting) and post-post networks (based on likes and comments), and bi-modal networks (based on user-post networks (based on likes and comments) ultimately did not result in any successful extractions.

An attempt was made to extract data using NCapture of NVivo, and while an extraction of the page's post stream resulted in well over 14,000 posts and 160,000-some comments, when an attempt was made to actually ingest the contents into an NVivo project, an error message was triggered. A screenshot of this effort may be seen in Figure 20.

Multiple additional attempts were made but were unsuccessful, as may be seen in Figure 21.

A third tool was tried—Maltego Chlorine—starting with an L2 footprinting of https://www.facebook. com/reddit and branching out to a number of transforms (Figure 22). This http network was shown to have 487 entities in a single run. The network showed broad ties across geographical regions, age groups, and interests—which speak to Reddit's popularity (across "silos" or group boundaries).

Another view shows this data with node size based on centrality (Figure 23). In an http network, linkages are created based on actual specified href links, not trace data based on ineractions (as on social media sites).

On Facebook, there are various types of metadata that may be used. These include descriptive data about shared imagery and multimedia.

Figure 19. An attempt to map the Reddit Facebook fan page with NodeXL

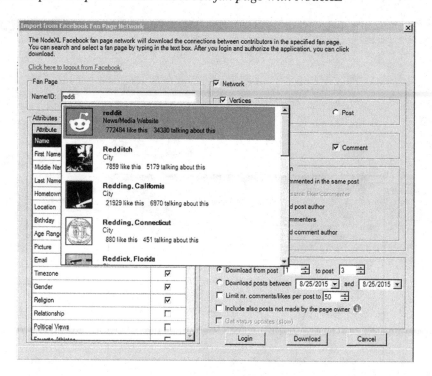

Figure 20. An attempt to capture Facebook posts in the Reddit Facebook page stream

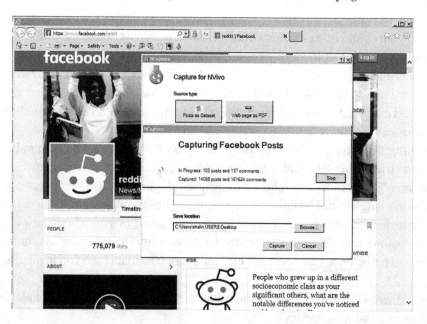

Figure 21. Importation of Reddit Facebook page post data failed in the NVivo Project

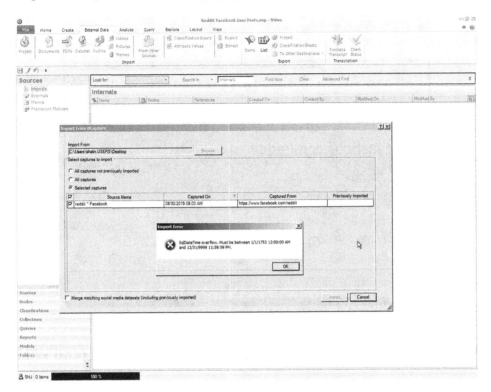

Figure 22. Mapping the Reddit presence on Facebook on the Web and Internet with Maltego Chlorine

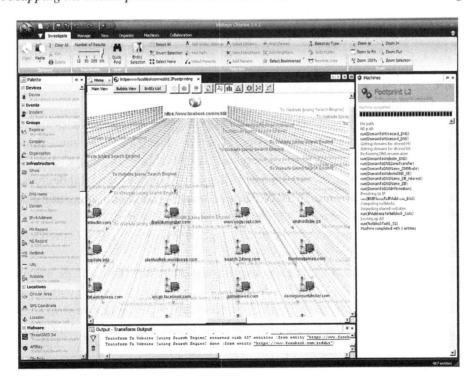

Figure 23. The https://www.facebook.com/reddit with high centrality connectivity on the WWW and Internet

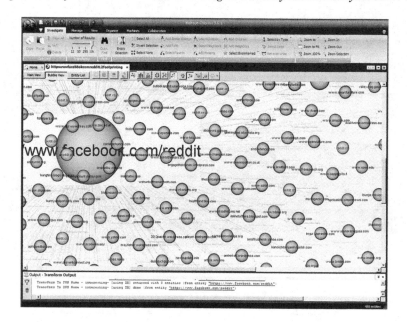

Crowd-Sourced and Open-Access Online Encyclopedia Sites (and Wiki Sites)

Websites built on the free and open-source MediaWiki understructure may be explored for messaging and shared contents (textual data, images, URLs, and others); relational or link data (such as article-article networks based on page relationships on a domain, user-page relationships, co-editing networks, and others), and metadata (descriptive data about the respective pages and multimedia artifacts). Some data extractions from MediaWiki-based sites are enabled through a third-party data exporter integrated with NodeXL.

On Wikipedia

The English Wikipedia, a crowd-sourced online encyclopedia, has 5 million articles and "averages 750 new articles per day" ("Wikipedia:Statistics," Aug. 21, 2015). There are other stand-alone Wikipedias in 291 languages, according to the Wikimedia Foundation ("List of Wikipedias," July 26, 2015). An article network on Wikipedia may be extracted at 1 degree, 1.5 degrees, and 2.0 degrees, or the basic direct-ties-based ego neighborhood at 1 degree, the ego neighborhood with transitivity between alters at 1.5 degrees, and inclusion of the alters' ego neighborhoods at 2 degrees.

A one-degree article-article network of the Reddit page on Wikipedia (https://en.wikipedia.org/wiki/Reddit) resulted 217 articles, as may be seen in Figure 24.

The "Reddit" article network at 1.5 degrees expands exponentially, with a large network of 24,035 articles, with 31,161 unique edges. Figure 25 shows the NodeXL data extraction with the labels to each of the vertices and analyses of the nodes in the respective groups in the tabbed worksheets to the left and a graph visualization (using the Fruchterman-Reingold force-based layout algorithm) to the right. The size of the graph was sufficiently large to deter labeling the vertices with the names of the respective articles (which would overlap and be hard to read without a lot of resizing and zooming in and out from the graph visualization).

Figure 24. "Reddit" article network on Wikipedia (1 deg.)

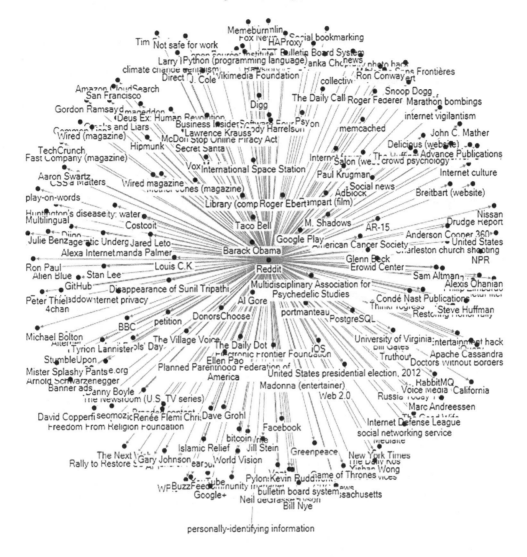

A two-degree extraction was too large and crashed during capture attempts. Each new degree adds exponentially more complexity

This same approach to mapping pages within the English Wikipedia domain also applies to user network. Users are the Wikipedians who often create and edit the various pages. Alongside human users are also approved robots who ensure that the spelling is correct on the site and that U.S. census statistics are accurate, and so on. Robots, which are identified and flagged as such on Wikipedia, also bolster human-made policies on the site, such as by cleaning off spam and heading off malicious posts. Some user accounts on Wikipedia may be cyborg ones, which are both human- and robot- (script).

Figure 26 shows the one-degree 11-vertex network of User:BurritoBazooka on Wikipedia. This indicates a small network of links to some images and some page topics of interest. BurritoBazooka was a member of the Reddit Wikipedia page history. At 1.5 degrees, User:BurritoBazooka had a graph with 2,344 vertices and 2,408 unique edges, and 6 groups, as may be seen in Figure 27. The groups were

Figure 25. "Reddit" article network on Wikipedia (1.5 deg.)

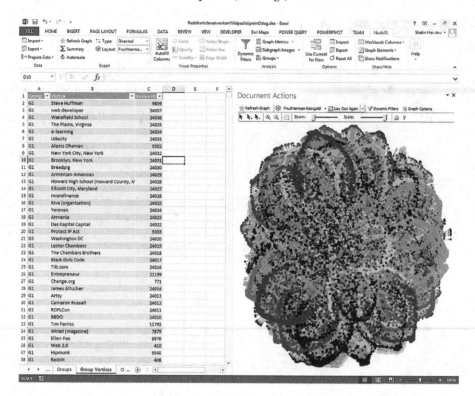

Figure 26. User:BurritoBazooka network on Wikipedia (1 deg.)

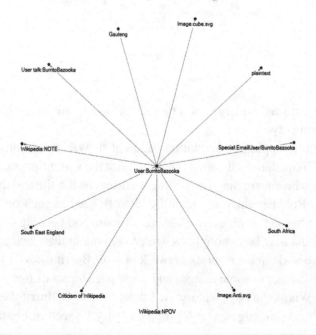

Figure 27. User:BurritoBazooka network on Wikipedia (1.5 deg.)

extracted using the Clauset-Newman-Moore clustering algorithm; the graph layout was created using the Harel-Koren Fast Multiscale layout algorithm and partitions to show the groups with more clarity. To partially alleviate the challenges with overlap, the vertex label sizes were scaled down to show the groups related to User:BurritoBazooka. The electronic versions of the graphs—in color—read better than the print ones.

Image- and Video-Sharing Sites

Some egos and entities also sign on for image- and video-sharing sites. A range of content, trace, and metadata may be extracted from such sites.

Figure 28. "reddit" related tags network on Flickr (1 deg.)

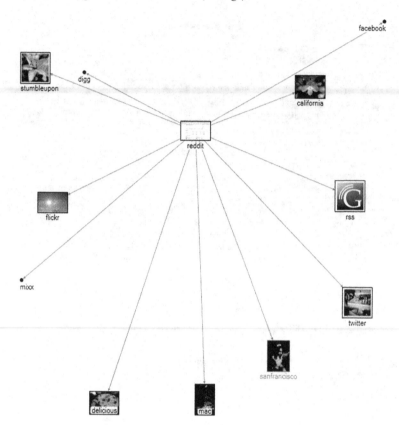

On Flickr

Reddit has a group space on Flickr (https://www.flickr.com/groups/reddit/). Researchers may join the group to access the collection of 12,200 photos, its 1,117 members, and 3 ongoing discussions. The messaging (comments) and imagery may be analyzed through various forms of content analysis. User networks may be mapped on Flickr, to examine both formal follower-following networks and group co-memberships but also more *ad hoc* networks created through replies and co-commenting. Flickr's image tagging may be applied for related tags analysis (based on metadata).

Of special interest here are related tags networks because these offer a way to use folksonomic tagging (metadata) of imagery (and other multimedia) to better understand the seeding term (a tag) and related co-occurring tags in terms of macro-level ties, which may be hidden or invisible otherwise.

A one-degree related tags network, seeded with "reddit," captures 12 vertices with 11 unique edges. The graph in Figure 28 was created using the Girvan-Newman clustering algorithm for smaller graphs (which identified two groups) and laid out using the Harel-Koren Fast Multiscale layout algorithm. Some sample images linked to each vertex is displayed. (Flickr uses recurrent placeholder images for each of the tags, so the same images are pulled every time the tag is pulled.) With related tags networks, the relationships are more diffuse and possibly semantically elusive. One way to think about this is, How do the tags interrelate, and why would they necessarily co-occur around the labeling of images on Flickr?

Figure 29. "reddit" related tags network on Flickr (1.5 deg.)

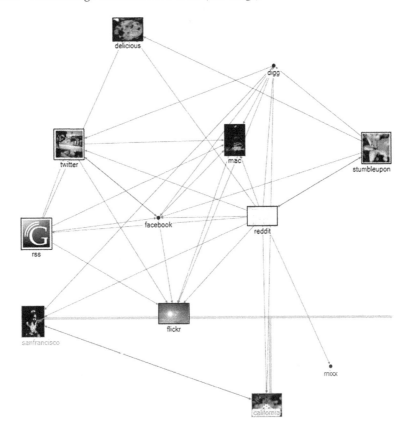

A 1.5 degree related tags network of "reddit" on Flickr captures a graph with 12 vertices and 35 unique edges, in three groups. This graph may be seen in Figure 29. The Girvan-Newman clustering algorithm was used on the data to extracted the three related tags clusters.

The Reddit group's user network was not extractable on Flickr, possibly due to protections issues. So to explore the user network feature on Flickr, one of the more popular contributors to the Reddit photo group on Flickr was selected, a member named "Grotos" (https://www.flickr.com/photos/grotos/). He had 27 followers and 35 following. At the time of the capture, the account had 417 photos shared to the Reddit group on Flickr.

This individual's one-degree user network consisted of 121 vertices and 105 unique edges, as may be seen in Figure 30. There are direct ties to other individuals based on various forms of interrelationships on Flickr's site, based on the contacts of the user and the persons who commented on the user's photos (these two sets may be joined or treated as separate), based on the NodeXL tool used for the data extraction.

The one-degree Grotos user network on Flickr, with available thumbnail images for each vertex, may be seen in Figure 31. This graph was scaled down for increased visibility and lessened overlap.

A subset of the grotos user network on Flickr, one based just on follower-following relationships, identified 36 users (vertices) with 124 edges. Among these users, there were four clusters or groups. These formal contacts of the "grotos" user network (expressed as "screen names") are viewable in Figure 32.

Figure 30. Grotos user network (with commenting networks) from reddit group on Flickr (1 deg.)

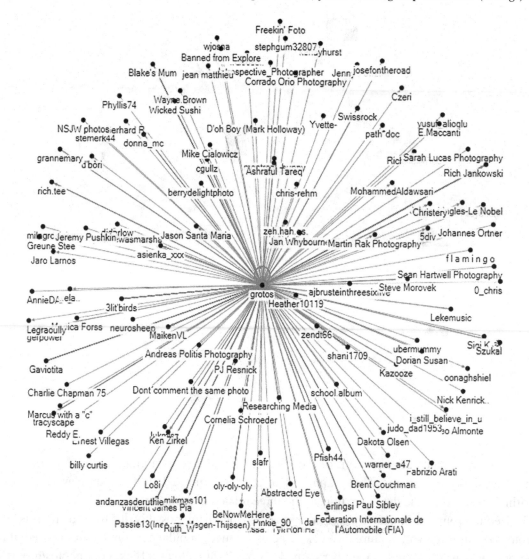

Image-Sharing Sites

Images may be scraped from public websites using a range of command-line tools and web-browser-based add-ins. DownThemAll, an add-in to the Mozilla Firefox web browser (a software program that retrieves web pages from web servers and displays them for users on their computing devices), was used to scrape the following Reddit-account images. Various browser-based downloaders have built-in accelerators for the speed of downloads; some include futures that enable pausing and resuming downloads that are particularly numerous. There are ways to select and categorize various types of scraped information including URLs, text, imagery, and videos.

Figure 31. Grotos user network (with commenting networks) from Reddit group on Flickr with account-related thumbnail imagery (1 deg.)

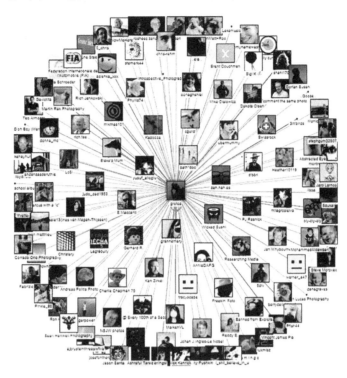

Figure 32. Grotos user network ("contact of the user") from Flickr group on Flickr (1.5 deg.)

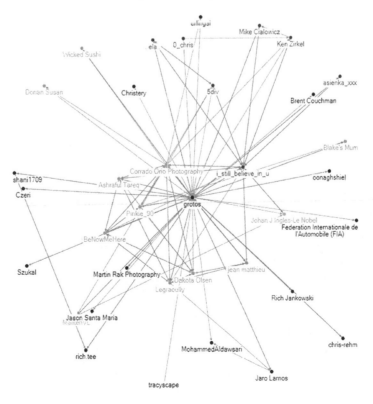

Figure 33. A Screenshot of images scraped from the Reddit account on Instagram

On Instagram

Instagram launched on Oct. 6, 2010. It was acquired by Facebook in April 2012, and user information on Instagram is shared directly with Facebook (Stretton & Aaron, January 2015). It hosts over billions of photographs. On its site, some 300 million people are what the company calls "monthly actives". Over 70 percent of its users are outside the U.S. More than 30 billion photos are shared. Every day, there are 2.5 billion likes on Instagram. There are 70 million average photos uploaded per day. ("Layout Instagram, Press News," 2015). A fifth of Internet users are said to use Instagram (Smith, Aug. 31, 2015).

The @reddit account on Instagram contains 180 posts, 43,200 followers, and 50 following. A data scrape of the page (located at https://instagram.com/reddit/?hl=en) resulted in 130 images. A screenshot of some of the extracted images, with numerical image identifiers used by Instagram, may be seen in Figure 33. In terms of content analysis of imagery, there are often both quantitative and qualitative methods applied. Image content analysis has been used diagnostically—to determine the presence or absence of a particular indicator of health, for example. While content analysis has traditionally been considered an objective and quantitative analysis approach, more recent focuses have been on "interpretive content analysis" and even "latent content analysis"—beyond what is manifestly and denotatively observed (Ahuvia, 2001).

A simple grounded theory image analysis approach involves placing the collected imagery into various categories and then coding them based on emergent themes. This approach enables the application of human insight for semantic (meaning-based) content analysis of digital imagery and enables potential extraction of subtle and hidden messaging. Various analytical frameworks may be applied instead of a wholly emergent grounded theory approach. In fields that are more developed in this area, the image analysis may draw on a theory or even multiple theories.

At the ego or individual level, shared imagery may be analyzed at the ego level as indicators of psychological features like personality, intelligence, cognition, and emotions; objectives; education; character; culture and social norms; skills; background, and resources. For example, researchers have explored Facebook profile pictures for insights about college student identity construction (Hum, Chamberlin, Hambright, Portwood, Schat, & Bevan, 2011). How males 18 – 40 edited their images on posted photos on social networking sites and shared selfies were linked to various character traits: "Self-objectification and narcissism predicted time spent on SNSs. Narcissism and psychopathy predicted the number of selfies posted, whereas narcissism and self-objectification predicted editing photographs of oneself posted on SNSs" (Fox & Rooney, 2015, p. 161). Selfie photos—of the self, of the self with romantic partners, and of the self with a group—were linked to narcissism in men but not with women (Sorokowski, Sorokowska, Oleszkiewicz, Frackowiak, Huk, & Pisanski, 2015).

At the entity or group level, shared imagery or image streams may be analyzed for objectives, strategies, group capabilities, group membership, and other features. Particular types of groups—for example, special interest political groups—may have unique image features typical of those shared by such groups; in that context, a particular political SIG may be analyzed in a more granular, refined, and specific way.

Analysts may examine images as data representations, as expressions of self and of culture, as parts of narratives, and so on. How images are understood may be based on ingrained cultural understandings and professional training. There may be coding based on the extraction of particular features or feature sets.

For example, it may be of interest to see how Snoo, the Reddit alien, is depicted and in what scenarios. It may be of interest to see how Redditors depict themselves in imagery. The image-linked geographical features and geolocational information may be informative, and EXIF metadata may be extracted for details about technologies used in the image capture, dates and times, and spatial and lighting information. If there is a hot trending issue with an image dimension, maybe it is helpful to code for expressed opinions and emotions in the imagery. Visual semantics and aesthetics (style issues) may be translated into textual terms, and those metadata labels or tags may be further analyzed as related tags networks.

Machine vision may be applied for object identification and facial recognition. Of late, there are also a number of computer algorithms applied for editing and analysis of visual contents—with machine learning based on (human-) supervised, semi-supervised, and fully automated means. For example, machine-based analysis of a big data set of images for a social media platform could capture summary data based on object identification, human faces, and general depictions.

Approaches to content analysis of imagery differs depending on the research domain, the research interests, the research tools, the researchers, and the available images. If structured correctly, content analysis may enable rich insights and theorizing.

Video-Sharing Sites

Video sharing sites also provide fodder for the profiling of egos and entities. One way to explore such sites is to view the video and examine the commenting linked to each one.

On YouTube

The YouTube API enabled the extraction of video networks and user networks through NodeXL, but at the time of this writing, the third-party data importer had been non-functioning for almost half a year. The Reddit page on YouTube is at https://www.youtube.com/user/reddit. At the top level were videos for the popular "Explain Like I'm Five" series. One useful insight here is that the tools and platforms are in dynamic interaction, and data extraction and data analysis capabilities are in a state of constant change. This means that what was available before may not be the next day, and unfunded software tools may have brief periods of access.

World Wide Web (WWW) and Internet

Several of the prior graphs showed "http networks" from the World Wide Web and the Internet. Hyperlinks, indicating webpage interlinkage, are considered "external marker(s) of source influence" (Meraz, 2009, p. 683). While the Web and Internet are the spaces where social media platforms actually reside, it is important to observe that there is still a lot of exploitable knowledge on the Web and Net. (Technically, the Web resides on the Internet.) In this conceptualization, a web page is also part of online human sociality because the information on web pages brings together people and enhances some types of intercommunications, cooperation, coordination, and collaboration. As with the other sections, there may be extracted messaging and shared multimedia contents, trace data, and metadata.

On the World Wide Web (WWW) and Internet

Researchers are able to map the technological understructure used to create the main Reddit website presence on the WWW and Internet. One example is a Level 1, 2 or 3 footprinting of the https://www.reddit.com/ site, using the penetration testing tool Maltego Chlorine. This footprinting collects a wide variety of information about a website's understructure, its linked domains, its IP addresses, its netblocks, its built-with technologies, and other data. A "Company Stalker" machine links a URL to a number of names of people and email addresses, ostensibly to enable social engineering (a form of deception used to compromise sensitive information and enable unauthorized access to an organization or company's valuables). Additional "transforms" enable de-aliasing names to personally identifiable information (with varying degrees of effectiveness), the capturing of images and documents related to a website, identifying geolocational information related to online data, mapping the electronic entities (of an Internet domain) in a physical location, and other types of affordances. There are ways to tap into social media sites, such as capturing Tweets and then linking those back to an identity, location, website, and other social media accounts, across the Web and Internet.

Figure 34 shows the use of Maltego Chlorine to link the www.reddit.com URL to network and domain information, which are transformed also to locations, individuals, and individual information.

Metadata may be observed for the respective captured nodes and contents. This may be seen in Figure 35.

Figure 34. www.reddit.com URL to network and domain information (with additional transforms)

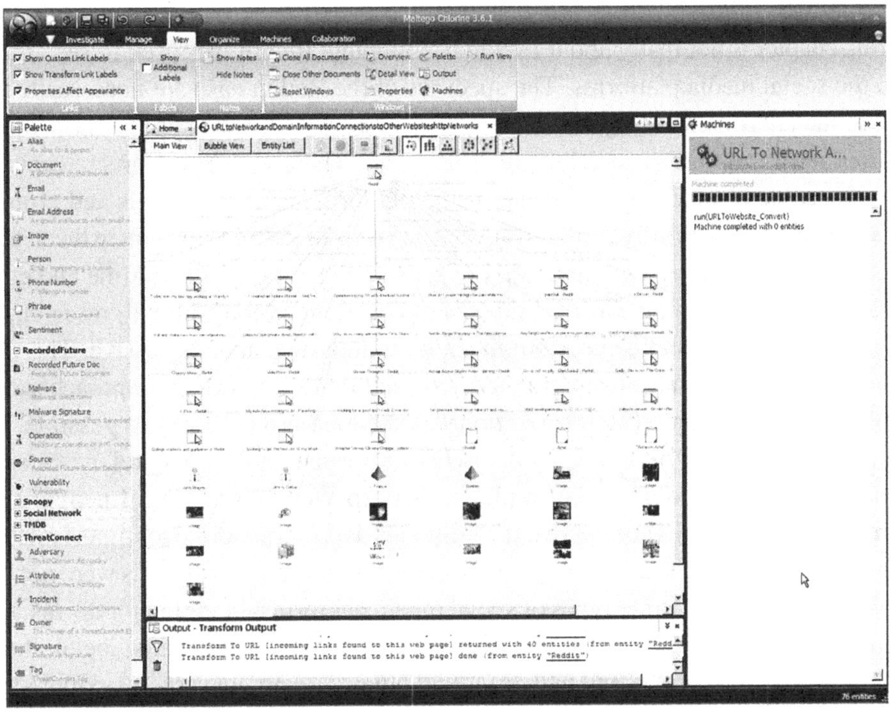

Figure 35. Expanded window for an image node in the "Reddit" URL to network and domain search (with transforms)

DISCUSSION

To be clear, this chapter is not really about Reddit even though Reddit was used to seed the various explorations on the social media platforms. The specifics of the Reddit case are necessarily vague in this context because the analysis was only conducted to serve as an exemplar case to show the profiling of egos and entities across a range of social media "channels". There were no efforts to capture and apply a wide range of seeding terms to extract social media platform data. Individuals and groups (egos and entities) within Reddit were not fully explored at various levels of granularity. Given the need for focused attention, this is pick-and-shovel work and fairly expensive in terms of human time and effort. The approach towards Reddit was not in the form of adversarial or "oppo" (oppositional) research, which seeks to find "dirt" about the target and is therefore much more thorough and aggressive. The wide range of data visualizations that could have been graphed were not done so; such an approach would enable a wider range of analyses. Text-based summarization was not done as thoroughly as possible. The captured data was not compared against other known datasets of information for cross-reference and additional learning. (One example may be the use of pipl.com, a deep Web search tool of people's names to all public government documents.) There were not continuous data extractions over time, and there were not iterated captures of data. While the main target was accessed, the peripheral leads were not pursued with any tenacity. A large number of other types of social media platforms—tagging platforms, pinning sites, massive gaming sites, immersive virtual worlds, fund-raising platforms, dedicated social sites (such as job search and dating sites), intranets, email networks, and others—were not actually explored because of a lack of middleware tools to easily capture data for analysis or a general lack of access (such to protected information). Proprietary systems in a number of countries were not explored, again, due to challenges with access. In this context, a light approach was applied to meet the objectives of this chapter. In other words, an actual and thorough profiling of egos and entities across social media platforms would entail the capture of even more information with more data capture and more in-depth analyses.

What makes this work innovative is that it combines a number of tools to extract information about an entity across various social media platforms and the WWW and Internet in order to create a deeper composite understanding of the distributed organization. The intuition here is that egos and entities manifest in different ways on different social media platforms, and this knowledge may provide insights on different facets of identity and membership (and they extend the sense of boundaries of belongingness).

Some of the more useful takeaways exist outside of the particular case. It may be helpful to conceptualize data in the three main types:

1. Messaging and shared contents,
2. Trace data, and
3. Metadata (in Table 1 "Types of Extractable Information about Egos and Entities across Social Media Platforms and the Web and Internet").

It may help to conceptualize a fourth type of data:

4. Coding data, which is added by researchers based on their knowledge and skills.

The research, social media data extraction, data analytics, and data visualization methods and technologies described may be valuable.

Astute readers may extrapolate the chaining of data from across social media platforms to seed further data extractions and to create additional research strategies and tactics. Such approaches are very amenable to finding other leads. For example, individual nodes with high centrality in a network may be targeted for profiling; bridging nodes may also be profiled because of their critical roles in connecting disparate networks. Clusters or groups of special interest may be probed for members, content, and interaction dynamics. Images and documents of interest captured during data scraping may be probed for contents, creators, geolocational information, and other data.

The data extraction sequences may be activated using macros on the respective tools, which means this work is repeatable. Some data extractions may be set up to run continuously. Computers may be brought in to enhance the analysis of data. There are software programs that enable sophisticated data mining (from text, quantitative, survey, and other data). For example, computational methods have been applied to classify the participants on Reddit based on their text-based public messaging, and gender and citizenship have been able to be extracted with fairly high levels of accuracy (Fabian, Baumann, & Keil, 2015). In most cases, while technologies may be used to extract and possibly organize and probe information, there is a need for human eyes to assess and analyze—at some points in the process.

FUTURE RESEARCH DIRECTIONS

One future direction in research may be about ways to ask (and answer) specific questions about egos and entities across social media platforms, in particular domains or contexts. For example, researchers have long asked: Where is this ego or entity on a continuum running from benevolent to malicious? A continuum from safe to dangerous? A continuum from honest to deceptive? Is the ego or entity fully human, 'bot, or cyborg, or some mix? Is there a "hidden hand" at play among agents on social media, and if so, what are their objectives? Such profiling may complement what is knowable based on more traditional lines of research.

CONCLUSION

This chapter provides an overview of some of the types of information that may be practically extracted from social media platforms and the WWW and Internet given widely available tools and popular methods available today. This remote profiling approach based on social media information was constructed around three types of data:

1. Messaging and shared contents,
2. Trace data, and
3. Metadata.

The software tools used (NodeXL, Maltego Chlorine, NCapture of NVivo, and others) are widely available ones, and the social media platforms tapped (Twitter, Facebook, Wikipedia, Flickr, Instagram, and YouTube) have wide usage and broad name recognition. The focus was on what is generally knowable, without an actual focus on specific types of applied questions that may interest researchers. The environment is highly dynamic, with changes to the functionalities of software tools, social media platforms, people's behaviors on social media, and so forth—resulting in grounds for new research.

ACKNOWLEDGMENT

I am grateful to the anonymous reviewer(s) who provided feedback on this chapter.

REFERENCES

Ahuvia, A. (2001). Traditional, interpretive, and reception based content analyses: Improving the ability of content analysis to address issues of pragmatic and theoretical concern. *Social Indicators Research*, *54*(2), 139–172. doi:10.1023/A:1011087813505

Arnaboldi, V., Conti, M., Passarella, A., & Dunbar, R. (2013). Dynamics of personal social relationships in online social networks: A study on Twitter. In *Proceedings of COSN '13*. doi:10.1145/2512938.2512949

Atig, M. F., Cassel, S., Kaati, L., & Shrestha, A. (2014). Activity profiles in online social media. In *Proceedings of the 2014 IEEE/ACM International Conference on Advances in Social Networks Analysis and Mining* (ASONAM 2014). doi:10.1109/ASONAM.2014.6921685

Bagozzi, R. P., & Dholakia, U. M. (2002). Intentional social action in virtual communities. *Journal of Interactive Marketing*, *16*(2), 2–21. doi:10.1002/dir.10006

Balani, S., & De Choudhury, M. (2015). Detecting and characterizing mental health related self-disclosure in social media. In *Proceedings of CHI 2015, Crossings*. doi:10.1145/2702613.2732733

Bazarova, N. N., Choi, Y. H., Sosik, V. S., Cosley, D., & Whilock, J. (2015). Social sharing of emotions on Facebook: Channel differences, satisfaction, and replies. In *Proceedings of CSCW*.

Benson, V., Saridakis, G., Tennakoon, H., & Ezingeard, J. N. (2015). The role of security notices and online consumer behaviour: An empirical study of social networking users. *International Journal of Human-Computer Studies*, *80*, 36–44.

Bergstrom, K. (2011). 'Don't feed the troll': Shutting down debate about community expectations on Reddit.com. *First Monday*, 1–16. Retrieved from http://firstmonday.org/ojs/index.php/fm/article/view/3498/3029

Boger, T., & Wernersen, R. (2014). How 'social' are social news sites? Exploring the motivation for using red.com. In iConference 2014 Proceedings. doi:10.9776/14108

Buntain, C., & Golbeck, J. (2014). Identifying social roles in reddit using network structure. In *Proceedings of the International World Wide Web Conference Committee* (IW3C2). doi:10.1145/2567948.2579231

Burke, J., & Wagner, B. (2015). RedNet, a different perspective of Reddit. In *5th IEEE Integrated STEM Conference*. doi:10.1109/ISECon.2015.7119910

Carmagnola, F., Osborne, F., & Torre, I. (2010). User data distributed on the social web: How to identify users on different social systems and collecting data about them. In Proceedings of HetRec '10.

Coscia, M., Rossetti, G., Giannotti, F., & Pedreschi, D. (2014). Uncovering hierarchical and overlapping communities with a local-first approach. *ACM Transactions on Knowledge Discovery from Data, 9*(1), 6:1 – 6:27.

Creese, S., Goldsmith, M., Nurse, J. R. C., & Phillips, E. (2012). A data-reachability model for elucidating privacy and security risks related to the use of online social networks. In *Proceedings of 2012 IEEE 11th International Conference on Trust, Security and Privacy in Computing and Communications.* doi:10.1109/TrustCom.2012.22

Das, S., & Lavoie, A. (2014). The effects of feedback on human behavior in social media: An inverse reinforcement learning model. In *Proceedings of the 13th International Conference on Autonomous Agents and Multiagent Systems* (AAMAS 2014).

Dennen, V. P. (2009). *Constructing academic alter-egos: Identity issues in a blog-based community. In Identity in the Information Society (IDIS).* Springer; doi:10.1007/s12394-009-0020-8

Duggan, M., & Smith, A. (2013). *6% of online adults are reddit users.* Pew Research Center. Retrieved from http://www.pewinternet.org/2013/07/03/6-of-online-adults-are-reddit-users/

Escobar, M. L., Kommers, P. A. M., & Beldad, A. (2014). Using narratives as tools for channeling participation in online communities. *Computers in Human Behavior, 37,* 64–72. doi:10.1016/j.chb.2014.04.013

Fabian, B., Baumann, A., & Keil, M. (2015). Privacy on Reddit? Towards large-scale user classification. Association for Information Systems Electronic Library. *ECIS 2015 Proceedings.* Retrieved August 2, 2015, from http://aisel.aisnet.org/ecis2015_cr/43

Fox, J., & Rooney, M. C. (2015). The Dark Triad and trait self-objectification as predictors of men's use and self-presentation behaviors on social networking sites. *Personality and Individual Differences, 76,* 161–165. doi:10.1016/j.paid.2014.12.017

Gagnon, T. (2013). The disinhibition of Reddit users. *Stylus Knights Write Showcase,* 49 – 55.

Geiger, R. S. (2013). Are computers merely 'supporting' cooperative work? Towards an ethnography of bot development. In *Proceedings of CSCW '13 Companion.*

Gilbert, E. (2013). Widespread underprovision on Reddit. In *Proceedings of CSCW '13.* doi:10.1145/2441776.2441866

Graham, J. (2015, July 11). Can Reddit be tamed? Probably not. *USA Today.*

Griffin, C., Mercer, D., Fan, J., & Squicciarini, A. (2012). Two species evolutionary game model of user and moderator dynamics. In *Proceedings of the 2012 International Conference on Social Informatics.* doi:10.1109/SocialInformatics.2012.95

Hai-Jew, S. (2015, Nov. 12). Profiling an entity across multiple social media platforms. *C2C Digital Magazine.* Retrieved Nov. 18, 2015, from http://scalar.usc.edu/works/c2c-digital-magazine-fall-winter-2016/profiling-an-entity-across-multiple-social-media-platforms

Haralabopoulos, G., Anagnostopoulos, I., & Zeadally, S. (2015). Lifespan and propagation of information in on-line social networks: A case study based on Reddit. *Journal of Network and Computer Applications,* 88 – 100.10.1016/j.jnca.2015.06.006

Hempel, J. (2015, Oct. 6). Inside Reddit's plan to recover from its epic meltdown. *Wired Magazine.*

Hum, N. J., Chamberlin, P. E., Hambright, B. L., Portwood, A. C., Schat, A. C., & Bevan, J. L. (2011). A picture is worth a thousand words: A content analysis of Facebook profile photographs. *Computers in Human Behavior, 27*(5), 1828–1833. doi:10.1016/j.chb.2011.04.003

Jain, P., Rodrigues, T., Magno, G., Kumaraguru, P., & Almeida, V. (2011). Cross-pollination of information in online social media: A case study on popular social networks. In *Proceedings of the 2011 IEEE International Conference on Privacy, Security, Risk, and Trust, and IEEE International Conference on Social Computing.* IEEE Computer Society.

Johansson, F., Kaati, L., & Shrestha, A. (2013). Detecting multiple aliases in social media. In *Proceedings of the 2013 IEEE/ACM International Conference on Advances in Social Networks Analysis and Mining.* doi:10.1145/2492517.2500261

Kamath, K. Y., & Caverlee, J. (2012). Content-based crowd retrieval on the real-time Web. In *Proceedings of CIKM '12.* doi:10.1145/2396761.2396789

Kim, J., Ko, E.-Y., Jung, J., Lee, C. W., Kim, N. W., & Kim, J. (2015). Factful: Engaging taxpayers in the public discussion of a government budget. In *CHI 2015. Crossings. HCI for Civic Engagement.*

Kivran-Swaine, F., Govindan, P., & Naaman, M. (2011). The impact of network structure on breaking ties in online social networks: Unfollowing on Twitter. In *Proceedings of CHI 2011.*

Krishnamurthy, B. (2013, May-June). Privacy and online social networks: Can colorless green ideas sleep furiously? *IEEE Computer and Reliability Societies,* 14 – 20.

Kumar, N., & Benbasat, I. (2002). Para-social presence: A re-conceptualization of 'social presence' to capture the relationship between a web site and her visitors. In *Proceedings of the 35th Hawaii International Conference on System Sciences.*

Layout Instagram, Press News. (2015). *Instagram.* Retrieved August 30, 2015, from https://instagram.com/press/

Leavitt, A. (2015). 'This is a throwaway account': Temporary technical identities and perceptions of anonymity in a massive online community. In *Proceedings of CSCW 2015.*

List of Wikipedias. (2015, July 26). *Wikimedia.* Retrieved Aug. 30, 2015, from https://meta.wikimedia.org/wiki/List_of_Wikipedias

Luchman, J. N., Bergstrom, J., & Krulikowski, C. (2014). A motives framework of social media website use: A survey of young Americans. *Computers in Human Behavior, 38,* 136–141. doi:10.1016/j.chb.2014.05.016

Mayande, N., & Weber, C. (2012). *Directed interaction networks and their impact on social media. In Proceedings of PICMET '13.* San Jose, CA: Slideshow.

McDermid, V. (2014). *Forensics: What Bugs, Burns, Prints, DNA, and More Tell Us about Crime.* New York: Grove Press.

Meraz, S. (2009). Is there an elite hold? Traditional media to social media agenda setting influence in blog networks. *Journal of Computer-Mediated Communication, 14*(3), 682–707. doi:10.1111/j.1083-6101.2009.01458.x

Moniz, K., & Yuan, Y. (2015). Reaching critical mass: The effect of adding new content on website visitors and user registration. In the proceedings of ISCTCS 2014. *CCIS, 520,* 359–369.

Mori, J., Gibbs, M., Arnold, M., Nansen, B., & Kohn, T. (2012). Design considerations for after death: Comparing the affordances of three online platforms. In *Proceedings of OZCHI '12.*

Number of monthly active Facebook users worldwide as of 2nd quarter 2015 (in millions). (2015). Statista, the Statistics Portal. Retrieved August 30, 2015, from http://www.statista.com/statistics/264810/number-of-monthly-active-facebook-users-worldwide/

Pavalanathan, U., & De Choudhury, M. (2015). Identity management and mental health discourse in social media. In *Proceedings of WWW 2015 Companion.* doi:10.1145/2740908.2743049

Peled, O., Fire, M., Rokach, L., & Elovici, Y. (2013). Entity matching in online social networks. In *Proceedings of SocialCom/PASSAT/BigData/Econcom/BioMedCom 2013.* IEEE. DOI 10.1109/Social-Com.2013.53

Potts, L., & Harrison, A. (2013). Interfaces as rhetorical constructions: reddit and 4chan during the Boston Marathon bombings. In *Proceedings of SIGDOC '13.*

r/bitcoin. (2015). *Reddit.* Retrieved Aug. 28, 2015, from https://www.reddit.com/r/Bitcoin/comments/zqocl/exchange_your_karma_for_bitcoin_reddit_bitcoin

Reddit. (2015, Aug. 18). *Wikipedia.* Retrieved Aug. 22, 2015, from https://en.wikipedia.org/wiki/Reddit

Reddit content policy. (2015). *Reddit.* Retrieved Aug. 28, 2015, from https://www.reddit.com/help/contentpolicy

Richterich, A. (2014, Jan.). 'Karma, precious karma!' Karmawhoring on Reddit and the Front Page's Econometrisation. *Journal of Peer Production, (4),* 1 – 12.

Shelton, M., Lo, K., & Nardi, B. (2015). Online Media Forums as Separate Social Lives: A Qualitative Study of Disclosure within and beyond Reddit. In iConference 2015 Proceedings.

Singer, P., Flöck, F., Meinhart, C., Zeitfogel, E., & Strohmaier, M. (2014). Evolution of Reddit: From the front page of the Internet to a self-referential community? In *Proceedings of the WWW '14 Companion.*

Smith, A. W. (2014). Porn architecture: User tagging and filtering in two online pornography communities. *Communication Design Quarterly, 3*(1), 17–22. doi:10.1145/2721882.2721885

Smith, C. (2015, Aug. 31). *By the numbers: 150+ interesting Instagram statistics (August 2015)*. DMR. Digital Marketing Stats / Strategy / Gadgets. Retrieved August 31, 2015, from http://expandedramblings. com/index.php/important-instagram-stats/

Sohn, D. (2013). Coping with information in social media: The effects of network structure and knowledge on perception of information value. Computers in Human Behavior, 145 – 151.

Sorokowski, P., Sorokowska, A., Oleszkiewicz, A., Frackowiak, T., Huk, A., & Pisanski, K. (2015). Selfie posting behaviors are associated with narcissism among men. *Personality and Individual Differences, 85*, 123–127. doi:10.1016/j.paid.2015.05.004

Stretton, T., & Aaron, L. (2015, January). The dangers in our trail of digital breadcrumbs. *Computer Fraud & Security, 2015*(1), 13–14. doi:10.1016/S1361-3723(15)70006-0

Traffic statistics for /r/AskReddit. (2015, Aug. 27). *AskReddit*. Retrieved Aug. 27, 2015, from https://www.reddit.com/r/AskReddit/about/traffic

Turkle, S. (1998). Identity in the age of the Internet: Living in the MUD. In *Composing Cyberspace: Identity, Community, and Knowledge in the Electronic Age* (pp. 5–11). Boston: McGraw Hill.

Vella, M. (2015, July 20). Reddit reboots. *Time Magazine*, 46 – 50.

Wang, X., Tang, L., Gao, H., & Liu, H. (2010). Discovering overlapping groups in social media. In *Proceedings of 2010 IEEE International Conference in Data Mining*. doi:10.1109/ICDM.2010.48

Weninger, T., Zhu, X. A., & Han, J. (2013). An exploration of discussion threads in social news sites: A case study of the Reddit community. In *Proceedings of the 2013 IEEE/ACM International Conference on Advances in Social Networks Analysis and Mining* (ASONAM '13). doi:10.1145/2492517.2492646

What can a Reddit user do about a Reddit-wide shadowban?. (2015). *Quora*. Retrieved Aug. 28, 2015, from https://www.quora.com/What-can-a-Reddit-user-do-about-a-Reddit-wide-shadowban

Wikipedia: Statistics. (2015, Aug. 21). *Wikipedia*. Retrieved Aug. 30, 2015, from https://en.wikipedia.org/wiki/Wikipedia:Statistics

Yang, C., Lin, K. H.-Y., & Chen, H. H. (2009). Writer meets reader: Emotion analysis of social media from both the writer's and reader's perspectives. In *Proceedings of the 2009 IEEE/WIC/ACM International Conference on Web Intelligence and Intelligent Agent Technology – Workshops*.

Zhu, Y.-Q., & Chen, H.-G. (2015). Social media and human need satisfaction: Implications for social media marketing. *Business Horizons, 58*(3), 335–345. doi:10.1016/j.bushor.2015.01.006

ADDITIONAL READING

Hansen, D., Schneiderman, B., & Smith, M. A. (2011). *Analyzing Social Media Networks with NodeXL: Insights from a Connected World*. Burlington, MA: Elsevier.

KEY TERMS AND DEFINITIONS

Bursty: Occurring in short episodes, indicated by sharp spikes in a linegraph.

Centrality: Measures of influence of a node in a social context (such as with closeness centrality, degree centrality, eigenvector centrality, network centrality, and others).

Data Analytics: The analysis of raw data for valuable information.

Ego: An individual represented as an independent node.

Entity: A group represented as a node or a cluster or a graph.

EULAs (End User License Agreements): A legally binding policy that informs users of a company's policies in relationship to them.

Eventgraphs: Network graphs based on an event (an occurrence with distinct start- and end- times) to capture participants, microblogging and other conversations, multimedia, and other details.

Graph: A node-link diagram that depicts egos and entities in relationship.

Latent: Hidden, invisible, non-obvious.

Node-Link Diagram: A two-dimensional (2D) depiction of nodes (as egos or entities) and links (as edges or ties or relationships), usually visualized as circles and lines.

Open-Source Intelligence (OSINT): Publicly available data and information which may be harnessed for knowability and analysis.

Profile: A description of an individual or group.

Social Media: Various online platforms that enable people to create profiles and to interact with others in various ways.

Social Network Analysis (also "Electronic Social Network Analysis): The exploration of the structure of people's inter-relationships and interactions to understand power dynamics, culture, information sharing, and other factors.

Social Norms: People's shared rules of behavior.

Text Summarization: A computer affordance that reduces data dimensionality by selecting out salient main points.

Chapter 20
Finding Information Faster by Tracing My Colleagues' Trails:
A Reference Algorithm for Enterprise Search

Patrick Winter
University of Marburg, Germany

Michael Schulz
University of Marburg, Germany

Tobias H. Engler
University of Marburg, Germany

ABSTRACT

Knowledge workers are confronted with the challenge of efficient information retrieval in enterprises, which is one of the most important barriers to knowledge reuse. This problem has been intensified in recent years by several organizational developments such as increasing data volume and number of data sources. In this chapter, a reference algorithm for enterprise search is developed that integrates aspects from personalized, social, collaborative, and dynamic search to consider the different natures and requirements of enterprise and web search. Because of the modular structure of the algorithm, it can easily be adapted by enterprises to their specificities by concretization. The components that can be configured during the adaptation process are discussed. Furthermore, the performance of a typical instance of the algorithm is investigated through a laboratory experiment. This instance is found to outperform rather traditional approaches to enterprise search.

INTRODUCTION

The ability of an enterprise to integrate and reuse the sometimes highly specialized knowledge of its employees has been identified as a major chance for gaining competitive advantages (Grant, 1996). Therefore, many enterprises have established internal repositories to support the explication of this

DOI: 10.4018/978-1-5225-0559-4.ch020

knowledge, its storage, its transfer, and, eventually, its reuse (Alavi & Leidner, 2001). However, only few employees utilize the knowledge stored in these repositories (Davenport et al., 2003; Desouza, 2003). In search for an explanation, difficulties in finding suitable documents efficiently have been identified as the major barrier to knowledge reuse (Davenport & Prusak, 2000), leading to high search costs and opportunity costs for enterprises (Feldman & Sherman, 2003). Functionalities for information retrieval within an enterprise (enterprise search) have long been undeveloped and highly inefficient (Hawking, 2004). In addition, recent changes in the organizational environment such as the availability of more data and data sources (McAfee & Brynjolfsson, 2012), the greater number of employees working with data (Hänel & Schulz, 2014), and the democratization of information in the enterprise (Li et al., 2014) further emphasize the need for new enterprise search functionalities that can help to overcome this barrier in addition to alternative approaches (e.g., improved information storage, (Schulz et al., 2015)). This can also be seen by the fact that three out of six constituting technology characteristics of Enterprise 2.0 (search, links, and tags) directly relate to enterprise search (McAfee, 2006).

Early search algorithms have mostly relied on a simple pattern matching between the search query and a document's content. Later, search engines have improved this approach by incorporating the link structure to rank the relevance of web content (Page et al., 1999). In the last years, four streams have emerged that each address one of the disadvantages of this approach: *Personalized* and *social search* taking into account the querying user's personal characteristics and social relationships (resp.) to adjust the ranking of the results, *collaborative search* aiming to exploit the information provided by historic search sessions (by potentially other users), and *dynamic search* considering search sessions which consist of multiple search queries. However, most of the algorithms originating from these streams were designed especially for web search. Attempts have been made to transfer such algorithms to enterprise search, but it soon has been recognized that this is hard to accomplish (O'Leary, 1997) given the different nature of these domains (e.g., the strongly differing numbers of potential users and results, no organic link structure on the intranet, etc. (McAfee, 2006)). The few algorithms that have especially been designed for enterprise search (e.g., Ronen et al., 2009) have two important limitations:

First, while some of them combine more than one of the four search streams described above, the unique chance to do so in the domain of enterprise search is often overlooked. In the environment of an enterprise search engine (ESE), users can easily be identified by their account, so that their activities can be tracked and logged across various systems. This enables a special form of collaborative search: For a search session, it can be predicted using historical information on previous search sessions:

1. Whether it will be successful,
2. Which document the querying user is likely to search for, and
3. How she will refine her search queries (integrating dynamic search).

The available information can be weighted by the strength of her similarity and relationship with the previous querying users (integrating personalized and social search).

Second, many existing enterprise search algorithms were designed specifically for the enterprise in which they are deployed. They often are proprietary and, therefore, kept a secret. Even if their code is disclosed they still cannot simply be deployed in other enterprises if the latter exhibit different characteristics (e.g., use a different file structure). Thus, elaborate transfer processes are necessary to adapt the algorithm.

In this paper, the authors address both limitations by developing a reference algorithm for enterprise search that integrates facets of personalized, social, collaborative, and dynamic search. The algorithm is based on a rather general and modular architecture that allows to control for each of these components separately. Enterprises can adapt the reference algorithm to their specificities easily by concretization. The authors discuss the choices that can be made during this adaption process and describe one sample instance of their algorithm. Furthermore, the authors evaluate this instance using data from a laboratory experiment. The results indicate that their algorithm is better suited to rank search results compared to traditional ESEs.

Summarizing, the algorithm exploits the social network of an employee in order to deliver her the information she requires faster. This is enabled by tracing the trails of her colleagues and other users in her social network who had a similar informational need and found a matching document. The time she saves by jumping directly to this document can be used for other tasks, so that the opportunity costs decrease.

The remainder of this paper is organized as follows: First, the authors briefly review the four major streams of search in the next section. Then, they present their reference enterprise search algorithm and discuss how it can be adapted by enterprises. The authors then evaluate the sample instance by an experiment and summarize the benefits and limitations of their algorithm, where they also give an outlook for possible future research.

BACKGROUND

Besides keyword-based search paradigms that are based on the premise that documents are more relevant if their content or their attributes match the search query to a higher degree, researchers and practitioners have looked for possibilities to improve search algorithms in both web and enterprises. This has led to four major streams that search has evolved into during the last years: personalized search, collaborative search, social search, and dynamic search. The premises derived from these trends should serve as a guideline to build a reference algorithm for enterprise search that combines these approaches.

Personalized Search

The actual goal of any search is to find documents that are relevant to the querying user's current informational need, not to the search query (e.g., Chirita et al., 2004; Shapira & Zabar, 2011). Thus, search algorithms should be based on a relevance concept that incorporates subjective relevance instead of being based on an objective relevance concept (such as mere pattern matching) only. This can easily be seen by the fact that different users searching with the same search query (e.g., "revenue report") might have different informational needs (e.g., the revenue report for their country). Personalization is an approach to alleviate this issue by considering information available on the querying user assuming that this information provides valuable insights on the relevance of documents. In the given example, her physical location could be used to decide which revenue report is most relevant to her. As a consequence, users with similar characteristics can be expected to have similar informational needs.

Social Search

A social search engine enriches the traditional keyword-based approach with information about the querying user's relationships with other users (the social graph) to personalize the search results (Shapira & Zabar, 2011). This approach is based on the assumption that users which are closely connected with each other tend to have similar informational needs. In contrast to personalized search, where the users' personal attributes are crucial to evaluate the similarity between users, social search measures this similarity based on the type and strength of connections within the users' social network (Watts et al., 2002). Note that in the context of enterprise search, personalized and social search are strongly linked because employees with similar characteristics (e.g., the same location) are often also socially connected (e.g., being colleagues).

Collaborative Search

Search engines are used by more than one person. This soon led to the idea of collaboration, that is, the hypothesis that the querying user can benefit from the experience of users who have searched earlier. This can happen either explicitly or implicitly (Papagelis & Zaroliagis, 2007).

Users can explicitly annotate documents they have found (e.g., with ratings, comments, or tags, (Bao et al., 2007)). This information can then be incorporated into a search algorithm to re-rank the results in accordance with other users' explicit feedback (Shapira & Zabar, 2011). The assumption behind this idea is that documents with good ratings are more relevant to the querying user than poorly rated documents because good ratings indicate a high quality.

Implicit collaboration takes place when search histories and logs of other users are utilized to identify similar search patterns among similar users. A search algorithm that takes implicit collaboration into account assumes that users searching with the same search query often have the same informational need. At its simplest, each document's relevance estimate can be adjusted by the number of searches starting with the querying user's search query and ending with the document.

Dynamic Search

Early search algorithms have assumed the search process of a user to be static, that is, starting with a user entering a search query and ending with her selecting one of the documents returned by the algorithm in response to this query. In the last decade, it has been recognized that search processes are rather dynamic, with users refining their initial search query until they are satisfied with the ranking of the results (e.g., Rich & Xie, 2006). In particular, prior research has argued that users start with a rather short search query consisting of only a few keywords and extend it step by step if necessary (Aula et al., 2010). The assumption behind the combination of collaborative and dynamic search is that users prefer search paths that have already been used by other users.

REFERENCE ALGORITHM

The authors next present a reference enterprise search algorithm that enterprises can adapt to their individual specificities (e.g., their organizational structure) by concretization. An exemplary instance is given and evaluated using data from a laboratory experiment later on.

General Approach

The development of the algorithm begins with some general considerations. Each time a user u with an informational need in (e.g., the revenue for Germany in 2014) enters a search query q (e.g., "revenue") into an ESE, the goal of its underlying algorithm is to rank all available documents by their estimated relevance (and possibly to discard documents with an estimated relevance below some critical value). "Relevance" here often is interpreted as "relevance to q"; however, one should more precisely speak of "relevance to the ESE's estimate $\widehat{in}$ of in". While $\widehat{in}$ is usually based on q, additional factors may be included in its calculation. In particular, personalized search, that is the incorporation of data describing u, has been found to improve the precision of $\widehat{in}$ (e.g., Qiu & Cho, 2006).

The precision of $\widehat{in}$ is also affected by its specificity, which in turn is largely determined by the specificity of q. This implies a trade-off: If q is chosen too unspecific, $\widehat{in}$ is less specific than in. Thus, documents that are not relevant to in may falsely be considered relevant and, therefore, rank high. If q is chosen too specific, on the other hand, $\widehat{in}$ is more specific than in. Documents being relevant to in may falsely be considered not relevant and rank low or even get discarded. Furthermore, the number of words u has to enter (and hence, her work) tends to increase with the specificity of q. Users for these reasons usually employ several queries during one search session. More precisely, they often begin a session with a rather unspecific query q_0, which they then refine in several rounds $t = 1, 2, \ldots$ to more specific queries q_t (Aula et al., 2010). This process continues until they either find a document fulfilling in through the ranking displayed by the ESE or decide to cancel the session.

The state s_t of a user's session in round t is completely determined by the query history $\mathbf{q}_t = \left(q_0, \ldots, q_t \right)$ up to this round. However, it is often reasonable to use a *query history transformation function* state to map $\mathbf{q}_t$ to s_t; that is, to set $s_t = \text{state}\left(\mathbf{q}_t \right)$. While state can always simply be chosen as $\text{state}\left(\mathbf{q}_t \right) = \mathbf{q}_t$, enterprises should benefit from choosing a more elaborated transformation function on the basis of their individual characteristics. This choice will be discussed later on. After the last query refinement round T, the final state s_{T+1} of the session can be indicated by the resulting document if the search ended successfully and by a special state for cancelled searches otherwise.

A single finished session can be visualized as a graph containing its states as nodes and its state transitions as edges (Figure 1). Different node types can be used to distinguish the states s_t for $t = 0, \ldots, T$ (query nodes, drawn elliptical) from s_{T+1} (either a document node, drawn rectangular, or the cancel node, drawn rhombic). By construction, query nodes always have at least one outgoing edge, while document nodes and the cancel node can only have ingoing edges.

The behavior of u (which queries she employs during one session, which document she finally opens, and when she decides to cancel the search) depends on in. E.g., if u begins the search session with the query "revenue", she is more likely to refine this query to "revenue Germany" than to "revenue France"

Figure 1. Graph visualizing a single search session

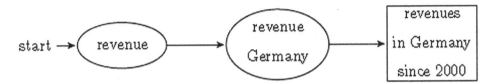

if her informational need is the revenue for Germany. Formally, this corresponds to the probability $P_u(x \rightarrow y)$ for a transition from a state x to a state y of u's search session depending on in; that is, $P_u(x \rightarrow y \mid in) \neq P_u(x \rightarrow y)$. As can easily be shown using Bayes' theorem, a direct consequence of this assumption is $P(in \mid x \rightarrow y) \neq P(in)$; that is, the knowledge about u using the edge from x to y changes the probability distribution $P(in)$ of in. This, in turn, leads to the fact that the queries u has employed up to round t of her search session provide information on in. However, by construction, this information is completely contained in $\mathbf{q}_t$ and, thus, for appropriate query history transformation functions $state$, also in the current state s_t (Markov property).

$P(in)$ can differ between users; that is, $P(in)$ has to be replaced by a user-specific probability distribution $P_u(in)$. E.g., an employee of a German subsidiary is usually more likely to search for the revenue for Germany than for the revenue for France. This example demonstrates that it often makes sense to let $P(in)$ differ only between groups of users than between all users. The proposed algorithm is valid for both approaches (since it allows for defining groups that consist of a single user). To which group g_u a user u belongs is determined by her characteristics $\mathbf{x}_u$ (e.g., her position in the organizational hierarchy and her country) through a *group assignment function* group ($g_u - \text{group}(\mathbf{x}_u)$). By incorporating $\mathbf{x}_u$ this way, the algorithm becomes personalized. For the integration of social search, the authors define a *group proximity function* prox that reflects the social proximity between u and the members of other groups. E.g., the proximity of the manager of a German subsidiary to the group of her employees may be higher than to the group of employees of a French subsidiary. For the reference algorithm, prox assigns to the combination of $\mathbf{x}_u$ and a group g a propensity score from the interval $[0;1]$ with $\text{prox}(\mathbf{x}_u, g) = 1$ if and only if $g = \text{group}(\mathbf{x}_u) = g_u$. Appropriate choices of group and prox are discussed later on.

An important consequence of the behavior of u depending on in and the probability distribution of in depending on u's group proximities is that the latter can be used to forecast u's behavior. E.g., when u has searched for "revenue" and belongs to a group of employees of a German subsidiary, she is more likely to search for "revenue Germany" next than for "revenue France". Thus, the ESE should rank documents higher that relate to "revenue Germany" when u has searched for "revenue". This is the essential idea on which the proposed reference algorithm is based. Formally,

$$P_u(x \Rightarrow y) = \begin{cases} 1 & \text{if } y = x \\ \sum_z P_u(x \rightarrow z) \cdot P_u(z \Rightarrow y) & \text{otherwise} \end{cases} \tag{1}$$

with z indexing all states that can be reached from x in one step. $P_u\left(x \Rightarrow y\right)$ is the probability that a search session that is in a state x will eventually reach a state y (after any number of further rounds). $P_u\left(x \Rightarrow y\right)$ accounts for the fact that some potential states (e.g., the document nodes and the cancel node) can be reached via several ways. In the given example, u may refine her initial query to "revenue 2014" instead of "revenue Germany". Nevertheless, she may eventually reach the same document (e.g., "revenues in Germany since 2000"), so that both ways have to be considered to calculate the relevance of this document when u has entered "revenue". Note that $P_u\left(x \Rightarrow y\right) = 0$ for all y if x is a document node or the cancel node, as these nodes end the search session. Besides, the authors set $P_u\left(x \Rightarrow x\right) = 1$ because in state x, state x already has been reached. Now the central assumption can be formalized as

$$\pi\left(\widehat{in_t}\right) = \left(P_u\left(s_t \Rightarrow y\right), y \in TC\left(s_t\right)\right)' \tag{2}$$

with $TC\left(s_t\right)$ characterizing the transitive closure of s_t (that is, all states that can be reached from s_t). (2) means that the vector of the probabilities with which a search session of a user u will reach the accessible states given its current state s_t reflects an estimate $\widehat{in_t}$ of u's informational need in through a representation π. In other words, this vector provides information on how much each state that is accessible from s_t fits in. $\pi\left(\widehat{in_t}\right)$ can be used to calculate the relevancies of the available documents to in and, hence, to rank them.

The definition of the total relevance TR_d of a document d contains three factors, which are discussed next. First, the subjective relevance SR_d is considered, which the authors operationalize as

$$SR_d = \frac{1}{\lambda} \cdot \pi\left(\widehat{in_t}\right) * \left(P_u\left(y \Rightarrow d\right), y \in TC\left(s_t\right)\right), \tag{3}$$

where * symbolizes the scalar product and $\lambda = \pi\left(\widehat{in_t}\right) * 1$ is a normalization constant. SR_d combines the information on how much each state y fits in with the information on how probable it is that u will eventually open d given that her search session has reached y. Since the latter is subjective to (the group proximities of) u, d's objective relevance OR_d has also be taken into account. For this purpose, the authors define a function $\text{match}\left(y, d\right)$ as $\text{match}\left(y, d\right) = \text{query\_match}\left(y, d\right)$ if y is a query state, $\text{match}\left(y, d\right) = \text{doc\_match}\left(y, d\right)$ if y is a document state, and $\text{match}\left(y, d\right) = 0$ if y is the cancel state. query_match and doc_match are *query and document matching functions* that express the degree of match between y and d for query and document states y (resp.) through a value from the interval $\left[0; 1\right]$. OR_d is then operationalized similarly to SR_d as

$$OR_d = \frac{1}{\lambda} \cdot \pi\left(\widehat{in_t}\right) * \left(\text{match}\left(y, d\right), y \in TC\left(s_t\right)\right). \tag{4}$$

It combines the information on how much each state y fits in with the degree of match between y and d. The third component the authors utilize is the quality Q_d of d that is determined on a scale from 0 to 1 through a *quality evaluation function* qual by d's characteristics $\mathbf{z}_d$; that is, $Q_d = \text{qual}\left(\mathbf{z}_d\right)$. Since $\mathbf{z}_d$ can include characteristics attributed to d by other users (e.g., a star rating), its incorporation represents a form of explicit collaborative search. Finally, a vector $\mathcal{TR}$ is calculated from the vectors $\mathcal{SR} = \left(\mathcal{SR}_d, \forall d\right)'$, $\mathcal{OR} = \left(\mathcal{OR}_d, \forall d\right)'$, and $\mathcal{Q} = \left(\mathcal{Q}_d, \forall d\right)'$ through a vector-valued *scoring function* score. The total relevance $\mathcal{TR}_d$ of d is then given by the d-th row of this vector. By this approach, the authors allow for $\mathcal{TR}_d$ depending on the total relevancies of all other documents. The choice of query_match, doc_match, qual, and score will be discussed later on.

Ant Algorithm

So far, the proposed reference algorithm is purely conceptual, since in practice, $\pi\left(\widehat{in_t}\right)$ cannot be determined. This is because the probabilities $P_u\left(x \Rightarrow y\right)$ are based on the transition probabilities $P_u\left(x \rightarrow y\right)$, which are not known. As explained earlier, the latter characterize the user u's behavior, that is, what she will do in the next round when the search session is in state x. The authors now integrate implicit collaborative search as the final component of their algorithm, which means that they assume that $P_u\left(x \rightarrow y\right)$ can be estimated on the basis of previous search sessions that also have been in state x. This is moderated by the group of u and u's proximities to other groups. E.g., if a high proportion of users from the same group as u who had searched for "revenue" have searched for "revenue Germany" next, it is likely that u also will refine her search query in this way.

A straightforward approach to express this idea in a formula would be to estimate $P_u\left(x \rightarrow y\right)$ by (a weighted average of) the relative frequencies of the usage of edge $x \rightarrow y$ from state x by all user groups. The authors employ Ant Colony Optimization (ACO, (Dorigo et al., 1996)) as a more general approach, which recently has been introduced in dynamic search (Albakour et al., 2011) and includes the usage of relative frequencies as a special case. In the terminology of ACO, a search session a corresponds to an ant travelling to a food source (a document fulfilling the searching user's informational need). During its journey, it drops a certain amount of pheromones on each way (edge) it passes. For the edge $x \rightarrow y$, this amount $\Delta\tau^a_{x \rightarrow y}$ is given by

$$\Delta\tau^a_{x \rightarrow y} = \begin{cases} \dfrac{Q}{C^a} & if \ \exists t : s^a_t = x \wedge s^a_{t+1} = y \\ 0 & otherwise \end{cases} \tag{5}$$

where s^a_t marks the states of a for all its rounds t, Q is a constant, and C^a is the "cost" of a's complete way. After a defined period W (e.g., a day or one hundred ants), the total amount of pheromones dropped on $x \rightarrow y$ by a user group g (with $\tau^g_{x \rightarrow y}$ initially being 0 for each g) is updated as

Figure 2. Graph visualizing a set of search sessions with pheromones of two user groups

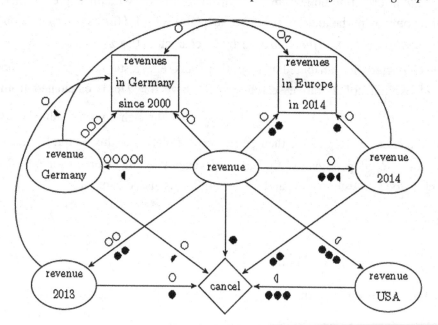

$$\tau^{g}_{x \to y} \leftarrow \left(1 - \rho^{g}\right) \cdot \tau^{g}_{x \to y} + \sum_{a \mid g_{u}a = g} {}^{,,} \tau^{a}_{x \to y},$$ (6)

where u^{a} is the user who has instanced a. $\rho^{g} \in \left[0;1\right]$ are group-specific evaporation coefficients that specify the percentage of pheromones that evaporate within the duration of W. The choice of Q, C^{a}, W, and ρ^{g} will be discussed later on.

A set of finished search sessions can be visualized by combining their individual graphs. The nodes and edges of the resulting graph (Figure 2) represent the states and state transitions that have occurred in at least one session (resp.). On each edge $x \to y$, the amount of pheromones can be drawn for each group. In the given example, two different groups exist (indicated by white and black pheromones) that obviously have different informational need distributions: While group 1 (white) seems to be mainly interested in the revenue for Germany and Europe, for which two matching documents exist, group 2 (black) seems rather to search for the revenues in the USA, for which no document exists (leading to a high rate of cancelled searches). As will become clearer later, the amount of pheromones dropped by each ant can be smaller than 1, which is symbolized in the figure by half circles.

Now the transition probability $P_{u}\left(x \to y\right)$ can be estimated by the total amount of the pheromones dropped on $x \to y$ relative to the total amount of pheromones dropped on all outgoing edges $x \to z$ of x, both weighted by the group proximity function prox:

$$\widehat{P}_{u}\left(x \to y\right) = \frac{\sum_{g} \text{prox}\left(u, g\right) \cdot \tau^{g}_{x \to y}}{\sum_{g} \text{prox}\left(u, g\right) \cdot \sum_{z} \tau^{g}_{x \to z}}.$$ (7)

Replacing the probabilities $\mathrm{P}_u\left(x \to y\right)$ with their estimates $\widehat{\mathrm{P}}_u\left(x \to y\right)$ in (1), one gets estimates $\widehat{\mathrm{P}}_u\left(x \Rightarrow y\right)$ of $\mathrm{P}_u\left(x \Rightarrow y\right)$, from which an estimate $\hat{\pi}\left(\widehat{in_t}\right)$ of $\pi\left(\widehat{in_t}\right)$ can be derived. $\hat{\pi}\left(\widehat{in_t}\right)$ can, in turn, be used to get estimates of the subjective and objective relevance of each document, which in combination with the documents' qualities lead eventually to estimates $\widehat{TR}_d$ of their total relevancies TR_d. Finally, the ranking of documents presented by the ESE is given by sorting them according to $\widehat{TR}_d$ in descending order.

ADAPTATION

The authors now outline how enterprises can adapt the proposed reference algorithm in dependence on their individual characteristics.

The Query History Transformation Function

Enterprises have to choose a query history transformation function state that converts the searching user's query history $\mathbf{q}_t = \left(q_0, \ldots, q_t\right)$ in round t to a state s_t of her search session; $s_t = \mathrm{state}\left(\mathbf{q}_t\right)$. This choice is very important since the number of states generated, the interweaving of different search sessions, and the compliance of search sessions with the Markov property depend on state. These factors entail a trade-off between

1. How fast the algorithm learns, and
2. How precise its results are.

In the following, some examples are given to illustrate this.

As mentioned earlier, the simplest option is to choose $\mathrm{state}\left(\mathbf{q}_t\right) = \mathbf{q}_t$. This function always complies with the Markov property since s_t contains, by construction, the whole information of $\mathbf{q}_t$ when it is employed. Using this function, one does not need to care manually about whether, e.g., the order of queries contained in $\mathbf{q}_t$ makes a difference. This is because state would assign different states to differently ordered query histories, so that the algorithm would account for potential differences automatically. However, this desirable property comes at a high price: By assigning two query histories to the same state only if they are exactly identical, the number of states created in total becomes extremely high. This results not only in a computationally intensive calculation of $\pi\left(\widehat{in_t}\right)$ but also in a very loose interweaving of different search sessions. E.g., if the initial queries of two sessions are "revenue Germany" and "Germany revenue", these sessions would not share any state despite their obvious similarity. The amount of pheromones deposited on each edge is, thus, usually very low, so that the algorithm may learn only very slowly and the variance of the estimator $\widehat{\mathrm{P}}_u\left(x \to y\right)$ may be rather high.

For almost all other transformation functions, the Markov property is not fulfilled by construction but rather imposes an assumption. The consequences can be illustrated by the extreme choice of $\mathrm{state}\left(\mathbf{q}_t\right) = q_t$ (that is, ignoring all queries except the current one). This function is valid in an environment where users cumulate keywords (e.g., search for "revenue" first, "revenue 2014" second, and "revenue 2014 Germany" third) since the last query in this case contains the information of the former queries. Otherwise (e.g., if they search for "revenue" first and "Germany" second), the information that s_t provides may not suffice to estimate the user's informational need correctly. $\widehat{in}_t$ and, hence, the ranking of documents may, therefore, be biased.

A multi-purpose transformation function that seems appropriate for most ESEs is

$$\text{state}\left(\mathbf{q}_t\right) = \bigcup_{r=1}^{t} kw\left(q_r\right) \tag{8}$$

where $kw\left(q_r\right)$ denotes the set of keywords contained in q_r. E.g., for two queries $q_0 = \text{"revenue"}$ and $q_1 = \text{"revenue2014"}$, $\text{state}\left(\mathbf{q}_1\right) = \left\{\text{"revenue"},\text{"2014"}\right\}$. (8) has three properties: First, it ignores the order of queries within a query history and the order of keywords within a query. This reduces the number of potential states by a number much greater than the faculty of t. Second, it regards keywords entered redundantly (such as "revenue" in the given example) as if they had been entered only once. Third, it automatically cumulates keywords, so that the Markov property is fulfilled by construction if the assumption holds that the order and frequency of queries and keywords do not make a difference. As a consequence of these properties, similar search sessions easily can get interweaved, so that the algorithm learns fast and $\widehat{P}_u\left(x \rightarrow y\right)$ has a low variance. Note that (8) could still be improved by incorporating a dictionary for synonyms, misspellings, etc.

The Group Functions

Ideally, enterprises should choose the group assignment function group and the group proximity function prox in a way such that exactly all users u within a group have the same probability distribution $P_u\left(in\right)$ of their informational need and that prox reflects the similarity of these distributions between groups. In practice, however, this can hardly be accomplished since these distributions are unknown. Therefore, care has to be taken when choosing group and prox : On the one hand, too few groups can bias $\widehat{in}_t$ towards an average informational need. The extreme case of a single group would be a direct contradiction to the assumption of $P_u\left(in\right)$ differing between users. If the number of groups is chosen too high, on the other hand, differences between these distributions are assumed that do not exist, which leads to a loss of efficiency. Furthermore, the number of search sessions of users belonging to a certain group and, therefore, the amount of pheromones dropped by this group would be rather low. This again leads to a high variance of $\widehat{P}_u\left(x \rightarrow y\right)$. Generally, a higher (lower) number of users corresponds to a higher (lower) number of informational need distributions and should, therefore, be met by a higher (lower) number of groups.

We propose the following three-step procedure for choosing group and prox : First, all variables $x_1,\ldots,x_K$ that can be assumed to have an influence on $P_u\left(in\right)$ (e.g., organizational position, country, etc.) are selected from the intersection of all users' characteristics $\mathbf{x}_u \forall u$. Second, variables having a continuous domain or taking too many different values for the given set of users (e.g., a user's age) are replaced with clustered versions. Third, group and prox are defined as

$$\text{group}\left(\mathbf{x}_u\right) = \left(x_{1,u}, \dots, x_{K,u}\right) \quad \text{and} \tag{9a}$$

$$\text{prox}\left(u, g\right) = \frac{1}{K} \cdot \sum_{k=1}^{K} 1\left(x_{k,u} = x_{k,g}\right) \tag{9b}$$

where $x_{K,u}$ and $x_{k,g}$ represent the values of x_k for u and each member of group g (resp.) for $k = 1, \dots, K$ and $1(\cdot)$ symbolizes the indicator function. This procedure has two major advantages: First, it can be adjusted to most enterprises because their specificities can be easily taken into account by the selection of the variables $x_1, \dots, x_K$. Second, it does not require an explicit decision on the number of groups being created since this number results as an implicit consequence of the decision on $x_1, \dots, x_K$.

Further Functions

The matching functions query_match and doc_match measure the degree of match between a query state or a document state y and a document d (resp.). For this purpose, the content of a document is often summarized by so-called tags, which have been either assigned to the document by users manually or generated from the document's content automatically (e.g., Chirita et al., 2007). Assuming that all documents are characterized by a set of tags $tags(\cdot)$, query_match and doc_match can be defined as

$$\text{query\_match}\left(y, d\right) = \text{sim}\left(kw\left(y\right), tags\left(d\right)\right) \quad \text{and} \tag{10a}$$

$$\text{doc\_match}\left(y, d\right) = \text{sim}\left(tags\left(y\right), tags\left(d\right)\right). \tag{10b}$$

As a simple similarity measure sim, the Jaccard index

$$\text{sim}\left(A, B\right) = \frac{\left|A \cap B\right|}{\left|A \cup B\right|} \tag{10c}$$

for two sets A and B can be used. More elaborate similarity measures can take into account linguistic subtleties such as synonyms.

The choice on the quality evaluation function qual, which estimates a document d's quality q_d by d's characteristics $\mathbf{z}_d$, does largely depend on the nature of $\mathbf{z}_d$. Assuming for simplicity that $\mathbf{z}_d$ contains a single value z_d expressing the perceived quality of d through a star rating on a scale from z_{min} to z_{max}, qual can simply be defined as

$$\text{qual}\left(\mathbf{z}_d\right) = \frac{z_d - z_{min}}{z_{max} - z_{min}}. \tag{11}$$

qual may also be based on other variables expressing further explicit collaborative behavior, such as user comments, recommendations, etc.

The goal of the scoring function score is to weigh the subjective relevancies $\mathcal{SR}$ against the objective relevancies $\mathcal{OR}$ and to adjust the result by the documents' qualities $\mathcal{Q}$. For this purpose, the authors suggest a two-step procedure: In the first step, a vector $\mathcal{R}$ is calculated as a linear combination of $\mathcal{SR}$ and $\mathcal{OR}$:

$$\mathcal{R} = \alpha \cdot \mathcal{SR} + \left(1 - \alpha\right) \cdot \mathcal{OR}. \tag{12a}$$

The weight $\alpha \in \left[0;1\right]$ may differ between periods: In the beginning, when the total amount of pheromones is low and the algorithm has not learned much, it seems reasonable to use a low value for α (that is, to prefer $\mathcal{OR}$ over $\mathcal{SR}$). This value can be increased when the estimates $\widehat{P}_u\left(x \Rightarrow y\right)$ become more precise over time. In the second step, score is defined as

$$\mathcal{TR} = \text{score}\left(\mathcal{R}, \mathcal{Q}\right) = \mathcal{R} + \text{lex} \tag{12b}$$

with lex representing any vector-valued function that achieves a lexicographical ordering of documents by $\mathcal{R}$ first, query_match second, and $\mathcal{Q}$ third (e.g., by adding values based on query_match and $\mathcal{Q}$ that are small enough to retain the principal order of $\mathcal{R}$).

ACO Parameters

If Q in (5) is chosen as a constant not only over all ants (search sessions) but also over all periods, its value does not matter and can be normalized to 1. However, it may make sense to alter Q between time periods to adjust the learning process of the algorithm to seasonality. An extreme example is setting Q to 0 for a certain period, which results in the algorithm learning nothing in this period. Another example is setting Q in each period to the average pheromone level over all used edges of the previous period (Albakour et al., 2011), which basically corresponds to attributing higher importance to periods with more search sessions in the previous period.

When choosing a period duration W, enterprises face a trade-off: On the one hand, the algorithm $\tau_{x \to y}^g$ should learn as fast as possible. This advocates for frequent updates, that is, a short period duration. In the extreme case, an update could take place after every search session. However, this approach is suited only for enterprises with a low number of search sessions per time unit. This is because, on the other hand, updates of the total amount of pheromones dropped on an edge $x \to y$ for a group g implicate the necessity of updating also $\widehat{P}_u\left(x \to y\right)$ and $\widehat{P}_u\left(x \Rightarrow y\right)$ for all users u. This is computationally costly and prevents these values from being stored for a longer time. Thus, a period should ideally end as soon as the benefit from the algorithm learning from the incurred search sessions outweighs the additional computational costs.

For the cost C^a of ant a's way, two choices are reasonable. First, C^a can be set to a constant normalized to 1 for all ants. The pheromones dropped in total on an edge $x \to y$ correspond in this case to the number of ants travelling from x to y, which leads to (7) being equivalent to the usage of relative frequency mentioned earlier. This approach is suited for ESEs with users who do not change their searching behavior over time. However, prior research has shown that the latter usually is influenced by a user's experience (Hölscher & Strube, 2000) and by visual aids that the ESE provides, such as query completion. The second approach accounts for this by setting $C^a = T^a + 1$, where T^a denotes the number of query refinements in session a. That is, ants drop less pheromones on an edge $x \to y$ if their total way is longer. Thus, longer ways requiring more query refinements to the final state become less important in the long run. This corresponds to experienced users avoiding such ways.

The pheromone evaporation coefficients ρ^g determine how fast the algorithm forgets what it has learned from the behavior of users belonging to a group g. Ideally, they should be chosen in such a way that they reflect how fast

1.   The distribution of informational needs of the members of g, and
2.   Documents relating to their informational needs change (e.g., how often new documents are added).

If 1 and 2 change only slowly, ρ^g may be set to 0. This choice has yielded the best results in prior research analyzing a university search engine (Albakour et al., 2011), for which at least the informational needs (e.g., lecture material) can be expected to vary only slightly over time. For $\rho^g = 1$, no learning would take place since the algorithm would immediately forget what it has learned. Thus, even for enterprises and groups for which 1 and 2 change fast, moderate values for ρ^g should be chosen.

EVALUATION

In this section the authors evaluate an instance of their reference algorithm through an experiment. First, they describe the design of this experiment, the dataset they have obtained, and the instance of the reference algorithm that they have tested. Then, they explain how they have measured the algorithm's performance and present and discuss its results.

Experimental Setup and Dataset

A laboratory experiment with 146 students (76 undergraduate, 70 graduate; 60 female, 86 male) as participants has been conducted. Such a setup is more controllable than a field study in a real enterprise, what leads to a higher internal validity (Straub et al., 2004). Particularly, the participants are unbiased by experience made with specific enterprise search functions.

Every participant had to complete 10 search tasks from an enterprise context, leading to 146x10=1,460 search sessions in total. In 28 cases students did not answer a search tasks, so that 1,432 search sessions remain. The search tasks differed in both, difficulty and specificity. More precisely, the first five tasks were specific to two characteristics,

1. The location, and
2. The department of a fictitious employee identity randomly assigned to each student (e.g., *In the next five years, what are the biggest risks in the sales department in Saxony?*), while the remaining tasks were more general in regard to these characteristics (e.g., *Can the company you work for be expected to downsize soon?*).

On the basis of 1 and 2, the grouping functions group and prox were defined as in (9a) and (9b), with two possible values each. As a result, the students were assigned to one of 2x2=4 groups (40, 36, 36, and 34 members), with similarities of 0, 0.5, 0.5, and 1.

To create the set of documents the authors proceeded as follows: 32 other students (6 undergraduate, 26 graduate; 18 female, 14 male) were given the same search tasks before the actual experiment was carried out. For each task, they were asked to attribute tags to documents which contain the desired information (possibly among other things). Tags that were mentioned by at least 10% of the participants were used to create one target document for each search task. Thereby, the authors simulate that in the enterprise, documents are often tagged rather by standard users than by experts. Besides these 4x5 group-specific and 5 generic target documents, the authors created 975 additional "noise" documents that were tagged randomly using the set of tags assigned by the students and a set of added tags (e.g., other regions and departments). This resulted in 7.5806 tags per document on average. For all 1,000 documents, a rating was randomly drawn from a discrete uniform distribution on $\{1;...;5\}$, from which the document's quality was calculated by the quality function qual given in (11). No documents were added or removed during the experiment. Therefore, the pheromone evaporation coefficients p^g to 0 have been set for each group as reasoned earlier.

The search process was carried out as follows: First, the participants were asked to enter a search query into a Google-like search mask. They were given the possibility to adapt this search query up to two times under the premise that no document will be found when using their initial search query. Then, the search sessions of all users were sorted in random order to avoid potential sequential bias. For each search session, the authors proceeded as follows: First, the documents were ranked by the algorithm based on the user's initial search query. Further, the number of documents the user is willing to view at most in one round is drawn from a uniform distribution on $\{10;...;30\}$, reflecting one to three pages with ten results each. After that, the user is assumed to view every document in the order defined by the ranking until the target document is found (so that the search session ends successfully) or the number of maximum views is reached. In the latter case, this process is repeated with the user's second and third search query (if applicable). If the target document is still not found after the last round, the user is assumed to cancel the search session so that it ends unsuccessfully.

The query history transformation function state the authors employed is based on (8). To improve learning, stop words (e.g., "the", "and", etc.), punctuation marks (1,274 cases), differing grammatical forms (2,548 cases), and synonyms (909 cases) have been homogenized. This reduced the total number of keywords from 14,027 to 12,753 and the number of distinctive keywords from 867 to 285. The same rules were applied for the tagging of documents (146, 250, and 114 cases, resp.) reducing the total and distinctive numbers of tags from 1,028 to 914 and from 295 to 149 (resp.). The scoring function score was chosen as described in (12a) with equal weights of the subjective and the objective relevance component ($\alpha = 0.5$). The latter was calculated according to query_match and doc_match as given in (10a) and (10b) (resp.) with the similarity function sim of (10c). Furthermore, the cost C^a of a search session a was chosen as the number of its rounds, and the constant Q was normalized to 1. Finally, the pheromone levels were updated after each search session, focusing more on the speed of learning than on computational efficiency.

Performance Measures and Results

Several performance measures can be considered to evaluate the algorithm. The authors are mainly interested in the effort of the searching user to find a document, which the authors operationalize by how often she has to refine her search query and by the number of documents she has to view until she finds a document fulfilling her informational need. Furthermore, accounting for the maximum number of documents a user is willing to view before she decides to cancel her search session, the authors also consider the percentage of successful search sessions. Since all of the former performance measures evaluate the algorithm's ranking only in the range up to the number of the user's maximum document views, a common approach to evaluate the complete ranking is the mean reciprocal rank (MRR) (e.g., Albakour et al., 2011). Here, MRR can be defined as

$$MRR = \frac{1}{n} \cdot \sum_{a=1}^{n} \left(\frac{1}{T^a + 1} \cdot \sum_{t=0}^{T^a} \frac{1}{r_{a,t}} \right) \tag{13}$$

where $r_{a,t}$ is the rank of a (by construction always existing) document d fulfilling the querying user's informational need in one of the $n=1{,}432$ search sessions (ants) a in response to its state in round t.

Figure 3 illustrates the performance of the tested reference algorithm instance in comparison to a traditional pattern matching algorithm as a benchmark. The latter was implemented by ranking the results according to query_match only. The graphic shows that the algorithm performs significantly better than the benchmark as measured by the MRR ($t=28.8729$, $p<0.001$). The difference becomes the more pronounced the more searches have been carried out, that is, the more the algorithm has learned. Consequently, both the average numbers of query refinements and document views decrease over time. After the last search, the algorithm has reduced them by 50.7010% ($t=-31.5766$, $p<0.001$) and 48.3790% ($t=-26.3605$, $p<0.001$) compared to the benchmark. Since the numbers of documents the users are willing to view at most were kept constant for the algorithm and the benchmark, the number of cancelled searches also decreases and more searches end successfully. In the end, the percentage of successful searches is 23.8129 points higher using the algorithm than when using the benchmark ($t=28.8729$, $p<0.001$).

The proposed algorithm performed better for the group-specific tasks 1 to 5 than for the generic tasks 6 to 10 regarding all performance measures expect the MRR (see Table 1). When restricting the evaluation to successful search sessions, however, the performance is better for generic search tasks than for group-specific search tasks for all performance measures (query refinements: 0.1802 vs. 0.2129, views: 8.7275 vs. 10.8211, MRR: 0.5089 vs. 0.3624). This may be because the number of prior search sessions (ant trails) that are exploited is higher for generic than for group-specific tasks. Given that they do not lead to a wrong document (unsuccessful search sessions), the performance should be improved.

Next, the authors have compared the tested algorithm instance to another instance for which the distinction between groups was deactivated by changing group to a constant function, so that all users

Figure 3. Algorithm performance

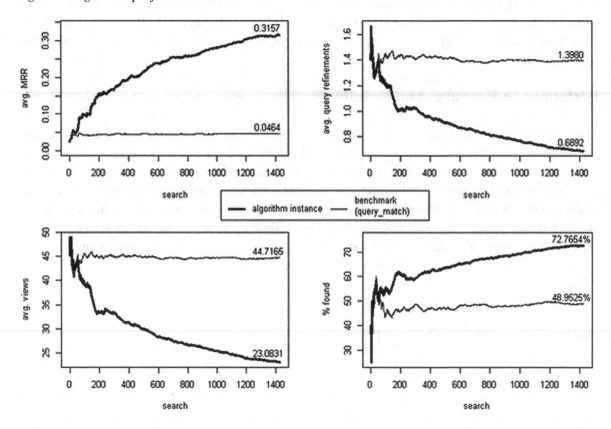

effectively are assigned to the same group. This approach can be compared to previous ACO-based search algorithms (Albakour et al., 2011). The single-group instance performs significantly worse regarding all performance measures (MRR: t=-11.0000, p<0.001). This is as expected and can be explained by the ranking being influenced by information which does not match the searching user's group.

Table 1. Comparison of dataset restrictions and algorithm variants

	Avg. MRR	Avg. Query Refinements	Avg. Views	% Found
Main algorithm instance	0.3157	0.6892	23.0831	72.7654%
Group-specific tasks (1 to 5) only	0.2981	0.5531	19.4290	80.9655%
Generic tasks (6 to 10) only	0.3338	0.8289	26.8303	64.3564%
No distinction between groups	0.1854	1.0573	34.4253	49.0922%
Objective relevance only ($\alpha = 0$)	0.3079	0.7060	23.5440	71.9274%
Subjective relevance only ($\alpha = 1$)	0.3142	0.6760	22.7528	73.0447%
Relative frequencies ($C^a = 1$)	0.3167	0.6920	23.1103	72.7654%

The authors also have explored the robustness of their algorithm by altering its parameters. First, they deactivated the subjective relevance component by setting $\alpha = 0$. This worsened the algorithm's performance significantly across all performance measures (MRR: $t=1.8549$, $p=0.0319$). The authors also tried the opposite and deactivated the objective relevance component by setting $\alpha = 1$. This did not lead to any significant changes (MRR: $t=0.3047$, $p=0.7607$). Finally, the authors replaced the ACO's pheromones with relative frequencies by setting the costs C^a to 1 for all search sessions. This also did not lead to any significant changes (MRR: $t=-0.2767$, $p=0.7820$). These results underline the necessity to make the exact specification of the algorithm's instance dependent on the environment.

DISCUSSION AND CONCLUSION

The field of knowledge management in enterprises currently faces various challenges that can prevent knowledge workers from finding the information they are searching for. To overcome this barrier, the authors have presented a reference algorithm for enterprise search, which enterprises can adapt by tailoring it to their specificities. The algorithm combines four current streams of search (personalized, social, collaborative, and dynamic), relying on information that is available in organizations since the advent of social knowledge management.

Some examples help to highlight the benefits of this integrated approach: First, the algorithm automatically accounts for different vocabularies between querying users and the creators of documents (and misspellings). To see this, consider a user searching with the keyword "Germany" in an environment where documents are tagged with "Deutschland" (the German word for "Germany") instead. This user may not find a suited document not until she reformulates her search query. This is learned by the algorithm, which in the long run will attribute a higher rank to this document when another user searches for "Germany" again (since the algorithm anticipates that she will search for "Deutschland" next). Second, the algorithm also accounts for different vocabularies between different groups of users (Cleverly, 2012) because it learns group-specifically. Third, it provides logs that could also be used for a group-specific query completion.

Enterprises can deploy the algorithm to reduce the search costs of their employees and, thus, opportunity costs. Our algorithm is self-learning; therefore, the effort of doing so is basically given by the one-time effort of implementing it. This also provides a basis for making implicit knowledge, which accrues over time due to the recording of search behavior, explicit later on. Furthermore, enterprises can adopt our algorithm to their specificities by following the instructions given in this work. This is a clear advantage over other algorithms which are ready-to-use from the beginning but inflexible.

However, in practice, there are also restrictions to our algorithm that have to be considered before implementation. Most importantly, as it is based on information on search behavior, this information must be accessible. This may be not the case for all enterprises, as some employees may not be willing to share it due to privacy concerns. Furthermore, our algorithm may be less efficient in very small enterprises because it learns relatively slow in this case.

FUTURE RESEARCH DIRECTIONS

Investigating a reference algorithm through a laboratory experiment leads to some limitations that can be seen as starting points for future research: First, while the authors have evaluated a typical instance of their algorithm by an experiment with students, they have not evaluated its performance in a real environment of an enterprise. This is because the search logs typically collected by most existing ESEs do not suffice for an evaluation. Instead, the algorithm first has to be implemented in a real environment before it can be evaluated with the data from the resulting log files.

Second, the authors did not optimize their algorithm with respect to computational efficiency. While it can be argued that ESEs often run on high-performance servers, so that the absolute computational costs can be expected to be relatively low, (2) involves multiple recursive calculations and could, therefore, probably be improved regarding speed.

Third, the authors have not explored the behavior of their algorithm for different settings (e.g., number of users, etc.), leaving space for future research. This could be particularly interesting when the proposed algorithm is employed in different enterprises, as mentioned earlier.

REFERENCES

Alavi, M., & Leidner, D. E. (2001). Review: Knowledge management and knowledge management systems: Conceptual foundations and research issues. *Management Information Systems Quarterly, 25*(1), 107–136. doi:10.2307/3250961

Albakour, M. D., Kruschwitz, U., Nanas, N., Song, D., Fasli, M., & De Roeck, A. (2011). Exploring ant colony optimisation for adaptive interactive search. In *Advances in Information Retrieval Theory* (pp. 213–224). Berlin: Springer. doi:10.1007/978-3-642-23318-0_20

Aula, A., Khan, R. M., & Guan, Z. (2010). How does search behavior change as search becomes more difficult? In *Proceedings of the SIGCHI Conference on Human Factors in Computing Systems.* doi:10.1145/1753326.1753333

Bao, S., Xue, G., Wu, X., Yu, Y., Fei, B., & Su, Z. (2007). Optimizing web search using social annotations. In *Proceedings of the 16th international conference on World Wide Web.* doi:10.1145/1242572.1242640

Chirita, P. A., Costache, S., Nejdl, W., & Handschuh, S. (2007). P-tag: Large scale automatic generation of personalized annotation tags for the web. In *Proceedings of the 16th international conference on World Wide Web.* doi:10.1145/1242572.1242686

Chirita, P. A., Olmedilla, D., & Nejdl, W. (2004). Pros: A personalized ranking platform for web search. In *Adaptive Hypermedia and Adaptive Web-Based Systems* (pp. 34–43). Berlin: Springer. doi:10.1007/978-3-540-27780-4_7

Cleverly, P. H. (2012). Improving enterprise search in the upstream oil and gas industry by automatic query expansion using a non-probabilistic knowledge representation. *International Journal of Applied Information Systems, 1*(1), 25–32.

Davenport, T. H., & Prusak, L. (2000). *Working knowledge: How organizations manage what they know*. Boston: Harvard Business Press.

Davenport, T. H., Thomas, R. J., & Desouza, K. C. (2003). Reusing intellectual assets. *Industrial Management (Des Plaines)*, *45*, 12–17.

Desouza, K. C. (2003). Facilitating tacit knowledge exchange. *Communications of the ACM*, *46*(6), 85–88. doi:10.1145/777313.777317

Dorigo, M., Maniezzo, V., & Colorni, A. (1996). Ant system: Optimization by a colony of cooperating agents. *IEEE Transactions on Systems, Man, and Cybernetics. Part B, Cybernetics*, *26*(1), 29–41. doi:10.1109/3477.484436 PMID:18263004

Feldman, S., & Sherman, C. (2003). *The high cost of not finding information*. IDC Whitepaper 29127.

Grant, R. M. (1996). Toward a knowledge-based theory of the firm. *Strategic Management Journal*, *17*(S2), 109–122. doi:10.1002/smj.4250171110

Hänel, T., & Schulz, M. (2014). Is there still a need for multidimensional data models? In *Proceedings of the Twenty Second European Conference on Information Systems*.

Hawking, D. (2004). Challenges in enterprise search. In *Proceedings of the 15th Australasian database conference*.

Hölscher, C., & Strube, G. (2000). Web search behavior of internet experts and newbies. *Computer Networks*, *33*(1), 337–346. doi:10.1016/S1389-1286(00)00031-1

Li, Y., Liu, Z., & Zhu, H. (2014). Enterprise search in the big data era: Recent developments and open challenges. *Proceedings of the VLDB Endowment*, *7*(13), 1717–1718. doi:10.14778/2733004.2733071 PMID:26167358

McAfee, A. P. (2006). Enterprise 2.0: The dawn of emergent collaboration. *MIT Sloan Management Review*, *47*(3), 21–28.

McAfee, A. P., & Brynjolfsson, E. (2012). Big data: The management revolution. *Harvard Business Review*, *90*(10), 60–66. PMID:23074865

O'Leary, D. E. (1997). The internet, intranets, and the AI renaissance. *IEEE Computer*, *30*(1), 71–78. doi:10.1109/2.562929

Page, L., Brin, S., Motwani, R., & Winograd, T. (1999). *The PageRank Citation Ranking: Bringing Order to the Web*. Technical Report. Stanford InfoLab.

Papagelis, A., & Zaroliagis, C. (2007). Searchius: A collaborative search engine. In *Proceedings of the 8th Mexican International Conference on Current Trends in Computer Science*.

Qiu, F., & Cho, J. (2006). Automatic identification of user interest for personalized search. In *Proceedings of the 15th International Conference on World Wide Web*. doi:10.1145/1135777.1135883

Rieh, S. Y., & Xie, H. I. (2006). Analysis of multiple query reformulations on the web: The interactive information retrieval context. *Information Processing & Management, 42*(3), 751–768. doi:10.1016/j.ipm.2005.05.005

Ronen, I., Shahar, E., Ur, S., Uziel, E., Yogev, S., Zwerdling, N., & Ofek-Koifman, S. et al. (2009). Social networks and discovery in the enterprise (SaND). In *Proceedings of the 32nd International ACM SIGIR Conference on Research and Development in Information Retrieval.* doi:10.1145/1571941.1572156

Schulz, M., Winter, P., & Choi, S.-K. T. (2015). On the relevance of reports – Integrating an automated archiving component into a business intelligence system. *International Journal of Information Management, 25*(6), 662–671. doi:10.1016/j.ijinfomgt.2015.07.005

Shapira, B., & Zabar, B. (2011). Personalized search: Integrating collaboration and social networks. *Journal of the American Society for Information Science and Technology, 62*(1), 146–160. doi:10.1002/asi.21446

Straub, D., Boudreau, M., & Gefen, D. (2004). Validation guidelines for IS positivist research. *Communications of the Association for Information Systems, 13*(1), 24.

Watts, D. J., Dodds, P. S., & Newman, M. E. J. (2002). Identity and search in social networks. *Science, 296*(5571), 1302–1305. doi:10.1126/science.1070120 PMID:12016312

KEY TERMS AND DEFINITIONS

Ant Colony Optimization: A probabilistic technique for reducing computational problems to finding shortest paths through graphs, mimicking the behaviour of ants.

Collaborative Search: A form of information retrieval in which users can utilize the experience of other users who have searched previously.

Dynamic Search: A form of information retrieval in which it is accounted for search sessions consisting of more than a single search query.

Enterprise Search: Searching for documents etc. in enterprises.

Enterprise Search Engine: A search engine specifically tailored to enterprise search (in contrast to, e.g., web search engines).

Personalized Search: A form of information retrieval that allows to incorporate information on the querying user in the search process in addition to the query she has entered.

Social Search: A form of information retrieval in which the relationship of the querying user to other users is taking into account.

Chapter 21
Professional and Business Applications of Social Media Platforms

Kijpokin Kasemsap
Suan Sunandha Rajabhat University, Thailand

ABSTRACT

This chapter provides an overview of the challenges and benefits of social media across various industries. The use of social media has created the highly effective communication platforms where any user, virtually anywhere in the world, can freely create the content and disseminate this information in real time to a global audience. The chapter argues that professional and business applications of social media platforms can enhance business performance toward reaching strategic goals in the digital age. What are keeping various industries awake these days? Why are social media applications important to various industries? How do social media platforms apply for professional and business perspectives across various industries?

INTRODUCTION

The diffusion of social media has opened the new possibilities for the targeted stakeholder communication (Saxton & Guo, 2014). Social media is recognized as a new platform which can be used as a competitive marketing tool by business organizations (Hassan, Nadzim, & Shiratuddin, 2015). Social media is used as an information source, including information related to risks and crises (Westerman, Spence, & van der Heide, 2014). Social media technology initiates the new ways of consumers' interactions in modern business with firms (Olsen & Christensen, 2015). Social media tools can be used by business organizations of various sizes and types as a marketing tool (Birkner, 2011). Carr et al. (2015) found that social media information is useful for marketers as they can directly track the consumer responses to marketing campaigns, product performance, and the changes in consumer sentiment toward a brand.

DOI: 10.4018/978-1-5225-0559-4.ch021

This chapter aims to offer a consolidated view of the business applications of social media. The extensive literature of social media applications provides a contribution to practitioners and researchers by describing the professional and business applications of social media platforms to maximize the business impact of social media applications in terms of customer relationship management, customer retention, product marketing, cost control initiatives, public relations, and sales.

BACKGROUND

In recent years, social media has gained popularity and attracted a great deal of attention among researchers and practitioners (Gan & Wang, 2015). According to Bernabe-Moreno et al. (2015), social media started as a space where could interact with other users, share content, and express their personal views. Social media comes in various forms, such as social networking sites (Facebook), blogs, microblogs (Twitter), collaborative projects (Wikipedia), content communities (YouTube), virtual social worlds (Second Life), and virtual game worlds (World of Warcraft) (Olsen & Christensen, 2015). Social media has changed the way that people interact with each other and with companies (Hanna, Rohm, & Crittenden, 2011).

Social media is the major component of social applications in organizations (Atzmueller, 2012). As the Internet users experience the usefulness of social media, it encourages the immense adoption of the medium and enables the Internet users to gain the power over information selection, thus affecting their behavior and attitude (Durukan, Bozaci, & Hamsioglu, 2012). Internet users have many options concerning their intention to use social media, due to the availability of hundreds of social media sites with the different features and user groups (Zolkepli & Kamarulzaman, 2015). Social media space becomes a common place for communication, networking, and content sharing (Paniagua & Sapena, 2014).

SOCIAL MEDIA PLATFORMS IN BUSINESS PRACTICE

Overview of Social Media

Social media provides a participatory media environment based on the interactive Web 2.0 platform (Hwang & Kim, 2015). The application of Web 2.0 has helped in the growth and public popularity of social networks and has created a new world of collaboration and communication (Pookulangara & Koesler, 2011). The rise of Web 2.0 has enabled customers to effectively act and react on what companies are doing (O'Reilly, 2007). Web 2.0 promotes the interactive information sharing, interoperability, user-centered design, and collaboration on the World Wide Web, thus allowing users to interact with other users (Click & Petit, 2010). Berthon et al. (2012) indicated that Web 2.0 technologies have three effects: a shift in the locus of activity from the desktop to the Web, a shift in the locus of value production from the firm to the consumer, and a shift in the locus of power away from the firm to the consumer.

As social media becomes the popular news platforms, journalists and news organizations have been keen to capitalize on their potential to build and maintain audiences (Lee, 2015). Organizations need to use social media sites to communicate with their audiences and to engage in dialogue on a regular basis (Sisco & McCorkindale, 2013). Social media can serve as platforms to address sustainability issues (Nwagbara, 2013). Twitter, Facebook, and other social media sites are recognized as the platforms for the networks of friends (Auer, 2011). Talent management makes a company more competitive in business competition. A company that has super talented employees always produces better products or services compare to competitors that only have employees with average talent. The right use of social media can strengthen talent management programs to create social and cooperative work environments in modern organizations.

Social media includes seven resources: identity, conversations, sharing, presence, relationships, reputation, and groups (Kietzmann, Hermkens, McCarthy, & Silvestre, 2011). As people spend more time on the Internet, managing reputation on social media becomes crucial for public relations (Ott & Theunissen, 2015). The Internet of Things (IoT) is all about connecting physical objects to the Internet and enabling them to communicate with each other. The IoT in social media context can be used to bring people together based on their needs toward increasing business performance. Communication organizations (e.g., advertising and public relations agencies) try to incorporate social media into their campaigns to catch up with the new media trend (Li & Tsai, 2015). Social media has had a significant impact on human resource practices and has been the basis for employment decisions that have resulted in litigation (Drouin, O'Connor, Schmidt, & Miller, 2015).

Employers are using social media as a mechanism to screen the potential job candidates (Curran, Draus, Schrager, & Zappala, 2014). The increasing use of social media at work offers organizations new opportunities for employee learning on the job (van Puijenbroek, Poell, Kroon, & Timmerman, 2014). Social media is the new communication channel in migration networks (Dekker & Engbersen, 2014). Motivations regarding individuals' use of social media develop social relationships and gain information (Nadkarni & Hofmann, 2012). Because of the range of motivations, the diversity of social relationships, and the vast quantity of subscribers, personal social media usage has become intertwined with the workplace (Drouin et al., 2015).

Social media serves as the important tools for facilitating interpersonal communication, business, and educational activities (Ephraim, 2013). Facebook and other social media platforms have been recognized as delivering the promise of the socially educational experiences for students in undergraduate, self-directed, and other educational sectors (Friesen & Lowe, 2012). In education, web-based social media applications can be applied to knowledge management, organizational learning, electronic learning (e-learning), mobile learning (m-learning), educational computer games, game-based learning, distance education, teacher education, and teacher professional development. Teaching strategy plays a key role in supporting students in moving from using social media in order to support coordination and information retrieval to also using such media for collaborative learning, when appropriate (Hrastinski & Aghaee, 2012).

Purposive value, self-discovery, entertainment value, social enhancement, and interpersonal connectivity are the fundamental requirements that are broadly adopted for the online media (Cheung, Chiu, & Lee, 2010). Social media technology can enhance the improved organizational productivity by fostering the communication and collaboration of employees which aids knowledge transfer and makes organizations more profitable (Kasemsap, 2014a). The use of social media creates the opportunity to turn organization-wide knowledge sharing in the workplace from an intermittent, centralized knowledge management process to a continuous online knowledge conversation of strangers, unexpected interpretations, and dynamic emergence (Majchrzak, Faraj, Kane, & Azad, 2013).

Social media is the boundary-spanning tool that can be used to build and increase the companies' absorptive capacity (Ooms, Bell, & Kok, 2015). The capability of social media in building brand in the global marketplace is practically important in modern advertising (Kasemsap, 2015a). Social media marks a huge range of the personalized cloud computing platforms and functions of interaction on the Web

(Bianco, 2009). Many benefits of social media can be achieved through the utilization of technologies, such as cloud computing and virtualization (Kasemsap, 2015b). Researchers and practitioners should recognize the importance of cloud computing toward gaining sustainable competitive advantage in global supply chain (Kasemsap, 2015c). Applying data mining techniques to social media can help provide insights into group behavior and divulge a group's characteristics by identifying a group, developing a profile for a group, revealing the sentiment of a group, and detailing a group's composition (Barbier, Tang, & Liu, 2011).

Health science literature has seen a surge in research on social media (Lis, Wood, Chiniara, Biskin, & Montoro, 2015). Social media provides patients a platform to exchange their drug use experiences (Yang, Kiang, & Shang, 2015). The nature of health communication globally changes as more people rely on the Internet for health information (Gallant, Irizarry, Boone, & Kreps, 2011). The use of social media for health information sharing is expanding among patients, physicians, and other health care professionals (Shcherbakova & Shepherd, 2014). Greaves et al. (2013) stated that young adults post on physician or health care rating sites (e.g., Yelp.com and Healthgrades.com) to indicate the opinions on the areas for improvement in the health care industry. Social media allows patients to discuss and rate their satisfaction with health care procedures (Domanski & Cavale, 2012).

Public health professionals can use social media in their efforts to assess health needs, set policy, and communicate health concerns as they focus on protecting and improving the health of the community (Smith & Denali, 2014). Physicians and patients increasingly use social media technologies, such as Facebook, Twitter, and blogs, both professionally and personally (DeCamp, 2013). Social media constitutes a major part of the online search results for information about health and medical matters (Yang, Li, & Kiang, 2011). Health care research can benefit from taking advantage of the social media-related rich information resource (Fichman, Kohli, & Krishnan, 2011). Web-based communication tool development that engages the electronic patients can better guide the effective health care strategies and promote the participatory medicine (Batta & Iwokwagh, 2015). In health care, the utilization of social media is beneficial to health information technology (HIT), electronic health record (EHR), and telemedicine.

In today's new media environment, publics are increasingly connecting with the political groups through the new media technologies (Sweetser, 2011), while social media platforms have been promoted as a mechanism for engaging the key stakeholder groups, disseminating campaign messages, and increasing the candidate support (LaMarre & Suzuki-Holbrecht, 2013). Informational uses of social media are expected to explain the political expression on social media platforms and to promote the political participation (Gil de Zúñiga, Molyneux, & Zheng, 2014). Social media technology provides individuals and small groups with the powerful resources for the rapid political mobilization (Bekkers, Moody, & Edwards, 2011).

The adoption of social media appears to have engendered the new paradigms of public engagement (Lovejoy & Saxton, 2012). The potential for social media to enhance, support, and motivate the engagement in the political process generates the excitement among the political elites (Housholder & LaMarre, 2015). Social media predicts the traditional offline engagement, such as voting (Bakker & de Vreese, 2011). Twitter is an important medium for political activity recognized as a predictor of election outcomes (Tumasjan, Sprenger, Sandner, & Welpe, 2010). Social media is associated with the online debates (Williams, McMurray, Kurz, & Lambert, 2015). For example, social network analyses of bloggers (Adamic & Glance, 2005) and Twitter users (Conover, Goncalves, Flammini, & Menczer, 2012) have revealed that online political debates are often highly polarized.

Professional and Commercial Impact of Social Media

Social media affects business performance through four channels: social capital, revealed preferences, social marketing, and social corporate networking (Paniagua & Sapena, 2014). Business performance focuses on the financial, operational, and corporate social performance capabilities (Venkatraman & Ramanujam, 1986). Financial performance indicators include sales level and growth, profitability, and stock price. Financial performance indicators (e.g., share prices) depend on the market's information and expectations on the firm (Froot, 1989). Corporate social performance depends on the firm's ability to establish the honest relations with society, with the special attention to reputation and brand (Paniagua & Sapena, 2014).

Many companies seek marketing and business opportunities through social media platforms (Paniagua & Sapena, 2014). Social media has changed how society communicates and organizes itself (Aral, Dellarocas, & Godes, 2013). Social media has dramatically changed how people obtain the information (Liu, Wu, Li, & Li, 2015). Social media users' activities can be used to predict the firms' financial performances (Yu, Duan, & Cao, 2013). Companies have embraced social media because of its potential for engagement and collaboration with consumers (Hudson, Roth, Madden, & Hudson, 2015). Through social media, marketers can gain the rich, unmediated customer insights, faster than ever before, and can foster the customer loyalty through networking (Hudson et al., 2015). Increasing customer loyalty obtains greater profitability because loyal customers provide long-term revenues and reduced costs in the retail supply chain (Kasemsap, 2016a). Managing social networking sites is high on the list of priorities for a lot of businesses that are eager to find more effective ways to reach, learn about, and engage customers in the new product development (Roberts & Candi, 2014).

Organizations place a high value on social media tools as an important part of the strategic marketing mix (Dixon, Martinez, & Martin, 2015). Many researchers have suggested ways that managers can leverage social media by shaping the customer discussions (Kaplan & Haenlein, 2010), and others have offered strategies for measuring the success of social media marketing campaigns (Hoffman & Fodor, 2010). Luo et al. (2013) discovered that social media metrics are the major indicators of firm's equity value. Sul et al. (2014) collected data from public Twitter posts about S&P 500 firms and stated that the positive or negative emotion of tweets about a specific firm are correlated with the firm's stock returns. Yu et al. (2013) indicated that overall social media metrics have a stronger relationship with the firm's stock performance than do the conventional media.

Social media preserves the relevantly valuable portions of life, especially reasoning, play, and exchange of ideas (Elder, 2014). While Facebook service is free, its business model is based on advertising (Ballings & den Poel, 2015). Consumers tend to trust their friends and contacts in social media over the advertisement displayed by business organizations (Woodcock & Green, 2011). Mangold and Faulds (2009) indicated that social media tools combine the features of traditional integrated marketing communications tools (IMC) (business organizations communicate with the users) with word of mouth (WOM) marketing (users communicate with each other) in which marketing managers cannot control the content of some information.

Social media has resulted in the changes to the strategies and tools utilized by business organizations to communicate with users (Hassan et al., 2015). The implications of the social media platforms for public relations and marketing are to improve the visibility, image, and branding (Neill & Moody, 2015). Interaction in social media is much more attractive forum in which information can be presented in various forms, such as the sharing of experiences, videos, and comments from friends. Forums for sharing information and experiences can shape the customer's perceptions of the product offered by business organizations (Hassan et al., 2015). Social media is valuable due to the potential to increase the product demand (Moran & Gossieaux, 2010).

Channels in Social Media and Its Impact on Business Performance

Social media affects business performance through four channels: social capital, revealed preferences, social marketing, and social corporate networking (Paniagua & Sapena, 2014). The social capital channel represents the extent to which social media affects the firms' relationships with society. Although companies are now less constrained by a single social order, corporations face the public scrutiny through social media (Fieseler, Fleck, & Meckel, 2010). Brammer and Pavelin (2006) tied the corporate reputation to the online platforms and corporate social performance. The revealed preferences channel represents the extent to which social media exposes the customers' likings.

Social media enables the development of knowledge value chain to customize information and delivery for a technological business growth (Kasemsap, 2014b). Firms have adopted social media as an essential part of their marketing mix (Mangold & Faulds, 2009). Regarding social marketing channel, social networks, blogs, microblogs, and communities approach customers with the interactive objectives, such as conversation, sharing, collaboration, and engagement (Weinberg & Pehlivan, 2011). The social corporate networking channel represents the extent to which social corporate resources (e.g., relationships and groups) are transformed into operational performance capabilities.

Regarding social media-related online reputation management, corporate reputation is the significant parameter in the supplier selection process by the potential customers (Walsh, Mitchell, Jackson, & Beatty, 2009). Customers are more likely to select companies with a positive corporate reputation, and are willing to pay more for their products (Graham & Moore, 2007). A positive corporate reputation can establish the market entry barriers for competitors, promote the customer loyalty and retention (Nguyen & Leblanc, 2001), and enable a company to attract more customers (Gardberg & Fombrun, 2002) toward gaining the higher market value (Smith, Smith, & Wang, 2010). A positive corporate reputation can protect a company in the times of crisis (Shamma, 2012). An effective reputation increases the stakeholders' willingness to invest in a company, since it enables the company to attract higher quality employees and to gain the better returns (Chun, 2005).

Social media establishes a great opportunity to develop and maintain relationships with customers (Yadav & Arora, 2012). Engagement in the social media activities is correlated with corporate reputation (Dijkmans, Kerkhof, & Beukeboom, 2015). Accomplishing a high level of customer engagement enhances the company's reputation and brand loyalty (Hollebeek, 2011) and purchase decisions (Patterson, Yu, & de Ruyter, 2006). The relational consequences of customer engagement include commitment, trust, customers' emotional brand attachment, and customer loyalty (Brodie, Ilic, Juric, & Hollebeek, 2013). Tourism firms can utilize the customer engagement as a counterweight to competition on price only, to attract more customers, and to develop the customer loyalty (Bowden, 2009). Regarding social media, tourism firms are empowered with more real-time customer insight in order to personalize and localize their interactions with customers and increase the effectiveness of their marketing strategies (Sigala, 2015).

Twitter and microblogging are the significant social media channels regarding business information sharing among individuals, firms, and public. Twitter and microblog conversations can easily be gathered from Internet services to create graphs representing the interactions between the entities in the online community (Corley, Farber, & Reynolds, 2012). Microblogging platforms play a critical role in information dissemination (Alexander & Gentry, 2014). Microblogging platforms allow users to bypass the intermediate channel of information distribution between firms and public (Liu et al., 2015). Blogging and social media play an important role in the recent calls for reform and change (Aman & Jayroe, 2013). YouTube is a public video-sharing website where people can experience varying degrees of engagement with videos in order to maintain social relationships (Lange, 2007).

Tourism is a main industry that is at the forefront of Internet adoption and online transactions in global business (Werthner & Ricci, 2004). The changes of visitors' needs and attitudes have increased the volume of information that tourism destinations have to analyze in order to stay competitive in a changing tourism market (Kiráľová & Pavliceka, 2015). If the tourism destination wants to enforce on the highly competitive global tourism market, it must be observable from the competition (Porter, 1996). Tourism destination will be effectively appreciable with the well-developed communications strategy with the focus on social media (Kiráľová & Pavliceka, 2015). The content of blogs and stories is extensively generated by visitors who have experienced the tourism destination, so that the information is based on the visitors' opinions and perceived experiences (Kiráľová & Pavliceka, 2015).

To develop information connections, individuals are using a variety of technologies to access content and join virtual communities on various social networking sites (Heinrichs, Lim, & Lim, 2011). With the development of IT, social media plays an important role in crisis communication (Veil, Buehner, & Palenchar, 2011). Social media creates the interactive platform that allows various hospitality suppliers and guests to stay connected during the times of crisis (Sigala, 2011). Social media can link the hospitality organizations with the key decision makers in the industry and general public during the times of crisis (Sellnow, Ulmer, Seeger, & Littlefield, 2008).

Understanding the content generated on social media is required for both marketing and crisis management purposes (Coombs, 2014). Many hospitality organizations have to develop their presence in the digital environment, in order to build the favorable brand image and manage the customer relationships (O'Connor, 2010). The effective interactions and conversations on social media can considerably contribute to the co-creation process of guests' service experience, and influence other people's travel decisions through electronic word of mouth (eWOM) (Park & Allen, 2013). Social media acts as the influential source to detect the signals for potential crises, the meaningful tool to monitor the public discourse, and references to understand how the public perceives the crisis (Pennington-Gray, London, Cahyanto, & Klages, 2011).

Facets of Social Media Applications in Business

Social media provides companies a new platform to interact with their customers (Wu, Sun, & Tan, 2013). While traditional commercial information (e.g., advertisement and promotion) is becoming decreasingly effective (Sethuraman, Tellis, & Briesch, 2011), customers tend to increasingly rely on the peer customer opinions available online (Park, Lee, & Han, 2007). Social media can effectively support the marketing of performing arts organizations with regard to promotion and communication, stimulation of WOM, market research and innovation management as well as reputation management (Hausmann & Poellmann, 2013). Social media is the use of Web-based and mobile technologies to turn communication into interactive dialogue (Bhanot, 2012). Social media technology has enabled blogs and other social networking forums to rapidly develop (Mucan & Özeltürkay, 2014). Through social media, potential customers express their likes or the tastes that rationalize an agent's observed actions (Beshears, Choi, Laibson, & Madrian, 2008).

Social media enables consumers to access product-related information from commercial and non-commercial sources (Cao, Meister, & Klante, 2014). Social corporate networking tools (e.g., customer relationship management and electronic business) are the major assets to increase the operational performance (Trainor, Andzulis, Rapp, & Agnihotri, 2014). Customer relationship management becomes one of the most important competitive business strategies in the digital age, thus involving organizational capability of managing business interactions with customers in an effective manner (Kasemsap, 2015d). Regarding social corporate networking channel, electronic business (e-business) revolutionizes the procedure of effective communication between internal and external customers in modern business (Kasemsap, 2015e).

The adoption of social media as a marketing tool is a marketing strategy that can save the business costs (Kirtis & Karahan, 2011). Social media performance focuses on new product development, product quality, product marketing, operating efficiency, and customer satisfaction (Paniagua & Sapena, 2014). Social media-related information affects the product marketing performance and branding in global marketing (Woodcock & Green, 2011). In tourism industry, social media allows the tourism destinations to contact visitors at the relatively low cost and higher levels of efficiency that can be achieved with more traditional communication tools (Kaplan & Haenlein, 2010). The social marketing channel represents the extent to which social marketing resources (e.g., conversations, sharing, and presence) are transformed into financial performance capabilities (e.g., sales) (Paniagua & Sapena, 2014). Customers' social media activities and interactions can affect their consumption intentions toward influencing the firms' sales (Phang, Zhang, & Sutanto, 2013).

Social media platforms are extensively used for the purpose of information seeking (Kim, Sin, & He, 2013). The most prevalent motives for companies to use social media involve enhancing trustworthiness, brand attitude, and customer commitment (Weinberg & Pehlivan, 2011). Customers have shifted their information seeking behavior related to products and services from offline sources to electronic word of mouth eWOM, such as social networking and review sites (Gruen, Osmonbekov, & Czaplewski, 2006). In today's world of Web 2.0, eWOM has materialized as a phenomenon of critical interest to marketers (Williams, Crittenden, Keo, & McCarty, 2012). Social media platforms (e.g., Facebook and Twitter) provide a substantive part of eWOM (Dijkmans et al., 2015). Social media-based relationships lead to the desired outcomes, such as positive WOM (Hudson et al., 2015).

Regarding public relations, Breakenridge (2012) indicated that the eight roles related to public relations' management of social media involve the developing employee policies, internal collaboration, technology testing, pre-crisis management, relationship analyzer, reputation task force, and master of metrics. Public relations' reputation management includes five core components: predicting potential problems, anticipating threats to the organization, minimizing surprises, resolving any issues that do arise, and preventing crises (Wilcox & Cameron, 2012). Gurau (2008) suggested a cross-functional approach to managing social media activities should collaborate with customers, employees, investors, the media, and social community.

Challenges and Implications of Social Media for Practice

Social media is increasingly implemented in the business organizations as tools for communication among employees (Leonardi, Huysman, & Steinfield, 2013). Active social customers set the social trends and agendas in the various range of topics, from economics to the environment and the entertainment industry (Shirky, 2011). With the enormous interest in social media sites, customers are assumed to be actively contributing to marketing content (Heinonen, 2011). Marketing through social media has an impact on the customer equity and intentions to purchase the product (Kim & Ko, 2011). Social media marketing, which uses social networks to enable the content sharing, information diffusion, relationship building, and fans cohesion (Cheung & Lee, 2010), is an influential marketing method. Social media marketing programs usually center on efforts to create content that attracts attention and encourages readers to share it across their social networks toward competition in the global marketplace (Kasemsap, 2016b).

Executives should be aware of the origination of the social media threats from the complaining process (Benson & Morgan, 2015) and should extend their resources toward reaching targets to manage various forms of social media complaints (Gregoire, Salle, & Tripp, 2015). Social media presents challenges and risks to reputation and security, such as confidentiality breaches (Johnston, 2015). The increasing progress of social media over privacy in the digital age has provided an opportunity to introduce students to the legal risks of using social media in the workplace (Binder & Mansfield, 2013). Online reputation management involves interacting with people online, creating shareable content, monitoring what stakeholders are saying, keeping track of their dialogue, addressing negative content found online, and following up on ideas that are shared through social media (Dijkmans et al., 2015).

Effective dissemination of information becomes an essential factor in the success of social media marketing (Chang, Yu, & Lu, 2015). Communication technologies are bidirectional (Camarero & San Jose, 2011). Both marketing managers and Internet users provide messages, targeting individuals and social alignments that include their links or relationships (Chang et al., 2015). Communication technologies (e.g., bulletin board systems for collecting public opinion, blogs for sharing personal messages, and interactive social media) can gain the message diffusion and cohesion through social media marketing (Karnik, Saroop, & Borkar, 2013). Search engines are the foundation of the Internet. Links to individual's content on Facebook, Twitter, LinkedIn, Google+, YouTube, and other social media sites help the search engines understand what websites are credible and should be ranked for what keyword phrases.

Social media makes the global communication easier and cheaper than ever (Gillin, 2007). With the widespread adoption of mobile devices and location-based services, social media allows users to share the information of daily activities (e.g., check-ins and taking photos), thus promoting the role of social media as a proxy for understanding the human behaviors and complex social dynamics in the geographic spaces (Cao et al., 2015). Content sharing, personal commentary, and private life broadcasting have emerged as the distinct elements of social media (Özgüven & Mucan, 2013). Companies are building and maintaining the social media public pages to improve their social network salience, promote the interest in their organizations, and establish the relationships with the online public (Parveen, Jaafar, & Ainin, 2015). Social media becomes less complex and more accessible where young and older people can share the content and interact through social media (Alabdulkareem, 2015).

Social media platforms are necessary for leaders toward promoting leadership, leadership development, and leadership communication in modern business. Social media gives leaders the power to greatly increase this level of engagement by really listening to the voices of stakeholders, then taking tangible actions based on those suggestions. The activities of social media aiming at achieving these goals are referred to as online reputation management, which can be recognized as the development of positioning, monitoring, measuring, talking, and listening as the organization engages in a transparent and ethical dialogue with its online stakeholders (Jones, Temperley, & Lima, 2009).

FUTURE RESEARCH DIRECTIONS

The classification of the extensive literature in the domains of social media platforms will provide the potential opportunities for future research. The topic of social media-related information security will be the important future research direction. Social media platforms are universal for personal and professional settings (Benson & Morgan, 2015). Practitioners and researchers should further study the applicability of a more multidisciplinary approach toward research activities in implementing social media in terms of knowledge management-related variables (e.g., knowledge-sharing behavior, knowledge creation, organizational learning, human capital, and collaborative competency). Concerning business education, collaborative competencies in professional social networking are significant at all ages. Younger students can gain business opportunities, while older graduates are less confident in utilizing social media platforms (Benson & Filippaios, 2015).

CONCLUSION

This chapter aimed to highlight the importance of social media in commercial domain and the multifaceted applications of social media. The differences between traditional and social media are defined by the level of interaction and interactivity available to the consumer. Business units (e.g., marketing, supply chain, retail, finance, IT, human resources, sales, hospitality, tourism, and customer service) should realize the potential for applying social media tools to facilitate organizational innovation, create brand recognition, hire employees, gain profits, improve customer satisfaction, enhance customer loyalty, and promote customer lifetime value. Social media becomes a powerful tool in the way businesses reach, attract, and engage customers, employees, and other stakeholders in a timely and effective manner.

With the advent of Web 2.0, social media platforms (e.g., Facebook, Twitter, and blog) are the advanced technology and can be utilized to encourage various functions, such as customer relationship management, customer service, entrepreneurship, internationalization, branding, marketing, tourism marketing, product development, advertising, cloud computing, electronic commerce (e-commerce), e-business, electronic retailing (e-retailing), electronic procurement (e-procurement), electronic government (e-government), mobile commerce (m-commerce), mobile payment (m-payment), human resource management (HRM), digital libraries, and education.

The adoption of social media introduces a new communication channel that must be monitored and managed. Depending on the number and type of social media sites, executives and social media users should be educated and trained to have digital literacy and IT competency to effectively manage social media platforms. Utilizing social media is required for modern organizations that seek to serve suppliers and customers, improve business performance, strengthen competitiveness, and obtain consistent success in the digital age. Therefore, it is required for modern organizations to investigate their social media, establish a strategic plan to regularly check their practical advancements, and immediately respond to the social media needs of customers in modern organizations. Professional and business applications of social media platforms can enhance business performance toward reaching strategic goals in the digital age.

REFERENCES

Adamic, L. A., & Glance, N. (2005). *The political blogosphere and the 2004 US election: Divided they blog*. Paper presented at the 3rd International Workshop on Link Discovery, Chicago, IL. doi:10.1145/1134271.1134277

Alabdulkareem, S. A. (2015). Exploring the use and the impacts of social media on teaching and learning science in Saudi. *Procedia: Social and Behavioral Sciences, 182*, 213–224. doi:10.1016/j.sbspro.2015.04.758

Alexander, R. M., & Gentry, J. K. (2014). Using social media to report financial results. *Business Horizons, 57*(2), 161–167. doi:10.1016/j.bushor.2013.10.009

Aman, M. M., & Jayroe, T. J. (2013). ICT, social media, and the Arab transition to democracy: From venting to acting. *Digest of Middle East Studies, 22*(2), 317–347. doi:10.1111/dome.12024

Aral, S., Dellarocas, C., & Godes, D. (2013). Introduction to the special issue–social media and business transformation: A framework for research. *Information Systems Research, 24*(1), 3–13. doi:10.1287/isre.1120.0470

Atzmueller, M. (2012). Mining social media: Key players, sentiments, and communities. *Wiley Interdisciplinary Reviews: Data Mining and Knowledge Discovery, 2*(5), 411–419. 10.1002/widm.1069

Auer, M. R. (2011). The policy sciences of social media.Policy Studies Journal, 39(4),709–736. doi:10.1111/j.1541-0072.2011.00428.x

Bakker, T. B., & de Vreese, C. H. (2011). Good news for the future? Young people, Internet use and political participation. *Communication Research, 38*(4), 451–470. doi:10.1177/0093650210381738

Ballings, M., & den Poel, D. V. (2015). CRM in social media: Predicting increases in Facebook usage frequency. *European Journal of Operational Research, 244*(1), 248–260. doi:10.1016/j.ejor.2015.01.001

Barbier, G., Tang, L., & Liu, H. (2011). Understanding online groups through social media. *Wiley Interdisciplinary Reviews: Data Mining and Knowledge Discovery, 1*(4), 330–338. doi: 10.1002/widm.37

Batta, H. E., & Iwokwagh, N. S. (2015). Optimising the digital age health-wise: Utilisation of new/social media by Nigerian teaching hospitals. *Procedia: Social and Behavioral Sciences, 176*, 175–185. doi:10.1016/j.sbspro.2015.01.459

Bekkers, V., Moody, R., & Edwards, A. (2011). Micro-mobilization, social media and coping strategies: Some Dutch experiences. *Policy & Internet, 3*(4), 1–29. doi:10.2202/1944-2866.1061

Benson, V., & Filippaios, F. (2015). Collaborative competencies in professional social networking: Are students short changed by curriculum in business education? *Computers in Human Behavior, 51*(B), 1331–1339. doi: 10.1016/j.chb.2014.11.031

Benson, V., & Morgan, S. (2015). *Implications of social media in personal and professional settings*. Hershey, PA: IGI Global. doi:10.4018/978-1-4666-7401-1

Bernabe-Moreno, J., Tejeda-Lorente, A., Porcel, C., Fujita, H., & Herrera-Viedma, E. (2015). CARE-SOME: A system to enrich marketing customers acquisition and retention campaigns using social media information. *Knowledge-Based Systems*, *80*, 163–179. doi:10.1016/j.knosys.2014.12.033

Berthon, P. R., Pitt, L. F., Plangger, K., & Shapiro, D. (2012). Marketing meets Web 2.0, social media, and creative consumers: Implications for international marketing strategy. *Business Horizons*, *55*(3), 261–271. doi:10.1016/j.bushor.2012.01.007

Beshears, J., Choi, J. J., Laibson, D., & Madrian, B. C. (2008). How are preferences revealed? *Journal of Public Economics*, *92*(8/9), 1787–1794. doi:10.1016/j.jpubeco.2008.04.010 PMID:24761048

Bhanot, S. (2012). Use of social media by companies to reach their customers. *SIES Journal of Management*, *8*(1), 47–55.

Bianco, J. S. (2009). Social networking and cloud computing: Precarious affordances for the "prosumer." *WSQ: Women's Studies Quarterly*, *37*(1/2), 303–312. doi:10.1353/wsq.0.0146

Binder, P., & Mansfield, N. R. (2013). Social networks and workplace risk: Classroom scenarios from a U.S. and EU perspective. *Journal of Legal Studies Education*, *30*(1), 1–44. doi:10.1111/j.1744-1722.2013.01113.x

Birkner, C. (2011). Sharing the love. *Marketing News*, *45*(3), 11–12.

Bowden, J. L. H. (2009). The process of customer engagement: A conceptual framework. *Journal of Marketing Theory and Practice*, *17*(1), 63–74. doi:10.2753/MTP1069-6679170105

Brammer, S. J., & Pavelin, S. (2006). Corporate reputation and social performance: The importance of fit. *Journal of Management Studies*, *43*(3), 435–455. doi:10.1111/j.1467-6486.2006.00597.x

Breakenridge, D. K. (2012). *Social media and public relations: Eight new practices for the PR professional*. Upper Saddle River, NJ: Pearson Education.

Brodie, R. J., Ilic, A., Juric, B., & Hollebeek, L. (2013). Consumer engagement in a virtual brand community: An exploratory analysis. *Journal of Business Research*, *66*(1), 105–114. doi:10.1016/j.jbusres.2011.07.029

Camarero, C., & San Jose, R. (2011). Social and attitudinal determinants of viral marketing dynamics. *Computers in Human Behavior*, *27*(6), 2292–2300. doi:10.1016/j.chb.2011.07.008

Cao, G., Wang, S., Hwang, M., Padmanabhan, A., Zhang, Z., & Soltani, K. (2015). A scalable framework for spatiotemporal analysis of location-based social media data. *Computers, Environment and Urban Systems*, *51*, 70–82. doi:10.1016/j.compenvurbsys.2015.01.002

Cao, P., Meister, S., & Klante, O. (2014). How social media influence apparel purchasing behavior. *Marketing Review St. Gallen*, *31*(6), 77–86. doi:10.1365/s11621-014-0427-y

Carr, J., Decreton, L., Qin, W., Rojas, B., Rossochacki, T., & Yang, Y. W. (2015). Social media in product development. *Food Quality and Preference*, *40*, 354–364. doi:10.1016/j.foodqual.2014.04.001

Chang, Y. T., Yu, H., & Lu, H. P. (2015). Persuasive messages, popularity cohesion, and message diffusion in social media marketing. *Journal of Business Research, 68*(4), 777–782. doi:10.1016/j.jbusres.2014.11.027

Cheung, C. M. K., Chiu, P. Y., & Lee, M. K. O. (2010). Online social networks: Why do students use Facebook? *Computers in Human Behavior, 27*(4), 1337–1343. doi:10.1016/j.chb.2010.07.028

Cheung, C. M. K., & Lee, M. K. O. (2010). A theoretical model of intentional social action in online social networks. *Decision Support Systems, 49*(1), 24–30. doi:10.1016/j.dss.2009.12.006

Chun, R. (2005). Corporate reputation: Meaning and measurement. *International Journal of Management Reviews, 7*(2), 91–109. doi:10.1111/j.1468-2370.2005.00109.x

Click, I. A., & Petit, J. (2010). Social networking and Web 2.0 in information literacy. *The International Information & Library Review, 42*(2), 137–142. doi:10.1080/10572317.2010.10762855

Conover, M. D., Goncalves, B., Flammini, A., & Menczer, F. (2012). Partisan asymmetries in online political activity. *EPJ Data Science, 1*(1), 1–19. doi:10.1140/epjds6

Coombs, W. T. (2014). *Ongoing crisis communication*. Thousand Oaks, CA: Sage Publications.

Corley, C. D., Farber, R. M., & Reynolds, W. N. (2012). Thought leaders during crises in massive social networks. *Statistical Analysis and Data Mining: The ASA Data Science Journal, 5*(3), 205–217. doi:10.1002/sam.11147

Curran, M. J., Draus, P., Schrager, M., & Zappala, S. (2014). College students and HR professionals: Conflicting views on information available on Facebook. *Human Resource Management Journal, 24*(4), 442–458. doi:10.1111/1748-8583.12033

DeCamp, M. (2013). Physicians, social media, and conflict of interest. *Journal of General Internal Medicine, 28*(2), 299–303. doi:10.1007/s11606-012-2251-x PMID:23129160

Dekker, R., & Engbersen, G. (2014). How social media transform migrant networks and facilitate migration. *Global Networks, 14*(4), 401–418. doi:10.1111/glob.12040

Dijkmans, C., Kerkhof, P., & Beukeboom, C. J. (2015). A stage to engage: Social media use and corporate reputation. *Tourism Management, 47*, 58–67. doi:10.1016/j.tourman.2014.09.005

Dixon, A. W., Martinez, J. M., & Martin, C. L. L. (2015). Employing social media as a marketing strategy in college sport: An examination of perceived effectiveness in accomplishing organizational objectives. *International Review on Public and Nonprofit Marketing, 12*(2), 97–113. doi:10.1007/s12208-015-0134-7

Domanski, M. C., & Cavale, N. (2012). Self-reported "worth it" rating of aesthetic surgery in social media. *Aesthetic Plastic Surgery, 36*(6), 1292–1295. doi:10.1007/s00266-012-9977-z PMID:23052381

Drouin, M., O'Connor, K. W., Schmidt, G. B., & Miller, D. A. (2015). Facebook fired: Legal perspectives and young adults' opinions on the use of social media in hiring and firing decisions. *Computers in Human Behavior, 46*, 123–128. doi:10.1016/j.chb.2015.01.011

Durukan, T., Bozaci, I., & Hamsioglu, A. B. (2012). An investigation of customer behaviours in social media. *European Journal of Economics, Finance and Administrative Sciences, 44*, 148–158.

Elder, A. (2014). Excellent online friendships: An Aristotelian defense of social media. *Ethics and Information Technology, 16*(4), 287–297. doi:10.1007/s10676-014-9354-5

Ephraim, P. E. (2013). African youths and the dangers of social networking: A culture-centered approach to using social media. *Ethics and Information Technology, 15*(4), 275–284. doi:10.1007/s10676-013-9333-2

Fichman, R. G., Kohli, R., & Krishnan, R. (2011). The role of information systems in healthcare: Current research and future trends. *Information Systems Research, 22*(3), 419–428. doi:10.1287/isre.1110.0382

Fieseler, C., Fleck, M., & Meckel, M. (2010). Corporate social responsibility in the blogosphere. *Journal of Business Ethics, 91*(4), 599–614. doi:10.1007/s10551-009-0135-8

Friesen, N., & Lowe, S. (2012). The questionable promise of social media for education: Connective learning and the commercial imperative. *Journal of Computer Assisted Learning, 28*(3), 183–194. doi:10.1111/j.1365-2729.2011.00426.x

Froot, K. A. (1989). New hope for the expectations hypothesis of the term structure of interest rates. *The Journal of Finance, 44*(2), 283–305. doi:10.1111/j.1540-6261.1989.tb05058.x

Gallant, L. M., Irizarry, C., Boone, G., & Kreps, G. (2011). Promoting participatory medicine with social media: New media applications on hospital websites that enhance health education and e-patients' voices. *Journal of Participatory Medicine, 3*, e49.

Gan, C., & Wang, W. (2015). Research characteristics and status on social media in China: A bibliometric and co-word analysis. *Scientometrics, 105*(2), 1167–1182. doi:10.1007/s11192-015-1723-2

Gardberg, N., & Fombrun, C. J. (2002). The global reputation quotient project: First steps towards a cross-nationally valid measure of corporate reputation. *Corporate Reputation Review, 4*(4), 303–307. doi:10.1057/palgrave.crr.1540151

Gil de Zúñiga, H., Molyneux, L., & Zheng, P. (2014). Social media, political expression, and political participation: Panel analysis of lagged and concurrent relationships. *Journal of Communication, 64*(4), 612–634. doi:10.1111/jcom.12103

Gillin, P. (2007). *The new influencers: A marketer's guide to the new social media*. Sanger, CA: Quill Driver Books.

Graham, M. E., & Moore, J. (2007). Consumers' willingness to pay for corporate reputation: The context of airline companies. *Corporate Reputation Review, 10*(3), 189–200. doi:10.1057/palgrave.crr.1550052

Greaves, F., Ramirez-Cano, D., Millett, C., Darzi, A., & Donaldson, L. (2013). Harnessing the cloud of patient experience: Using social media to detect poor quality healthcare. *BMJ Quality & Safety, 22*(3), 251–255. doi:10.1136/bmjqs-2012-001527 PMID:23349387

Gregoire, Y., Salle, A., & Tripp, T. M. (2015). Managing social media crises with your customers: The good, the bad, and the ugly. *Business Horizons, 58*(2), 173–182. doi:10.1016/j.bushor.2014.11.001

Gruen, T. W., Osmonbekov, T., & Czaplewski, A. J. (2006). eWOM: The impact of customer-to-customer online know-how exchange on customer value and loyalty. *Journal of Business Research, 59*(4), 449–456. doi:10.1016/j.jbusres.2005.10.004

Gurau, C. (2008). Integrated online marketing communication: Implementation and management. *Journal of Communication Management, 12*(2), 169–184. doi:10.1108/13632540810881974

Hanna, R., Rohm, A., & Crittenden, V. L. (2011). We're all connected: The power of the social media ecosystem. *Business Horizons, 54*(3), 265–273. doi:10.1016/j.bushor.2011.01.007

Hassan, H., Nadzim, S. Z. A., & Shiratuddin, N. (2015). Strategic use of social media for small business based on the AIDA model. *Procedia: Social and Behavioral Sciences, 172*, 262–269. doi:10.1016/j.sbspro.2015.01.363

Hausmann, A., & Poellmann, L. (2013). Using social media for arts marketing: Theoretical analysis and empirical insights for performing arts organizations. *International Review on Public and Nonprofit Marketing, 10*(2), 143–161. doi:10.1007/s12208-013-0094-8

Heinonen, K. (2011). Consumer activity in social media: Managerial approaches to consumers' social media behavior. *Journal of Consumer Behaviour, 10*(6), 356–364. doi:10.1002/cb.376

Hoffman, D. L., & Fodor, M. (2010). Can you measure the ROI of your social media marketing? *MIT Sloan Management Review, 52*(1), 41–49.

Hollebeek, L. D. (2011). Demystifying customer brand engagement: Exploring the loyalty nexus. *Journal of Marketing Management, 27*(7/8), 785–807. doi:10.1080/0267257X.2010.500132

Housholder, E., & LaMarre, H. L. (2015). Political social media engagement: Comparing campaign goals with voter behavior. *Public Relations Review, 41*(1), 138–140. doi:10.1016/j.pubrev.2014.10.007

Hrastinski, S., & Aghaee, N. M. (2012). How are campus students using social media to support their studies? An explorative interview study. *Education and Information Technologies, 17*(4), 451–464. doi:10.1007/s10639-011-9169-5

Hudson, S., Roth, M. S., Madden, T. J., & Hudson, R. (2015). The effects of social media on emotions, brand relationship quality, and word of mouth: An empirical study of music festival attendees. *Tourism Management, 47*, 68–76. doi:10.1016/j.tourman.2014.09.001

Hwang, H., & Kim, K. O. (2015). Social media as a tool for social movements: The effect of social media use and social capital on intention to participate in social movements. *International Journal of Consumer Studies, 39*(5), 478–488. doi:10.1111/ijcs.12221

Johnston, J. (2015). "Loose tweets sink fleets" and other sage advice: Social media governance, policies and guidelines. *Journal of Public Affairs, 15*(2), 175–187. doi:10.1002/pa.1538

Jones, B., Temperley, J., & Lima, A. (2009). Corporate reputation in the era of Web 2.0: The case of Primark. *Journal of Marketing Management, 25*(9/10), 927–939. doi:10.1362/026725709X479309

Kaplan, A. M., & Haenlein, M. (2010). Users of the world, unite! The challenges and opportunities of social media. *Business Horizons, 53*(1), 59–68. doi:10.1016/j.bushor.2009.09.003

Karnik, A., Saroop, A., & Borkar, V. (2013). On the diffusion of messages in on-line social networks. *Performance Evaluation, 70*(4), 271–285. doi:10.1016/j.peva.2012.12.002

Kasemsap, K. (2014a). The role of social networking in global business environments. In P. Smith & T. Cockburn (Eds.), *Impact of emerging digital technologies on leadership in global business* (pp. 183–201). Hershey, PA: IGI Global. doi:10.4018/978-1-4666-6134-9.ch010

Kasemsap, K. (2014b). The role of social media in the knowledge-based organizations. In I. Lee (Ed.), Integrating social media into business practice, applications, management, and models (pp. 254–275). Hershey, PA: IGI Global. doi:10.4018/978-1-4666-6182-0.ch013

Kasemsap, K. (2015a). The role of social media in international advertising. In N. Taşkıran & R. Yılmaz (Eds.), *Handbook of research on effective advertising strategies in the social media age* (pp. 171–196). Hershey, PA: IGI Global. doi:10.4018/978-1-4666-8125-5.ch010

Kasemsap, K. (2015b). The role of cloud computing adoption in global business. In V. Chang, R. Walters, & G. Wills (Eds.), *Delivery and adoption of cloud computing services in contemporary organizations* (pp. 26–55). Hershey, PA: IGI Global. doi:10.4018/978-1-4666-8210-8.ch002

Kasemsap, K. (2015c). The role of cloud computing in global supply chain. In N. Rao (Ed.), *Enterprise management strategies in the era of cloud computing* (pp. 192–219). Hershey, PA: IGI Global. doi:10.4018/978-1-4666-8339-6.ch009

Kasemsap, K. (2015d). The role of customer relationship management in the global business environments. In T. Tsiakis (Ed.), *Trends and innovations in marketing information systems* (pp. 130–156). Hershey, PA: IGI Global. doi:10.4018/978-1-4666-8459-1.ch007

Kasemsap, K. (2015e). The role of e-business adoption in the business world. In N. Ray, D. Das, S. Chaudhuri, & A. Ghosh (Eds.), *Strategic infrastructure development for economic growth and social change* (pp. 51–63). Hershey, PA: IGI Global. doi:10.4018/978-1-4666-7470-7.ch005

Kasemsap, K. (2016a). Encouraging supply chain networks and customer loyalty in global supply chain. In N. Kamath & S. Saurav (Eds.), *Handbook of research on strategic supply chain management in the retail industry* (pp. 87–112). Hershey, PA: IGI Global. doi:10.4018/978-1-4666-9894-9.ch006

Kasemsap, K. (2016b). The roles of social media marketing and brand management in global marketing. In W. Ozuem & G. Bowen (Eds.), *Competitive social media marketing strategies* (pp. 173–200). Hershey, PA: IGI Global. doi:10.4018/978-1-4666-9776-8.ch009

Kietzmann, J. H., Hermkens, K., McCarthy, I. P., & Silvestre, B. S. (2011). Social media? Get serious! Understanding the functional building blocks of social media. *Business Horizons*, *54*(3), 241–251. doi:10.1016/j.bushor.2011.01.005

Kim, A. J., & Ko, E. (2011). Do social media marketing activities enhance customer equity? An empirical study of the luxury fashion brand. *Journal of Business Research*, *65*(10), 1480–1486. doi:10.1016/j.jbusres.2011.10.014

Kim, K. S., Sin, S. C. J., & He, Y. (2013). Information seeking through social media: Impact of user characteristics on social media use. *Proceedings of the American Society for Information Science and Technology*, *50*(1), 1–4. doi:10.1002/meet.14505001155

Kiráľová, A., & Pavliceka, A. (2015). Development of social media strategies in tourism destination. *Procedia: Social and Behavioral Sciences, 175*, 358–366. doi:10.1016/j.sbspro.2015.01.1211

Kirtis, A. K., & Karahan, F. (2011). *To be or not to be in social media arena as the most cost-efficient marketing strategy after the global recession.* Paper presented at the 7th International Strategic Management Conference, Paris, France. doi:10.1016/j.sbspro.2011.09.083

LaMarre, H. L., & Suzuki-Holbrecht, Y. (2013). Tweeting democracy? Twitter as a voter mobilization strategy for congressional campaigns. *Public Relations Review, 39*(4), 360–368. doi:10.1016/j.pubrev.2013.07.009

Lange, P. G. (2007). Publicly private and privately public: Social networking on YouTube. *Journal of Computer-Mediated Communication, 13*(1), 361–380. doi:10.1111/j.1083-6101.2007.00400.x

Lee, J. (2015). The double-edged sword: The effects of journalists' social media activities on audience perceptions of journalists and their news products. *Journal of Computer-Mediated Communication, 20*(3), 312–329. doi:10.1111/jcc4.12113

Leonardi, P. M., Huysman, M., & Steinfield, C. (2013). Enterprise social media: Definition, history, and prospects for the study of social technologies in organizations. *Journal of Computer-Mediated Communication, 19*(1), 1–19. doi:10.1111/jcc4.12029

Li, C., & Tsai, W. H. S. (2015). Social media usage and acculturation: A test with Hispanics in the U.S. *Computers in Human Behavior, 45*, 204–212. doi:10.1016/j.chb.2014.12.018

Lis, E., Wood, M. A., Chiniara, C., Biskin, R., & Montoro, R. (2015). Psychiatrists' perceptions of Facebook and other social media. *The Psychiatric Quarterly, 86*(4), 597–602. doi:10.1007/s11126-015-9358-2 PMID:25791472

Liu, L., Wu, J., Li, P., & Li, Q. (2015). A social-media-based approach to predicting stock comovement. *Expert Systems with Applications, 42*(8), 3893–3901. doi:10.1016/j.eswa.2014.12.049

Lovejoy, K., & Saxton, G. D. (2012). Information, community, and action: How nonprofit organizations use social media. *Journal of Computer-Mediated Communication, 17*(3), 337–353. doi:10.1111/j.1083-6101.2012.01576.x

Luo, X., Zhang, J., & Duan, W. (2013). Social media and firm equity value. *Information Systems Research, 24*(1), 146–163. doi:10.1287/isre.1120.0462

Majchrzak, A., Faraj, S., Kane, G. C., & Azad, B. (2013). The contradictory influence of social media affordances on online communal knowledge sharing. *Journal of Computer-Mediated Communication, 19*(1), 38–55. doi:10.1111/jcc4.12030

Mangold, W. G., & Faulds, D. J. (2009). Social media: The new hybrid element of the promotion mix. *Business Horizons, 52*(4), 357–365. doi:10.1016/j.bushor.2009.03.002

Moran, E., & Gossieaux, F. (2010). Marketing in a hyper-social world. *Journal of Advertising Research, 50*(3), 232–239. doi:10.2501/S0021849910091397

Mucan, B., & Özeltürkay, E. Y. (2014). Social media creates competitive advantages: How Turkish banks use this power? A content analysis of Turkish banks through their webpages. *Procedia: Social and Behavioral Sciences, 148*, 137–145. doi:10.1016/j.sbspro.2014.07.027

Nadkarni, A., & Hofmann, S. G. (2012). Why do people use Facebook? *Personality and Individual Differences, 52*(3), 243–249. doi:10.1016/j.paid.2011.11.007 PMID:22544987

Neill, M. S., & Moody, M. (2015). Who is responsible for what? Examining strategic roles in social media management. *Public Relations Review, 41*(1), 109–118. doi:10.1016/j.pubrev.2014.10.014

Nguyen, N., & Leblanc, G. (2001). Corporate image and corporate reputation in customers' retention decisions in services. *Journal of Retailing and Consumer Services, 8*(4), 227–236. doi:10.1016/S0969-6989(00)00029-1

Nwagbara, U. (2013). The effects of social media on environmental sustainability activities of oil and gas multinationals in Nigeria. *Thunderbird International Business Review, 55*(6), 689–697. doi:10.1002/tie.21584

O'Reilly, T. (2007). What is Web 2.0: Design patterns and business models for the next generation of software.Communications & Strategies, *65*(1), 17–37.

O'Connor, P. (2010). Managing a hotel's image on TripAdvisor. *Journal of Hospitality Marketing & Management, 19*(7), 754–772. doi:10.1080/19368623.2010.508007

Olsen, N. V., & Christensen, K. (2015). Social media, new digital technologies and their potential application in sensory and consumer research. *Current Opinion in Food Science, 3*, 23–26. doi:10.1016/j.cofs.2014.11.006

Ooms, W., Bell, J., & Kok, R. A. W. (2015). Use of social media in inbound open innovation: Building capabilities for absorptive capacity. *Creativity and Innovation Management, 24*(1), 136–150. doi:10.1111/caim.12105

Ott, L., & Theunissen, P. (2015). Reputations at risk: Engagement during social media crises. *Public Relations Review, 41*(1), 97–102. doi:10.1016/j.pubrev.2014.10.015

Özgüven, N., & Mucan, B. (2013). The relationship between personality traits and social media use. *Social Behavior and Personality, 41*(3), 517–528. doi:10.2224/sbp.2013.41.3.517

Paniagua, J., & Sapena, J. (2014). Business performance and social media: Love or hate? *Business Horizons, 57*(6), 719–728. doi:10.1016/j.bushor.2014.07.005

Park, D. H., Lee, J., & Han, I. (2007). The effect of on-line consumer reviews on consumer purchasing intention: The moderating role of involvement. *International Journal of Electronic Commerce, 11*(4), 125–148. doi:10.2753/JEC1086-4415110405

Park, S., & Allen, P. J. (2013). Responding to online reviews problem solving and engagement in hotels. *Cornell Hospitality Quarterly, 54*(1), 64–73. doi:10.1177/1938965512463118

Parveen, F., Jaafar, N. I., & Ainin, S. (2015). Social media usage and organizational performance: Reflections of Malaysian social media managers. *Telematics and Informatics*, *32*(1), 67–78. doi:10.1016/j.tele.2014.03.001

Patterson, P., Yu, T., & de Ruyter, K. (2006). *Understanding customer engagement in services*. Paper presented at the 2006 Australian & New Zealand Marketing Academy Conference (ANZMAC 2006), Brisbane, Australia.

Pennington-Gray, L., London, B., Cahyanto, I., & Klages, W. (2011). Expanding the tourism crisis management planning framework to include social media: Lessons from the deepwater horizon oil spill, 2010. *International Journal of Tourism Anthropology*, *1*(3/4), 239–253. doi:10.1504/IJTA.2011.043708

Phang, C. W., Zhang, C., & Sutanto, J. (2013). The influence of user interaction and participation in social media on the consumption intention of niche products. *Information & Management*, *50*(8), 661–672. doi:10.1016/j.im.2013.07.001

Pookulangara, S., & Koesler, K. (2011). Cultural influence on consumers' usage of social networks and its' impact on online purchase intentions. *Journal of Retailing and Consumer Services*, *18*(4), 348–354. doi:10.1016/j.jretconser.2011.03.003

Porter, M. E. (1996). What is strategy? *Harvard Business Review*, *74*(6), 61–78. PMID:10158474

Roberts, D. L., & Candi, M. (2014). Leveraging social network sites in new product development: Opportunity or hype? *Journal of Product Innovation Management*, *31*(s1), 105–117. doi:10.1111/jpim.12195

Saxton, G. D., & Guo, C. (2014). Online stakeholder targeting and the acquisition of social media capital. *International Journal of Nonprofit and Voluntary Sector Marketing*, *19*(4), 286–300. doi:10.1002/nvsm.1504

Sellnow, T. L., Ulmer, R. R., Seeger, M. W., & Littlefield, R. (2008). *Effective risk communication: A message-centered approach*. New York, NY: Springer–Verlag.

Sethuraman, R. A. J., Tellis, G. J., & Briesch, R. (2011). How well does advertising work? Generalizations from a meta-analysis of brand advertising elasticity.JMR, Journal of Marketing Research, 48(3), 457–471. doi: 10.1509/jmkr.48.3.457.

Shamma, H. M. (2012). Toward a comprehensive understanding of corporate reputation: Concept, measurement and implications. *International Journal of Business and Management*, *7*(16), 151–169. doi:10.5539/ijbm.v7n16p151

Shcherbakova, N., & Shepherd, M. (2014). Community pharmacists, Internet and social media: An empirical investigation. *Research in Social & Administrative Pharmacy*, *10*(6), e75–e85. doi:10.1016/j.sapharm.2013.11.007 PMID:24388002

Shirky, C. (2011). The political power of social media: Technology, the public sphere, and political change. *Foreign Affairs*, *90*(1), 28–41.

Sigala, M. (2011). Social media and crisis management in tourism: Applications and implications for research. *Information Technology & Tourism*, *13*(4), 269–283. doi:10.3727/109830512X13364362859812

Sigala, M. (2015). Social media marketing in tourism and hospitality. *Information Technology & Tourism, 15*(2), 181–183. doi:10.1007/s40558-015-0024-1

Sisco, H. F., & McCorkindale, T. (2013). Communicating "pink": An analysis of the communication strategies, transparency, and credibility of breast cancer social media sites. *International Journal of Nonprofit and Voluntary Sector Marketing, 18*(4), 287–301. doi:10.1002/nvsm.1474

Smith, K. T., Smith, M., & Wang, K. (2010). Does brand management of corporate reputation translate into higher market value? *Journal of Strategic Marketing, 18*(3), 201–221. doi:10.1080/09652540903537030

Smith, M. K., & Denali, D. L. (2014). Social media in health education, promotion, and communication: Reaching rural Hispanic populations along the USA/Mexico border region. *Journal of Racial and Ethnic Health Disparities, 1*(3), 194–198. doi:10.1007/s40615-014-0025-3

Sul, H. K., Dennies, A. R., & Yuan, L. I. (2014). *Trading on Twitter: The financial information content of emotion in social media.* Paper presented at the 47th Hawaii International Conference on System Sciences (HICSS 2014), Big Island, HI.

Sweetser, K. D. (2011). Digital political public relations. In J. Stromback & S. Kiousis (Eds.), *Political public relations principles and applications* (pp. 293–313). New York, NY: Routledge.

Trainor, K. J., Andzulis, J., Rapp, A., & Agnihotri, R. (2014). Social media technology usage and customer relationship performance: A capabilities-based examination of social CRM. *Journal of Business Research, 67*(6), 1201–1208. doi:10.1016/j.jbusres.2013.05.002

Tumasjan, A., Sprenger, T. O., Sandner, P. G., & Welpe, I. M. (2010). *Predicting elections with Twitter: What 140 characters reveal about political sentiment.* Paper presented at the 4th International Conference on Weblogs and Social Media (ICWSM 2010), Washington, DC.

van Puijenbroek, T., Poell, R. F., Kroon, B., & Timmerman, V. (2014). The effect of social media use on work-related learning. *Journal of Computer Assisted Learning, 30*(2), 159–172. doi:10.1111/jcal.12037

Veil, S. R., Buehner, T., & Palenchar, M. J. (2011). A work-in-process literature review: Incorporating social media in risk and crisis communication. *Journal of Contingencies and Crisis Management, 19*(2), 110–122. doi:10.1111/j.1468-5973.2011.00639.x

Venkatraman, N., & Ramanujam, V. (1986). Measurement of business performance in strategy research: A comparison of approaches. *Academy of Management Review, 11*(4), 801–814. doi: 10.2307/258398

Walsh, G., Mitchell, V. W., Jackson, P., & Beatty, S. E. (2009). Examining the antecedents and consequences of corporate reputation: A customer perspective. *British Journal of Management, 20*(2), 187–203. doi:10.1111/j.1467-8551.2007.00557.x

Weinberg, B. D., & Pehlivan, E. (2011). Social spending: Managing the social media mix. *Business Horizons, 54*(3), 275–282. doi:10.1016/j.bushor.2011.01.008

Werthner, H., & Ricci, F. (2004). E-commerce and tourism. *Communications of the ACM, 47*(12), 101–105. doi:10.1145/1035134.1035141

Westerman, D., Spence, P. R., & van der Heide, B. (2014). Social media as information source: Recency of updates and credibility of information. *Journal of Computer-Mediated Communication*, *19*(2), 171–183. doi:10.1111/jcc4.12041

Wilcox, D. L., & Cameron, G. T. (2012). *Public relations strategies and tactics*. Glenview, IL: Pearson Education.

Williams, D. L., Crittenden, V. L., Keo, T., & McCarty, P. (2012). The use of social media: An exploratory study of usage among digital natives. *Journal of Public Affairs*, *12*(2), 127–136. doi:10.1002/pa.1414

Williams, H. T. P., McMurray, J. R., Kurz, T., & Lambert, F. H. (2015). Network analysis reveals open forums and echo chambers in social media discussions of climate change. *Global Environmental Change*, *32*, 126–138. doi:10.1016/j.gloenvcha.2015.03.006

Woodcock, N., Green, A., & Starkey, M. (2011). Social CRM as a business strategy: The customer framework. *Journal of Database Marketing & Customer Strategy Management*, *18*(1), 50–64. doi:10.1057/dbm.2011.7

Wu, J., Sun, H., & Tan, Y. (2013). Social media research: A review. *Journal of Systems Science and Systems Engineering*, *22*(3), 257–282. doi:10.1007/s11518-013-5225-6

Yadav, V., & Arora, M. (2012). The product purchase intentions in Facebook using analytical hierarchical process. *Radix International Journal of Economics and Business Management*, *1*(4), 26–54.

Yang, M., Kiang, M., & Shang, W. (2015). Filtering big data from social media: Building an early warning system for adverse drug reactions. *Journal of Biomedical Informatics*, *54*, 230–240. doi:10.1016/j.jbi.2015.01.011 PMID:25688695

Yang, M., Li, Y., & Kiang, M. (2011). *Uncovering social media data public health surveillance*. Paper presented at the 15th Pacific Asia Conference on Information System (PACIS 2011), Brisbane, Australia.

Yu, Y., Duan, W., & Cao, Q. (2013). The impact of social and conventional media on firm equity value: A sentiment analysis approach. *Decision Support Systems*, *55*(4), 919–926. doi:10.1016/j.dss.2012.12.028

Zolkepli, I. A., & Kamarulzaman, Y. (2015). Social media adoption: The role of media needs and innovation characteristics. *Computers in Human Behavior*, *43*, 189–209. doi:10.1016/j.chb.2014.10.050

ADDITIONAL READING

Agerdal-Hjermind, A. (2014). Organizational blogging: A case study of a corporate weblog from an employee perspective. *Corporate Communications: An International Journal*, *19*(1), 34–51. doi:10.1108/CCIJ-09-2012-0066

Ali, H. (2011). Exchanging value within individuals' networks: Social support implications for health marketers. *Journal of Marketing Management*, *27*(3/4), 316–335. doi:10.1080/0267257X.2011.547075

Andre, P., Bernstein, M., & Luther, K. (2012). What makes a great tweet? *Harvard Business Review*, *90*(5), 36–37.

Babaesmailli, M., Arbabshirani, B., & Golmah, V. (2012). Integrating analytical network process and fuzzy logic to prioritize the strategies: A case study for tile manufacturing firm. *Expert Systems with Applications, 39*(1), 925–935. doi:10.1016/j.eswa.2011.07.090

Baird, H. C., & Parasnis, G. (2011). From social media to social customer relationship management. *Strategy and Leadership, 30*(5), 30–37. doi:10.1108/10878571111161507

Bertoni, M., & Chirumalla, K. (2011). Leveraging Web 2.0 in new product development: Lessons learned from a cross-company study. *Journal of Universal Computer Science, 17*(4), 548–564.

Brown, V. R., & Vaughn, E. D. (2012). The writing on the (Facebook) wall: The use of social network sites in hiring decisions. *Journal of Business and Psychology, 26*(2), 219–225. doi:10.1007/s10869-011-9221-x

Chen, Y., Fay, S., & Wang, Q. (2011). The role of marketing in social media: How online consumer reviews evolve. *Journal of Interactive Marketing, 25*(2), 85–94. doi:10.1016/j.intmar.2011.01.003

Chikandiwa, S. T., Contogiannis, E., & Jembere, E. (2013). The adoption of social media marketing in South African banks. *European Business Review, 25*(4), 365–381. doi:10.1108/EBR-02-2013-0013

Christou, E. (2015). Branding social media in the travel industry. *Procedia: Social and Behavioral Sciences, 175*, 607–614. doi:10.1016/j.sbspro.2015.01.1244

Gopsill, J. A., McAlpine, H. C., & Hicks, B. J. (2013). A social media framework to support engineering design communication. *Advanced Engineering Informatics, 27*(4), 580–597. doi:10.1016/j.aei.2013.07.002

Green, E. (2011). Pushing the social media buttons. *Media Development, 58*(1), 12–15.

Grieve, R., Indian, M., Witteveen, K., Tolan, G. A., & Marrington, J. (2013). Face-to-face or Facebook: Can social connectedness be derived online? *Computers in Human Behavior, 29*(3), 604–609. doi:10.1016/j.chb.2012.11.017

Hall, R., & Lewis, S. (2014). Managing workplace bullying and social media policy: Implications for employee engagement. *Academy of Business Research Journal, 1*, 128–138.

Hansen, D. L., Shneiderman, B., & Smith, M. A. (2011). *Analyzing social media networks with Nodexl.* Burlington, MA: Elsevier.

Hsu, Y. H., & Tsou, H. T. (2011). Understanding customer experiences in online blog environments. *International Journal of Information Management, 31*(6), 510–523. doi:10.1016/j.ijinfomgt.2011.05.003

Hughes, D. J., Rowe, M., Batey, M., & Lee, A. (2011). A tale of two sites: Twitter vs. Facebook and the personality predictors. *Computers in Human Behavior, 28*(2), 561–569. doi:10.1016/j.chb.2011.11.001

Kietzmann, J. H., Silvestre, B. S., McCarthy, I. P., & Pitt, L. F. (2012). Unpacking the social media phenomenon: Towards a research agenda. *Journal of Public Affairs, 12*(2), 109–119. doi:10.1002/pa.1412

Kim, Y. A., & Ahmad, M. A. (2013). Trust, distrust and lack of confidence of users in online social media-sharing communities. *Knowledge-Based Systems, 37*(1), 438–450. doi:10.1016/j.knosys.2012.09.002

Kuksov, D., Shachar, R., & Kangkang, W. (2013). Advertising and consumers' communications. *Marketing Science*, *32*(2), 294–309. doi:10.1287/mksc.1120.0753

Lau, R. Y. K., Xia, Y., & Ye, Y. (2014). A probabilistic generative model for mining cybercriminal networks from online social media. *IEEE Computational Intelligence Magazine*, *9*(1), 31–43. doi:10.1109/MCI.2013.2291689

Lee, T. Y., & BradLow, E. T. (2011). Automated marketing research using online customer reviews. *JMR, Journal of Marketing Research*, *48*(5), 881–894. doi:10.1509/jmkr.48.5.881

Moe, W. M., & Schweidel, D. A. (2012). Online product opinions: Incidence, evaluation, and evolution. *Marketing Science*, *31*(3), 372–386. doi:10.1287/mksc.1110.0662

Oh, O., Agrawal, M., & Rao, H. R. (2013). Community intelligence and social media services: A rumor theoretic analysis of tweets during social crises. *Management Information Systems Quarterly*, *37*(2), 407–426.

Okazaki, S., & Taylor, C. R. (2013). Social media and international advertising: Theoretical challenges and future directions. *International Marketing Review*, *30*(1), 56–71. doi:10.1108/02651331311298573

Onishi, H., & Manchanda, P. (2012). Marketing activity, blogging and sales. *International Journal of Research in Marketing*, *29*(3), 221–234. doi:10.1016/j.ijresmar.2011.11.003

Smock, A. D., Ellison, N. B., Lampe, C., & Wohn, D. Y. (2011). Facebook as a toolkit: A uses and gratification approach to unbundling feature use. *Computers in Human Behavior*, *27*(6), 2322–2329. doi:10.1016/j.chb.2011.07.011

Sun, M., Chen, Z. Y., & Fan, Z. P. (2014). A multi-task multi-kernel transfer learning method for customer response modeling in social media. *Procedia Computer Science*, *31*, 221–230. doi:10.1016/j.procs.2014.05.263

Wang, X., Yu, C., & Wei, Y. (2012). Social media peer communication and impacts on purchase intentions: A consumer socialization framework. *Journal of Interactive Marketing*, *26*(4), 198–208. doi:10.1016/j.intmar.2011.11.004

Yuan, Y., Zhao, X., Liao, Q., & Chi, C. (2013). The use of different information and communication technologies to support knowledge sharing in organizations: From e-mail to micro-blogging. *Journal of the American Society for Information Science and Technology*, *64*(8), 1659–1670. doi:10.1002/asi.22863

KEY TERMS AND DEFINITIONS

Blog: The website, similar to an online journal that includes chronological entries made by individuals.
Facebook: The name of a social networking service and website, launched in 2004.
Internet: The worldwide computer network that provides information on many subjects and enables users to exchange messages.

Social Media: The website and application considered as collectively constituting a medium by which people share messages, photographs, and other information, especially in the online communities based on shared interests.

Social Media Marketing: The methods for advertising products, services, or brands using the Internet, by attracting the interest of groups of people who discuss them, make suggestions about them.

Technology: The use of scientific knowledge to solve practical problems, especially in industry and commerce.

Twitter: The website where people can post short messages about their current activities.

Web 2.0: The name for all the Internet features and websites that allow users to create, change, and share the Internet content.

Compilation of References

Aaker, J., & Smith, A. (2010). *The Dragonfly Effect.* San Francisco: Jossey-Bass.

Aaker, L. J. (1997). Dimensions of brand personality. *JMR, Journal of Marketing Research, 14*(1), 347–356. doi:10.2307/3151897

Adamic, L. A., & Glance, N. (2005). *The political blogosphere and the 2004 US election: Divided they blog.* Paper presented at the 3rd International Workshop on Link Discovery, Chicago, IL. doi:10.1145/1134271.1134277

Adelman, M. B., Ahuvia, A., & Goodwin, C. (1994). Beyond Smiling: Social Support and Service Quality. In R. T. Rust & R. L. Oliver (Eds.), *Service Quality: New Directions in Theory and Practice* (pp. 139–171). London: Sage. doi:10.4135/9781452229102.n7

Adner, R. (2012). *The wide lens. A new strategy for innovation.* London: Penguin Group.

Adorno, T. W. (2005). *Minima Moralia: Reflections on a Damaged Life.* London: Verso.

Agnihotri, R., Kothandaraman, P., Kashyap, R., & Singh, R. (2012). Bringing "Social" into Sales: The Impact of Salespeople's Social Media Use on Service Behaviors and Value Creation. *Journal of Personal Selling & Sales Management, 32*(3), 333–348. doi:10.2753/PSS0885-3134320304

Aguirre-Rodriguez, A., Bosnjak, M., & Sirgy, J. (2012). Moderators of the self-congruity effect on consumer decision-making: A meta-analysis. *Journal of Business Research, 65*(8), 1179–1188. doi:10.1016/j.jbusres.2011.07.031

Ahlquist, L., & Shukoff, P. (2015). *YouTube.* Retrieved from Epic Rap Battles of history: https://www.youtube.com/user/ERB

Ahmed, I., & Qazi, T. F. (2011). Deciphering the social costs of Social Networking Sites (SNSs) for university students. *African Journal of Business Management, 5*(14), 5664–5674. Retrieved from http://www.academicjournals.org/article/article1380721081_Ahmed%20and%20Qazi.pdf

Ahuja, K., Galletta, D., & Carley, D. (2003). Individual centrality and performance in virtual R&D groups: An empirical study. *Management Science, 49*(1), 21–38. doi:10.1287/mnsc.49.1.21.12756

Ahuvia, A. (2001). Traditional, interpretive, and reception based content analyses: Improving the ability of content analysis to address issues of pragmatic and theoretical concern. *Social Indicators Research, 54*(2), 139–172. doi:10.1023/A:1011087813505

Akçay, D. (2013). *The effects of interaction design in mobile publishing: Research on newspaper web pages compatibility to mobile devices.* (Unpublished doctoral dissertation). Yeditepe University's Graduate Institute Of Social Sciences, Istanbul.

Alabdulkareem, S. A. (2015). Exploring the use and the impacts of social media on teaching and learning science in Saudi. *Procedia: Social and Behavioral Sciences, 182,* 213–224. doi:10.1016/j.sbspro.2015.04.758

Alavi, M., & Leidner, D. E. (2001). Review: Knowledge management and knowledge management systems: Conceptual foundations and research issues. *Management Information Systems Quarterly*, *25*(1), 107–136. doi:10.2307/3250961

Albakour, M. D., Kruschwitz, U., Nanas, N., Song, D., Fasli, M., & De Roeck, A. (2011). Exploring ant colony optimisation for adaptive interactive search. In *Advances in Information Retrieval Theory* (pp. 213–224). Berlin: Springer. doi:10.1007/978-3-642-23318-0_20

Alcázar, P. (2010). *Estrategias de marketing en las redes sociales*. Retrieved from http://www.emprendedores.es/gestion/marketing-en-redes-sociales/sumario

Aldrich, H. E., Rosen, B., & Woodward, W. (1987). The impact of social networks on business foundings and profit: a longitudinal study. In Frontiers of Entrepreneur-ship Research. Wellesley, MA: Babson College.

Alexander, R. M., & Gentry, J. K. (2014). Using social media to report financial results. *Business Horizons*, *57*(2), 161–167. doi:10.1016/j.bushor.2013.10.009

Al-Rahmi, W. M., Othman, M. S., & Musa, M. A. (2014). The improvement of students' academic performance by using social media through collaborative learning in Malaysian higher education. *Asian Social Science*, *10*(8), 210–221.

Al-Saggaf, Y., & Islam, M. Z. (2012). Privacy in Social Network Sites (SNS): The threats from data mining. *Ethical Space: The International Journal of Communication Ethics*, *9*(4), 32–40.

Al-Saggaf, Y., & Islam, M. Z. (2015). Data Mining and Privacy of Social Network Sites' Users: Implications of the Data Mining Problem. *Science and Engineering Ethics*, *21*(4), 941–966. doi:10.1007/s11948-014-9564-6 PMID:24916538

Al-Shawabkeh, A., & Lim, A. (2014). The Use of Social Media In Higher Education Learning: SWOT Analysis of Using Social Media for Learning. In *Proceedings of the European Conference on Social Media (ECSM)*. University of Brighton.

Aman, M. M., & Jayroe, T. J. (2013). ICT, social media, and the Arab transition to democracy: From venting to acting. *Digest of Middle East Studies*, *22*(2), 317–347. doi:10.1111/dome.12024

Amichai-Hamburger, Y. (2002). Internet and Personality. *Computers in Human Behavior*, *18*(1), 1–10. doi:10.1016/S0747-5632(01)00034-6

Amichai-Hamburger, Y., & Vinitzky, G. (2010). Social network use and personality. *Computers in Human Behavior*, *26*(6), 1289–1295.

Anderson, D. G. (2002). Biotechnology and the quaternary industrial sector. *Australasian Biotechnology*, *12*(1), 21–21.

Anderson, E. W., Fornell, C., & Lehmann, D. R. (1994). Customer Satisfaction, Market Share, and Profitability: Findings from Sweden. *Journal of Marketing*, *58*(3), 53–66. doi:10.2307/1252310

Anderson, E., & Weitz, B. (1992). The Use of Pledges to build and Sustain Commitment in Distribution Channels. *JMR, Journal of Marketing Research*, *29*(1), 18–34. doi:10.2307/3172490

Anderson, J. C., & Narus, J. A. (1984). A Model of the Distributor's Perspective of Distributor- Manufacturer Working Relationships. *Journal of Marketing*, *48*(4), 62–74. doi:10.2307/1251511

Anderson, K. (2011, December26). The Protester. *Time*, 38–68.

Anderson, L., & Taylor, R. (1995). McCarthy's 4PS: Timeworn or time-tested? *Journal of Marketing Theory and Practice*, *3*(3), 1–9. doi:10.1080/10696679.1995.11501691

Andzulis, J. M., Panagopoulos, N. G., & Rapp, A. (2012). A Review of Social Media and Implications for the Sales Process. *Journal of Personal Selling & Sales Management*, *32*(3), 305–316. doi:10.2753/PSS0885-3134320302

Appadurai, A. (2011). *Disjuncture and Difference in the Global Cultural Economy*. Retrieved October 15, 2011 from http://www.intcul.tohoku.ac.jp/~holden/MediatedSociety/Readings/2003_04/Appadurai.html

Aral, S., Dellarocas, C., & Godes, D. (2013). Social Media and Business Transformation: A Framework for Research. *Information Systems Research, 24*(1), 3–14. doi:10.1287/isre.1120.0470

Arboledas, J. R., Ferrero, M. L., & Vidal-Ribas, I. S. (2001). *Internet recruiting power: opportunities and effectiveness*. University of Navarra.

Arche, K. (2013). *Postinternet Observations*. Retrieved November 20, 2015, from https://artaftertheinternet.files.wordpress.com/2013/10/eeadf-postinternetessay.pdf

Arendt, H. (1998). *The Human Condition*. Chicago: University of Chicago Press. doi:10.7208/chicago/9780226924571.001.0001

Armiani, M., Badii, A., De Liddo, A., Georgi, S., Passani, A., Piccolo, L. S. G., & Teli, M. (2014). Collective Awareness Platform for Sustainability and Social Innovation: An Introduction. France/Nice.

Armstrong, L. (2013). Twitterfeed @lancearmstrong.

Armstrong, L. (2015). Twitterfeed @lancearmstrong.

Arnaboldi, V., Conti, M., Passarella, A., & Dunbar, R. (2013). Dynamics of personal social relationships in online social networks: A study on Twitter. In *Proceedings of COSN '13*. doi:10.1145/2512938.2512949

Arnett, D. B., & Badrinarayanan, V. (2005). Enhancing Customer-Needs--Driven CRM Strategies: Core Selling Teams, Knowledge Management Competence, and Relationship Marketing Competence. *Journal of Personal Selling & Sales Management, 25*(4), 329–343.

Arnold, N., & Paulus, T. (2010). Using a social networking site for experiential learning: Appropriating, lurking, modeling and community building. *The Internet and Higher Education, 13*(4), 188–196. doi:10.1016/j.iheduc.2010.04.002

Arnstein, S. R. (1969). A ladder of citizen participation. *Journal of the American Planning Association, 35*(4), 216. Retrieved from http://openurl.library.dmu.ac.uk/stxlcl3?sid=google&auinit=SR&aulast=Arnstein&atitle=Aladderofcitizenparticipation&id=doi:10.1080/01944366908977225&title=JournaloftheAmericanInstituteofPlanners&volume=35&issue=4&date=1969&spage=216&issn=0002-8991

Arquilla, J., & Ronfeldt, D. (1998). Preparing for the Information-Age Conflict: Part 1 Conceptual and Organizational Dimensions. *Information Communication and Society, 1*(1), 1–22. doi:10.1080/13691189809358951

Ashton, K. (2009, June 22). The Internet of Things Thing. *RFID Journal*.

Associated Press. (2012). *Lance Armstrong says he's champ*. Retrieved October 13, 2015, from http://espn.go.com/olympics/cycling/story/_/id/8315779/lance-armstrong-introduces-7-time-tour-de-france-champ

Atig, M. F., Cassel, S., Kaati, L., & Shrestha, A. (2014). Activity profiles in online social media. In *Proceedings of the 2014 IEEE/ACM International Conference on Advances in Social Networks Analysis and Mining* (ASONAM 2014). doi:10.1109/ASONAM.2014.6921685

Atzmueller, M. (2012). Mining social media: Key players, sentiments, and communities. *Wiley Interdisciplinary Reviews: Data Mining and Knowledge Discovery, 2*(5), 411–419. 10.1002/widm.1069

Auer, M. R. (2011). The policy sciences of social media.Policy Studies Journal, 39(4),709–736. doi:10.1111/j.1541-0072.2011.00428.x

Aula, A., Khan, R. M., & Guan, Z. (2010). How does search behavior change as search becomes more difficult? In *Proceedings of the SIGCHI Conference on Human Factors in Computing Systems*. doi:10.1145/1753326.1753333

Avaaz. (2014). Retrieved October 15, 2014 from Avaaz: http://www.avaaz.org/en/about.php

Avis, M. (2012). Brand personality factor based models: A critical review. *Australasian Marketing Journal*, *20*(1), 89–96. doi:10.1016/j.ausmj.2011.08.003

Baars, H., & Kemper, H.-G. (2008). Management Support with Structured and Unstructured Data — An Integrated Business Intelligence Framework. *Information Systems Management*, *25*(2), 132–148. doi:10.1080/10580530801941058

Bachelor, A. (2015). *Vine*. Retrieved from King Bach: https://vine.co/u/934940633704046592

Bagozzi, R. P., & Dholakia, U. M. (2002). Intentional social action on virtual communities. *Journal of Interactive Marketing*, *16*(2), 2–21. doi:10.1002/dir.10006

Bakker, P. (2014). Mr Gates returns: Curation, community management and new roles for journalists. *Journalism Studies*, *15*(5), 596–606. doi:10.1080/1461670X.2014.901783

Bakker, T. B., & de Vreese, C. H. (2011). Good news for the future? Young people, Internet use and political participation. *Communication Research*, *38*(4), 451–470. doi:10.1177/0093650210381738

Balani, S., & De Choudhury, M. (2015). Detecting and characterizing mental health related self-disclosure in social media. In *Proceedings of CHI 2015, Crossings*. doi:10.1145/2702613.2732733

Balkundi, P., Kilduff, M., & Harrison, D. (2011). Centrality and charisma: Comparing how leader networks and attribution affect team performance. *The Journal of Applied Psychology*, *96*(6), 1209–1222. doi:10.1037/a0024890 PMID:21895351

Ballinger, C. (2015, September 23). *You Tube*. Retrieved September 23, 2015, from Miranda Sings: https://www.youtube.com/user/mirandasings08

Ballings, M., & den Poel, D. V. (2015). CRM in social media: Predicting increases in Facebook usage frequency. *European Journal of Operational Research*, *244*(1), 248–260. doi:10.1016/j.ejor.2015.01.001

Banesto Fundación. (2011). Observatorio sobre el uso de las redes sociales en las PYMEs españolas (F. Banesto, Ed.). Author.

Banesto Fundación. (2013). Observatorio sobre el uso de las redes sociales en las PYMEs españolas (F. Banesto, Ed.). Author.

Bao, S., Xue, G., Wu, X., Yu, Y., Fei, B., & Su, Z. (2007). Optimizing web search using social annotations. In *Proceedings of the 16th international conference on World Wide Web*. doi:10.1145/1242572.1242640

Barahona, M., García, C., Gloor, P., & Parraguez, P. (2012). *Tracking the 2011 Student-led Movement in Chile through Social Media Use*. MIT.

Baran, P. (1962). *On Distributed Communications Networks*. Rand.

Barbier, G., Tang, L., & Liu, H. (2011). Understanding online groups through social media. *Wiley Interdisciplinary Reviews: Data Mining and Knowledge Discovery*, *1*(4), 330–338. doi: 10.1002/widm.37

Barker, M., Barker, D., Bormann, N., & Neher, K. (2012). Social Media Marketing. A Strategic Approach. CENGAGE Learning South-Western.

Baron, S., Warnaby, G., & Hunter-Jones, P. (2014). Service(s) marketing research: Developments and directions. *International Journal of Management Reviews*, *16*(2), 150–171. doi:10.1111/ijmr.12014

Barreto, A. (2013). The word-of-mouth phenomenon in the social media era. *International Journal of Market Research*, *56*(5), 632.

Barry, T. E. (1987). The Development of the Hierarchy of Effects: An Historical Perspective. *Current Issues and Research in Advertising*, *1987*, 251–295.

Bartes, F. (2010). Competitive Intelligence. *Acta Universitatis Agriculturae et Silviculturae Mendelianae Brunensis*, *58*(6), 43–50. doi:10.11118/actaun201058060043

Bartram, D. (2000). Internet recruitment and selection: Kissing frogs to find princes. *International Journal of Selection and Assessment*, *8*(4), 261–274. doi:10.1111/1468-2389.00155

Bates, D. (2013). *Lance Armstrong: I'm like Bill Clinton and people will forgive me*. Retrieved October, 13, 2015, from http://www.dailymail.co.uk/news/article-2292248/Lance-Armstrong-Im-like-Bill-Clinton-people-forgive-me.html

Batta, H. E., & Iwokwagh, N. S. (2015). Optimising the digital age health-wise: Utilisation of new/social media by Nigerian teaching hospitals. *Procedia: Social and Behavioral Sciences*, *176*, 175–185. doi:10.1016/j.sbspro.2015.01.459

Bazarova, N. N., Choi, Y. H., Sosik, V. S., Cosley, D., & Whilock, J. (2015). Social sharing of emotions on Facebook: Channel differences, satisfaction, and replies. In *Proceedings of CSCW*.

Beatson, A., Lee, N., & Coote, L. V. (2007). Self-Service Technology and the Service Encounter. *Service Industries Journal*, *27*(1), 75–89. doi:10.1080/02642060601038700

Beatty, R. P., & Ritter, J. R. (1986). Investment Banking, Reputation, and the Underpricing of Initial Public Offerings. *Journal of Financial Economics*, *15*(1-2), 213–232. doi:10.1016/0304-405X(86)90055-3

Beatty, S. E., Coleman, J. E., Ellis Reynolds, K., & Lee, J. (1996). Customer-sales associate retail relationships. *Journal of Retailing*, *72*(3), 223–247. doi:10.1016/S0022-4359(96)90028-7

Bekkers, V., Moody, R., & Edwards, A. (2011). Micro-mobilization, social media and coping strategies: Some Dutch experiences. *Policy & Internet*, *3*(4), 1–29. doi:10.2202/1944-2866.1061

Bell, D. R. (2005). Liberal Environmental Citizenship. *Environmental Politics*, *14*(2), 179–194. doi:10.1080/09644010500054863

Benckendorff, P., Moscardo, G., & Pendergast, D. (2010). *Tourism and Generation Y*. Cambridge: CAB International.

Benkler, Y. (2006). *The Wealth of Networks: How Social Production Transforms Markets and Freedom*. New Haven, CT: Yale Universty Press.

Bennett, S., Bishop, A., Dalgarno, B., Waycott, J., & Kennedy, G. (2012). Implementing Web 2.0 technologies in higher education: A collective case study. *Computers & Education*, *59*(2), 524–534. doi:10.1016/j.compedu.2011.12.022

Benson, V., & Filippaios, F. (2015). Collaborative competencies in professional social networking: Are students short changed by curriculum in business education? *Computers in Human Behavior*, *51*(B), 1331–1339. doi: 10.1016/j.chb.2014.11.031

Benson, V., & Filippaios, F. (2015). Collaborative competencies in professional social networking: Are students short changed by curriculum in business education?. *Computers in Human Behavior*, *51*(B), 1331-1339.

Benson, V., Saridakis, G., & Tennakoon, H. (2015). Information disclosure of social media users: does control over personal information, user awareness and security notices matter? *Information Technology & People*.

Benson, V. (2014). *Cutting-edge technologies and social media use in higher education*. IGI Global. doi:10.4018/978-1-4666-5174-6

Benson, V., & Morgan, S. (2015). *Implications of Social Media Use in Personal and Professional Settings*. Hershey, PA: IGI Global; doi:10.4018/978-1-4666-7401-1

Benson, V., Morgan, S., & Filippaios, F. (2010). Online Social Networks: Changing the Face of Business Education and Career Planning. *International Journal of Business and Management*, *40*(1), 20–33.

Benson, V., Morgan, S., & Filippaios, F. (2014). Social career management: Social media and employability skills gap. *Computers in Human Behavior*, *30*, 519–525. doi:10.1016/j.chb.2013.06.015

Benson, V., Morgan, S., & Tennakoon, H. (2012). A framework for knowledge management in higher education using social networking. *International Journal of Knowledge Society Research*, *3*(2), 44–54. doi:10.4018/jksr.2012040104

Benson, V., Saridakisa, G., Tennakoonb, H., & Ezingeard, J. N. (2015). The role of security notices and online consumer behaviour: An empirical study of social networking users. *International Journal of Human-Computer Studies*, *80*, 36–44. doi:10.1016/j.ijhcs.2015.03.004

Benson, V., Saridakis, G., & Tennakoon, H. (2015). Information disclosure of social media users: Does control over personal information, user awareness and security notices matter? *Information Technology & People*, *28*(Iss: 3), 426–441. doi:10.1108/ITP-10-2014-0232

Berelson, B. (1952). *Content analysis in communication research*. Glencoe, IL: The Free Press Publishers.

Bergstrom, K. (2011). 'Don't feed the troll': Shutting down debate about community expectations on Reddit.com. *First Monday*, 1–16. Retrieved from http://firstmonday.org/ojs/index.php/fm/article/view/3498/3029

Bernabe-Moreno, J., Tejeda-Lorente, A., Porcel, C., Fujita, H., & Herrera-Viedma, E. (2015). CARESOME: A system to enrich marketing customers acquisition and retention campaigns using social media information. *Knowledge-Based Systems*, *80*, 163–179. doi:10.1016/j.knosys.2014.12.033

Berners-Lee, T. (2015, September 14). *World Wide Consortium*. Retrieved September 14, 2015, from Berners-Lee: https://www.w3.org/People/Berners-Lee/

Berry, L. L. (1983). *Relationship Marketing*. Paper presented at the Emerging Perspectives on Services Marketing, Chicago, IL.

Berry, B. (2004). Recruiting and retaining 'highly qualified teachers' for hard-to-staff schools. *NASSP Bulletin*, *88*(638), 5–27. doi:10.1177/019263650408863802

Berry, L. L. (1995). Relationship Marketing of Services-Growing Interest, Emerging Perspectives. *Journal of the Academy of Marketing Science*, *23*(4), 236–245. doi:10.1177/009207039502300402

Berthon, P., Pitt, L. F., Plangger, K., & Shapiro, D. (2012). Marketing meets Web 2.0, social media, and creative consumers: Implications for international marketing strategy. *Business Horizons*, *55*(3), 261–271. doi:10.1016/j.bushor.2012.01.007

Beshears, J., Choi, J. J., Laibson, D., & Madrian, B. C. (2008). How are preferences revealed? *Journal of Public Economics*, *92*(8/9), 1787–1794. doi:10.1016/j.jpubeco.2008.04.010 PMID:24761048

Bessom, R. M., & Jackson, D. W. Jr. (1975). Service Retailing: A Strategic Marketing Approach. *Journal of Retailing*, *51*(2), 75–85.

Bhanot, S. (2012). Use of social media by companies to reach their customers. *SIES Journal of Management*, *8*(1), 47–55.

Bianco, J. S. (2009). Social networking and cloud computing: Precarious affordances for the "prosumer." *WSQ: Women's Studies Quarterly, 37*(1/2), 303–312. doi:10.1353/wsq.0.0146

Biasutti, M., & El-Deghaidy, H. (2015). Interdisciplinary project-based learning: An online wiki experience in teacher education. *Technology, Pedagogy and Education, 24*(3), 339–355. doi:10.1080/1475939X.2014.899510

Bickerstaff, K., & Walker, G. (2005). Shared Visions, Unholy Alliances: Power, Governance and Deliberative Processes in Local Transport Planning. *Urban Studies (Edinburgh, Scotland), 12*(42), 2123–2144. doi:10.1080/00420980500332098

Bierema, L. L., & Merriam, S. B. (2002). E-mentoring: Using Computer Mediated Communication to Enhance the Mentoring Process. *Innovative Higher Education, 26*(3), 211–227. doi:10.1023/A:1017921023103

Binder, P., & Mansfield, N. R. (2013). Social networks and workplace risk: Classroom scenarios from a U.S. and EU perspective. *Journal of Legal Studies Education, 30*(1), 1–44. doi:10.1111/j.1744-1722.2013.01113.x

Birkner, C. (2011). Sharing the love. *Marketing News, 45*(3), 11–12.

Birley, S. (1985). The Role of Networks in the Entrepreneurial Process. *Journal of Business Venturing, 1*(1), 107–117. doi:10.1016/0883-9026(85)90010-2

Bitner, M. J., Booms, B. H., & Tetreault, M. S. (1990). The service encounter: Diagnosing favourable and unfavourable incidents. *Journal of Marketing, 54*(1), 71–84. doi:10.2307/1252174

Bitner, M. J., Brown, S. W., & Meuter, M. L. (2000). Technology infusion in service encounters. *Journal of the Academy of Marketing Science, 28*(1), 138–149. doi:10.1177/0092070300281013

Bjerregaard, M. (2014, March 5). What Indonesians really think about The Act of Killing. *The Guardian*.

Blau, P. (1964). *Power and exchange in social life.* John Wiley & Sons. Retrieved September 2, 2015, from http://garfield.library.upenn.edu/classics1989/A1989CA26300001.pdf

Bloom, B., Englehart, M., Furst, E., Hill, W., & Krathwohl, D. (1956). *Taxonomy of educational objectives: The classification of educational goals. In Handbook I: Cognitive domain.* New York: Longmans, Green.

Bloomberg. (2014). Retrieved April 1, 2014, from http://www.bloomberg.com/markets/stocks/http://www.bloomberg.com/markets/stocks/

Blythe, J. (2008). *Consumer Behaviour.* London: Thomson Learning.

Boder, A. (2006). Collective Intelligence: A Keystone in Knowledge Management. *Journal of Knowledge Management, 10*(1), 81–93. doi:10.1108/13673270610650120

Boger, T., & Wernersen, R. (2014). How 'social' are social news sites? Exploring the motivation for using red.com. In iConference 2014 Proceedings. doi:10.9776/14108

Bohmova, L., & Malinova, L. (2013). Facebook User's Privacy in Recruitment Process. In P. Doucek, G. Chroust, V. Oskrdal (Eds.), *Proceedings of the 21st Interdisciplinary Information Management Talks* (pp 159-168). Linz: Trauner Verlag.

Bolt, Beranek, & Newman. (1981). *A History of the ARPANET.* Arlington, VA: BNN, Inc.

Bolter, J. D., & Grusin, R. (1999). *Remediation: Understanding New Media.* Cambridge, MA: MIT Press.

Bolton, R. N., Hoefnagels, A., Migchels, N., Kabadayi, S., Gruber, T., Loyreiro, Y. K., & Solnet, D. (2013). Understanding generation Y and their use of social media: A review of research agenda. *Journal of Service Management, 24*(3), 245–267. doi:10.1108/09564231311326987

Bonabeau, E. (2009). Decisions 2.0: The Power of Collective Intelligence. *MIT Sloan Management Review, 50*(2), 45–52.

Bonnemaizon, A., Cova, B., & Louyot, M. (2007). Relationship marketing in 2015: A Delphi approach. *European Management Journal, 25*(1), 50–59. doi:10.1016/j.emj.2006.12.002

Borgatti, S., Brass, A., & Labianca, D. (2009). Network Analysis in Social Sciences. *Science, 323*(5916), 892–895. doi:10.1126/science.1165821 PMID:19213908

Boshmaf, Y., Muslukhov, I., Beznosov, K., & Ripeanu, M. (2013). Design and analysis of a social botnet. *International Journal of Computer and Telecommunications Networking, 57*(2), 556–578.

Bosse, T., Jonker, C. M., Schut, M. C., & Treur, J. (2006). Collective Representational Content for Shared Extended Mind. *Cognitive Systems Research, 7*(2-3), 151–174. doi:10.1016/j.cogsys.2005.11.007

Bothos, E., Apostolou, D., & Mentzas, G. (2009). Collective Intelligence for Idea Management with Internet-based Information Aggregation Markets. *Internet Research, 19*(1), 26–41. doi:10.1108/10662240910927803

Bove, L. L., & Johnson, L. W. (2000). A customer-service worker relationship model. *International Journal of Service Industry Management, 11*(5), 491–511. doi:10.1108/09564230010360191

Bowden, J. L. H. (2009). The process of customer engagement: A conceptual framework. *Journal of Marketing Theory and Practice, 17*(1), 63–74. doi:10.2753/MTP1069-6679170105

boyd, d. (2011). Social Network Sites as Networked Publics. In Z. Papacharissi (Ed.), *A Networked Self*. New York: Routledge.

Boyd, A. (2002). The Goals, Questions, Indicators, Measures (GQIM) Approach to the Measurement of Customer Satisfaction with e-commerce Web sites. *Aslib Proceedings, 54*(3), 177–187. doi:10.1108/00012530210441728

Boyd, D. M., & Ellison, N. B. (2007). Social Network Sites: Definition, History, and Scholarship. *Journal of Computer-Mediated Communication, 13*(1), 210–230. doi:10.1111/j.1083-6101.2007.00393.x

Boyd, D. M., & Ellison, N. B. (2007). Social network sites: Definition, history, and scholarship. *Journal of Computer-Mediated Communication, 13*.

Boyle, D. (2003). *Athenticity*. Hammersmith: Harper Collins.

Boyle, R. (2013). Reflections on Communication and Sport: On journalism and digital culture. *Communication & Sport, 1*(2), 88–99. doi:10.1177/2167479512467978

Brady, M., Saren, M., & Tzokas, N. (2002). *Integrating information technology into marketing practice - the IT reality of contemporary marketing practice*. Academic Press.

Brammer, S. J., & Pavelin, S. (2006). Corporate reputation and social performance: The importance of fit. *Journal of Management Studies, 43*(3), 435–455. doi:10.1111/j.1467-6486.2006.00597.x

Brandtzaeg, P. B., & Heim, J. (2011). A typology of social networking sites users. *International Journal of Web Based Communities, 7*(1), 28–51. doi:10.1504/IJWBC.2011.038124

Breakenridge, D. K. (2012). *Social media and public relations: Eight new practices for the PR professional*. Upper Saddle River, NJ: Pearson Education.

Brennan, R., & Croft, R. (2012). The use of social media in B2B marketing and branding: An Exploratory Study. *Journal of Customer Behaviour, 11*(2), 101–115. doi:10.1362/147539212X13420906144552

Briones, R. L., Kuch, B., Liu, B. F., & Jin, Y. (2011). Keeping up with the digital age: How the American Red Cross uses social media to build relationships. *Public Relations Review, 37*(1), 37–43. doi:10.1016/j.pubrev.2010.12.006

Brodie, R. J., Ilic, A., Juric, B., & Hollebeek, L. (2011). Consumer engagement in a virtual brand community: An exploratory analysis. *Journal of Business Research, 66*(1), 105–114. doi:10.1016/j.jbusres.2011.07.029

Broersma, M. (2014). *Techweek Europe*. Retrieved from IBM Watson Powers Natural-Language Analytics: http://www.techweekeurope.co.uk/workspace/ibm-watson-analytics-152450

Brogan, R. J., & Smith, J. (2009). *Trust agents: Using the Web to build influence, improve reputation, and earn trust.* Hoboken, NJ: John Wiley & Sons.

Bronstein, J. (2013). Like me! Analyzing the 2012 presidential candidates' Facebook pages. *Online Information Review, 37*(2), 173–192. doi:10.1108/OIR-01-2013-0002

Brooksbank, R. W. (1991). Successful Marketing Practice: A Literature Review and Checklist for Marketing Practitioners. *European Journal of Marketing, 25*(5), 20–29. doi:10.1108/EUM0000000000619

Brown, N., & Billings, A. (2013). Sports fans as crisis communicators on social media websites. *Public Relations Review, 39*(1), 74–81. doi:10.1016/j.pubrev.2012.09.012

Bruns, A. (2008). *Blogs, Wikipedia, Second Life, and Beyond: From Production to Produsage.* New York: Peter Lang.

Bughin, J., Chui, M., & Miller, A. (2009). *How companies are benefiting from web 2.0: McKinsey global survey results.* Retrieved from: www.mckinsey.com

Buhalis, D., & Law, R. (2008). Progress in information technology and tourism management: 20 years on and 10 years after the Internet – the state of etourism research. *Tourism Management, 29*(4), 609–623. doi:10.1016/j.tourman.2008.01.005

Bull, R., Petts, J., & Evans, J. (2008). Social learning from public engagement: Dreaming the impossible? *Journal of Environmental Planning and Management, 51*(5), 701–716. doi:10.1080/09640560802208140

Bültmann, R. (2012). Social Media – A Splendid Opportunity for Fund Promoters and Asset Managers, Performance. Bath, UK: Deloitte Financial Services.

Buntain, C., & Golbeck, J. (2014). Identifying social roles in reddit using network structure. In *Proceedings of the International World Wide Web Conference Committee (IW3C2)*. doi:10.1145/2567948.2579231

Burke, J., & Wagner, B. (2015). RedNet, a different perspective of Reddit. In *5th IEEE Integrated STEM Conference*. doi:10.1109/ISECon.2015.7119910

Burrows, R., Johnson, H., & Johnson, P. (2013). *Influencing Values, Attitudes and Behaviour via Interactive and Social-Media Technology: The Case of Energy Usage.* Unpublished. Bath, UK.

Burt, R. (2003). The social capital of structural holes. In *The new economic sociology: developments in an emerging field* (pp. 148-189). New York, NY: Russell Sage Foundation. Retrieved September 2, 2015, from http://www.arschile.cl/moodledata/2/Mod3/Propiedades/SocialCapitalStructureHole-Burt.pdf

Burt, R., Kilduff, M., & Tasselli, S. (2013). Social networks Analysis: Foundations and frontiers of advantage. *Annual Review of Psychology, 64*(1), 527–547. doi:10.1146/annurev-psych-113011-143828 PMID:23282056

Buzzetto-More, N. A. (2012). Social networking in undergraduate education. *Interdisciplinary Journal of Information, Knowledge, and Management, 7*, 63–90.

Bynum, R. (2008). The Myth Of Equality. *New English Review*. Retrieved September 30, 2015, from http://newenglishreview.org/Rebecca_Bynum/The_Myth_Of_Equality/

Camarero, C., & San Jose, R. (2011). Social and attitudinal determinants of viral marketing dynamics. *Computers in Human Behavior*, *27*(6), 2292–2300. doi:10.1016/j.chb.2011.07.008

Camprubí, R., Guia, J., & Comas, J. (2013). The new role of tourists in destination image formation. *Current Issues in Tourism*, *16*(2), 203–209. doi:10.1080/13683500.2012.733358

Canada, E. (2004). *An environmental citizen... who me?*. Academic Press.

Cao, G., Wang, S., Hwang, M., Padmanabhan, A., Zhang, Z., & Soltani, K. (2015). A scalable framework for spatiotemporal analysis of location-based social media data. *Computers, Environment and Urban Systems*, *51*, 70–82. doi:10.1016/j.compenvurbsys.2015.01.002

Cao, P., Meister, S., & Klante, O. (2014). How social media influence apparel purchasing behavior. *Marketing Review St. Gallen*, *31*(6), 77–86. doi:10.1365/s11621-014-0427-y

Cappelli, P. (2001). On-line recruiting. *Harvard Business Review*, *79*(3). PMID:11246921

Carlson, M. (2007). Blogs and journalistic authority: The role of blogs in US Election Day 2004 coverage. *Journalism Studies*, *8*(2), 264–279. doi:10.1080/14616700601148861

Carmagnola, F., Osborne, F., & Torre, I. (2010). User data distributed on the social web: How to identify users on different social systems and collecting data about them. In Proceedings of HetRec '10.

Carr, J., Decreton, L., Qin, W., Rojas, B., Rossochacki, T., & Yang, Y. W. (2015). Social media in product development. *Food Quality and Preference*, *40*, 354–364. doi:10.1016/j.foodqual.2014.04.001

Cary, T. (2015). *Too soon to forgive and forget but Lance Armstrong is right about hypocrisy and need for a grown-up debate: cycling's Voldemort remains a compelling story, for better or for worse*. Retrieved October 13, 2015, from http://www.telegraph.co.uk/sport/othersports/cycling/lancearmstrong/11668810/Too-soon-to-forgive-and-forget-but-Lance-Armstrong-is-right-about-hypocrisy-and-need-for-a-grown-up-debate.html

Casaló, L. V., Flavián, C., & Guinalíu, M. (2011). Understanding the intention to follow the advice obtained in an online travel community. *Computers in Human Behavior*, *27*(2), 622–633. doi:10.1016/j.chb.2010.04.013

Castells, M., Fernandez-Ardevol, M., Qiu, J. L., & Sey, A. (2009). *Mobile communication and society: A global perspective*. University of Southern California. Retrieved September 28, 2015, from http://hack.tion.free.fr/textes/MobileCommunicationSociety.pdf

Castells, M. (2000). *The Rise of the Network Society* (S. Edition, Ed.). Blackwell Publishing.

Castells, M. (2007). Communication, power and counter-power in the network society. *International Journal of Communication*, *1*(1), 29.

Castells, M., & Cardoso, G. (2005). *The Networked Society: from Knowledge to Policy*. Washington, DC: Johns Hopkins Center for Transatlantic Relations.

Catone, J. (2010), *Should Employers Use Social Network Profiles in the Hiring Process?* Retrieved May 7, from http://www.readwriteweb.com/archives/should_employers_use_social_netowrking_when_hiring.php

Cecere, G., Le Guel, F., & Soulie, N. (2015). Perceived Internet privacy concerns on social networks in Europe. *Technological Forecasting and Social Change*, *96*, 277–287. doi:10.1016/j.techfore.2015.01.021

Cedrola, E. (2005). *Il marketing internazionale per le piccole e medie imprese*. Milano: McGraw-Hill.

Cermak, R. (2015). Multicultural Web Design: A Review. In P. Doucek, G. Chroust, V. Oskrdal (Eds.), *Proceedings of the 23nd Interdisciplinary Information Management Talks* (pp. 303–310), Linz: Trauner Verlag.

Cermak, R., Smutny, Z., & Janoscik, V. (2014). Analysis of the Facebook Privacy Settings of Young People with an Emphasis on the Czech Republic and France. In A. Rospigliosi & S. Greener (Eds.), *The Proceedings of the European Conference on Social Media ECSM 2014* (pp. 613-621). Reading: ACPI.

CERN. (2015, September 14). *Berners-Lee posts a summary of the project on alt.hypertext*. Retrieved September 14, 2015, from CERN: http://timeline.web.cern.ch/berners-lee-posts-a-summary-of-the-project-on-althypertext

Chae, J. H., & Lee, Y. J. (2015). A Study on the Impact of Apprehension for Privacy concern and Attitude for Social Network Game Advertisement on the Use of Promotion Advertisement of SNG. *Journal of the Korean Society for Computer Game*, *28*(2), 151–157.

Chang, Y. T., Yu, H., & Lu, H. P. (2015). Persuasive messages, popularity cohesion, and message diffusion in social media marketing. *Journal of Business Research*, *68*(4), 777–782. doi:10.1016/j.jbusres.2014.11.027

Chaputula, A. H., & Majawa, F. P. (2013). Use of social network sites by mass media organisations in Malawi. *Aslib Proceedings*, *65*(5), 534–557. doi:10.1108/AP-06-2012-0055

Chen, C. (2007). Holistic Sense-making: Conflicting Opinions, Creative Ideas, and Collective Intelligence. *Library Hi Tech*, *25*(3), 311–327. doi:10.1108/07378830710820907

Chen, C., & Knight, K. (2014). Energy at work: Social psychological factors affecting energy conservation intentions within Chinese electric power companies. *Energy Research & Social Science*, *4*, 23–31. doi:10.1016/j.erss.2014.08.004

Chen, T. J. (2003). Network resources for internationalization: The case of Taiwan's electronics firms*. *Journal of Management Studies*, *40*(5), 1107–1130. doi:10.1111/1467-6486.t01-1-00373

Chesbrough, H. W. (2003). *Open Innovation, the New Imperative for Creating and Profiting from Technology*. Harvard Business School Press.

Chesbrough, H. W., & Crowther, A. K. (2006). Beyond high-tech: Early adopters of Open Innovation in other industries. *R & D Management*, *36*(3), 229–236. doi:10.1111/j.1467-9310.2006.00428.x

Chetty, S., & Campbell-Hunt, C. (2004). A strategic approach to internationalisation: A traditional versus a born-global approach. *Journal of International Marketing*, *12*(1), 57–81. doi:10.1509/jimk.12.1.57.25651

Cheunga, C. M. K., & Thadani, D. R. (2012). The impact of electronic word-of-mouth communication: A literature analysis and integrative model. *Decision Support Systems*, *54*(1), 461–470. doi:10.1016/j.dss.2012.06.008

Cheung, C. M. K., Chiu, P. Y., & Lee, M. K. O. (2010). Online social networks: Why do students use Facebook? *Computers in Human Behavior*, *27*(4), 1337–1343. doi:10.1016/j.chb.2010.07.028

Cheung, C. M. K., & Lee, M. K. O. (2010). A theoretical model of intentional social action in online social networks. *Decision Support Systems*, *49*(1), 24–30. doi:10.1016/j.dss.2009.12.006

Chikhaouia, B., Wanga, S., Xionga, T., & Pigot, H. (2014). Pattern-based causal relationships discovery from event sequences for modeling behavioral user profile in ubiquitous environments. *Information Sciences*, *285*, 204–222. doi:10.1016/j.ins.2014.06.026

Chirita, P. A., Costache, S., Nejdl, W., & Handschuh, S. (2007). P-tag: Large scale automatic generation of personalized annotation tags for the web. In *Proceedings of the 16th international conference on World Wide Web.* doi:10.1145/1242572.1242686

Chirita, P. A., Olmedilla, D., & Nejdl, W. (2004). Pros: A personalized ranking platform for web search. In *Adaptive Hypermedia and Adaptive Web-Based Systems* (pp. 34–43). Berlin: Springer. doi:10.1007/978-3-540-27780-4_7

Christina, S., Dainty, A., Daniels, K., & Waterson, P. (2013). How organisational behaviour and attitudes can impact building energy use in the UK retail environment: A theoretical framework. *Architectural Engineering and Design Management, 10*(1-2), 164–179. doi:10.1080/17452007.2013.837256

Chui, M., Manyika, J., Bughin, J., & Dobbs, R. (2012). *The social economy: Unlocking value and productivity through social technologies.* McKinsey Global Institute.

Chun, R. (2005). Corporate reputation: Meaning and measurement. *International Journal of Management Reviews, 7*(2), 91–109. doi:10.1111/j.1468-2370.2005.00109.x

Churches, A. (2008). Bloom's taxonomy blooms digitally. *Tech & Learning, 1*, 1-6. Retrieved September 13,2015 https://edorigami.wikispaces.com/file/view/bloom's+Digital+taxonomy+v3.01.pdf

Chu, S., & Kim, Y. (2011). Determinants of consumer engagement in electronic word-of-mouth (eWOM) in social networking sites. *International Journal of Advertising, 30*(1), 47–75. doi:10.2501/IJA-30-1-047-075

Cialdini, R. B., Borden, R. J., Thorne, A., Walker, M. R., Freeman, S., & Sloan, L. R. (1976). Basking in reflected glory: Three (football) field studies). *Journal of Personality and Social Psychology, 34*(3), 366–375. doi:10.1037/0022-3514.34.3.366

Cinemalaya. (2012). *Cinemalaya.* (F. Kohle, Producer, & Tiny Little Doclab). Retrieved from Screening Schedule: http://cinemalaya.org/schedules_calendar.htm

Clark, B. H. (1999). Marketing Performance Measures: History and Interrelationships. *Journal of Marketing Management, 15*(8), 711–732. doi:10.1362/026725799784772594

Clarke, R. (1994). The digital persona and its application to data surveillance. *The Information Society: An International Journal, 10*(2).

Clemons, E. K. (2008). How information changes consumer behavior and how consumer behavior determines corporate strategy. *Journal of Management Information Systems, 25*(2), 13–40. doi:10.2753/MIS0742-1222250202

Cleverly, P. H. (2012). Improving enterprise search in the upstream oil and gas industry by automatic query expansion using a non-probabilistic knowledge representation. *International Journal of Applied Information Systems, 1*(1), 25–32.

Click, I. A., & Petit, J. (2010). Social networking and Web 2.0 in information literacy. *The International Information & Library Review, 42*(2), 137–142. doi:10.1080/10572317.2010.10762855

Cohen, C. (2011). Interconnections: Brand Reputation And Free Online Monitoring Tools. *Franchising World, 43*(7), 18.

Cohen, D., & Prusak, N. (2001). *In Good Company: How Social Capital Makes Organizations Work.* Boston: Harvard Business School Press.

Cokley, J., & Eeles, S. (2003). The origin of a species: 'The distributed newsroom'. *Australian Studies in Journalism, 12*, 240–261.

Cole, M. (2009). Using Wiki technology to support student engagement: Lessons from the trenches. *Computers & Education, 52*(1), 141–146. doi:10.1016/j.compedu.2008.07.003

Coleman, M. J., Irvine, K. N., Lemon, M., & Shao, L. (2013). Promoting behaviour change through personalized energy feedback in offices. *Building Research and Information*, *41*(6), 637–651. doi:10.1080/09613218.2013.808958

Collin, A. (1979). Notes on some typologies of management development and the role of the mentor in the proof of adaption of the individual to the organization. *Personnel Review*, *8*(4), 10–14. RetrievedSeptember262015. doi:10.1108/eb055392

Conover, M. D., Goncalves, B., Flammini, A., & Menczer, F. (2012). Partisan asymmetries in online political activity. *EPJ Data Science*, *1*(1), 1–19. doi:10.1140/epjds6

Constantinides, K. (2006). The marketing mix revisited: Towards the 21st century marketing. *Journal of Marketing Management*, *22*(3-4), 407–438. doi:10.1362/026725706776861190

Coombs, W. T. (2012). *Ongoing Crisis Communication. Planning, Managing and Responding.* Thousand Oaks, CA: Sage.

Coombs, W. T. (2014). *Ongoing crisis communication.* Thousand Oaks, CA: Sage Publications.

Corley, C. D., Farber, R. M., & Reynolds, W. N. (2012). Thought leaders during crises in massive social networks. *Statistical Analysis and Data Mining: The ASA Data Science Journal*, *5*(3), 205–217. doi:10.1002/sam.11147

Cornelissen, J. (2004). *Corporate communications: Theory and practice.* London: Sage Publications.

Coscia, M., Rossetti, G., Giannotti, F., & Pedreschi, D. (2014). Uncovering hierarchical and overlapping communities with a local-first approach. *ACM Transactions on Knowledge Discovery from Data*, *9*(1), 6:1 – 6:27.

Court, D., Elzinga, D., Mulder, S., & Vetvik, O. J. (2009). The Consumer Decision Journey. *McKinsey Quarterly*. Retrieved September 30, 2015, from http://www.mckinsey.com/insights/marketing_sales/the_consumer_decision_journey

Cova, B. (1997). Community and consumption: Towards a definition of the linking value of product or services. *European Journal of Marketing*, *31*(3/4), 297–316. doi:10.1108/03090569710162380

Coviello, N. E., & Brodie, R. J. (2001). Contemporary marketing practices of consumer and business- to-business firms: How different are they? *Journal of Business and Industrial Marketing*, *16*(5), 382–400. doi:10.1108/08858620110400223

Coviello, N. E., & McAuley, A. (1999). Internationalization of smaller firm: A review of contemporary empirical research. *Management International Review*, *39*, 223–256.

Coviello, N. E., & Munro, H. J. (1997). Network relationships and the internationalisation process of small software firms. *International Business Review*, *6*(4), 361–386. doi:10.1016/S0969-5931(97)00010-3

Creese, S., Goldsmith, M., Nurse, J. R. C., & Phillips, E. (2012). A data-reachability model for elucidating privacy and security risks related to the use of online social networks. In *Proceedings of 2012 IEEE 11th International Conference on Trust, Security and Privacy in Computing and Communications.* doi:10.1109/TrustCom.2012.22

Cross, R., & Parker, A. (2004). *The Hidden Power of Social Networks.* Boston: Harvard Business School Press.

Crowley, D. N., Curry, E., & Breslin, J. G. (2014). Leveraging Social Media and IoT to Bootstrap Smart Environments In N. Bessis & C. Dobre (Eds.), *Big Data and Internet of Things: A Roadmap for Smart Environments* (pp. 379–399). Spinger International Publishing Switzerland. doi:10.1007/978-3-319-05029-4_16

Cruz, M., Varajao, J., & Goncalves, P. (2012). The perceived potential of business social networking sites. *International Journal of Web Portals*, *4*(1), 1–15. doi:10.4018/jwp.2012010101

Csordas, T., & Gati, M. (2014). The new (marketing) role of firms as media content providers: The case of SME's strategic social media presence. *Budapest Management Review*, *45*(2), 22–32.

Curran, M. J., Draus, P., Schrager, M., & Zappala, S. (2014). College students and HR professionals: Conflicting views on information available on Facebook. *Human Resource Management Journal*, *24*(4), 442–458. doi:10.1111/1748-8583.12033

Czepiel, J. A., Solomon, M. R., Surprenant, C. F., & Gutman, E. G. (1985). Service encounters: An overview. In J. A. Czepiel, M. R. Solomon, & C. F. Surprenant (Eds.), *The service encounter: Managing employee/customer interaction in service businesses* (pp. 3–15). Toronto: Lexington Books.

Dabbish, L., Stuart, C., Tsay, J., & Herbsleb, J. (2014). Social Coding in GitHub: Transparency and Collaboration in an Open Software Repository. *Collective Intelligence 2014*. Boston: MIT Center for Collective Intelligence.

Daft, R., & Lengel, R. (1986). Organisational Information requirements, Media Richness and Structural Design'. *Management Science*, *32*(5), 554–571. doi:10.1287/mnsc.32.5.554

Dahlberg, L. (2001). The Internet and democratic discourse: Exploring the prospects of online deliberative forums extending the public sphere. *Information Communication and Society*, *4*(4), 615–633. doi:10.1080/13691180110097030

Dahlgren, P. (2005). The Internet, Public Spheres, and Political Communication: Dispersion and Deliberation. *Political Communication*, *22*(2), 147–162. doi:10.1080/10584600590933160

Dalziel, N. (2007). *The impact of marketing communications on customer relationships: an investigation into the UK banking sector*. (Unpublished doctoral dissertation). The Open University Business School.

Dalziel, N. (2014). Customer Complaints and Service Recovery on Social Media: An Investigation into Barclays Bank Facebook Page. In *Proceedings of European Conference on Social Media (ECSM2014)*, (pp. 111-119). University of Brighton.

Dalziel, N., Harris, F., & Laing, A. (2011). A multidimensional typology of customer relationships: From faltering to affective. *International Journal of Bank Marketing*, *29*(4-5), 398–432. doi:10.1108/02652321111152918

Danaher, P. J., Wilson, I. W., & Davis, R. A. (2003). A comparison of online and offline consumer brand loyalty. *Marketing Science*, *22*(4), 461–476. doi:10.1287/mksc.22.4.461.24907

Darby, S. (2010). Smart metering: What potential for householder engagement? *Building Research and Information*, *38*(5), 442–457. doi:10.1080/09613218.2010.492660

Das, S., & Lavoie, A. (2014). The effects of feedback on human behavior in social media: An inverse reinforcement learning model. In *Proceedings of the 13th International Conference on Autonomous Agents and Multiagent Systems (AAMAS 2014)*.

Davenport, T. H., & Prusak, L. (2000). *Working knowledge: How organizations manage what they know*. Boston: Harvard Business Press.

Davenport, T. H., Thomas, R. J., & Desouza, K. C. (2003). Reusing intellectual assets. *Industrial Management (Des Plaines)*, *45*, 12–17.

Davidson, M. M. (2001). The computerization of career services: Critical issues to consider. *Journal of Career Development*, *27*(3), 217–228. doi:10.1177/089484530102700308

Davidsson, P., & Honig, B. (2003). The role of social and human capital among nascent entrepreneurs. *Journal of Business Venturing*, *18*(3), 301–331. doi:10.1016/S0883-9026(02)00097-6

Davies, D. W. (1966). *Proposal for a Digital Communication Network*. Retrieved from NPL: www.archive.org/details/NationalPhysicalLaboratoryProposalForADigitalCommunicationNetwork

Davis, R., & Piven, I. (2013). *Social media branding: Manifesto for the branding revolution* (1st ed.). Available from https://books.google.co.nz/

Davis, R., Piven, I., & Breazeale, M. (2014). Conceptualising brand consumption in social media community. In *Proceedings of the European Conference on Social Media* (pp.128-135). Reading, UK: Academic Conferences and Publishing.

Davis, R., & Sajtos, L. (2008). Measuring consumer interactivity in response to campaigns coupling mobile and television media. *Journal of Advertising Research, 48*(3), 2008–2391. doi:10.2501/S0021849908080409

De Certeau, M. (1984). *Practice of everyday life*. Berkeley: University of California Press.

de Groot, M., & Robinson, T. (2008). Sport fan attachment and the psychological continuum model: A case study of an Australian league fan. *Leisure/Loisir, 32*(1), 117-138.

de Wet, J., & Erasmus, Z. (2005). Towards rigour in qualitative analysis. *Qualitative Research Journal, 5*(1), 27–40.

De Wever, B., Hämäläinen, R., Voet, M., & Gielen, M. (2015). A wiki task for first-year university students: The effect of scripting students' collaboration. *The Internet and Higher Education, 25*, 37–44. doi:10.1016/j.iheduc.2014.12.002

De Wit, B., & Meyer, R. (1998). *Strategy: Process, content, context*. London: Thomson Business Press.

de Wulf, K., Odekerken-Schröder, G., & Iacobucci, D. (2001). Investments in consumer relationships: A cross-country and cross-industry exploration. *Journal of Marketing, 65*(4), 33–50. doi:10.1509/jmkg.65.4.33.18386

Deans, K. R., Gray, B. J., Ibbotson, P., Osborne, P., & Knightbridge, K. (2003). Web Marketing Practices of Service Providers. *Service Industries Journal, 23*(3), 82–102. doi:10.1080/714005119

DeCamp, M. (2013). Physicians, social media, and conflict of interest. *Journal of General Internal Medicine, 28*(2), 299–303. doi:10.1007/s11606-012-2251-x PMID:23129160

Deibert, R., & Rohozinski, R. (2008). Good for Liberty, Bad for Security? Global Civil Society and the Securitization of the Internet. In R. Deibert, J. Palfrey, R. Rohozinski, & J. Zittrain (Eds.), *Access Denied: The Paractice and Policy of Global Internet Filtering* (pp. 123–150). Cambridge, MI: The MIT Press.

Dekker, R., & Engbersen, G. (2014). How social media transform migrant networks and facilitate migration. *Global Networks, 14*(4), 401–418. doi:10.1111/glob.12040

della Porta, D., & Diani, M. (2006). *Social Movements: An Introduction*. New York: Blackwell Publishing.

DeMars, W. (2005). *NGOs and Transnational Networks*. London: Pluto Press.

Democratic Socialist Women of the Philippines. (2010). *Democratic Socialist Women of the Philippines*. (E. Angsioco, Producer). Retrieved from Democratic Socialist Women of the Philippines: https://vimeo.com/105547859

Dennen, V. P. (2009). *Constructing academic alter-egos: Identity issues in a blog-based community. In Identity in the Information Society (IDIS)*. Springer. doi:10.1007/s12394-009-0020-8

Dery, K., Tansley, C., & Hafermalz, E. (2014). Games people play: social media and recruitment.*Proceedings of the 25th Australasian Conference on Information Systems*. ACIS.

Desouza, K. C. (2003). Facilitating tacit knowledge exchange. *Communications of the ACM, 46*(6), 85–88. doi:10.1145/777313.777317

Deuze, M. (2005). What is journalism? Professional identity and ideology of journalists reconsidered. *Journalism, 6*(4), 442–464. doi:10.1177/1464884905056815

Dickie, V. A., & Meier, H. (2015). The facebook tutor: Networking education. *Ubiquitous Learning, 8*(2), 1–12.

Dijkmans, C., Kerkhof, P., & Beukeboom, C. J. (2015). A stage to engage: Social media use and corporate reputation. *Tourism Management, 47*, 58–67. doi:10.1016/j.tourman.2014.09.005

Dinev, T. (2014). Why would we care about privacy? *European Journal of Information Systems, 23*(2), 97–102. doi:10.1057/ejis.2014.1

Dinev, T., Bellotto, M., Hart, P., Russo, V., Serra, I., & Colautti, C. (2006). Privacy calculus model in e-commerce – A study of Italy and the United states. *European Journal of Information Systems, 15*(4), 389–402. doi:10.1057/palgrave. ejis.3000590

Dinev, T., Goo, J., Hu, Q., & Nam, K. (2009). User behaviour towards protective information technologies: The role of national cultural differences. *Information Systems Journal, 19*(4), 391–412. doi:10.1111/j.1365-2575.2007.00289.x

Dixon, A. W., Martinez, J. M., & Martin, C. L. L. (2015). Employing social media as a marketing strategy in college sport: An examination of perceived effectiveness in accomplishing organizational objectives. *International Review on Public and Nonprofit Marketing, 12*(2), 97–113. doi:10.1007/s12208-015-0134-7

Dixon, G. N., Deline, M. B., McComas, K., Chambliss, L., & Hoffmann, M. (2015). Saving energy at the workplace: The salience of behavioral antecedents and sense of community. *Energy Research & Social Science, 6*, 121–127. doi:10.1016/j.erss.2015.01.004

DMC11. (2013). *DMCii imagery – Halting Deforestation in Argentina.* Retrieved October 15 from http://www.dmcii. com/?p=9215

Dobson, A. (2010). Environmental citizenship and pro-environmental behaviour. Rapid research and evidence review. London: Academic Press.

Domanski, M. C., & Cavale, N. (2012). Self-reported "worth it" rating of aesthetic surgery in social media. *Aesthetic Plastic Surgery, 36*(6), 1292–1295. doi:10.1007/s00266-012-9977-z PMID:23052381

Donath, J. (2008). Signals in social supernets. *Journal of Computer-Mediated Communication, 13*(1), 231–251. doi:10.1111/j.1083-6101.2007.00394.x

Doney, P. M., & Cannon, J. P. (1997). An examination of the nature of trust in buyer-seller relationships. *Journal of Marketing, 61*(2), 35–51. doi:10.2307/1251829

Donlan, L. (2014). Exploring the views of students on the use of Facebook in university teaching and learning. *Journal of Further and Higher Education, 38*(4), 572–588. doi:10.1080/0309877X.2012.726973

Donnelly, D. F., & Hume, A. (2015). Using collaborative technology to enhance pre-service teachers' pedagogical content knowledge in Science. *Research in Science & Technological Education, 33*(1), 61–87. doi:10.1080/02635143.2014.977782

Dorigo, M., Maniezzo, V., & Colorni, A. (1996). Ant system: Optimization by a colony of cooperating agents. *IEEE Transactions on Systems, Man, and Cybernetics. Part B, Cybernetics, 26*(1), 29–41. doi:10.1109/3477.484436 PMID:18263004

Downes, E. J., & McMillan, S. J. (2000). Defining interactivity: A qualitative identification of key dimensions. *New Media & Society, 2*(2), 157–179. doi:10.1177/14614440022225751

Dropbox. (2009). *Dropbox.* Retrieved from Dropbox: www.dropbox.com

Drouin, M., O'Connor, K. W., Schmidt, G. B., & Miller, D. A. (2015). Facebook fired: Legal perspectives and young adults' opinions on the use of social media in hiring and firing decisions. *Computers in Human Behavior, 46*, 123–128. doi:10.1016/j.chb.2015.01.011

Drucker, P. F. (1954). *The Practice of Management*. New York: Harper and Row.

Duarte, P. (2015). The use of a group blog to actively support learning activities. *Active Learning in Higher Education*, *16*(2), 103–117. doi:10.1177/1469787415574051

Dubini, P., & Aldrich, H. (1991). Personal and Extended Networks are Central to the Entrepreneurial Process. *Journal of Business Venturing*, *6*(5), 305–313. doi:10.1016/0883-9026(91)90021-5

Duggan, M., & Smith, A. (2013). *6% of online adults are reddit users*. Pew Research Center. Retrieved from http://www.pewinternet.org/2013/07/03/6-of-online-adults-are-reddit-users/

Dullaart, C. (2014). Balconism. *Art Papers*. Retrieved September 15, 2015, from http://artpapers.org/feature_articles/feature3_2014_0304.html

Dunbar, R. (2012). *Social Networks*. Reed Business Info. Ltd. Available: http://search.ebscohost.com/login.aspx?direct=true&db=a9h&AN=74134004&site=ehost-live

Durkheim, E. (1893). *De la division du travail social: étude sur l'organisation des sociétés supérieures*. Paris: ALCAN.

Durkin, M., Howcroft, B., O'Donnell, A., & McCartan-Quinn, D. (2003). Retail bank customer preferences: Personal and remote interactions. *International Journal of Retail & Distribution Management*, *31*(4), 177–189. doi:10.1108/09590550310469176

Durukan, T., Bozaci, I., & Hamsioglu, A. B. (2012). An investigation of customer behaviours in social media. *European Journal of Economics, Finance and Administrative Sciences*, *44*, 148–158.

Dutta, S., Narasimhan, O., & Rajiv, S. (1999). *Success in High-Technology Markets: Is Marketing Capability Critical?*. Academic Press.

Dwyer, F. R., Schurr, P. H., & Oh, S. (1987). Developing Buyer-Seller Relationships. *Journal of Marketing*, *51*(2), 11–27. doi:10.2307/1251126

Edelman, D. C. (2010).Branding in the Digital Age: You're Spending Your Money in All the Wrong Places. *Harvard Business Review*.

El Ouirdi, M., (2014). Social Media Conceptualization and Taxonomy: A Lasswellian Framework. *Journal of Creative Communications*, *9*(2), 107–126. doi:10.1177/0973258614528608

Elder, A. (2014). Excellent online friendships: An Aristotelian defense of social media. *Ethics and Information Technology*, *16*(4), 287–297. doi:10.1007/s10676-014-9354-5

Elenurm, T. (2014). Combining social media and collaborative e-learning for developing personal knowledge management. In *Proceedings of the European Conference of Social Media: ECSM 2104* (pp. 185-192). Reading, UK: Academic Conferences and Publishing International.

Elenurm, T. (2008). Applying cross-cultural student teams for supporting international networking of Estonian enterprises'. *Baltic Journal of Management*, *3*(2), 145–158. doi:10.1108/17465260810875488

Elenurm, T., Ennulo, J., & Laar, J. (2007). Structures of Motivation and Entrepreneurial Orientation in Students as the Basis for Differentiated Approaches in Developing Human Resources for Future Business Initiatives. *EBS Review*, *23*(2), 50–61.

Ellison, N., Steinfield, C., & Lampe, C. (2000). Ensuring service quality for campus career services centers: A modified SERVQUAL scale. *Journal of Marketing Education*, *22*(3), 236–245. doi:10.1177/0273475300223007

Ellison, N., Steinfield, C., & Lampe, C. (2007). The benefits of Facebook "friends:" Social capital and college students' use of online social network sites. *Journal of Computer-Mediated Communication, 12*(4), 12–25. doi:10.1111/j.1083-6101.2007.00367.x

Emerson, S. L. (1983). Usenet: A Bulletin Board for Unix Users. *Byte Magazine, 8*(10).

Emirates Fleet & Seats. (n.d.). Retrieved from http://www.airreview.com/Emirates/Fleet.htm,15.09.2015

Enli, G. S., & Ihlebaek, K. A. (2011). 'Dancing with the audience': Administrating vote-ins in public and commercial broadcasting. *Media Culture & Society, 33*(6), 953–962. doi:10.1177/0163443711412299

Ephraim, P. E. (2013). African youths and the dangers of social networking: A culture-centered approach to using social media. *Ethics and Information Technology, 15*(4), 275–284. doi:10.1007/s10676-013-9333-2

Eriksson, K., Johanson, J., Majkgård, A., & Sharma, D. D. (2000). Effect of variation on knowledge accumulation in the internationalization process. *International Studies of Management & Organization, 30*(1), 26–44. doi:10.1080/002 08825.2000.11656781

Escobar, M. L., Kommers, P. A. M., & Beldad, A. (2014). Using narratives as tools for channeling participation in online communities. *Computers in Human Behavior, 37*, 64–72. doi:10.1016/j.chb.2014.04.013

Etherington, T. (2015). *Micro-moments: how to survive the new mobile battleground for brands.* Retrieved August 27, 2015, http://www.marketingmagazine.co.uk/article/1359653/micro-moments-survive-new-mobile-battleground-brands

Ettenson, R., Corado, E., & Knowles, J. (2013). Rethinking the 4 P's. *Harvard Business Review.* Retrieved from https://hbr.org/2010/12/branding-in-the-digital-age-youre-spending-your-money-in-all-the-wrong-places

European Commission. (2015). *Fifteenth annual report of the Article 29 Working Party on Data Protection.* Luxembourg: Publications Office of the European Union.

Eye for Travel. (2015, September 12). *Airlines to sell the majority of tickets direct to passengers by 2013: Survey.* Retrieved from http://www.eyefortravel.com/mobile-and-technology/airlines-sell-majority-tickets-direct-passengers-2013-survey

Ezumah, B. A. (2013). College students' use of social media: Site preferences, uses and gratifications theory revisited. *International Journal of Business and Social Science, 4*(5), 27-34. Retrieved November, 30, 2015, from http://ijbssnet.com/journals/Vol_4_No_5_May_2013/3.pdf

Fabian, B., Baumann, A., & Keil, M. (2015). Privacy on Reddit? Towards large-scale user classification. Association for Information Systems Electronic Library. *ECIS 2015 Proceedings.* Retrieved August 2, 2015, from http://aisel.aisnet.org/ecis2015_cr/43

Facebook. (2011, January 18). *Unfriend Coal.* Retrieved March 5, 2012 from http://www.facebook.com/unfriendcoal

Fauld, D., & Mangold, W. (2014). Developing a Social Media and Marketing Course. *Marketing Education Review, 24*(2), 127–144. doi:10.2753/MER1052-8008240204

Fayolle, A., Gailly, B. T., & Lassas-Clerc, N. (2006). Assessing the impact of entrepreneurship education programmes: A new methodology. *Journal of European Industrial Training, 30*(8/9), 701–720. doi:10.1108/03090590610715022

Feldman, S., & Sherman, C. (2003). *The high cost of not finding information.* IDC Whitepaper 29127.

Ferro, E., & Molinari, F. (2010). Framing Web 2.0 in the process of public sector innovation: Going down the participation ladder. *European Journal of ePractice, 9*, 1–15.

Fichman, R. G., Kohli, R., & Krishnan, R. (2011). The role of information systems in healthcare: Current research and future trends. *Information Systems Research*, *22*(3), 419–428. doi:10.1287/isre.1110.0382

Fieseler, C., Fleck, M., & Meckel, M. (2010). Corporate social responsibility in the blogosphere. *Journal of Business Ethics*, *91*(4), 599–614. doi:10.1007/s10551-009-0135-8

Films, K. (2015, Sept. 30). *Indiegogo*. Retrieved Sept. 30, 2015, from Life Itself - A feature documentary based on Roger Ebert's memoir: https://www.indiegogo.com/projects/life-itself-a-feature-documentary-based-on-roger-ebert-s-memoir#/

Financial Times – Markets/Equities. (2014). Retrieved April 1, 2014, from: http://www.ft.com/intl/markets/equitieshttp://www.ft.com/intl/markets/equities

Firat, A. F. (2014). Marketing challenges: A personal history. *Journal of Historical Research in Mar-keting*, *6*(3), 414–429. doi:10.1108/JHRM-11-2013-0062

Fischer, E., & Reuber, A. R. (2011). Social interaction via new social media: (How) can interactions on Twitter affect effectual thinking and behavior? *Journal of Business Venturing*, *26*(1), 1–18. doi:10.1016/j.jbusvent.2010.09.002

Fisher, M., & Baird, D. (2005). Online Learning Design that Fosters Student Support, Self-Regulation, and Retention. Campus Wide Information Systems. *International Journal on E-Learning*, *22*. Retrieved from https://pantherfile.uwm.edu/simonec/public/Motivation%20retention%20articles/Articles/Fisher_OnlineLearningDesign.pdf

Fisher, T. (2009). ROI in Social Media: A look at the Arguments. *Journal of Database Marketing & Customer Strategy Management*, *16*(3), 189–195. doi:10.1057/dbm.2009.16

Fogues, R., Such, J. M., Espinosa, A., & Garcia-Fornes, A. (2015). Open Challenges in Relationship-Based Privacy Mechanisms for Social Network Services. *International Journal of Human-Computer Interaction*, *31*(5), 350–370. doi:10.1080/10447318.2014.1001300

Ford, D., Gadde, L. E., Håkansson, H., & Snehota, I. (2002). Managing networks. In *18th IMP Conference*, Perth, Australia.

Ford, D., & Mouzas, S. (2013). The theory and practice of business networking. *Industrial Marketing Management*, *42*(3), 433–442. doi:10.1016/j.indmarman.2013.02.012

Ford, W. S. Z. (2001). Customer expectations for interactions with service providers: Relationships versus encounter orientation and personalised service communication. *Journal of Applied Communication Research*, *29*(1), 1–29. doi:10.1080/00909880128098

Foster, D., Lawson, S., Wardman, J., Blythe, M., & Linehan, C. (2012). "Watts in It for Me?": Design Implications for Implementing Effective Energy Interventions in Organisations. In *Proceedings of the SIGCHI Conference on Human Factors in Computing Systems* (pp. 2357–2366). New York: ACM. doi:10.1145/2207676.2208396

Foster, D., Linehan, C., Kirman, B., Lawson, S., & James, G. (2010). Motivating Physical Activity at Work: Using Persuasive Social Media for Competitive Step Counting. In *Proceedings of the 14th International Academic MindTrek Conference: Envisioning Future Media Environments* (pp. 111–116). New York: ACM. doi:10.1145/1930488.1930510

Foucault, M. (1976). Histoire de la sexualité, 3 volumes: La volonté de savoir, L'usage des plaisirs, and Le souici de soi. Paris: Gallimard.

Foucault, M. (1963). *Naissance de la clinique*. Paris: Presses Universitaires de France.

Foucault, M. (1972). *L'histoire de la folie à l'âge classique*. Paris: Gallimard.

Foucault, M. (1975). *Surveiller et punir*. Paris: Gallimard.

Fournier, S. (1998). Consumers and their brands: Developing relationship theory in consumer research. *The Journal of Consumer Research, 24*(4), 343–373. doi:10.1086/209515

Fournier, S., & Lee, L. (2009, April). Getting brand communities right. *Harvard Business Review, 87*(4), 105–111. PMID:19736854

Foutz, N. Z., & Jank, W. (2010). Research Note-Prerelease Demand Forecasting for Motion Pictures Using Functional Shape Analysis of Virtual Stock Markets. *Marketing Science, 29*(3), 568–579. doi:10.1287/mksc.1090.0542

Fox, J., & Rooney, M. C. (2015). The Dark Triad and trait self-objectification as predictors of men's use and self-presentation behaviors on social networking sites. *Personality and Individual Differences, 76*, 161–165. doi:10.1016/j.paid.2014.12.017

Franklin, B. (2012). The future of journalism. Developments and debates. *Journalism Studies, 13*(5-6), 663–681. doi:10.1080/1461670X.2012.712301

Franklin, B. (2014). The future of journalism in an age of digital media and economic uncertainty. *Digital Journalism, 2*(3), 254–272. doi:10.1080/21670811.2014.930253

Frederick, E., Lim, C. H., Clavio, G., Pedersen, P., & Burch, L. M. (2014). Choosing between the one-way or two-way street: An exploration of relationship promotion by professional athletes on Twitter. *Communication & Sport, 2*(1), 80–99. doi:10.1177/2167479512466387

Fredriksson, M., & Johansson, B. (2014). The dynamics of professional identity. *Journalism Practice, 8*(5), 585–595. doi:10.1080/17512786.2014.884746

Freeman, S. (2002). *A comprehensive model of the process of small firm internationalisation: A network perspective.* Competitive Paper for IMO Conference, Dijon, Francia.

Freeman, L. C. (1978, January). Centrality in Social Networks Conceptual Clarification. *Social Networks, 1*(3), 215–239. doi:10.1016/0378-8733(78)90021-7

Freeway, F. (2011). *Film Freeway.* Retrieved from Film Freeway: https://filmfreeway.com

Fretzin, S. (2009). Get terworking. *Benefits Canada, 33*(10), 7–10.

Friesen, N., & Lowe, S. (2012). The questionable promise of social media for education: Connective learning and the commercial imperative. *Journal of Computer Assisted Learning, 28*(3), 183–194. doi:10.1111/j.1365-2729.2011.00426.x

Froome, C. (2014). *The Climb: The Autobiography.* London: Viking.

Froot, K. A. (1989). New hope for the expectations hypothesis of the term structure of interest rates. *The Journal of Finance, 44*(2), 283–305. doi:10.1111/j.1540-6261.1989.tb05058.x

Fruchter, G. E., & Sigué, S. P. (2005). Transactions vs. Relationships: What Should the Company Emphasize? *Journal of Service Research, 8*(1), 18–36. doi:10.1177/1094670505276629

Fuero, A., & García, J. M. (2008). Redes sociales. contextualización de un fenómeno "dos-punto-cero" [Social Networks. Contextualizing the Phenomenon of Web 2.0]. *TELOS Cuadernos De Innvación y Comunicación, 76.*

Fuller-Love, N., & Thomas, E. (2004). Networks in small manufacturing firms. *Journal of Small Business and Enterprise Development, 11*(2), 244–253. doi:10.1108/14626000410537182

Funk, D., & James, J. (2006). Consumer loyalty: The meaning of attachment in the development of sport team allegiance. *Journal of Sport Management, 20*, 189–217.

Furnes V., (2007, January). The new frontier. *Personnel Today.*

Furtado, V., Ayres, L., Oliveira, M., Vasconcelos, E., & Caminha, C. (2010). Collective Intelligence in Law Enforcement – The WikiCrimes System. *Inf. Sci., 180*(1), 4–17. doi:10.1016/j.ins.2009.08.004

Gagnon, T. (2013). The disinhibition of Reddit users. *Stylus Knights Write Showcase, 49 – 55.*

Galanaki, E. (2002). The decision to recruit online: A descritive study. *Career Development International, 17*(4).

Gallant, L. M., Irizarry, C., Boone, G., & Kreps, G. (2011). Promoting participatory medicine with social media: New media applications on hospital websites that enhance health education and e-patients' voices. *Journal of Participatory Medicine, 3*, e49.

Gan, C., & Wang, W. (2015). Research characteristics and status on social media in China: A bibliometric and co-word analysis. *Scientometrics, 105*(2), 1167–1182. doi:10.1007/s11192-015-1723-2

Gantz, W. (2012). Reflections on Communication and Sport: On Fanship and Social Relationships. *Communication & Sport, 1*(2), 176–187.

Garcia, E., Elbeltagi, I., Brown, M., & Dungay, K. (2015). The implications of a connectivist learning blog model and the changing role of teaching and learning. *British Journal of Educational Technology, 46*(4), 877–894. doi:10.1111/bjet.12184

Gardberg, N., & Fombrun, C. J. (2002). The global reputation quotient project: First steps towards a cross-nationally valid measure of corporate reputation. *Corporate Reputation Review, 4*(4), 303–307. doi:10.1057/palgrave.crr.1540151

Garratt, D. (2010). Sporting citizenship: The rebirth of religion? *Pedagogy, Culture & Society, 18*(2), 123–143. doi:10.1080/14681366.2010.488040

Gates, B. (2015, Sept 28). *Digibarn.* Retrieved Sept 28, 2015, from Digibarn - Bill Gates' letter to Hobbyists: http://www.digibarn.com/collections/newsletters/homebrew/V2_01/homebrew_V2_01_p2.jpg

Geho, P. R., & Dangelo, J. (2012). The Evolution of Social Media as a Marketing Tool for Entrepreneurs. *Entrepreneurial Executive, 17*, 61–68.

Geiger, R. S. (2013). Are computers merely 'supporting' cooperative work? Towards an ethnography of bot development. In *Proceedings of CSCW '13 Companion.*

Geohive. (2015). *Geohive.* Retrieved from Geohive - Projected World Population by year 1950-2100: http://www.geohive.com/earth/his_history3.aspx

Ghonim, W. (2012). *Revolution 2.0.* Fourth Estate.

Gibb, A. A. (1997). Small firms training and competitiveness: Building upon the small business as a learning organisation. *International Small Business Journal, 15*(3), 13–30. doi:10.1177/0266242697153001

Gil de Zúñiga, H., Molyneux, L., & Zheng, P. (2014). Social media, political expression, and political participation: Panel analysis of lagged and concurrent relationships. *Journal of Communication, 64*(4), 612–634. doi:10.1111/jcom.12103

Gilbert, E. (2013). Widespread underprovision on Reddit. In *Proceedings of CSCW '13.* doi:10.1145/2441776.2441866

Gilbert, E., Bergstrom, T., & Karahalios, K. (n.d.). Blogs Are Echo Chambers: Blogs Are Echo Chambers. *Proceedings of the 42nd Hawaii International Conference on System Sciences – 2009.* Retrieved October 15, 2014, from http://ieeexplore.ieee.org/stamp/stamp.jsp?tp=&arnumber=4755503

Gillin, P. (2007). *The new influencers: A marketer's guide to the new social media.* Sanger, CA: Quill Driver Books.

Giridharadas, A. (2013, September 20). Draining the life from 'community'. *The New York Times*. Retrieved from http://www.nytimes.com/2013/09/21/us/draining-the-life-from-community.html?_r=0

Gladwell, M. (2010, October 4). Small Change: Why the Revolution Will Not Be Tweeted. *The New Yorker*.

Glaser, B. G., & Strauss, A. L. (1999). *The discovery of grounded theory: strategies for qualitative research*. New York: Aldine de Gruyter.

Glasius, M. (2002). *Global Civil Society Yearbook 2002*. London School of Economics.

Gloor, P. (2006). *Swarm Creativity, Competitive advantage through collaborative innovation networks*. Oxford, UK: Oxford University Press. doi:10.1093/acprof:oso/9780195304121.001.0001

Gloor, P. A., Paasivaara, M., Schoder, D., & Willems, P. (2008). Finding Collaborative Innovation Networks through Correlating Performance with Social Network Structure. *International Journal of Production Research*, *46*(5), 1357–1371. doi:10.1080/00207540701224582

Glynn, P. (2013). *Super league referees answer fans' Twitter questions*. BBC. Retrieved October 13, 2015, from http://www.bbc.com/sport/0/rugby-league/22384383

Google. (2013). *Project Loon*. Retrieved from Google: http://www.google.com/loon/

Google. (2015). *Cloud Storage*. Retrieved from Google: https://cloud.google.com/storage/docs/overview

Goyal, A., & Akhilesh, K. B. (2007). Interplay among Innovativeness, Cognitive Intelligence, Emotional Intelligence and Social Capital of Work Teams. *Team Performance Management*, *13*(7/8), 206–226. doi:10.1108/13527590710842538

Graham, J. (2015, July 11). Can Reddit be tamed? Probably not. *USA Today*.

Graham, M. E., & Moore, J. (2007). Consumers' willingness to pay for corporate reputation: The context of airline companies. *Corporate Reputation Review*, *10*(3), 189–200. doi:10.1057/palgrave.crr.1550052

Granovetter, M. (1973). The strength of weak ties. *American Journal of Sociology*, *78*(6), 1360–1380. doi:10.1086/225469

Granovetter, M. (1983). The Strength of Weak Ties: A Network Theory Revisited. *Sociological Theory*, *1*, 201–233. doi:10.2307/202051

Grant, R. M. (1996). Toward a knowledge-based theory of the firm. *Strategic Management Journal*, *17*(S2), 109–122. doi:10.1002/smj.4250171110

Gravili, G. (2015). Social communication in management: implications in recruitment processes of Latin American countries. In *ECMLG Proceeding*.

Gravili, G. (2008). *La cooperazione conveniente: I virtual social networks*. Bari, Italy: Cacucci Editore.

Gravili, G. (2011). *Il social recruitment*. Bari, Italy: Cacucci Editore.

Gray, D., Ekinci, Y., & Goregaokar, H. (2011). Coaching SME Managers: Business development or personal therapy? A mixed methods approach. *International Journal of Human Resource Management*, *22*(4), 862–881. doi:10.1080/09585192.2011.555129

Greaves, F., Ramirez-Cano, D., Millett, C., Darzi, A., & Donaldson, L. (2013). Harnessing the cloud of patient experience: Using social media to detect poor quality healthcare. *BMJ Quality & Safety*, *22*(3), 251–255. doi:10.1136/bmjqs-2012-001527 PMID:23349387

Greenpeace. (2014). *Green Gadgets: Designing the future The path to Greener electronice.* Retrieved October 15, 2014, from http://www.greenpeace.org/international/Global/international/publications/toxics/2014/Green%20Gadgets.pdf

Greenwald, G. (2014). *The Intercept.* Retrieved from How Covert Agents Infiltrate the Internet to Manipulate, Deceive, and Destroy Reputations: https://firstlook.org/theintercept/2014/02/24/jtrig-manipulation/

Gregg, D. G. (2010). Designing for Collective Intelligence. *Communications of the ACM, 53*(4), 134–138. doi:10.1145/1721654.1721691

Gregoire, Y., Salle, A., & Tripp, T. M. (2015). Managing social media crises with your customers: The good, the bad, and the ugly. *Business Horizons, 58*(2), 173–182. doi:10.1016/j.bushor.2014.11.001

Gregory, S. (2009). *Twitter craze is rapidly changing the face of sports.* Retrieved October 13, 2015, from http://www.si.com/more-sports/2009/06/05/twitter-sports

Gregory. (2013). *How sports fans engage with social media.* Retrieved October, 13, 2015, from http://mashable.com/2013/10/03/sports-fans-social-media/#DumUh1plUkqz

Griffin, C., Mercer, D., Fan, J., & Squicciarini, A. (2012). Two species evolutionary game model of user and moderator dynamics. In *Proceedings of the 2012 International Conference on Social Informatics.* doi:10.1109/SocialInformatics.2012.95

Griffith, E. (2015 August 25). Brands are using social media more than ever, and users are ignoring them more than ever. *Fortune.* Retrieved from http://fortune.com/2015/08/25/social-media-brands-ignore/

Griffiths, G. (2015, June 19). *Rugby World Cup 2015: James Hook launches Emirates hunt to find official tournament flag bearers.* Retrieved from http://www.walesonline.co.uk/sport/rugby/rugby-news/rugby-world-cup-2015-james-9482006

Grönroos, C. (2001). The perceived service quality concept - a mistake? *Managing Service Quality, 11*(3), 150–152. doi:10.1108/09604520110393386

Groundwire. (2012). *Home Page.* Retrieved March 1, 2012 from Groundwire: http://groundwire.org/

Gruber, T. (2008). Collective Knowledge Systems: Where the Social Web Meets the Semantic Web. *Journal of Web Semantics, 6*(1), 4–13. doi:10.1016/j.websem.2007.11.011

Gruen, T. W., Osmonbekov, T., & Czaplewski, A. J. (2006). eWOM: The impact of customer-to-customer online know-how exchange on customer value and loyalty. *Journal of Business Research, 59*(4), 449–456. doi:10.1016/j.jbusres.2005.10.004

Guerin, C., Carter, S., & Aitchison, C. (2015). Blogging as community of practice: Lessons for academic development? *The International Journal for Academic Development, 20*(3), 212–223. doi:10.1080/1360144X.2015.1042480

Gundclach, G., & Wilkie, W. (2009). The American Marketing Association's new definition of marketing: Perspective and commentary on the 2007 revision. *Journal of Public Policy & Marketing, 28*(2), 259–264. doi:10.1509/jppm.28.2.259

Gupta, S., & Zeithaml, V. (2006). Customer Metrics and Their Impact on Financial Performance. *Marketing Science, 25*(6), 718–739. doi:10.1287/mksc.1060.0221

Gurau, C. (2008). Integrated online marketing communication: Implementation and management. *Journal of Communication Management, 12*(2), 169–184. doi:10.1108/13632540810881974

Habermas, J. (1979). *Communication and the Evolution of Society, translated by Thomas McCarthy.* Boston: Beacon Press.

Hadnagy, C. (2010). *Social Engineering: The Art of Human Hacking.* New York: Wiley.

Haeckel, S. H. (1998). About the nature and future of interactive marketing. *Journal of Interactive Marketing, 12*(1), 63–71. doi:10.1002/(SICI)1520-6653(199824)12:1<63::AID-DIR8>3.0.CO;2-C

Hai-Jew, S. (2015, Nov. 12). Profiling an entity across multiple social media platforms. *C2C Digital Magazine*. Retrieved Nov. 18, 2015, from http://scalar.usc.edu/works/c2c-digital-magazine-fall-winter-2016/profiling-an-entity-across-multiple-social-media-platforms

Hair, J. F., Black, W. C., Babin, B. J., & Anderson, R. E. (2010). *Multivariate data analysis* (7th ed.). Upper Saddle River, NJ: Pearson Prentice Hall.

Ha, J., & Shin, D. H. (2014). Facebook in a standard college class: An alternative conduit for promoting teacher-student interaction. *American Communication Journal, 16*(1), 36–52.

Hakansson, H., & Snehota, I. (1989). No Business is an Island: The Network Concept of Business Strategy. *Scandinavian Journal of Management, 4*(3), 187–200. doi:10.1016/0956-5221(89)90026-2

Hambrick, M., Frederick, E., & Sanderson, J. (2013). From Yellow to Blue: Exploring Lance Armstrong's Image Repair Strategies Across Traditional and Social Media. *Communication & Sport, 00*(0), 1–23.

Hambrick, M., Simmons, J., Greenhalgh, G., & Greenwell, T. C. (2010). Understanding Professional Athletes' Use of Twitter: A Content Analysis of Athlete Tweets. *International Journal of Sports Communication, 3*, 454–471.

Hamburg, I. (2012). eLearning and social networking in mentoring processes to support active ageing. *eLearning Papers, 29*(4). Retrieved December 1, 2015, from http://portal.sio.si/uploads/media/e-Learning_in__druzbeno_mrezenje_From-Field_29_1.pdf

Hammond, M. S. (2001). Career centers and needs assessments: Getting the information you need to increase your success. *Journal of Career Development, 27*(3), 187–197. doi:10.1177/089484530102700305

Hänel, T., & Schulz, M. (2014). Is there still a need for multidimensional data models? In *Proceedings of the Twenty Second European Conference on Information Systems*.

Hanna, R., Rohm, A., & Crittenden, V. L. (2011). We're all connected: The power of the social media ecosystem. *Business Horizons, 54*(3), 265–273. doi:10.1016/j.bushor.2011.01.007

Hanoi International Film Festival. (2012). *Hanoi International Film Festival*. (F. Kohle, Producer, & Tiny Little Doclab). Retrieved from Short Documentary & Animation: http://www.haniff.vn/en/giai-thuong-va-ban-giam-khao/ban-giam-khao-phim-truyen/9-main-news/88-short-documentary-animation.html

Hanusch, F. (2011). A profile of Australian travel journalists' professional views and ethical standards. *Journalism, 13*(5), 668–686. doi:10.1177/1464884911398338

Hanusch, F., & Fürsich, E. (2014). On the relevance of travel journalism: An introduction. In F. Hanusch & E. Fürsich (Eds.), *Travel Journalism: Exploring Production, Impact and Culture* (pp. 1–17). Basingstoke, UK: Palgrave Macmillan. doi:10.1057/9781137325983.0005

Haralabopoulos, G., Anagnostopoulos, I., & Zeadally, S. (2015). Lifespan and propagation of information in on-line social networks: A case study based on Reddit. *Journal of Network and Computer Applications, 88 – 100.*10.1016/j.jnca.2015.06.006

Hargreaves, T., Nye, M., & Burgess, J. (2013). Keeping energy visible? Exploring how householders interact with feedback from smart energy monitors in the longer term. *Energy Policy, 52*(0), 126–134. doi:10.1016/j.enpol.2012.03.027

Harker, M. J., & Egan, J. (2006). The Past, Present and Future of Relationship Marketing. *Journal of Marketing Management, 22*(1/2), 215–242. doi:10.1362/026725706776022326

Harris, L., & Rae, A. (2009). Social networks: The future of marketing for small business. *The Journal of Business Strategy, 30*(5), 24–31. doi:10.1108/02756660910987581

Harris, R., Harris, K., & Baron, S. (2003). Theatrical service experiences: Dramatic script development with employees. *International Journal of Service Industry Management, 14*(2), 184–199. doi:10.1108/09564230310474156

Hart, C. W. L., Heskett, J. L., & Sasser, W. E. Jr. (1990). The profitable art of service recovery. *Harvard Business Review*, (July-August), 148–156. PMID:10106796

Hart, S., & Diamantopoulos, A. (1993). Marketing Research Activity and Company Performance: Evidence from Manufacturing Industry. *European Journal of Marketing, 27*(5), 54–72. doi:10.1108/03090569310039723

Harvard Business Review., (2010). *The New Conversation: Taking Social Media from Talk to Action.* Boston, MA: Harvard Business School Publishing.

Hassan, H., Nadzim, S. Z. A., & Shiratuddin, N. (2015). Strategic use of social media for small business based on the AIDA model. *Procedia: Social and Behavioral Sciences, 172*, 262–269. doi:10.1016/j.sbspro.2015.01.363

Hausmann, A., & Poellmann, L. (2013). Using social media for arts marketing: Theoretical analysis and empirical insights for performing arts organizations. *International Review on Public and Nonprofit Marketing, 10*(2), 143–161. doi:10.1007/s12208-013-0094-8

Hawking, D. (2004). Challenges in enterprise search. In *Proceedings of the 15th Australasian database conference.*

Heallam-Wells, J. (2004). Mentoring for aspiring women managers. *Gender in Management, 19*(4), 212-218. Retrieved September 27, 2015, from http://www.emeraldinsight.com/doi/full/10.1108/09649420410541281

Heinonen, K. (2011). Consumer activity in social media: Managerial approaches to consumers' social media behavior. *Journal of Consumer Behaviour, 10*(6), 356–364. doi:10.1002/cb.376

Heirati, N., O'Cass, A., & Ngo, L. V. (2013). The Contingent Value of Marketing and Social Networking Capabilities in Firm Performance. *Journal of Strategic Marketing, 21*(1), 82–98. doi:10.1080/0965254X.2012.742130

Helgeson, J. M., & Supphellen, M. (2004). A conceptual and measurement comparison of self-congruity and brand personality: The impact of socially desirable responding. *International Journal of Market Research, 46*(2), 205–233.

Hempel, J. (2015, Oct. 6). Inside Reddit's plan to recover from its epic meltdown. *Wired Magazine.*

Hennig-Thurau, T., Malthouse, E. C., Friege, C., Gensler, S., Lobschat, L., Rangaswamy, A., & Skiera, B. (2010). The impact of new media on customer relationships. *Journal of Service Research, 13*(3), 311–330. doi:10.1177/1094670510375460

Herbert, J. (2004). *Journalism in the Digital Age: Theory and Practice for Broadcast, Print and On-Line Media.* Oxford, UK: Focal Press.

Hermida, A., & Thurman, N. (2008). A clash of cultures: The integration of user-generated content within professional journalistic frameworks at British newspaper websites. *Journalism Practice, 2*(3), 343–356. doi:10.1080/17512780802054538

Hew, K. F., & Cheung, W. S. (2013). Use of Web 2.0 technologies in K-12 and higher education: The search for evidence-based practice. *Educational Research Review, 9*, 47–64. doi:10.1016/j.edurev.2012.08.001

Highfield, T., Harrington, S., & Bruns, A. (2013). Twitter as a technology for audiencing and fandom. *Information Communication and Society, 16*(3), 315–339. doi:10.1080/1369118X.2012.756053

Hills, S. B., & Sarin, S. (2003). From Market Driven to Market Driving: An Alternate Paradigm for Marketing in High Technology Industries. *Journal of Marketing Theory and Practice, 11*(3), 13–24. doi:10.1080/10696679.2003.11658498

Hoffman, D. L., & Novak, T. P. (2012). *Why do people use social media? Empirical findings and a new theoretical framework for social media goal pursuit.* Retrieved From Social Science Research Network: http://Papers.Ssrn.Com/Sol3/Papers.Cfm?Abstract_Id=1989586

Hoffman, D. L., & Fodor, M. (2010). Can you measure the ROI of your social media marketing? *MIT Sloan Management Review, 52*(1), 41–49.

Hoffman, D. L., & Novak, T. P. (1996). Marketing in hypermedia computer-mediated environments: Conceptual foundations. *Journal of Marketing, 60*(3), 50–68. doi:10.2307/1251841

Hofstaetter, C., & Egger, R. (2009). The importance and use of weblogs for backpackers. In Information and Communication Technologies in Tourism. New York: Springer-Verlag.

Hofstede, G. (1991). *Cutures and Organizations: Software of the Mind.* New York, NY: McGraw-Hill.

Hollebeek, L. D. (2011). Demystifying customer brand engagement: Exploring the loyalty nexus. *Journal of Marketing Management, 27*(7/8), 785–807. doi:10.1080/0267257X.2010.500132

Holmlund, M., & Kock, S. (1998). Relationships and the internationalization of finnish small and medium-sized companies. *International Small Business Journal, 16*(4), 46–63. doi:10.1177/0266242698164003

Hölscher, C., & Strube, G. (2000). Web search behavior of internet experts and newbies. *Computer Networks, 33*(1), 337–346. doi:10.1016/S1389-1286(00)00031-1

Homitz, D. J., & Berge, Z. L. (2008). Using e-mentoring to sustain distance training and education. *The Learning Organization, 15*(4), 326–335. doi:10.1108/09696470810879574

Hong, L., & Page, S. (2004). Groups of Diverse Problem-solvers Can Outperform Groups of High-ability Problem-solvers. *Proceedings of the National Academy of Sciences of the United States of America, 101*(46), 16385–16389. doi:10.1073/pnas.0403723101 PMID:15534225

Hopwood, M. (2007). The sport integrated marketing communications mix. In J. Beech & S. Chadwick (Eds.), *The Marketing of Sport* (pp. 213–238). Harlow: Pearson Education Limited.

Housholder, E., & LaMarre, H. L. (2015). Political social media engagement: Comparing campaign goals with voter behavior. *Public Relations Review, 41*(1), 138–140. doi:10.1016/j.pubrev.2014.10.007

Howarth, A. (2015). Exploring a curatorial turn in journalism. *Media/Culture Journal, 18*(4).

Howcroft, B., Hewer, P., & Durkin, M. (2003). Banker-Customer Interactions in Financial Services. *Journal of Marketing Management, 19*(9/10), 1001–1020. doi:10.1080/0267257X.2003.9728248

Howe, J. (2008). *Crowdsourcing: Why the Power of the Crowd Is Driving the Future of Business.* New York: Crown Business.

Hoy, G. M., & Milne, G. (2010). Gender Differences in Privacy-Related Measures for Young Adult Facebook Users. *Journal of Interactive Advertising, 10*(2), 28–45. doi:10.1080/15252019.2010.10722168

Hrastinski, S., & Aghaee, N. M. (2012). How are campus students using social media to support their studies? An explorative interview study. *Education and Information Technologies, 17*(4), 451–464. doi:10.1007/s10639-011-9169-5

Hsu, C. H. C., & Song, H. (2013). Destination image in travel magazines: A textual and pictorial analysis of Hong Kong and Macau. *Journal of Vacation Marketing*, *19*(3), 253–268. doi:10.1177/1356766712473469

Huang, H.-Y. (2014). *Self-presentation Tactics in Social Media*. Xiamen University, School of Journalism and Communication. doi:10.2991/icss-14.2014.76

Hubspot. (2012). *LinkedIn 277% more effective for lead generation than facebook & twitter*. Retrieved from http://blog.hubspot.com/blog/tabid/6307/bid/30030/LinkedIn-277-More-Effective-for-Lead-Generation-Than-Facebook-Twitter-New-Data.aspx

Hudson, S., Roth, M. S., Madden, T. J., & Hudson, R. (2015). The effects of social media on emotions, brand relationship quality, and word of mouth: An empirical study of music festival attendees. *Tourism Management*, *47*, 68–76. doi:10.1016/j.tourman.2014.09.001

Hulpia, H., & Devos, G. (2010). How Distributed Leadership Can Make a Difference in Teachers' Organizational Commitment? *Teaching and Teacher Education*, *26*(3), 565–575. doi:10.1016/j.tate.2009.08.006

Hum, N. J., Chamberlin, P. E., Hambright, B. L., Portwood, A. C., Schat, A. C., & Bevan, J. L. (2011). A picture is worth a thousand words: A content analysis of Facebook profile photographs. *Computers in Human Behavior*, *27*(5), 1828–1833. doi:10.1016/j.chb.2011.04.003

Hung, H., & Wong, Y. H. (2007). Organisational Perception of Customer Satisfaction: Theories and Evidence. *Service Industries Journal*, *27*(4), 495–507. doi:10.1080/02642060701346540

Hunt, D. M., & Michael, C. (1983). Mentorship: A career training and development tool. *Academy of Management Review*, *8*, 475–485.

Hurrell, S., & Scholarios, A. D. (2013). The people make the brand: Reducing social skills gaps through person-brand fit and human resource management practices. *Journal of Service Research*, *17*(1), 54–67. doi:10.1177/1094670513484508

Hwang, H., & Kim, K. O. (2015). Social media as a tool for social movements: The effect of social media use and social capital on intention to participate in social movements. *International Journal of Consumer Studies*, *39*(5), 478–488. doi:10.1111/ijcs.12221

IAB. (2013). IV estudio anual de redes sociales. IAB.

Ibbotson, R. G., Sindelar, J. L., & Ritter, J. R. (1994). The Market's Problems with the Pricing of Initial Public Offerings. *Journal of Applied Corporate Finance*, *7*(1), 66–74. doi:10.1111/j.1745-6622.1994.tb00395.x

IBC. (2015, Sept 30). *IBC Content Everywhere*. Retrieved Sept 30, 2015, from IBC Content Everywhere Hub Programme: http://www.ibc.org/

IBM. (2015). *Watson Developer Cloud*. Retrieved from Personality Insights: https://watson-pi-demo.mybluemix.net/

Ibrahim, S. Z., Blandford, A., & Bianchi-Berthouze, N. (2012). Privacy Settings on Facebook: Their Roles and Importance. In *IEEE/ACM International Conference on Green Computing and Communications* (pp. 426-433). IEEE. doi:10.1109/GreenCom.2012.67

ICO. (2015). *Guide to data protection*. Information Commissioner's Office. Retrieved November 20, 2015, from https://ico.org.uk/for-organisations/

IMDB. (2012). *IMDB*. (F. Kohle, Producer). Retrieved from God, Church, Pills & Condoms: http://www.imdb.com/title/tt2170682

IMDB. (2013). *IMDB*. (J. Oppenheimer, Producer). Retrieved from The Act of Killing: http://www.imdb.com/title/tt2375605/

IMDB. (2015a). *IMDB*. Retrieved from Koen Suidgeest: http://www.imdb.com/name/nm0837639/

Index Reporting – Solactive Social Media Index. (2014). Solactive AG. Retrieved March 31, 2014, from: http://www.solactive.com/indexing-en/indices/equity/solactive-indices/

Indiegogo. (2008). *Indiegogo*. Retrieved from Indiegogo: www.indiegogo.com

Internet Live Stats. (2015, September 15). *Internet Live Stats*. Retrieved September 15, 2015, from Internet Users: http://www.internetlivestats.com/internet-users/#trend

Ipsos/Mrbi. (2015a). *Joint National Listenership and Readership: Third Quarter 2015*. Dublin: Ipsos/Mrbi.

Ipsos/Mrbi. (2015b). *Social Media Quarterly: August 2015*. Dublin: Ipsos/Mrbi.

Jablonski, S., & Yakup, D. (2012). Integrated Approach to Factors Affecting Consumers Purchase Behavior in Poland and an Empirical Study. *Global Journal of Management and Business Research*, *12*(15), 94–115.

Jacobs, I. (2015). Take social customer service beyond your own walled garden. *Forrester Research Brief*. Retrieved 19 February 2015 from: https://www.forrester.com/Brief+Take+Social+Customer+Service+Beyond+Your+Own+Walled+Garden/fulltext/-/E-res119674

Jagers, S. C. (2009). In search of the Ecological citizen. *Environmental Politics*, *18*(1), 18–26. doi:10.1080/09644010802624751

Jahn, B., & Kunz, W. (2012). How to transform consumers into fans of your brand. *Journal of Service Management*, *23*(3), 344–361. doi:10.1108/09564231211248444

Jain, P., Rodrigues, T., Magno, G., Kumaraguru, P., & Almeida, V. (2011). Cross-pollination of information in online social media: A case study on popular social networks. In *Proceedings of the 2011 IEEE International Conference on Privacy, Security, Risk, and Trust, and IEEE International Conference on Social Computing*. IEEE Computer Society.

Janoscik, V., Smutny, Z., & Cermak, R. (2015). Integrated Online Marketing Communication of Companies: Survey in Central and Eastern Europe. In A. Kocourek (Ed.), *The Proceedings of the 12th International Conference Liberec Economic Forum* (pp. 376–383). Liberec: Technical University of Liberec.

Jarvey, N., & Svetkey, B. (2015). Yes, Hollywood this is your future. Variety, p. 88.

Jasek, P. (2015). Impact of Customer Networks on Customer Lifetime Value Models. In R. P. Dameri, & L. Beltrametti (Eds.), *Proceedings of the 10th European Conference on Innovation and Entrepreneurship* (pp. 759-764), Reading: ACPI.

Jaworski, B. J., & Kohli, A. K. (1993). Market Orientation - Antecedents and Consequences. *Journal of Marketing*, *57*(3), 53–70.

Jayachandran, S., Sharma, S., Kaufman, P., & Raman, P. (2005). The role of relational information processes and technology use in customer relationship management. *Journal of Marketing*, *69*(4), 177–192.

Jeacle, I., & Carter, C. (2011). In TripAdvisor we trust: Rankings, calculative regimes and abstract systems. *Accounting, Organizations and Society*, *36*(4–5), 293–309. doi:10.1016/j.aos.2011.04.002

Jenkins, H. W. (2013, April 12). Will Google's Ray Kurzweil Live Forever? *The Wall Street Journal*.

Jerin, K. (Ed.). (2015). *Nowi mieszczanie, raport trendowy*. Retrieved September 21, 2015, from http://www.fpiec.pl/nowi_mieszczanie_f5_analytics.pdf

Jobs, S. (2007). Retrieved March 25, 2012, from http://www.apple.com/hotnews/agreenerapple/

Johannisson, B. (1987). Anarchists and Organizers: Entrepreneurs in a Network Perspective. *International Studies of Management & Organization*, *17*(1), 49–63. doi:10.1080/00208825.1987.11656445

Johanson, J., & Mattsson, L. G. (1987). Interorganizational relations in industrial systems: A network approach compared with the transaction-cost approach. *International Studies of Management & Organization*, *17*(1), 34–48. doi:10.1080/00208825.1987.11656444

Johansson, F., Kaati, L., & Shrestha, A. (2013). Detecting multiple aliases in social media. In *Proceedings of the 2013 IEEE/ACM International Conference on Advances in Social Networks Analysis and Mining*. doi:10.1145/2492517.2500261

Johnsen, R. E., & Johnsen, T. E. (1999). International market development through networks: The case of the ayrshire knitwear sector. *International Journal of Entrepreneurial Behavior & Research*, *5*(6), 297–312. doi:10.1108/13552559910306114

Johnson, W. B., & Ridley, C. R. (2008). *The elements of mentoring*. New York, NY: Palgrave Macmillan.

Johnstone, J. W. C., Slawski, E. J., & Bowman, W. B. (1972). The professional values of American newsmen. *Public Opinion Quarterly*, *36*(4), 522–540. doi:10.1086/268036

Johnston, J. (2015). "Loose tweets sink fleets" and other sage advice: Social media governance, policies and guidelines. *Journal of Public Affairs*, *15*(2), 175–187. doi:10.1002/pa.1538

Jones, B., Temperley, J., & Lima, A. (2009). Corporate reputation in the era of Web 2.0: The case of Primark. *Journal of Marketing Management*, *25*(9/10), 927–939. doi:10.1362/026725709X479309

Jones, H., & Farquhar, J. D. (2003). Contact management and customer loyalty. *Journal of Financial Services Marketing*, *8*(1), 71–78. doi:10.1057/palgrave.fsm.4770108

Jonsson, P. (2014). *Ericson Mobility Report*. Ericsson. Ericsson.

Jung, C. G. (2011). Die Archetypen und das kollektive Unbewusste. London: Patmos.

Jung, C. (1928). *Two Essays on Analytical Psychology*. London: Baillière, Tindall and Cox.

Juvonen, J., & Gross, E. F. (2008). Extending the School Grounds?—Bullying Experiences in Cyberspace. *The Journal of School Health*, *78*(9), 496–505. doi:10.1111/j.1746-1561.2008.00335.x PMID:18786042

Kabilan, M. K., Ahmad, N., & Abidin, M. J. Z. (2010). Facebook: An online environment for learning of English in institutions of higher education? *The Internet and Higher Education*, *13*(4), 179–187. doi:10.1016/j.iheduc.2010.07.003

Kaldor, M. (2003). Civil Society and Accountability. *Journal of Human Development*, *4*(1), 5–27. doi:10.1080/1464988032000051469

Kamath, K. Y., & Caverlee, J. (2012). Content-based crowd retrieval on the real-time Web. In *Proceedings of CIKM '12*. doi:10.1145/2396761.2396789

Kameda, T., Ohtsubo, Y., & Takezawa, M. (1997). Centrality in sociocognitive networks and social influence: An illustration in a group decision-making context. *Journal of Personality and Social Psychology*, *73*(2), 296–309. doi:10.1037/0022-3514.73.2.296

Kane, G. C., Alavi, M., Lacianca, G., & Borgatti, S. P. (2014). What's different about social media networks? A framework and research agenda. *Management Information Systems Quarterly*, *38*(1), 275–304.

Kapetanios, E. (2008). Quo Vadis Computer Science: From Turing to Personal Computer, Personal Content and Collective Intelligence. *Data & Knowledge Engineering*, *67*(2), 286–292. doi:10.1016/j.datak.2008.05.003

Kaplan, & Haenlein. (2010). Users of the world, unite! The challenges and opportunities of Social Media. *Science Direct, 53*, 59-68.

Kaplan, A. M., & Haenlein, M. (2010). Users of the world, unite! The challenges and opportunities of Social Media. *Business Horizons, 53*(1), 59–68. doi:10.1016/j.bushor.2009.09.003

Kaplan, A. M., & Haenlein, M. (2010). *Users of the world, unite! The challenges and opportunities of Social Media.* Elsevier.

Kapp, E. (1877). *Grundlinien einer Philosophie der Technik.* Braunschweig: Westermann.

Karahan, E., & Roehrig, G. (2014). Constructing Media Artifacts in a Social Constructivist Environment to Enhance Students' Environmental Awareness and Activism. *Journal of Science Education and Technology, 24*(1), 103–118. doi:10.1007/s10956-014-9525-5

Karim, J. (2005). *Me at the Zoo.* Retrieved from Youtube: https://www.youtube.com/watch?v=jNQXAC9IVRw

Karnik, A., Saroop, A., & Borkar, V. (2013). On the diffusion of messages in on-line social networks. *Performance Evaluation, 70*(4), 271–285. doi:10.1016/j.peva.2012.12.002

Kasemsap, K. (2014b). The role of social media in the knowledge-based organizations. In I. Lee (Ed.), Integrating social media into business practice, applications, management, and models (pp. 254–275). Hershey, PA: IGI Global. doi:10.4018/978-1-4666-6182-0.ch013

Kasemsap, K. (2014a). The role of social networking in global business environments. In P. Smith & T. Cockburn (Eds.), *Impact of emerging digital technologies on leadership in global business* (pp. 183–201). Hershey, PA: IGI Global. doi:10.4018/978-1-4666-6134-9.ch010

Kasemsap, K. (2015a). The role of social media in international advertising. In N. Taşkıran & R. Yılmaz (Eds.), *Handbook of research on effective advertising strategies in the social media age* (pp. 171–196). Hershey, PA: IGI Global. doi:10.4018/978-1-4666-8125-5.ch010

Kasemsap, K. (2015b). The role of cloud computing adoption in global business. In V. Chang, R. Walters, & G. Wills (Eds.), *Delivery and adoption of cloud computing services in contemporary organizations* (pp. 26–55). Hershey, PA: IGI Global. doi:10.4018/978-1-4666-8210-8.ch002

Kasemsap, K. (2015c). The role of cloud computing in global supply chain. In N. Rao (Ed.), *Enterprise management strategies in the era of cloud computing* (pp. 192–219). Hershey, PA: IGI Global. doi:10.4018/978-1-4666-8339-6.ch009

Kasemsap, K. (2015d). The role of customer relationship management in the global business environments. In T. Tsiakis (Ed.), *Trends and innovations in marketing information systems* (pp. 130–156). Hershey, PA: IGI Global. doi:10.4018/978-1-4666-8459-1.ch007

Kasemsap, K. (2015e). The role of e-business adoption in the business world. In N. Ray, D. Das, S. Chaudhuri, & A. Ghosh (Eds.), *Strategic infrastructure development for economic growth and social change* (pp. 51–63). Hershey, PA: IGI Global. doi:10.4018/978-1-4666-7470-7.ch005

Kasemsap, K. (2016a). Encouraging supply chain networks and customer loyalty in global supply chain. In N. Kamath & S. Saurav (Eds.), *Handbook of research on strategic supply chain management in the retail industry* (pp. 87–112). Hershey, PA: IGI Global. doi:10.4018/978-1-4666-9894-9.ch006

Kasemsap, K. (2016b). The roles of social media marketing and brand management in global marketing. In W. Ozuem & G. Bowen (Eds.), *Competitive social media marketing strategies* (pp. 173–200). Hershey, PA: IGI Global. doi:10.4018/978-1-4666-9776-8.ch009

Kaske, F., Kugler, M., & Smolnik, S. (2012). Return on Investment in Social Media – Does the Hype Pay Off? Towards an Assessment of the Profitability of Social Media in Organizations. *45th Hawaii International Conference on System Sciences* (pp. 3898-3907). IEEE Computer Society. doi:10.1109/HICSS.2012.504

Kassarjian, H. H. (1977). Content analysis in consumer research. *The Journal of Consumer Research, 4*(June), 8–18. doi:10.1086/208674

Kaye, J., & Quinn, S. (2010). *Funding Journalism in the Digital Age: Business Models, Strategies, Issues and Trends.* New York: Peter Lang.

Kerbel, M., & Bloom, J. (2005). Blog for America and Civic Involvement. *The International Journal of Press/Politics, 10*(4), 3–27. doi:10.1177/1081180X05281395

Khalaf, S. (2014). *The Rise of the Mobile Addict.* Retrieved September 6, 2015: http://flurrymobile.tumblr.com/post/115191945655/the-rise-of-the-mobile-addict#.VPA77_mG-W5

Kickstarter. (2008). *Kickstarter.* Retrieved from Kickstarter: www.kickstarter.com

Kietzmann, J. H., Hermkens, K., McCarthy, I. P., & Silvestre, B. S. (2011). Social media? Get serious! Understanding the functional building blocks of social media. *Business Horizons, 54*(3), 241–251. doi:10.1016/j.bushor.2011.01.005

Kim, J., Ko, E.-Y., Jung, J., Lee, C. W., Kim, N. W., & Kim, J. (2015). Factful: Engaging taxpayers in the public discussion of a government budget. In *CHI 2015. Crossings. HCI for Civic Engagement.*

Kim, A. J., & Ko, E. (2011). Do social media marketing activities enhance customer equity? An empirical study of the luxury fashion brand. *Journal of Business Research, 65*(10), 1480–1486. doi:10.1016/j.jbusres.2011.10.014

Kim, K. S., Sin, S. C. J., & He, Y. (2013). Information seeking through social media: Impact of user characteristics on social media use. *Proceedings of the American Society for Information Science and Technology, 50*(1), 1–4. doi:10.1002/meet.14505001155

King, B. (2008). Stardom, celebrity and the para-confession. *Social Semiotics, 18*(2), 115–132. doi:10.1080/10350330802002135

King, W. R. (2008). An integrated architecture for the effective knowledge organization. *Journal of Knowledge Management, 12*(2), 29–41. doi:10.1108/13673270810859497

Kinkade, S., & Verclas, K. M. (2008). Text Messaging to Save Trees (Argentina). Wireless Technologies for Social Change: Trends in Mobile Use by NGOs, 45-47.

Kiráľová, A., & Pavliceka, A. (2015). Development of social media strategies in tourism destination. *Procedia: Social and Behavioral Sciences, 175*, 358–366. doi:10.1016/j.sbspro.2015.01.1211

Kiron, D., Palmer, D., Phillips, A. N., & Kruschwitz, N. (2012). *Social business: What are companies really doing.* MIT Sloan Management Review.

Kirtis, A. K., & Karahan, F. (2011). *To be or not to be in social media arena as the most cost-efficient marketing strategy after the global recession.* Paper presented at the 7th International Strategic Management Conference, Paris, France. doi:10.1016/j.sbspro.2011.09.083

Kishner, I., & Crescenti, B. (2010). The Rise of Social Media. *The Entertainment and Sports Lawyer, 27*(4), 24–26.

KISS debuts "KISS Liveshare ". (2010). Retrieved from http://www.kissonline.com/news?n_id=51273

Kivran-Swaine, F., Govindan, P., & Naaman, M. (2011). The impact of network structure on breaking ties in online social networks: Unfollowing on Twitter. In *Proceedings of CHI 2011.*

Kleinrock, L. (2011, April 6). *The Day the Infant Internet Uttered its First Words*. Retrieved September 14, 2015, from UCLA: http://www.lk.cs.ucla.edu/internet_first_words.html

Kleinrock, L. (2010). *An Early History of the Internet. IEEE Communications Magazine*.

Kliegr, T., Svatek, V., Ralbovsky, M., & Simunek, M. (2011). SEWEBAR-CMS: Semantic analytical report authoring for data mining results. *Journal of Intelligent Information Systems, 37*(3), 371–395. doi:10.1007/s10844-010-0137-0

Klimis, C. (2010). Digital marketing: the gradual integration in retail banking. *EFMA Journal,* (226), 16-19.

Knappenberger, B. (2014, December 30). *Kickstarter*. Retrieved September 17, 2015, from Aaron Swartz Documentary - The Internet's Own Boy: https://www.kickstarter.com/projects/26788492/aaron-swartz-documentary-the-internets-own-boy-0

Kohle, F. (2009). *Tiny Little Doclab*. Retrieved 7 16, 2015, from Facebook: https://www.facebook.com/tinylittledoclab

Kohle, F. H. (2015). The Social Media "Information Explosion" Spectacle: Perspectives for Documentary Producers. In J. Sahlin (Eds.), Social Media and the Transformation of Interaction in Society (pp. 173-187). London: Academic Press.

Kohle, F., & Raj, S. (2015). Implications of Social Media Use in Personal and Professional Settings. In S. M. Vladlena Benson (Ed.), Abuse of the social media brain: Implications for media producers and educators (pp. 102-117)). IGI-Global.

Kolin, K. K. (2011). Social informatics today and tomorrow: Status, problems and prospects of development of complex lines in the field of science and education. *TripleC: Communication. Capitalism & Critique, 9*(2), 460–465.

Korhonen, H., Luostarinen, R., & Welch, L. (1996). Internationalization of SMEs: Inward-outward patterns and government policy. *Management International Review*, 315–329.

Korn, M. (2011, October 24). Top 'Innovators' Rank Low in R&D Spending. *Wall Street Journal*.

Kotler, P. (2003). *Marketing mix*. Hoboken, NJ: John Wiley & Sons, Inc.

Kotler, P., Armstrong, G., Saunders, J., & Wong, V. (2000). *Principles of Marketing* (2d Russian Ed). Moscow: Williams Publishing House.

Kotler, P., & Keller, K. L. (2007). *Marketing Management*. Praha: Grada Publishing.

Kozinets, R. (2015). *Netnography: Redefined*. London: SAGE. doi:10.1002/9781118767771.wbiedcs067

Kramer, S. D. (2004). CBS scandal highlights tension between bloggers and news media. *Online Journalism Review*. Retrieved from http://www.ojr.org/ojr/workplace/1096589178.php

Krause, S., James, R., Faria, J. J., Ruxton, G. D., & Krause, J. (2011). Swarm Intelligence in Humans: Diversity Can Trump Ability. *Animal Behaviour, 81*(5), 941–948. doi:10.1016/j.anbehav.2010.12.018

Kreutzer, R. T., & Land, K.-H. (2015). *The Necessity of Change Management: Why Our Traditional Communication and Organizational Structures Are Becoming Obsolete. In Digital Darwinism* (pp. 209–248). Springer.

Krishnamurthy, B. (2013, May-June). Privacy and online social networks: Can colorless green ideas sleep furiously? *IEEE Computer and Reliability Societies*, 14 – 20.

Krishnamurthy, B., & Cormode, G. (2008). Key differences between Web 1.0 and Web 2.0. *First Monday, 13*(6).

Kuhn, T. S. (1996). *The Structure of Scientific Revolutions* (3rd ed.). The University of Chicago Press. doi:10.7208/chicago/9780226458106.001.0001

Kumar, N., & Benbasat, I. (2002). Para-social presence: A re-conceptualization of 'social presence' to capture the relationship between a web site and her visitors. In *Proceedings of the 35ᵗʰ Hawaii International Conference on System Sciences.*

Kuratko, D. F., Goodale, J. C., & Hornsby, J. S. (2001). Quality Practices for a Competitive Advantage in Smaller Firms. *Journal of Small Business Management, 39*(4), 293–311.

Kurzweil, R. (2009, April 28). *Youtube.* Retrieved September 15, 2015, from Big Think - Ray Kurzweil: The Coming Singularity: https://www.youtube.com/watch?v=1uIzS1uCOcE

Kushner, M. (2015, May 18). *Why the buildings of the future will be shaped by ... you* [Video]. Retrieved from https://www.ted.com/talks/marc_kushner_why_the_buildings_of_the_future_will_be_shaped_by_you

Lahtinen, H. J. (2012). Young people's ICT role at home – A descriptive study of young Finnish people's ICT views in the home context. *Quality & Quantity, 46*(2), 581–597. doi:10.1007/s11135-010-9409-6

Laine, A., & Kock, S. (2000). *A process model of internationalization-new times demands new patterns.* 16th IMP-Conference, Bath, UK.

Laister, J. (2012). *Creativity & Innovation Training in SME I-Create.* Paper presented at the International Conference The Future of Education, Florence, Italy.

LaMarre, H. L., & Suzuki-Holbrecht, Y. (2013). Tweeting democracy? Twitter as a voter mobilization strategy for congressional campaigns. *Public Relations Review, 39*(4), 360–368. doi:10.1016/j.pubrev.2013.07.009

Lampe, C., Ellison, N., & Steinfield, C. (2007). A familiar Face(book): Profile elements as signals in an online social network. In *Proceedings of the SIGCHI Conference on Human Factors in Computing Systems* (pp. 435-444). New York: ACM Press.

Lange, P. G. (2007). Publicly private and privately public: Social networking on YouTube. *Journal of Computer-Mediated Communication, 13*(1), 361–380. doi:10.1111/j.1083-6101.2007.00400.x

Lankes, R. D. (2008). Trusting the Internet: New approaches to credibility tools. In M. J. Metzger & A. J. Flanagin (Eds.), *Digital Media, Youth and Credibility* (pp. 101–122). Cambridge, MA: MIT Press.

Lanoue, S. (2015). *How to Win on Mobile: Understanding Micro-Moments and Consumer Behavior.* Retrieved from https://www.usertesting.com/blog/2015/07/02/how-to-win-on-mobile-understanding-micro-moments-and-consumer-behavior/

Lashkari, A. H., Parhizkar, B., Ramachandran, A., & Navaratnam, S. (2010). Privacy and Vulnerability Issues of Social Networks (Facebook). In H. Xie (Ed.), *Proceedings of the International Conference on Internet Technology and Security* (pp. 157-163). New York: ASME. doi:10.1115/1.859681.paper31

Latour, B. (1987). *Science in Action. How to follow Scientists and Engineers through Society.* Milton Keynes, UK: Open University Press.

Latour, B. (1999). *Science's Blood Flow; An Example from Joliot's Scientific Intelligence. In Pandora's Hope: Essays on the Reality of Science Studies* (pp. 80–112). Cambridge, MA. Harvard University Press.

Lauterborn, B. (1990). New Marketing Litany: Four Ps Passé: C-Words Take Over. *Advertising Age, 61*(4), 26.

Lawson-Body, A., Willoughby, L., & Logossah, K. (2010). Developing an Instrument for Measuring E-Commerce Dimensions. *Journal of Computer Information Systems, 51*(2), 2–13.

Layout Instagram, Press News. (2015). *Instagram.* Retrieved August 30, 2015, from https://instagram.com/press/

Lazarsfeld, P., & Merton, R. (1954). Friendship as a social process: a substantive and methodological analysis. In M. Berger, T. Abel, & C. H. Page (Eds.), *Freedom and Control in Modern Society* (pp. 18–66). New York: Van Nostrand.

Le Sourd, V. (2007). *Performance Measurement for Traditional Investment - Literature Survey*. Nice, France: EDHEC Business School.

Leavitt, A. (2015). 'This is a throwaway account': Temporary technical identities and perceptions of anonymity in a massive online community. In *Proceedings of CSCW 2015*.

Lederer, K. (2012). Pros and cons of social media in the classroom. *Campus Technology*, 25(5), 1–2.

Lee, J. (2015). The double-edged sword: The effects of journalists' social media activities on audience perceptions of journalists and their news products. *Journal of Computer-Mediated Communication*, 20(3), 312–329. doi:10.1111/jcc4.12113

Leek, S., Turnbull, P., & Naudé, P. (2003). How is information technology affecting business relationships? Results from a UK survey. *Industrial Marketing Management*, 32(2), 119–126. doi:10.1016/S0019-8501(02)00226-2

Lehrer, D., & Vasudev, J. (2010). *Visualizing Information to Improve Building Performance: A study of expert users*. Center for the Built Environment.

Lehtinen, U. (2011). Combining Mix and Relationship marketing. *Marketing Review*, 11(2), 117–136.

Leibnitz, M. (1703). Essai d'une nouvelle science des nombres. Paris: Académie royale des sciences.

Leichteris, E. (2011). Mokslo ir technologijų parkai socialinių technologijų kontekste. *Social Technologies*, 1(1), 139–150.

Leimeister, J. M. (2010). Collective Intelligence. *Business & Information Systems Engineering*, 4(2), 245–248. doi:10.1007/s12599-010-0114-8

Leonardi, P. M., Huysman, M., & Steinfeld, C. (2013). Enterprise social media: Definition, history, and prospects for the study of social technologies in organizations. *Journal of Computer-Mediated Communication*, 19(1), 1–19. doi:10.1111/jcc4.12029

Leonidou, L. C., & Katsikeas, C. S. (1996). The export development process: An integrative review of empirical models. *Journal of International Business Studies*, 27(3), 517–551. doi:10.1057/palgrave.jibs.8490846

Lesser, E. L., & Fontaine, M. A. (2004). Overcoming knowledge barriers with communities of practice: Lessons learned through practical experience. *Knowledge networks: Innovation through communities of practice*, 14-23.

Lesser, E., Ransom, D., Shah, R., & Pulver, B. (2012). *Collective Intelligence. Capitalizing on the Crowd*. IBM Global Services.

Levesque, T., & McDougall, G. H. G. (1996). Determinants of customer satisfaction in retail banking. *International Journal of Bank Marketing*, 14(7), 12–20. doi:10.1108/02652329610151340

Levitt, T. (1983). The globalization of markets. *Harvard Business Review*, 26(3), 92–102.

Levy, S. (2001). *Hackers: Heroes of the Computer Revolution*. Penguin.

Lewine, S. S., & Prietula, M. J. (2015). Open Collaboration for Innovation: Principles and Performance. Collective intelligence 2015.

Lewin, J. E., & Johnston, W. J. (1997). Relationship Marketing Theory in Practice: A Case Study. *Journal of Business Research*, 39(1), 23–31.

Lewis, B. R., & Spyrakopoulos, S. (2001). Service failures and recovery in retail banking: The customers' perspective. *International Journal of Bank Marketing*, *19*(1), 37–47. doi:10.1108/02652320110366481

Li, C., & Tsai, W. H. S. (2015). Social media usage and acculturation: A test with Hispanics in the U.S. *Computers in Human Behavior*, *45*, 204–212. doi:10.1016/j.chb.2014.12.018

Licklider, J. (1960). Man-Computer Symbiosis. *IRE Trans. Human Factors in Electronics*, 4-11.

Licklider, J., & Clarke, W. (1962, May). On-line Man `computer Communication.*Spring Joint Comp. Conf.*, 21, 113-28.

Liedtke, M. (2013). *Twitter's Founders Differ On The Creation Of The Social Network*. Retrieved from Huffington Post: http://www.huffingtonpost.com/2013/11/06/twitter-creation-founders_n_4228473.html

Liesch, P. W., & Knight, G. A. (1999). Information internalization and hurdle rates in small and medium enterprise internationalization. *Journal of International Business Studies*, *30*(2), 383–394. doi:10.1057/palgrave.jibs.8490075

Lindstrom, M. (2009). *The real decision makers*. Retrieved: September 30, 2015 http://juicecompany.net/development1/the-real-decision-makers/

Linkedin. (2015). *A brief history of Linkedin*. Retrieved from Linkedin: https://ourstory.linkedin.com/

Lis, E., Wood, M. A., Chiniara, C., Biskin, R., & Montoro, R. (2015). Psychiatrists' perceptions of Facebook and other social media. *The Psychiatric Quarterly*, *86*(4), 597–602. doi:10.1007/s11126-015-9358-2 PMID:25791472

List of Wikipedias. (2015, July 26). *Wikimedia*. Retrieved Aug. 30, 2015, from https://meta.wikimedia.org/wiki/List_of_Wikipedias

Littleton, C. (2014, October 15). *Variety*. Retrieved September 23, 2015, from HBO to Launch Standalone Over-the-Top Service in U.S. Next Year: http://variety.com/2014/tv/news/hbo-to-launch-over-the-top-service-in-u-s-next-year-1201330592/

Littleton, T. (2013). Social media and customer service. *eModeration Report*. Retrieved May 2013 from: http://www.emoderation.com/social-media-publications/download-a-guide-to-social-media-and-customer-service

Liu, B. (2012). *Sentiment analysis and opinion mining*. San Rafael: Morgan.

Liu, L., Wu, J., Li, P., & Li, Q. (2015). A social-media-based approach to predicting stock comovement. *Expert Systems with Applications*, *42*(8), 3893–3901. doi:10.1016/j.eswa.2014.12.049

Livestrong Foundation. (2013). *Our Founder*. Retrieved October 13, 2015, from http://www.livestrong.org/Our-Founder

Li, X., Hess, T. J., McNab, A. L., & Yu, Y. (2009). Culture and Acceptance of Global Web Sites: A Cross-Country Study of the Effects of National Cultural Values on Acceptance of a Personal Web Portal. *ACM SIGMIS Database*, *40*(4), 62–87. doi:10.1145/1644953.1644959

Li, Y., Liu, Z., & Zhu, H. (2014). Enterprise search in the big data era: Recent developments and open challenges. *Proceedings of the VLDB Endowment*, *7*(13), 1717–1718. doi:10.14778/2733004.2733071 PMID:26167358

Li, Y., Li, Y. J., Yan, Q., & Deng, R. H. (2015). Privacy leakage analysis in online social networks. *Computers & Security*, *49*, 239–254. doi:10.1016/j.cose.2014.10.012

Lloyd, B. A. (2009). Profesional networking on the internet.*IEEE Conference Record of 2009 Anual Pulp and Paper Industry*, Birmingham, AL. doi:10.1109/PAPCON.2009.5185427

Loewenstein, G. (1994). The Psychology of curiosity: A review and reinterpretation. *Psychological Bulletin*, *116*(1), 75–98. doi:10.1037/0033-2909.116.1.75

Long, M., & McMellon, C. (2004). Exploring the determinants of retail service quality on the Internet. *Journal of Services Marketing*, *18*(1), 78–90. doi:10.1108/08876040410520726

Long, N. H., & Jung, J. J. (2015). Privacy-Aware Framework for Matching Online Social Identities in Multiple Social Networking Services. *Cybernetics and Systems*, *46*(1-2), 69–83. doi:10.1080/01969722.2015.1007737

Lopes, J. L., Souza, R. S., Gadotti, G. I., Pernas, A. M., Yamin, A. C., & Geyer, C. F. (2014). An Architectural Model for Situation Awareness in Ubiquitous Computing. *IEEE Latin America Transactions*, *12*(6), 1113–1119. doi:10.1109/TLA.2014.6894008

Lopez, B. (2010). Doping as Technology: A Re-Reading of the History of Performance-Enhancing Substance Use. *Institute for Culture and Society Occasional Paper Series*, *1*(4), 1-17.

López, F. (2008). *El poder del networking. trabaja tu red de contactos. España: NETBIBLO S.L.*

Lorenz, J., Rauhut, H., Schweitzer, F., & Helbing, D. (2011). How Social Influence Can Undermine the Wisdom of Crowd Effect. *Proceedings of the National Academy of Sciences of the United States of America*, *108*(22), 9020–9025. doi:10.1073/pnas.1008636108 PMID:21576485

Lovejoy, K., & Saxton, G. D. (2012). Information, community, and action: How nonprofit organizations use social media. *Journal of Computer-Mediated Communication*, *17*(3), 337–353. doi:10.1111/j.1083-6101.2012.01576.x

Lovelock, C., & Wright, L. (1999). *Principles of Service Marketing and Management* (2nd ed.). Prentice Hall.

Lowrey, W. (2011). Institutionalism, news organizations and innovation. *Journalism Studies*, *12*(1), 64–79. doi:10.1080/1461670X.2010.511954

Lowry, M., Officer, M., & Schwert, G. (2010). The Variability of IPO Initial Returns. *The Journal of Finance*, *65*(2), 425–465. doi:10.1111/j.1540-6261.2009.01540.x

Luchman, J. N., Bergstrom, J., & Krulikowski, C. (2014). A motives framework of social media website use: A survey of young Americans. *Computers in Human Behavior*, *38*, 136–141. doi:10.1016/j.chb.2014.05.016

Lund, D., & Marinova, D. (2014). Managing revenue across retail channels: The interplay of service performance and direct marketing. *Journal of Marketing*, *78*(5), 99–118. doi:10.1509/jm.13.0220

Luo, S., Xia, H., Yoshida, T., & Wang, Z. (2009). Toward Collective Intelligence of Online Communities: A Primitive Conceptual Model. *Journal of Systems Science and Systems Engineering*, *18*(2), 203–221. doi:10.1007/s11518-009-5095-0

Luo, X., Zhang, J., & Duan, W. (2013). Social media and firm equity value. *Information Systems Research*, *24*(1), 146–163. doi:10.1287/isre.1120.0462

Lykourentzou, I., Vergados, D. J., Kapetanios, E., & Loumos, V. (2011). Collective Intelligence Systems: Classification and Modelling. *Journal of Emerging Technologies in Web Intelligence*, *3*(3), 217–226. doi:10.4304/jetwi.3.3.217-226

Łysik, Ł., Kutera, R., & Machura, P. (2014). Zero Moment of Truth: a new Marketing Challenge in Mobile Consumer Communities. *Proceedings of the European Conference on Social Media: ECSM 2014*. Academic Conferences Limited.

Łysik, Ł., Kutera, R., & Machura, P. (2014, November). Behavioural and technical factors of influence on purchase behaviour of mobile consumers. In *Proceedings of the 18th International Academic MindTrek Conference: Media Business, Management, Content & Services* (pp. 110-117). ACM.

Macaskill, E., & Dance, G. (2013). *The Guardian.* Retrieved from NSA Files decoded: What the revelations mean for you.: http://www.theguardian.com/world/interactive/2013/nov/01/snowden-nsa-files-surveillance-revelations-decoded#section/1

Mačiulienė, M., Leichteris, E., & Mačiulis, A. (2013). The perspectives of developments of virtual communities in Lithuania. In *Proceedings of Social Technologies'2013 conference*. Vilnius: MRU.

Maclaran, P., & Catterall, M. (2002). Analysing qualitative data: Computer software and the market research practitioner. *Qualitative Market Research: An International Journal, 5*(1), 28–39. doi:10.1108/13522750210414490

Madhok, A. (1997). Cost, value and foreign market entry mode: The transaction and the firm. *Strategic Management Journal, 18*(1), 39–61. doi:10.1002/(SICI)1097-0266(199701)18:1<39::AID-SMJ841>3.0.CO;2-J

Magrath, A. (1986). When marketing services, 4Ps are not enough. *Business Horizons, 29*(3), 44–50. doi:10.1016/0007-6813(86)90007-8

Majchrzak, A., Faraj, S., Kane, G. C., & Azad, B. (2013). The contradictory influence of social media affordances on online communal knowledge sharing. *Journal of Computer-Mediated Communication, 19*(1), 38–55. doi:10.1111/jcc4.12030

Makarem, S. C., Mudambi, S. M., & Podoshen, J. S. (2009). Satisfaction in Technology-enabled Service Encounters. *Journal of Services Marketing, 23*(2-3), 134–143. doi:10.1108/08876040910955143

Malär, L., Krohmer, H., Hoyer, W. D., & Nyffenegger, B. (2011). Emotional brand attachment and brand personality: The relative importance of the actual and the ideal self. *Journal of Marketing, 75*(4), 35–52. doi:10.1509/jmkg.75.4.35

Malhotra, N. K. (2010). *Marketing Research: An Applied Orientation* (6th ed.). Upper Saddle River, NJ: Pearson Education. doi:10.1108/S1548-6435(2010)6

Malone, T. W. (2006). *What is Collective Intelligence and What Will We Do About it?* Edited transcript of remarks presented at the official launch of the MIT Center for Collective Intelligence, October 13, Cambridge, MA.

Maloney, S., Moss, A., & Ilic, D. (2014). Social media in health professional education: A student perspective on user levels and prospective applications. *Advances in Health Sciences Education: Theory and Practice, 19*(5), 687–697. doi:10.1007/s10459-014-9495-7 PMID:24566977

Mangold, W. G., & Faulds, D. J. (2009). Social Media: The New Hybrid Element of the Promotion Mix. *Business Horizons, 52*(4), 357–365. doi:10.1016/j.bushor.2009.03.002

MarketWatch. (2014). Retrieved April 1, 2014, from: http://www.marketwatch.com/investing/stocks?link=MW_Nav_INVhttp://www.marketwatch.com/investing/stocks?link=MW_Nav_INV

Markoff, J. (2006, November 12). Entrepreneurs See a Web Guided by Common Sense. *New York Times.*

Maryska, M., & Doucek, P. (2012). ICT Specialists Skills and Knowledge – Business Requirements and Education. *Journal on Efficiency and Responsibility in Education and Science, 5*(3), 157–172. doi:10.7160/eriesj.2012.050305

Mason, M., & Hacker, K. (2003). Applying Communication Theory to Digital Divide Research. *IT & Society, 1*(5), 40–55.

Mason, P. (2015). *Post Capitalism: A Guide to Our Future.* London: Penguin.

Massie, W., & Underhill, C. (1908). The Future of the Wireless Art. *Wireless Telegrpahy and Telephony*, 67-71.

Mattila, A. S. (2004). The impact of service failures on customer loyalty. *International Journal of Service Industry Management, 15*(2), 134–149. doi:10.1108/09564230410532475

Mayande, N., & Weber, C. (2012). *Directed interaction networks and their impact on social media. In Proceedings of PICMET '13*. San Jose, CA: Slideshow.

McAfee, A. P. (2006). Enterprise 2.0: The dawn of emergent collaboration. *MIT Sloan Management Review, 47*(3), 21–28.

McAfee, A. P., & Brynjolfsson, E. (2012). Big data: The management revolution. *Harvard Business Review*, *90*(10), 60–66. PMID:23074865

McCarthy, B. (2014). A sports journalism of their own: An investigation in the motivations, behaviors and media attitudes of fan sports bloggers. *Communication & Sport*, *2*(1), 65–79. doi:10.1177/2167479512469943

McCollough, M. A., Berry, L. L., & Yadav, M. S. (2000). An empirical investigation of customer satisfaction after service failure and recovery. *Journal of Service Research*, *32*(2), 121–137. doi:10.1177/109467050032002

McDaniel, C. D., & Gates, R. H. (2010). *Marketing Research Essentials* (7th ed.). Hoboken, NJ: John Wiley & Sons.

McDermid, V. (2014). *Forensics: What Bugs, Burns, Prints, DNA, and More Tell Us about Crime*. New York: Grove Press.

McDonald, G. (2010). Networking in an icy community. *Stuff*. Retrieved from http://www.stuff.co.nz/business/small-business/3501543/Networking-in-an-icy-community

McDonald, L., Sparks, B., & Glendon, A. (2010). Stakeholder reactions to company crisis communication and causes. *Public Relations Review*, *36*(2), 263–271. doi:10.1016/j.pubrev.2010.04.004

McGuire, S. (2013). *Social Media and Markets: The New Frontier (whitepaper) GNIP*. Boulder, CO: GNIP.

McLean, H. (2014). Crisis and Issues Management. In J. Johnston & M. Sheehan (Eds.), Public Relations Theory and Practice. Crows Nest: Allen & Unwin.

McLuhan, M. (1962). *The Gutenberg Galaxy: The Making of Typographic Man*. Toronto: University of Toronto Press.

McMahon, D. (2013). *The Role of Social Media in Audience Engagement with Irish Radio*. Paper presented at the ECREA Radio Research Conference, London.

McMahon, D. (2015). *Old Dog, New Tricks: Can Social Media Help Youth Radio Stations Grow Their Audience?* Presented at the MeCCSA Conference, Newcastle.

McMillan, S. J., & Hwang, J. (2002). Measure of perceived interactivity: An exploration of the role of direction of communication, user control, and time in shaping perceptions of interactivity. *Journal of Advertising*, *31*(3), 29–42. doi:10.1080/00913367.2002.10673674

Meikle, J. (2011). *Facebook 'Unfriends' Coal and 'Likes' Clean Power*. Retrieved from http://www.guardian.co.uk/environment/2011/dec/15/facebook-coal-clean-power-energy-greenpeace

Mejri, K., & Umemoto, K. (2010). Small-and medium-sized enterprise internationalization: Towards the knowledge-based model. *Journal of International Entrepreneurship*, *8*(2), 156–167. doi:10.1007/s10843-010-0058-6

Memmi, D. (2010). Sociology of Virtual Communities and Social Software Design. In S. Murugesan (Ed.), *Web 2.0, 3.0, and X.0: Technologies, Business, and Social Applications* (Vol. 2, pp. 790–803). New York: Information Science Reference. doi:10.4018/978-1-60566-384-5.ch045

Meraz, S. (2009). Is there an elite hold? Traditional media to social media agenda setting influence in blog networks. *Journal of Computer-Mediated Communication*, *14*(3), 682–707. doi:10.1111/j.1083-6101.2009.01458.x

Merton, R. (1961). *Phenomenon of independent scientific discoveries*. Academic Press.

Meyer, K., & Skak, A. (2002). Networks, serendipity and SME entry into eastern Europe. *European Management Journal*, *20*(2), 179–188. doi:10.1016/S0263-2373(02)00028-2

Meyers, L. S., Gamst, G., & Guarino, A. J. (n.d.). Applied multivariate Research: Design and Interpretation (2nd ed.). Thousand Oaks, CA: SAGE Publications.

Miles, M. B., & Huberman, A. M. (1994). *Qualitative data analysis: An expanded sourcebook.* London: Sage.

Milliyet. (2015, September 22). *Thy which fly to Roma,* Retrieved from http://www.milliyet.com.tr/roma-ya-ucan-thy-/ekonomi/detay/2105730/default.htm

MillwardBrown. (2012). *How social technologies drive business success. European survey results.* Retrieved from http://www.millwardbrown.com/docs/default-source/insight-documents/articles-and-reports/Googe_MillwardBrown_How-Social-Technologies-Drive-Business-Success_201205.pdf

Miltgen, C. L., & Peyrat-guillard, D. (2014). Cultural and generational influences on privacy concerns: A qualitative study in seven european countries. *European Journal of Information Systems, 23*(2), 103–125. doi:10.1057/ejis.2013.17

Ministry of Statistics & Programme Implementation. India. (2011). *Value Addition and Employment Generation in the ICT Sector in India.* Retrieved from http://mospi.nic.in/mospi_new/upload/val_add_ict_21june11.pdf

Min, J., & Kim, B. (2015). How Are People Enticed to Disclose Personal Information Despite Privacy Concerns in Social Network Sites? The Calculus Between Benefit and Cost. *Journal of the Association for Information Science and Technology, 66*(4), 839–857. doi:10.1002/asi.23206

Minkov, M., & Hofstede, G. (2011). The evolution of Hofstede's doctrine. *Cross Cultural Management: An International Journal, 18*(1), 10–20. doi:10.1108/13527601111104269

Minniti, M., & Bygrave, W. (2001). A dynamic model of entrepreneurial learning. *Entrepreneurship: Theory and Practice, 23*(4), 41–52.

Mintzberg, H. (2015, October 5). Networking and communities. *Harvard Business Review.* Retrieved from https://hbr.org/2015/10/we-need-both-networks-and-communities

Mislove, A., Marcon, M., Gummadi, K. P., Druschel, P., & Bhattacharjee, B. (2007). Measurement and analysis of online social networks. *IMC '07 Proceedings of the 7th ACM SIGCOMM Conference on Internet Measurement.*

Mitic, M., & Kapoulas, A. (2012). Understanding the role of social media in bank marketing. *Marketing Intelligence & Planning, 30*(7), 668–686. doi:10.1108/02634501211273797

Mobli.com. (2015). *Back in Austin and just layin' around.* Retrieved October 13, 2015, from http://www.mobli.com/media/show/id/22700756?referer=tw17

Moen, O., Endresen, I., & Gavlen, M. (2003). Executive insights: Use of the Internet in International Marketing: A Case Study of Small Computer Software Firms. *Journal of International Marketing, 11*(4), 129–149. doi:10.1509/jimk.11.4.129.20146

Moen, O., Madsen, T. K., & Aspelund, A. (2008). The Importance of the Internet in International Business-to-Business Markets. *International Marketing Review, 25*(5), 487–503. doi:10.1108/02651330810904053

Moen, Ø., & Servais, P. (2002). Born global or gradual global? examining the export behavior of small and medium-sized enterprises. *Journal of International Marketing, 10*(3), 49–72. doi:10.1509/jimk.10.3.49.19540

Moezzi, M., & Janda, K. B. (2014). From "if only" to "social potential" in schemes to reduce building energy use. *Energy Research & Social Science, 1*(0), 30–40. doi:10.1016/j.erss.2014.03.014

Mohr, J. J., Fisher, R. J., & Nevin, J. R. (1996). Collaborative communication in interfirm relationships: Moderating effects of integration and. *Journal of Marketing, 60*(3), 103. doi:10.2307/1251844

Mohr, J., Slater, S., & Sengupta, S. (2010). *Marketing of High-Technology Products and Innovations* (3rd ed.). Upper Saddle River, Prentice Hall.

Mollen, A., & Wilson, H. (2010). Engagement, telepresence and interactivity in online consumer experience: Reconciling scholastic and managerial perspectives. *Journal of Business Research, 63*(9/10), 919–925. doi:10.1016/j.jbusres.2009.05.014

Möller, K., & Halinen, A. (2000). Relationship Marketing Theory: Its Roots and Direction. *Journal of Marketing Management, 16*(1-3), 29–54. doi:10.1362/026725700785100460

Mongay, J. (2006). Strategic Marketing. A literature review on definitions, concepts and boundaries. MPRA Paper No. 41840.

Monica, P. L. (2006). *Google to buy YouTube for $1.65 billion.* Retrieved from CNN Money: http://money.cnn.com/2006/10/09/technology/googleyoutube_deal/index.htm?cnn=yes

Moniz, K., & Yuan, Y. (2015). Reaching critical mass: The effect of adding new content on website visitors and user registration. In the proceedings of ISCTCS 2014. *CCIS, 520,* 359–369.

Moorman, C., Zaltman, G., & Deshpande, R. (1992). Relationships Between Providers and Users of Market Research: The Dynamics of Trust Within and Between Organizations. *JMR, Journal of Marketing Research, 29*(3), 314–328. doi:10.2307/3172742

Moran, E., & Gossieaux, F. (2010). Marketing in a hyper-social world. *Journal of Advertising Research, 50*(3), 232–239. doi:10.2501/S0021849910091397

Morgan, B. (2015, August 31). When brands try too hard on social media. *Forbes.* Retrieved from http://www.forbes.com/sites/blakemorgan/2015/08/31/when-brands-try-too-hard-on-social-media/

Morgan-Thomas, A., & Veloutsou, C. (2013). Beyond technology acceptance: Brand relationships and online brand experience. *Journal of Business Research, 66*(1), 21–27. doi:10.1016/j.jbusres.2011.07.019

Mori, J., Gibbs, M., Arnold, M., Nansen, B., & Kohn, T. (2012). Design considerations for after death: Comparing the affordances of three online platforms. In *Proceedings of OZCHI '12.*

Morozov, E. (2013). *To Save Everything Click Here.* New York: Public Affairs.

Morris, T. (2010). *All a twitter: a personal and professional guide to social networking with Twitter.* Indianapolis, IN: Pearson Education.

Moutinho, L., & Smith, A. (2000). Modelling bank customer satisfaction through mediation of attitudes towards human and automated banking. *International Journal of Bank Marketing, 18*(3), 124–134. doi:10.1108/02652320010339699

Mucan, B., & Özeltürkay, E. Y. (2014). Social media creates competitive advantages: How Turkish banks use this power? A content analysis of Turkish banks through their webpages. *Procedia: Social and Behavioral Sciences, 148,* 137–145. doi:10.1016/j.sbspro.2014.07.027

Muniz, J. A. Jr, & O'Guinn, T. C. (2001). Brand community. *The Journal of Consumer Research, 27*(4), 412–432. doi:10.1086/319618

Murdick, R. G., Render, B., & Russell, R. S. (1990). *Service operations management.* Allyn and Bacon.

Murphy, T. (2000). *Web rules: How the Internet is changing the way consumers make choices.* Chicago: Dearborn Financial Publishing, Inc.

Murray, K. (1991). A test of services marketing theory: Consumer information acquisition activities. *Journal of Marketing, 55*(1), 10–25. doi:10.2307/1252200

Murray, L., Durkin, M., Worthington, S., & Clark, V. (2014). On the potential for Twitter to add value in retail bank relationships. *Journal of Financial Services Marketing, 19*(4), 277–290. doi:10.1057/fsm.2014.27

Murtagh, N., Nati, M., Headley, W. R., Gatersleben, B., Gluhak, A., Imran, M. A., & Uzzell, D. (2013). Individual energy use and feedback in an office setting: A field trial. *Energy Policy, 62*(0), 717–728. doi:10.1016/j.enpol.2013.07.090

Nadkarni, A., & Hofmann, S. G. (2012). Why do people use Facebook? *Personality and Individual Differences, 52*(3), 243–249. doi:10.1016/j.paid.2011.11.007 PMID:22544987

Nahapiet, J., & Ghoshal, S. (1998). Social Capital, Intellectual Capital, and the Organizational Advantage. *Academy of Management Review, 23*(2), 242–266. Retrieved from https://www.uzh.ch/iou/orga/ssl-dir/wiki/uploads/Main/v26.pdf

Nah, S., & Chung, D. S. (2012). When citizens meet both professional and citizen journalists: Social trust, media credibility, and perceived journalistic roles among online community news readers. *Journalism, 13*(6), 714–730. doi:10.1177/1464884911431381

Nambisan, P., & Watt, J. H. (2011). Managing customer experiences in online product communities. *Journal of Business Research, 64*(8), 889–895. doi:10.1016/j.jbusres.2010.09.006

National Association of Software and Services Companies. India. (2013). *Indian IT-BPO Industry*. Retrieved from http://www.nasscom.in/impact-indias-growth

Nationbuilder. (2015). *Nationbuilder*. Retrieved from Jeff Dunne: http://nationbuilder.com/jeffdunne

Naudé, P., & Holland, C. P. (2004). The Role of Information and Communications Technology in Transforming Marketing Theory and Practice. *Journal of Business and Industrial Marketing, 19*(3), 165–166. doi:10.1108/08858620410531298

Negi, R., & Ketema, E. (2010). Relationship Marketing and Customer Loyalty: The Ethiopian Mobile Communications Perspective. *International Journal of Mobile Marketing, 5*(1), 113–124.

Negroponte, N. (1995). *Being Digital*. London: Hodder and Stoughton.

Neil, A. (2015, September 23). *ibTV*. (IBC, Producer). Retrieved September 23, 2015, from Facing the Internet Era keynote forum: http://site-73.bcvp0rtal.com/detail/videos/2015-keynotes/video/4501428165001/thursday-facing-the-internet-era-keynote?autoStart=true

Neill, M. S., & Moody, M. (2015). Who is responsible for what? Examining strategic roles in social media management. *Public Relations Review, 41*(1), 109–118. doi:10.1016/j.pubrev.2014.10.014

Netflix. (2015). *Netflix*. Retrieved from A brief history of Netflix: https://pr.netflix.com/WebClient/loginPageSalesNetWorksAction.do?contentGroupId=10477

Networks, A. M. C. (2015, September 23). *AMZ Networks*. Retrieved September 23, 2015, from Bruce Tucman, President, AMC Global and Sundance Channel Global: http://www.amcnetworks.com/about-us/leadership/bruce-tuchman

Newman, M. (2003). The structure and function of complex networks. *SIAM Review, 45*(2), 167–256. doi:10.1137/S003614450342480

Nguyen, N., & Leblanc, G. (2001). Corporate image and corporate reputation in customers' retention decisions in services. *Journal of Retailing and Consumer Services, 8*(4), 227–236. doi:10.1016/S0969-6989(00)00029-1

Nonaka, I., & Takeuchi, H. (1995). *The knowledge-creating company: How japanese companies create the dynamics of innovation*. Oxford University Press.

Norvaišas, S., Mažeika, A., Paražinskaitė, G., Skaržauskienė, A., Šiugždaitė, R., & Tamošiūnaitė, R. (2011). Networked business informatics studies: methodical guidelines. Lithuania: Mykolo Romerio universiteto Leidybos centras.

Number of monthly active Facebook users worldwide as of 2ⁿᵈ quarter 2015 (in millions). (2015). Statista, the Statistics Portal. Retrieved August 30, 2015, from http://www.statista.com/statistics/264810/number-of-monthly-active-facebook-users-worldwide/

Nwagbara, U. (2013). The effects of social media on environmental sustainability activities of oil and gas multinationals in Nigeria. *Thunderbird International Business Review*, *55*(6), 689–697. doi:10.1002/tie.21584

Nyce, J., & Kahn, P. (1991). *From Memex to Hypertext - Vannevar Bush and the Mind's Machine*. Academic Press Inc.

O'Boyle, I. (2014). Mobilising social media in sport management education. *Journal of Hospitality, Leisure, Sport and Tourism Education*, *15*(1), 58–60. doi:10.1016/j.jhlste.2014.05.002

O'Connor, D. (2010). Apomediation and ancillary care: Researchers' responsibilities in health-related online communities. *International Journal of Internet Research Ethics*, *12*, 87–103.

O'Connor, P. (2010). Managing a hotel's image on TripAdvisor. *Journal of Hospitality Marketing & Management*, *19*(7), 754–772. doi:10.1080/19368623.2010.508007

O'Leary, D. E. (1997). The internet, intranets, and the AI renaissance. *IEEE Computer*, *30*(1), 71–78. doi:10.1109/2.562929

O'Leary, D. E. (2008). Wikis: From Each According to His Knowledge. *Computer*, *41*(2), 34–41.

O'Loughlin, D., Szmigin, I., & Turnbull, P. (2004). From relationships to experiences in retail financial services. *International Journal of Bank Marketing*, *22*(7), 522–539. doi:10.1108/02652320410567935

O'Reilly, T. (2005). *What is Web 2.0? Design patterns and business models for the next generation of software*. Retrieved 25 February 2014 from: http://oreilly.com/web2/archive/what-is-web-20.html

Oeberst, A., Halatchliyski, I., Kimmerle, J., & Cress, U. (2014). Knowledge Construction in Wikipedia: A Systemic-Constructivist Analysis. *Journal of the Learning Sciences*, *23*(2), 149–176. doi:10.1080/10508406.2014.888352

Olkkonen, R., Tikkanen, H., & Alajoutsijärvi, K. (2000). The role of communication in business relationships and networks. *Management Decision*, *38*(6), 403–409. doi:10.1108/EUM0000000005365

Olsen, N. V., & Christensen, K. (2015). Social media, new digital technologies and their potential application in sensory and consumer research. *Current Opinion in Food Science*, *3*, 23–26. doi:10.1016/j.cofs.2014.11.006

Onis, P. d. (2006, September 9). *Skylight Pictures*. Retrieved September 18, 2015, from Quechua 2.0 - A Film Reborn: http://skylight.is/2008/09/quechua-2-0-a-film-reborn/

Onis, P. D. (2009). Documentary Film and Social Networking in Human Rights: Producing and Distributing a Quechua-Language Version of 'State of Fear' in Pero. *Journal of Human Rights Practice*, *1*(2), 308–314. doi:10.1093/jhuman/hup010

Ooms, W., Bell, J., & Kok, R. A. W. (2015). Use of social media in inbound open innovation: Building capabilities for absorptive capacity. *Creativity and Innovation Management*, *24*(1), 136–150. doi:10.1111/caim.12105

Ooyala. (2015). *Ooyala*. Retrieved from Ooyala: http://www.ooyala.com/ott-tv

Oppenheimer, J. (2014, February 28). The Act of Killing. (R. Salam, Interviewer). *Vice*.

O'Reilly, T. (2007). What Is Web 2.0 - Design Patterns and Business Models for the Next Generation of Software. *Communications & Stratégies*, *1*. Retrieved from https://mpra.ub.uni-muenchen.de/4578/1/MPRA_paper_4578.pdf

O'Reilly, T. (2007). What is Web 2.0: Design patterns and business models for the next generation of software.Communications & Strategies, *65*(1), 17–37.

Orsman, B. (2005, March 18). Readers nominate Auckland's ugliest buildings. *New Zealand Herald*. Retrieved from http://www.nzherald.co.nz/nz/news/article.cfm?c_id=1&objectid=10116020

Osborne, A., & Coombs, D. (2013). Performative Sport Fandom: an approach to retheorizing sport fans. *Sport in society: Cultures, Commerce, Media. Politics*, *16*(5), 672–681.

Ott, L., & Theunissen, P. (2015). Reputations at risk: Engagement during social media crises. *Public Relations Review*, *41*(1), 97–102. doi:10.1016/j.pubrev.2014.10.015

Ouchi, W. (1980). Markets, bureaucracies and clans. *Administrative Science Quarterly*, *25*(1), 129–141. doi:10.2307/2392231

Oviatt, B. M., & McDougall, P. P. (1994). Towards a theory of international new ventures. *Journal of International Business Studies*, *25*(1), 45–64. doi:10.1057/palgrave.jibs.8490193

Owens, S., & Driffill, L. (2008). How to change attitudes and behaviours in the context of energy. *Energy Policy*, *36*(12), 4412–4418. doi:10.1016/j.enpol.2008.09.031

Özgüven, N., & Mucan, B. (2013). The relationship between personality traits and social media use. *Social Behavior and Personality*, *41*(3), 517–528. doi:10.2224/sbp.2013.41.3.517

Page, K. L., & Reynolds, N. (2015). Learning from a wiki way of learning. *Studies in Higher Education*, *40*(6), 988–1013. doi:10.1080/03075079.2013.865158

Page, L., Brin, S., Motwani, R., & Winograd, T. (1999). *The PageRank Citation Ranking: Bringing Order to the Web*. Technical Report. Stanford InfoLab.

Palmatier, R. W., Gopalakrishna, S., & Houston, M. B. (2006). Returns on Business-To-Business Relationship Marketing Investments: Strategies For Leveraging Profits. *Marketing Science*, *25*(5), 477–493. doi:10.1287/mksc.1060.0209

Paniagua, J., & Sapena, J. (2014). Business performance and social media: Love or hate? *Business Horizons*, *57*(6), 719–728. doi:10.1016/j.bushor.2014.07.005

Papagelis, A., & Zaroliagis, C. (2007). Searchius: A collaborative search engine. In *Proceedings of the 8th Mexican International Conference on Current Trends in Computer Science*.

Parasuraman, A., Zeithaml, V. A., & Berry, L. L. (1988). SERVQUAL: A Multiple-Item Scale for Measuring Consumer Perceptions of Service Quality. *Journal of Retailing*, *64*(1), 12–40.

Park, D. H., Lee, J., & Han, I. (2007). The effect of on-line consumer reviews on consumer purchasing intention: The moderating role of involvement. *International Journal of Electronic Commerce*, *11*(4), 125–148. doi:10.2753/JEC1086-4415110405

Park, M., & Park, J. (2009). Exploring the influences of perceived interactivity on consumers' e-shopping effectiveness. *Journal of Customer Behaviour*, *8*(4), 361–379. doi:10.1362/147539209X480990

Park, N., Kee, K. F., & Valenzuela, S. (2009). Being Immersed in Social Networking Environment: Facebook Groups, Uses and Gratifications, and Social Outcomes. *Cyberpsychology & Behavior*, *12*(6), 729–733. doi:10.1089/cpb.2009.0003 PMID:19619037

Park, S., & Allen, P. J. (2013). Responding to online reviews problem solving and engagement in hotels. *Cornell Hospitality Quarterly*, *54*(1), 64–73. doi:10.1177/1938965512463118

Parry, E., Professor Stefan Strohmeier, D., Guillot-Soulez, C., & Soulez, S. (2014). On the heterogeneity of Generation Y job preferences. *Employee Relations, 36*(4), 319–332. doi:10.1108/ER-07-2013-0073

Parsons, S. (1991). *Qualitative Methods for Reasoning under Uncertainty.* Cambridge, MA: The MIT Press.

Partridge, C. (2008, April). The Technical Development of Internet Email. *IEEE Annals of the History of Computing,* 9.

Parveen, F., Jaafar, N. I., & Ainin, S. (2015). Social media usage and organizational performance: Reflections of Malaysian social media managers. *Telematics and Informatics, 32*(1), 67–78. doi:10.1016/j.tele.2014.03.001

Patel, A., & Balakrishnan, A. (2009). *Generic framework for recommendation system using collective intelligence.* Internet Technology and Secured Transactions, 2009. ICITST 2009. International Conference for, London, UK.

Patienkin, D. (1983). Multiple Discoveries and the Central Message. *American Journal of Sociology, 89*(2), 306–323. doi:10.1086/227867

Patterson, P., Yu, T., & de Ruyter, K. (2006). *Understanding customer engagement in services.* Paper presented at the 2006 Australian & New Zealand Marketing Academy Conference (ANZMAC 2006), Brisbane, Australia.

Patterson, A. (2011). Social-networkers of the world, unite and take over: A meta-introspective perspective on the Facebook brand. *Journal of Business Research, 65*(4), 527–534. doi:10.1016/j.jbusres.2011.02.032

Patterson, P. G., & Ward, T. (2000). Relationship marketing and management. In T. A. Swartz & D. Iacobucci (Eds.), *Handbook of Services Marketing and Management* (pp. 317–342). Sage. doi:10.4135/9781452231327.n22

Patton, M. Q. (2002). *Qualitative research & evaluation methods.* Thousand Oaks, CA: Sage.

Patton, M. Q. (2002). *Qualitative Research and Evaluation Methods.* Thousand Oaks, CA: Sage.

Paulussen, S., & Ugille, P. (2008). User generated content in the newsroom: Professional and organisational constraints on participatory journalism. *Westminster Papers in Communication and Culture, 5*(2), 24–41.

Pavalanathan, U., & De Choudhury, M. (2015). Identity management and mental health discourse in social media. In *Proceedings of WWW 2015 Companion.* doi:10.1145/2740908.2743049

Pavlicek, A., & Novak, R. (2015). Big data from the perspective of data sources. In R. Nemec, F. Zapletal (Eds.), *Proceedings of the 11th international conference on Strategic Management and its Support by Information Systems* (pp. 454–462). Ostrava: VSB-TU FE.

Pavlou, P. A. (2011). State of the information privacy literature: Where are we now and where should we go? *Management Information Systems Quarterly, 35*(4), 977–988.

Peláez, M., & Rodenes, M. (2009). La internacionalización de empresas: Relación entre el capital social, las tecnologías de la información relacional y la innovación. *Redalyc, 12*(25), 111–138.

Peled, O., Fire, M., Rokach, L., & Elovici, Y. (2013). Entity matching in online social networks. In *Proceedings of SocialCom/PASSAT/BigData/Econcom/BioMedCom 2013.* IEEE. DOI 10.1109/SocialCom.2013.53

Pels, J., Möller, K., & Saren, M. (2009). Do we really understand business marketing? Getting beyond the RM and BM matrimony. *Journal of Business and Industrial Marketing, 24*(5/6), 322–336. doi:10.1108/08858620910966219

Peluchette, J., & Karl, K. (2010). Examining Students' Intended Image on Facebook: "What Were They Thinking?! *Journal of Education for Business, 85*(1), 30–37. doi:10.1080/08832320903217606

Pendergast, D. (2010). Getting to know the Generation Y. In P. Benckendorff, G. Moscar, & D. Pendergast (Eds.), *Tourism and Generation Y* (pp. 1–15). Wallingford: CABI.

Pennington-Gray, L., London, B., Cahyanto, I., & Klages, W. (2011). Expanding the tourism crisis management planning framework to include social media: Lessons from the deepwater horizon oil spill, 2010. *International Journal of Tourism Anthropology*, *1*(3/4), 239–253. doi:10.1504/IJTA.2011.043708

Perreau F. (2013). *4 factors influencing consumer behavior*. Retrieved September 1, 2015, from http://theconsumerfactor.com/en/4-factors-influencing-consumer-behavior/

Pesout, P., & Matustik, O. (2012). On a Modeling of Online User Behavior Using Function Representation. *Mathematical Problems in Engineering*, *784164*. doi:10.1155/2012/784164

Peterson, K. (2012). How social media and emerging technologies influence passenger flow. *Airport Business*. Retrieved from. http://www.aviationpros.com/article/10815625/how-social-media-and-emerging-technologies-influence-passenger-flow,29.08.2015

Petrevska, B. (2015). Assessing tourism development: The case of Krusevo, Macedonia. *Economic Development*, *17*(1–2), 261–275.

Petts, J., & Brooks, C. (2006). Expert conceptualisations of the role of lay knowledge in environmental decisionmaking: Challenges for deliberative democracy. *Environment & Planning A*, *38*(6), 1045–1059. doi:10.1068/a37373

Pew Research Center. (2012). *Why Most Facebook Users Get More Than They Give*. Pew Internet and American Life Project.

Peytchev, A., Conrad, F. G., Couper, M. P., & Tourangeau, R. (2010). Increasing Respondents' Use of Definitions in Web Surveys. *Journal of Official Statistics*, *26*(4), 633–650. PMID:23411499

Pfeiffer, M., & Zinnbauer, M. (2010). Can Old Media Enhance New Media?: How Traditional Advertising Pays off for an Online Social Network. *Journal of Advertising Research*, *50*(1), 42–49. doi:10.2501/S0021849910091166

Phang, C. W., Zhang, C., & Sutanto, J. (2013). The influence of user interaction and participation in social media on the consumption intention of niche products. *Information & Management*, *50*(8), 661–672. doi:10.1016/j.im.2013.07.001

Philips, S. (2007). *A brief history of Facebook*. Retrieved from The Guardian: http://www.theguardian.com/technology/2007/jul/25/media.newmedia

Philips, A. (2005). Who's to make journalists? In H. de Burgh (Ed.), *Making Journalists* (pp. 227–244). Abingdon: Routledge.

Phillips, S. (2007, July 25). A brief History of Facebook. *The Guardian*.

Picard, R. G. (2014). Twilight or new dawn of journalism? *Digital Journalism*, *2*(3), 1–11. doi:10.1080/21670811.2014.895531

Piccolo, L., Alani, H., De Liddo, A. & Baranauskas, C. (2013). Motivating Online Engagement and Debates on Energy Consumption. In *Proceeding of WebSci 2014*.

Pilger, J. (2015, Sept. 30). *Indiegogo*. Retrieved Sept. 30, 2015, from John Pilger - The Coming War documentary: https://www.indiegogo.com/projects/john-pilger-the-coming-war-documentary#/

Piper, D. L. A. (2014). *Laws of the World Handbook: Third Edition*. Retrieved September 15, 2015, from http://dlapiperdataprotection.com/#handbook/

Pirolli, B. (2014). Travel journalism in flux: New practices in the blogosphere. In F. Hanusch & E. Fürsich (Eds.), *Travel Journalism: Exploring Production, Impact and Culture* (pp. 83–98). Basingstoke, UK: Palgrave Macmillan. doi:10.1057/9781137325983.0011

Piven, I. (2012). *Conceptual model of consumer service brand consumption in a social media community*. (Masters dissertation). Unitec Institute of Technology, Auckland, New Zealand.

Plouffe, C. R., & Barclay, D. W. (2007). Salesperson navigation: The Intraorganizational Dimension of the Sales Role. *Industrial Marketing Management, 36*(4), 528–539. doi:10.1016/j.indmarman.2006.02.002

Polipulse. (2011). *Amercia Reacts to Armstrong Confession*. Retrieved November 15 2013 http://polipulse.com/america-reacts-armstrong-confession

Pookulangara, S., & Koesler, K. (2011). Cultural influence on consumers' usage of social networks and its' impact on online purchase intentions. *Journal of Retailing and Consumer Services, 18*(4), 348–354. doi:10.1016/j.jretconser.2011.03.003

Popesku, S. (2014). *Social media as a tool of destination marketing organizations*. E-Business in Tourism and Hospitality Industry.

Porter, M. E. (1996). What is strategy? *Harvard Business Review, 74*(6), 61–78. PMID:10158474

Poster, M. (1995). *CyberDemocracy: Internet and the Public Sphere*. Irvine, CA: From University of California. http://www.hnet.uci.edu/mposter/writings/democ.html

Potts, L., & Harrison, A. (2013). Interfaces as rhetorical constructions: reddit and 4chan during the Boston Marathon bombings. In *Proceedings of SIGDOC '13*.

Pour, J., Maryska, M., & Novotny, O. (2012). *Business intelligence v podnikové praxi*. Praha: Professional Publishing.

Powell, W. W. (1990). Neither market nor hierarchy: Network forms of organization. *Research in Organizational Behavior, 12*, 295–336. Retrieved from http://www.uvm.edu/~pdodds/files/papers/others/1990/powell1990a.pdf

Powell, W. W., Kenneth, W. K., & Smith-Doerr, L. (1996). Interorganizational Collaboration and the Locus of Innovation: Networks of Learning in Biotechnology. *Administrative Science Quarterly, 41*(1), 116–145. doi:10.2307/2393988

Prahalad, C. K., & Ramaswamy, V. (2004). Co-creation Experiences: The Next Practice in Value Creation. *Journal of Interactive Marketing, 18*(3), 5–14. doi:10.1002/dir.20015

Pranjic, G. (2011). Influence of Business and Competitive Intelligence on Makong Right Business Decisions. *Economic Thought and Practice, 20*(1), 271–288.

Preece, J., & Shneiderman, B. (2009). The Reader-to-leader Framework: Motivating Technology-mediated Social Participation. *AIS Transactions on Human-Computer Interaction, 1*(1), 13–32.

Prensky, M. (2001). Digital Natives, Digital Immigrants Part 1. *On the Horizon, 9*(5), 1–6. doi:10.1108/10748120110424816

Preston, P. (2002, January 6). Sic transit Andre Neil. *The Observer*.

Preston, P. (2008). The curse of introversion. *Journalism Studies, 9*(5), 642–649. doi:10.1080/14616700802207516

Prić, J., Taeihagh, A., & Melton, J. (2014). Crowdsourcing the Policy Cycle. *Collective Intelligence 2014*. Boston: MIT Center for Collective Intelligence.

Provost, F., & Fawcett, T. (2013). *Data science for business: What you need to know about data mining and data-analytic thinking*. Sebastopol, CA: O'Reilly.

Pry, C. G. (2010). Social Media: The Less-Noticed Risks. *ABA Bank Marketing, 42*(7), 22–27.

Puddephatt, A., Mendel, T., Wagner, B., Hawtin, D., & Torres, N. (2012). *Global survey on Internet privacy and freedom of expression*. Paris: United Nations Educational, Scientific, and Cultural Organization.

Pugh, K., & Prusak, L. (2013). Designing effective knowledge networks. *MIT. Sloan Management Review, 55*(1), 79–88. Retrieved from http://web.stanford.edu/~woodyp/Rso1.pdf

Purcell, J. (2013). Keynote Address. Paper presened at the IBI Radio: Future Shock Conference, Dublin, Ireland.

Qiu, F., & Cho, J. (2006). Automatic identification of user interest for personalized search. In *Proceedings of the 15th International Conference on World Wide Web*. doi:10.1145/1135777.1135883

Quinton, K. (2013). The community brand paradigm: A response to brand management's dilemma in the digital era. *Journal of Marketing Management, 29*(7–8), 912–932. doi:10.1080/0267257X.2012.729072

r/bitcoin. (2015). *Reddit*. Retrieved Aug. 28, 2015, from https://www.reddit.com/r/Bitcoin/comments/zqocl/exchange_your_karma_for_bitcoin_reddit_bitcoin

Radeljic, K. (2013). *Look before you tweet. How asset managers can use social media to their advantage*. New York: EY Financial Services.

Rafaeli, S. (1988). Interactivity from new media to communication. In R. P. Hawkins, J. M. Wiemann, & S. Pingree (Eds.), *Advancing Communication Science: Merging Mass and Interpersonal Processes* (pp. 110–134). Beverly Hills, CA: Sage.

Rajaei, M., Haghjoo, M. S., & Miyaneh, E. K. (2015). Ambiguity in Social Network Data for Presence, Sensitive – Attribute, Degree and Relationship Privacy Protection. *PLoS ONE, 10*(6), e0130693. doi:10.1371/journal.pone.0130693 PMID:26110762

Rajan, R., & Servaes, H. (2002). *The Effect of Market Conditions on Initial Public Offerings*. University of Chicago and NBER/London Business School and CEPR.

Raman, U., & Choudary, D. (2014). Have travelled, will write: User-generated content and new travel journalism. In F. Hanusch & E. Fürsich (Eds.), *Travel Journalism: Exploring Production, Impact and Culture* (pp. 116–133). Basingstoke, UK: Palgrave Macmillan.

Ramaswamy, & Namakumari. (2013). *Marketing Management: Indian Context* (5th ed.). McGraw Hill Education (India) Private Limited.

Ramaswamy, S. (2015). Outside Voices: Why Mobile Advertising May Be All About Micro-Targeting Moments. *The Wall Street Journal*. Retrieved September 3, 2015 http://blogs.wsj.com/cmo/2015/04/08/outside-voices-why-mobile-advertising-may-be-all-about-micro-targeting-moments/

Ramaswamy, V., & Ozcan, K. (2013). Strategy and co-creation thinking. *Strategy and Leadership, 41*(6), 5–10. doi:10.1108/SL-07-2013-0053

Ramirez de la Piscina, T., Zabalondo, B., Aisteran, A., & Agirre, A. (2015). *The future of journalism—who to believe? Different perceptions among European professionals and internet users*. Journalism Practice.

Ranaweera, C., & Prabhu, J. (2003). On the relative importance of Customer Satisfaction and Trust as Determinants of Customer Retention and Positive Word Of Mouth. *Journal of Targeting. Measurement & Analysis for Marketing, 12*(1), 82–90. doi:10.1057/palgrave.jt.5740100

Random House Dictionary. (2015, September 30). *Dictionary.com*. Retrieved September 30, 2015, from Random House Dictionary: http://dictionary.reference.com/browse/application programming interface

Ransbotham, S., & Kane, G. C. (2011). Membership Turnover and Collaboration Success in Online Communities: Explaining Rises and Falls from Grace in Wikipedia. *MIS Quarterly-Management Information Systems, 35*(3), 613.

Rauch, J. (2013). *Observational Calculi and Association Rules*. Berlin: Springer-Verlag. doi:10.1007/978-3-642-11737-4

Rebillard, F., & Touboul, A. (2010). Promises unfulfilled? Journalism 2.0, user participation and editorial policy on newspaper websites. *Media Culture & Society, 32*(2), 323–334. doi:10.1177/0163443709356142

Reddit content policy. (2015). *Reddit*. Retrieved Aug. 28, 2015, from https://www.reddit.com/help/contentpolicy

Reddit. (2015, Aug. 18). *Wikipedia*. Retrieved Aug. 22, 2015, from https://en.wikipedia.org/wiki/Reddit

Reid, K. (2015). *Social media and your business: How to approach this marketing channel with balance and control.* Retrieved from https://www.highbeam.com/doc/1G1-413779851.html, 02.09.2015

Rexha, N., Kingshott, R. P. J., & Aw, A. S. S. (2003). The impact of the relational plan on adoption of electronic banking. *Journal of Services Marketing, 17*(1), 53–67. doi:10.1108/08876040310461273

Reyneke, M., Pitt, L., & Berthon, P. R. (2011). Luxury wine brand visibility in social media: An exploratory study. *International Journal of Wine Business Research, 23*(1), 21–35. doi:10.1108/17511061111121380

Rheingold, H. (2002). *Smart Mobs: The Next Social Revolution.* Cambridge, MA: Perseus Publishing.

Richards, J. (2007). *Workers are doing it for themselves: Examining creative employee application of Web 2.0 communication technology.* Paper presented at the Work, Employment and Society (WES), Aberdeen, UK. Retrieved from http://www.scribd.com/doc/6873217/JRichardsWES2007

Richterich, A. (2014, Jan.). 'Karma, precious karma!' Karmawhoring on Reddit and the Front Page's Econometrisation. *Journal of Peer Production,* (4), 1 – 12.

Rieh, S. Y., & Xie, H. I. (2006). Analysis of multiple query reformulations on the web: The interactive information retrieval context. *Information Processing & Management, 42*(3), 751–768. doi:10.1016/j.ipm.2005.05.005

Rigby, B. (2008). *Mobilizing Generation 2.0: A Practical Guide to Using Web 2.0.* San Francisco: Jossey-Bass.

Robert Half -Technology. (2009). *Whistle-but-don't tweet-while you work.* Retrieved from http://rht.mediaroom.com/index.php?s=131&item=790

Roberts, M. L., Zahay, D. L. (2012). *Internet Marketing: Integrating Online and Offline Strategies.* Mason, OH: South-Western Cengage Learning.

Roberts, D. L., & Candi, M. (2014). Leveraging social network sites in new product development: Opportunity or hype? *Journal of Product Innovation Management, 31*(s1), 105–117. doi:10.1111/jpim.12195

Robertus, T. H. (2015). Grown Up Digital: Effect Social Media Usage on Consumer Behavior. Advanced Science Letters, 21(4), 1035-1038.

Rogers, E. M. (2003). *Diffusion of Innovations.* New York: The Free Press, A Division of Simon&Schuster.

Rollason, H. (2012). *Why Social Media Makes Customer Service Better.* Retrieved 30 Sept 2013 from: http://mashable.com/2012/09/29/social-media-better-customer-service/

Ronen, I., Shahar, E., Ur, S., Uziel, E., Yogev, S., Zwerdling, N., & Ofek-Koifman, S. et al. (2009). Social networks and discovery in the enterprise (SaND). In *Proceedings of the 32nd International ACM SIGIR Conference on Research and Development in Information Retrieval.* doi:10.1145/1571941.1572156

Ronfeldt, D., Arquilla, J., Fuller, G., & Fuller, M. (1999). *The Zapatista 'Social Netwar' in Mexico.* RAND.

Rosenzweig, R. (1998, December). Wizards, Beureaucrats, Warriors, and Hackers: Writing the History of the Internet. *The American Historical Review, 103*(5), 1530–1552. doi:10.2307/2649970

RTL Group. (2015, April 9). *RTL Group*. Retrieved September 23, 2015, from RTL Group invests in Clypd: http://www.rtlgroup.com/en/news/2015/15/rtl_group_invests_in_clypd.cfm

Rudolf, R. S., Elfriede, P., & Pervez, N. G. (2005). Analysing textual data in international marketing research. *Qualitative Market Research: An International Journal*, *8*(1), 9–38. doi:10.1108/13522750510575426

Rust, R. T., Moorman, C., & Dickson, P. R. (2002). Getting Return on Quality: Revenue Expansion, Cost Reduction, or Both? *Journal of Marketing*, *66*(4), 7–24. doi:10.1509/jmkg.66.4.7.18515

Ruzzier, M., Hisrich, R. D., & Antoncic, B. (2006). SME internationalization research: Past, present, and future. *Journal of Small Business and Enterprise Development*, *13*(4), 476–497. doi:10.1108/14626000610705705

Ryan, T., & Xenos, S. (2011). Who uses Facebook? An investigation into the relationship between the Big Five, shyness, narcissism, loneliness, and Facebook usage. *Computers in Human Behavior*, *27*(5), 658–1664. doi:10.1016/j.chb.2011.02.004

Ryssel, R., Ritter, T., & Gemunden, H. G. (2004). The impact of information technology deployment on trust, commitment and value creation in business relationships. *Journal of Business and Industrial Marketing*, *19*(3), 197–207. doi:10.1108/08858620410531333

Salminen, J. (2012). Collective Intelligence in Humans: A Literature Review. *Collective Intelligence 2012*. Boston: MIT Center for Collective intelligence.

Sanderson, J. (2010). "The nation stands behind you": Mobilising social support on 38pitches.com. *Communication Quarterly*, *58*(2), 188–201. doi:10.1080/01463371003717884

Sanderson, J. (2013). From loving the hero to despising the villain: Sport fans, Facebook and social identity threats. *Mass Communication & Society*, *16*(4), 487–509. doi:10.1080/15205436.2012.730650

Sanderson, J., & Emmon, B. (2014). Extending and withholding forgiveness to Josh Hamilton: Exploring forgiveness within parasocial interaction. *Communication & Sport*, *2*(1), 24–47. doi:10.1177/2167479513482306

Sands, S., Harper, E., & Ferraro, C. (2011). Customer-to-noncustomer interactions: Extending the 'social' dimension of the store environment. *Journal of Retailing and Consumer Services*, *18*(5), 438–447. doi:10.1016/j.jretconser.2011.06.007

Sandström, S., Edvardsson, B., Kristensson, P., & Magnusson, P. (2008). Value in use through service experience. *Managing Service Quality*, *18*(2), 112–126. doi:10.1108/09604520810859184

Sapuppo, A., & Seet, B. C. (2015). Privacy and technology challenges for ubiquitous social networking. *International Journal of Ad Hoc and Ubiquitous Computing*, *18*(3), 121–138. doi:10.1504/IJAHUC.2015.068127

Sarin, S. (2012). My Years with B2B Marketing in India: Reflections and Learnings from a Journey of 40 years. *Journal of Business and Industrial Marketing*, *27*(3), 160–168. doi:10.1108/08858621211207199

Sashi, C. M. (2012). Customer engagement, buyer-seller relationships, and social media. *Management Decision*, *50*(2), 253–272. doi:10.1108/00251741211203551

Satariano, A. (2014). *WhatsApp's Founder Goes From Food Stamps to Billionaire*. Retrieved from Bloomberg Business: http://www.bloomberg.com/news/articles/2014-02-20/whatsapp-s-founder-goes-from-food-stamps-to-billionaire

Savage, S. (2011). Making sense of Generation Y: The world view of 15-25 year olds. London: Church House Publishing.

Saxton, G. D., & Guo, C. (2014). Online stakeholder targeting and the acquisition of social media capital. *International Journal of Nonprofit and Voluntary Sector Marketing*, *19*(4), 286–300. doi:10.1002/nvsm.1504

Sayer. (2011). *Facebook Unfriends Coal, Friends Greenpeace in Clean Energy Campaign*. Retrieved from http://www.computerworld.com/s/article/9222721/Facebook_unfriends_coal_friends_Greenpeace_in_clean_energy_campaign

Schadler, T., Bernoff, J., & Ask, J. (2014).*The Mobile Mind Shift: Engineer Your Business To Win in the Mobile Moment*. Forrester Research.

Schlicht, P. (2013). Turning the digital divide into digital dividends through free content and open networks: Wikieducator learning4content (l4c) initiative. *Journal of Asynchronous Learning Networks, 17*(2), 87–100.

Schlinke, J., & Crain, S. (2013). Social media from an integrated marketing and compliance perspective. *Journal of Financial Service Professionals, 67*(2), 85–92.

Schoen, P. M. (2009). *Der Mensch auf dem Weg der Individuation*. Muenchen: Herbert Utz Verlag.

Schouten, J. W. (1991). Selves in transition: Symbolic consumption in personal rites of passage and identity reconstruction. *The Journal of Consumer Research, 17*(4), 412–425. doi:10.1086/208567

Schouten, J. W., & Mcalexander, J. H. (1995). Subcultures of consumption: An ethnography of the New Bikers. *The Journal of Consumer Research, 22*(1), 43–61. doi:10.1086/209434

Schramm, J. (2007). Internet connection. *HRMagazine, 52*(9).

Schreiber, E. S. (2015). Intelligence is collective, Collective Innovation: The Known and the Unknown. Collective Intelligence 2015.

Schultz, R. J., Schwepker, C. H., & Good, D. J. (2012). An Exploratory Study of Social Media in Business-To-Business Selling: Salesperson Characteristics, Activities and Performance. *Marketing Management Journal, 22*(2), 76–89.

Schulz, M., Winter, P., & Choi, S.-K. T. (2015). On the relevance of reports – Integrating an automated archiving component into a business intelligence system. *International Journal of Information Management, 25*(6), 662–671. doi:10.1016/j.ijinfomgt.2015.07.005

Schut, M. C. (2010). On Model Design for Simulation of Collective Intelligence. *Information Sciences, 180*(1), 132–155. doi:10.1016/j.ins.2009.08.006

Seimiene, E. (2012). Emotional connection of consumer personality traits with brand personality traits: Theoretical considerations. *Economics and Management, 17*(4), 1477–1478. doi:10.5755/j01.em.17.4.3016

Sellnow, T. L., Ulmer, R. R., Seeger, M. W., & Littlefield, R. (2008). *Effective risk communication: A message-centered approach*. New York, NY: Springer–Verlag.

Selva, S., Kuflik, T. & Gustavo, S. (2012). Changes in the discourse of online hate blogs: The effect of Barack Obama's election in 2008. *First Monday, 17*(11).

Senge, P. (1990). *The Fifth Discipline*. New York: Currency Doubleday.

Sethuraman, R. A. J., Tellis, G. J., & Briesch, R. (2011). How well does advertising work? Generalizations from a meta-analysis of brand advertising elasticity.JMR, Journal of Marketing Research, 48(3), 457–471. doi: 10.1509/jmkr.48.3.457.

Shachtman, N. (2010). Exclusive: Google, CIA invest in 'Future' of Web Monitoring. *Wired*.

Shamma, H. M. (2012). Toward a comprehensive understanding of corporate reputation: Concept, measurement and implications. *International Journal of Business and Management, 7*(16), 151–169. doi:10.5539/ijbm.v7n16p151

Shanker, R. (2008).*Services Marketing*. New Delhi: Excel Books.

Shapira, B., & Zabar, B. (2011). Personalized search: Integrating collaboration and social networks. *Journal of the American Society for Information Science and Technology, 62*(1), 146–160. doi:10.1002/asi.21446

Sharma, D. D., & Blomstermo, A. (2003). *The internationalization process of born globals: A network view.* Academic Press.

Sharma, N., & Patterson, P. G. (1999). The impact of communication effectiveness and service quality on relationship commitment in consumer, professional services. *Journal of Services Marketing, 13*(2/3), 151–170. doi:10.1108/08876049910266059

Shaw, S. (2007). *Airline Marketing and Management.* Ashgate Publishing Limited.

Shcherbakova, N., & Shepherd, M. (2014). Community pharmacists, Internet and social media: An empirical investigation. *Research in Social & Administrative Pharmacy, 10*(6), e75–e85. doi:10.1016/j.sapharm.2013.11.007 PMID:24388002

Sheldon, P. (2008). Student Favorite: Facebook and Motives for its Use. *Southwestern Mass Communication Journal, 23*, 39–53.

Shelton, M., Lo, K., & Nardi, B. (2015). Online Media Forums as Separate Social Lives: A Qualitative Study of Disclosure within and beyond Reddit. In iConference 2015 Proceedings.

Shemen, J. (2013). *The Story Behind Social Media Valuations.* Stern School of Business New York University.

Shirky, C. (2010a). *SXSW: South by SouthWest.* Retrieved March 15, 2011, from Why Would We Think Social Media Is Revolutionary?: http://schedule.sxsw.com/2011/events/event_IAP000246

Shirky, C. (2010b). *The Political Power of Social Media. Foreign Affairs.* Retrieved October 15 from https://www.foreignaffairs.com/articles/2010-12-20/political-power-social-media

Shirky, C. (2008). *Here Comes Everybody.* Penguin Books.

Shirky, C. (2011). The political power of social media: Technology, the public sphere, and political change. *Foreign Affairs, 90*(1), 28–41.

Shneiderman, B. A. (2009). National Initiative for Social Participation. *Science, 323*(5920), 1426–1427. doi:10.1126/science.323.5920.1426 PMID:19286535

Shostack, G. L. (1977). Breaking Free from Product Marketing. *Journal of Marketing, 41*(2), 73–80.

Shostack, G. L. (1985). Planning the service encounter. In J. A. Czepiel, M. R. Solomon, & C. F. Surprenant (Eds.), *The service encounter: Managing employee/customer interaction in service businesses* (pp. 243–253). Toronto: Lexington Books.

Sickert, A. (2011). Airline marketing and service quality: Foundations for growing nonaeronautical revenue — An Indian perspective. *Journal of Airport Management, 5*(3), 213–225.

Sigal, I. (2009). *Digital Media in Conflict-Prone Societies.* Center for International Media Assistance, National Endowerment for Democracy.

Sigala, M. (2011). Social media and crisis management in tourism: Applications and implications for research. *Information Technology & Tourism, 13*(4), 269–283. doi:10.3727/109830512X13364362859812

Sigala, M. (2015). Social media marketing in tourism and hospitality. *Information Technology & Tourism, 15*(2), 181–183. doi:10.1007/s40558-015-0024-1

Sigmund, T. (2015). The Relationship of Ethical and Economic Behaviour. *Politicka Ekonomie, 63*(2), 223–243. doi:10.18267/j.polek.998

Siles, I., & Boczkowski, P. J. (2012). Making sense of the newspaper crisis: A critical assessment of existing research and an agenda for future work. *New Media & Society, 14*(8), 1375–1394. doi:10.1177/1461444812455148

Singer, P., Flöck, F., Meinhart, C., Zeitfogel, E., & Strohmaier, M. (2014). Evolution of Reddit: From the front page of the Internet to a self-referential community? In *Proceedings of the WWW '14 Companion.*

Singer, J. B. (2003). Who are these guys? The online challenge to the notion of journalistic professionalism. *Journalism, 4*(2), 139–163.

Singer, J. B. (2007). Contested autonomy: Professional and popular claims on journalistic norms. *Journalism Studies, 8*(1), 79–95. doi:10.1080/14616700601056866

Singer, J. B. (2010). Quality control: Perceived effects of user-generated content on newsroom norms, values and routines. *Journalism Practice, 4*(2), 127–142. doi:10.1080/17512780903391979

Sin, L. Y. M., Tse, A. C. B., Yau, O. H. M., Chow, R. P. M., Lee, J. S. Y., & Lau, L. B. Y. (2005). Relationship Marketing Orientation: Scale Development and Cross-Cultural Validation. *Journal of Business Research, 58*(2), 185–194.

Sirgy, J. M. (1982). Self-concept in consumer behaviour: A critical review. *The Journal of Consumer Research, 9*(3), 287–300. doi:10.1086/208924

Sirkkunen, E., & Cook, C. (Eds.). (2012). *Chasing Sustainability on the Net: International Research on 69 Journalistic Pure Players and Their Business Models.* Tampere, Finland: Tampere Research Centre for Journalism, Media and Communication, University of Tampere.

Sisco, H. F., & McCorkindale, T. (2013). Communicating "pink": An analysis of the communication strategies, transparency, and credibility of breast cancer social media sites. *International Journal of Nonprofit and Voluntary Sector Marketing, 18*(4), 287–301. doi:10.1002/nvsm.1474

SITA. (2015, September 10). *The social journey.* Retrieved from http://www.sita.aero/resources/air-transport-it-review/air-transport-it-review,issue-3-2014/the-social-journeya-bigger-role-for-social-media

Skarzauskiene, A., Ewart, J., Krzywosz-Rynkiewizc, B., Zalewska, A. M., Leichteris, E., Mačiulis, A., … Valys, T. (2015). *Social technologies and collective intelligence.* Vilnius: Baltijos kopija.

Skaržauskienė, A., Pitrėnaitė-Žilienė, B., & Leichteris, E. (2013). Following Traces of Collective Intelligence in Social Networks: Case of Lithuania. In *Proceedings of ICICKM 2013: the 10th international conference on intellectual capital knowledge management and organisational learning* (vol. 2, pp. 411-419). The George Washington University.

Slater, S. F., Hult, G. T. M., & Olson, E. M. (2007). On the Importance of Matching Strategic Behavior and Target Market Selection to Business Strategy in High-Tech Markets. *Journal of the Academy of Marketing Science, 35*(1), 5–17. doi:10.1007/s11747-006-0002-4

Smith, C. (2015, Aug. 31). *By the numbers: 150+ interesting Instagram statistics (August 2015).* DMR. Digital Marketing Stats / Strategy / Gadgets. Retrieved August 31, 2015, from http://expandedramblings.com/index.php/important-instagram-stats/

Smith, A. W. (2014). Porn architecture: User tagging and filtering in two online pornography communities. *Communication Design Quarterly, 3*(1), 17–22. doi:10.1145/2721882.2721885

Smith-Jentsch, K. A., & Scielzo, S. A. (2007). *Exploring gender-based differences in e-mentoring. In Refining familiar constructs: Alternative views in OB, HR, and I/O, research in organizational science* (Vol. 2). Greenwich, CT: Information Age Publishing.

Smith, K. T., Smith, M., & Wang, K. (2010). Does brand management of corporate reputation translate into higher market value? *Journal of Strategic Marketing*, *18*(3), 201–221. doi:10.1080/09652540903537030

Smith, M. K., & Denali, D. L. (2014). Social media in health education, promotion, and communication: Reaching rural Hispanic populations along the USA/Mexico border region. *Journal of Racial and Ethnic Health Disparities*, *1*(3), 194–198. doi:10.1007/s40615-014-0025-3

Smith, R. E., & Wright, W. F. (2004). Determinants of Customer Loyalty and Financial Performance. *Journal of Management Accounting Research*, *16*(1), 183–205. doi:10.2308/jmar.2004.16.1.183

Smith, T. (2009). The social Media Revolution. *International Journal of Market Research*, *51*(4), 559–561. doi:10.2501/S1470785309200773

Smutny, Z. (2015). Analysis of Online Marketing Management in Czech Republic. *Organizacija – Journal of Management. Informatics and Human Resources*, *48*(2), 99–111. doi:10.1515/orga-2015-0010

Sohn, D. (2013). Coping with information in social media: The effects of network structure and knowledge on perception of information value. Computers in Human Behavior, 145 – 151.

Solactive. (2012). *Guideline relating the Solactive Social Media Total Return Index*. Structured Solutions AG.

Solactive. (2015). *Solactive Social Media Index*. Solactive AG.

Solis, B. (2013). *What's the Future of Business: Changing the Way Businesses Create Experiences*. John Wiley & Sons.

Solomon, A. (2014). *The question of social media and air cargo*. Retrieved from http://aircargoworld.com/the-question-of-social-media-and-air-cargo-9822/

Solomon, M. R. (1983). The role of products as social stimuli: A symbolic interactionism perspective. *The Journal of Consumer Research*, *10*(3), 319–329. doi:10.1086/208971

Solomon, M. R., Surprenant, C. F., Czepiel, J. A., & Gutman, E. G. (1985). A role theory perspective on Dyadic interactions: The service encounter. *Journal of Marketing*, *49*(1), 99–111. doi:10.2307/1251180

Sony, U. K. (2015, March 2). *Sony UK*. Retrieved September 23, 2015, from Sony appoints strategic media industry expert to lead European Professional AV & Media solutions marketing team: http://www.sony.co.uk/pro/press/sony-michael-harrit-appointment

Sorokowski, P., Sorokowska, A., Oleszkiewicz, A., Frackowiak, T., Huk, A., & Pisanski, K. (2015). Selfie posting behaviors are associated with narcissism among men. *Personality and Individual Differences*, *85*, 123–127. doi:10.1016/j.paid.2015.05.004

Sovacool, B. K. (2014). What are we doing here? Analyzing fifteen years of energy scholarship and proposing a social science research agenda. *Energy Research & Social Science*, *1*, 1–29. doi:10.1016/j.erss.2014.02.003

Spangler, T. (2015). *Netflix Adds Record 4.9 Million Subscribers in Q1*. Retrieved 7 31, 2015, from Variety: http://variety.com/2015/digital/news/netflix-adds-record-4-9-million-subscribers-in-q1-1201473151/

Sperkova, L., & Skola, P. (2015). E-WoM Integration to the Decision-Making Process in Bank Based on Business Intelligence. In P. Doucek, G. Chroust, V. Oskrdal (Eds.), *Proceedings of the 23nd Interdisciplinary Information Management Talks* (pp. 207–216). Linz: Trauner Verlag.

Spyridou, L.-P., Matsiola, M., Veglis, A., Kalliris, G., & Dimoulas, C. (2013). Journalism in a state of flux: Journalists as agents of technology innovation and emerging news practices. *The International Communication Gazette*, *75*(1), 76–98. doi:10.1177/1748048512461763

Stark, B., & Weichselbaum, P. (2013). What attracts listeners to Web radio? A case study from Germany. *Radio Journal: International Studies in Broadcast & Audio Media, 11*, 185–202.

Starwood, H. (2010). Starwood Hotels pilots e-mentoring: Success depends on mutual trust. *Human Resource Management International Digest, 18*(7), 29–31. doi:10.1108/09670731011083798

Statista. (2015a). *Number of monthly active Facebook users worldwide as of 2nd quarter 2015 (in millions).* Retrieved from Statista: http://www.statista.com/statistics/264810/number-of-monthly-active-facebook-users-worldwide/

Statista. (2015b). *Number of monthly active Twitter users worldwide from 1st quarter 2010 to 2nd quarter 2015 (in millions).* Retrieved from Statista: http://www.statista.com/statistics/282087/number-of-monthly-active-twitter-users/

Statista. (2015c). *Number of monthly active WhatsApp users worldwide from April 2013 to April 2015 (in millions).* Retrieved from Statista: http://www.statista.com/statistics/260819/number-of-monthly-active-whatsapp-users/

Statista. (2015d). *Numbers of LinkedIn members from 1st quarter 2009 to 1st quarter 2015 (in millions).* Retrieved from Statista: http://www.statista.com/statistics/274050/quarterly-numbers-of-linkedin-members/

Stefanone, M. A., Lackaff, D., & Rosen, D. (2010). The Relationship between Traditional Mass Media and "Social Media": Reality Television as a Model for Social Network Site Behavior. *Journal of Broadcasting & Electronic Media, 54*(3), 508–525. doi:10.1080/08838151.2010.498851

Stengel, R. (2011, December26). 2011 Person of the Year. *Time*, 36.

Stewart, A., Ambrose-Oji, B., & Morris, J. (2012). *Social Media and Forestry: A Scoping Report*. Academic Press.

St-Jean, E. (2011). Mentor functions for novice entrepreneurs. *Academy of Entrepreneurship Journal, 17*(2), 65-84. Retrieved December 3, 2015, from http://crawl.prod.proquest.com.s3.amazonaws.com/fpcache/8d9db01cfd5e3c33cc9 3a5c3fef393d3.pdf?AWSAccessKeyId=AKIAJF7V7KNV2KKY2NUQ&Expires=1449270707&Signature=%2Be79k 4vrQ7gzYZ%2Bv4sin5F%2BoR%2BA%3D

Stokes, A. (2001). Using tele-mentoring to deliver training to SMEs: A pilot study. *Education + Training, 43*(6), 317–324. doi:10.1108/00400910110406833

Stone, M. (2009). Staying customer-focused and trusted: Web 2.0 and Customer 2.0 in financial services. *Journal of Database Marketing & Customer Strategy Management, 16*(2), 101–131. doi:10.1057/dbm.2009.13

Stratford, P. (2013). Asset management and social media. In EY EMEIA Asset Management Viewpoint. London: Ernst & Young Global Limited.

Straub, D., Boudreau, M., & Gefen, D. (2004). Validation guidelines for IS positivist research. *Communications of the Association for Information Systems, 13*(1), 24.

Stretton, T., & Aaron, L. (2015, January). The dangers in our trail of digital breadcrumbs. *Computer Fraud & Security, 2015*(1), 13–14. doi:10.1016/S1361-3723(15)70006-0

Sui-Hua, Y. (2007). An Empirical Investigation on the Economic Consequences of Customer Satisfaction. *Total Quality Management & Business Excellence, 18*(5), 555–569. doi:10.1080/14783360701240493

Sul, H. K., Dennies, A. R., & Yuan, L. I. (2014). *Trading on Twitter: The financial information content of emotion in social media.* Paper presented at the 47th Hawaii International Conference on System Sciences (HICSS 2014), Big Island, HI.

Suleman, K. (2015). *PR war over Chris Froome doping allegations boils over during Tour de France 2015.* Retrieved October 18, 2015, from http://www.prweek.com/article/1357129/pr-war-chris-froome-doping-allegations-boils-during-tour-de-france-2015

Sunstein, C. (2001). *Republic.com*. Princeton, NJ: Princeton University Press.

Surman, M., & Reilly, K. (2003). *Appropriating the Internet for Social Change: Towards the Strategic Use of Networked Technologies by Transnational Civil Society Organizations*. Social Sciences Research Council, Information Technology and International Cooperation Program.

Surowiecki, J. (2005). *The Wisdom of Crowds*. New York: Random House.

Surowiecki, J. (2005). *Wisdom of Crowds*. New York: Anchor Books.

Surprenant, C. F., & Solomon, M. R. (1987). Predictability and Personalization in the Service Encounter. *Journal of Marketing, 51*(2), 86–96. doi:10.2307/1251131

Sweetser, K. D. (2011). Digital political public relations. In J. Stromback & S. Kiousis (Eds.), *Political public relations principles and applications* (pp. 293–313). New York, NY: Routledge.

Swisher, P., & Kasten, G. W. (2005). *Post-Modern Portfolio Theory*. FPA Journal.

Syn, S. Y., & Oh, S. (2015). Why do social network site users share information on Facebook and Twitter? *Journal of Information Science, 41*(5), 553–569. doi:10.1177/0165551515585717

Szmigin, I. (1997). *Cognitive style and the use of payment methods: An interpretative study of consumer initiator behaviour*. (Unpublished doctoral dissertation). University of Birmingham.

Szuba, T. (2001). A Formal Definition of the Phenomenon of Collective Intelligence and its IQ Measure. *Future Generation Computer Systems, 17*(4), 489–500. doi:10.1016/S0167-739X(99)00136-3

Szymanski, D. M., & Henard, D. H. (2001). Customer Satisfaction: A Meta-analysis of the Empirical Evidence. *Journal of the Academy of Marketing Science, 29*(1), 16–35. doi:10.1177/0092070301291002

Tabachnick, B. G., & Fidel, L. S. (2013). *Using Multivariate Statistics* (6th ed.). Boston: Pearson Education.

Tadajewski, M., & Jones, D. G. (2014). Historical research in marketing theory and practice: A review essay. *Journal of Marketing Management, 30*(11-12), 1239–1291. doi:10.1080/0267257X.2014.929166

Taker, I. (2012). *Social media & sport – the importance of interacting with, not just talking at fans*. Retrieved October 13, 2015, from, http://www.theuksportsnetwork.com/social-media-interaction

Talpau, A. (2014). The marketing mix in the online environment. *Bulletin of the Transylvania University of Braşov. Series V. Economic Sciences, 7*(56), 53–58.

Tandoc, E. (2014). The roles of the game: The influence of news consumption patterns on the role conceptions of journalism students. *Journalism and Mass Communication Educator, 69*(3), 256–270. doi:10.1177/1077695813520314

Tapscott, D. (2008). *Grown Up Digital: How the Net Generation is Changing Your World*. New York, NY: McGraw-Hill.

Tapscott, D., & Williams, A. D. (2006). *Wikinomics: How Mass Collaboration Changes Everything*. New York: Portfolio.

Taylor, R., King, F., & Nelson, G. (2012). Student learning through social media. *Journal of Sociological Research, 3*(2), 29–35. doi:10.5296/jsr.v3i2.2136

Tej Adidam, P., Gajre, S., & Kejriwal, S. (2009). Cross-cultural competitive intelligence strategies. *Marketing Intelligence, 27*(5), 666–680. doi:10.1108/02634500910977881

ten Brink, J. (2014). Joram ten Brink, Personal Communication. *Breda*.

The Argentina Independent. (2014). *Salta Governor closes Deforestation Loophole*. Retrieved October 15 from http://www.argentinaindependent.com/tag/forest-law/

The Climate Group. (2008). *SMART 2020: Enabling the Low Carbon Economy in the Information Age*. Global e-Sustainability Initiative.

The Guardian. (2014). *Google, Facebook and Apple lead on green data centers*. Retrieved October 15, 2014, from http://www.theguardian.com/sustainable-business/greenpeace-report-google-facebook-apple-green-data-centers

TheCityUK. (2013). *Fund Management*. Retrieved April 1, 2014, from: http://www.thecityuk.com/research/our-work/reports-list/fund-management-2013/http://www.thecityuk.com/research/our-work/reports-list/fund-management-2013/

Thompson, C. J. (1997). Interpreting consumers: A hermeneutical framework for deriving marketing insights from the texts of consumers' consumption stories. *JMR, Journal of Marketing Research*, *34*(4), 438–455. doi:10.2307/3151963

Thornton, P. H., Ocasio, W., & Lounsbury, M. (2012). *The Institutional Logics Perspective: A New Approach to Culture, Structure and Process*. Oxford: OUP. doi:10.1093/acprof:oso/9780199601936.001.0001

Tiny Little Doclab. (2011). *God, Church, Pills & Condoms*. Retrievedfrom Indiegogo.com: https://www.indiegogo.com/projects/go-forth-and-multiply-a-documentary/x/243560#/story

Tiny Little Doclab. (2012). *Vimeo*. (A. Cuevas, Producer, & Tiny LIttle Doclab). Retrieved from God, Pills, Church & COndoms: https://vimeo.com/105547859

Toffler, A. (1980). *The Third Wave*. New York: Morrow.

Toh, R., & Raven, P. (2003). Perishable asset revenue management: Integrated internet marketing strategies for the airlines. *Transportation Journal Press*, *42*(4), 30–43.

Tomiuk, D., & Pinsonneault, A. (2001). Customer Loyalty and Electronic-Banking: A Conceptual Framework. *Journal of Global Information Management*, *9*(3), 4–14. doi:10.4018/jgim.2001070101

Tomlinson, R. (2015, September 14). *The First Network Email*. Retrieved September 14, 2015, from Raytheon / BBN: http://www.raytheon.com/news/rtnwcm/groups/public/documents/content/rtn12_tomlinson_email.pdf

Tomoson Research Institute. (2015). *Influencer marketing study*. Retrieved from http://blog.tomoson.com/influencer-marketing-study/,02.12.2015

Tönnies, F. (1887). Gemeinschaft und Gesellschaft. Leipzig: Fues' Verlag.

Toral, S. L., Martinez-Torres, M. R., Barrero, F., & Cortes, F. (2009). An empirical study of the driving forces behind online communities. *Internet Research*, *19*(4), 378–392. doi:10.1108/10662240910981353

Traffic statistics for /r/AskReddit. (2015, Aug. 27). *AskReddit*. Retrieved Aug. 27, 2015, from https://www.reddit.com/r/AskReddit/about/traffic

Trainor, K. J., Andzulis, J., Rapp, A., & Agnihotri, R. (2014). Social media technology usage and customer relationship performance: A capabilities-based examination of social CRM. *Journal of Business Research*, *67*(6), 1201–1208. doi:10.1016/j.jbusres.2013.05.002

Trappey, R. J., & Woodside, A. (2005). Consumer responses to interactive advertising campaigns coupling short-message-service direct marketing and TV commercials. *Journal of Advertising Research*, *45*(4), 382–401.

Traynor, K., & Traynor, S. (2004). A Comparison of Marketing Approaches used by High-tech Firms: 1985 versus 2001. *Industrial Marketing Management*, *33*(5), 457–461. doi:10.1016/j.indmarman.2003.08.013

TripAdvisor. (2015). Accessed at http://www.tripadvisor.com.sg/PressCenter-c6-About_Us.html

Tugend, T. (1969). *UCLA*. Retrieved from UCLA Press: www.lk.cs.ucla.edu/LK/Bib/REPORT/press.html

Tumasjan, A., Sprenger, T. O., Sandner, P. G., & Welpe, I. M. (2010). *Predicting elections with Twitter: What 140 characters reveal about political sentiment*. Paper presented at the 4th International Conference on Weblogs and Social Media (ICWSM 2010), Washington, DC.

Turkish Airlines. (2010, September 15). *Turkish Airlines annual report2010*. Retrieved from http://investor.turkishairlines.com/documents/ThyInvestorRelations/kurumsal/faaliyet-raporu/2010/tr/m-6-8-1.html

Turkle, S. (1998). Identity in the age of the Internet: Living in the MUD. In *Composing Cyberspace: Identity, Community, and Knowledge in the Electronic Age* (pp. 5–11). Boston: McGraw Hill.

Udland, M. (2015, February 27). The internet is losing its composure over this dress that might be white and gold or black and blue". *Business Insider*. Retrieved from http://www.businessinsider.com.au/white-and-gold-black-and-blue-dress-2015-2

UNED. (2011). *Un community manager: ¿Qué son las redes sociales profesionales?* Retrieved from http://www.uncommunitymanager.es/redes-profesionales/

United States Anti-Doping Agency. (2013). *Statement from USADA CEO Travis T. Tygart Regarding Lance Armstrong Interview*. Retrieved October, 13, 2015 from http://www.usada.org/statement-from-usada-ceo-travis-t-tygart-regarding-lance-armstrong-interview/

UNWTO. (2014). *Tourism Highlights*. Retrieved 30 September 2015 from: www.unwto.org/pub

Urry, J. (1990). *The Tourist Gaze: Leisure and Travel in Contemporary Societies*. London: Sage.

USADA. (2012). *Statement from USADA CEO Travis T. Tygart Regarding The U.S. Postal Service Pro Cycling Team Doping Conspiracy*. Retrieved October, 13, 2015, from http://cyclinginvestigation.usada.org/

Uslay, C., Malhotra, N. K., & Citrin, A. V. (2004). Unique Marketing Challenges at the Frontiers of Technology: An Integrated Perspective. *International Journal of Technology Management, 28*(1), 8–30. doi:10.1504/IJTM.2004.005050

Usui, K. (2008). *The development of marketing management: The case of U.S.A 1910–1940*. Ashgate Publishing Limited.

Utterback, J. (2003). The Dynamics of Innovation. In *The Internet and the University* (pp. 81-103). Aspen Institute Forum, Educause.

Valentine, D. B., & Powers, T. L. (2013). Generation Y values and lifestyle segments. *Journal of Consumer Marketing, 30*(7), 597–606. doi:10.1108/JCM-07-2013-0650

Valenzuela, S., Park, N., & Kee, K. F. (2009). Is there social capital in a social network site?: Facebook use and college students' life satisfaction, trust, and participation. *Journal of Computer-Mediated Communication, 14*(4), 875–901. doi:10.1111/j.1083-6101.2009.01474.x

van de Donk, W., Loader, B., Nixon, P., & Rucht, D. (2004). Social Movements and ICTs. In W. van de Donk, B. Loader, P. Nixon, & D. Rucht (Eds.), *Cyberprotest: New Media, citizens and social movements* (pp. 1–25). London: Routledge.

Van Dijck, J. (2012). Facebook as a Tool for Producing Sociality and Connectivity. *Television & New Media, 13*(2), 160–176. doi:10.1177/1527476411415291

van Puijenbroek, T., Poell, R. F., Kroon, B., & Timmerman, V. (2014). The effect of social media use on work-related learning. *Journal of Computer Assisted Learning, 30*(2), 159–172. doi:10.1111/jcal.12037

VanAuken, K. (2015). Using social media to improve customer engagement and promote products and services. *Journal of Airport Management, 9*(2), 109–117.

Vargo, S. L., & Lusch, R. F. (2004). Evolving to a New Dominant Logic for Marketing. *Journal of Marketing, 68*(1), 1–17. doi:10.1509/jmkg.68.1.1.24036

Veil, S. R., Buehner, T., & Palenchar, M. J. (2011). A work-in-process literature review: Incorporating social media in risk and crisis communication. *Journal of Contingencies and Crisis Management, 19*(2), 110–122. doi:10.1111/j.1468-5973.2011.00639.x

Vella, M. (2015, July 20). Reddit reboots. *Time Magazine,* 46 – 50.

Venkataramani, V., Green, S., & Schleicher, D. (2010). Well-connected leaders: The impact of leaders' social network ties on LM and members' work attitude. *The Journal of Applied Psychology, 95*(6), 1071–1084. doi:10.1037/a0020214 PMID:20718519

Venkatraman, N., & Ramanujam, V. (1986). Measurement of business performance in strategy research: A comparison of approaches. *Academy of Management Review, 11*(4), 801–814. doi: 10.2307/258398

Vis, F. (2013). A critical reflection on Big Data: Considering APIs, researches and tools as data makers. *First Monday, 18*(10), 1–14. doi:10.5210/fm.v18i10.4878

Vivacqua, A. S. B., & Marcos, R. S. (2010). Collective Intelligence for the Design of Emerge ncy Response, In *Proceedings of 14th International Conference on Computer Supported Cooperative Work in Design (CSCWD)* (pp. 623–628).

Vladica, F. (2009). *Business Innovation and New Media Practices in Documentary Film Production and Distribution: Conceptual Framework and Review of Evidence.* Retrieved 7 21, 2015, from Digital Value Lab, Rogers Communications Centre: http://www.ryerson.ca/~c5davis/publications/Vladica-Davis%20business%20innovation%20and%20new%20media%20pracitices%20in%20documentaries%20FINAL%2013%20October%2008.pdf

Vlasic, G., & Kesic, T. (2007). Analysis of consumers' attitudes toward interactivity and relationship personalization as contemporary developments in interactive marketing communication. *Journal of Marketing Communications, 13*(2), 109–129. doi:10.1080/13527260601070417

Volo, S. (2010). Bloggers' reported tourist experiences: Their utility as a tourism data source and their effect on prospective tourists. *Journal of Vacation Marketing, 16*(4), 297–311. doi:10.1177/1356766710380884

Von Hippel, E., & Von Krogh, G. (2003). Open Source Software and the "Private-collective" Innovation Model: Issues for Organization Science. *Organization Science, 14*(2), 209–223. doi:10.1287/orsc.14.2.209.14992

Von Krogh, G. (1998). Care in knowledge creation. *California Management Review, 40*(3), 133–154. doi:10.2307/41165947

Vorhies, D. W., Harker, M., & Rao, C. P. (1999). The Capabilities and Performance Advantages of Market-driven Firms. *European Journal of Marketing, 33*(11/12), 1171–1202. doi:10.1108/03090569910292339

Vuori, M. (2012). Exploring Uses of Social Media in a Global Corporation. *Journal of Systems and Information Technology, 14*(2), 155–170. doi:10.1108/13287261211232171

Vyncke, F., & Bergman, M. (2010). Are culturally congruent websites more effective?: An overview of a decade of empirical evidence. *Journal of Electronic Commerce Research, 11*(1), 14–29.

W3C. (2015, September 23). *W3C.* Retrieved September 23, 2015, from Semantic Web: http://www.w3.org/standards/semanticweb/

Walsh, G., Mitchell, V. W., Jackson, P., & Beatty, S. E. (2009). Examining the antecedents and consequences of corporate reputation: A customer perspective. *British Journal of Management*, *20*(2), 187–203. doi:10.1111/j.1467-8551.2007.00557.x

Wang, K. (2014). Collective Innovation: The Known and the Unknown. *Collective Intelligence 2014*. Boston: MIT Center for Collective Intelligence.

Wang, X., Tang, L., Gao, H., & Liu, H. (2010). Discovering overlapping groups in social media. In *Proceedings of 2010 IEEE International Conference in Data Mining*. doi:10.1109/ICDM.2010.48

Wang, Y., Hou, J., Xia, Y., & Li, H. Z. (2015). Efficient privacy preserving matchmaking for mobile social networking. *Concurrency and Computation*, *27*(12), 2924–2937. doi:10.1002/cpe.3284

Warrington, T. B., Abgrab, N. J., & Caldwell, H. M. (2000). Building trust to develop competitive advantage in e-business relationships. *Competitiveness Review*, *10*(2), 160–168. doi:10.1108/eb046409

Wasan, P., & Tripathi, G. (2014). Revisiting social marketing mix: A socio-cultural perspective. *Journal of Service Research*, *14*(2), 128.

Watts, D. J., Dodds, P. S., & Newman, M. E. J. (2002). Identity and search in social networks. *Science*, *296*(5571), 1302–1305. doi:10.1126/science.1070120 PMID:12016312

Weaver, D. H. (Ed.). (1998). *The Global Journalist*. Hampton Press.

Webler, T. (1995). `Right` discourse in citizen participation: an evaluative yard-stick. In O. Renn, T. Webler, & P. Wiedemann (Eds.), *Fairness and Competence in Citizen Participation: Evaluating Models for Environmental Discourse*. Dordrecht: Kluver Academic Press. doi:10.1007/978-94-011-0131-8_3

Webler, T., Tuler, S., & Krueger, R. (2001). What is a good public participation process? Five perspectives from the public. *Environmental Management*, *27*(3), 435–450. doi:10.1007/s002670010160 PMID:11148768

Webster, J. F. E. (1992). The Changing role of Marketing in the Corporation. *Journal of Marketing*, *56*(4), 1. doi:10.2307/1251983

Weigley, S. (2011, August 5). Employers recruiting off-campus. *Wall Street Journal*.

Weinberg, B. D., & Pehlivan, E. (2011). Social spending: Managing the social media mix. *Business Horizons*, *54*(3), 275–282. doi:10.1016/j.bushor.2011.01.008

Wellman, B. (2001). Physical Place and Cyberplace: The Rise of Personalized Networking. *International Journal of Urban and Regional Research*, *25*(2), 227–252. doi:10.1111/1468-2427.00309

Wells, H. (1938). *World Brain*. Methuen & Co.

Weninger, T., Zhu, X. A., & Han, J. (2013). An exploration of discussion threads in social news sites: A case study of the Reddit community. In *Proceedings of the 2013 IEEE/ACM International Conference on Advances in Social Networks Analysis and Mining* (ASONAM '13). doi:10.1145/2492517.2492646

Wertheim, L. J. (2011). *Tweet smell of #success*. Retrieved October, 13, 2015 from http://www.si.com/vault/2011/07/04/106084755/tweet-smell-of-success

Werthner, H., & Ricci, F. (2004). E-commerce and tourism. *Communications of the ACM*, *47*(12), 101–105. doi:10.1145/1035134.1035141

Westaby, J., Pfaff, D., & Redding, N. (2014, April). A Dynamic Network Theory Perspective. *The American Psychologist*, *69*(3), 269–284. doi:10.1037/a0036106 PMID:24750076

Westerman, D., Spence, P. R., & van der Heide, B. (2014). Social media as information source: Recency of updates and credibility of information. *Journal of Computer-Mediated Communication, 19*(2), 171–183. doi:10.1111/jcc4.12041

What can a Reddit user do about a Reddit-wide shadowban?. (2015). *Quora*. Retrieved Aug. 28, 2015, from https://www.quora.com/What-can-a-Reddit-user-do-about-a-Reddit-wide-shadowban

White, M. (2010, August 12). *Clicktivism is ruining leftist activism*. Retrieved December 16, 2011, from http://www.guardian.co.uk/commentisfree/2010/aug/12/clicktivism-ruining-leftist-activism

White, D., & Houseman, M. (2003). The Navigability of Strong Ties: Small Worlds, Tie Strength, and Network Topology. *WileyPeriodicals, 8*(1), 72–81.

Wigley, S. (2011). Telling your own bad news: Eliot Spitzer and a testing of stealing thunder strategy. *Public Relations Review, 37*(1), 50–56. doi:10.1016/j.pubrev.2011.01.003

Wikipedia: Statistics. (2015, Aug. 21). *Wikipedia*. Retrieved Aug. 30, 2015, from https://en.wikipedia.org/wiki/Wikipedia:Statistics

Wilcox, D. L., & Cameron, G. T. (2012). *Public relations strategies and tactics*. Glenview, IL: Pearson Education.

Wilkinson, I., & Young, L. (2002). On cooperating: Firms, relationships, networks. *Journal of Business Research, 55*(2), 123–132. doi:10.1016/S0148-2963(00)00147-8

Williams, D. L., Crittenden, V. L., Keo, T., & McCarty, P. (2012). The use of social media: An exploratory study of usage among digital natives. *Journal of Public Affairs, 12*(2), 127–136. doi:10.1002/pa.1414

Williams, H. T. P., McMurray, J. R., Kurz, T., & Lambert, F. H. (2015). Network analysis reveals open forums and echo chambers in social media discussions of climate change. *Global Environmental Change, 32*, 126–138. doi:10.1016/j.gloenvcha.2015.03.006

Williams, K. D., Bourgeois, M. J., & Croyle, R. T. (1993). The effects of stealing thunder in criminal and civil trials. *Law and Human Behavior, 17*(6), 597–609. doi:10.1007/BF01044684

Williams, M. R., & Attaway, J. S. (1996). Exploring salespersons' customer orientation as a mediator of organisational culture's influence on buyer-seller relationships. *Journal of Personal Selling & Sales Management, XVI*(4), 33–52.

Wilson, S. (2015, January 22). The city's shame: Why is Auckland's urban design so bad? *The Metro*. Retrieved from http://www.metromag.co.nz/metro-archive/citys-shame-aucklands-urban-design-bad/

Wincent, J. (2005). Does size matter? A study of firm behavior and outcomes in strategic SME networks. *Journal of Small Business and Enterprise Development, 12*(3), 437–453. doi:10.1108/14626000510612330

Wise, S., Paton, R. A., & Gegenhuber, T. (2012). Value Co-creation through Collective Intelligence in the Public Sector: A Review of US and European Initiatives. *Vine, 42*(2), 251–276. doi:10.1108/03055721211227273

Wise, S., Valliere, D., & Miric, M. (2010). Testing the Effectiveness of Semi-predictive Markets: Are Fight Fans Smarter than Expert Bookies? *Procedia: Social and Behavioral Sciences, 2*(4), 6497–6502. doi:10.1016/j.sbspro.2010.04.059

Wiśniewski, P. (2015). Intellectual Capital (IC) in Social Media Companies: Its Positive and Negative Outcomes. In A. Rospigliosi & S. Greeder (Eds.), *Leading Issues in Social Media* (pp. 71–88). Reading, UK: Academic Conferences & Publishing International.

Without a Box. (2011). *Without a box*. Retrieved from Without a box: http://withoutabox.com

Witten, I. H., Frank, E., & Hall, M. A. (2011). *Data Mining: Practical Machine Learning Tools and Techniques.* Burlington, MA: Morgan Kaufmann.

Wolf, J. (2011). Ecological Citizenship as Public Engagement with Climate Change. In L. Whitmarsh, S. O'Neill, & I. Lorenzoni (Eds.), *Engaging the Public with Climate Change. Behaviour Change and Communication.* London: Earthscan.

Wolf, J., Brown, K., & Conway, D. (2009). Ecological citizenship and climate change: Perceptions and practice. *Environmental Politics, 18*(4), 503–521. doi:10.1080/09644010903007377

Woodcock, N., Green, A., & Starkey, M. (2011). Social CRM as a business strategy: The customer framework. *Journal of Database Marketing & Customer Strategy Management, 18*(1), 50–64. doi:10.1057/dbm.2011.7

Woolley, A. W., Chabris, C. F., Pentland, A., Hashmi, N., & Malone, T. W. (2010). Evidence for a Collective Intelligence Factor in the Performance of Human Groups. *Science, 330*(6004), 686–688. doi:10.1126/science.1193147 PMID:20929725

Wright, D. K., & Hinson, M. D. (2012). *A four-year longitudinal analysis measuring social and emerging media use in public relations practice.* Paper presented to the 15th Annual International Public Relations Research Conference, Coral Gables, FL.

Wu, J., Sun, H., & Tan, Y. (2013). Social media research: A review. *Journal of Systems Science and Systems Engineering, 22*(3), 257–282. doi:10.1007/s11518-013-5225-6

Xiang, Z., & Gretzel, U. (2010). Role of social media in online travel information search. *Tourism Management, 31*(2), 179–188. doi:10.1016/j.tourman.2009.02.016

Yadav, N., Swami, S., & Pal, P. (2006). High Technology Marketing: Conceptualization and Case Study. *Vikalpa: The Journal for Decision Makers, 31*(2), 57–74.

Yadav, V., & Arora, M. (2012). The product purchase intentions in Facebook using analytical hierarchical process. *Radix International Journal of Economics and Business Management, 1*(4), 26–54.

Yahoo Finance. (2015a). Retrieved October 9, 2015 from: http://finance.yahoo.com/q?s=socl&ql=1

Yahoo Finance. (2015b). Retrieved October 9, 2015, from: http://finance.yahoo.com/http·//finance.yahoo.com/

Yahoo Help Central. (2015). Retrieved October 19, 2015, from https://help.yahoo.com/kb/SLN2347.htmlhttps://help.yahoo.com/kb/SLN2347.html

Yakup, D. (2014). The Impact of Psychological Factors on Consumer Buying Behavior and an Empirical Application in Turkey. *Asian Social Science, 10*(6), 194-204.

Yang, C., Lin, K. H.-Y., & Chen, H. H. (2009). Writer meets reader: Emotion analysis of social media from both the writer's and reader's perspectives. In *Proceedings of the 2009 IEEE/WIC/ACM International Conference on Web Intelligence and Intelligent Agent Technology – Workshops.*

Yang, M., Li, Y., & Kiang, M. (2011). *Uncovering social media data public health surveillance.* Paper presented at the 15th Pacific Asia Conference on Information System (PACIS 2011), Brisbane, Australia.

Yang, G. (2009). *The Power of the Internet in China.* New York: Columbia University Press.

Yang, M., Kiang, M., & Shang, W. (2015). Filtering big data from social media: Building an early warning system for adverse drug reactions. *Journal of Biomedical Informatics, 54*, 230–240. doi:10.1016/j.jbi.2015.01.011 PMID:25688695

Yaros, R. A. (2008). Digital natives: following their lead on a path to a new journalism, *Nieman Reports,* 13–15.

Yates, P. (Director). (2005). *Stae of Fear* [Motion Picture].

Yen, H. J. R., & Gwinner, K. P. (2003). Internet retail customer loyalty: The mediating role of relational benefits. *International Journal of Service Industry Management, 14*(5), 483–500. doi:10.1108/09564230310500183

Yin, R. K. (2003). *Case Study Research Design and Methods.* London: Sage Publications.

Yoon, D., Choi, S. M., & Sohn, D. (2008). Building customer relationships in an electronic age: The role of interactivity of E-commerce web sites. *Psychology and Marketing, 25*(7), 602–618. doi:10.1002/mar.20227

Yoo, W., Lee, Y., & Park, J. (2010). The role of interactivity in E-tailing: Creating value and increasing satisfaction. *Journal of Retailing and Consumer Services, 17*(2), 89–96. doi:10.1016/j.jretconser.2009.10.003

Young, S. (2013). *Lance Armstrong – Everybody's doing it: A case study about a leader's ethics and use of power.* Retrieved October 13, 2015, from https://www.researchgate.net/publication/245024505_Young_-_Lance_Armstrong_2013_v1-4

Young, A. L., & Quan-Haase, A. (2013). Privacy protection strategies on Facebook: The Internet privacy paradox revisited. *Information Communication and Society, 16*(4), 479–500. doi:10.1080/1369118X.2013.777757

Youtube. (2015). *Statistics.* Retrieved from Youtube: https://www.youtube.com/yt/press/statistics.html

Yukawa, J. (2006). Co-reflection in online learning: Collaborative critical thinking as narrative. *International Journal of Computer-Supported Collaborative Learning, 1*(2), 203–228. doi:10.1007/s11412-006-8994-9

Yu, Y., Duan, W., & Cao, Q. (2013). The impact of social and conventional media on firm equity value: A sentiment analysis approach. *Decision Support Systems, 55*(4), 919–926. doi:10.1016/j.dss.2012.12.028

ZDF. (2015). *Schoene digitale Welt.* Retrieved 7 17, 2015, from Diskussionsveranstaltung Evangelischer Kirchentag 2015: http://www.zdf.de/ZDF/zdfportal/programdata/3c6207e5-5373-4524-870d-7e7c80b6e84f/20443602?generateCanonicalUrl=true

Zeithaml, V. A., Parasuraman, A., & Berry, L. L. (1985). Problems and strategies in services marketing. *Journal of Marketing, 49*, 33–46.

Zelizer, B. (2004). When facts, truth and reality are God-terms: On journalism's uneasy place in cultural studies. *Communication and Critical Cultural Studies, 1*(1), 100–119.

Zettsu, K., & Kiyoki, Y. (2006). Towards Knowledge Management Based on Harnessing Collective Intelligence on the Web. *Lecture Notes in Artificial Intelligence, 4248*, 350–357.

Zhang, W., Johnson, T., Seltzer, T., & Bichard, S. (2009). The revolution will be networked: The influence of social networking sites on political attitudes and behavior. *Social Science Computer Review, 28*(1), 75–92. doi:10.1177/0894439309335162

Zheng, B., Niiya, M., & Warschauer, M. (2015). Wikis and collaborative learning in higher education. *Technology, Pedagogy and Education, 24*(3), 357–374. doi:10.1080/1475939X.2014.948041

Zheng, Y., Zhang, L., Xie, X., & Ma, W. (2009). Mining interesting locations and travel sequences from gps trajectories. In *Proceedings of the 18th International Conference on World Wide Web* (pp. 791-800). New York, NY: ACM. doi:10.1145/1526709.1526816

Zhu, Y.-Q., & Chen, H.-G. (2015). Social media and human need satisfaction: Implications for social media marketing. *Business Horizons, 58*(3), 335–345. doi:10.1016/j.bushor.2015.01.006

Zikmund, W. G., & Babin, B. J. (2012). Marketing Research (10th ed.). South-Western/Cengage Learning.

Zikmund, W. G., Babin, B. J., Carr, J. C., & Griffin, M. (2010). *Business Research Methods.* South-Western Cengage Learning.

Zimmerman, A. S., & Blythe, J. (2013). *Business to business marketing management: a global perspective* (2nd ed.). New York: Routledge.

Zineldin, M. (2000). Beyond relationship marketing: Technologicalship marketing. *Marketing Intelligence & Planning, 18*(1), 9–23. doi:10.1108/02634500010308549

Zolkepli, I. A., & Kamarulzaman, Y. (2015). Social media adoption: The role of media needs and innovation characteristics. *Computers in Human Behavior, 43*, 189–209. doi:10.1016/j.chb.2014.10.050

Zuse, D.-I. H. (2015, September 14). *Konrad Zuse*. Retrieved September 14, 2015, from Z1: http://www.konrad-zuse.de/

About the Contributors

Vladlena Benson works as an Associate Professor at the Kingston Business School in Kingston University. She earned her PhD in 2001 from the University of Texas in Dallas.

Ronald Tuninga is the Dean of the Faculty of Business and Law at Kingston University, and is also Dean of the AVT Business School in Denmark. He earned his PhD in 1987 from Temple University. He has experience in publishing journal articles, and has also edited conference proceedings.

George Saridakis works as a Professor at Kingston University in the Small Business Research Center. He earned his PhD in 2006 from the University of Essex.

* * *

Michael Breazeale is a Marketing educator, researcher, and consultant. Assistant Professor of Marketing at Mississippi State University, he received his Ph.D. from Mississippi State University in 2010 and has taught at Indiana University Southeast and University of Nebraska at Omaha. His primary areas of research encompass consumer-brand connections, branding for nontraditional organizations, the consumption of experiences, and retail atmospherics. Mike has published several articles in publications that include International Journal of Market Research, Marketing Management Journal, Journal of Retailing, and Journal of Business Research, and has made numerous conference presentations relating to his research. He has won multiple awards for both teaching and research, and serves as reviewer for several top marketing journals. Mike is a founding member and organizer of the Institute for Brands and Brand Relationships, which sponsors an annual gathering of marketing scholars and practitioners from around the globe. Mike is co-editor of Consumer-Brand Relationships: Theory and Practice (2012) and Strong Brands, Strong Relationships (2015), both from Routledge Publishing.

Richard Bull is a social scientist with a diverse background in energy, behaviour change, waste management and the digital economy. His PhD was an ESRC Case award with Veolia exploring the role of business in society through an examination of whether public engagement and deliberative processes can generate 'social learning' and environmental citizenship. Over the last 7 years he has led a range of UK and EU research projects (£500k+) around public engagement and behaviour change and has an ongoing interest in the benefits of public engagement to behaviour change, governance and environmental and corporate citizenship.

Radim Cermak graduated from applied informatics. Currently, he is PhD student at the Faculty of Informatics and Statistics, University of Economics, Prague, where he deals with the issue of cultural differences in the sphere of Internet.

Nurdilek Dalziel started her career as a banker working for financial institutions in Istanbul and Ankara at various levels. In her last banking role, she was in charge of a Marketing and Product Development unit. In 2002, Nurdilek decided to transform her financial services background into an academic career in the UK, which resulted in the award of a PhD in 2007. Nurdilek has developed her teaching, supervisory and research experiences as a result of work undertaken with several British universities. Currently she is a Lecturer for Staffordshire University Business School with a particular research interest on relationship marketing, social media, marketing communications and financial services marketing. She also contributes to distance learning programmes at the University of Leicester. Additionally, Nurdilek is a reviewer for International Journal of Bank Marketing and Service Industries Journal, and an editorial board member of American Journal of Economics and Business Administration.

Andrew Duffy is an Assistant Professor in the Wee Kim Wee School of Communication and Information at Nanyang Technological University in Singapore. His research interests include travel journalism and User-generated content, and the next generation of journalists.

Tiit Elenurm is head of the entrepreneurship department at the Estonian Business School. Ph. D. in 1980 for the dissertation "Management of the Process of Implementation of New Organizational Structures". Professor Elenurm is manager of the Entrepreneuship MBA programme at the Estonian Business School. Author of more than 120 research publications. Lecturing experince in Germany, France, Poland, Czech Republic and Finland. Research interests include knowledge management, cross-border virtual networking, innovative entrepreneurship and international transfer of management knowledge.

Tobias H. Engler received his PhD in business administration from University of Marburg where he is a member of the research group Information Systems. His research on the use of social media in enterprises for collaboration, communication and knowledge management was published in various international journals such as Information Processing and Management and Journal of Retailing & Consumer Services as well as proceedings of conferences such as ECIS.

Ginevra Gravili was born in Lecce on 07 October 1969. She graduated in Economic Studies in 1992, and she achieved PHD in Management and Organization in 1996. Since 2002, she is professor of Organization Theory at University of Salento, Department of Economics and Management, Lecce, Italy. She has written numerous books and articles on sme's, knowledge sharing, social recruitment, HRM of public administration, ICT, social media and organizations.

Shalin Hai-Jew works as an instructional designer at Kansas State University (K-State). She has taught at university and college levels for many years (including four years in the People's Republic of China) and was tenured at Shoreline Community College but left tenure to pursue instructional design work. She has Bachelor's degrees in English and psychology, a Master's degree in Creative Writing from the University of Washington (Hugh Paradise Scholar), and an Ed.D in Educational Leadership with a focus on public administration from Seattle University (where she was a Morford Scholar). She reviews for a number of publications and is editor of several IGI Global titles. Hai-Jew was born in Huntsville, Alabama, in the U.S.

Janet Hontoir, BSc(Econ), PGCE, FCIB, RSA Cert (TEFL), is Senior Lecturer in Financial Markets & Risk at ifs University College. She graduated in Economics from the University of London in 1972 and specialises in monetary and financial economics. She is also interested in financial sustainability and bank-customer relationships.

Maria Hopwood, MA, MSc, is a highly experienced academic and lecturer in the fields of sport public relations, marketing and business and is a published author, accomplished researcher and conference presenter. Prior to joining SMWW, Maria enjoyed a lengthy career in University education having taught at UCFB Wembley, the University of Northampton (UK), Leeds Beckett University (UK), Bond University (Queensland, Australia) and the University of Teesside (UK). Maria has gained extensive experience working with professional sports organisations in both Australia and the UK such as Durham County Cricket Club, Middlesbrough Football Club, Brisbane Roar Football Club and Gold Coast United Football Club. She has also worked with UEFA as an academic consultant. She is a member of the editorial boards for the journals Public Relations Review, the International Journal of Sport Communication and the International Journal of Sport Marketing and Sponsorship.

Vaclav Janoscik graduated from philosophy, history and law. He received his doctorate at the Academy of Arts, Architecture and Design in Prague. He deals with applying philosophy within humanities and its methodology with focus on how do certain discourses establish the concept of subjectivity.

Kijpokin Kasemsap received his BEng degree in Mechanical Engineering from King Mongkut's University of Technology Thonburi, his MBA degree from Ramkhamhaeng University, and his DBA degree in Human Resource Management from Suan Sunandha Rajabhat University. He is a Special Lecturer at Faculty of Management Sciences, Suan Sunandha Rajabhat University based in Bangkok, Thailand. He is a Member of International Association of Engineers (IAENG), International Association of Engineers and Scientists (IAEST), International Economics Development and Research Center (IEDRC), International Association of Computer Science and Information Technology (IACSIT), International Foundation for Research and Development (IFRD), and International Innovative Scientific and Research Organization (IISRO). He also serves on the International Advisory Committee (IAC) for International Association of Academicians and Researchers (INAAR). He has numerous original research articles in top international journals, conference proceedings, and book chapters on business management, human resource management, and knowledge management published internationally.

Alexander K. Kofinas received his PhD in Organisational Management from Manchester Metropolitan University in 2008. In October 2008 he joined the University of Greenwich as a Senior Lecturer. In 2013 he joined the Department of Strategy and Management as a Principal Lecturer in Management and he is currently programme leader for the Business Management Portfolio. His current interests lie in social media as well as the development of a sound game-based pedagogy of learning.

Fritz Kohle studied at the Surrey Institute of Art and Design and as a postgraduate at the Northern Media School, Sheffield Hallam University. He currently studies for a PhD at the University of Edinburgh investigating how social media is changing the production value chain in documentary production. In 2009 he obtained tenure at NHTV, University of Applied Sciences, Breda, Netherlands, as a senior lecturer teaching Film & TV production, while continuing his professional production practice. Kohle began his career as a production assistant at companies such as the The Weather Channel UK, working his way up to become Location Manager for a Channel 4 UK feature film (Prometheus), Head of Productions at the Lux Centre London, and Field Producer for iBeam Europe. As a freelance Producer and Production Manager he has produced episodes for Marienhof, one of Germany's most popular soaps, with a daily viewership exceeding 6 million. In collaboration with the Ludwigsburg Film Academy in Germany, he published the media handbook Medienmacher Heute. Kohle's projects include post-production management for Studio Babelsberg features in Berlin, such as Wim Wender's Soul of a Man, and Jackie Chan's 80 Days Around the World. In addition, he was also involved in various German soaps such as Notruf 110 and Tatort. Kohle was Bigfoot Entertainment's Head of Post Production until 2007. In June 2007 he joined New York Universities Tisch School of the Arts as Assistant Director for the Production and Post-production Centre, significantly contributing to the establishment of the NYU Singapore Campus.

Robert Kutera is currently holding a position of business analyst in an international research project entitled ActGo-Gate (Active Retiree and Golden Workers Gate) under the Ambient Assisted Living program) at Wroclaw University of Economics; Since 2007 he has given lectures and classes at the Wroclaw University of Economics and the University of Business in Wroclaw. His research interests are concentrating on e-business communications and e-marketing, business implications of social media and mobile technologies, online consumer behavior analysis as well as different aspects of information society development. Author of 38 scientific articles and speaker at many scientific conferences, both national and international in the area of business informatics; the beneficiary and participant in 12 research projects in the area of business communications, e-business and social media (including four individual projects) financed from EU funds and grants of Polish Ministry of Science and Higher Education. Privately passionate of motor sports and recreational fishing. In his spare time he likes to get away from the noise of the city to the nature with a fishing rod and a good book, especially a good fantasy one.

Andriew Lim is Professor of Technopreneurship and Innovation in Hospitality at, Hotelschool The Hague in the Netherlands. His current research interests include technology innovation and entrepreneurship in hospitality industry, where he also teaches strategy and innovation courses as well. He holds a bachelor degree in Mechanical Engineering, a master degree in International Business and PhD in Technology Management.

Lukasz Lysik, PhD, is currently working as lecturer and researcher at University of Economics based in Wroclaw Poland in the Department of Information Systems. His main field of interest are mobile technologies, social media, marketing and application of new technologies in omnichannel. He is an active researcher involved in many projects.

Piotr Machura is a science and new technology researcher, experienced both in the academic field as well as in business practice. CEO & Founder of Unitee – advertising agency.

Manoj Maharaj is a Professor of Information Systems in the School of Management, Information Technology and Governance, in the College of Law and Management Studies, UKZN

Hamish McLean lectures in risk and crisis communication at Griffith University, Australia. He has 30 years' professional experience in emergency management, journalism and police media, along with operating a crisis and media consultancy for more than a decade with international clients in the health, aviation, law and allied sectors. His PhD is in media and disasters and his research interests are in political communication during disasters and risk communication involving community resilience and disaster planning, response and recovery.

Daithí McMahon is currently writing his doctoral thesis in Media Studies at Mary Immaculate College, University of Limerick where he also earned his MA in the same discipline. Daithí's research interests include mass media audience participation in particular the convergence of radio and social media, the political economy of media industries and online communities. He is a leading writer and radio producer and winner of several national and international radio awards. He currently lectures in media writing at Institute of Technology, Tralee, Ireland.

Sergio Monge-Benito teaches subjects as "Advertising Effectiveness" or "Marketing: Concepts, Strategies and Tactics" at the University of the Basque Country (UPV/EHU). His lines of research includes commercial communication though Internet (blogs, social networks, SEO, ecommerce) and neuromarketing (psychophysiological measures used in market research). He has published several articles in peer reviewed journals and regularly works as consultant in university-enterprise contracts. Publications: MONGE, Sergio; OVELAR, Ramón; AZPEITIA, Iker. Repository 2.0: Social dynamics to support community building in learning object repositories.Interdisciplinary Journal of E-Learning and Learning Objects, 2008, vol. 4, no 1, p. 191-204. MONGE-BENITO, Sergio; OLABARRI-FERNÁNDEZ, María Elena. Uses and perceptions of Tuenti and Facebook among students from the University of the Basque Country. Revista Latina de Comunicación Social, 2011, vol. 66, p. 079. OLABARRI-FERNÁNDEZ, Elena; MONGE-BENITO, Sergio. Autoexpresión y privacidad de los universitarios en las redes sociales. Los estudiantes de la Universidad del País Vasco como caso de estudio. Doxa Comunicación: revista interdisciplinar de estudios de comunicación y ciencias sociales, 2011, no 13, p. 89-113. MONGE-BENITO, Sergio; OLABARRI-FERNÁNDEZ, Elena. Recuerdo y recomendación de las marcas en Facebook. Investigación y marketing, 2013, no 118, p. 24-33

Aitziber Nunez is a professor at Business Studies School, at University of Basque Country in San Sebastian (UPV/EHU). She teaches in the field of Strategic Management and Marketing. Research interests include: Business communication through social media, professional networking, sharing knowledge and new ideas in search of business opportunities through Web 2.0 tools.

Maria Elena Olabarri has a grade in Sociology (1980), a PhD in Political Science and Sociology (1989) and a Full Professor position in Audiovisual Communication and Advertising (2001) at the University of the Basque Country. She teaches "Consumer Psychosociology" in undergraduate courses and "Communication Marketing" for graduate students. Her main lines of research are Consumer Behavior and Advertising Research. Regarding the first line, she has been invited to several congress, received an award to the best research methodology from "La Asociación Europea de Estudios de Mercado,

Marketing y Opinión Publica" and co-written a book: "El Comportamiento del Consumidor". In the second line of research, she has made annual evaluations of touristic advertising campaigns of the local government of the Autonomous Region of the Basque Country (in Spain). She has several recent publications in academic journals.

Monica Pianosi is a PhD student with a multidisciplinary education in the built environment, sustainable development, behaviour change and social media. She is finalising a thesis that investigates the impacts of social media campaigns on the up taking of pro-environmental behaviours in the non-domestic environment. At the same time, she is working in the social media industry, applying and testing different marketing theories to brand communication.

Kiru Pillay received his PhD in 2012. He is a visiting academic and researcher, based at the LINK Centre, University of the Witwatersrand, which focuses on electronic communications policy.

Inna P. Piven is a Learning Designer at Unitec Institute of Technology, Auckland, New Zealand. She also teaches Services Marketing and Managing for Growth papers as well as supervises student projects on social media strategies in business. She received her Master of Business from Unitec Institute of Technology and is currently pursuing a PhD in Education at Australian Curtin University. In addition to her teaching, Inna writes journal and conference articles on consumer-brand communications on social media. Prior to teaching, Inna was a brand manager for a leading media holding in the Russian Far East. After moving to New Zealand in 2005, Inna started a family business that she still successfully runs together with her husband. Last year Inna developed a strong interest in education research, specifically on the applicability of social media in the intensive business course delivery. The intent of her PhD research is to investigate what social media has to offer when it comes to student learning experiences, and their academic progress.

Michael Schulz is a doctoral student and a member of the research group Information Systems at the University of Marburg. He earned a M. Sc. degree in Business Information Systems from the AKAD Hochschule Pinneberg. His research interest is in Business Intelligence (BI), especially in Self-Service BI.

A. Skarzauskiene is an initiator and scientific leader of a priority research program for "Social technologies" at Mykolas Romeris University (MRU). Her research field is application of new technologies in different fields of society life focusing on innovative leadership and management approaches in knowledge society (distributed leadership, collective intelligence etc.). Prof. Skarzauskiene's research is based on principles of system theory, scientific research publications cover the topics of networked structures, clusters and networked organizations. A.Skarzauskiene was leading the Project for development of Self-managing teams in European Parliament in Luxembourg and Brussels with DEMOS Group Belgium (www.demosgroup.com) 2007-2008.

Zdenek Smutny is teaching assistant at the Department of Systems Analysis, University of Economics, Prague and also project manager at Telematix Group. He graduated in applied informatics and media studies. He deals with a wide concept of social informatics: interaction between ICT and humans at the organizational (micro) and society (macro) level and ICT applications in the social sciences.

Thelma Solomon is an emerging researcher who has recently completed her doctoral degree in Massey University, Wellington, New Zealand. Her research explored the strategic marketing practices of the Information and Communication Technology firms. Her areas of interest include strategic Marketing Practices and Social Media in the B2B sector. She has taught in tertiary institutions in India, Singapore and New Zealand. Currently she is working for SYSMAN ICT Ltd in New Zealand.

Oliana Sula is a full-time lecturer at the Department of Management at the University of Durres in Durres, Albania. She is a guest lecturer and a PhD student at the Department of Entrepreneurship at the Estonian Business School. Her thesis focuses on the role of international networks in establishing a youth entrepreneurial culture a comparison between Albania and Estonia. Her research interests include social innovation, social business, social entrepreneurship, youth entrepreneurship, entrepreneurial culture, social media, online social networks, virtual teams, philanthropy and CRS.

Rūta Tamošiūnaitė is a lecturer and researcher at Mykolas Romeris Univeristy, Lithuania. She is active in science communication: managing editor of research paper journal "Social Technologies", member of Academic association of Management and Administration (AVADA) with responsibilities in external communication sphere. Her interest fields are decision making and communication in digital environment.

Patrick Winter is a doctoral student and a member of the research group Information Systems at the University of Marburg. He earned two B. Sc. degrees with distinction from the University of Osnabrück, where he studied Information Systems and Business Administration/Economics. His research areas cover quantitative methods and their applications, primarily in the domain of E-Marketing.

Piotr Wisniewski is Associate Professor at the Warsaw School of Economics (Poland). His interests in social media (SM) concentrate on publicly listed SM companies and the takeup of SM by financial institutions. Piotr brings two decades of executive experience in financial services; memberships of the Chartered Institute for Securities & Investment and the Professional Risk Managers' International Association.

Index

A

Action Learning 248-249, 255, 258-260
Actor-Network Theory 267, 282
Adaptivity 135
Advocacy 59-61, 65, 67, 69-71, 75
airline company 218, 220-222, 226
Airline Marketing 215-217
Ant Colony Optimization 413, 426
Anti-Doping Agency 49, 54
Attitudes 27, 82-83, 85, 90, 95, 98, 108, 111, 173, 178, 182, 213, 255, 355-356, 433
Audience Interaction 162, 164
Audience Participation 168
Authenticity 197-199, 359

B

B2B Marketing 328
Banking Channel 145, 155
Basque Country 334-335, 339, 344, 349-350
Behavioural Factors 23, 29-32, 36, 43
Blog 52, 60, 81, 178-179, 181, 270, 274, 291, 340-341, 436, 449
Brand Community 284, 290-291, 296-297, 313
Brand Community on Social Media 313
Brand Consumption 283-286, 291, 293-294, 297, 306
Brand Value 283-284, 286, 288, 290-292, 295, 298-299, 302, 304-306
Brand Value Creation 284, 286, 302, 305-306
build value 23-24, 44
Bursty 362, 405
Business Networking 252, 258, 260-262, 334-335, 338, 344
Business students 248-249, 255-256, 259, 261
Business-to-Business (B2B) 339, 348

C

Capabilities 71, 120, 124-125, 127, 130, 146, 316, 327, 337, 352, 365, 372, 395-396, 431-432, 434
Centrality 62, 195, 197, 201, 204, 360, 377, 383, 386, 399, 405
Channels 3, 23, 25, 28-29, 32, 35, 37, 39-41, 51, 53, 62, 77, 82, 120, 122, 137-138, 140, 142-144, 146-148, 155, 164, 168, 215-216, 218, 236, 287, 355, 398, 431-432
City Council 81, 86, 88-89
Civil Society 59-62, 67-72, 75
Click Activism 75
Co-Creation 122, 248-249, 253-254, 261, 301-302, 306, 318, 433
Collaborative Search 407-409, 413, 426
Collective Intelligence 120-125, 130, 135, 250, 356
Collective Intelligence System 125, 135
collective investment 5
Communication 22-23, 25-26, 28-29, 32, 38, 41, 44-48, 51, 58, 61-62, 68, 76-77, 79-80, 86-87, 98-100, 103, 105, 109-110, 121-125, 138-140, 142, 144, 146, 155, 158-159, 161-162, 164, 168, 188-189, 212, 215, 218-219, 229, 235-236, 238, 242-244, 249, 254-255, 258-259, 261, 267-269, 272-273, 276, 278-279, 283-284, 287-288, 291, 296, 300, 306, 313-315, 317, 321, 324, 326, 427-430, 433-436
Community 8, 23, 31-32, 36, 47-48, 54, 61, 66-67, 72, 78-79, 81, 100, 103, 120-121, 123-125, 127-130, 135, 167, 180, 188, 190, 194-195, 197, 200-202, 240, 252, 256, 269, 275-276, 282, 284-286, 290-291, 294-298, 301-302, 313, 336, 342-344, 355-356, 359, 362, 366, 371, 430, 432, 434
Competencies 71, 248-249, 251-256, 259-261, 436
Consumer Behaviour 22-23, 25, 27-29, 35, 40-41, 43-44
Consumer Journey 23-24, 33, 35, 37, 40-41

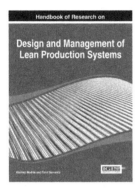

Printed in the United States
By Bookmasters